Children's Early Understanding of Mind: Origins and Development

edited by

Charlie Lewis
Lancaster University, UK

Peter Mitchell
University College, Swansea, UK

 LAWRENCE ERLBAUM ASSOCIATES, PUBLISHERS
Hove (UK)   Hillsdale (USA)

Lawrence Erlbaum Associates Ltd., Publishers
27 Palmeira Mansions
Church Road
Hove
East Sussex, BN3 2FA
UK

British Library Cataloguing in Publication Data

A catalogue record for this book is available from the British Library

ISBN 0-86377-333-8 (Hbk)
ISBN 0-86377-352-4 (Pbk)

Typeset by DP Photosetting, Aylesbury, Bucks.
Printed and bound by BPC Wheatons Ltd., Exeter

This book is dedicated to Rita and Andrew Mitchell, and Alex Moore

Contents

List of Contributors

Dare A. Baldwin, Department of Psychology, University of Oregon, Eugene, OR 97403, USA.

Sarah Baker, Laboratory of Experimental Psychology, University of Sussex, Falmer, Brighton BN1 9QG, UK.

Simon Baron-Cohen, Departments of Psychology & Child Psychiatry, Institute of Psychiatry, University of London, De Crespigny Park, London SE5 8AF, UK.

Karen Bartsch, Department of Psychology, University of Wyoming, PO Box 3415, Room 135, Biological Sciences, Laramie, Wyoming 82071-3415, USA.

George Butterworth, Division of Psychology, Arts D Building, University of Sussex, Falmer, Brighton BN1 9QN, UK.

Michael Chandler, Department of Psychology, University of British Columbia, Vancouver, Canada V6T 1W5.

Judy Dunn, S-211 Henderson Building, Pennsylvania State University, University Park, PA 16802, USA.

Norman H. Freeman, Department of Psychology, University of Bristol, 8 Woodland Road, Bristol BS8 1TN, UK.

Alison Gopnik, Department of Psychology, University of California at Berkeley, Berkeley, CA 94720, USA.

Suzanne Hala, Department of Psychology, University of British Columbia, Vancouver, Canada V6T 1W5.

Paul L. Harris, Department of Experimental Psychology, University of Oxford, South Parks Road, Oxford OX1 3UD, UK.

R. Peter Hobson, Developmental Psychopathology Research Unit, Adult Department, The Tavistock Clinic, 120 Belsize Lane, London NW3 5BA, UK.

Deborah Hutton, Laboratory of Experimental Psychology, University of Sussex, Falmer, Brighton BN1 9QG, UK.

Charlie Lewis, Department of Psychology, Lancaster University, Fylde College, Lancaster LA1 4YF, UK.

Angeline Lillard, Department of Psychology, University of San Francisco, Ignatian Heights, 2130 Fulton Street, San Francisco, CA 94117-1080, USA.

Andrew Meltzoff, Child Development & Mental Retardation Center, University of Washington, Seattle, Washington, USA.

Peter Mitchell, School of Psychology, University of Birmingham, PO Box 363, Birmingham B15 2TT, UK.

Louis J. Moses, Department of Psychology, University of Oregon, Eugene, OR 94703, USA.

Josef Perner, Laboratory of Experimental Psychology, University of Sussex, Falmer, Brighton BN1 9QG, UK.

Candida C. Peterson, Department of Psychology, University of Queensland, Brisbane, Queensland 4072, Australia.

Howard Ring, Department of Neuropsychiatry, Raymond Way Suite, Institute of Neurology, University of London, Queen Square, London WC1 3BG, UK.

Elizabeth J. Robinson, School of Psychology, University of Birmingham, Edgbaston, Birmingham B15 2TT, UK.

Marilyn Shatz, Cognition & Perception, Department of Psychology, University of Michigan, 330 Packard Road, Ann Arbor, MI 48104-2994, USA.

Michael Siegal, Department of Psychology, University of Queensland, Brisbane, Queensland 4072, Australia.

Virginia Slaughter, Department of Psychology, University of California at Berkeley, CA 94720, USA.

Beate Sodian, Universität München, Institut für Empirische Pädagogik und Pädagogische Psychologie, Leopoldstr. 13, 80802 München, Germany.

Henry M. Wellman, Centre for Human Growth & Development, University of Michigan, 300 N. Ingalls Bldg., 10th Level, Ann Arbor, MI 48109-0406, USA.

Andrew Whiten, School of Psychology, University of St. Andrews, St. Andrews, Fife KY16 9JU, Scotland, UK.

Preface

The origin of this book can be traced back to a workshop on the acquisition of a theory of mind in normally developing children and individuals with autism, which took place in Swansea, March, 1992. The event was financially supported by the Welsh Branch of the British Psychological Society, which we gratefully acknowledge. The enthusiasm of the participants and the full-capacity audience persuaded us that there was ample interest, plus an abundance of key findings and new ideas, to merit the present volume.

Theory of mind symposia continue to feature prominently in conferences on developmental psychology and there is an avalanche of articles being published on this topic at the present time. Given this background, perhaps it is no longer wise to create a general text on the topic, but instead identify a specific theme. This was certainly the case in the books by Baron-Cohen, Tager-Flusberg and Cohen (1993) and Whiten (1991). In the former, the theme was autism, whereas in the latter, common links with a socio-biological perspective were explored.

In this book, the focus is on the origins of an understanding of mind, and the authors present interesting ideas and evidence from research on children largely under the age of four. One of the main questions asked by many of the authors is: "What are the precursors of a fully fledged understanding of the representational mind?" It is obvious from the answers to this question that there are no grounds for supposing that a theory of mind is suddenly installed in the child's cognition at a specified time—such as her fourth birthday—akin to upgrading the RAM of one's personal computer with the addition of a new microchip. Instead, we see that prior to passing a standard test of false belief, the child has already acquired a spectrum of foundational abilities. The existence of these no longer assumes that the eventual ability to acknowledge false belief on a standard test is the result of a radical conceptual shift in cognition. In this respect, it would appear that the work reported in this book represents a genuine advance over previous research in what we know about the development of an understanding of mind.

While working on this book, both of us were assisted financially by the Economic and Social Research Council (CL in collaboration with Norman Freeman, Grant No. R-000-23-2330; and PM in collaboration with Elizabeth Robinson, Grant No. R-000-23-3313). We gratefully acknowledge this support. Additionally, PM received much support from the Department of Psychology, University College of Swansea, particularly a sabbatical period spent at the School of Psychology, University of Birmingham, during the Lent term of 1993. Meanwhile, CL spent the summer of 1993 at the Department of Psychology, University of British Columbia, allowing him to apply the finishing touches to the book. Finally, we are grateful to Michael Forster, Jane Charman and Corinna Lord of Lawrence Erlbaum Associates Ltd. for their tireless work in ensuring that everything in the preparation of this book ran smoothly.

Charlie Lewis and
Peter Mitchell, December 1993

REFERENCES

Baron-Cohen, S., Tager-Flusberg, H., & Cohen, D.J. (Eds.). (1993). *Understanding other minds: Perspectives from autism.* Oxford: Oxford University Press.
Whiten, A. (Ed.). (1993). *Natural theories of mind: Evolution, development and simulation of everyday mindreading.* Oxford: Basil Blackwell.

1

Critical Issues in Children's Early Understanding of Mind

Peter Mitchell
University College, Swansea, UK

Charlie Lewis
Lancaster University, UK

INTRODUCTION

A fascination with mind and psychological states is fundamental to human intellectual functioning. For example, the diversity of literary genres, from Shakespeare to soap opera, share a common theme: exploring the reasons why people act as they do. There has been an ambivalence towards the concept of mind over the course of 20th-century psychology, but over the past couple of decades there has been an increasing consensus that our passion for dwelling upon psychological matters forms a central feature of the human condition. It is perhaps no mere coincidence that humans are unique both in their creation of culture and in their expertise in contemplating the psychological (see Crook, 1980, for a detailed socio-biological view of the emergence of culture). In this respect, we adopt the role of the "intuitive psychologist" (Humphrey, 1983).

What is the fundamental cognitive basis of our theory of mind? It is an understanding of the mind–world distinction, and that behaviour is the product of belief and desire rather than just desire (cf. Bartsch & Wellman, 1989; Wellman & Bartsch, 1988; this volume). So if we wish to triumph over someone in the game of life, or at least manoeuvre them to fulfil our needs, it is greatly advantageous to understand that misinformation instils a false belief in others, leading them to act as we want them to. So, we endeavour to influence others' behaviour by manipulating the content of their beliefs. This is an activity premised on the assumption that people hold their beliefs

1

as being true of reality and act on them accordingly (cf. Perner, 1991; Perner, Baker, & Hutton, this volume).

This fascination with mental states has become a major focus of attention within psychology over the past 15 years. It is now widely recognised that an ability to make inferences about others' representational states, and to predict behaviour accordingly, is a fundamental human ability, and this topic now rightly assumes a central position in human experimental psychology. The cornerstone issue concerns the development of understanding that people, including oneself, can hold false beliefs. Such understanding liberates the individual from immediate reality, and enables a grasp of the concept that behaviour is the product of what people believe to be true rather than of what is really true. Investigating how a theory of mind develops potentially offers great insight into the character of social cognition. An explosion of research has shown that by the end of their preschool years children come to take many of these skills for granted (e.g. Astington, Harris, & Olson, 1988; Frye & Moore, 1991; Whiten, 1991). This book attempts to take the next step towards an understanding of how these developments occur. It examines what happens before as well as during the period when the child comes to demonstrate an understanding of possible discrepancies between events in the world, and people's differential understanding of those events. So with reference to early competencies the authors of this volume ask: "How primitive is this ability?"; "Are some elements innate?"; "How do the child's experiences feature in the emergence and refinement of a theory of mind?"

TESTS OF THEORY OF MIND COMPETENCE: THE RESEARCH LEGACY

Perhaps as a legacy of the previously dominant Piagetian approach to cognitive development, many investigators have assumed that theory of mind develops in stages (e.g. Gopnik & Wellman, 1992; Perner, 1991; Sullivan & Winner, 1991; Wimmer & Hartl, 1991), an assumption made in many of the chapters of this volume. This claim is based to a considerable extent on three-year-old children's failure to acknowledge false belief, as demonstrated in the two following complimentary experimental paradigms.

1. The Unexpected Transfer Test. This can be regarded as the seminal demonstration in contemporary research on theory of mind that young children have difficulty acknowledging false belief. The task, devised by Wimmer and Perner (1983), is as follows. The child subject observes a story enacted with a pair of dolls. One of these is a boy called Maxi, who leaves chocolate in a kitchen cupboard (location A), and then departs from the scene. In his absence, the other doll (his mother) enters and transfers the chocolate to another cupboard in the kitchen (location B).

Maxi did not witness this transfer due to his absence, and therefore is ignorant that the chocolate has moved to a new location. The observing child is then informed by the experimenter that Maxi is returning to the kitchen to get his chocolate, and is invited to judge where Maxi will look. In the seminal study, children below age five years, unlike most older children, often gave realist judgements that Maxi would look where the chocolate was stored at the time of asking, rather than in the location Maxi last saw the chocolate.

Since that initial finding, most published studies report that children of four years are proficient in acknowledging false belief, with the accompanying claim that it is specifically children below this age who are yet to develop a fully fledged theory of mind. Perner (1991) accounts for the discrepancy between earlier and later findings by noting that, in later procedures, a convention emerged for explicitly pointing out to the observing child that Maxi was ignorant of the chocolate being transferred.

2. The Deceptive Box Test. For whatever reason children fail to acknowledge false belief in the unexpected transfer test, it certainly is not merely because it is a hypothetical scenario enacted with dolls. This was demonstrated by results of the deceptive box test (Perner, Leekam, & Wimmer, 1987), which typically does not involve dolls. In this task, the experimenter will show the child a box whose exterior proclaims its content (e.g. a Smarties tube), and asks the child what she thinks is inside. After the child has replied "Smarties," the experimenter reveals surprisingly that the contents are pencils, returns them to the tube and asks what another child will think is in the tube. As in the unexpected transfer task, children aged around three years often give the wrong answer of "pencils" (a realist judgement.

This task has been adapted to ask children to comment on their own initial belief about the deceptive box's content (Gopnik & Astington, 1988). In doing so, children are at least as likely to commit a realist error. Having seen the true contents of the box, they judge that when they had *first* seen the tube they had thought it contained pencils. This finding carries important theoretical implications, since it suggests that development of a theory of mind pertains also to knowledge of one's own mind. Firstly, it argues against the Cartesian position that the mind is transparent to itself, which implied that development takes the form of introspecting and applying insights into one's own mind to others' minds (Wimmer & Hartl, 1991). Secondly, it makes it inappropriate to characterise young children's difficulty acknowledging false belief merely as a symptom of egocentrism. Young children's difficulty is more general than one of confusing their own with others' beliefs, since they even seem ignorant of the representational quality of their own mental states.

THE SPECIAL CASE OF AUTISM

Research into theory of mind assumed even greater significance with the advent of the "theory of mind hypothesis of autism" (e.g. Frith, 1989). This hypothesis presents autism as a disorder of social cognition, where the unfortunate individual lacks the insight into mind that most of us take for granted. Supporting evidence arose from a milestone study by Baron-Cohen, Leslie, and Frith (1985). They presented an unexpected transfer task to children with autism, and found realist errors in abundance. The finding was subsequently replicated using a deceptive box procedure (Perner, Frith, Leslie, & Leekam, 1989).

What made these findings especially relevant is that a theory of mind deficiency seemed specific to autism among children above four years of age. For example, Baron-Cohen et al. (1985) showed that children with Down's syndrome were unimpaired in their ability to acknowledge false belief. Moreover, children with autism apparently did not experience difficulty acknowledging false belief merely because of their delayed language development. Baron-Cohen et al. selectively chose children with autism who had a verbal mental age in excess of four years, yet failure to acknowledge false belief remained rife. Emerging from the early research (e.g. Baron-Cohen et al., 1985) was a prevailing impression that children with autism lacked a theory of mind, as was hypothesised to be the case in normal three-year-olds. However, it now looks as though autism is better construed as aberrant, or different, rather than absent development (e.g. Leekam & Perner, 1991; Leslie & Thaiss, 1992).

From a research standpoint, the relation between investigations into the development of a theory of mind in normal children and in children with autism has been mutually beneficial. As well as shifting attention away from the Piagetian focus on egocentrism, research on developing theories of mind has injected new impetus into the study of autism as a developmental disorder. In particular, the creation of a framework for normal development of social cognition has provided a fruitful point of comparison for abnormal development in this domain. Conversely, studies examining how the autistic theory of mind differs from that of the normal young child's allows us to specify a variety of cognitive components underlying the facets of theory of mind phenomena (e.g. Leslie & Thaiss, 1992).

THEORETICAL DIVISIONS AND A MOVE
TOWARDS RECONCILIATION

Towards the end of the 1980s and into the early 1990s, researchers studying normal development polarised into two opposing camps. One group of researchers published converging data, suggesting that a watershed occurred around the time of the child's fourth birthday, amounting to a radical conceptual shift (e.g. Gopnik & Astington, 1988; Gopnik & Slaughter, 1990; Perner, 1988; 1991; Perner & Ogden, 1988; Sullivan & Winner, 1991; Wimmer & Hartl, 1991). Meanwhile, another group of researchers accumulated data pointing to early acknowledgment of false belief (e.g. Chandler, Fritz, & Hala, 1989; Bartsch & Wellman, 1989; Lewis & Osborne, 1990; Mitchell & Lacohée, 1991; Siegal & Beattie, 1991; Zaitchik, 1991). Ostensibly, these latter research efforts were to shed light on the progression of development, but sadly are often cited only for their challenge to the received wisdom on the age that the child first acknowledges false belief.

However, as this volume will freely attest, there now prevails a serious and concerted effort to explain how development takes place. The aim is to ask the question "What is the origin of development and how does it progress?" and to begin to answer it. Although the authors of each chapter may ask this question, it does not follow that issues of controversy concerning whether we are underestimating young children's competence have now vanished. Siegal and Peterson (this volume), for example, remain vociferous in their warning that much speculation on the development of a theory of mind can be questioned because of its failure to consider the clash between the conversational worlds of children and adults that occurs during testing. This valuable point should always be at the forefront of researchers' minds when devising tests and questions for young children.

Nonetheless, there is a prevailing consensus that we must get down to the task of devising means of assessing and theorising about early competencies. In this volume, a creatively wide variety of different views are expressed. At least four themes seem to emerge from this. One examines general conceptual or innate prerequisites for a theory of mind (chapters by Baron-Cohen & Ring, Butterworth, Hobson, Mitchell, Whiten). The second focuses specifically on the developmental role of early perceptual experience (chapters by Baron-Cohen & Ring, Butterworth, Gopnik et al., Hobson). This issue is also addressed in Freeman's analysis of the use of pictures in facilitating children's grasp of mental representation. A third theme concerns the role of pretence in early theory of mind development (Harris, Lillard, Perner). The fourth focuses on linguistic and communication factors, both in terms of how these might play a causal role in development (Baldwin & Moses, Dunn, Robinson, Wellman & Bartsch) and in how we might avoid communication failure with young children, either in tasks (Lewis; Siegal & Peterson) or in facilitating performance by requiring children to create the conditions for false belief in another person (Chandler & Hala, *pace*, Sodian). Next we expand briefly on these contributions, in chapter order.

PREREQUISITES OF A THEORY OF MIND

Mitchell's chapter challenges the stage view of development by showing that various manipulations can either decrease or increase the age threshold at which children acknowledge false belief. This evidence gives the impression that age of success is task-specific rather than due to some radical conceptual shift intrinsic to the child's cognitive development.

Yet it is still necessary to explain why young children are inclined to refer to reality when invited to judge about belief. Mitchell accounts for this by arguing that early realist judgments are not a default consequence of not knowing about belief. Rather, he turns the issue on its head to suggest that failure to acknowledge false belief is a function of an early bias to consult reality in a variety of domains. What changes with age, therefore, is not the ability to understand belief but a diminution in the prominence that reality holds in the child's cognition. Mitchell argues that an early reality focus could actually be adaptive for a young child whose first mission is to come to grips with the physical aspects of reality.

Of relevance to the third chapter, by Andrew Whiten, is a long-standing debate on the extent to which we should infer mentalism from overt behaviour. Lloyd Morgan's canon warns that we should avoid such inferences if a behavioural explanation can be presented. In his chapter, Whiten points out that at least in some false belief tests we can explain children's success in terms of behavioural explanations. For example, Maxi may simply search for the chocolate in the place he last saw it. That is, we can identify an heuristic for correct judgements without invoking the concept of an understanding of false belief.

However, Whiten goes on to argue that, although success can be achieved with complex behaviourism of this kind, it can be achieved much more simply with a cognitivism revolving around the concept of false belief. As such, a complex behaviourism can better be construed as a simple cognitivism. This analysis applies not only to the false belief test, but also to other theory of mind tasks, like the ignorance versus knowledge distinction in level-1 perspective taking (Flavell, Shipstead, & Croft, 1978). In sum, Whiten shows that there is no easily identifiable threshold that can mark the existence of a theory of mind.

Hobson's chapter discusses the developmental role of perceiving others' attitudes. He notes that attitudes have both behavioural and mentalistic components. That is, attitudes can be conveyed by a distinctive posture, which in turn conveys a certain frame of mind or mental orientation. As observers, we frequently see what it is in the world that provokes the attitude. For example, the presence of a snake may provoke a posture that we could describe as fear or profound anxiety. We may also see that a single event in the world provokes different reactions in different people. For example, a snake handler presumably appears at peace in the presence of a snake.

In this context, Hobson describes a special kind of attitude that is fundamental to the emergence of an understanding of the representational mind: the propositional attitude, which is captured by phrases such as, "He's pretending that X," or "She believes that X." In the case of propositional attitudes, the child comes to understand that the attitude must hold a special relation with reality, particularly the attitude associated with belief. He or she will learn that beliefs are defined as propositions held to be true (though obviously a young child would not be able to express this understanding explicitly). The child might learn this from events arising in a family context; for example, disputes about who should be admonished for a misdemeanour. In sum, the child will learn that propositional attitudes are locked into reality. However, special cases could then arise where an individual is misinformed about reality, so the construct of false belief becomes pertinent to accommodate this. Hobson goes on to argue how abnormalities in autistic perception of attitudes could give rise to the well-known socially debilitating condition central to this syndrome.

Freeman's chapter begins with a theme that has been held, albeit tacitly in some cases, by increasing numbers of researchers in this field since Chandler's (1988) critical analysis: Perhaps too much weight has been given to the standard tests of false belief. This has been regarded as a litmus test for the possession of a theory of mind. Of the standard tests, Freeman argues that the best is that which probes children's acknowledgement of their own prior false belief because, unlike other tasks, this actually implants a false belief in the child's mind. In the other standard tests, the child has to infer false belief, so we cannot be sure whether the child's difficulty is with inferring or accessing the false belief.

Freeman goes on to present some intriguing data, suggesting that pictures serve as an especially effective aid to acknowledgement of own false belief. In particular, getting the child to select a picture of her initial belief (e.g. a picture of Smarties) seems to facilitate subsequent acknowledgement of that belief, more so than getting the child to select a sample of the initial belief (e.g. a Smartie). Freeman argues that pictures are especially effective memory tracers of the initial false belief. He assumes that being in the same representational domain as the belief, they provide the child with a representational head start.

EARLY PERCEPTUAL EXPERIENCE

In the first of the chapters dedicated to examining the role of early perceptual experiences, Butterworth argues that mind is embodied in behaviour, and is thus available to be perceived. He makes a further point that consciousness can be regarded transitively, that to be conscious is to be conscious *of* something. Bringing these two issues together, it then becomes pertinent to ask whether and when infants are conscious of people attending to certain objects in their environment.

Butterworth's own data show that by 12 months, infants have acquired a geometric conception of shared attention, calculating what a person is looking at from the direction of their gaze. This ability implies that they understand that their own visual field is shared with others. Importantly, however, infants understand the possibility but not the inevitability of a shared focus of attention and thus knowledge within that space. This is implied by the infant's striving to focus on whatever the other person is gazing at.

Baldwin and Moses demonstrate even more impressive competencies in infants aged around 18 months. Their chapter begins by suggesting that infants must be highly attuned to adults' attentional focus, otherwise it would be difficult to explain rapid expansion of vocabulary development with only a few errors along the way. For example, suppose the adult is fixating on one object and names it, while the infant attends to a different object. Will this result in the infant wrongly associating the name with the object she herself attended to?

Baldwin and Moses show that infants seldom commit such an error. The reason for their success, apparently, is because infants are highly proficient in perceiving the adult's attentional focus. As Baldwin and Moses put it, it seems that infants perform a mentalistic analysis of others' communicative behaviour. The authors report parallel findings in similar-aged infants in the domain of social referencing.

In their chapter, Gopnik, Slaughter, and Meltzoff argue that an understanding of the representational mind is founded in early visual experiences, particularly those concerned with level-1 perspective taking (Flavell et al., 1978). This is the ability to judge that what can be seen by oneself may not be seen by another person. Children aged three years are easily able to succeed on this task. From an understanding that objects are not inevitably visible to everybody, children construct the idea that a viewer who experiences a restricted view will remain in a state of ignorance. A step beyond this is an understanding of the general concept of perceptual misrepresentation. Perceptual misrepresentation can then serve as an analogy for mental misrepresentation, and the young child will succeed in acknowledging false belief.

From this argument, Gopnik et al. predict that acknowledgment of misrepresentation should first be apparent in the perceptual domain. Their supporting data show that, as predicted, young children enjoy considerable success in acknowledging misrepresentation in contexts where this results from visual distortion. For example, somebody might think that a stick, which appears bent on being half-submerged in water, is broken. Children performed better on this task compared with a standard test of false belief. Gopnik et al. point out that the hypothesised perceptual origin of our ability to understand misrepresentation is characterised in certain common expressions we use when referring to representational change: "I saw it in a new light; I changed my view."

Baron-Cohen and Ring attempt to specify a different mechanism of early perceptual experience in playing a vital role in the emergence of a theory of mind. They invoke a hypothetical construct which they call the "Eye Direction Detector" (EDD), and ambitiously proceed to locate this within the architecture of the brain. EDD informs the child what people look at, allowing him or her to formulate a triadic representation of "agent-sees-object." Following a process of generalisation, the child subsequently learns that the agent seeing an object can be equated in some contexts with the agent wanting that object or intending to refer to it. Consequently, EDD supplies the child with a basis for inferring mental states in others.

Additional to EDD, Baron-Cohen and Ring grant the existence of a "Theory of Mind Mechanism" (TOMM), as suggested by Leslie and Thaiss (1992). This construct putatively allows the child to process propositional attitudes (e.g. pretend, believe). Baron-Cohen and Ring propose that since EDD developmentally predates the emergence of TOMM, TOMM need only fill in the middle slot, X, in the triadic relation "agent–X–object" with the appropriate propositional attitude. For example, John (agent) believes that (propositional attitude) Smarties are in the tube (object). In this sense, EDD paves the way for the successful operation of TOMM.

THE ROLE OF PRETENCE

In the first of the three chapters on pretence, Lillard presents a review of background literature on this topic. From this, she concludes that by age three years, children are able to make the real–pretend distinction. She argues that evidence suggesting that young children are frightened of pretend monsters is not confusion between pretence and reality, but is an expression of a desire in the child to distance him or herself from an aversive stimulus.

Although Lillard credits young children with an ability to draw the real–pretend distinction, she argues that this should not be equated with an ability to reflect on pretence as a mental state. She proceeds to present persuasive data in support of this claim. Her studies show, surprisingly, that not until about six years of age do children use the word "pretend" to refer exclusively to contexts where the agent knows what it is he or she is supposed to be pretending. For example, prior to this age, children say that an agent is pretending to be a rabbit when hopping around, irrespective of whether that agent is depicted as knowing or not knowing anything about rabbits. In other words, it seems that children below about six years use "pretend" to mean "behaving as if."

Harris describes some recent investigations into early pretence, with the revelation that children as young as two years can exhibit a sustained grasp of a complex pretend scenario. In particular, they apparently understand the experimenter's reference to make-believe substance (e.g. pretend tea) and the effects this can have within the pretence. For example, if Naughty Teddy spills the (pretend) "tea" over another character, then, in the child's words, that character would become 'teasy"! Remarkably (or perhaps not), the child is able to hold on to the pretend identify of an object through a sequence of pretend events.

Contrary to the position taken by Lillard, Harris suggests that a capacity for pretence in young children should be construed as a symptom of an ability to reflect on mental states. He sympathises with the view espoused by Leslie (1987), that the child must treat pretence as being a set of propositions detached from reality, given that it is reasonable to suppose the child draws the pretend–reality distinction effectively (which his data suggest they do). In particular, Harris' data show that the young pretender can take into account another person's distinctive mental stance, though Harris concedes that this in itself is not sufficient to acknowledge false belief. Harris concludes that early pretence should be regarded as a manifestation of the constructive activity children bring to the interpretation of ordinary world-related activity.

Perhaps falling somewhere in between the positions adopted by Lillard and Harris, the authors of the next chapter, Perner, Baker, and Hutton, accept that young children do understand pretence as a mental state, but nonetheless that they conceptualise pretence (along with belief) as "behaving as if." This is a development of Perner's (1988; 1991) previous position that young children should be regarded as what he calls 'situation theorists"; meaning that they have an understanding that people behave in certain ways in certain situations. Yet this contrasts with the state of what Perner et al. call "behaving as is," which is the more mature understanding that people behave according to the beliefs that they hold as being true.

In this context, Perner et al. argue that young children do not hold distinct concepts of belief and pretence, but instead possess a protoconcept that amalgamates the two, labelling this as "prelief." Their supporting data show that children who fail a standard test of false belief use the words "think" and "pretend" apparently interchangeably when referring to the behaviour of an agent who acts in a way not conducive to satisfying any goal in reality. Most importantly, children do not discriminate in their use of "think" and "pretend" whether the agent is depicted as knowing reality (and should be correctly described as pretending X) or not knowing reality (and should correctly be described as wrongly thinking X).

The section ends with a brief commentary written by the contributing authors, who attempt to show how their views and data might be reconciled.

EARLY CONVERSATION AND COMMUNICATION

Moving on to conversation and communication, Dunn's chapter provides an overview of her longitudinal research into precursors of an ability to acknowledge belief as distinct from reality. In the process, Dunn introduces valuable ecological validity to her work by showing how changes in cognitive development, relating to the emergence of theory of mind skills, influence changes in relationship with others, hence the title of her chapter. Three precursors that stand out are (1) young children seem predisposed in their conversations with each other to refer to internal (including mental) states; (2) around 33–40 months there is typically an increase in causal talk explaining phenomena (including the behaviour of others); (3) around 33–47 months there is an increase in self-oriented argument. This latter development is where the young child marshals justifications as a means to satisfying his or her own self interest.

These precursors in themselves testify to the emergence of a theory of mind, but Dunn goes further, to make an explicit link between at least one of these developments and subsequent ability to acknowledge false belief. She reports that children who are notable for engaging in discussions of causality around the time of their third birthday are typically the ones who are proficient in acknowledging false belief in a standard test six months later in development. Dunn ends her chapter by warning that, since an understanding of mind develops in certain contexts, it follows that ability to acknowledge belief as distinct from reality might well be context-specific.

Continuing with this theme, Shatz depicts the development of an understanding of mind as intertwined with budding communicative competence. She characterises this as a blossoming of social-linguistic intelligence, in which a conception of mind is founded on the emerging verbal ability to understand and explain the behaviour of self and others. The special value of language in this case is that it provides a vehicle for making internal states public and therefore accessible.

Shatz proceeds to document the case of her grandson, Ricky, between 17 and 36 months. Even at 17 months he apparently understood that what he was attending to may not be noticed by another person. Ricky came to utilise his emerging verbal communication skills for establishing a mutual focus on things. Despite this, Ricky had not yet developed an ability to include in his conversation topics concerned with mental states such as "think." The latter appeared first as an expression of uncertainty, but later, by about 33 months, served explicitly to characterise false belief, among other things. Shatz's persuasive account shows how Ricky's participation in discourse acquainted him firstly with his own uniqueness and subsequently with the mental worlds of other people. In turn, these insights seemed to boost his ability and desire to communicate.

Wellman and Bartsch also look for precursors of an ability to acknowledge false belief in early conversations. Following their previous work, investigating early belief-desire psychology in young children, the authors argue that before entertaining a belief-desire psychology, young children possess a simple desire psychology. A belief-desire psychology assumes that people act to satisfy their desires, providing that their beliefs about the appropriate means to this end are accurate. If not, then ironically people might behave in a way that thwarts their desire.

Yet why should we suppose that young children who lack a concept of belief possess a concept of desire? Perhaps they merely judge that people act according to what is true. However, archive data analysed by Wellman and Bartsch suggest that children aged about two years do understand desire on a level that merits the label "psychological." For example, they understand that what is wanted will not always be satisfied (the desire-reality distinction) and that a particular desire might not be shared by everyone (desires are subjective). It thus seems that two-year-olds regard desires in a psychological way in several key respects that will later characterise their conception of beliefs. Consequently, an early understanding of desire could be a vital precursor of a later developing understanding of belief.

Robinson's chapter gives an overview of research investigating young children's understanding of verbal utterances as sources of knowledge. As Robinson points out, utterances present a special kind of information about the world, which "hits" the listener after filtering through the cognition of the speaker. As such, utterances provide a window into the representational mind of speakers; these are representations that the child listener can then compare and contrast with what she knows of reality from a direct source of information, such as seeing. Experiencing a discrepancy between what is said to be true and what is known to be true thus presents an interesting contrast that the child can resolve by invoking the concept of the representational mind. For example, "He said X (but I know Y is true) because he thinks the wrong thing."

Robinson presents a wide variety of data germane to this issue, beginning with investigations into how young children resolve conflicting information derived from direct and indirect sources. Her evidence shows that young children, even those who fail a standard test of false belief, give different weightings to direct and indirect sources. In particular, they are inclined not to update their knowledge of the true content of a deceptive box when they are merely informed what it is (pencils), as opposed to when they are shown the contents. As such, it seems that young children are sensitive to the tentative status of information emanating from another person. This could serve as an important developmental precursor of a more sophisticated understanding of the representational mind that enables correct judgements on a standard test of false belief.

BROADER ISSUES IN FALSE BELIEF COMPREHENSION

Sodian begins the final section by assessing young children's ability to deceive. Previous research on this topic by Chandler et al. (1989) seemed to suggest that even children as young as two years are capable of deceiving a competitor in a game situation. This ability suggests that children understand that misinformation gives rise to a state of misrepresentation. Putting it another way, presumably children would not generate false information if they did not understand that it would create a false belief in a recipient.

Since Chandler et al.'s early work, more recent research, much of it carried out by Sodian and her colleagues, elegantly demonstrates that only by about four years of age do children come to grasp the representational impact of misinformation. Prior to that age, although children might give misleading information, they fail to do this specifically in contexts where it would be appropriate to deceive; they also give misleading information in co-operative contexts. Sodian thus argues that a genuine insight into deception only emerges at around the time the child is able to acknowledge false belief in a standard test. She presents this as persuasive evidence in favour of a radical conceptual change occurring around the time of the child's fourth birthday, marked by an ability to engage in insightful deception and acknowledgement of false belief on a standard test.

Chandler and Hala take an opposing view to Sodian, touching on a theme raised in several other chapters: They challenge the status of standard false belief tests as tools for detecting a watershed conceptual revolution in the emergence of a theory of mind. They argue eloquently that the "one miracle" approach to the development of a theory of mind is at best seriously lacking in merit and at worst downright misleading. The authors argue instead that more important developments occur well before success on the standard test of false belief and also well after.

Chandler and Hala go on to present data that further challenge the value of the standard test of false belief. They suggest that children perform badly on this test because they are not actively involved in effecting the circumstances that would give rise to false belief in another person. They remedy this state of affairs by comparing children's ability to acknowledge false belief in both unexpected transfer and deceptive box tasks where the child subject either instigates the transfer (or the exchange of expected for surprise contents) or passively observes the same effected by the experimenter. As Chandler and Hala predicted, only in the former conditions did young children show proficiency in acknowledging false belief, suggesting that standard tests of false belief seriously underestimate young children's competence.

Continuing with the theme that young children's abilities have been underestimated by standard tests of false belief, Siegal and Peterson argue in their chapter that a clash in the conventional worlds of children and adults (including experimenters) gives a misleading impression that young children are incompetent. Specifically, they argue that, whereas the experimenter has a scientific purpose to her questioning, the child imposes a conversational interpretation. In developing their argument, the authors appeal to Gricean conversational maxims.

Siegal and Peterson proceed to analyse conversational dynamics of false belief tests, and specify precisely how children might misinterpret the test question. For example, in the unexpected transfer task, the child might interpret the experimenter to mean, "Where will Maxi have to look to get the chocolate?" They report their own previously published data, showing that when the question is modified to, "Where will Maxi look first of all?" children are significantly more likely to judge correctly that he will search in the place where he last saw the chocolate. In the case of the deceptive box task, Siegal and Peterson argue that children privately question why the experimenter goes to the trouble of showing them the unexpected content of pencils. They rationalise this behaviour by supposing that the experimenter wants them to refer to this content when answering the test question—hence young children's realist answers. Although a fair proportion of this chapter rests on plausible argument without supporting data, the authors succeed in presenting a highly thought-provoking thesis, which researchers in this field will dismiss at their own peril.

The final chapter, by Lewis, compares both the researcher and the child with a detective trying to solve a specified problem. As indicated in the previous chapter, the child is engaged in an attempt to identify which information is salient and relevant to the problem's solution. In that light, it would not be surprising if a young child attended to a misleading aspect of the information presented, such as the present reality rather than a protagonist's false belief. If so, this would not necessarily mean that the child has a deficient theory of mind.

Lewis investigated his hypothesis by getting the child to repeat back the elements of an unexpected transfer false belief story, before answering the test questions. This simple manipulation massively facilitated children's correct judgements. It seems that ensuring all the relevant information was stored in the child's memory was sufficient to allow the child to make the inference of false belief. However, when the false belief story was a familiar one, namely Goldilocks and the Three Bears, there was considerable reluctance to acknowledge the three bears' ignorance concerning who ate their porridge. Lewis suggests that this narrative is so well known to the child that she assumes everybody knows who did what, including the protagonists themselves! From these findings we see that how children answer questions in a false belief task is at least partly a product of how they process the stream of information mentally. Any problems are not just due to a deficiency they have in conceptualising representation.

This collection of chapters offers both complimentary and contrasting views on the origins of an understanding of mind. The authors have made admirable efforts to generate imaginative and highly original suggestions on how early theory of mind develops, and in what contexts we are most likely to witness early acknowledgement of false belief in particular. This does not mean to say that a fully fledged theory of mind is up and running by the child's fourth birthday. Many of the authors take the view that what is achieved in early childhood, although momentous, is but the first part of an odyssey in becoming acquainted with the greatest mystery: the human mind.

REFERENCES

Astington, J.W., Harris, P.L., & Olson, D.R. (1988). *Developing theories of mind*. Cambridge: Cambridge University Press.

Baron-Cohen, S., Leslie, A.M., & Frith, U. (1985). Does the autistic child have a "theory of mind?" *Cognition, 21*, 37–46.

Bartsch, K., & Wellman, H. (1989). Young children's attribution of action to beliefs and desires. *Child Development, 60*, 946–964.

Chandler, M. (1988). Doubt and developing theories of mind. In J.W. Astington, P.L. Harris, & D.R. Olson (Eds.), *Developing theories of mind*. Cambridge: Cambridge University Press.

Chandler, M., Fritz, A.S., & Hala, S. (1989). Small-scale deceit: Deception as a marker of two-, three-, and four-year-olds' early theories of mind. *Child Development, 60*, 1263–1277.

Crook, J.H. (1980). *The evolution of human consciousness*. Oxford: Clarendon Press.

Flavell, J.H., Shipstead, S.G., & Croft, K. (1978). Young children's knowledge about visual perception: Hiding objects from others. *Child Development, 49*, 1208–1211.

Frith, U. (1989). *Autism: Explaining the enigma*. Oxford: Blackwell.

Frye, D., & Moore, C. (1991). *Children's theories of mind*. Hove: Lawrence Erlbaum Associates Ltd.

Gopnik, A., & Astington, J.W. (1988). Children's understanding of representational change and its relation to the understanding of false-belief and the appearance-reality distinction. *Child Development, 62*, 98–110.

Gopnik, A., & Slaughter, V. (1991). Young children's understanding of changes in their mental states. *Child Development, 62*, 98–110.

Gopnik, A., & Wellman, H. (1992). Why the child's theory of mind really is a theory. *Mind and Language, 7*, 145–171.

Humphrey, N.K. (1983). *Consciousness regained*. Oxford: Oxford University Press.

Leekam, S.R., & Perner, J. (1991). Does the autistic child have a "metarepresentational" deficit? *Cognition, 40*, 203–218.

Leslie, A.M. (1987). Pretence and representation: The origins of "theory of mind." *Psychological Review, 94*, 412–426.

Leslie, A.M., & Thaiss, L. (1992). Domain specificity in conceptual development: Neuropsychological evidence from autism. *Cognition, 43*, 225–251.

Lewis, C., & Osborne, A. (1990). Three-year-olds' problems with false belief: Conceptual deficit or linguistic artifact? *Child Development, 61*, 1514–1519.

Mitchell, P., & Lacohée, H. (1991). Children's early understanding of false belief. *Cognition*, *39*, 107–127.

Perner, J. (1988). Developing semantics for theories of mind: From propositional attitudes to mental representation. In J.W. Astington, P.J. Harris, & D.R. Olson (Eds.), *Developing theories of mind*. Cambridge: Cambridge University Press.

Perner, J. (1991). *Understanding the representational mind*. London: MIT Press.

Perner, J., Frith, U., Leslie, A.M., & Leekam, S.R. (1989). Exploration of the autistic child's theory of mind: Knowledge, belief and communication. *Child Development*, *60*, 689–700.

Perner, J., Leekam, S.R., & Wimmer, H. (1987). Three-year-olds' difficulty with false belief: The case for a conceptual deficit. *British Journal of Developmental Psychology*, *5*, 125–137.

Perner, J., & Ogden, J.E. (1988). Knowledge for hunger: Children's problem with representation in imputing mental states. *Cognition*, *29*, 47–61.

Siegal, M., & Beattie, K. (1991). Where to look first for children's knowledge of false beliefs. *Cognition*, *38*, 1–12.

Sullivan, K., & Winner, E. (1991). When three-year-olds understand ignorance, false belief, and representational change. *British Journal of Developmental Psychology*, *9*, 159–172.

Wellman, H.M., & Bartsch, K. (1988). Young children's reasoning about beliefs. *Cognition*, *30*, 239–277.

Whiten, A. (1991). *Natural theories of mind*. Oxford: Blackwell.

Wimmer, H., & Hartl, M. (1991). Against the Cartesian view on mind: Young children's difficulty with own false beliefs. *British Journal of Developmental Psychology*, *9*, 125–138.

Wimmer, H., & Perner, J. (1983). Beliefs about beliefs: Representation and constraining function of wrong beliefs in young children's understanding of deception. *Cognition*, *13*, 103–128.

Zaitchik, D. (1991). Is only seeing really believing? Sources of the true belief in the false belief task. *Cognitive Development*, *6*, 91–103.

ONTOGENESIS OF AN
UNDERSTANDING OF MIND

2 Realism and Early Conception of Mind: A Synthesis of Phylogenetic and Ontogenetic Issues

Peter Mitchell
University College, Swansea, UK

INTRODUCTION

It is well documented that children aged three years seldom acknowledge false belief, either in themselves or in others. Instead, they typically judge the content of belief by reference to whatever maintains presently in reality. Acknowledging false belief is of great theoretical importance, serving as a litmus test for crediting an individual with a theory of mind. Many researchers prominent in this field of investigation argue that the emergence of an understanding of false belief is stage-like and due to a radical conceptual shift occurring around the time of the child's fourth birthday. Contrary to this prevailing view, I wish to argue that development takes the form of children gradually coming to attach more weight to a representational criterion rather than a realist one when judging about belief. Yet we would still need to account for the presence of early realist errors. Paradoxically, from an ecological/evolutionary perspective, realism could be adaptive in that it might be vital for the very young child to have a preoccupation with reality. In this light, it is not that realist errors are a default consequence of the child's failing to understand about belief. Rather, such errors mask a theory of mind competence that remains largely dormant in the early years. A couple of implications of this view are that: (1) the rudiments of a theory of mind owe more to genetic inheritance than world experience, and (2) development in this domain takes the form of smooth evolution rather than conceptual revolution.

HUMAN THEORY OF MIND: SOME SUGGESTIONS
ON UTILITY AND EVOLUTIONARY ORIGIN

Understanding of belief (as distinct from reality) is highly relevant to our Darwinian fitness, with the implication that an individual who possessed a cognition well suited to this kind of reasoning would thrive in immediate survival and reproduction (cf. Krebs & Dawkins, 1984). Consider humans in their natural state, in the absence of all the familiar features of society and culture. Suppose that in this stage we are unfortunate enough to face interpersonal conflict. A capability to understand mind would be advantageous in acquiring allies and influencing them to fight alongside us. Alternatively, perhaps we could put our diplomatic skills to good effect and appease our adversary without recourse to aggression, maintaining honour despite turning away from battle. Should it come to combat, then the better we understand the enemy, the better we are able to predict his behaviour and deploy evasive, defensive, or offensive strategies accordingly. It would be especially useful in this respect to understand that misinformation gives rise to misrepresentation, as a cognitive underpinning of effective manipulation of deceptive strategies.

Insofar as deception affords a fundamental and perhaps primitive value of a theory of mind, we might witness instances of elementary deception in non-human primates. Such evidence certainly is accumulating in the case of chimpanzees in the form of their deployment of deceptive tactics directed at other chimps (Whiten & Byrne, 1988; 1991). Humphrey (1980; see also Krebs & Dawkins, 1984) reinforces this view with the argument that any individual who had the qualities of a "natural psychologist" would enjoy considerable advantage in this context: Correctly assessing others' intentions, attitudes, and beliefs enables the individual to prepare a state of readiness, which is far preferable to reacting only when the other person's behaviour is enacted. A conception of mind is also useful for forming alliances, both in dealing with potential conflict and in identifying and wooing potential reproductive partners (Whiten, 1992), as expanded next.

Tantamount to preserving the immortality of our genes in the distal sense is effective reproduction. In this matter, the better we understand a potential partner's mind, the better equipped we are to do things to please that person, and so become attractive to him or her. However, people, especially females, need to be discerning in their choice of partner. For example, if they procreated with one who had unviable genes, this would be a serious threat to their Darwinian fitness: There would be the usual enormous health, time, and energy cost in pregnancy followed by many years of investment in nurturing, but with no ultimate payoff in terms of an offspring who would carry their genes henceforth in perpetuity. This matter is not so chronic for males because, conscience and immunity from life-threatening diseases permitting, they are able to spread their seeds far and wide in the absence of such big investments and therefore with relative impunity.

There is thus an onus on us (especially if we are female) to seek a partner who behaves in a way conducive to survival, and we would be inclined to interpret such behaviour as emanating from personal traits if the concept of the representational mind was prominent to us. This is because the trait concept serves as a useful vehicle for conceptualising the mind behind the behaviour. Interestingly, then, we could predict a fundamental attribution error (that people tend to explain behaviour by reference to trait rather than situation), and this is precisely what is found (e.g. Hewstone, 1989). The better insight we have into the traits behind the behaviour, the more likely we are to choose a partner worthy of investment in our genetic future. The asymmetry between male and female investment in their partner leads to the provocative prediction that the female theory of mind might be more refined and better developed than the male's in some respects. One possible consequence of this is that the male theory of mind might be more fragile than the female's and less well established. Consistent with this is the finding that children with autism (who are supposedly deficient in their theory of mind: Baron-Cohen, Leslie, & Frith, 1985) are seldom girls (Frith, 1989), suggesting that girls have a more robust basis to their theory of mind.

Understanding mind is also intimately linked with interpreting others' speech. To illustrate, consider this example from Robinson and Mitchell (1992, 1994; Mitchell & Robinson, in press; see also Robinson, this volume): Mum is tidying away two bags of material, and she puts bag A into the drawer and B into the cupboard. Subsequently, John swaps over the bags, so that A is now in the cupboard and B in the drawer. John did this in Mum's absence, so we can assume she is ignorant of the swap and that her belief concerning the bags' locations is obsolete. Now Mum wants one of the bags, and requests the bag in the drawer. By taking into account Mum's false belief on the whereabouts of the bags, we can infer that she really wants the bag in the cupboard.

Therefore, an ability to understand that the mind represents and can misrepresent reality gives an extra dimension to our ability to interpret others' messages. There are obvious implications in terms of whether we thrive in situations depending on how effective we are at interpreting speech. Being an effective speech interpreter opens the door to the accumulated wisdom of previous generations of minds. One who was effective at this would thus have much better prospects than one who did not consider the mind behind the speech.

Robinson and Mitchell (1992; 1994; Mitchell & Robinson, in press) report surprisingly early competence in children's ability to interpret messages nonliterally by taking into account the speaker's false belief: Some children aged only three years and many aged four years succeeded in imposing the appropriate nonliteral interpretation; that Mum really wants the bag in the cupboard. The demonstration appeared especially impressive thanks to a control condition employing a story schematically identical to that described, except after John removed the bags he returned them to the same places, resulting in Mum's belief remaining a true one. Under this condition children nearly always judged correctly that Mum wanted the bag in the drawer, as she said. In other words, it seems that when children imposed a nonliteral interpretation when the bags swapped locations, this interpretation was dependent upon the speaker entertaining a false belief; they treated the message as a product of mental (mis)representation. This is a particularly important finding, because it forces us to revise previous suppositions; that not until children reach approximately six years of age do they come to understand that verbal messages emanate from the mind (e.g. Beal, 1988; Beal & Flavell, 1984; Bonitatibus, 1988; Robinson, this volume; Robinson & Whittaker, 1987).

How did we acquire this mind theorising capability phylogenetically? My suggestion on this is highly speculative, but nonetheless it is an important issue and we should rise to the challenge it presents. We can begin with the assumption that natural selection operates at the level of the individual rather than the species (Hamilton, 1964). A second assumption is that increasing cognitive sophistication is driven by adaptation to the environment, especially an environment that is changing (e.g. Dawkins, 1989). We can make the further assumption that, to some extent, cognitive abilities are compartmentalised. For example, children with Downs' syndrome are mentally retarded according to many measures on standard intelligence tests, yet perform reasonably well on tests designed to probe their understanding of mind (e.g. Baron-Cohen, 1991; Baron-Cohen et al., 1985). In contrast, we see the converse in children with autism: Some of these children perform very well on certain subscales of intelligence tests, usually those designed to probe spatial abilities, yet typically perform badly on tests that probe understanding of the mind. This goes to show that troughs and peaks in performance can be specific to domains of cognition, consistent with these domains possessing modular characteristics.

Somewhere in the murky past of our ancestry, cognition apparently blossomed as tool using evolved. This could have been in the form of expansion in imagination and insight; for example, insight into how an item normally associated with one situation could be used to good effect for a novel purpose in a completely different one: A small branch may usually serve as a handle while the individual eats the fruit from it, but could subsequently serve as a device for poking or measuring in another situation.

The imagination and insight in question might have taken the form of enhanced foresight and planning; for example, refraining from discarding a stick once it has been stripped of food, thanks to foresight that it could be exploited in a forthcoming situation, and then planning in detail (a process we might call "mental stimulation," cf. Harris, 1991; Humphrey, 1986) how best it could be used. We can see, then, that as foresight and planning are at the disposal of the individual, so the individual's behaviour would be predicted better on the basis of cognition rather than from external stimuli. This contrasts with the behaviour of a simple organism: It is highly predictable on the basis of external stimuli, in which case the organism's information processing offers little more than a relay service from stimulus to response. In order to understand behaviour from a simple organism, it is more useful to attend to stimuli that might elicit a response than to contemplate the role of mind in making a decision about which behaviour to execute. In other words, when predicting such behaviour one need only be a behaviourist, but this would be insufficient for predicting the behaviour of a cognitively complex organism such as a human.

A capacity for mental simulation, which could be necessary for competence in using tools, might not only serve as a stimulus provoking reasoning about the mind behind the behaviour, but could also confer upon the individual the cognitive machinery for contemplating mind. Whiten and Byrne (1991) note that the facility for mental simulation employed in tool using would also lend itself to simulating mind-states, such as beliefs. Chimpanzees are pre-eminent in tool using among nonhuman primates, and perhaps it is for this reason that they have the best theory of mind credentials besides humans (Whiten & Byrne, 1991). In this light, we see that the emergence of the mental simulation necessary for tool using provides both the stimulus and the instrument for the arrival of a theory of mind in humans.

We can suppose that as cognition became more prominent through the millennia, in planning and decision making (which presumably coincided with the ballooning of the brain), so behaviour became less predictable from external stimuli. Therefore, the mind of others became an increasingly important feature in predicting one's immediate environment. A change in the social environment in terms of behaviour becoming less predictable from external stimuli would therefore exert an evolutionary challenge to individuals, provoking the emergence of a capacity to understand the cognition that determines the behaviour of others. Meanwhile, the emergence of a more sophisticated mental simulation cognition would allow an ever more complex theory of mind reasoning.

An additional factor, as indicated previously, is the arrival of language in our species. Once language has evolved, there is evolutionary pressure for us to treat messages as expressions of internal representations, so that we may interpret messages more effectively by taking into account the speaker's representational state. The other side of the coin is that we would anticipate that people who severely lack understanding of mind would be poor communicators. Children with autism are putatively lacking in a theory of mind (e.g. Baron-Cohen et al., 1985), and in the framework presented here, it comes as no surprise that they are also notoriously poor at communication (Frith, 1989). In particular, unlike clinically normal children aged around four years, they do not take account of the speaker's false belief when interpreting her message; instead, they impose literal interpretations, just like many clinically normal three-year-olds (Mitchell & Isaacs, in press).

In sum, initial expansion of the brain, particularly the frontal cortex, may have resulted from the advantage given by increased faculty in planning, foresight, decision making, and language. It is perhaps no coincidence that the listed abilities are located in the frontal cortex, which has expanded more than other cortical regions in our recent evolutionary history. This increase in cognition would then make the social environment predictable more from mental representations and less from external stimuli. Therefore, an increased planning capability necessarily engenders accompanying evolutionary pressure for even further expansion of the brain in developing a potential to understand itself. The same applies regarding the emergence of language. Rudiments of the requisite cognition should have been ready-installed in the form of the mental simulation processes necessary for tool using. These pressures would be less prominent in other species because their behaviour is more predictable from external stimuli, they are usually not tool users, and they lack language. So it follows that humans would have the most impressive theory of mind in the animal kingdom.

ACKNOWLEDGEMENT OF MISREPRESENTATION IN YOUNG CHILDREN

If possession of a theory of mind is the product of evolutionary forces, then we might (but might not) expect an incipient manifestation of this very early in life, more as the product of genetic endowment than of experience (Fodor, 1992; Leslie & Thaiss, 1992; Mitchell, 1992). However, many researchers present evidence in support of the idea that not until children are aged four years do they acknowledge one fundamental feature of mind (e.g. Astington & Gopnik, 1988; 1991; Flavell, 1988; Perner, 1991; Wellman, 1990). They argue that young children fail to acknowledge that the mind can misrepresent, raising the possibility that they do not draw a distinction between mind and world so far as belief is concerned (though very young children do make some kind of distinction between mental and physical entities: Wellman & Bartsch, 1988; Wellman & Estes, 1986; Wellman & Woolley, 1990). Much of the evidence comes from the deceptive box test of false belief (Perner, Leekam, & Wimmer, 1987). According to this, many four-year-olds acknowledge false belief and therefore have a fundamental requisite for the possession of a mature theory of mind; they draw the mind–world distinction so far as belief is concerned. The same cannot be said of many three-year-olds.

Researchers have thus claimed that the emergence of a theory of mind is stage-like, taking the form of a radical conceptual shift, and that an understanding of false belief can be grasped (Sullivan & Winner, 1991, p. 170) "only after the age of 3:7." Gopnik and Wellman (1992) add that any early acknowledgment of false belief would merely be the product of an "auxiliary hypothesis" attached to the young child's nonrepresentational theory of mind. It is thus claimed (Astington & Gopnik, 1988, p. 204) that three-year-olds' difficulties in acknowledging misrepresentation in various guises "reflect a deep-seated and profound conceptual difference between three- and five-year-olds, and do not simply involve the demands of . . . specific tasks." These researchers apparently regard the absence of a correct judgement of false belief as mirroring a corresponding absence in a theory of mind intellect or capacity. Even if we accept the stage theory, the emergence of a theory of mind could still owe much to genetic inheritance, but with a stage-like development resulting from genetically controlled maturational forces.

However, other researchers (perhaps a minority) favour the idea of early theory of mind competence (e.g. Chandler, Fritz, & Hala, 1989; Fodor, 1992; Freeman, Lewis, & Doherty, 1991; Leslie, 1987; Lewis & Osborne, 1990; Mitchell & Lacohée, 1991; Robinson & Mitchell, 1992; Robinson, Mitchell, & Nye, 1992; Siegal & Beattie, 1991; Zaitchik, 1991), and some of these see early acknowledgement of false belief as evidence for the nativist hypothesis (e.g. Fodor, 1992; Leslie & Thaiss, 1992; Mitchell, 1992; Mitchell & Lacohée, 1991). These researchers are divided in opinion according to whether the classic test of false belief underestimates children because (1) its administration has not been sufficiently child based (Lewis, this volume; Lewis & Osborne, 1990; Siegal & Beattie, 1991; Siegal & Peterson, this volume), (2) it provides an insensitive measure of understanding misrepresentation (Chandler & Hala, this volume; Chandler et al., 1989; Freeman et al., 1991; Hala, Chandler, & Fritz, 1991), or (3) that understanding of misrepresentation is not the primary cause of children's failure and that another distinctive aspect of early cognition accounts for failure on the false belief task (Mitchell, 1992; Mitchell & Lacohée, 1991; Robinson, this volume; Robinson et al., 1992; Russell, Mauthner, Sharpe, & Tidswell, 1991). These latter authors focus on the salience reality holds for young children, and propose that this could mask a fledgling grasp of misrepresentation. This view maintains that we should not attend exclusively to the idea of absence of a correct false belief judgment reflecting an absence in underlying cognition, but rather we should be concerned with the presence of the realist judgement reflecting an underlying excessive reality orientation as a distinctive feature of early cognition.

Later, I argue that the third view has much greater merit than the other two. This is partly because the first two do not always stand up well to empirical test and partly because the third view offers a richer and more ecologically valid account of how and why development apparently takes place in the child's conception of misrepresentation. This is a view premised on the assumption that an understanding of belief is developmentally very primitive, probably innate. It also challenges the stage concept of theory of mind development, with the corollary that there is no radical conceptual shift occurring late in the child's fourth year. I shall expand on these ideas subsequently.

Regarding the first view expressed earlier, that children err on the false belief test because it is presented in a non-child-based way, researchers have focused on the possibility that children misinterpret the test question (Lewis & Osborne, 1990; Siegal & Beattie, 1991; Siegal & Peterson, this volume). The standard version is something to the effect, "What will Johnny think is in the tube?" or "What did you think was in the tube?" (e.g. Perner et al., 1987). Lewis and Osborne suggested that young children might interpret the question to mean, "What did you think was (or "What does Johnny think is ...) in the tube *after you (he) opened the lid and peeped inside*?" These authors correctly point out that in many test questions the time reference is vague. When they presented questions with more specific wording, by suffixing them with "first of all" and "before we opened the lid," they observed a considerable increase in correct judgements of "Smarties."

Although it is possible that in previous studies children sometimes failed to acknowledge misrepresentation due to misinterpretation of the test question, there must also be another factor influencing their judgements. First, many procedures have specific time reference thanks to the inclusion of the words "before" and "first" or other precise temporal markers, yet realist errors remained in abundance (Gopnik & Astington, 1988; Gopnik & Slaughter, 1991; Mitchell & Lacohée, 1991).

Second, children's errors are specific to cases of misrepresentation when the wording of the test question is held constant. This was demonstrated most elegantly by Wimmer and Hartl (1991). They assessed children's acknowledgement of their own false belief and, importantly, compared their performance on this with a control condition that was identical except that initially the Smarties tube contained Smarties, as one would normally expect. Having elicited a comment from the child that she thought the tube contained Smarties as it was first presented, the experimenter proceeded to confirm the child's supposition correct by revealing the familiar confectionery. At this point, while the child watched, the experimenter moved the Smarties from view and put pencils in the tube instead, closed the lid, and asked the standard test question. Under this control condition, many children judged correctly that when they first saw the tube they had thought there were Smarties inside.

The only difference between this control condition and that where the tube contained the unexpected content of pencils all along is that, in the control condition, making a correct judgement need not require the child to acknowledge misrepresentation. If the child misinterpreted the time reference in the test question, she would judge "pencils" under both these conditions, yet it turned out that many only gave such a realist judgement under the condition that engendered misrepresentation. It seems, then, that children's difficulty was specific to misrepresentation, rather than general to any incidental feature of the procedure such as misinterpretation of the question. In addition to this finding, the misinterpretation hypothesis is weakened further in view of a study by Lewis, Freeman, and Smith (1992), in which a temporarily specific test question failed to yield facilitation over one that did not include such explicit temporal reference.

The second view expressed earlier was that the classic test of false belief provides only an insensitive measure of the child's incipient insight into misrepresentation. Chandler and colleagues (Chandler, Fritz, & Hala, 1989; Hala, Chandler & Fritz, 1991; see also Chandler & Hala, this volume) have argued for evidence of early false belief reasoning via another route. They explored young children's ability to deceive in the form of manipulation of clues that would have the effect either of withholding information, misinforming, or both. In their procedure, a doll went to one of several locations where she deposited treasure that she was trying to hide from a second experimenter. The doll left tell-tale inky footprints, giving a clue to which of the locations she visited. Chandler alerted the observing child subject to these footprints and asked whether she could think of doing anything to prevent the second experimenter knowing the whereabouts of the treasure. On this cue, even children as young as two years promptly wiped away the footprints, and many proceeded to lay false trails to a location that was empty.

This seemed like powerful evidence to the effect that young children understand that misinformation gives rise to misrepresentation. The obvious interpretation of children's manipulation of clues seemed to be that they acted in order to make the second experimenter think the wrong thing regarding the location of the treasure. Putting it another way, presumably children would not manipulate clues if they did not grasp the significance of misrepresentation.

However, it now looks possible that young children manipulate clues without understanding the effect this would have on another person's representational state. Sodian, Taylor, Harris, and Perner (1991) repeated Chandler et al.'s (1989) procedure and began by confirming that very young children do indeed wipe away trails then make false ones when prompted to do so. Despite this, children made realist judgements about the other person's knowledge, saying that he would think the treasure was located where it really was located, thereby apparently failing to appreciate the relevance of false trails for misrepresentation. Moreover, they even laid false trails under a co-operative condition, when encouraged to assist the other person to find the treasure because he would then offer it to the child as a reward!

A control condition devised by Sodian (1991) suggests that children's difficulty with this task is specific to processing misrepresentation. This control task required the child to engage in sabotage, in the form of locking the container that housed the treasure, to prevent the other person procuring it. Young children were able to succeed at this, and selectively engaged in sabotage under a competitive condition, but refrained from doing so under a co-operative one. Yet they were unable to restrict their laying of false trails to a competitive condition. This shows that, despite young children apparently entering into the spirit of the game by attempting to prevent the other person getting the treasure, they failed to understand how manipulation of clues relates to this endeavour; it seems they did not understand that misinformation can give rise to misrepresentation.

Young children's difficulty with deception remains apparent even when they are given feedback over a series of trials, and even when reward is made contingent on their success. This was demonstrated by Russell, Mauthner, Sharpe, & Tidswell (1991; see also Boysen & Raskin, 1990). In their task, children were deprived of reward if they pointed to the location that actually housed a desirable item, because the other person would swiftly proceed to search at the indicated location, take out the item and then keep it for herself. If, however, the child pointed to the empty location, the other person would look there, not find the item, and so it would remain for the child to keep. Interestingly, children who pointed to the location that housed the item tended to persevere with this behaviour over all 20 trials, even though they were repeatedly confronted with the negative consequence of truthfully informing the other person. Evidently, failure to deceive is resistant to the effects of feedback and reward. Yet again the possibility of early understanding of misrepresentation via deception looks like a false alarm.

Freeman et al. (1991) also devised a procedure that they supposed would be more sensitive to early understanding of misrepresentation, compared with the classic task. This procedure employed the game of hide and seek, where the seeker peeped and, in doing so, witnessed the hider go into location A. Subsequently, unknown to the seeker, the hider then moved to B (compare with the tasks presented by Chandler & Hala, this volume). Young children observing the task frequently judged correctly that the seeker would first look for the hider in the empty location A. This could indeed be genuine evidence of early acknowledgement of misrepresentation, but it might be wise to reserve judgement on this until we know whether the children acknowledge verbally that the seeker thinks the wrong thing in connection with the hider's location. It is possible that children would make a realist error of judging that the seeker *thinks* the hider is in B, even if they judge correctly that the seeker would look in A. If so, it might be that children succeeded in a correct prediction of the protagonist's behaviour via some nonmetarepresentational route. In any case, Freeman et al. had difficulty generating the facilitation in their second experiment. Although they present a plausible explanation for this, a possibility remains that the facilitation was not genuine or robust.

We now turn to the third account of early understanding of misrepresentation. This is the idea that inability to grasp misrepresentation is not the primary cause of children's failure on the false belief task, but rather such errors are attributable to another cognitive characteristic: Namely, early childhood realism. In other words, when we say that children commit realist errors on the false belief task, this is not merely a convenient label, but is actually an explanatory concept: We assume that reality is highly salient to the young child, and this could mask a fledgling grasp of misrepresentation. The point here is that many researchers have focused on the idea of the absence of a correct judgement mirroring a certain absence in underlying cognitive functioning (lack of a capacity for acknowledging misrepresentation). What we ought to do, however, is focus on the presence of the distinctive realist judgement as a feature peculiar to early cognition, which raises the possibility that this intrudes on, and therefore masks or replaces, the child's reasoning about belief. In other words, the proposal is that realist errors are not a default option that appears in the absence of the child being able to generate a correct judgement of misrepresentation, but rather *prevent* the child from acknowledging misrepresentation.

Primitive versions of the reality-masking hypothesis are articulated by Mitchell and Lacohée (1991) and Russell et al. (1991), whereas more elaborated and polished versions are stated by Robinson et al. (1992) and Robinson and Mitchell (1994; see also Robinson, this volume). Briefly, the evidence for masking is as follows. Procedures that either enhance the salience of belief by identifying it with a physical characteristic, or those that reduce the salience of reality by de-emphasising its physical characteristic, should engender facilitation in terms of children's early acknowledgement of false belief. A corpus of evidence supports such a prediction.

Beliefs are provided with a physical counterpart when the behaviour based on false belief has already happened (Bartsch & Wellman, 1989; Moses & Flavell, 1990; Robinson & Mitchell, 1992). The first study listed was open to criticism (Perner, 1991; Wellman, 1990) and the second showed only a very weak effect, but Robinson and Mitchell report that children were much more effective at inferring which of two identical twins had gone to the wrong place to get his ball (the one who saw it move or the one who didn't), then at predicting where the twin who had been absent would go to look for his ball. Control experiments showed that the facilitation was not due to the reasoning being backwards (*pace* Bartsch & Wellman, 1989), from behaviour to belief. Rather, it became apparent that facilitation was generally due to the child making a link between physical evidence of wrong belief (in the form of wrong search) and conditions giving rise to false belief (being absent when the ball was transferred to its final location).

False beliefs were also provided with a physical counterpart, and thus presumably enhanced in salience, in Mitchell and Lacohée's (1991; also, see Freeman, this volume, for a development of this task) posting procedure. In this, children posted a picture that matched their expectation about the contents of the deceptive box. The picture then remained out of sight in a closed postbox until the end of the procedure. Meanwhile, the deceptive box was opened and the unexpected content revealed. Children were then asked what they had thought was in the box when they posted their picture. These children were better at reporting their prior belief than controls who posted an irrelevant picture and asked an identical test question. One might be tempted to criticise this study by supposing that children gave the "right" answer (e.g. "Smarties") by misinterpreting the question to refer to the picture on the posted card. However, this possibility can be rejected on the grounds that children never stated the item on the posted picture in the control condition, which involved a representationally irrelevant image.

Usually, misrepresentation has no contemporary basis in reality, and it might be that young children are led into judging wrongly because they are inclined to consult reality when evaluating belief. In the posting experiment, we endorsed the misrepresentation with a reality status, in the form of a picture residing in the postbox, and the test question directed the child to attend to this fact. We propose that it is for this reason that children were enabled to acknowledge their own misrepresentation. Under this condition, children could consult the reality of the content of the postbox, yet this would not lead them to a wrong judgement.

Another procedure we are presently exploring takes the posting idea a stage further. In the last experiment, the physicality of the belief was embodied in a posted picture. In a new procedure, a similar situation is effected with the help of video apparatus (Saltmarsh & Mitchell, in preparation). In this, the camera is credited with anthropomorphic qualities and, on initially seeing the deceptive box, the child is instructed to "tell the camera what's inside," and replies dutifully "Smarties." Then the experimenter ostentatiously switches off the camera, points it away, covers it with a hood and declares that it can no longer see or hear. The true content of pencils is revealed and then returned to the deceptive box.

Finally, children are invited to comment on their initial (mis)representation of the box's content.

Under one variant of this procedure, the experimenter played part of the video back to the child but, crucially, paused it just prior to the child saying "Smarties" on the video. Under the other condition, the experimenter did not do this. Under both conditions, however, the experimenter reminded the child that she (the child) had told the camera what was in the box earlier on (but without stating what the child had said in that utterance).

The findings were that only under the condition where the film was played back did facilitation occur. In contrast, under the nonplayback video procedure, realist errors were just as common as in a standard nonvideo test of false belief. We interpret this result to suggest that the video rigmarole in itself was insufficient to generate facilitation; only when the child was alerted to the possibility that her earlier behaviour (which involved articulating a misrepresentation) was preserved in a kind of artificial reality (i.e. stored in the video machine) did facilitation occur.

In a sense, this experiment goes some way to form a bridge between the posting procedure (Mitchell & Lacohée, 1991) and procedures that offer physical evidence of false belief in the form of the protagonist's wrong search (Bartsch & Wellman, 1989; Moses & Flavell, 1990; Robinson & Mitchell, 1993). The video procedure provided the child with a physical replay, or reminder in the pictorial domain, of behaviour immediately preceding her initial misrepresentation of the deceptive box. In the posting procedure, the posted picture provides a physical pictorial reminder, whereas in the procedure where wrong search has already taken place when the false belief judgement is made, the evidence of the wrong search serves as a physical anchor of the false belief.

Arguably, these procedures generate facilitation in children's correct judgements by raising the salience of belief, specifically by linking it with a physical counterpart so that it would no longer be masked by the child's preference to attend to a reality criterion. An alternative approach following the same theme would be to facilitate false belief acknowledgement by reducing the salience of certain physical characteristics of reality. This was effected by removing the desired object altogether in a variant of an unexpected transfer procedure (Wimmer & Perner, 1983; Russell & Jarrold, 1991). In a standard procedure, a protagonist witnessed a desired object in location A, but this was then moved to B in the protagonist's absence. Young children typically committed a realist judgement, saying that on his return the protagonist would think the object is in B. The modified procedure involved annihilating the object (the experimenter ate it!) instead of transferring it to B, and many young children then judged correctly that the protagonist would search in the empty location A.

Another way of de-emphasising the physical salience of reality is to communicate to the child subject what the reality is indirectly: via a verbal message or a picture (Robinson et al., 1992; Zaitchik, 1991). For example, the experimenter merely tells the child that the tube contains a pencil rather than show her. Again, under these protected conditions, children apparently find it easier to acknowledge false belief than they do in the classic task.

Moreover, when physical reality is absent and therefore prevented from intruding on the child's belief reasoning, we see impressive competence in the latter. This was demonstrated by Wellman and Bartsch (1988), who told children that Sam's puppy was either in the garage or under the porch. They then invited children to guess where the puppy was, which they were perfectly content to do. Suppose the child stated "garage," then Wellman and Bartsch would say that Sam thinks it is under the porch, and asked the child where Sam would look. If children egocentrically confused their own knowledge with Sam's, they would judge that he would look in the garage because that is where the child subject thinks it is. However, children rarely judged in this way, and instead they often judged correctly that Sam would look where he thinks the puppy is. It was only when Sam's belief contrasted with reality that children judged incorrectly. This example shows that young children can contrast their own thoughts with another person's, but only run into difficulty when required to contrast their thoughts with reality.

An additional finding of interest reported by Wellman and Bartsch (1988) was that young children were perfectly capable of judging that Sam's behaviour would be in accordance with his belief when reality was uncertain. For example, "Sam's puppy could either be in the garage or under the porch, but Sam thinks it's in the garage. Where will be look?" Children judged correctly that he would look in the garage. Once again, when reality was denied its usual prominence, due to a state of uncertainty surrounding it being imposed, children were able to engage in belief reasoning.

The reality-masking hypothesis does not predict that any manipulation that focuses the child's attention on belief would produce facilitation. Rather, it specifies the role of the physical: that normally this is a characteristic of reality but not the representational (compare with Butterworth, this volume). We might predict, therefore, that realist errors would remain even if the child's attention is alerted to the content of the belief. This manipulation was actually effected by Wellman and Bartsch (1988), already mentioned earlier, though with a view to testing a hypothesis other than the one being explored here. In the condition where it was communicated that Sam's puppy was really in the garage, children still committed very many realist errors when told explicitly that Sam thought it was under the porch: They judged that he would search in the garage. Lillard and Flavell (1992) followed a similar procedure, except they asked children where Sam thought the puppy was. In this case, all the child needed to do to get the correct answer was parrot the experimenter regarding Sam's belief, without reflecting on the misrepresentational implication of what was being said, yet they still made a realist judgement; they could have unthinkingly echoed the experimenter, yet did not do so. These authors did not contrast the explicit false belief condition with a classic task, so it remains possible that the former would generate facilitation over the latter. Nonetheless, according to an absolute criterion, the findings are consistent with the possibility that alerting children to the content of the false belief in the absence of a physical token is an ineffective method of yielding early false belief acknowledgement.

Another nonphysical way of alerting children to misrepresentation is to ask not what they thought was in the deceptive box but rather what they had said was inside (Gopnik & Slaughter, 1991; Wimmer & Hartl, 1991). Even in this procedure, realist judgements prevail, and this time a comparison has been made with the classic test, revealing no difference: Realist errors are in abundance. It is interesting that children should make a realist judgement when all they need do is echo what they said earlier without acknowledging the implications this has for mental misrepresentation (it is only an acknowledgement of verbal misrepresentation). In this case, the child is reminded of the content of her own false belief because the test question refers her back to her statement on the box's content when it was first presented. Again, however, highlighting the content of false belief in this way proves to be insufficient, perhaps because it lacks the crucial physical enhancement ingredient.

Although the reality-masking hypothesis suggests that many young children can acknowledge misrepresentation, we do not seek to claim that young children are competent mind theorists. On the contrary, the masking hypothesis helps to pinpoint the deficiency in the fledgling theory of mind. The child is loath to deviate from reality when contemplating representation: In other words, it reveals the nature of the child's problem rather than suggesting that the child does not have a problem.

How can we square this claim with the well-known fact that young children not only engage in pretence, but apparently have an appetite for it? In pretence, young children actively seek an alternative, nonreal way of representing common objects. The famous example presented by Leslie (1987; 1988) is of the two-year-old child pretending that a banana is a telephone. Leslie argues that such pretence demonstrates that the young child is capable of mentally creating an alternative reality, where the banana stands in for "telephone," whilst keeping track of the item's identity in true reality. In other words, when the child pretends that the banana is a telephone, she does not confuse the identity of this fruit with the thing that it stands in for. If there were such confusion, then we may find children attempting to eat the telephone, but they never do this!

Leslie (1987; 1988) argued that, if young children can entertain an alternative reality in pretence, then in principle they ought to be able to acknowledge misrepresentation, since (according to Leslie) the main cognitive challenge this poses is the giving of joint attention to two conflicting mental representations of a single situation. In this context, one of the mental representations has to be "decoupled" from reality, and considered strictly in relation to a distinctive propositional attitude, for example, "I believe that ..." or "I pretend that ...' Leslie suggested that the reason children have difficulty with misrepresentation, then, is because they fail to infer it on the premise of insufficient or misleading information. However, that argument now seems untenable (e.g. Pratt & Bryant, 1990; Wellman, 1990; Wimmer & Hartl, 1991).

Perner (1988; 1991; Perner, Baker, & Hutton, this volume) advanced an alternative account to help clear up the controversy. He pointed out that the pretender does not hold the representation of telephone in relation to the real item of banana as being true of the world, whereas when one holds a false belief, one does hold it as being true. That is, pretence is usually (but not always: Leslie & Frith, 1990) held as being untrue, whereas by definition beliefs (including veridically false ones) are held as being true; only in the latter case does it make sense to say that there is misrepresentation of reality. According to Perner, this difference accounts for the discrepancy in age of onset between pretence and acknowledgment of false belief. He suggests that acknowledging false belief entails representing the representational relation between mind and world, whereas that is not true of pretence.

Although it is possible to argue, as Perner does, that the reality criterion is relevant to acknowledgement of false belief but not to pretence, it still seems odd that children should engage in pretence if fundamentally they are realists; why do they actively seek a world that lacks a reality status if they are so concerned with reality?

One rather ironic possibility is that pretence is itself an expression of the child's concern about reality. This could even be evident in the banana/telephone example. Let us assume that, being a realist, the young child is naturally motivated to discover through her senses, and explore through her actions, what reality is all about. One common event that the child wishes to investigate is the mother speaking into the telephone. If the child is to get to grips with this feature of reality (speaking into telephones) then it would be useful to try out the activity (a behavioural simulation). The child may therefore pick up the handset and speak into it. This is a very common occurrence in families with young children. If the child is deprived of this experience, either by being reprimanded or by the phone being moved out of reach, then the child will switch to practising telephone skills with a substitute item, which in Leslie's example is a banana.

The case of the Olympic skier who practises her sport on a synthetic ski slope helps to illustrate the point. The skier is concerned with the reality of the snow, not with the synthetic material that she practices on. The latter just serves as a prop to help develop skills that hopefully will transfer to her activities on the piste. In this case, although the skier is deprived of full access to real snow, she nonetheless seeks to develop her skill in a substitute situation; a situation that does not provide an end in itself, given the skier's goal, but which does give a clue to the nature of the skier's concern about reality.

The case of the skier serves as an allegory of how we should view the young child's pretence. In pretence, the child is concerned with exploration of the reality that she is imitating rather than the alternative world she appears to create in the pretence mode; that the child has created an alternative world is not the central issue, rather the child's appetite for pretence is better described as an appetite for imitation of behaviour in others that is prominent in the real world. A difference between the child pretender and the skier is that the latter is explicitly motivated to practise, whereas the child apparently finds pretence intrinsically motivating. This suggests that, unlike the skier, the child's practice and exploration through pretence should be characterised as an automatic process, resulting from natural inclination (compare with Harris, this volume).

The possibility that pretence is geared towards practice in the form of "behaving as if" gets support from recent findings reported by Lillard (in 1993; this volume; Lillard & Flavell, 1992). She found that four-year-olds were able to acknowledge pretence when it was accompanied by action. Children judged that Jane was pretending there was a kitten in the box when Jane went through the motions of preparing the kitten's dinner. In contrast, children were unwilling to ascribe pretence to Jane, even when told explicitly that this was what she was doing, when her pretence was not accompanied by any behaviour. These contrasting findings raise the possibility that young children do not code pretence primarily as a mental state in which an alternative world is created. In this light, there is no contradiction between claiming that young children fail to acknowledge misrepresentation because they are realists, and the fact that they have an appetite for engaging in pretence.

Nonetheless, although we can view early pretence as an aid for exploring reality, its presence suggests that the child is able to make the real–mental distinction (Harris, this volume). Just as it is vital for the skier to identify the differences between the synthetic ski slope and real snow, so it must be that the child does not confuse pretence with reality. As Leslie (1987; 1988) argues, this could be a primitive yet useful test-run of the young child's metarepresentational machinery.

HOW DOES A THEORY OF MIND DEVELOP?

Finally, and importantly, we need to address ourselves to the developmental processes involved in children's transition from giving realist judgements to giving correct judgements of false belief. In particular, if they are competent to acknowledge misrepresentation before four years of age, as we claim they are, why do they not do so in practice—why would there be such a competence-performance discrepancy?

The child should be viewed as searching for a criterion by which to answer the false belief question. When contemplating belief, two criteria are pertinent. One is the state of the person's representational mind and the other is the aspect of reality that the belief is about. The latter is necessary, since a defining feature of "belief" is that it is held to be about reality. If it were a representation not concerned with reality, then it would be appropriate to call it fantasy or hypothesis. In most cases, the content of the representation and the state of reality actually coincide, so we can focus on the reality criterion and suppose this also applies for the representational criterion. We can thus treat beliefs as though they are transparent to reality, effectively conceptualising "belief" as factual.

In the case of false belief, however, one criterion cannot be matched for content with the other, and each has to be treated as substantive. For we adults, a representational criterion holds prominence, and we are able to attend to this in the case of false belief. It seems that many researchers tacitly suppose that the young child's failure to acknowledge false belief in a symptom of absence of a representational criterion (e.g. Gopnik & Wellman, 1992; Perner, 1991; Sullivan & Winner, 1991). However, it is conceivable that a representational criterion is already installed and operational very early in development, but failure to acknowledge false belief is due to a representational criterion holding low prominence relative to a realist one.

In this respect, we see development as the representational criterion gradually beginning to assume more prominence and indeed precedence over the reality criterion when appropriate. As such, development takes the form of a smooth transition rather than conceptual revolution, with the corollary that it would be possible to bias the child to attend to one criterion in preference to the other with certain experimental manipulations. In terms of early realist judgements, then, to put it most simply, the child knows about misrepresentation yet prefers to answer according to a physical reality criterion because that is more salient or relevant to her. This raises the question of why a physical reality criterion should be prominent in the young child's cognition.

The reason, we suggest, is because the issue of reality has great relevance to the existence of the young child relative to that of the older one.

Conversely, mind as a modeller of reality holds much greater relevance to the older child compared with the younger.

Reality holds great relevance for the young child because she will be unable to sustain an independent existence if she does not master the nature of her physical environment. For example, in Western culture, the child has to learn how to use utensils for eating, how to use the toilet, how to get in and out of her cot or bed without doing herself a serious injury, and so on. The physical environment is far from static and predictable so far as human infants are concerned. This is so for at least two reasons. First, humans have a nomadic characteristic, and show a flexibility in preference for their habitat that is seldom seen in other creatures. Humans live in a wide variety of geographical terrains and climatic regions, venturing well beyond the rain forest of their immediate ancestors.

Second, humans have an aptitude for imposing change on their environment, sometimes to a detrimental degree, and enjoy introducing gadgets. The latter is no doubt a legacy of our Homo habilis ancestry. The scale of this intervention far exceeds anything we witness in other creatures. Humans, then, both seek novel environments and are instrumental in change to their environment. For these reasons, human newborns must have a flexibility that allows them to attune and adapt rapidly to whatever manifestation their environment takes. This would not be necessary in the case of animals, which survive in a more predictable habitat. Information written in the genetic material of such creatures can be premised on a predictable environment. This could, of course, lead to the threat of extinction should a change of environment be imposed on these creatures, such as that introduced by industrial development.

In the case of humans, in contrast, the prospect of a changing environment is apparently built into the constitution. This might take the form of the very young child entertaining a heavy focus on reality, an heuristic serving to establish rapidly what reality is like. As hinted earlier, one manifestation of this could be in the child's engagement in pretence, where she apparently explores aspects of reality not immediately available, through a behavioural simulation (e.g. exploring the telephone by using a banana as a substitute).

Giving such priority to physical matters of the environment could result in a corresponding low priority to misrepresentation that lacks a reality status, even if the cognitive faculty for processing this should be available to the child. Additionally, however, we could argue that not only is physical reality dominant in the child's cognition, but also the concept of misrepresentation would, independently, hold little relevance. Indeed, attending to the possibility of misrepresentation could be a disadvantage, as expanded later.

As proposed earlier, understanding misrepresentation is of relevance to us in several respects. Two of these are: (1) it gives an advantage in our relationships with others, both in dealing with enemies and in making friends; (2) it enables us to interpret the mind that resides behind the message, resulting in successful communication (Robinson & Mitchell, 1992). Although misrepresentation is highly relevant to older children and adults for the reasons stated earlier, it is less relevant, and indeed could be a disadvantage, for young children.

Misrepresentation lacks relevance for young children where relationships with others are concerned. A young child has neither the psychological or physical capability, nor the world knowledge, to sustain an existence independently of a caregiver, whereas that is not necessarily true of an older child. The primary caregiver will be highly motivated to act in the child's best interests, due to a bond of attachment having formed between her and the infant (e.g. Ainsworth, Blehar, Waters, & Wall, 1978; Klaus & Kennell, 1976). Note that this is presumably a mechanism selected naturally because it is likely to ensure that parents provide the necessary care to promote the health and development of a child in whom they would almost certainly have considerable genetic investment. As such, the caregiver's mind (motives, intentions, attitudes, beliefs, etc.) would not be relevant to the child, since the caregiver will spontaneously provide an umbrella of protection and care. That is, the child need not actively go to any lengths to please or manipulate the caregiver, and the caregiver will usually (though not always) feel pleased with the child almost regardless of what the child does.

Since the child is so dependent on the caregiver, she will rarely venture beyond the boundary of protection offered by her. In this sense, the very young child has not yet entered the social realm of people who have no special investment in her well-being. When the child enters the social domain she will then, perhaps for the first time, be confronted with the opposing interests of potential adversaries. Until that time, it is usually of no relevance to the child to reason about the psychological states of adversaries.

Acknowledging misrepresentation not only lacks relevance but could actually be a disadvantage so far as the child's language development is concerned. As already mentioned, understanding misrepresentation in others is an advantage to adults insofar as they can interpret the message correctly (i.e. nonliterally) by taking into consideration the speaker's misrepresentation concerning the thing he is trying to communicate about. For example, if the speaker says the food is in the cupboard, we may infer that really it is in the fridge on recognising that the speaker did not know that the food had transferred from the cupboard to the fridge. In doing this reinterpretation of the message's literal meaning, we substitute "cupboard" with "fridge." That is, we take the speaker's word "cupboard" to refer to the thing that keeps food cold, has an enamelled metal exterior, periodically makes a buzzing noise, plugs into a power point, has plastic-coated wire shelves, and so on. In other words, when we reinterpret an utterance on the basis of the speaker's misrepresentation, we necessarily assume that there is no inevitable correspondence between a word articulated by another person and a given item in the world that he means.

However, if a young child operated on this assumption, it could pose a serious impediment to her vocabulary development. For example, if the child experienced uncertainty about whether the word "cupboard" referred to a cupboard or a fridge or both, then she would be disadvantaged in her vocabulary development compared with a child who felt no doubt about the relation between words and objects. The latter child necessarily would not consider the speaker's cognition when interpreting his message.

Once the child has achieved considerable consolidation in her vocabulary, then she would be at liberty to consider special circumstances of a speaker uttering words that only map onto a model of reality residing inside the speaker's mind (cf. Karmiloff-Smith, 1986). In other words, the child first has to make most of the important discoveries about her environment, including the names people give to things, and only then would she feel disposed to consider misrepresentation, whether verbal or mental.

Young children could, perhaps, be pressed into attending more to misrepresentation if they have an early confrontation with other minds that entertain interests conflicting with the child's own. Although the child is certain to meet unrelated individuals when venturing beyond the bounds of the immediate family at an age appropriate to do this, it does not necessarily follow that a conflict of interests will be absent within the family. If the child has siblings, then despite shared genetic constitution, there will still be competition for attention and resources. This could sharpen an ability to reason about mind in a quest to avoid being duped and exploited. In other words, the social conflict could serve to direct attention to the psychology residing behind the behaviour.

We predict, then, that theory of mind activity would be better developed in young children who have siblings. This prediction gets support from a study by Perner, Ruffman, and Leekam (in press), who found a significant relation between acknowledging false belief and having siblings. This emerges as an intriguing finding, because it suggests that the kind of cognition involved in theory of mind abilities is of a different order compared with that involved in other intellectual feats. For example, Zajonc (1983) reports a negative correlation between number of siblings and performance on an IQ test.

Development of a shift in attention away from a reality criterion and towards a representational one might be stimulated by ways other than encountering people who entertain conflicting interests. Dunn, Brown, Slomkowski, Tesla, and Youngblade (1991; see also Dunn, this volume) conducted a longitudinal study attempting to identify factors that precipitated acknowledgement of misrepresentation. They found that children who were most effective at this, especially in the form of explaining wrong search by reference to false belief, tended to be the ones who, six months previously, had been engaged by their mothers in conversations about causality of behaviour.

The findings reported by Dunn et al. (1991) could be interpreted within a Vygotskian framework (Kozulin, 1990). The parent who engages her child in conversation about causality could be viewed as providing a tutoring service, not necessarily consciously, on the psychology that lies behind human action. This could help the child to recognise the relevance of a representational criterion such that it does not always take second place to a physical reality criterion.

Continuing with the Vygotskian theme, perhaps we ought to concern ourselves with the child's expression of competence with adult help. That is, we should seek to identify the zone of proximal development. Early false belief reasoning, elicited by prompting, would give weight to the claim that a capability to cognise misrepresentation is present from a very early age. The absence of its expression, however, reflects the possibility that it is not a relevant tool for the child to have at her disposal until such time that the child is projected more into the social realm.

Perhaps the simplest and most obvious way to provide adult assistance is to tell the child what the correct answer is. For example, in a deceptive box procedure, we could replace the usual test question with a suggestion of the form, "When you first saw this box, you thought there were Smarties inside, didn't you?" Using this procedure, we (Steverson & Mitchell, 1992) have discovered that very nearly all children aged three years, including those who fail a classic test of false belief, are perfectly willing to accept the suggestion of misrepresentation.

Superficially, one might suppose that the force of the suggestion was such that children would accept it no matter what the content. Fortunately, we ruled out such a possibility with the following control. In an "untrue suggestion" condition, the experimenter said, "When you first saw this box, you thought there were Jelly Babies inside, didn't you?" Children nearly always correctly rejected this suggestion. Importantly, those who failed a classic test of false belief were significantly much more likely to accept the true suggestion (Smarties) than the false one (Jelly Babies).

Although children were easily able to identify a true suggestion while rejecting a false one, we subsequently found that this did not extend to all false suggestions, for instance, a suggestion that indicated the realist option (Steverson & Mitchell, 1993). Indeed, even quite old children accepted this kind of false suggestion. In this variant, we said, "When you first saw this tube, you thought there were pencils inside, didn't you?", and even children aged four and five years, who had no difficulty with the classic test of false belief, tended to agree. Meanwhile, as with the earlier study, children rejected an untrue suggestion that did not mention the realist option.

These findings provide strong evidence to suggest that how children answer false belief questions depends on what criterion (realist versus representational) they attend to. Various procedures can bias children to attend early to a representational criterion, but it is also possible to bias them later in development to revert to a reality criterion. This makes children's performance on false belief tests seem most unlike their performance on other age-dependent tests. For example, it is extremely difficult to make children revert to a nonconserving judgement even when one is suggested to the child (e.g. Russell, 1982). This provides credibility for the idea that development is stage-like in the case of conservation. It thus follows that reversion to realist judgements in the case of false belief testifies to a non-stage-like characteristic of development in this domain.

The account I present shows that human infants should be characterised primarily as realists according to the ethological and ecological perspective adopted. Despite special reasons for supposing that humans in particular should be born with a realist bias, it would not be surprising if our closest animal cousins shared this bias to some extent, merely due to proximity on the evolutionary tree. Evidence we can interpret as realism in chimps is reported by Boysen and Raskin (1990). Using a task similar to that employed by Russell et al. (1991, see earlier), chimp Sara played a competitive game with a second chimp, Sheba. Sweets were in two locations. In one of these was four sweets and in another only two. Sara was obliged to inform Sheba about one, but only one, of these locations. Sheba would act upon the information by searching there and devour the goodies. The remaining sweets in the other location then became available for Sara. In other words, Sara was effectively rewarded for informing Sheba about the smaller quantity. Despite this, Sara persevered in informing Sheba about the larger quantity, thus depriving herself of this prize.

However, when the game was played symbolically, where tokens served to represent two and four sweets in the two locations, Sara now successfully informed Sheba about the location, which resulted in the latter gaining the smaller prize. Interestingly, Sara reverted to informing Sheba of the location of the larger prize when the game with real objects resumed. These findings suggest that Sara had difficulty detaching herself from the reality of the larger prize that she was attempting to misinform Sheba about. When the symbolic version of the game had the effect of detaching her from that reality, Sara was then able to succeed. It seems, then, that a realist bias resembling that seen in humans might exist also in chimps, disrupting their ability to manipulate the mind and behaviour of adversaries. This gives a further evolutionary credibility to the reality-masking hypothesis presented in this chapter.

CONCLUSION

To sum up, the view I have tried to advocate is that children possess the machinery for processing misrepresentation very early in life and that certain rudiments of this ability are more the product of genetic endowment than world experience. However, such ability is not much in evidence until the child is typically aged around four years. This is because the child prefers to refer to a reality criterion when making judgements, which is the consequence of an excessive but adaptive focus on reality early in development; focus on psychological matters, especially those pertaining to misrepresentation, only assumes relevance later, particularly when the child is projected into the social realm.

Procedures can reveal early acknowledgement of false belief by artificially adjusting the salience of reality relative to belief, by manipulating the physical characteristics of either belief or reality. In doing so they simultaneously reveal an early theory of mind reasoning and that young children have a preference for a reality criterion when making judgements. Theory of mind reasoning can be identified independently by the experimenter by explicitly suggesting misrepresentation as the appropriate criterion. Similarly, reversion to the immature response will result from explicit suggestion of reality as an appropriate criterion for judgement.

With this account, we see that development is not stage-like, at least in terms of a cognitive revolution at the age of four years. We are also able to square the claim that young children do indeed possess fundamentals of a theory of mind yet spontaneously give a realist judgement when performing on a classic test of false belief. We also see that early failure to acknowledge false belief should be viewed not as an absence (of reasoning about representations) but as a presence (of finding the realist criterion irresistible).

ACKNOWLEDGEMENTS

Thanks are due to John Archer, Paul Harris, Elizabeth Robinson, Rebecca Saltmarsh, and Andrew Whiten for their expert comments on an earlier draft.

REFERENCES

Ainsworth, M.D.S., Blehar, M., Waters, E., & Wall, S. (1978). *Patterns of attachment*. London: Lawrence Erlbaum Associates Ltd.

Astington, J.W., & Gopnik, A. (1988). Knowing you've changed your mind: Children's understanding of representational change. In J.W. Astington, P.L. Harris, & D.R. Olson (Eds.), *Developing theories of mind* (pp. 193–206). Cambridge: Cambridge University Press.

Astington, J.W., & Gopnik, A. (1991). Theoretical explanations of children's understanding of the mind. *British Journal of Developmental Psychology, 9*, 7–32.

Baron-Cohen, S. (1991). The theory of mind deficit in autism: How specific is it? *British Journal of Developmental Psychology, 9*, 301–314.

Baron-Cohen, S., Leslie, A.M., & Frith, U. (1985). Does the autistic child have a "theory of mind"? *Cognition, 21*, 37–46.

Bartsch, K., & Wellman, H.M. (1989). Young children's attribution of action to beliefs and desires. *Child Development, 60*, 946–964.

Beal, C.R. (1988). Children's knowledge about representations of intended meaning. In J.W. Astington, P.L. Harris, & D.R. Olson (Eds.), *Developing theories of mind* (pp. 315–325). Cambridge: Cambridge University Press.

Beal, C.R., & Flavell, J.H. (1984). Development of the ability to distinguish between communicative intention and literal message meaning. *Child Development, 55*, 920–928.

Bonitatibus, G. (1988). What is said and what is meant in referential communication. In J.W. Astington, P.L. Harris, & D.R. Olson (Eds.), *Developing theories of mind* (pp. 326–338). Cambridge: Cambridge University Press.

Boysen, S.T., & Raskin, L.S. (1990). Symbolically facilitated discrimination of quantities by chimpanzees. *Bulletin of the Psychonomic Society, 28*, 500.

Chandler, M., Fritz, A.S., & Hala, S. (1989). Small-scale deceit: Deception as a marker of two-, three-, and four-year-olds' early theories of mind. *Child Development, 60*, 1263–1277.

Crook, J.H. (1980). *The evolution of human consciousness.* Oxford: Clarendon Press.

Dawkins, R. (1989). *The selfish gene* (2nd edn.). Oxford: Oxford University Press.

Dunn, J., Brown, J., Slomkowski, C., Tesla, C., & Youngblade, L. (1991). Young children's understanding of other people's feelings and beliefs: Individual differences and their antecedents. *Child Development, 62*, 1352–1366.

Flavell, J.H. (1988). The development of children's knowledge about the mind: From cognitive connections to mental representations. In J.W. Astington, P.L. Harris, & D.R. Olson (Eds.), *Developing theories of mind* (pp. 244–267). Cambridge: Cambridge University Press.

Fodor, J.A. (1992). A theory of the child's theory of mind. *Cognition, 44*, 283–296.

Freeman, N.H., Lewis, C., & Doherty, M.J. (1991). Preschoolers' grasp for a desire for knowledge in false-belief prediction: Practical intelligence and verbal report. *British Journal of Developmental Psychology, 9*, 139–158.

Frith, U. (1989). *Autism: Explaining the enigma.* Oxford: Blackwell.

Gopnik, A., & Astington, J.W. (1988). Children's understanding of representational change and its relation to the understanding of false-belief and the appearance-reality distinction. *Child Development, 59*, 26–37.

Gopnik, A., & Slaughter, V. (1991). Young children's understanding of changes in their mental states. *Child Development, 62*, 98–110.

Gopnik, A., & Wellman, H.M. (1992). Why the child's theory of mind really is a theory. *Mind and Language, 7*, 145–171.

Hala, S., Chandler, M., & Fritz, A.S. (1991). Fledgling theories of mind: Deception as a maker of three-year-olds' understanding of false belief. *Child Development, 62*, 83–97.

Hamilton, W.D. (1964). The genetic theory of social behaviour. I and II. *Journal of Theoretical Biology, 7*, 1–52.

Harris, P.L. (1991). The work of the imagination. In A. Whiten (Ed.), *Natural theories of mind.* Oxford: Blackwell.

Hewstone, M. (1989). *Causal attribution: From cognitive processes to collective beliefs.* Oxford: Basil Blackwell.

Humphrey, N.K. (1980). Nature's psychologists. In B. Josephson & V. Ramachandran (Eds.), *Consciousness and the physical world.* London: Pergamon.

Humphrey, N.K. (1983). *Consciousness regained.* Oxford: Oxford University Press.

Humphrey, N.K. (1986). *The inner eye*. London: Faber & Faber.

Karmiloff-Smith, A. (1986). From meta processes to conscious access: Evidence from children's metalinguistic and repair data. *Cognition, 23*, 95–147.

Klaus, H.M., & Kennell, J.H. (1976). *Maternal infancy bonding*. St. Louis: Mosby.

Kozulin, A. (1990). *Vygotsky's psychology: A biography of ideas*. London: Harvester Wheatsheaf.

Krebs, J.R., & Dawkins, R. (1984). Animal signals: Mind reading and manipulation. In J.R. Krebs & N. Davies (Eds.), *Behavioural ecology: An evolutionary approach*. Oxford: Blackwell.

Leslie, A.M. (1987). Pretence and representation: The origins of "theory of mind." *Psychological Review, 94*, 412–426.

Leslie, A.M. (1988). Some implications of pretence for mechanisms underlying the child's theory of mind. In J.W. Astington, P.L. Harris, & D.R. Olson (Eds.), *Developing theories of mind*. Cambridge: Cambridge University Press.

Leslie, A.M., & Frith, U. (1990). Prospects for a cognitive neuropsychology of autism: Hobson's choice. *Psychological Review, 97*, 122–131.

Leslie, A.M., & Thaiss, L. (1992). Domain specificity in conceptual development: Neuropsychological evidence from autism. *Cognition, 43*, 225–251.

Lewis, C., & Osborne, A. (1990). Three-year-olds' problems with false belief: Conceptual deficit or linguistic artifact? *Child Development, 61*, 1514–1519.

Lewis, C.N., Freeman, N.H., & Smith, C. (1992). *Dissociation of inferences about beliefs and pictures in preschoolers*. Unpublished manuscript, University of Lancaster.

Lillard, A.S. (1993). Young children's conceptualization of pretence: Action or mental representational state? *Child Development, 64*, 372–386.

Lillard, A.S., & Flavell, J.H. (1992). Young children's understanding of different mental verbs. *Developmental Psychology, 28*, 626–634.

Mitchell, P. (1992). Réalité et représentation du monde, une distinction innée? *La Recherche, 23*, 1332–1333.

Mitchell, P., & Isaacs, J.E. (in press). Understanding of verbal representation in children with autism: The case of referential opacity. *British Journal of Developmental Psychology*.

Mitchell, P., & Lacohée, H. (1991). Children's early understanding of false belief. *Cognition, 39*, 107–127.

Mitchell, P., & Robinson, E.J. (in press). Discrepant messages resulting from a false belief: Children's evaluations. *Child Development*.

Moses, L.J., & Flavell, J.H. (1990). Inferring false beliefs from actions and reactions. *Child Development, 61*, 929–945.

Perner, J. (1988). Developing semantics for theories of mind: From propositional attitudes to mental representation. In J.W. Astington, P.L. Harris, & D.R. Olson (Eds.), *Developing theories of mind*. Cambridge: Cambridge University Press.

Perner, J. (1991). *Understanding the representational mind*. London: MIT Press.

Perner, J., Leekam, S.R., & Wimmer, H. (1987). Three-year-olds' difficulty with false belief: The case for a conceptual deficit. *British Journal of Developmental Psychology, 5*, 125–137.

Perner, J., Ruffman, T., & Leekam, S.R. (in press). Theory of mind is contagious: You catch it from your sibs. *Child development*.

Pratt, C., & Bryant, P. (1990). Young children understand that looking leads to knowing (so long as they are looking down a single barrel). *Child Development, 91*, 973–982.

Robinson, E.J., & Mitchell, P. (1992). Children's interpretation of messages from a speaker with a false belief. *Child Development, 63*, 639–652.

Robinson, E.J., & Mitchell, P. (1993) *Masking of children's early understanding of the representational mind: Backwards explanation versus prediction*. Unpublished manuscript, University of Birmingham.

Robinson, E.J., & Mitchell, P. (1994). Young children's false belief reasoning: Interpretation of messages is no easier than the classic task. *Developmental Psychology*.

Robinson, E.J., Mitchell, P., & Nye, R. (1992). *Young children's understanding of indirect sources of knowledge*. Paper presented at the BPS Developmental Section Conference, September, Edinburgh.

Robinson, E.J., & Whittaker, S.J. (1987). Children's conceptions of relations between messages, meanings, and reality. *British Journal of Developmental Psychology*, 5, 81–90.

Russell, J. (1982). Propositional attitudes. In M. Beveridge (Ed.), *Children thinking through language*. London: Edward Arnold.

Russell, J., & Jarrold, C. (1991). *The role of the object in deception and false belief tasks*. Unpublished manuscript, University of Cambridge.

Russell, J., Mauthner, N., Sharpe, S., & Tidswell, T. (1991). The "windows task" as a measure of strategic deception in preschoolers and autistic subjects. *British Journal of Developmental Psychology*, 90, 331–350.

Saltmarsh, R., & Mitchell, P. (in preparation). *Being confronted by a film of oneself: Videoing as an aid to false belief acknowledgment*. Work in preparation, University College, Swansea.

Siegal, M., & Beattie, K. (1991). Where to look first for children's knowledge of false beliefs. *Cognition*, 38, 1–12.

Sodian, B. (1991). The development of deception in young children. *British Journal of Developmental Psychology*, 9, 173–188.

Sodian, B., Taylor, C., Harris, P.L., & Perner, J. (1991). Early deception and the child's theory of mind: False traits and genuine markers. *Child Development*, 62, 468–483.

Steverson, E.J., & Mitchell, P. (1992). *The suggestibility of false belief*. Paper presented at the BPS Developmental Section Conference, September, Edinburgh.

Steverson, E.J., & Mitchell, P. (1993). *Late realist judgments on a false belief task: Reversion provoked by suggestion*. Unpublished manuscript, University College, Swansea.

Sullivan, K., & Winner, E. (1991). When three-year-olds understand ignorance, false belief and representational change. *British Journal of Developmental Psychology*, 9, 159–172.

Wellman, H.M. (1990). *The child's theory of mind*. London: MIT Press.

Wellman, H.M., & Bartsch, K. (1988). Young children's reasoning about beliefs. *Cognition*, 30, 239–277.

Wellman, H.M., & Estes, D. (1986). Early understanding of mental entities: A re-examination of childhood realism. *Child Development*, 57, 910–923.

Wellman, H.M., & Woolley, J.D. (1990). From simple desires to ordinary beliefs: The early development of everyday psychology. *Cognition*, 35, 245–275.

Whiten, A. (1992). Evolving theories of mind: The nature of non-verbal mentalism in other primates. In S. Baron-Cohen, H. Tager-Flusberg, D. Cohen, & F. Volkmar (Eds.), *Understanding other minds: Perspectives from autism*. Oxford: Oxford University Press.

Whiten, A., & Byrne, R.W. (1988). Tactical deception in primates. *Behavioural and Brain Sciences*, 11, 233–273.

Whiten, A., & Byrne, R.W. (1991). The emergence of metarepresentation in human ontogeny and primate phylogeny. In A. Whiten (Ed.), *Natural theories of mind*. Oxford: Blackwell.

Wimmer, H., & Hartl, M. (1991). Against the Cartesian view on mind: Young children's difficulty with own false beliefs. *British Journal of Developmental Psychology*, 9, 125–138.

Wimmer, H., & Perner, J. (1983). Beliefs about beliefs: Representation and constraining function of wrong beliefs in young children's understanding of deception. *Cognition*, 13, 103–128.

Zaitchik, D. (1991). Is only seeing really believing? Sources of the true belief in the false belief task. *Cognitive Development*, 6, 91–103.

Zajonc, R.B. (1983). Validating the confluence model. *Psychological Bulletin*, 93, 457–480.

3

Grades of Mindreading

Andrew Whiten
University of St. Andrews, UK

INTRODUCTION

The origins of an understanding of mind can be sought on several different timescales. One scale is that of human development, perhaps the most accessible to empirical investigation and certainly the area of most vigorous research in recent years, as demonstrated by this volume and its ancestors (Astington, Harris, & Olson, 1988; Butterworth, Harris, Leslie, & Wellman, 1991; Frye & Moore, 1991; Whiten, 1991). At the other extreme is the evolutionary timescale. The ability to understand mind, which develops in our species, did not spring out of nowhere: it must have had more primitive evolutionary beginnings. Although many details of these origins may be lost to empirical study, comparative research, particularly on our closest primate relatives, is beginning to shed light on the roots of mindreading (Whiten, 1993). So we should be thinking about origins on at least these two very different timescales. In addition, we should remember that the two are not separate, but interactive processes. Evolutionary change is moulded through successive developmental cycles and therefore influenced by the processes and products of ontogeny (Baldwin, 1902): Conversely, developmental processes are themselves the products of evolution and their nature may therefore often be understood in functional terms—as taking the particular ontogenetic course they do for adaptive reasons. For example, it may be beneficial for the human infant initially to be focused on the reading of certain mental states, rather than others, in its caretakers (see Mitchell, this volume; Dunn, this volume).

Between these two timescales, there is the historical one. We shall be less concerned with it here, but its existence should be remembered. The "folk psychology" or "folk theory of mind" (Heider, 1958; Wundt, 1916) that children appear to acquire itself has origins in historical and cultural processes. These have shaped the language in which we talk about states of mind and, presumably, unlike the processes we may distinguish as evolutionary, have led to divergent understandings of mind in different cultures (Heelas & Lock, 1981). These understandings can hardly fail to influence what the children of each culture learn; but in turn we must acknowledge that the cultural processes must have built on and interacted with social cognitive abilities that evolution bequeathed our species. I suggest, therefore, that the origins of understanding of mind lie in a complex web of ontogenetic, historical, and evolutionary factors. We cannot understand the first of these adequately if we neglect the other two.

We should also recognise diversity—the main theme of this paper (and arguably, of this book)—when we consider what counts as an "understanding of mind." The answer depends, of course, on what we mean by "understanding" and by "mind" (Whiten & Perner, 1991). Neither of these are neatly circumscribed concepts: But this is for good reason, and I am going to advocate that we acknowledge and indeed exploit the fact that grades of both can be discriminated, which is of obvious relevance when we are interested in processes of developmental or evolutionary elaboration. If we seek the origins of an understanding of mind, we shall need to examine a range of phenomena, from potential precursors, through marginal and superficial cases of mindreading, to the deep and sophisticated diagnoses of others' mental lives, which may eventually be built on such foundations.

My aim in this chapter is to map the scope of what needs to go into the melting pot if we seek to understand the origins of people's everyday "understanding of mind." What different ideas, concepts, types of experiment and observations, species of animals, and ages of children do we need to entertain? I shall start by sketching what I see as some of the extremes in analyses of the nature of mindreading, to emphasise the potentially enormous—not to mention fascinating—breadth of our subject matter.

MINDREADING, INTERSUBJECTIVITY, THEORY OF MIND—DIFFERENT APPROACHES TO A COMMON THEME

One way to begin to appreciate this breadth is to list some of the many terms and concepts—variations on the theme of mindreading—that have proliferated in the literature (Table 3.1). Some of these are sufficiently similar in meaning to be used interchangeably, as synonyms. Others appear to express very different ideas of what shall count as reading the mind.

TABLE 3.1
Alternative Labels for, and Concepts about, Mindreading (a Partial List)

FOLK PSYCHOLOGY (Wundt, 1916)

CONSCIOUSNESS OF THE FEELING OF THEIR
FELLOWS (Thorndike, 1911)

IMPUTATION TO OTHERS OF FIRST-HAND
EXPERIENCE (Lloyd Morgan, 1930)

NAIVE PSYCHOLOGY (Heider, 1958)

SECOND-ORDER INTENTIONALITY (Dennett, 1971)

INTERSUBJECTIVITY (Trevarthen, 1977)

THEORY OF MIND (Premack & Woodruff, 1978)

METAREPRESENTATION (Pylyshyn, 1978)

BELIEF-DESIRE REASONING (Davidson, 1980)

NATURAL PSYCHOLOGY (Humphrey, 1980)

SOCIAL REFERENCING (Feinman, 1982)

MINDREADING (Krebs & Dawkins, 1984)

MENTAL SIMULATION (Gordon, 1986)

MENTALISING (Morton, 1989)

PERCEPTION OF INTENTIONALITY (Dasser et al., 1989)

(MENTAL) ATTRIBUTION (Cheney & Seyfarth, 1990)

MENTALISTIC THEORY OF BEHAVIOUR (Perner, 1991)

REPRESENTATIONAL THEORY OF MIND (Perner, 1991)

Theory of Mind

The most familiar expression to students of developmental psychology will be "theory of mind," as used by Premack and Woodruff (1978, p. 515), who first asked "Does the chimpanzee have a theory of mind?": "In saying that an individual has a theory of mind, we mean that the individual imputes mental states to himself and to others... A system of inferences of this kind is properly viewed as a theory, first, because such states are not directly observable, and second, because the system can be used to make predictions, specifically about the behaviour of other organisms."

The expression "theory of mind" has been adopted enthusiastically by a network of researchers in child development (e.g. Butterworth et al., 1991). On the basis of Premack and Woodruff's paper and suggestions made by the philosophers Bennett, Dennett, and Harman in the peer commentary on the paper, Wimmer and Perner (1983) designed tests for children's ability to ascribe one particular mental state—(false) belief—which has come to assume special significance in this research area (see Mitchell & Lewis, this volume). This is because a child's recognition that others may hold beliefs that are false (about states of the world that the child knows to be true) entails an appreciation that others may represent the state of the world in a way different to that used by the child itself. Perner (1991) thus refers to such a child as achieving a "representational theory of mind," and it can be argued that such a representational theory expresses a deep grasp of the nature of mind. In the classic test of false belief attribution (what Mitchell & Lewis, this volume, distinguish as the "unexpected transfer test"), the child-mentalist will recognise that, even though she herself believes an object is in locus A, another person may represent reality differently, believing the object is in locus B because, unlike the child, he did not witness the shift from B to A (Wimmer & Perner, 1983).

Tests of such false-belief attribution have been used to legislate on whether the child "has a theory of mind." For example, failure on such tests was the basis for a negative answer to the question "Does the autistic child have a theory of mind?" (Baron-Cohen, Leslie, & Frith, 1985), and to many researchers it is the ability to attribute false belief that marks the average four-year-old's acquisition of an explicit theory of mind (Light, 1993; and see Mitchell & Lewis, this volume).

There are grades of complexity within this idea of a "Theory of Mind" (T-o-M), which will beg closer scrutiny later. At this point, however, I want to contrast the concept of T-o-M with other concepts which, although sharing the central focus of interest, are nevertheless drastically different. For these comparative purposes it is sufficient to emphasise two things in the story so far. First, the basic ability is seen as recognising states of mind (or mental states). This is taken to be inherent in the everyday folk psychology utilised by adults, the function of which appears to lie in the provision of a scheme that facilitates powerful prediction and explanation of others' actions. Second, the ability has been argued by many to be a quite sophisticated cognitive achievement, emerging clearly only in four-year-old children. No nonhuman primate has yet passed a test for the attribution of false belief (Premack, 1988; Whiten, 1993). Compare, then, two further concepts that emerged in ethology between the time of the Premack and Woodruff paper and the beginnings of the present explosion of research in child development.

Natural Psychology and Mindreading

For ethologists, the starting point of any journey of scientific discovery must be the natural behaviour of the organisms concerned, and this is no less true in the present case. Humphrey (1976) sought an answer to the question of why monkeys and apes are so intelligent in the problems they had to deal with in their everyday lives. His observations led him to the hypothesis that the answer lay not in the complexity of their physical ecology, such as the nature and distribution of their food sources, but rather in their social complexity. Subsequent research has dissected this social complexity and revealed anthropoid primates to be skilled social operators (Byrne & Whiten, 1988), using tactics ranging from deception (Whiten & Byrne, 1988a), to alliances with powerful others (Harcourt & de Waal, 1992), which manipulate the social environment to their advantage. Of course each individual is playing out such tactics in a social environment made up of skilled, like-minded others, so that we must envisage these social interactions as an escalating "game." As in many formalised human games, from chess to basketball, the optimal tactics will vary according to the intentions, knowledge, and motivations of one's opponents: in a word, their states of mind. We might therefore expect these societies to be evolutionary hotbeds selecting for the cognitive abilities that would allow the recognition of such states, as suggested by Humphrey (1980; 1986). A primate who, in Humphrey's expression, could act as one of "nature's psychologists," reading the true intentions of others before they acted, might get one step ahead in the game (see Mitchell, this volume, for further discussion of the utility of mentalism).

Humphrey's speculations were grounded in the everyday lives of anthropoid primates and other socially complex mammals like wolves and elephants. Dawkins and Krebs' (1978) analyses were set in a yet wider ethological perspective. The first step in their analysis involved pointing out that the classic assumption about the nature of animal communication signals, that their function has evolved to facilitate the transfer of information about the animal's motivational state (e.g. its intentions), is not so consistent with evolutionary theory as was first thought. Instead, we should expect natural selection to have favoured information transmission that manipulates others to the (reproductive, or genetic) benefit of the self. Although in some, or many, cases this can be achieved by co-operative and honest communication, the fact that the "bottom line" is manipulation of others to the self's benefit means that, wherever it pays, communication will be selected not to correspond with the true internal state. The relevance to the subject matter of this paper is clear: Once this lack of correspondence emerges, a selection pressure will exist for animals to avoid such manipulation by attempting to discern the true internal state—the true state of mind—of the protagonist. Krebs and Dawkins (1984) and Dawkins (1992) thus present a very general argument for natural selection to favour the emergence of an ability for what they called "mindreading." The argument would appear to apply in principle to all animals who communicate with their conspecifics: to all those vertebrates and invertebrates, who, for example, either threaten or court other animals.

We thus appear to have a vast difference amongst concepts of what might be involved in taking account of states of mind in others, and which organisms might have such capacities. At one extreme, amongst some researchers there is debate about whether a true "theory of mind" is the province of any children less than four years of age (e.g. Chandler, Fritz, & Hala, 1989), or whether it can be ascribed to such an intelligent animal as our closest living relative, the chimpanzee (Whiten, 1993). At the other extreme, in the ethologists' theorising just reviewed, we appear to have a general argument for the reasons that the recognition of mental states should be widespread in nature (Krebs & Dawkins, 1984; Dawkins, 1992 are coy of being too specific about just which animals might deserve the label "mindreader").

There could be several reasons for this apparent gulf. One is that, theoretical arguments notwithstanding, nonhuman animals and very young humans are not, in fact, mindreaders. That might be (for example) because mindreading requires cognitive processes unique to the size and/or organisation of the human brain in middle childhood. Another possibility is that people are really talking about different things: That it is misleading to think of all the expressions in Table 3.1 as anything like close synonyms. I think that there is some truth in each of these answers. There are important differences between some of the concepts labelled in Table 3.1, although these have yet to be made explicit: When they are, we may well find ontogenetic and phylogenetic differences in their expression. However, equally important is that the concepts share sufficient meaning such that all of them are of potential relevance to understanding developmental and evolutionary transitions. If the ethologists' term "mindreading" is justified at all, it must in some sense involve taking into account "states of mind!"

We shall therefore scrutinise the meaning and significance of these concepts further in the following paragraphs. In particular, we need to examine more closely just what is the difference between what is implied by the expressions in Table 3.1 and the most obvious alternative to them: In the absence of mindreading, it is "just behaviour" that is read. "Mentalism" is the term in Table 3.1 which most precisely expresses this contrast with "behaviourism." However, the distinction is not so straightforward as it looks on first sight (Whiten, 1993). Whenever I say that I can read the mind of my daughter, I am not claiming telepathy: However well I do it, the achievement has to be based on direct observations of behaviour (the actions of my daughter and perhaps others) and its context (the world within which she perceives and acts). We therefore need to consider rather carefully just where the analysis of states of behaviour/world becomes the analysis of states of mind. Before doing that, however, there are still other major frontiers in the landscape of mindreading which should be mentioned at the outset.

Intersubjectivity

Some who have studied the micro-structure of social interactions in human infancy carefully—the vocalisations, gestures, and facial expressions that occur when babies and their parents "talk" to each other—have concluded that these scenes are best described as a meeting of minds. Intersubjectivity literally means the sharing of subjective states: It is a term borrowed from philosophy of mind and, applied to parent–infant interactions, it has been defined (Trevarthen, 1977) as "the mutual adjustments of conscious voluntary agents (subjects) to one another's mental states." Primary intersubjectivity refers to an early and "purely social" mental meshing of the infant directly with the parent: Secondary intersubjectivity is distinguished when infant and parent are able to incorporate objects into this sensitivity, as in the case of achieving joint attention on some locus in their environment (Trevarthen & Hubley, 1978).

The reference to mental states in the definition of intersubjectivity implies that it is within our remit: It is some grade of mindreading—but what? Attempts to relate the work in this area to the new T-o-M literature are so far few, tentative, and controversial (Karmiloff-Smith, 1993; Leekam, 1991; 1993; Perner, 1991; Reddy, 1991). You will not even find "intersubjectivity" in the index of principal T-o-M monographs (Harris, 1989; Perner, 1991; Wellman, 1990). In the present volume, however, see especially Butterworth, and Baldwin and Moses, on the related concept of "social referencing."

Perception of Intentionality

Many years ago, Michotte showed that our recognition of physical causality could be manipulated by small changes in visual displays: For example, the tendency to see the movement of an object A as being caused by object B can be reduced or eliminated by delays between impact and movement, and by physical separation (Michotte, 1963), and such phenomena have been investigated in human infants (Leslie, 1982). Heider and Simmel (1944) and, more recently, Dasser, Ulbaek, and Premack (1989) showed that similar effects can be obtained for the perception of intentional states, or "psychological causality." Abstract objects enacted what could be seen as a narrative sequence. In one example from Dasser et al., a ball fell down a small incline, and was "helped" up again by another ball. Young children were shown to attend differentially to such patterns, versus control patterns in which the movement of the balls were the same, but displayed in a different order such that intentions (helping, in the example above) would not be apparent. Such results raise similar questions to those provoked by some other concepts in Table 3.1. They seem to imply some form of mentalism, which in this case involves imputing automatically certain intentional states, normally associated only with living beings, to abstract shapes that move in the right way.

WHEN DOES READING BEHAVIOUR BECOME READING MIND?

The question of whether a child or a nonhuman animal has reached the stage of truly recognising states of mind is typically contrasted with the likelihood that the organism concerned is instead merely reacting to the behaviour of others. Cheney and Seyfarth (1990a; 1990b), for example, conclude from negative results of tests for knowledge attribution in macaques that these monkeys are poor psychologists, even though excellent ethologists: They are very good at making fine distinctions only at the level of the behaviour of their companions. Likewise, Perner (1991, p. 128) suggests that human infants, in allowing their mother's expression of fear to influence their decision about crossing a potentially dangerous ledge (Sorce, Emde, Campos, & Klinnert, 1985), are not applying an implicit theory of mind in which fear is recognised as a mental state: rather, they may be following a behavioural rule that "when you see something dubious and your mother is watching you and shows a fearful face, then avoid that object or area."

However, we noted earlier that mindreading is not telepathy: The minds of others have to be read in observables, which inevitably brings us back to behaviour. Indeed, Krebs and Dawkins (1984, p. 386) make quite explicit reference to the way in which the predictive function of mindreading, as they conceive of it, must be based on behavioural analysis:

> Animals can, in principle, forecast the behaviour of other animals, because sequences of animal behaviour follow statistical rules. Ethologists discover the rules systematically by recording long sequences of behaviour and analysing them statistically, for example by transition matrices, and in the same way an animal can behave as if it is predicting another individual's future behaviour ... we may use the term mindreading as a catch-word to describe what we are doing when we use statistical laws to predict what an animal will do next. [Or, presumably, when any organism makes these predictions.]

In one sense, I must agree with this analysis. The possibility of reading others' mental states must be based on certain statistical patterns in what is directly observable in the world (behaviour and environmental context): These would seem to offer the only data available. However, if the trick of prediction were to lie only in analysing linear sequences—"fear-expression predicts withdrawal behaviour," for example—then behaviour-reading would be as apt a description as mindreading. In other words, the pattern of observations that underlies the recognition of mental states has to be of a certain special character. I have suggested elsewhere (Whiten, 1993) that the key pattern must be akin to that which begged the recognition of "intervening variables" in an earlier phase in the development of the science of psychology.

Mental States as Intervening Variables

A well-known example of the original rationale for recognising intervening variables is shown in Fig. 3.1. The first diagram represents the fact that it is possible to show that any of a rat's behavioural tendencies listed on the right can be predicted from the conditions listed on the left: Thus, nine stimulus-response links need to be represented, as indicated by the arrows. In the second diagram, a more economical representation of this knowledge is offered by replacing the nine links with only six, together with an intervening variable interposed as shown. The value of the posited intervening variable is influenced by changes in the states of the variables on the left, and in turn influences those on the right. We can think of this intervening variable as a state the animal can be in, which can take different values. In this case an apt label for the variable is "thirst."

My suggestion is that the recognition of a mental state—whether this is achieved by a human adult, an infant, or a monkey—shares key similarities with the recognition of such intervening variables by behavioural scientists. In particular, the important difference between a mental state (e.g. fear) and a behavioural one (e.g. looking scared, fleeing) is similar to that between an intervening variable like thirst in Fig. 3.1b, and any one of the variables on the left or right: The mental state must lie at the centre of some web of observed conditions and predicted outcomes. Precisely because it stands here at the centre, it provides an *economical* representation of the state of the observed organism. This economy seems one likely reason why everyday psychology is mentalist rather than behavioural. However, this eminently plausible proposition presents a paradox. If mental states are the most economical units in which to code the action pattern of others, shouldn't this be the primitive way of operating, observable in animals and infants? After all, millions of years of hominid evolution and thousands of years of human history passed before "behaviourism" got invented. The answer to this conundrum may lie in distinguishing two aspects of cognitive mechanisms underlying mindreading. The ability to detect state patterns (fear, knowledge, and so on) in the first place may require extensive cognitive resources. By contrast, the routine classification of further events into such a framework may be efficient of cognitive resources. In addition, mental states as intervening variables are potentially powerful, productive representations. If all predictions were done on the basis of recognising

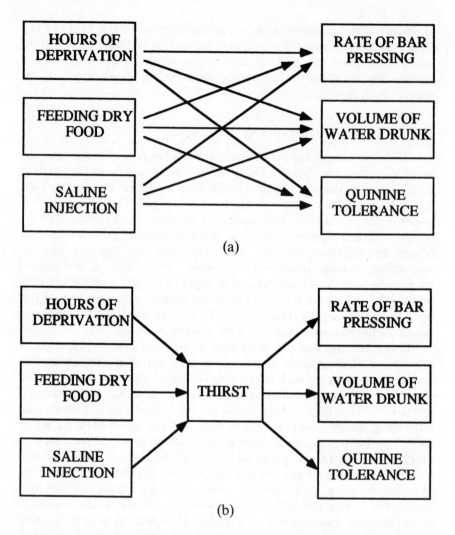

FIG. 3.1   (a) shows relationships between three independent and three dependent variables relating to rats' drinking behaviour; (b) shows a more economical representation incorporating an intervening variable, here labelled "thirst" (after Miller, 1959; Hinde, 1970).

individual S–R links, as in Fig. 3.1a, then only those specific contingencies can be handled. By contrast, once an intervening state like thirst is posited, novel predictions can be generated. For example, a new input condition, observed to be correlated with only some of the outcomes on the right, leads us to predict that the new input condition will also affect other output conditions not yet observed to be linked with this input.

Figure 3.2 shows a hypothetical example for a mental state of wanting: A baboon Y codes various different specific observations of baboon X (on the left) in the same way: The equivalence class is "X wants the meat." Irrespective of the basis on which this state of meat-wanting is recognised, it then predicts various consequences (on the right) that Y can utilise in making adaptive decisions about how to behave, according to the local circumstances (e.g. Y might be in naked competition with X, or alternatively may be seeking to befriend X: in each case the coding of X as wanting the meat can be put to appropriate, but different, effect). It follows that mindreading, as defined in this way, will only be of use (i.e. it would be

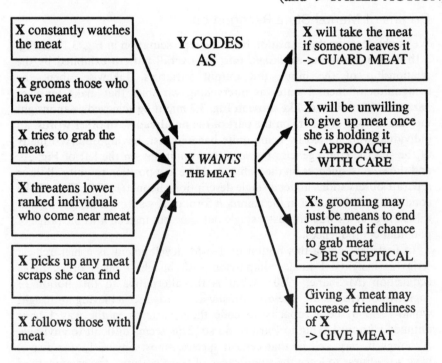

FIG. 3.2 A hypothetical example of mindreading as the recognition of an intervening variable in the course of repeated and varied interactions of two baboons, X and Y, over a meat carcass, which is generally a source of significant competition. In this example a mental state of *wanting* is recognised in X by a mindreader Y, permitting various predictions about X and appropriate courses of action on Y's part. Here *wanting* has the status of an intervening variable that economically represents the relationships between observations of X listed on the left, and outcomes for X listed on the right.

expected to develop/evolve) in a creature with a certain degree of intelligence and potential for flexibility of action: Otherwise, prediction of others' further actions and generation of appropriate responses can be handled by a small set of linear sequences.

This analysis of what mental states "are" to the mindreader suggests that any attempt simply to dichotomise mentalism and behaviourism is likely to dissolve into gradations. If mentalism can be boiled down to a kind of complex behaviour/context pattern recognition, the process of recognising a mental state can, in principle, always be described alternatively in terms of the pattern of behaviour/context on which it rests: It is just that as the pattern becomes more complex, it becomes uneconomic to do so. Simple mentalism would thus appear to grade into complex behaviourism.

Origins of Mental State Recognition

We might describe the transition from the representation in Fig. 3.1a to Fig. 3.1b as demonstrating an *insight* into the overall pattern exhibited by the relationship of the input and output variables. Likewise, then, the recognition of mental states as intervening variables that make sense of patterns of correlations like those in Fig. 3.2 might be achieved as an insight into the actions of others on the part of the mindreader. In other words, an individual who started by being quite behaviourist, having observed many of the specific contingencies between the conditions on the left of Fig. 3.2 and those consequences on the right, would be in a position to unite all these separate observations under a single description (Bennett, 1991): That all the conditions can be coded in the common form of X wanting a thing, and that this state of X affords not just a single outcome but instead a whole range of potential consequences.

In first developing this notion of T-o-M development as a hierarchical series of insights, I made comparison with insight models of language acquisition (McShane, 1980). What is the alternative to this notion of cognitive development? The only drastic alternative to achieving an insight would seem to be a capacity to code these patterns in the way I have outlined without having to learn to do so. This seems difficult to envisage. Although it may well be that certain species—most obviously our own— have a readiness to learn the significance of these patterns, the exemplars of conditions and consequences (as in Fig. 3.2) are so local and concrete that their recognition would probably be achieved through active information processing, rather than be given. This is supported by the circumstantial evidence that mental state attribution is accelerated in children's development in richer social contexts (Dunn, Brown, & Beardsall, 1991a; Dunn et al., 1991; Perner, Ruffman, & Leekam, in press).

However, in the case of the language-acquiring human child, the situation is of course different to that for preverbal infants or nonverbal animals. The child appears to acquire a folk psychology, which is richly described in the terms of everyday language—Johnson-Laird and Oatley (1989) list 590 English terms that describe emotions alone—and the child develops her ability to mentalise in the context of such talk. To whatever extent the recognition of mental states depends on the achievement of insights into the causal structure of human action, the language of mental states has the capacity to point the child towards selection of the most productive intervening variables. Andrew Lock (1980) aptly titled a treatise on language acquisition "The guided reinvention of language": Most children probably exemplify "the guided reinvention of mentalism." Any non-human primate who discriminates a mental state must, by contrast, achieve this without any such cultural, linguistic guide. That this is not necessarily a very radical possibility, is suggested by the likelihood that in the course of human history/evolution, the naming of these states postdated the initial recognition of them, which would therefore have been preverbal by definition (Whiten, 1993).

Implications for the Identification of Mentalism

The logic of the intervening variables account of mental states is that the identification of mindreading is unlikely to lie in the one-shot experiment (Heyes, 1993). Even a classic false belief test can be solved by the use of a behavioural rule—"people tend to search for an object in the place they last saw it hidden." That the subject is discriminating a mental state as an intervening variable can really only be established in a variety of contexts, which yield convergent evidence. Ideally, the mental state should be created in a number of ways, and evidence sought that the candidate mindreader can discriminate this state as a means to achieving different ends. An example of the first of these requirements comes from a study by Povinelli, Nelson, and Boysen (1990) on chimpanzees' ability to discriminate between potential helpers who are either knowledgeable or ignorant of the location of a reward. In a first series of tests, ignorance was created by absence from the scene, but a critical transfer test created the ignorant state in a different way, by covering the eyes. An example of the second requirement, applying the hypothesised attribution to different contexts for which that mental state is appropriate, comes from Wimmer and Perner's (1983) original experiments on false belief attribution, where the child was tested for appropriate application of false belief recognition to very different contexts of competition versus co-operation with others.

All too few experiments have manipulated variations of both ends of the web in the centre of which mental states sit logically. However, even though this may not be done in the case of individual studies, convergence of evidence has occurred in a more general way, so that particular mindreading competence is becoming pinpointed for children at a certain age (or, in Heyes' [in press] terms, "triangulated"); the "unexpected transfer" and "deceptive box" tests representing two alternative contexts for revealing the attribution of false belief (see Mitchell & Lewis, this volume).

IMPLICIT VERSUS EXPLICIT MINDREADING

It is sometimes suggested that a distinction can be made between an advanced grade of mindreading that is *explicit*, and an *implicit* grade that precedes and perhaps gives rise to it: In other words, what is initially implicit may become explicit, either in development (e.g. Bretherton, McNew, & Beeghly-Smith, 1981) or in evolution (e.g. Gomez, 1991). However, I suspect that two different types of distinction are at stake here, in what is meant by implicit versus explicit. I shall consider each in turn.

What is Read–Implicit Mind or Explicit Mind?

Gomez (1991) has described the development of a young gorilla's techniques for getting a human to unlatch a door. In the earliest phase the gorilla treated the human like an object, merely attempting to drag to the door and even climbing on them to release the latch. However, with time, the youngster developed communication strategies, during which she would more gently guide the human towards the door, alternating her gaze at the latch and at the humans' eyes. As Gomez says (1991, p. 201): "she seemed to use eye contact to monitor if the human was *attending* to her request that he act. Thus, she seemed to understand that in subjects perceiving is causally related to acting. And here is where the mind appears, since the co-ordination between perceptions and actions is carried out by the mind." Gomez compares this to the stage of secondary intersubjectivity in human infancy, because (1991, p. 202) it is: "based on an understanding of people as subjective entities, whose autonomous behaviour can be influenced through a special kind of causal contact: mutual attention. This development seems to coincide with that of preverbal human infants at around 12 months, when they begin to communicate with adults about external objects."

Gomez is making an important point with respect to the origins of an understanding of mind. Even though what the gorilla (or human infant) is recognising can be described in fairly straightforward external terms, such as direction of eye gaze and unlatching actions, her recognition of the significance of the integrated pattern of these means that she is attending to crucial perceptual foundations of a more advanced model of mind.

However, the difficulty in calling this an implicit theory of mind (or in another of Gomez's expressions, a "latent hypothesis of mind") lies in the very ease of redescription in simple behavioural terms: We are brought back to our discussion of mentalism versus behaviourism. "Mindreading," as defined by Krebs and Dawkins and discussed at the start of this paper, seems to suffer the same difficulty, insofar as it reflects merely the ability of organism A to predict what B will do next on the basis of a previously observed sequence of behaviour. One can object that, in the end, not only known sequences but *all* sequences of behaviour are organised by a mind, so that to read behaviour is always implicitly to read mind! This, of course, makes a mockery of any attempt to make an interesting distinction between behaviourism and mentalism. What is special about cases such as that described by Gomez is that the observables the animal is attending to constitute a pattern that incorporates causally connected evidence of perceptions and actions.

Still, the Gomez gorilla example fits the Krebs and Dawkins formulation of mindreading, in that what was described appeared to be a specific technique for getting a particular job done—opening the latch. If such an animal were to go further and utilise attention to others' gaze patterns for other purposes, then one would be more justified in talking of the ape recognising attention as a mental state; and if the candidate mindreader also utilised other evidence of attention, such as pointing or talking, to similar ends, then one would be more justified still (I suspect that this appeal to convergent evidence is what we do when, in everyday life and without any experiments, we confidently talk of a child having come to distinguish when others are attending to things). What this amounts to is that the organism is classifying a mental state (in this case, attention) as unifying a web of input conditions and outcomes in the manner of an intervening variable, as described in an earlier section of this chapter. And once this happens, it becomes appropriate to talk of a state of mind being read not only as implicit in behaviour, but as explicitly recognised, coded as a unique state in the mindreaders' brain. So that is one sense in which a distinction between implicit and explicit mindreading should be made. *Explicit* means there is a mental coding in the mindreader that, uniquely, picks out the mental state as the unifying factor in very diverse observations. *Implicit* means that the only mind being read is implicit in others' actions and it is only the latter that the observer is mentally coding: So, given the extent to which mind is always implicit in animals' behaviour, other criteria need to be applied to justify why some mindreading in this category is of interest. One such case is where what is discriminated is a perception-action cluster, like that described earlier for Gomez's gorilla.

Is Mindreading Implicated or Explicated?

The second dichotomy that can be labelled implicit/explicit hinges on the more advanced, explicit grade being distinguished by the individual's ability to represent the underlying mindreading rule independently. In operational terms, this translates into whether they can verbally explain an understanding underlying their actions. An example comes from the work of Povinelli and deBlois (1991), who repeated the tests described earlier for chimpanzees, with children. In these tests, success depended on an ability to discriminate knowledgeable helpers from ignorant ones who could only guess about the location of a hidden reward. Four-year-old children usually succeeded where three-year-olds failed, and the successful children were able to offer verbal explanations for their choice; these exemplified explicit mentalism. In this experiment, there was no obvious case of implicit mentalism—those who succeeded could give explanations, whereas those who failed tended not to be able to do so. In other experiments, however, children have been found to be capable of taking the right course of nonverbal action according to the belief state of another individual, and yet to fail in verbal responses (Freeman, Lewis, & Doherty, 1991). The verbalisations in this case were not explanations as such, but the results suggest that there may be cases where children can take a course of action that proves they recognise a certain mental state, yet cannot explain how they do so: their mentalism would then be implicit in the sense I am discussing it here. In the case of the chimpanzees tested by Povinelli et al., their lack of language means we cannot decide the issue either way. For these animals, the implicit/explicit distinction discussed in the previous section is the one that can be pursued empirically.

GRADES OF MENTAL STATE THAT CAN BE READ

There are theoretical reasons why certain mental states would be expected to be more difficult to diagnose, and results of a now extensive catalogue of experiments and observations on children and nonhuman animals appear to fit with theory—although, compared to the number of mental states folk psychology covers (e.g. D'Andrade, 1987), the list of those whose ascription has been investigated is small. The special significance of false belief recognition was outlined early in this chapter. Accordingly, it has been the most studied attribution. Many studies have concurred in the conclusion that this is difficult to demonstrate in children younger than about four years of age (Astington & Gopnik, 1991; Leekam, 1993 for reviews; Perner, 1991), although a growing literature documents controversies and conditions that appear to facilitate expression at earlier ages (Chandler et al., 1989; Dunn, 1991; Freeman et al., 1991; McGregor & Whiten, 1993; and see Mitchell & Lewis, this volume).

Children can recognise other mental states at earlier ages, however, and there is convergent evidence that autistic children who fail to attribute false belief can succeed with some of those states. Such states include other epistemic categories like knowledge (versus ignorance) (Leslie & Frith, 1988; Pratt & Bryant, 1990); intention (Astington & Gopnik, 1991; Shultz & Shamash, 1981; wanting (Wellman, 1991) emotions like happy and sad (Harris, 1989; 1991); and seeing (Baron-Cohen, 1991; Flavell, Everett, Croft, & Flavell, 1981). There appear to be parallels here with evidence for mindreading in primates, as reviewed by Whiten (1991b; 1993). Thus, experiments (Premack, 1988) and observations of tactical deception in chimpanzees (Whiten & Byrne, 1988a; 1988b; Byrne & Whiten, 1992) have failed to provide convincing evidence of the attribution or intentional creation of false beliefs in others: However, there is evidence from these same sources for the recognition of wanting/intention (see also Premack & Woodruff, 1978) and the seeing–knowing complex (see also Povinelli et al., 1990; Whiten, 1993). Monkeys, much more distantly related to us than are chimpanzees, have yielded only negative evidence on these counts (Cheney & Seyfarth, 1990a; 1990b; Povinelli, Parks, & Novak, 1992), although records of deception provide tentative support for their ability to compute the visual perspective of others (to recognise that sometimes others cannot see what they themselves can see)—what Flavell et al. (1981) labelled Level-1 understanding of seeing.

Thus, amongst these folk psychology states of mind, there appear to be grades of cognitive difficulty when it comes to reading them. Very crudely, one might say this gradation corresponds to the depth of penetration that the mindreader makes into the mind of the other: Level-1 seeing is very much on the behavioural surface, wanting and intention less clearly so, and false belief much less so—the conditions for this last state not even requiring the person acquiring the belief to twitch a muscle.

Perner (1991), arguing that it is only at the level of false belief ascription that children achieve a truly "representational theory of mind," has classed the earlier achievements as those of a "mentalistic theory of behaviour." In the terms I used earlier in this paper, this idea of a mentalistic theory of behaviour translates into the gaining of an insight into states of mind acting as intervening variables. The achievement of the higher grade of mindreading, in which the nature of representation is appreciated, could represent a further insight that older children, and perhaps not other animals, achieve (see Robinson, this volume).

READING ONE'S OWN MIND VERSUS OTHERS'

I have couched much of the foregoing discussion as if the only minds a mindreader reads are those of other individuals. However, the ethologist

Humphrey (1980) suggested that individuals might be able to use their own privileged access to their mental states to model the way the mind works in a way useful to the trick of reading the apparently less accessible minds of others. This idea was developed by philosophers (e.g. Gordon, 1986) and psychologists (Harris, 1991) and, now dubbed the "simulation theory" of mind, has been contrasted with the "theory theory" of mind in vigorous theoretical and empirical debates (see the journal *Mind and Language*, *Volume 7*). The theory theory suggests that, rather than use her own mind to simulate others', the mindreader employs mental states as theoretical constructs that predict and explain others' actions. I will not dwell on this controversy because it is dealt with in other chapters (Freeman, Harris, this volume). However, it demands mention here because of the implication that, if the simulation theory is right, reading one's own mind is a different grade of mindreading to that of reading others': It should be easier, and one apparent prediction is that specific mental states, such as ignorance, would be recognised in self before others. However, this is disputed (Gopnik, 1993).

COUSINS OF MINDREADING

Two phenomena that have been discussed recently in the theory of mind literature are pretence and imitation. These are marginal instances of mindreading per se, insofar as folk psychology does not tend to talk about a child indulging in pretend play by itself, or imitating another, in terms of their attributing any mental states to either self or other. However, psychologists have suggested that links exist in both cases.

In the case of pretence, Leslie (1987) argued that, as in T-o-M, metarepresentation is implicated: The child engaged in pretend play must hold in mind both the primary representation of the reality before it, and the pretend representation derived from the primary one. Perner (1991) has argued against this, that a distinction should be made between what is achieved in pretence, which as Leslie noted occurs in two-year-olds, and the achievement in four-year-olds of a representational theory of mind. In the latter, the nature of representation is grasped by the child in a way that Perner proposes is unnecessary for explaining pretence. Instead, Perner proposes that, in the prior stage of the child's mentalistic theory of behaviour, the level of representation achieved is best thought of as secondary representation rather than metarepresentation in the strong sense. Secondary representations are about hypothetical situations (the child is a "situation theorist") rather than about the representational power of certain mental states.

I find Perner's dissection of representational development into these three levels—primary, secondary, and meta—compelling. Whereas previous papers (Whiten, 1988; Whiten & Byrne, 1991) followed up Leslie's insight by arguing that certain records of elaborate pretend play documented in chimpanzees are consistent with their mindreading because metarepresentation is implicated, Perner's analysis leads me to the more modest interpretation that the chimps' pretence and mindreading are at the secondary level, which would be consistent with the pretence and mindreading of two- to three-year-old children.

Whiten and Byrne (1991), having noted the pretence-mindreading linkage in both nonhuman primates and children (and the linked deficit/delay in both and in autistic children), went on to observe that, amongst nonhuman primates, the pattern appears to extend to imitation, in which chimpanzees again outperform monkeys (Whiten & Ham, 1992). It is therefore of interest that a recent review showed that accumulating evidence in autistic children suggests difficulties in imitation, which includes the copying of acts that should not be difficult just because they have an intentional or pretence component (Rogers & Pennington, 1991).

Whiten (1992) suggested two alternative explanations for why imitation might be linked to mindreading abilities: One is that imitation requires a transposition of visual perspective in translating the acts of the model into those of the imitator; the other is that it depends, in many cases, on some understanding of what the model's intentions are.

According to these analyses, one could argue that imitation is a grade of mindreading in its own right. In addition, because both pretence and imitation can vary from simple acts to very complex ones, grades of difficulty are to be expected in their performance, and thus in their mastery by different species and children of different ages.

GRADES OF INTEGRATION

Although the question of whether a child "has a theory of mind" has often been diagnosed through one-shot tests, particularly for the recognition of false belief, it seems over-grand to equate the attribution of any one mental state with a "theory of mind." A distinctive feature of mind as seen by folk psychology lies in the way it integrates a number of mental states, and only through this integration does a theory of mind become useful in explanation and prediction. The integration between two states in particular have been emphasised by philosophers (Bennett, 1991; Davidson, 1980; and investigated by psychologists (Wellman, 1990; 1991). These states are beliefs and desires, and in combination they are used to explain and/or predict much rational action. However, young children integrate other states. Two-year-olds, for example, can predict emotional reactions to the fulfilment or frustration of desires (Wellman, 1991). I suggest that only when children use their ascriptions of mental states in some combinatorial fashion could we reasonably say they have a theory of mind rather than just an ability to recognise one or more mental states. When they first combine two simple states they have a primitive theory, we might say, and when they combine several, including complex states like belief, they have a more sophisticated theory. There are obviously many grades of integration between (see Lewis, this volume).

GRADES OF EMBEDDING

Five-year-olds can usually attribute false beliefs, but only older children can successfully take account of another individual's beliefs about someone else's beliefs. It is one of the logical features of mental states that they can embed in this way indefinitely, but as Dennett (1983, p. 345) so nicely put it: "I suspect that you wonder whether I realise how hard it is for you to be sure that you understand whether I mean to be saying that you can recognise that I can believe you to want me to explain that most of us can keep track of only about five or six orders, under the best of circumstances." Nevertheless, the ability to handle embeddings is plausibly the basis of sophisticated social manoeuvring, as, for example, in deception and escalating counter-deception (Whiten & Byrne, 1988b; see also Mitchell, this volume), and distinguishing jokes and lies (Leekam, 1991). There are thus important developmental questions about the number of embeddings a child can handle (although care has to be taken in the counting procedure: Whiten & Perner, 1991), and what permits developmental progress to higher grades.

GRADES OF MINDREADING AND GRADES OF MIND

Finally, we should remember that one factor contributing to the grading of mindreading is the grade of mind that is being read. Chimpanzees may have at best a primitive capacity for mindreading, but then they have not such complex minds to read as we do.

There are many grades of interplay between the mindreader and the mind being read. In the case of social competition, we may have deceptive minds trying not to be read: Conversely, in the case of parental scaffolding behaviour we may have a parent offering their mind to be read. A different type of interplay arises when the minds are very different, as in the case of parent and infant, or scientist and chimpanzee.

Of course, the most challenging of these combinations comes in the scientific efforts of the psychologist to read the mind of the mindreader reading minds commonsensically.

ACKNOWLEDGEMENTS

I am grateful to P. Mitchell and C. Lewis for their comments on an earlier draft: Also, to the organisers and participants for their support and criticism in two meetings where some of the issues in this paper were discussed: New College Interdisciplinary Symposium on Mindreading, Oxford, 1992; Symposium on the Mental Life of Animals, Georgia State University, 1993.

REFERENCES

Astington, J.W., & Gopnik, A. (1991). Developing understanding of desire and intention. In A. Whiten (Ed.), *Natural theories of mind: Evolution, development and simulation of everyday mindreading*. Oxford: Basil Blackwell.

Astington, J.W., Harris, P.L., & Olson, D.R. (Eds.) (1988). *Developing theories of mind*. Cambridge: Cambridge University Press.

Baldwin, J.M. (1902). *Development and evolution*. New York: Macmillan.

Baron-Cohen, S. (1991). Precursors to a theory of mind: Understanding attention in others. In A. Whiten (Ed.), *Natural theories of mind: Evolution, development and simulation of everyday mindreading*. Oxford: Basil Blackwell.

Baron-Cohen, S., Leslie, A.M., & Frith, U. (1985). Does the autistic child have a "theory of mind?" *Cognition, 21*, 37–46.

Bennett, J. (1991). How to read minds in behaviour: A suggestion from a philosopher. In A. Whiten (Ed.), *Natural theories of mind: Evolution, development and simulation of everyday mindreading*. Oxford: Basil Blackwell.

Bretherton, I., McNew, S., & Beeghly-Smith, M. (1981). Early person knowledge as expressed in gestural and verbal communication: When do infants acquire a "theory of mind?" In M.E. Lamb & L.R. Sherrod (Eds.), *Infant social cognition*. Hillsdale, NJ: Lawrence Erlbaum Associates Inc.

Butterworth, G., Harris, P.L., Leslie, A.M., & Wellman, H.M. (Eds.) (1991). *Perspectives on the child's theory of mind*. Oxford: BPS and Oxford University Press.

Byrne, R.W., & Whiten, A. (1988). *Machiavellian intelligence: Social expertise and the evolution of intellect in monkeys, apes and humans*. Oxford: Oxford University Press.

Byrne, R.W., & Whiten, A. (1991). Computation and mindreading in primate tactical deception. In A. Whiten (Ed.), *Natural theories of mind: Evolution, development and simulation of everyday mindreading*. Oxford: Basil Blackwell.

Byrne, R.W., & Whiten, A. (1992). Cognitive evolution in primates: Evidence from tactical deception. *Man, 27*, 609–627.

Chandler, M., Fritz, A.S., & Hala, S. (1989). Small-scale deceit: Deception as a marker of two-, three- and four-year-olds' early theories of mind. *Child Development, 60*, 1263–1277.

Cheney, D.L., & Seyfarth, R.M. (1990a). Attending to behaviour versus attending to knowledge: Examining monkey's attribution of mental states. *Animal Behaviour, 40*, 742–753.

Cheney, D.L., & Seyfarth, R.M. (1990b). *How monkeys see the world*. Chicago: Chicago University Press.

D'Andrade, R.G. (1987). A folk model of the mind. In D. Holland & N. Quinn (Eds.), *Cultural models in language and thought*. Cambridge: Cambridge University Press.

Davidson, D. (1980). Psychology as philosophy. In D. Davidson (Ed.), *Essays on actions and events*. Oxford: Oxford University Press.

Dasser, V., Ulbaek, I., & Premack, D. (1989). The perception of intention. *Science, 243*, 365–367.

Dawkins, R. (1992). *The theories of mind used by animals and children.* Paper read at New College Interdisciplinary Symposium on Mindreading, Oxford.

Dawkins, R., & Krebs, J.R. (1978). Animal signals: Information or manipulation? In J.R. Krebs & N.B. Davies (Eds.), *Behavioural ecology: An evolutionary approach.* Oxford: Blackwell.

Dennett, D.C. (1971). Intentional systems. *Journal of Philosophy, 8*, 87–106.

Dennett, D.C. (1983). Intentional systems in cognitive ethology: The "Panglossian paradigm" defended. *Behavioral and Brain Sciences, 6*, 343–390.

Dunn, J. (1991). Understanding others: Evidence from naturalistic studies of children. In A. Whiten (Ed.), *Natural theories of mind: Evolution, development and simulation of everyday mindreading.* Oxford: Basil Blackwell.

Dunn, J., Brown, J., & Beardsall, L. (1991a). Family talk about emotions, and children's later understanding of others' emotions. *Developmental Psychology, 27*, 448–455.

Dunn, J., Brown, J., Slomowski, C., Tesla, C., & Youngblade, L. (1991b). Young children's understanding of other people's feelings and beliefs. *Child Development, 91* (62), 1352–1366.

Feinman, S. (1982). Social referencing in infancy. *Merrill-Palmer Quarterly, 28*, 445–470.

Flavell, J.H., Everett, B.A., Croft, K., & Flavell, E.R. (1981). Young children's knowledge about visual perception: Further evidence for the Level 1–Level 2 distinction. *Developmental Psychology, 17*, 99–103.

Freeman, N.H., Lewis, C., & Doherty, M.J. (1991). Preschoolers' grasp of a desire for knowledge in false belief prediction: Practical intelligence and verbal report. *British Journal of Developmental Psychology, 9*, 139–157.

Frye, D., & Moore, C. (Eds.) (1991). *Children's theories of mind: Mental states and social understanding.* Hillsdale, NJ: Lawrence Erlbaum Associates Inc.

Gomez, J.C. (1991). Visual behaviour as a window for reading the mind of others in primates. In A. Whiten (Ed.), *Natural theories of mind: Evolution, development and simulation of everyday mindreading.* Oxford: Basil Blackwell.

Gopnik, A. (1993). How we know our minds: The illusion of first-person knowledge of intentionality. *Behavioural and Brain Sciences, 16*, 1–14.

Gordon, R.M. (1986). Folk psychology as simulation. *Mind and Language, 1*, 158–171.

Harcourt, A.H., & de Waal, F.B.M. (1992). *Coalitions and alliances in humans and other animals.* Oxford: Oxford University Press.

Harris, P.L. (1989). *Children and emotion: The development of psychological understanding.* Oxford: Basil Blackwell.

Harris, P.L. (1991). The work of the imagination. In A. Whiten (Ed.), *Natural theories of mind: Evolution, development and simulation of everyday mindreading.* Oxford: Basil Blackwell.

Heelas, P., & Lock, A. (Eds.) (1981). *Indigenous psychologies.* London: Academic Press.

Heider, F. (1958). *The psychology of interpersonal relations.* New York: Wiley.

Heider, F., & Simmel, M. (1944). An experimental study of apparent behaviour. *American Journal of Psychology, 57*, 243–259.

Heyes, C.M. (1993). Anecdotes, training, trapping, and triangulating: Do animals attribute mental states? *Animal Behaviour, 46*, 177–188.

Hinde, R.A. (1970). *Animal behaviour: A synthesis of ethology and comparative psychology* (2nd edn.). London: McGraw-Hill.

Humphrey, N. (1976). The social function of intellect. In P.P.G. Bateson & R.A. Hinde (Eds.), *Growing points in ethology.* Cambridge: Cambridge University Press.

Humphrey, N.K. (1980). Nature's psychologists. In B. Josephson & V. Ramachandran (Eds.), *Consciousness and the physical world.* London: Pergamon Press.

Humphrey, N.K. (1983). *Consciousness regained.* Oxford: Oxford University Press.

Humphrey, N.K. (1986). *The inner eye.* London: Faber & Faber.

Johnson-Laird, P.N., & Oatley, K. (1989). The meaning of emotions: Analysis of a semantic field. *Cognition and Emotion, 3*, 81–123.

Karmiloff-Smith, A. (1993). *Beyond modularity: A developmental perspective on cognitive science.* Cambridge, Mass.: Bradford/MIT.

Krebs, J.R., & Dawkins, R. (1984). Animal signals: Mind reading and manipulation. In J.R. Krebs & N.B. Davies (Eds.), *Behavioural ecology: An evolutionary approach.* Oxford: Blackwell

Leekam, S.R. (1991). Jokes and lies: Children's understanding of intentional falsehood. In A. Whiten (Ed.), *Natural theories of mind: Evolution, development and simulation of everyday mindreading.* Oxford: Basil Blackwell.

Leekam, S.R. (1993). Children's understanding of mind. In M. Bennet (Ed.), *The child as psychologist: An introduction to the development of social cognition.* London: Harvester Wheatsheaf.

Leslie, A.M. (1982). The perception of causality in infants. *Perception, 11,* 173–186.

Leslie, A.M. (1987). Pretence and representation in infancy: The origins of "theory of mind." *Psychological Review, 94,* 84–106.

Leslie, A.M., & Firth, U. (1988). Autistic children's understanding of seeing, knowing and believing. *British Journal of Developmental Psychology, 6,* 315–324.

Light, P. (1993). Developing psychologies. In M. Bennett (Ed.), *The child as psychologist: An introduction to the development of social cognition.* London: Harvester Wheatsheaf.

Lloyd Morgan, C. (1930). *The animal mind.* London: Edward Arnold.

Lock, A. (1980). *The guided reinvention of language.* New York: Academic Press.

McGregor, E., & Whiten, A. (1993). *Factors affecting young children's recognition of others' false beliefs: Do actions speak louder than words?* Unpublished manuscript, University of St. Andrews.

McShane, J. (1980). *Learning to talk.* Cambridge: Cambridge University Press.

Michotte, A. (1963). *The perception of causality.* London: Methuen.

Miller, N.E. (1959). Liberalisation of basic S-R concepts. In S. Koch (Ed.), *Psychology: A study of a science.* New York: McGraw-Hill.

Morton, J. (1989). The origins of autism. *New Scientist, 1964,* 44–7.

Perner, J. (1991). *Understanding the representational mind.* Cambridge, Mass.: Bradford/MIT.

Perner, J., Ruffman, T., & Leekam, S.R. (in press). *Theory of mind is contagious: You catch it from your sibs. Child Development.*

Povinelli, D.J., & deBlois, S. (1991). Young children's (*Homo sapiens*) understanding of knowledge formation in themselves and others. *Journal of Comparative Psychology, 106,* 228–238.

Povinelli, D.J., Nelson, K.E., & Boysen, S.T. (1990). Inferences about guessing and knowing by chimpanzees (*Pan troglodytes*). *Journal of Comparative Psychology, 104,* 203–210.

Povinelli, D.J., Parks, K.A., & Novak, M.A. (1992). Do rhesus monkeys (*Macaca mulatta*) attribute knowledge and ignorance to others? *Journal of Comparative Psychology, 105,* 318–325.

Pratt, C., & Bryant, P.E. (1990). Young children understand that looking leads to knowing (so long as they are looking into a single barrel). *Child Development, 61,* 973–982.

Premack, D. (1988). "Does the chimpanzee have a theory of mind?" revisited. In R.W. Byrne & A. Whiten (Eds.), *Machiavellian intelligence: Social expertise and the evolution of intellect in monkeys, apes and humans.* Oxford: Oxford University Press.

Premack, D., & Woodruff, G. (1978). Does the chimpanzee have a theory of mind? *The Behavioural and Brain Sciences, 1,* 515–526.

Pylyshyn, Z.W. (1978). When is attribution of belief justified? *Behavioral and Brain Sciences, 1,* 592–593.

Reddy, V. (1991). Playing with other's expectations: Teasing and mucking about in the first year. In A. Whiten (Ed.), *Natural theories of mind: Evolution, development and simulation of everyday mindreading.* Oxford: Basil Blackwell.

Rogers, S.J., & Pennington, B.F. (1991). A theoretical approach to the deficits in infantile autism. *Development and Psychopathology, 3,* 137–162.

Shultz, T.R., & Shamash, F. (1981). The child's conception of intending act and consequence. *Canadian Journal of Behavioural Science, 13*, 368–372.

Sorce, J.F., Emde, R.N., Campos, J., & Klinnert, M.D. (1985). Maternal emotional signalling: Its effect on the visual cliff behaviour of infants and young children. *Journal of Experimental Child Psychology, 35*, 369–390.

Thorndike, E.L. (1911). *Animal intelligence.* New York: MacMillan.

Trevarthen, C. (1977). Descriptive analyses of infant communicative behaviour. In H.R. Schaffer (Ed.), *Studies in mother–infant interaction.* London: Academic Press.

Trevarthen, C., & Hubley, P. (1978). Secondary intersubjectivity: Confidence, confiders and acts of meaning in the first year. In A. Lock (Ed.), *Action, gesture and symbol.* New York: Academic Press.

Wellman, H.M. (1990). *Children's theories of mind.* Cambridge, Mass.: Bradford/MIT Press.

Wellman, H.M. (1991). From desires to beliefs: Acquisition of a theory of mind. In A. Whiten (Ed.), *Natural theories of mind: Evolution, development and simulation of everyday mindreading.* Oxford: Basil Blackwell.

Whiten, A. (1988). *From literal to non-literal social knowledge in human ontogeny and primate phylogeny.* [Abstracted in *Primate Eye 37, 11* (1989).] Paper presented at Primate Society of Great Britain meeting on Social Knowledge in Primates, London.

Whiten, A. (Ed.) (1991a). *Natural theories of mind: Evolution, development and simulation of everyday mindreading.* Oxford: Basil Blackwell.

Whiten, A. (1991b). The emergence of mindreading: Steps towards an interdisciplinary enterprise. In A. Whiten (Ed.), *Natural theories of mind: Evolution, development and simulation of everyday mindreading.* Oxford: Basil Blackwell.

Whiten, A. (1992). Mindreading, pretence, and imitation in monkeys and apes. *The Behavioral and Brain Sciences, 15*, 170–171.

Whiten, A. (1993). Evolving a theory of mind: The nature of nonverbal mentalism in other primates. In S. Baron-Cohen, H. Tager-Flusberg, & D.J. Cohen (Eds.), *Understanding other minds.* Oxford: Oxford University Press.

Whiten, A., & Byrne, R.W. (1988a). Tactical deception in primates. *Behavioral and Brain Sciences, 11*, 233–273.

Whiten, A., & Byrne, R.W. (1988b). Taking (Machiavellian) intelligence apart. In R.W. Byrne & A. Whiten (Eds.), *Machiavellian intelligence: Social expertise and the evolution of intellect in monkeys, apes and humans.* Oxford: Oxford University Press.

Whiten, A., & Byrne, R.W. (1991). The emergence of metarepresentation in human ontogeny and primate phylogeny. In A. Whiten (Ed.), *Natural theories of mind: Evolution, development and simulation of everyday mindreading.* Oxford: Basil Blackwell.

Whiten, A., & Ham, R. (1992). On the nature and evolution of imitation in the animal kingdom: Reappraisal of a century of research. In P.J.B. Slater, J.S. Rosenblatt, C. Beer, & M. Milinski (Eds.), *Advances in the study of behaviour, 21.* New York: Academic Press.

Whiten, A., & Perner, J. (1991). Fundamental issues in the multidisciplinary study of mindreading. In A. Whiten (Ed.), *Natural theories of mind: Evolution, development and simulation of everyday mindreading.* Oxford: Basil Blackwell.

Wimmer, H., & Perner, J. (1983). Beliefs about beliefs: Representation and constraining function of wrong beliefs in young children's understanding of deception. *Cognition, 13*, 103–128.

Wundt, W. (1916). *Elements of folk psychology: Outlines of a psychological history of the development of mankind.* London: Allen & Unwin.

4 Perceiving Attitudes, Conceiving Minds

R. Peter Hobson
The Tavistock Clinic and University College, London, UK

INTRODUCTION

One of the most challenging theoretical tasks for developmental psychology is to characterise the transition between an infant's modes of communicating with other people in the first year of life, and the emergence of a young child's increasingly sophisticated concepts of mind over the ensuing three or four years. In this chapter I shall offer an account that begins with the infant's abilities to perceive certain forms of "attitude" in the behaviour of other people, and ends with the young child's insight into the nature of intentional mental states. I shall be emphasising not only the special qualities of personal relatedness and interpersonal engagement that make this progression possible, but also the significance of a one-year-old's ability to perceive the directness of another person's attitudes towards a visually specified world. I shall argue that the child's capacity to disembed from his or her own perspective vis-à-vis the world, and to engage in creative symbolic play, are important stepping-stones along this social-development pathway.

I shall proceed by analysing each of the terms I have employed in the title of my chapter. I shall need to introduce a further notion to weld together the business of perceiving attitudes on the one hand, and conceiving of minds on the other—the young child's developing concept of "persons."

71

PERCEIVING ATTITUDES

In the Beginning

Let me begin with the notion of perception, as this applies to the period of infancy. Perception is relational. By this I mean that the very act of perceiving is bound up with the infant's propensities to action and feeling towards the world-as-perceived. Heinz Werner (1948) tried to capture this by writing of the "things of action" or "signal things" in the primitive world of animals or young children. The signal-qualities in the environment depend not only on the biologically relevant characteristics of what is perceived, but also on an organism's readiness for action. Correspondingly (Werner, 1948, pp. 65–6; see also Piaget, 1972): "the affective and motor behavior of the child impresses itself on the world of things and fashions it ... In fact, things are often not known at all unless they are known motor-affectively, that is, according to their pragmatic value for the subject." Werner emphasises how physiognomic as opposed to matter-of-fact perception has special importance in the social domain (1948, pp. 69, 76): "In our own sphere there is one field where objects are commonly perceived as directly expressing an inner life. This is in our perception of the faces and bodily movements of human beings and higher animals ... The relatively early understanding of human expressions and gestures is possible because of the early development of physiognomic perception." So for example, when an infant (or an older child or adult, come to that) perceives another person's infectious smile *as* a smile, or perceives someone's angry growl *as* a personally meaningful event, this mode of apprehending emotional meaning entails that the individual has an inclination to respond to the person concerned with appropriate motor-affective behaviour and attitudes. A child's understanding of what people's emotional expressions *are*— expressions of subjective mental life, as well as gestures that occur when a person faces emotion-arousing circumstances and reacts with emotion-typical styles of action—is grounded in such biologically provided perceptual-affective processes.

These considerations give prominence to the role of "attitudes" in establishing interpersonal relatedness. Not only does the infant have perceptible attitudes of its own, but also from around two months of age, the infant appears to react to certain of the bodily expressed attitudes of another person who is engaged with the infant in face-to-face exchanges (Haviland & Lelwica, 1987; Murray & Trevarthen, 1985). Of course, this is not to say that an infant has a conception of what attitudes are, any more than he or she has a conception of what things are. Rather, the infant can be observed to respond to meanings perceived in the bodies and behaviour of other people, meanings that we as adults know to have significance as expressions of a person's psychological state.

Now it is essential to the nature of attitudes that they have a subjective dimension. We know "what it is like" to be angry about something, jealous of someone, interested in events, and so on (Nagel, 1979). It is also the case that *certain* attitudes have overt behavioural manifestations. Indeed, Warren and Jahoda (1973) suggest that, a little over one hundred years ago, the term "attitude" was used exclusively to refer to a person's posture, for instance the posture associated with a threatening attitude. As a class, therefore, attitudes have *both* mental *and* bodily attributes. This is significant for our account of how a child's understanding of the mind, as well as the child's ability to read the mind in a person's expressions and other behaviour, originates. More specifically, it suggests that we might characterise the earliest stages of interpersonal perception not in terms of an infant perceiving (what we call) bodies, nor in terms of the infant perceiving (what we call) minds, but rather in terms of the infant perceiving and relating to person-anchored attitudes that the older child comes to conceptualise as having bodily and mental aspects.

Thus far, I have focused upon person-to-person perception and relatedness. Before I move on to consider more sophisticated forms of "perceiving attitudes," I need to amplify the implications of what I have described. I have been dealing with what Werner and Kaplan (1984) call the primordial sharing situation between infant and caretaker, and what Trevarthen (1979) calls primary intersubjectivity. I have drawn attention to the way in which an infant's attitudes may be configured in accordance with his or her perception of the attitudes of other people. Such interpersonal co-ordination often, but by no means always, involves a sharing of similar feelings between infant and caretaker; for example, an infant might be angry when the caretaker is disapproving and restraining. Nor do the means to emotional contact between infant and caretaker always involve the mutual sharing and perceiving of universal facial and vocal expressions of affect such as those of happiness, anger, or fear (Ekman & Friesen, 1975; Izard, 1977). There are more subtle but equally significant patterns in the timing and strength of a person's bodily gestures that influence the affective states of someone else (Stern, 1985). Having said this, we as adults observe (in behaviour) that the psychological states of infant and caretaker often correspond in one way or another, and there is indication that each member of the dyad registers and even seeks harmonious communion (e.g. Murray & Trevarthen, 1985). The crux is that there *is* such a thing as "emotional contact" between an infant and caretaker, just as there is between one adult and another, and human beings have the capacity to perceive when this occurs or fails to occur between themselves and others. Correspondingly, there are primitive mechanisms for establishing and registering psychological connectedness between one individual and another. These are givens of human psychology. It would also appear that infants can perceive when there is interpersonal disconnectedness, and this implies that they have the capacity to discriminate between states of self–other congruence and self-other disparity. In summary, therefore, intersubjective engagement and mental co-ordination between infant and caretaker entail that the infant's attitudes are altered and shaped by the infant's perception of those aspects of the caretaker's behaviour that we as adults conceptualise as manifestations of attitudes, especially emotional attitudes.

Attitudes involve more than bodily expressible feeling states, however. Attitudes are directed towards "objects." If an individual has a fearful attitude, this entails not only that her behaviour and subjective experience has a quality of fearfulness about it, but also that there is something that is feared. The complication is that what is feared may "exist" only in the mind of the individual. Here we encounter the fact that, being mental states, attitudes have intentionality (Brentano, 1874/1973, p. 88):

> Every mental phenomenon is characterized by what the Scholastics of the Middle Ages called the intentional (or mental) inexistence of an object, and what we might call, though not wholly unambiguously, reference to a content, direction toward an object (which is not to be understood here as meaning a thing), or immanent objectivity. Every mental phenomenon includes something as object within itself, although they do not all do so in the same way. In presentation something is presented, in judgment something is affirmed or denied, in love loved, in hate hated, in desire desired and so on. This intentional in-existence is characteristic exclusively of mental phenomena.

On the one hand, we can often perceive what it is that another person fears, loves and so on. As Bechtel (1988) notes, the intentionality of mental states has to do with their ability to be about events in the world, and we can often *see* what is at the focus of someone else's attitude. On the other hand, the object or focus of an attitude may exist only in the mind of the person who has the attitude. Moreover, what a person judges, loves, or hates is something that falls under a particular description *for* that person. For example, a person may be afraid of his shadow, thinking that it is a menacing pursuer; or another might fear eternal damnation. One way of characterising this aspect of mental states is to say that a person can "misrepresent" one thing as another, or can represent something as having properties it does not have, or can (re)present something that does not exist (Leslie, 1987). What a single object or event is represented *as*, may differ from person to person.

Therefore, if children are going to acquire an understanding of what attitudes are, they will need to grasp at least two things: Firstly, they must understand the kinds of subjectively experienced and qualitatively distinct psychological-cum-behavioural states that characterise each of a range of attitudes, not only different states of feeling (whether fear, envy, competitiveness, love, or whatever), but also attitudes that are implicated in pretending, believing and knowing; and secondly, they must understand the ways in which such states are directed towards actual or merely potential situations and events in the world, as these fall under descriptions for the individual whose states they are.

I shall come to some special properties of propositional attitudes, attitudes such as pretending or believing *that* such-and-such is the case, when I come to consider a child's growing conception of mind. For now, I want to argue (as I have in earlier papers: Hobson, 1990a; 1991) that a critical stage in the elaboration of interpersonal, and therefore psychological, understanding occurs when, towards the end of the first year of life, an infant begins to relate to another person's attitudes as these are "directed" to objects and events in a shared, visually specified world.

The Relatedness Triangle

The period from about eight months of age, what Trevarthen and Hubley (1978) call the phase of secondary intersubjectivity, is one in which an infant acquires new ways of relating to the care giver as a person. In particular, the infant co-ordinates object-directed actions and attitudes with interpersonal sharing and exchange (Bakeman & Adamson, 1982; Sugarman, 1984). I am going to speak of the "relatedness triangle" when referring to such instances of person-with-person co-reference in relation to things. Examples are when the infant shows things to another person, checking whether the person is attending by looking to the person's eyes; when the infant engages in "social referencing," seeking out another person's emotional attitude to events in the environment, and altering her own attitudes to these events accordingly; when the infant follows the eye-gaze or point of someone else, again with checking-back; or when he or she requests help with something or responds to simple requests. In each case, infants not only relate to another person and to the nonpersonal world of objects and events, but they also relate to the *other person's* relatedness towards the world and towards themselves— the relatedness triangle among self, other, and the environment. Around the end of the first year of life, the infant also initiates as well as accepts invitations to games such as peek-a-boo, gives a shake of the head to express refusal, imitates conventional gestures (e.g. hugging) as well as actions on objects, begins to pretend-copy others' activities such as telephoning or mopping the floor, and utters greetings and uses name-like words (Bretherton, McNew, & Beeghly-Smith, 1981; Klinnert, Campos, Sorce, Emde, & Svejda, 1983; Trevarthen & Hubley, 1978).

I have already emphasised that in the months leading up to this time, the infant is able to register forms of one-to-one, intersubjective "sharing" with another person (Hobson, 1989a; Mundy & Sigman, 1989; Rogers & Pennington, 1991). What is new beyond the age of eight months or so is that the infant shares experiences of the world "out there," both intending to establish such interpersonally co-ordinated attitudes in showing things to someone else and monitoring that person's reactions, and being interested in following another person's focus of attention in order to establish psychological "co-orientation" vis-à-vis objects and events in the surroundings. In requesting actions, initiating games, communicating refusal, making greetings, and so on, infants are also engaging with and relating to the other person's attitudes and intentions towards themselves. The infants' capacity to imitate conventional actions and gestures reveals how they can identify with and assume the attitudes and actions of another person. Infants appreciate not only that they and others have the capacity to share, but that they are also psychologically distinct (Bretherton et al., 1981; Hobson, 1990b).

It is not clear how we should account for the transition into the phase of secondary intersubjectivity. It may very well be the case that at this time in infancy, endogenous factors to do with maturation of the nervous system play an important role in furthering both cognitive and social development. However, there is also evidence for a newly established linkage across two relatively distinct lines of development. Sugarman (1984) reported that only when infants could co-ordinate objects in an instrumental fashion at around eight to ten months of age, for example in using a support to reach an object, were they able to "use" someone else to reach something, or "use" an object to gain someone's attention (also Bates, 1979; Bates, Benigni, Bretherton, Camaioni, & Volterra, 1979). This suggests that some generalised ability associated with means-ends understanding finds special application in the social arena. Having said this, it is also obvious that another person is *not* used just like a mechanical tool or even a robot, for in such circumstances the child will often smile or vocalise towards the person without physically manipulating her. As Camaioni (1992) stresses, to engage with someone as a communicative partner is very different from attributing autonomous behaviour or mere "instrumentality" to others.

Comparative studies highlight what is at stake here. Gomez (1991) describes how the young hand-reared gorilla masters tool use several months *before* she is able to attract attention from and communicate requests to another person. This is similar to the developmental progression one sometimes observes in young children with autism, who may take hold of a person's hand and treat it as if it were a mechanical tool (albeit at times, like a tool with some agent-like properties such as a capacity to move itself). Kanner (1943, p. 247) portrays this impersonal attitude as follows:

If the adults did not try to enter the [autistic] child's domain, he would at times, while moving between them, gently touch a hand or a knee as on other occasions he patted the desk or the couch. But he never looked into anyone's face. If an adult forcibly intruded himself by taking a block away or stepping on an object that the child needed, the child struggled and became angry with the hand or the foot, which was dealt with per se and not as a part of a person. He never addressed a word or a look to the owner of the hand or foot. When the object was retrieved, the child's mood changed abruptly to one of placidity. When pricked, he showed fear of the *pin* but not of the person who pricked him.

Let us tentatively suppose that one constraint on person–person–object co-ordination is an infant's grasp of means-ends relations, or something related to this. What the above set of observations suggest is that, in the case of normal infants, an awareness of persons as subjects of experience is in place "ready and waiting" for the cognitive advance of means-ends understanding to usher in the stage of secondary intersubjectivity and person–person–object co-ordination. This is not so for gorillas, nor for autistic individuals. As Gomez (1991) argues for the case of the gorilla, and as I have argued for the case of the child with autism (Hobson, 1982; 1989b), it is just a sufficiently elaborated awareness of persons as "subjects of experience" that seems to be slow in developing and perhaps limited in depth in these individuals. It is a limitation that is rendered conspicuous by the dissociation between nonsocial and social abilities that emerge simultaneously in normal development.

The comparative perspective reveals something further. The specific constraints in social understanding amongst gorillas and autistic children are reflected at a succeeding stage of development, when such individuals *do* come to exhibit requesting behaviour that may involve eye-contact and communicative gestures to another person. In normal infants towards the end of the first year, communicative acts of requesting ("protoimperatives") emerge at roughly the same time as those aimed at sharing experiences ("protodeclaratives") (Bates et al., 1979). This is not the case with gorillas, who exhibit protoimperative but not protodeclarative gestures (Gomez, Sarria, & Tamarit, 1993). So, too, young autistic children who are able to regulate an adult's behaviour to achieve an environmental end such as getting food, typically do not try to direct the adult's attention towards themselves or to an object, as an end in and of itself (Curcio, 1978; Loveland & Landry, 1986; Sigman, Mundy, Sherman, & Ungerer, 1986; Wetherby & Prutting, 1984; also Baron-Cohen, 1989). To communicate requests is one thing; to communicate for the sake of communicating and sharing experiences is quite another.

There is something else that needs emphasis. This has to do with the infant's capacity to perceive the directedness of attitudes. There are probably a set of rather different mechanisms that enable and incline an infant (perhaps even an infant under eight months of age) to follow another person's line of regard or another person's directedness of action (Baron-Cohen & Cross, 1992; Butterworth & Jarrett, 1991; Scaife & Bruner, 1975). The significant point for the present discussion is that such mechanisms may lead an infant to share a focus of attitude with someone else, in the sense of attending to the same thing, *without* the infant apprehending that object or event *as* a shared focus. This changes with the advent of secondary intersubjectivity at the end of the first year of life, in that now the infant specifically demonstrates the desire to share experiences with others.

Once again in the domain of sharing, there appears to be a linkage between two rather different sets of processes in the infant. One is concerned with perceiving the directedness of another person's bodily orientation and action, and the other is concerned with apprehending the subjective, psychological orientation or attitude that accompanies such relatedness between a person and the world. I anticipate that there is something special about the perception of goal-directed agency (e.g. Premack & Dasser, 1991), something special about the perception of eye-direction (e.g. Baron-Cohen & Ring, this volume; Butterworth & Jarrett, 1991), and quite possibly other specialised perceptual mechanisms for detecting directedness in behaviour. At least certain of these mechanisms appear to be distinct from those that enable a child to perceive and become engaged with the subjectivity of others. For example, autistic children who are impaired in grasping the quality of a person's subjective orientations perform well in line-of-sight tasks such as hide-and-seek played out with miniature figures (Hobson, 1984). The important point is that to perceive goal-directedness or eye-direction is not the same as perceiving attitudes—consider our understanding of mobile robots—and that perceiving and subsequently conceiving of *attitudes* is at the core of interpersonal understanding. On the other hand, the mechanisms for perceiving "outer-directedness" conjoin with the mechanisms for perceiving "subjectivity" in such a way that an infant can perceive how another person's subjective attitudes are targeted. This means that the nine-month-old infant relates to a world that *is* a potentially shareable world, that is, a world that the infant itself recognises to be shared amongst persons who have attitudes towards the surroundings.

The question arises, how we should characterise the forms of interpersonal understanding that are present in normal nine- to ten-month-olds but relatively absent in gorillas and autistic children? It is tempting to suppose that we have to decide between two rather stark alternatives; *either* the infant is merely reacting to "behaviour," rather in the way one might react to the organised and goal-directed movements of a robot, *or* the infant has a concept of someone else's "mind" operating in the background of behaviour. In keeping with my argument thus far, I want to reject each of these alternatives. I suggest that we are simply one step further along the pathway from perceiving attitudes to conceptualising minds. Clearly, the infant does apprehend and react to signs that another person is attending to things, having emotional reactions to events, acting in a goal-directed manner, and so on. The mode of apprehension is such that the infant becomes engaged with these facets of human expression and conduct, in ways that are different to the infant's engagement with nonpersonal things. The kind of engagement not only influences the infant's own affective and motivational states and may influence his or her attitudes towards shared objects and events in the world, but it also prompts the infant to seek out how another person is orientated towards the world, and quite often to *imitate* the person's actions and to *assume* the person's attitudes. The notion of "engagement" is intended to capture the motivational and emotional as well as cognitive aspects of such interpersonal relatedness. All this is subsumed under what Bretherton et al. (1981) call the infant's implicit recognition of other persons. It does not require that infants *conceptualise* "minds," nor does it presuppose that infants have the degree of reflective self-awareness, to enable them knowingly to adopt or to try to adopt another person's psychological perspective. What it does require is that the infants have a kind of insight that other persons are special by virtue of affording these particular modes of interpersonal engagement. It also requires that infants register how people have psychological states that may differ from their own (why else would the infant need to show the person objects, or engage in social referencing?), and that another person's orientation may be aligned with (as in imitation), rebuffed (as in refusal or negation), shared (as in co-operative play), and so on. It is insofar as these modes of apprehending and identifying with other persons as sources of attitude are relatively absent in gorillas and autistic children, that gorillas and autistic children differ from normal infants of around one year old (see also Gomez et al., 1993; Tomasello, Kruger, & Ratner, 1993).

A little earlier I speculated that we shall need an account of several distinct mechanisms involved in an infant's capacities to perceive another person's goal-directed agency, to perceive the person's line of visual regard, and to perceive the quality of the person's subjective orientation. I am now suggesting that we need a complementary account of how the infant is drawn into acting like someone else, looking to the same place as someone else, and assuming a similar or correspondent psychological orientation to that of someone else. I pursue this line of thought because I believe there are forms of interpersonal "role taking" that antedate, and are developmental prerequisites for, the more sophisticated varieties of perspective taking in which children deliberately and self-consciously put themselves into someone else's shoes. My proposal is that it is partly through assuming another person's attitudes by processes of noninferential empathy, and perhaps through imitating another person's actions, that children come to experience and in due course to understand what it means to assume another's psychological viewpoint. It is only when the children achieve insight into the nature of "self" vis-à-vis "other," and have acquired the *concept* of a person as "someone in whose place I can put myself" (Bosch, 1970, p. 89), that they are in a position to adopt alternative perspectives *as* alternative perspectives. Shortly I shall offer some suggestions as to how this stage is attained around the middle of the second year of life.

THE CONCEPT OF PERSONS

I should like to recapitulate a part of what has gone before, from a different starting-point. The theoretical position I am advocating is sufficiently out of key with much contemporary developmental theory, that it may well seem ill-focused or confusing. In addition to this, I need to establish a bridge between the infant's capacities to perceive attitudes on the one hand, and the three-or four-year-old's new-found conception of the "representational mind" on the other. The bridge is constituted by the young child's developing concept of persons (also Hobson, 1993a; 1993b).

Wittgenstein (1958, p. 178) writes: "My attitude towards him is an attitude towards a soul. I am not of the *opinion* that he has a soul ... The human body is the best picture of the human soul." Wittgenstein's point is that there is something primary and irreducible about our attitudes toward a person, and the attitudes we adopt are what gives substance to our concept of a person who has her own subjective experiences. As Malcolm (1962, p. 91) explains: "I do not *believe* that the man is suffering who writhes before me—for to what facts would a 'belief' be related, such that a change in the facts would lead me to alter it? I *react* to his suffering. I look at him with compassion and try to comfort him." If one never experienced the kinds of attitude that are fitting for persons, what Hamlyn (1974, p. 34) calls "natural reactions of person to person," then one would not acquire the concept of what a person is. Such personal relatedness has anchorage in perceptual-affective propensities. To return to Wittgenstein (1980a, para. 570) again: " 'We *see* emotion'—As opposed to what?—We do not see facial contortions and *make the inference* that he is feeling joy, grief, boredom. We describe a face immediately as sad, radiant, bored, even when we are unable to give any other description of the features.—Grief, one would like to say, is personified in the face. This is essential to what we call 'emotion'." Such interpersonal relatedness is *not* primarily and essentially a matter of ascribing to others what one knows from one's own case (Wittgenstein, 1980b, para. 927): "Do you look within *yourself*, in order to recognize the fury in *his* face? It is there as clearly as in your own breast."

Suppose it is true that the attitudes involved in our relatedness towards persons are constitutive of our concepts of persons. What does this matter for our account of the origins of an understanding of mind?

I believe it matters a great deal. The reason is that it is through a child's apprehension of the nature of persons, that the child comes to conceptualise how persons *are* bodies-cum-minds, or if you like, how persons "have" bodies and minds. Just as attitudes have a subjective dimension as well as behavioural expression, so persons have mental as well as physical existence. As Strawson (1962, pp. 135–137) insists:

> What we have to acknowledge ... is the *primitiveness* of the concept of a person. What I mean by the concept of a person is the concept of a type of entity such that *both* predicates ascribing states of consciousness *and* predicates ascribing corporeal characteristics, a physical situation, etc. are equally applicable to a single individual of that single type ... The concept of a person is logically prior to that of an individual consciousness. The concept of a person is not to be analysed as that of an animated body or of an embodied anima.

Sure enough, we adults tend to maintain a radical disjunction between our concepts about the body and those that concern the mind. Although this conceptual apartheid is certainly justified and appropriate in many circumstances, it may prove an obstacle to evolving an adequate genetic epistemology in relation to the development of interpersonal understanding. As Cockburn (1990, p. 55) also has argued, notions of "body" and "mind" should not "displace the notion of the *human being* from its fundamental place in our ontology."

CONCEIVING (OF) MINDS

The title of this chapter contains the expression "conceiving minds," but I have mainly written about the child's progress towards conceiving *of* minds as a psychological property of persons. I believe that the two are intimately linked, in the sense that the developed, creative human mind is conceived (and subsequently born) through a phylogenetic and ontogenetic advance in human beings' capacity to conceive *of* the minds of others and themselves. I need to sketch my view of how this advance proceeds in normal child development.

An adequate treatment of the matter would begin with an analysis of what it means to acquire a concept of anything at all, and then to apply the results to the special case of "concepts of mind" (Hobson, 1993c). I shall gloss over the fact that, for an individual to acquire *the* concept of something, he or she needs to share that concept with others, and therefore needs to enter into relations with others that make agreement and correction possible (Hamlyn, 1978). Instead I shall adopt the stance that much, if not all, of our capacity for conceptual thought is bound up with the ability to symbolise, and suggest how this latter ability is founded upon a certain level of interpersonal understanding. In other words, I shall try to portray a kind of developmental bootstrapping in which interpersonal understanding yields symbolic functioning, and symbolic functioning affords the means to conceptualise mental life itself.

The basic idea is relatively simple. It is that, in the course of the second year of life, a child achieves an insight into the nature of the relationship between persons and the world, and along with this a further insight into the correspondences between self and others. The first insight is that objects and events in the world can be "given" meanings by people. The child discovers a fact of life: Any given object can be construed differently by different people, and any person can apprehend meanings that are person-dependent rather than object-specified. Not only may one person find alarming what another finds attractive, but also one person might construe something (say, a spoon) as a device for feeding, whereas another sees it as an instrument for banging. The second insight is that children themselves can choose to *confer* new meanings on objects and events, as in symbolic play. Children appreciate that a wooden block is a wooden block, but alongside this they can adopt an attitude towards the block that is in some way fitting for something else such as a house, and pretend-take the block to represent a house. A third advance (which I would hesitate to call an "insight") is that children come to adopt another person's stance towards themselves as a source of attitudes—they achieve self-reflective awareness (Mead, 1934). This is especially important because children can now "introspect" and confer on to others what they discover about the quality of their own mental life—children can take roles and apply analogy from their own case to that of others, on the basis of an earlier-established awareness of the nature of persons. An additional insight has to do with the nature of designation— people (including themselves) can concur in employing particular sounds or other symbols to "name" or otherwise to carry meanings, in such a way that meaning-for-self and meaning-for-others agree (Huttenlocher & Higgins, 1978). I believe that the notion of a "naming insight" (McShane, 1980) is both justified and necessary here, not least because, in order truly to symbolise in a communicative context, individuals must know that this is what they are doing, and for this they must have anticipated the meaning of the symbol for the receiver of the communication (Kaye, 1982).

I hope this makes it clear why the child's understanding of person-anchored attitudes, intentional symbolisation, and self-reflective awareness are so tightly knit together (if not, I hope it might become clearer from the more detailed account I give in Hobson, 1993c). In employing communicative and conventional symbols, children reorientate another person's attitude to correspond with the attitude that the symbol anchors for themselves. Such consciousness of self and others is possible only on the basis of the child's recognition of and responsiveness to a range of attitudes, including others' attitudes towards the child's own self.

It remains to explain how children acquire the critical insights I have described. What are the conditions that enable children to make the distinction between attitudes and the things to which those attitudes are directed; to appreciate that a given person may have (and be expressing) this, that, or the other attitude at a given point in time; to transfer attitudes across situations, as in symbolic play; to conceptualise their own attitudes, and to realise that attitudes with which children are familiar in their own case are ascribable to other persons as *their* first-person experiences; and to grasp the nature of intentional communication by symbols?

I believe that the answer lies in the "relatedness triangle" I described earlier. By the end of the first year of life, infants are already relating to people's psychological orientations to a shared world, and have the propensity not only to register but also to imitate and identify with alternative attitudes. A *given*, visually specified object has one meaning for the infant and a potentially different meaning for another person. Not only this, but at times the other person's attitudes are directed towards infants themselves, and often towards infants' own expressed attitudes. I have emphasised how infants can perceive the directedness of attitudes, and are in a position to "triangulate" two separable person-derived attitudes as these bear upon a single object or event that is related-to. That is, a particular object can begin with one meaning for the infant, but the infant can also perceive that it means something different to someone else. It is by registering this contrast that infants come to disembed from their own immediate apprehension of the world, and to distance thought from thing (Werner & Kaplan, 1984). If there are two attitudes to one thing, then attitudes-to-things are different from the things themselves. Out of the infant's experience of *inter*personal co-referential attitudes, the young child distils out an understanding of the nature of co-reference itself. The child discovers how it is possible to adopt more than a single attitude to *anything*, and soon may be observed to adopt attitudes towards his or her own attitudes and thus towards "himself"/"herself" (e.g. Kagan, 1982).

Once children understand that they have the potential as human beings to adopt more than one co-referential attitude to a given object or event, then they can apply alternative attitudes in creative symbolic play. At the same time, the child appreciates how attitudes are essentially to do with meanings-for-persons; as such, they pick out or even create particular *aspects* of meaning in whatever is at the focus of the attitude. The child has become aware of what it means for an object to fall under a particular description *for* a person. Correspondingly, the child is in a position to learn of symbols

(Langer, 1957, pp. 60–61) as *'vehicles for the conception of objects ... it is the conceptions, not the things, that symbols directly 'mean'.''* The point is that symbols capture particular aspects of what things mean to people, and what things mean have much to do with the attitudes that people adopt towards them. We psychologists may think of "symbolic thought" as a highly abstracted process, but the source of such thinking is in the infant's psychological engagement with the world. This is of critical importance for the referring and representational characteristics of symbolising. After all, it is *people*, not symbols or "representations," that represent things and situations. Here we fathom the profound insight in Vygotsky's (1962, p. 8) claim that: "every idea contains a transmuted affective attitude toward the bit of reality to which it refers."

Let me review where this condensed argument has led us. Perhaps it is fitting to do so by referring to Leslie's (1987) seminal article on the topic of "metarepresentation" (my reply to which fills out aspects of the present alternative approach: Hobson, 1990a). Leslie (1987, p. 412) drew attention to the: "striking isomorphism between the three fundamental forms of pretend play and three crucial logical properties of mental state expressions in language." The forms of play in question are object substitution, when one object is treated as if it were another object, the attribution of pretend properties, and the invention of imaginary objects. Correspondingly, mental state expressions have referential opacity (e.g. one may know of something under one description, without recognising the same referent when this falls under a different description), nonentailment of truth (one can believe something that is untrue), and nonentailment of existence (one can think about fairies that probably don't exist). Leslie's suggestion is that mental state expressions are akin to pretence in that they depend upon an innate ability to "decouple" representations from the world they represent, that is, upon the ability to "metarepresent." This metarepresentational capacity emerges towards the end of infancy at around 18 months of age, and underpins (Leslie, 1987, p. 416): "the human mind's ability to characterise and manipulate its own attitudes to information."

I have found this a very helpful *description* of what pretence entails, but I take a different approach to the "isomorphism" that Leslie maps out. Moreover, I question whether to posit a "decoupling mechanism" tells us any more than that somehow the infant has to distinguish attitudes from the objects of those attitudes, and I doubt whether the appeal to innatism is justified here (although in a personal communication, Alan Leslie has suggested that I do not offer a cognitive-process theory, and so do not experience the problem in the way that he does). According to the account I have presented, this critical ability to relate to one's own relatedness to the world is the developmental outcome of a prior ability to relate to *other people's* relatedness to the world. In other words, the process of "decoupling" or "distancing" of self from other, of thought from thing, and of symbol from referent is one that occurs through the interiorisation of the relatedness triangle (Vygotsky, 1978, p. 57): "An interpersonal process is transformed into an intrapersonal one." No wonder that the modes of symbolic play correspond with the characteristics of mental state understanding, because the capacity for creative symbolisation is the exercise of just such insight into the nature of psychological attitudes and their meaning-conferring properties. It is telling that Leslie compares pretending with holding a primary (veridical) representation in quotation marks. I think it is *more* like this than Leslie appreciates, because of the early forms of role taking that antedate and form the substrate for the capacity knowingly to assume an attitude to play materials "as if" the attitude were another person's. The child who symbolises is one who can play with the fact that an object or event can fall under "different descriptions" not only for different persons, but also for a single individual—the child him/herself.

Having said this, it will take another two or three years before a child fully appreciates what it means to have the particular attitude: "to take as true of reality," and thus what it means to entertain false beliefs (Forguson & Gopnik, 1988; Perner, 1988). Earlier I promised to say something about propositional attitudes, for example to pretend/believe/fear *that* such-and-such is the case. Once a child has recognised that people have attitudes, then there is development in the *kinds* of attitude that a child understands. It should be no surprise that emotional attitudes (including attention) and the pretend attitude are amongst the first to be understood as applicable to "intentional objects" (i.e. things and events as-represented), because there is evidence that such attitudes are both registered and adopted well before a child's first birthday (e.g. Reddy, 1991). What is new in the second year of life is that the child can pretend "that" one thing is another.

How should we characterise this achievement? I have argued that it corresponds with the child coming to understand that objects or events fall under descriptions-for-persons, or what is known as mental content. The child also grasps that an already-established attitude of pretending can be applied as a kind of "meta-attitude" in taking up the creative possibilities of adopting alternative attitudes to the world. That is, the child can now choose to adopt alternative attitudes to objects or situations pretendingly, over and above the ability to engage in infantile forms of playful, not-for-serious face-to-face transactions with others. The alternative attitudes entail corresponding mental contents. A child who pretend-takes a block as a house applies selected house-appropriate attitudes in a pretending, as-if manner to the object which she continues to treat as a wooden block. Thus the child chooses to subsume the block "under the description" of a house in a specifically playful and symbolic manner—that is, only *certain* house-meanings are applied, for the child knows the block is not literally a house!

It is the ability to understand the nature of attitudes, together with the ability to be playful (and to maintain the distinction between coexisting playful and serious attitudes) that enables the child to pretend *that* a block is a house. This kind of theoretical account has some affinity with that of Perner (1988), but it differs in emphasising the child's insight into the nature of person-to-world attitudes and what I have called descriptions-for-persons.

The child's understanding of the content of mental states, *what* is pretended/attended to/feared, becomes elaborated as the child learns more about how people construe the world. The child's grasp of the nature of mental states also becomes more sophisticated. Here we come to consider the child's conception of "belief."

There is something very special about the cases of knowing and believing, insofar as the nature of these mental states corresponds with a change in the status of the "objects" of the attitudes involved. In order to understand knowing and believing, the child must appreciate that there is a *privileged* description of the world, namely what is true or real or "what is the case," with which an attitude may be concerned. As I have suggested elsewhere (Hobson, 1993c), it may be partly because a child has to recognise what it means for a particular description of the world to be branded as "true" of reality, that it takes a relatively long time for the child to understand the nature of the particular attitude, "to hold as true" (i.e. to believe; Hobson, 1993c). I strongly suspect that children learn this in at least two ways (probably more): firstly, by observing how in their own case as well as that of others, successful action depends upon a person holding a "correct" view of the world, a view that may be derived from perceiving how things are; and secondly, by registering that there is a particular ("true") description of states of affairs concerning which people can reach agreement or be corrected, and over which people engage in passionate exchanges ("You took my sweets"; "I didn't!"; "Mummy, she *did*, she *did*!"). Once children recognise the significance of the attitude "to hold as true" (for example, whom did Mummy believe?), then they can work out the behavioural implications of holding "false beliefs." Reality (what is true) may be contrasted with mere appearance (what seems true to a person from a particular and perhaps deceptive viewpoint); knowledge (what is correctly held as true) may be contrasted with belief.

In order to acquire concepts of belief and false belief, therefore, the child needs to become oriented towards reality *as* "reality." My suggestion is that the concept of "reality" is a concept of the way things truly are, and the way human beings should agree they are, over and above any particular individual's potentially distorted viewpoint. (Think how often we argue about what is really the case, in the belief that if we are correct, others will eventually agree.) This account is in keeping with recent evidence that young

children who are in a position to have co-operative and conflictual
discussions with siblings are those who achieve success in false belief tasks
at a relatively early age (Dunn, this volume; Dunn, Brown, Slomkowski,
Tesla, & Youngblade, 1991; Perner, Ruffman, & Leekam, 1993). My
suggestion is that, through participating in and witnessing exchanges among
siblings and parents, such children are quicker to learn to how there is a
special, "true" description of states of affairs. For instance, reality serves as
the reference-point for agreement and dispute. I agree with Gopnik,
Slaughter, and Meltzoff (this volume) that here we witness a genuine
conceptual change in children's understanding of the relation between mind
and the world, and I too argue that certain forms of perceptual role taking
are important for prompting the recognition of contrasts in perspective that
are relevant for understanding "belief." I also think this conceptual change
corresponds with a shift away from what Mitchell (this volume) calls early
childhood realism. My point is that the revolution at around the age of three
or four years is one that occurs when the child's mental orientation alters
from that of merely distinguishing serious from pretend attitudes, "my
view" from "your view," and so on, to that of relating *any* individual views
to the supra-individual characterisation of the world that we call "reality."
Reality and truth command respect and acknowledgement—from anyone.
Four-year-olds have come to understand this, and they have come to focus
upon, register, and recall what a person holds to be true of reality.

Thus one can trace a developmental sequence from the infant perceiving
how people's attitudes have both qualitative characteristics (of emotional
tone, playfulness, etc.) and directedness towards the world, to the older child
conceiving how people have psychological states that entail a representational relationship between "the mind" and reality.

PERSPECTIVES FROM DEVELOPMENTAL PSYCHOPATHOLOGY

An important source of evidence concerning the position I have outlined is
that provided by developmental psychopathology, and specifically the
developmental psychopathology of early childhood autism and congenital
blindness. In each of these conditions, there is a striking coincidence
between limitations and/or delays in the development of interpersonal
understanding on the one hand, and in the emergence of creative symbolic
play on the other (e.g. Fraiberg & Adelson, 1977; Hobson, 1990a). How is
this coincidence to be explained?

Let me begin with autism. I believe that "autism" is essentially a failure
to engage in patterned intersubjective co-ordination and exchange with
other people (e.g. Hobson, 1989a; 1991). In many but probably not all cases,
this seems to include a relative incapacity to perceive and react to affective

attitudes in others, and therefore to "share experiences" (Hobson, 1989b). One result is that the autistic child suffers delay and often permanent limitation in engaging with and in understanding the nature of psychological attitudes, and with this in apprehending and comprehending the nature of persons who have subjective orientations towards the world. The child's lack of sharing and co-reference with others in the relatedness triangle deprives the child of the kinds of experience that promote (and may even be a prerequisite for) the *normal* disembedding of thought from thing, and thus the capacity to apply co-referential attitudes in symbolic play. At a more sophisticated level, the autistic child's inattentiveness towards and unengagement with the attitudes of other persons, coupled with his or her difficulty in comprehending what it might mean to arrive at a shared, "correct" description of the world, have serious consequences for the child's grasp of what it means to believe, to know, and so on (e.g. Baron-Cohen, Leslie, & Frith, 1985; Leslie & Frith, 1988).

The major differences between this and Leslie's "metarepresentation hypothesis" as applied to autism lie in the degree to which each style of account lends itself to the "computational metaphor" of psychological functioning—Leslie's certainly does, mine does only to a limited degree—and in the roles that Leslie ascribes to innate cognitive abilities and which I ascribe to social-developmental processes grounded in innate capacities for interpersonal and specifically intersubjective engagement.

I believe the phenomena of congenital blindness provide evidence against the view that there is a normally innate "decoupling mechanism" that is subject to autism-specific dysfunction. My thesis is that a critical component of a congenitally blind child's difficulties in developing creative symbolic play (and in mastering personal pronoun usage and becoming non-echolalic) lies in the child's inability to see the *directedness* of other people's attitudes towards a common, visually specified world. Once again, this time for reasons of visual impairment rather than because of essential deficits in intersubjective engagement, blind children have deficient experience of the relatedness triangle and of co-reference with others. The result is what Anderson, Dunlea, and Kekelis (1984) identify as an impairment in perspective taking, an impairment that may extend to those early forms of psychological co-orientation with others that are the roots of creative symbolic functioning. The impediment is not absolute, because vision is not the only means to interpersonal and thus intrapersonal co-reference, but it may nevertheless account for the blind child's difficulty (Fraiberg & Adelson, 1977, p. 249) in "representing the self as an 'I' in a universe of I's" and in appreciating the nature of person-anchored attitudes to the world. My suggestion is that this disability plays an important part in causing the impressive degree of overlap in the clinical presentation of congenitally blind and autistic children, especially with regard to abnormalities in creative symbolic play and specific aspects of linguistic role taking (e.g. Hobson, 1990a; in press). The children in each diagnostic group encounter an obstacle on the social-developmental pathway that normally leads to the capacity to conceptualise self and others as persons with attitudes vis-à-vis a shared world, and through this, to the capacity for creative symbolic play. In the case of children with autism, the obstacles have to do with intersubjective engagement and the perceiving and understanding of an important class of psychological attitudes; in the case of congenitally blind children, the obstacles include that of being unable to see the ways in which attitudes are directed from persons towards a given, visually specified world.

CONCLUSION

Perhaps I have been overambitious in trying to condense so much into a brief chapter. There are many gaps in the account, and several of my points are speculative. For example, I have stressed the significance of a young child's dawning understanding of what I have called descriptions-for-persons (or mental content). I have also emphasised the importance of the "for-persons" part of this phrase, partly because of the developmental background to the cognitive advance in question (especially, the infant's awareness of persons, and the subsequent recognition of co-orientations among persons), and partly because I am dealing with the child's understanding of *psychological* orientations, not merely "representations" or "metarepresentations" in the abstract, as for example in photographs (see relevant discussions in Leekam & Perner, 1991; Leslie & Thaiss, 1992; Perner, 1993). What I have only implied, and not properly dealt with, is the possibility that there may be alternative routes to at least a partial understanding of attitudes and thus descriptions-for-persons, routes that may be open even to children with autism (who after all do understand quite a lot about having visuo-spatial viewpoints and a range of other mental states, e.g. Baron-Cohen, 1991). Indeed, my treatment of approaches from developmental psychopathology has been distinctly unsubtle: It goes without saying that early childhood autism and congenital blindness are complex conditions, and there may well be alternative or additional explanations for the children's deficits.

Nevertheless, I hope that I have conveyed the thrust of my argument. A philosophical analysis of what it means to arrive at knowledge of persons with minds, and a conceptual analysis of what it means to symbolise and to designate-for-persons, combine with evidence from normal development and developmental psychopathology to suggest that a young child's conceptions of mind are founded on preconceptual forms of interpersonal understanding and "sharing" that depend upon innate capacities to perceive and react to attitudes in other people. The specifically human creative and symbolic capacities of mind are conceived by virtue of the young child's developing conception of the minds of persons, and the child's conceptions of mind are founded on abilities to perceive and to have attitudes towards the psychological attitudes of others.

ACKNOWLEDGEMENTS

I am most grateful to David Hamlyn for his patient help and criticism, and to Alan Leslie for offering comments on this chapter.

REFERENCES

Andersen, E.S., Dunlea, A., & Kekelis, L.S. (1984). Blind children's language: Resolving some differences. *Journal of Child Language, 11*, 645–664.

Bakeman, R., & Adamson, L.B. (1982). Co-ordinating attention to people and objects in mother–infant and peer–infant interaction. *Child Development, 55*, 1278–1289.

Baron-Cohen, S. (1989). Perceptual role-taking and protodeclarative pointing in autism. *British Journal of Developmental Psychology, 5*, 139–148.

Baron-Cohen, S. (1991). The development of a theory of mind in autism: Deviance and delay? *Psychiatric Clinics of North America, 14*, 33–51.

Baron-Cohen, S., & Cross, P. (1992). Reading the eyes: Evidence for the role of perception in the development of a theory of mind. *Mind and Language, 7*, 172–186.

Baron-Cohen, S., Leslie, A.M., & Frith, U. (1985). Does the autistic child have a "theory of mind?" *Cognition, 21*, 37–46.

Bates, E. (1979). The emergence of symbols: Ontogeny and phylogeny. In W.A. Collins (Ed.), *Children's language and communication. Minnesota Symposia on Child Psychology, Vol 12.* Hillsdale, NJ: Lawrence Erlbaum Associates Inc.

Bates, E., Benigni, L. Bretherton, I., Camaioni, L., & Volterra, V. (1979). Cognition and communication from 9–13 months: Correlational findings. In E. Bates (Ed.), *The emergence of symbols: Cognition and communication in infancy.* New York: Plenum.

Bechtel, W. (' 88). *Philosophy of mind: An overview for cognitive science.* Hillsdale, NJ: Lawrence Erlbaum Associates Inc.

Bosch, G. (1970). *Infantile autism* (translated by D. Jordan & I. Jordan). New York: Springer-Verlag.

Brentano, F. (1874/1973). *Psychology from an empirical standpoint* (translated by A.C. Rancurello, D.B. Terrell, & L.L. McAlister). London: Routledge & Kegan Paul.

Bretherton, I., McNew, S., & Beeghly-Smith, M. (1981). Early person knowledge as expressed in gestural and verbal communication: When do infants acquire a "theory of mind?" In M.E. Lamb & L.R. Sherrod (Eds.), *Infant social cognition: Empirical and theoretical considerations.* Hillsdale, NJ: Lawrence Erlbaum Associates Inc.

Butterworth, G., & Jarrett, N. (1991). What minds have in common in space: Spatial mechanisms serving joint visual attention in infancy. *British Journal of Developmental Psychology, 9*, 55–72.

Camaioni, L. (1992). Mind knowledge in infancy: The emergence of intentional communication. *Early Development and Parenting, 1*, 15–22.

Cockburn, D. (1990). *Other human beings.* London: Macmillan.

Curcio, F. (1978). Sensorimotor functioning and communication in mute autistic children. *Journal of Autism and Childhood Schizophrenia, 8*, 281–292.

Dunn, J., Brown, J., Slomkowski, C., Tesla, C., & Youngblade, L. (1991). Young children's understanding of other people's feelings and beliefs: Individual differences and their antecedents. *Child Development, 62,* 1352–1366.

Ekman, P., & Friesen, V.W. (1975). *Unmasking the face: A guide to recognizing emotions from facial cues.* Englewood Cliffs, NJ: Prentice-Hall.

Forguson, L., & Gopnik, A. (1988). The ontogeny of common sense. In J.W. Astington, P. Harris, & D.R. Olson (Eds.), *Developing theories of mind.* Cambridge: Cambridge University Press.

Fraiberg, S., & Adelson, S. (1977). *Insights from the blind.* London: Souvenir.

Gomez, J.-C. (1991). Visual behaviour as a window for reading the mind of others in primates. In A. Whiten (Ed.), *Natural theories of mind: Evolution, development and simulation of everyday mindreading.* Oxford: Blackwell.

Gomez, J.-C., Sarria, E., & Tamarit, J. (1993). The comparative study of early communication and theories of mind: Ontogeny, phylogeny, and pathology. In S. Baron-Cohen, H. Tager-Flusberg, & D. Cohen (Eds.), *Understanding other minds: Perspectives from autism.* Oxford: Oxford University Press.

Hamlyn, D.W. (1974). Person-perception and our understanding of others. In T. Mischel (Ed.), *Understanding other persons.* Oxford: Blackwell.

Hamlyn, D.W. (1978). *Experience and the growth of understanding.* London: Routledge & Kegan Paul.

Haviland, J.M., & Lelwica, M. (1987). The induced affect response: Ten-week-old infants' responses to three emotion expressions. *Developmental Psychology, 23,* 97–104.

Hobson, R.P. (1982). The autistic child's concept of persons. In D. Park (Ed.), *Proceedings of the 1981 International Conference on Autism, Boston, USA.* Washington, DC: National Society for Children and Adults with Autism.

Hobson, R.P. (1984). Early childhood autism and the question of egocentrism. *Journal of Autism and Developmental Disorders, 14,* 85–104.

Hobson, R.P. (1989a). On sharing experiences. *Development and Psychopathology, 1,* 197–203.

Hobson, R.P. (1989b). Beyond cognition: A theory of autism. In G. Dawson (Ed.), *Autism: Nature, diagnosis, and treatment.* New York: Guilford.

Hobson, R.P. (1990a). On acquiring knowledge about people and the capacity to pretend: Response to Leslie. *Psychological Review, 97,* 114–121.

Hobson, R.P. (1990b). On the origins of self and the case of autism. *Development and Psychopathology, 2,* 163–181.

Hobson, R.P. (1991). Against the theory of "Theory of Mind." *British Journal of Developmental Psychology, 9,* 33–51.

Hobson. R.P. (in press). Through feeling and sight to self and symbol. In U. Neisser (Ed.), *Ecological and interpersonal knowledge of self.* Cambridge: Cambridge University Press.

Hobson, R.P. (1993a). The emotional origins of interpersonal understanding. *Philosophical Psychology, 6,* 227–249.

Hobson, R.P. (1993b). Understanding persons: The role of affect. In S. Baron-Cohen, H. Tager-Flusberg, & D. Cohen (Eds.), *Understanding other minds: Perspectives from autism.* Oxford: Oxford University Press.

Hobson, R.P. (1993c). *Autism and the development of mind.* Hove: Lawrence Erlbaum Associates Ltd.

Huttenlocher, J., & Higgins, E.T. (1978). Issues in the study of symbolic development. In W.A. Collins (Ed.), *Minnesota Symposia on Child Psychology, Vol.11.* Hillsdale, NJ: Lawrence Erlbaum Associates Inc.

Izard, C.E. (1977). *Human emotions.* New York: Plenum.

Kagan, J. (1982). The emergence of self. *Journal of Child Psychology and Psychiatry, 23,* 363–381.

Kanner, L. (1943). Autistic disturbances of affective contact. *Nervous Child, 2,* 217–250.

Kaye, K. (1982). *The mental and social life of babies*. London: Methuen.

Klinnert, M.D., Campos, J.J., Sorce, J.F., Emde, R.N., & Svejda, M. (1983). Emotions as behavior regulators: Social referencing in infancy. In R. Plutchik & H. Kellerman. (Eds.), *Emotion: Theory, research and experience, Vol. 2. Emotions in early development*. New York: Academic Press.

Langer, S.K. (1957). *Philosophy in a new key* (3rd edn.). Cambridge, Mass.: Harvard University Press.

Leekam, S.R., & Perner, J. (1991). Does the autistic child have a metarepresentational deficit? *Cognition, 40*, 203–218.

Leslie, A.M. (1987). Pretence and representation: The origins of "theory of mind." *Psychological Review, 94*, 412–426.

Leslie, A.M., & Frith, U. (1988). Autistic children's understanding of seeing, knowing and believing. *British Journal of Developmental Psychology, 6*, 315–324.

Leslie, A.M., & Thaiss, L. (1992). Domain specificity in conceptual development: Neuropsychological evidence from autism. *Cognition, 43*, 225–251.

Loveland, K.A., & Landry, S.H. (1986). Joint attention and language in autism and developmental language delay. *Journal of Autism and Developmental Disorders, 16*, 335–349.

Malcolm, N. (1962). Wittgenstein's Philosophical Investigations. In V.C. Chappell (Ed.), *The philosophy of mind*, Englewood Cliffs, NJ: Prentice-Hall.

McShane, J. (1980). *Learning to talk*. Cambridge: Cambridge University Press.

Mead, G.H. (1934). *Mind, self and society*. Chicago and London: University of Chicago Press.

Mundy, P., & Sigman, M. (1989). The theoretical implications of joint-attention deficits in autism. *Development and Psychopathology, 1*, 173–183.

Murray, L., & Trevarthen, C. (1985). Emotional regulation of interactions between two-month-olds and their mothers. In T.M. Field & N.A. Fox (Eds.), *Social perception in infants*. Norwood, NJ: Ablex.

Nagel, T. (1979). *Mortal questions*. Cambridge: Cambridge University Press.

Perner, J. (1988). Developing semantics for theories of mind: From propositional attitudes to mental representation. In J.W. Astington, P.L. Harris, & D.R. Olson (Eds.), *Developing theories of mind*. Cambridge: Cambridge University Press.

Perner, J. (1993). The theory of mind deficit in autism: Rethinking the metarepresentation theory. In S. Baron-Cohen, H. Tager-Flusberg, & D. Cohen (Eds.), *Understanding other minds: Perspectives from autism*. Oxford: Oxford University Press.

Perner, J., Ruffman, T., & Leekam, S.R. (1993). *Theory of mind is contagious: You catch it from your sibs*. Unpublished manuscript, Department of Experimental Psychology, University of Sussex.

Piaget, J. (1972). *The principles of genetic epistemology* (translated by W. Mays). London: Routledge & Kegan Paul.

Premack, D., & Dasser, V. (1991). Perceptual origins and conceptual evidence for Theory of Mind in apes and children. In A. Whiten (Ed.), *Natural theories of mind: Evolution, development and simulation of everyday mindreading*. Oxford: Blackwell.

Reddy, V. (1991). Playing with others' expectations: Teasing and mucking about in the first year. In A. Whiten (Ed.), *Natural theories of mind: Evolution, development and simulation of everyday mindreading*. Oxford: Blackwell.

Rogers, S.J., & Pennington, B.F. (1991). A theoretical approach to the deficits in infantile autism. *Development and Psychopathology, 3*, 137–162.

Scaife, M., & Bruner, J. (1975). The capacity for joint visual attention in the infant. *Nature, 253*, 265–266.

Sigman, M., Mundy, P., Sherman, T., & Ungerer, J.A. (1986). Social interactions of autistic, mentally retarded, and normal children and their caregivers. *Journal of Child Psychology and Psychiatry, 27*, 647–656.

Stern, D.N. (1985). *The interpersonal world of the infant*. New York: Basic Books.

Strawson, P.F. (1962, originally 1958). Persons. In V.C. Chappell (Ed.), *The philosophy of mind*. Englewood Cliffs, NJ: Prentice-Hall.

Sugarman, S. (1984). The development of preverbal communication. In R.F. Schiefelbusch and J. Picker (Eds.), *The acquisition of communicative competence*. Baltimore: University Park Press.

Tomasello, M., Kruger, A.C., & Ratner, H.H. (1993). Cultural learning. *Behavioral and Brain Sciences, 16*, 495–552

Trevarthen, C. (1979). Communication and co-operation in early infancy: A description of primary intersubjectivity. In M. Bullowa (Ed.), *Before speech*. Cambridge: Cambridge University Press.

Trevarthen, C., & Hubley, P. (1978). Secondary intersubjectivity: Confidence, confiding and acts of meaning in the first year. In A. Lock (Ed.), *Action, gesture and symbol: The emergence of language*. London: Academic Press.

Vygotsky, L.S. (1962). *Thought and language* (translated by E. Hanfmann & G. Vakar). Cambridge, Mass: MIT Press.

Vygotsky, L.S. (1978). Internalisation of higher psychological functions. In M. Cole, V. John-Steiner, S. Scribner, & E. Souberman (Eds.), *Mind in society: The development of higher psychological processes*. Cambridge, Mass.: Harvard University Press.

Warren, N., & Jahoda, M. (1973). *Attitudes*. Harmondsworth, Middlesex: Penguin.

Werner, H. (1948). *Comparative psychology of mental development*. Chicago: Follett.

Werner, H., & Kaplan, B. (1984, originally 1963). *Symbol formation*. Hillsdale, NJ: Lawrence Erlbaum Associates Inc.

Wetherby, A.M., & Prutting, C.A. (1984). Profiles of communicative and cognitive-social abilities in autistic children. *Journal of Speech and Hearing Research, 27*, 364–377.

Wittgenstein, L. (1958). *Philosophical investigations* (translated by G.E.M. Anscombe). Oxford: Blackwell.

Wittgenstein, L. (1980a). *Remarks on the philosophy of psychology, Vol. 2*. In G.H. von Wright & H. Nyman (Eds.) (translated by C.G. Luckhardt & M.A.E. Aue). Oxford: Basil Blackwell.

Wittgenstein, L. (1980b). *Remarks on the philosophy of psychology, Vol. 1*. In G.E.M. Anscombe & G.H. von Wright (Eds.) (translated by G.E.M. Anscombe). Oxford: Basil Blackwell.

5 Associations and Dissociations in Theories of Mind

Norman H. Freeman
University of Bristol, UK

INTRODUCTION

Experimentation in child psychology seems to go through a cycle of methods whenever a new problem-domain is tackled. Typically, tests are given to age-matched groups of children, then, once the tools of the trade have been polished, a battery of tests is given to groups of children; and only then do researchers move on to longitudinal studies and to recombining parts of tests to see whether the standard indices of transfer and of dissociation of functions can be demonstrated within individuals. Such an agenda starts with a concentration on valid tests of whatever competence is under scrutiny and, hopefully, ends with a process model that is truly developmental. The bulk of the evidence on the child's theory of mind is still at the first stages, working out agreement over tests and the reasons for an association between tests in a battery: the lack of a process model has succinctly been noted by Perner (1991) and Wellman (1990).

To be fair, the body of research has been built up in only about a decade, a short time in which to tackle the vast topic of the child's grasp of *intentional psychology*—the child's grasp of the ways in which mental states relate to situations (e.g. "if I have a fear it must be a fear of something, or that something will occur," Searle, 1983, p. 1). In this volume, Gopnik, Slaughter, and Meltzoff report an elegant sort of training study that moves the research agenda on to a remarkable extent by showing that preschoolers can be brought to associate one type of problem with a supposedly more advanced problem. In the second half of this chapter I discuss another association-based attempt to move onto the second half of the empirical agenda (with a focus on pictures as intentional aids). But before trying out an empirical association method it is useful to take the complementary tack of examining some existing evidence for signs of dissociation, signs that *children can come up with the solution to a theory of mind problem but not realise the significance of what it is that they have come up with.* Not all competence is accessible to reflective awareness on demand. Maybe preschoolers develop a theory of mind before they realise its range of applications and utility. And when the realisation dawns, one can expect to find a surge of prowess as the new conceptual terrain is colonised, a surge that would appear to researchers as though a *contemporaneous* conceptual revolution had occurred in the children.

On the assumption that the proposal so far is roughly on the right lines, it would help us understand why the aftermath of the putative conceptual revolution bears so many hallmarks of the earlier stage, at which the requisite concepts were slowly differentiating out. If given half a chance preschoolers will translate a high-order problem into subroutines. Preschoolers thus reduce the problem of inferring what someone believes to (1) what someone sees (evidence in Perner, 1991), or to (2) what action someone wants to take (evidence in Wellman, 1990). Such reduction surely attests to some weakness in the children's theory of mind. Yet the lower order of thinking is surely a valuable resource base whence children could advance if they could only find the symbolic support for the endeavour. The contention in this chapter is that more conceptual resource is in place in three-year-olds than one would guess from their signal lack of success in coping with the problems that stage 1 methodology has devised.

GENERAL BACKGROUND

There is a sombre side to the literature on the child's conception of intentional psychology. The arguments and experiments are replete with references to the child's understanding of deception, ignorance, misrepresentation, conflicting desires, thwarted needs, unfulfilled intentions, disappointed expectations, and so forth. These destructive terms reflect researchers' need to take things apart: for example, to dissociate a belief from its truth value and to see whether children stand loyally by the belief (understanding that a belief is still a belief even when it is false). The rationale behind the endeavour is straightforward—one can only really probe children's competence by seeing whether they can rise to the challenge of dealing with situations in which something has gone wrong. Nonetheless, it is as well to bear in mind the admonition of Crystal (1984, p. 39) in his writing about dissociations and deficits in language: "We must beware of

Humpty Dumpty syndrome. We should never take language apart without the intention and ability to put it back together again." The same applies to intentional psychology. Indeed, as Sterelny (1993, p. 83) observed: "A theory of mind may be the next best candidate after language for a cultural universal. Like language, intentional psychology is not an obvious inductive generalisation from experience." We must take care lest we lose sight of the wood for the trees.

Along with the decomposition of beliefs, desires, and intentions, many theorists emphasise the necessity for young children to struggle with conflicting evidence and counter-instances in order to emerge as fully paid-up members of their community of folk psychologists. Such struggles are seen as being the child's chance to advance to a representational theory of mind (Pillow, 1993, p. 69): "Experiencing conflict between expectations and actual states of affairs may provide the data that lead to a representational understanding of belief." The suggestion is a powerful one. Yet one has to be careful here. Experiencing conflict can certainly provide data and be a window of opportunity for the advancement of a theory or the acquisition of a new concept; but something more is needed if one is to explain *how* the child resolves the conflict. The mere fact of the existence of counter-evidence does not provide a cue for what form a better theory should take (Bryant, 1982). To take a leaf from the book of psycholinguistics yet again, there is general agreement that preschool children master the language system on the basis of processing positive instances rather than via counter-instance and correction (see MacWhinney, 1987). Beckwith (1991) has presented a linguistically inspired analysis of how a grasp of the intentionality of desires can be "bootstrapped" from a lower to a higher level of representation by a sort of progressive abstraction. In order to be ready to accept challenging data and emerge with an understanding that eventually converts counter-instances to intelligible phenomena, children must mobilise their existing sources of strength. How are these recruited in the interests of conceptual advance?

The central concern in this chapter is to probe how far a "positive account" can bring to light a deeper continuity *underlying* the appearance of a conceptual revolution around four years of age. Although there is every reason to believe that conceptual revolutions do occur—conceptual revolutions are as real and as important as political revolutions—my focus is on the existing resources whence a revolution emerges. It is a possibility worth entertaining, that children's repeated confrontations with sombrely decomposed states of affairs merely force on the children's awareness the realisation that they know more than they know that they know about the workings of intentional psychology. To turn again to psycholinguistics, the '80s saw researchers gradually abandoning "linguistic revolution" formulations in favour of preschoolers' spontaneous generation of varieties of actions (at all levels, from phonological to syntactic) with a struggle for survival amongst the varieties. The generation of variety is a natural phenomenon whence advance occurs. There are positive formulations already available according to which a powerful mechanism of conceptual advance is the appropriation and reworking of existing mental resources (Plaut & Karmiloff-Smith, 1993, p. 70): "We believe that the developmental results are best interpreted in terms of increasing capability in using and generating symbolic representations that are sufficiently well elaborated to override the otherwise compelling interpretations generated by direct experience." These symbolic representations and their elaboration must come from somewhere. So any positive account of conceptual advance has to specify the foundations on which the child's newer conceptual structure rests.

In sum, we shall examine situations in which the child is exposed to informational conflict, but I shall focus on the productive potential of the child's detection of connectedness, coherence, and the creation of intelligibility in the situation (as does Lewis in this volume, though from a different angle). In the course of following the account, I shall consider some tantalising evidence that is only now emerging. Then, analysis of a new technique shows how a phenomenon that has been taken as evidence for advance-through-conflict still yields the advance when the degree of conflict is controlled.

There are now two agendas open in probing the case so cursorily laid out above. One agenda is to focus on a new use of existing resources, which can be supported sufficiently to result in a conceptual revolution. Thus Plaut and Karmiloff-Smith (1993, p. 70) suggested that: "Language is central to theory-of-mind processes precisely because it provides particularly effective 'scaffolding' for symbolic representations." Such an agenda involves regarding preschool children as acquiring language and acquiring intentional psychology such that the two systems of symbolic representations interact and support one another in the particular way that will sustain a conceptual revolution. The approach has appeal. Language is highly intentional (much of our discourse is directed to and is about states of affairs in the world), as is our psychology (we believe things about the world and desire things of the world); systematic development in both occurs before school age, neither is completely acquired during that period, and theory of mind tests are highly verbally loaded. The second agenda involves initially taking a step back by focusing on an analysis of what advance in the child's knowledge of the mind occurs before the proposed amplification by language makes the four-year-old advance manifest to researchers' eyes. In the following sections of this chapter we largely implement that second agenda, with consideration from language appealed to where necessary. In sum, we may regard the four-year-old advance as an amplification of the three-year-old advance—a dramatic amplification with far-reaching consequences, but not a single discontinuity whereby a concept of representation that was previously unavailable in the child's conceptual system suddenly comes on stream.

Karmiloff-Smith (1991, p. 193) argued that to capture the complexities of representational advance: "One needs to invoke several different levels, namely a level of implicit knowledge represented but embedded in procedures, a level of explicitly defined knowledge but not available to conscious access, a level of consciously accessible representations but not available to verbal report, and a level available to verbal report." In that light we can consider any traditional theory of mind test, such as that involving unexpected transfer (the agent thinks that an object is at location A because she does not know it has been transferred to location B). The child is asked to infer where the agent thinks the object is. From the fact that most three-year-olds fail to verbalise the agent's false belief, all that one can safely conclude is that the child's computations have not reached Karmiloff-Smith's highest level. On the one hand, if one takes the term "theory of mind" to label what the child herself knows that she knows about the agent's mind, it would be correct to say that the three-year-old has a poor theory of mind. On the other hand, it may be that the child has a good theory at some deep level, but has not yet appropriated the theory or consciously incorporated it into her worldview.

Karmiloff-Smith (1991) argued at length that the developing cognitive system operates by re-representing its internal representations recursively. It is no easy matter to discover phenomena that index cognitive organisation unambiguously at lower and lower levels. Yet the attempt must be made. Evidently the task involves (1) deciding how to *decompose* the notion of theory (whether into "levels" or "underlying concepts" are but two of the options), (2) *mapping* the account onto child development in such a way as to specify *what* it is that changes in the course of theory-change, and (3) devising a test to *detect* the point of change in children who cannot pass a theory of mind test by delivering a correct verbal report on demand.

LEVELS AND TYPES OF ANALYSIS

At about the time that the first theory of mind tests were being devised, Searle (1983, p. 1) produced his account of Intentionality: "As a preliminary formulation we might say: Intentionality is that property of many mental states and events by which they are directed at or about or of objects and states of affairs in the world. If, for example, I have a belief, it must be a belief that such and such is the case, if I have a desire, it must be a desire to do something or that something should happen or be the case ..." In view of the concentration in the theory of mind literature upon preschoolers' ability to engage in belief-desire reasoning it is interesting to note that Searle did not regard conceptions of beliefs and desires as the primary focus for explanatory work. He laid emphasis (1983, p. 36) on: "The biologically primary forms of Intentionality, perception and action. Beliefs and desires are not the primary forms, rather they are etiolated forms of more primordial experiences in perceiving and doing." These "biologically primary forms" are readily amenable to the kinds of representation on which Karmiloff-Smith concentrated as indexed by the first-person certainty they engender (Searle, 1983, p. 90): "Just as at any point in a man's conscious life he knows the answer to the question, 'What do you see now?', so he knows the answer to the question, 'What are you doing now?'" Searle's "he" may not find it so easy to verbalise what it is that he currently thinks or wants.

Accordingly, let us search for empirical data that might reveal a level of expertise in the child that comes from the "primordial level" and which current techniques are not usually designed to catch. We are looking for indications that there may be a degree of association in children's computations, whereby they solve the problem set them by the use of practical intelligence, yet fail to forward the solution to the secondary level, where that solution has to be packaged in the language of belief and desire.

The first suggestive fragment of data is anecdotal, and is certainly open to alternative interpretations. Freeman, Lewis, and Doherty (1991) tested preschoolers on an unexpected transfer false belief test, in which the child's task was to infer that an agent falsely thinks that his target of search is at location A, because he had not witnessed the target's subsequent move to location B. The authors noted (Freeman et al., 1991, p. 147):

> Three four-year-olds failed the ... test by predicting that the actor would search where the toy really was and not where his false belief represented it as being. One child spontaneously explained that that was because the actor would already have looked in the empty place and then gone on, and two children offered that explanation when questioned. Some false negatives may occur by children reporting on the end-state of the actor's search ... They had grasped the actor's plan and mentally run through it.

The observation might be of trivial noise in the data. But it might equally well be a first glimpse of something underlying the child's effective awareness of the actor's belief. Perhaps children compute the actor's relations to the situation in terms of what the actor has perceived and what he will then do. Only then would the children reflect on the computation to yield the verbal answers that are taken as evidence for their understanding of false belief. For a systematic attempt to give children directive questioning in such a situation, see Siegal and Beattie (1991).

The second fragment of evidence comes from the same paper by Freeman et al. (1991). Children were asked to take hold of the doll that represented the actor and physically move him through his search trajectory. Probing across all the data (including probe tests), there were 66 children (old three-year-olds and young four-year-olds) who failed to verbalise the actor's false belief yet then correctly acted out the actor's journey to the empty box (with only three counter-instances of a successful verbalisation of false belief followed by making the actor go straight to location B). The data seem to attest to an ability to *implement* an actor's mistaken actions before being able to verbalise the false belief that informs the actor's plan. However, one would like to see a systematic replication in which the acting-out was given at the first instruction, followed by verbal questioning about where *did* the agent first think the target was (a question that can be posed at the moment the child makes the actor reach the first box, whether that be box A or box B).

The third fragment of evidence was noticed by Lewis, Freeman, Hagestadt, and Douglas (1992) when they read three-year-old children a picture-book story of a false belief episode but refrained from posing a question. Instead, the book was turned back to the start and the children recounted the story, with prompting, and only then, when the experimenters could be sure that the children had grasped the narrative, was a question asked. Children were either asked to predict where the actor *would look* or where the actor *thought* the target was. The former group were reliably more successful (see Lewis, this volume). Of course, it may be that the design provoked the finding, in that the story was constructed of information about what the actor did. But it may be the case that three-year-olds compute the rationality of actions informed by the actor's perceptions before they themselves realise that the rationality is directly translatable into a *think*-statement.

Finally, Yoon and Yoon (1993) reported a rather complex experiment in which half of the children were asked where the actor, Betty, will look for the target (and why she will look there), followed by a question requiring an inference about where Betty *thinks* her doll is (and why she thinks that). The other half of the children were asked to infer where Betty *thinks* the doll is before predicting where Betty *will look*. The finding that concerns us is that, with 90 children tested, there were no less than 33/49 who could predict where Betty will look and not infer where Betty thinks the doll is. The data could not be attributed to question-order. Again it is possible that at some time (possibly 3 years 6 months or so) children become able to compute a correct prediction of action based on the actor's perception before they realise that they have computed the agent's false belief. Note that the advantage of *look* and *think* appeared only weakly in three of the four studies reported by Chandler and Hala in this volume, and not at all in two early studies (Hogrefe, Wimmer and Perner, 1986; Perner, Leekam and

Wimmer, 1987). An encouraging sign is that Perner (personal communication, May 1993) had observed that some preschoolers, when asked a critical test question, briefly turn their eyes to location A before giving location B as the (erroneous) answer.

What is to be made of the observations? On the one hand they all sustain the proposal that there is something amiss in preschoolers' theory of mind if they cannot reliably give verbal expression to some statement of the agent's false belief. But it may not be right to assert point blank that the children do not *have* a concept of representation, since the fragmentary observations indicate that children may *use* the concept without grasping the implications of what they are using sufficiently to deal with a *think*-question. Perhaps the concept is *available* for computations on information at the "primordial level" but not fully *accessible* for expression at the secondary level. What would be a sharp test of the possibility? Ideally, one would like to be able to take a new test off the shelf, a test that acts unambiguously as a "concept detector." One would apply the test to preschoolers, setting the test to detect a "concept of representation" in the children's conceptual system. Unfortunately, no one has yet invented the requisite conceptoscope. However, there are guidelines on how to devise the next best thing.

DEVISING A SYMBOLIC DETECTOR

The argument so far has served to table two questions. Can a competence be detected, at the level of practical intelligence about perception and action, that could be appropriated by symbolic means and fed into the secondary level, where the child needs the language of beliefs? That question was narrowed down to whether a concept of representation can be detected, whether or not the children can normally use the concept in answering a traditional *think*-question. The second question is whether a positive account can be sustained, rather than a conflict account, of the four-year-old conceptual advance. We concentrate here on the first question, and devise as close an approximation to a detector as we can, then evaluate the evidence in the light of conflict-resolution.

The first requirement of a detector test is that a false belief be implanted in the child's mind. One would then only have to trace what became of the belief as the child attempted to retrieve and use it. Fortunately, one of the traditional tests does indeed serve the requirement. In a "deceptive box test", the child is shown a tube of Smarties, asked what is in it, then shown that the contents are only pencils, and has to recall her prior false belief that the contents were Smarties. Samples of three-year-olds typically fail rather dramatically (see Astington & Gopnik, 1988; Wimmer & Hartl, 1991). It has been proposed that, once the child realises the truth about the contents, the memory of the earlier belief is completely overwritten so it is no longer available in the child's mind (Astington & Gopnik, 1988). Perner (1991) argued that, in order to succeed in the tasks, the child would have to be able to dissociate sense from reference: *How* the contents were represented in the mind as separate from *what* the referent really is. So the paradigm yields a fitting target for a detector test, since if one could detect that the child has the requisite record in the mind even after discovering the truth, that would be a first step in tracing what becomes of the representation when the child is asked to use it in an output.

The question now is what tracer of the belief state can be found. Many things can be used as tracers (e.g. metal detectors, truffle-pigs). What we need is something that the *children themselves* might classify along with beliefs as being "semantically evaluable" (see Fodor, 1992). That demands something that can *symbolise the referent of the belief and the belief itself.* Such a symbol must be recognisable independently of the entities it might symbolise, so that anyone who saw the tracer would recognise what a referent would be for it. Here, a picture would serve. If you see a drawing of Saskia, it is natural to recognise that the drawing forms a symbolic link between Saskia as a referent and the artist's relation to her. The artist could not have done the drawing without thinking of Saskia. Children come to regard pictures as targets of action and perception at a very young age— they make pictures and they are skilled at looking for what pictures depict. Pictures are targets of a "primordial" type of intentionality (Freeman, 1993). A picture of Smarties that is recognisable to anyone who knows what real Smarties are like, is dissociable from the real, has to be drawn and redrawn if necessary to fit the appearance of the real, is "about" or "directed towards" Smarties and not other referents, only comes into being once Smarties are invented as objects that can then be depicted, and so forth. In short, the characterisations of beliefs also apply to pictures, with two differences. One difference is that pictures exist independently of beliefs—they are in a different medium. The other difference is that pictures can be *used* by anyone to mislead, but cannot in themselves be *false*—they can only fail to serve an accurate representational function in some situation or other. Both of these are differences that are wanted in a proposed detector test, since the aim is to use something (a picture) to trace something of a different kind (belief) with which it has a clear affinity but enough difference so as not to be totally confusable. The affinity was ably expounded by Perner (1991), whereby the principles governing representing relations were shown to encompass pictures as well as beliefs (Perner, 1991, p. 9). Children come to "understand that the picture is an object in itself that represents something else. In other words, children understand that the picture needs to be interpreted." All we add for the proposed detector test is that children understand that the agent's relation to a picture needs interpreting (see Saskia, earlier).

In sum, we need a small modification to be made to the deceptive box test. When the child forms the false belief, a picture of Smarties will be provided, which can symbolise both the belief and the referent. After discovering the true contents of the box, the child can be reminded that something external has been held and asked for the then-current belief. Such a design has been reported by Mitchell and Lacohée (1991), in which children briefly held a picture of Smarties and then popped it in a postbox. The design can readily be adapted to become a detector test. The adaptation consists in varying the symbolic status of the tracer, in the following progressive steps. First, one group of children can be given a sample of real Smarties instead of a picture when they form the false belief. A sample is part of the real referential domain of Smarties, that is, a sample is not in itself readily dissociable into referent and representor, any more than any other Smarties are. So the child should regard the sample as belonging to the referential domain and not the symbolic domain. Therefore the first prediction is that being reminded of holding a picture of a few Smarties would help the child recall the false belief whereas being reminded of holding a sample of a few Smarties would be ineffectual.

The empirical results that now follow were written up by Freeman and Lacohée (1993). Hazel Lacohée tested children of mean age 3 years 8 months (SD = 3 months). There were 22/27 successful false belief recalls with the picture compared with 14/27 with the sample. So the initial probe had revealed a phenomenon in the predicted direction.

However, it is conceivable that the picture gave rise to false positives in the data because the Smartie box has Smarties depicted on it, and some children may have made a mechanical association between pictures of Smarties and saying "Smarties" in that particular situation. Accordingly, a much clearer test would be to use a plain eggbox (containing only a tomato) whereby a picture of an egg would not be seen until the child had said that there were eggs in the box. Some of the children could be asked to post a picture of an eggbox itself, so one can unconfound a symbolisation of the *contents* of the belief with a symbolisation of the stimulus that was the *causal origin* of the belief. Again, other groups of children could be asked to post a real egg or a real eggbox. Simon Coulton carried out the tests on four groups of children using unusually careful age-matching—1 child at each month of age between 35 and 50 months, inclusive.

The results were striking. Almost all (14/16) of the children who posted the picture of an egg recalled their prior false belief, whereas none of the other conditions gave more than 7/16 successes. So the suggestion is that the picture of an egg provides a sort of tracer of the false belief for the child to use. The failure of the eggbox cues seems to show that the children had no insight into how the false belief originated in an initial sight of the eggbox—

the children could not use a picture of an eggbox to retrace the route through which the misinterpretation had entered their minds.

But what of the failure of the sample egg? Perhaps that yielded false negatives in the data. Perhaps some children imposed the unwanted evaluation on the sample that *all* the eggs had been removed from the box, thus altering their initial interpretation of the contents of the eggbox to "nothing inside the box." True, not one child answered "nothing" when asked to report the prior false belief, but then "nothing" is perhaps a little odd as a reply to a *what*-question. The particular problem of assuming that the eggbox had been emptied does not seem to be applicable to the picture of an eggbox, and yet that failed as a cue. However, in the event, it was decided to run a test. Twelve children (one at almost each month of age between 34 and 48 months, inclusive) participated. After they said there were eggs in the eggbox, they were given a sample egg to post. Then each was asked "In this box (pushing forward the eggbox) are there eggs or is it empty?" (half the children had the reverse formulation "... is it empty or are there eggs?"). All bar one child said the box had eggs in it. So the danger of false negatives seems to be small. Ignoring that child who opted for "empty," it was noticeable that only 4/11 children succeeded in recalling their reiterated prior false belief when questioned immediately afterwards, replicating the weakness of the sample as a cue.

In the next experiment, in addition to posting a line-drawing or a sample, another group of children was given a plastic model of an egg to post, an object that is not usually to be found in a supermarket eggbox amongst a bag of shopping. A model is distinguishable from the reality that it is directed towards but is much more like the real 3-D object than is a line-drawing. DeLoache (1989) argued that young children grasp the symbolic status of a picture more easily than of a model, and we expected that the model would give success at an intermediate level between that of the picture and the sample.

Simon Coulton and Juliette Hall tested children aged between 33 and 52 months, inclusive. The line-drawings gave rise to 31/43 successes and the sample gave rise to 16/43 successes. The plastic model was almost identical to the sample at 18/43 successes. So it looks as though there is something special about a picture as a symbol. It seems fairly safe to conclude that a picture that is in *correspondence* with the target belief ("Smarties," "egg") can be used by the child to detect a false belief in the mind. The immediate suggestion is that the stark deficit accounts of Astington and Gopnik (1988) and Perner (1991) need amending. The developmental advance from ages three to four years seen in traditional unaided-recall tests does not readily translate into a lack of false belief competence followed by competence.

More recently, Perner (this volume) has ingeniously argued that the three-year-old deficit in traditional tests is due to a lack of differentiation between a concept of belief and a concept of pretence. His argument is that children will fail a rigorous false belief test until a concept of belief has emerged. It is possible that the very young children who succeeded in our tests did not really *believe that they had believed a falsity* about the contents of the container. If all the successful children were to maintain, on further questioning, that they had "only pretended" to think what they said they had thought, that would be congenial for Perner's revised account of development. Yet when we questioned children at the end of the study about whether they had "really thought" or "only pretended" when they had told us their prior belief, an interesting effect emerged. In the first experiment, with the Smartie box (pooling across the conditions we have noted and some others that occurred when systematically varying the administration of the test), 72% of those children who successfully recalled their false belief opted for "really thought" and 78% of those children who erroneously said they had thought there were pencils in the box opted for "only pretended!" The latter finding is queer, because there really were pencils in the box and yet the children were denying that their report of pencils was real enough to support the label "thought." Perhaps the children registered that there was something amiss with their reality-directed answer, but were unable to identify quite what it was that had gone awry.

But the pretend/think question had been asked at the very end of the experiment; after asking the traditional memory control and reality control questions "what is in the box?" and "what did you post?", so had to be prefaced with "when you told me there were Smarties/pencils [according to child's answer] in the box..." and that may have been confusing. In itself, the objection cannot explain away the cross-over, but it is desirable to consider asking the pretend/think question immediately after the child's reply to the critical test question. When this was done, in the eggbox experiments, the cross-over vanished in favour of virtually 50-50 answers. Perhaps Perner was right in supposing that children are confused over, or oblivious of, the difference between "pretend" and "think." However, it was noticed that a high number of children refused to answer or said "don't know." That suggested to us that the question, following as it did hard on their answer to the test question, may have been received as sceptical or hostile. In such a case, one is reluctant to put too much weight on what could well have been random choice by those who did answer. Yet one finding is suggestive: There were far more children who refused to answer or said "don't know" amongst those who gave an erroneous reality-directed answer than amongst those who succeeded in recalling their false belief, at 58% and 38% respectively ($\chi^2(1) = 7.61$, $P < 0.01$). Perhaps those who were reality-directed were aware that they were not properly giving a mental state report so were reluctant to attach an epistemic label to their report. Again, then, what evidence did emerge favoured the successful children.

To sum up, there were distinct indications that children in and around the first half of the age-group of three-year-olds can indeed recall a prior misinterpretation if they are given access to an iconic symbolic tracer. The doubt concerning the outcome of their pretend/think reflection on what they have done in recall suggests that such young children do not yet have an explicit theory of mind that encompasses their ability to re-present a misrepresentation in the form of a report. Indeed, the failure of the picture of an eggbox as a cue indicates that the children have not grasped the importance of the anchoring of a belief in its causal conditions. Such a grasp is surely crucial in a theory of beliefs because reality-directed beliefs arise in the mind from informational access to reality; unlike pretence, which arises by stipulation about an imaginary world, with objects in the real world selected as props to the drama (Harris & Kavanaugh, 1993).

The research pushes back the quest for the origins of an ability to deal with a situation in which a genuine misrepresentation arises to an earlier stage of development, at around the age of three years. The children's competence was manifest under the right sort of conditions for a symbolic account, namely where a semantically evaluable object served a symbolic role in associating a mental state with a referent. The children registered, at some level, an association between a belief as a misrepresentation and a picture as a vehicle of representation.

It is interesting that previous work on young children from within the theory of mind tradition has procedurally *dissociated* pictures and beliefs. Zaitchik (1990) invented a pictorial analogue of a false belief test in which a polaroid photograph of an object was taken, the object was moved from location A to location B, and the children were asked to predict what would appear on the developing photograph. Three-year-olds failed—they predicted that the photograph would show the object at location B. Zaitchik therefore suggested that three-year-olds have an across-the-board problem in inferring a "wrong" representation. Leslie and Thaiss (1992) showed that children with autism could pass the photograph test with ease yet still failed a false belief test, and suggested that pictorial and mentalistic processing was carried out in different modules. Yet, we suggest, by taking principles of representation literally and using the "tracer' metaphor as a disposable aid to launch the research, we have found an association between the two symbolic media at the requisite level for inferring the existence of a target competence. The research was focused on an adaptation of one particular form of false belief test but there is no reason why it should not be extended to other forms of testing.

IMPLICATIONS FOR EXPLANATION OF
CONCEPTUAL ADVANCE

The argument so far has been that three-year-olds possess a concept of representation that is acquired in the course of computations at the level of perception and action. What is a concept?

Carey (1991, p. 258) formulated the matter in the following way: "Concepts are units of mental representation roughly the grain of single lexical items, such as *object*, *matter* and *weight*. Beliefs are mentally represented propositions taken by the believer to be true, such as *Air is not made of matter*. Concepts are the constituents of beliefs" (original italics). It is possible to describe theory change in terms of change in a network of beliefs and in terms of the reorganisation of constituent concepts and an amplification of their domain of application (analogical reasoning can be a powerful amplification method—see Goswami, 1992). The two descriptions are complementary in accounting for theory-change, and the literature on theory of mind is full of accounts that stress either belief-construction or concept-differentiation as the more important aspect on which to focus for various purposes. A good example is in the work of Perner. In the early stages he emphasised the task of identifying children's beliefs about belief (Wimmer & Perner, 1983), then identified concept-belief relations as crucial to theory-change (Perner (1991, p. 11): "One can think of the concept of 'representation' as playing a catalytic role in children's reconceptualisation of what the mind is . . . . The understanding of representation helps children form a theory of mind out of their existing mentalistic theory", and, more recently in this volume, Perner emphasises the differentiation of a primitive concept "prelief" into "belief" and "pretence."

Congruent with Perner's suggestion is the powerful evidence adduced by Lillard (this volume), that many five-year-old children fail to identify the key distinction between pretence and belief. However, as was stated earlier on, it is quite acceptable to suggest that the child has a defective theory at the secondary level—the crucial question is whether one thence infers that the child lacks the requisite concepts or has the concepts in place but has not yet set them to work at a higher symbolic level. The child's understanding of perceptual representation is available as a template for her higher-order understanding of belief.

That formulation tallies well with that of Gopnik, Slaughter, and Meltzoff (this volume). Indeed, those authors cite remarkable initial evidence that solving certain perceptual problems can precipitate an advance in the child's understanding of false belief. The demonstration adds to the authors' compilation of evidence that when perceptual tasks and belief tasks are equated for representational difficulty, proficiency is greater with the perceptual tasks. The authors conclude that, some time around the age of four, the child is forced to generalise a concept of misrepresentation from its perceptual base by attempts to solve an accumulation of counter-evidence.

The focus of the account is well placed. But is it entirely right in its emphasis on counter-evidence as revelatory of the *mechanisms* of conceptual advance? It is, of course, possible to regard the posting technique as forcing children (Gopnik, 1991, p. 13): "To recognise the contradiction between the action they had just performed (picking a picture of candies), which was well within the scope of their memory, and their theoretical prediction about their past belief." But picking a real egg or a plastic model is no less of a "contradiction" in *content* than picking a line-drawing, and yet there was some evidence for the superiority of the drawing as a symbolic aid. To reiterate the position suggested earlier on in this chapter, it is important to keep sight of a positive formulation: The child registers the similarity between the picture as a vehicle of representation and the prior belief as a representation.

Kosslyn (1980, p. 455) noted that there was: "no obvious necessary reason for people to have imagery at all." Yet our species is noted for its iconophilia. Even two-year-olds need very little encouragement to produce pages of scribbles, which they stipulate as being recognisably representational. Two-year-olds also readily recognise the referents of pictures in the real world. There is no evidence that the capacity to regard icons as purportedly fictional or factual needs any special training beyond mere exposure to the opportunities to see pictures and to make them. We agree with Kosslyn (1980, p. 455) that: "Even if images are not the mother of all internal representations they may be important as an 'engineering' feature of the mind which is not necessary or fundamental so much as just convenient." Kosslyn added that imagery can be used to simulate transformations of the world. Pictures are tangible referents that warrant interpretation and can bridge the gap between fiction and fact in a saliently perceptible form. I suggest that two-year-olds take a decisive step towards understanding the mediating role of pictures between actuality and possibility in the pictures' capacity to form vehicles of representation. Young three-year-olds intuitively use an iconic mediator in accessing a misrepresentation. From that beginning, children start to develop beliefs about beliefs as representations: For all one knows, the children conceive of beliefs as something akin to pictures in the mind—the mental imagery studied by Kosslyn (1980). But one thing seems sure—when confronted by the miniature examinations that have developed in the theory of mind tradition, children's performance tends to go to pieces. Surely a search for competence should encompass a search for the public *symbolic aids* that children can use in understanding the mind of agents. Such research involves a shift from collating children's separate successes and failures to analysing what symbols *children themselves* associate together under what circumstances.

ACKNOWLEDGEMENTS

The work was supported by research grant R000-23-2330 from the Economics and Social Research Council, held jointly with Charlie Lewis. A great deal of help was also given by Hazel Lacohée (on an ESRC postgraduate grant), Simon Coulton, and Juliette Hall. John Morton and Jo Perner gave their own versions of sceptical solidarity at inconvenient stages in the development of the account.

REFERENCES

Astington, J.A., & Gopnik, A. (1988). Knowing you've changed your mind: Children's understanding of representational change. In J.W. Astington, P.L. Harris, & D.R. Olson (Eds.), *Developing theories of mind*. Cambridge: Cambridge University Press.

Beckwith, R.T. (1991). Language, emotion and nominalism. In D. Frye & C. Moore (Eds.), *Children's theories of mind*. Hove: Lawrence Erlbaum Associates Ltd.

Bryant, P.E. (1982). The role of conflict and agreement between intellectual strategies in children's ideas about measurement. *British Journal of Psychology, 73*, 243–251.

Carey, S. (1991). Knowledge acquisition: Enrichment or conceptual change? In S. Carey & R. Gelman (Eds.), *The epigenesis of mind*. Hillsdale, NJ: Lawrence Erlbaum Associates Inc.

Crystal, D. (1984). *Linguistic encounters with language handicap*. Oxford: Basil Blackwell.

DeLoache, J.S. (1989). Symbolic functioning in very young children: Understanding pictures and models. *Child Development, 62*, 736–752.

Fodor, J.A. (1992). A theory of the child's theory of mind. *Cognition, 44*, 283–296.

Freeman, N.H. (1993). Drawing: Public instruments of representation. In C. Pratt & A.F. Garton (Eds.), *Systems of representation in children: Development and use*. Chichester: John Wiley & Sons.

Freeman, N.H., & Lacohée, H. (1993). *Pictures as "representation tracers" for false beliefs in three-year-olds*. Unpublished manuscript, University of Bristol.

Freeman, N.H., Lewis, C., & Doherty, M. (1991). Preschoolers' grasp of a desire for knowledge in false-belief prediction: Practical intelligence and verbal report. *British Journal of Developmental Psychology, 9*, 139–157.

Gopnik, A. (1993). How we know our own minds: The illusion of first-person knowledge of intentionality. *Behavioral and Brain Sciences, 16*, 1–14.

Goswami, U. (1992). *Analogical reasoning in children*. Hove: Lawrence Erlbaum Associates Ltd.

Harris, P.L., & Kavanaugh, R.D. (1993). Young children's understanding of pretence. *Society for Research in Child Development Monographs* (Serial No. 237).

Hogrefe, G.J., Wimmer, H., & Perner, J. (1986). Ignorance versus false belief: A developmental lag in attribution of epistemic states. *Child Development, 57*, 567–582.

Karmiloff-Smith, A. (1991). Beyond modularity: Innate constraints and developmental change. In S. Carey & R. Gelman (Eds.), *The epigenesis of mind*. Hillsdale, NJ: Lawrence Erlbaum Associates Inc.

Kosslyn, S.M. (1980). *Image and mind*. Cambridge, Mass.: Harvard University Press.

Leslie, A.M., & Thaiss, L. (1992). Domain specificity in conceptual development: Neuropsychological evidence from autism. *Cognition, 43*, 225–251.

Lewis, C., Freeman, N.H., Hagestadt, C., & Douglas, H. (1992). *Narrative access and production: Necessary and sufficient conditions for preschoolers' false-belief reasoning*. Unpublished manuscript, University of Bristol.

MacWhinney, B. (1987). *Mechanisms of language acquisition*. Hillsdale, NJ: Lawrence Erlbaum Associates Inc.

Mitchell, P., & Lacohée, H. (1991). Children's early understanding of false belief. *Cognition, 29*, 107–127.

Perner, J. (1991). *Understanding the representational mind*. Cambridge, Mass.: MIT Press.

Perner, J., Leekam, S.R., & Wimmer, H. (1987) Three-year-olds' difficulty with false belief: The case for a conceptual deficit. *British Journal of Developmental Psychology, 5*, 125–137.

Pillow, B.H. (1993). Limitations on first-person experience: Implications of the "extent." *Behavioral and Brain Sciences, 16*, 69.

Plaut, D.C., & Karmiloff-Smith, A. (1993). Representational development and theory-of-mind computations. *Behavioral and Brain Sciences, 16*, 70–71.

Searle, J.R. (1983). *Intentionality*. Cambridge: Cambridge University Press.

Siegal, M., & Beattie, K. (1991). Where to look first for children's understanding of false beliefs. *Cognition, 18*, 1–12.

Sterelny, K. (1993). Categories, categorisation and development: Introspective knowledge is no threat to functionalism. *Behavioral and Brain Sciences, 16*, 81–83.

Wellman, H.M. (1990). *The child's theory of mind*. Cambridge, Mass.: MIT Press.

Wimmer, H., & Hartl, M. (1991). Against the Cartesian view on mind: Young children's difficulties with own false belief. *British Journal of Developmental Psychology, 9*, 125–138.

Wimmer, H., & Perner, J. (1983). Beliefs about beliefs: Representation and constraining function of wrong beliefs in young children's understanding of deception. *Cognition, 13*, 103–128.

Yoon, M.G., & Yoon, M. (1993). *Correct prediction of intentional action develops earlier than attribution of false belief in three-year-olds*. Unpublished manuscript, Dalhousie University.

Zaitchik, D. (1990). When representation conflicts with reality: The preschooler's problem with false beliefs and "false" photographs. *Cognition, 35*, 41–68.

ATTENTION, PERCEPTION, AND COGNITION: THE LEGACY OF INFANCY

6

Theory of Mind and the Facts of Embodiment

George Butterworth
University of Sussex, Brighton, UK

INTRODUCTION: ON MINDS AND CONSCIOUSNESS

Conceptual behaviourism is the thesis that behaviour can be the only observable basis for scientific psychology. This view held such sway in the past that psychologists in the vanguard of the cognitive revolution made the opposite mistake to the behaviourists, and they became conceptual cognitivists. They were so keen to promote a psychology of mental life that they were tempted to leave behaviour out of the explanation altogether. Cognitivists imported their own methodological strictures to be sure that they really were dealing with "pure" cognition. To study mental phenomena, for example to establish whether children or animals understand about beliefs or desires, it was thought necessary to eliminate any possibility of a behaviourist explanation.

One criterion adopted for "purely mental" phenomena is "intentional inexistence" (Chisholm, 1991). Psychological attitudes such as desires, hopes, wishes, and beliefs have objects, even though these objects do not necessarily exist, just as a child may believe that there are biscuits in the jar, even though the jar is empty. The unique characteristic of mental terms is that they can be related intentionally to nonexistent objects, for example, we can imagine fighting with dragons. Premack and Woodruff (1978) make use of the criterion of intentional inexistence in the "false belief" task. If the chimpanzee understands that another chimp has a false belief, or if it attempts to induce a false belief in a conspecific by deception, then it must ascribe mental states to other chimps. Similarly, the child who understands false beliefs at about four to five years, according to Wimmer and Perner (1983), must have at least a glimmer that others have mental lives not unlike the child's own. Thus, one of the central assumptions that has been made in the recent literature on the child's "theory of mind" is that an understanding of mental states can only satisfactorily be demonstrated independently of behaviour.

Demonstrating that chimpanzees and children comprehend the desires of their conspecifics by the ascription of mental states, rather than directly through overt behaviour, certainly suggests that a capacity to represent such states exists. However, it is as well to bear in mind that these tasks are methodological instruments for cognitive psychology, devised specifically to bypass explanations based on behaviourist reductionism. Correct perfor-mance on the tests should not necessarily be conceived as a watershed, or graduation ceremony, affording admittance either phylogenetically or ontogenetically to the world of the mind. Nor does the fact that children below a particular age fail on tasks which require them to reason about other minds necessarily mean that they have no earlier means to understand other minds.

Although reasoning about minds may be related systematically to theorising about minds (which is what psychologists do), the child's understanding of other minds may be misconstrued if she is considered first and foremost to be a folk psychologist, rather than a person in a social world. Leekam (1993) offers an excellent taxonomy of the various theories of "theory of mind." What all these theories have in common is the assumption that minds are unobservable entities that can only be known inferentially, or by imputing mental states to others. Hence, it is argued, the child constructs a systematic, although naive, theory of mind as her knowledge of mental states slowly accumulates. My own position is that minds are not theoretical entities and that mind can be perceived directly in behaviour. Theorising is not the ultimate source of knowledge about minds, rather information for mental events is available in social relationships. In real life, minds are situated in bodies and mental events are made manifest in social behaviour. If individual minds are socially constituted, then minds extend to, and are observable in, the social relations that constitute them. Ecological theorists, such as Gregory Bateson (1972a), maintain that it is a fundamental epistemological error to separate the mind from the ways in which it is evidenced through the body, and through human relationships, in society. Likewise, Coulter (1979) speaks of the "transparency of mind" in an attempt to get away from the conception of mind as a purely private, unobservable, inner mental state. These views taken on particular pertinence in the context of infant development, where the mind and body can be considered as one indivisible entity.

It is interesting to note that the antithesis between observable behaviour and unobservable minds has also been repeated in the recent history of the study of consciousness. This is not surprising, since states of mind inevitably imply states of consciousness. A small diversion into ways of defining consciousness will help to situate the ecological approach to mind that I should like to propose in this chapter. Just as the rise of cognitive psychology reintroduced mental events as a legitimate object of study, so too has consciousness been reintroduced in place of mechanistic explanations for behaviour. Hannay (1990) and Humphrey (1992) distinguish three uses of the word consciousness. Originally the word derives from the Latin *con*, meaning "together with," and *scire*, meaning "to know." In the original Latin the verb *conscire* (from which came the adjective *conscius*) meant literally to share knowledge with other people. In time, the circle with whom the knowledge was shared became tighter and tighter until it included just a single person, the subject who was conscious. That is, consciousness shifted from being a matter of public knowledge to one of private knowledge. Most recently, there was a further shift of definition to having knowledge to which, by its very nature, no one else could have access (knowledge of one's innermost thoughts and feelings). That is, consciousness became equated with subjective experience.

As Humphrey (1992) points out, the meaning of the word has not only become narrower and narrower, it has turned round. As he says, it is rather like the word "window," which has changed its meaning from "a hole where the wind comes in" to "a hole where the wind does not come in." Consciousness has changed from "having shared knowledge" to "having intimate knowledge not shared with anyone except oneself." Humphrey suggests that there has been a further shift from using the word transitively "I am conscious of such and such a thing" to using it intransitively, simply: "I am conscious." Just as the definition of consciousness as an attribute of mind has slipped from the public to the private domain, the notion that mind is unobservable encourages its definition as a theoretical construct. The definition of mind I should like to stress for very young babies is its transitive and shared public aspect, rather than the intransitive, private one.

Another distinction that may prove useful is that between "primary" consciousness, based on perception and "higher-order" consciousness, or reflective self-awareness, in early human development. I am borrowing the distinction between "primary" and "higher-order" consciousness from Edelman (1989), although I am using it here in a modified form. According to Edelman, primary consciousness is the state of being mentally aware of things in the world—of having mental images in the present—higher-order consciousness includes recognition by a thinking subject of his or her own thoughts, actions, and emotions. It embodies a model of the personal and of the past, future, and present and there is direct awareness of mental episodes. In essence, then, the distinction between primary and higher-order consciousness is one between consciousness of the products of perception (which, I will argue, may originate interoceptively or exteroceptively) and consciousness of mental events in themselves.

This chapter will pursue the argument that the embodied mind can be observed in human infants through their social behaviours, such as in imitation, in communication through joint visual attention, or in the comprehension of pointing. These phenomena reveal some direct under-standing of other minds as expressed through behaviour and as mediated through perception. These capacities do not require that the infant has a theory that other people have minds, nor does the baby perceive behaviour and then impute mental states to others (nor do we as adults perceive disembodied minds). From the infant's perspective there is no duality between the bodily and the mental. From the stance of ecological realism that will be adopted here, the expressive behaviour of other bodies reveals the presence of other minds, even to babies. The essence of the ecological approach, as recounted by Gibson (1966), is that perception is a means of obtaining information about reality, and this theoretical stance can be extended to include social information revelatory of other minds.

But perception is not the whole story. Developmental changes can also be observed in the infant's understanding of her own embodiment which are consistent with acquiring representational knowledge of self. Eventually, as the false belief task demonstrates, the child does become able to reason about the mental lives of other persons. I will attempt to make some links between these different levels of understanding of other bodies and their minds.

CONSCIOUSNESS AND THE NATURE OF EMBODIMENT

Traditional developmental psychology attributed little, if any, conscious awareness to the young infant. The assumption was that the newborn is merely a reflexive organism, all hungry body and little mind, responsive but with only the most limited ability to perceive. The earliest demonstrations of selective attention by Fantz (1956) showed that even newborns have visual preferences. He found that neonates prefer to look at patterned rather than plain stimuli, and also that newborns prefer face-like patterns. Subsequent research exploiting the preference technique has shown that babies, in the first few days outside the womb, prefer the sound of their own mother's voice to that of a stranger, they prefer the smell of their mother's breast milk to the breast milk of another nursing mother, and recently it has been shown that three-day-old babies prefer to look at their mother rather than a stranger (DeCaspar & Fifer, 1980; MacFarlane, 1975; Bushnell, Sai, & Mullin, 1989). Thus, even newborn babies discriminate important aspects of social reality from the outset. Such results certainly require a reappraisal of the perceptual abilities of newborn babies, with particular reference to their perception of persons.

Among the most challenging research of recent years has been the demonstration of imitation in newborn human infants. Neonatal imitation has now been shown for tongue protrusion, mouth opening, lip pursing, sequential finger movements, blinking, vocalisation of vowel sounds and emotional expressions (Field, Woodson, Greenberg, & Cohen, 1984; Kugiumutzakis, 1985; Maratos, 1973; Meltzoff & Moore, 1977; Reissland, 1988). Imitation is not reflexive. Newborns observe the model for several seconds and there is evident effort and progressive approximation to the model. Kugiumutzakis (1985) found imitation in many, but not all, neonates so long as the infants were in a quiet and alert state. Not all the models were imitated as statistically reliable levels: Among the facial models, tongue protrusion, mouth opening, eye blinking, and lip pursing were imitated usually after the fifth presentation. Among the acoustic models only the vowel sound "aah" and not the consonant "mmm" or the compound "ang" was reliably imitated.

Imitation in the newborn was called "participation" by Baldwin (1905), perhaps to emphasise the species recognition that it seems to imply. It has recently been shown that newborn infants imitate the dynamics (not the statics) of the acts they observe. Vinter (1986) showed that they need to see the act in progress in order to imitate it; they will not imitate if they merely observe a static protruded tongue. Toward the end of the first year of life, however, it is sufficient for the infant to see the end state (e.g. tongue protruded) in order to imitate it. That is, one-year-old infants can reproduce the dynamics of the movement given only the static end state. Newborn imitation also occurs within a relatively short reaction time, whereas Meltzoff (1988) has recently shown that, by eight months, babies are capable of deferred imitation over several days. By one year of age imitation can also take on symbolic properties; it is no longer merely literal, as in the neonate. Piaget (1962) showed this when his daughter tried to work out the modus operandi of the sliding drawer of a matchbox by moving her tongue in and out. Neonatal imitation is therefore the first level of a developing system of imitation, which comes to have the capacity for deferred and symbolic response. The thesis I wish to pursue here is that imitation in newborns is based on the operation of perceptual systems that give direct information about the correspondence between self and other. That is, the perceptual system specifies the equivalence between persons. In perceiving other persons the stage is set for perceiving other minds.

MECHANISMS AND MOTIVES FOR NEONATAL IMITATION

There are two important questions about neonatal imitation which will help develop our position further. How is neonatal imitation possible, especially when it involves parts of the body the infant cannot see, and secondly, why do babies imitate at all? The question of mechanism was first addressed by Sherrington (1906), when he distinguished between proprioception and exteroception. Proprioception is feedback that is specific to the activities of one's own body, whereas exteroception concerns the perception of the outside world. As elaborated by the perceptual psychologist, James Gibson (1964), proprioception is considered a general function, rather than a special sense, and it is normally a component of all perceptual systems. The argument I will elaborate briefly is that the mechanism of neonatal imitation depends on proprioceptive aspects of visual perception. That is, imitation depends on perceptual systems that provide information not only about one's own body, but also for the equivalence between self and other.

As to why infants imitate, Kugiumutzakis (1992) draws on evidence from neonatal preference for voice sounds, and other aspects of their sensitivity to sound and affective tone, to suggest that imitation reflects an innate motive for communication. He argues that newborns show an "innate inter-subjectivity" and also that they distinguish between self and others from the outset. Kugiumutzakis suggests that imitation is not a reflex act that lacks volition, since imitation clearly has the characteristic of selective and effortful behaviour. The variability and goal-seeking character of the infant's response suggests a proto-intentional act, which implies some conscious awareness of a goal. He also argues that it is true hetero-imitation, i.e. imitation of another person and not simply the cyclic repetition of activity, which was all the newborn infant was traditionally considered to be capable of.

Meltzoff and Borton (1979) have produced convergent evidence that there may be a perceptual basis for imitation in their studies of inter-sensory perception in babies aged one month. They have shown that babies can transfer information from oral touch to vision. In their study, infants first suck a smooth or knobbly pacifier, without having seen it, when it is inserted into their mouth. The pacifier is removed and they are then presented with two large models of the pacifiers on either side of the visual field. Babies prefer to look at the model of the same shape and texture as the one they previously had been sucking. This demonstrates that there is a mechanism that registers, at least in some basic ways, the correspondence between vision and oral touch.

Kuhl and Meltzoff (1982) have also shown that babies at three months can detect the correspondence between lip movements and speech sounds.

Babies prefer to look at whichever of two video-recorded speaking faces corresponds with the sound track played between the televised displays. The face mouthing "ah ah ah" is preferred when the sound track corresponds with it, whereas the face on the other side, mouthing "ba ba ba," is preferred when that sound track is played. The implication is that imitation may assist the infant to read the lips and voice of the social partner and assist in communication and the earliest aspects of language acquisition.

Neonatal imitation, therefore, seems to be based on the mechanisms of perception. Perception carries information for self and for the external environment and can be considered as if it were a phase of action, just as action can be considered as a phase of perception. Hence, perceiving the dynamics of tongue protrusion provides some of the necessary information for production of the action. Although memory is, in some sense, involved from the outset, it too develops. This is shown by the capacity for deferred imitation, which increases with age (Meltzoff, 1988), as does the capacity to reproduce actions having observed only their end states (Vinter, 1986). With those provisos we may wish to argue that neonatal imitation is evidence in newborns for primary consciousness of other persons, and that it is based on perception.

OTHER MINDS AND COMMUNICATION

Until now, we have not mentioned the infant's capacity for emotional expression and the role that it may play in early communication. The newborn can perform seven facial expressions, which are usually regarded as species-specific and universal (happiness, sadness, surprise, interest, disgust, fear, and anger). These facial expressions are reliably observed during standard hospital assessment procedures for newborns (Field et al., 1984). It is interesting, therefore, that newborns have been shown to be able to imitate happy, sad, and surprised facial expressions (but see Kaitz, Meschulach-Sarfaty, & Auerbach, 1988). They widen their lips when the model has a happy face, protrude the lower lip during modelling of a sad face, and open eyes and mouth wide during modelling of a surprised face.

Trevarthen has perhaps done most in recent years to study the role of emotional expression in early communication. He follows Sperry in arguing that consciousness is the highest-level organising principle of the mind and that it is present as a motivation for learning and mental development at birth (Sperry & Trevarthen, 1991; Trevarthen, 1990; 1992). Consciousness, he says, is most readily evidenced in the infant's responses to people. Trevarthen distinguishes innate primary intersubjectivity (infant's conscious awareness of mother, especially in relation to emotion) from secondary intersubjectivity (infant's conscious joint awareness with mother of the world of objects).

Primary intersubjectivity consists of the exchange of feelings, a common code of cooing noises, facial and hand movements, concentration, pleasure, and surprise, which manifest even in very early social interactions between the two-month-old infant and the mother (Trevarthen, 1990, p. 3): "The universal emotions are the natural bridge between minds at any age." Primary intersubjectivity, Trevarthen argues, can be thought of as a directly perceived, conversational consciousness where communication occurs through the dynamic, transient shifts of emotion, as revealed in emotional expression of infant and adult like. Once again, the innate perceptual abilities of the baby make possible the comprehension of such complex exchanges. Infants, Trevarthen argues, have the capacity for communication within them and this develops both for intrinsic reasons and through social interactions. Those properties of mind revealed through emotional expression are transparent to the infant precisely because they are embodied in emotional expression. This argument is applicable to the theory put forward by Hobson (this volume), who offers an extended discussion, based on Wittgenstein, of how mental states such as anger, grief, and joy are revealed in the expressions of the face. Emotional expressions are neither purely mental nor merely behavioural.

Trevarthen has shown, by various means, the effects on the infant of disrupting emotional engagement with the mother. For example, when a happily communicating mother–infant pair interact over a video-system it is possible to show the synchrony between their behaviours microanalytically. If the happily engaged infant is then shown the live video-image of the mother delayed by a few seconds, the baby becomes puzzled and withdraws. Trevarthen argues that emotional signalling in the young infant is primarily adapted to a loving and playful partner and that it is the confluence of emotions between infant and adult, in social interaction, that underlies social communication. For Trevarthen, then, social consciousness is primary to communication and the further development of the infant. The emotional and expressive capacities of young infants are considered to be species-typical ways in which mental events are manifest in systems of joint activity, in primary intersubjectivity.

JOINT VISUAL ATTENTION

According to Trevarthen (1992) the infant achieves secondary intersubjectivity, based on jointly construed meaning, the negotiation of conventional knowledge, common purposes, and communication through symbols, towards the end of the first year of life. These more advanced aspects of knowledge of the world and of other minds are nevertheless founded upon the direct awareness underlying primary intersubjectivity. Our own research on joint visual attention and the comprehension and production of manual pointing in babies complements Trevarthen's work on the emotional foundations of intersubjectivity. Stated simply, joint visual attention concerns how an infant knows where someone else is looking, how a baby knows where someone else is pointing, and how babies produce pointing for other people. Joint attention concerns the foundations of referential communication; how babies share objects with other people. The definition of mind that might apply here is a transitive one of joint awareness of public objects.

There is no doubt that babies as young as six months are able to change their own line of sight to follow a change in the attention of another person (see also Baldwin & Moses, this volume; Baron-Cohen & Ring, this volume). Contrary to the traditional assumption that infants are totally egocentric and therefore unaware of other minds, babies will take a change in the focus of attention of their social partner as indicating a potentially interesting sight for themselves and they will turn to look for it. In our carefully controlled studies, an adult turns, slowly and deliberately, to look at one of several targets positioned around the room. Babies can find the target the adult is looking at and we have described several different mechanisms for this, which arise during the first 18 months of life (Butterworth & Jarrett, 1991). The earliest mechanism, certainly apparent in six-month-olds, we call the ecological mechanism. The mother's change of gaze signals the direction in which to look (to the left or to the right) but it does not specify the precise location within the visual hemi-field. However, if the target is sufficiently attention-worthy, it will single itself out. Hence, the attractive characteristics of the object that initially led the mother to turn and look, and which led the infant to turn in the same direction, finally complete the reference triangle. The minds of the mother and baby meet in the self-same object, in the world.

Later in development, by about 12 months, a new mechanism appears, which we call geometric, because the mother's gaze or pointing hand specifies not only the direction but also, rather precisely, the location at which to look. The geometric mechanism does not replace the ecological one. Under normal circumstances both processes collaborate in singling out the object of mutual interest. From a developmental perspective something has been gained, since the geometric mechanism allows joint reference even where one object has no intrinsically more attention-worthy properties than any other. Definite reference can be made again to allow communication and a meeting of minds in the self-same object.

One of the most striking phenomena we have discovered, however, is that the ability to look where someone else is looking or pointing is limited by the boundaries of the infant's own visual field. At 12 months, when the laboratory is stripped bare of targets, babies do not search behind them (Butterworth & Cochran, 1980). Instead, on the adult's signal the baby turns through about 40° and, failing to encounter a target, gives up the search. Only at 18 months do babies succeed in searching in the invisible space behind themselves when the adult looks there (Butterworth & Jarrett, 1991). At the average age of 12 months, the baby begins to comprehend manual pointing, but this still does not extend the boundaries of joint attention. Grover (1988, see also Butterworth & Grover, 1988; 1989), showed that babies fail to search beyond the boundaries of the visual field even when the mother looks and points behind the baby.

These data suggest that the infant takes her own visual field to be held in common with others (which of course it is!). Perception necessarily originates at a particular viewpoint but, as the results show, the infant also perceives that others can have a perspective on a common space. Thus, the boundaries of the infant's visual consciousness are revealed by the joint attention task and, at the same time, the task shows that the infant is aware that others also perceive a world of objects. Objects serve as the public intermediaries between the infant and the adult. That joint visual attention does indeed serve the purposes of communication is revealed clearly in social referencing tasks, where the mother's emotional expression will influence the child's behaviour toward the object of joint attention. Where the mother expresses fear or disgust, the infant will avoid the object toward which the particular emotion has been directed (Bradshaw, Campos, & Klinnert, 1986).

Perhaps the clearest evidence that the infant is concerned with communicating comes from the study of manual pointing. Infants produce pointing at about 14 months and we know that this gesture bridges nonverbal and verbal communication. Pointing, with the typical extended index finger posture of the hand, is species-specific to humans (see Whiten, this volume, for further comparative evidence). In our most recent studies we have examined the production of pointing in babies. We use automated toys, either a toy truck that can move from place to place or remotely controlled doll figures that move their arms and legs. Babies find these objects very interesting and they will point at them. Noteworthy, for our argument about conscious awareness of other minds, they will often check that the adult has taken notice of their point. Checking reveals a concern for the effectiveness of communication (Franco & Butterworth, 1991). We were particularly interested to find that 14-month-old babies, when tested in pairs, also point for each other and check that their message has been received (Franco, Perruchini, & Butterworth, 1992). It seems unlikely that 14-month infants are theorising about each others' minds. It is simpler to say that they wish to communicate and that this necessarily entails some basic awareness of their success or lack of success, as revealed in the bodily orientation, facial expressions, and behaviours of the addressee.

William James (1947) argued that joint visual attention depends on expressive movements that lead unrelated minds to terminate in the same perception. Objects, he said, are coterminous, mutual aspects of experience. Indeed, he argued that other minds are known only by virtue of the body's expressive movements and their effects on one's own perception. A change in another person's visual orientation, or manual pointing, signals to the infant the possibility of an object, just as the changes in emotional expression we have just been discussing may refer transparently to the feeling states that accompany them. James argues that minds have external space in common. Visual space, for instance, acts as a public location, as a receptacle for experience. Both perception and emotion have their perceptible objects within this publicly accessible space. Thus, it is possible to observe properties of mind, in their earliest manifestation, in the social interaction between persons and in relation to objects. Mind and its objects are transparently revealed in expressive behaviours whose purpose is to communicate.

SELF-CONSCIOUSNESS AND THE TRANSITION FROM DIRECT PERCEPTION TO REPRESENTATION

By the second year, the baby is entering the linguistic community and beginning also to show evidence of reflective self-awareness, or higher-order consciousness. Recognising the self in a mirror is revealed by the infant removing a surreptitiously placed dab of odourless rouge from the nose, using the mirror reflection as a guide. Rouge removal has been taken as a particular index of self-consciousness. Human infants solve the task at about 15 months, which suggests that the infants, by this age, have a visual image of their own appearance.

Gordon Gallup (1970) showed that chimpanzees and orangutans are the only primates capable of solving this task. I have argued elsewhere that recognising oneself in a mirror is actually a complex intellectual task and that interest in the mirror image may be based on different mechanisms at different ages, ranging from simple awareness of the contingency between their own behaviour and that of the mirror image to knowledge of the visual appearance of the face (see Table 6.1 and Butterworth, 1992). Rouge removal may require comprehension of the reflective qualities of the mirror, a concept of self, self-identification by means of memorised distinctive features, plus comprehension of the identity of the reflected image with self and attribution of the reflected image to the self. On the evidence of the mirror task, these abilities are restricted to two higher primates other than man. It seems possible that this marks both an ontogenetic and phylogenetic boundary between primary and higher-order consciousness of the embodied self, although it would be a mistake to suppose that mirror awareness is the only possible index of self-knowledge applicable to other organisms. Nevertheless Gallup (1992) has suggested that performance on the rouge

TABLE 6.1
Main Stages in Mirror and Video Self Recognition Tasks During Infancy[1]

Developmental Stage	Age	Characteristics
Unlearned attraction to images of others	3–8 months	Interest in mirror, touches, smiles, behaves "socially" to reflection
Self as a permanent object	8–12 months	Aware of stable categorical features of self, locates objects attached to body using mirror image, differentiates contingent from noncontingent video-recordings of self[a]
Self-other differentiation	12–15 months	Uses mirror to locate others in space. Differentiates own video-image from that of others[a]
Facial feature detection	15–24 months	Recognition based on self-specific features. Success on "rouge removal" tasks

[1] After Butterworth (1992).

[a] These are actually very conservative measures of infants' social awareness. Using contingent and noncontingent video-feedback, Trevarthen has found that infants as young as three months show signs of distress and disengagement when shown noncontingent video-feedback of their own interaction with their mothers.

removal task predicts performance of monkeys and apes on introspectively based social strategies and on tasks that require the imputation of mental states to others. If this is true, then the mirror task may be taken as an early marker for the transition from direct perception to representation of self and others and perhaps the beginning of a differentiation of "mind" from "body" as cognitive processes become recursive upon themselves. This argument will be pursued further in relation to the classic diagnostic test for a representational "theory of mind," the false belief task, (also known as the unexpected transfer task).

THE FALSE BELIEF TASK

So far we have argued that very young babies show awareness of embodied minds by direct perception. If we accept the Gibsonian position on perception, the question becomes: How does development progress from direct perception of embodied minds to the representation of mental states? On a Gibsonian account, the developmental pathway would have to be from information about other minds obtained through perception, to a representation that preserves the information originally derived from perception. Furthermore, given the human capacity for symbolism and language, this information may be re-represented in different ways.

The unexpected transfer task ("false belief") is critical to this argument, since it supposedly gets at specifically mental states by incorporating the requirement of "intentional inexistence." To understand "misrepresentation" may require additional cognitive mechanisms to those of direct perception. However, it may not be necessary to argue that what is required is a theory of mind. Rather, a different type of representation may be necessary to ascribe false beliefs than for the ascription of true beliefs that can directly be observed in behaviour.

This argument can be illustrated through Wimmer and Perner's (1983) paradigm, where the young child is told a story, using props. The story concerns a child called Maxi who helps his mother unpack the shopping and places a bar of chocolate in a green cupboard, being careful to remember where he stored it, so that he can come back later and eat some. He then goes off to play. His mother then uses some of the chocolate in cooking and places the remainder in another, blue cupboard. Mother leaves the scene and Maxi returns. The child is asked where Maxi will search for the chocolate. Children of four years say that he will look for it in the blue cupboard, where it was most recently hidden, even though Maxi could not know this. Between four and five years, the child says Maxi will look for it in the green cupboard, where Maxi last saw it. They reveal knowledge of Maxi's false belief (there is, however, some evidence that children as young as three can solve similar problems under some circumstances: Bartsch & Wellman, 1989; Moses & Flavell, 1990). The younger child, who fails the test, egocentrically bases her judgment on her own knowledge of the visible movements of the object. She fails to take into account that some of these movements were not visible to Maxi.

The test depends on representing the information available to the visual perception of another observer. Understanding false belief is inferred from specifying the position of the object within a represented reality. It is striking that the task resembles, very closely, a series of physical search tasks devised by Piaget (1954) for assessing a baby's understanding of object permanence. According to Piaget, babies become able to search manually for an object hidden under a cloth at about 9 months, followed by mastery of visible movements of the object by about 12 months, and culminating at about 18 months, when the baby will search persistently for a hidden object after invisible displacements of the object. The stage IV task is particularly important since perseverative errors occur, where the infant persists in returning to the first place from which an object has been retrieved, rather than allowing for the perceived movement of the object to a new place. Piaget might have argued that the failure of four-year-olds and the success of five-year-olds on false belief tasks demonstrates a "vertical decalage" between the achievements of stages IV, V, and VI of the sensorimotor stage in object permanence. Between four and five years the child successively masters the consequences, for another observer, of visible and invisible movements of an object in represented reality.

I have argued that babies in the stage IV age range can search correctly for objects hidden at successive locations. Errors in search are not inevitable; they are, at least in part, a function of the spatial conditions of testing (Butterworth, 1981). Correct search for objects hidden at successive locations and looking where someone else is looking both reflect the unexpected perceptual competence of the baby (see also Gopnik et al., this volume). What is crucial to search tasks is the infant's perception of the continuing identity of the object hidden at successive places; what may be crucial to joint attention tasks is perceiving a change in someone else's focus of visual attention as signalling the "permanent possibility of an object" to enable otherwise unrelated minds to meet in referential communication. So why do older children consistently fail on the unexpected transfer task, which requires specification of place from a viewpoint in a represented reality?

One crucial difference between object search tasks of infancy and the unexpected transfer task may lie in the representation of negative information. Joint visual attention and searching for hidden objects are necessarily positive, in the sense that the object is always present (although it may be hidden), and we may surmise that the spatial location information as to its whereabouts is iconically represented. That is, it is represented as it would be perceived. The unexpected transfer task requires the child to reason that, since Maxi did not see the movement of the object, Maxi would represent the object where it was first seen. That is, the child must be able to act as if the same object simultaneously exists and does not exist at two locations, depending on the perspective of each observer in the story. It seems possible that children may have no difficulty in the representation of positive beliefs as expressed through behaviour. However, the unexpected transfer task presents them with the requirement to represent the non-existence of the object somehow. The child must represent the place where the object is symbolically located if he is to take the perspective of Maxi successfully. In other words, the four-year-old specifies the true physical location (where the object is really located) and fails the task, whereas the five-year-old specifies the symbolic location (where the object does not exist) and passes.

On this analysis, passing the unexpected transfer task may not reveal the child's first understanding of mental events. It may, however, reveal the beginning of the ability to reason about "non-existence at a place," or intentional inexistence. Bateson (1972b) discussed the "mysterious step from the iconic to the verbal" in describing the differences between the signalling systems of animals and men. The ability to solve false belief tasks may involve a first level of integration between an "iconic" system of representation, which is adequate for "positive representation," and for basic intentional communication and another "symbolic" type of representation, which can cope with "negative representation." That is, reasoning about the non-existence of objects at a place may require a symbolic (non-iconic) mode adequate to the task of simultaneously representing counterfactual (negative) and factual (positive) states of affairs.

Such an ecologically based developmental progression, involving the interco-ordination and hierarchical integration of iconic and symbolic representation, may still yield the conclusion that children have difficulties with unexpected transfer. The difference over previous accounts is that comprehension of false beliefs is not divorced from perception of true beliefs, nor does it distance the developing child from what is real about minds. Such an analysis raises the possibility that the problem for the child may be one of hierarchical co-ordination of different types of representation. This is not the same thing as constructing a theory that other people have minds, nor does it amount to introspection or simulation of other minds. Such a fine-grained analysis of the representational processes involved could enable us to reunite research on reasoning about mental life with the ecological tradition, which rightly insists that minds are embodied and in the world.

CONCLUSION

The evidence reviewed on imitation and joint attention in babies suggests some major conclusions. First, there is evidence for primary consciousness in human infants that is based on the direct perception of mental states as revealed in behaviour, emotional expressions, and in bodily and other forms of orientation to objects. Furthermore, human social communication may be of central importance to the development of specifically human consciousness, and for knowledge of other minds, both in its primary and higher-order forms. Joint visual attention and the production and comprehension of pointing necessarily entail a meeting of minds in processes of referential communication. Although it is possible to demonstrate a variety of perceptual and cognitive mechanisms that come into play during early development, none of them need entail postulating that the infant communicates through the intermediary of a theory of mind. If development does not begin by constructing the rudiments of a theory of other minds, it is hardly necessary to postulate that subsequent development is a matter of acquiring a theory of mind. The perceptual abilities of the infant play an important and hitherto neglected part in primary consciousness and in perceiving other minds, and this is sufficient to provide the basic information for subsequent representation. The evidence from infancy may lead us to concur with Sperry and Trevarthen (1990) that: "Consciousness appears in the causal chain in the form of emergent properties in which motives and emotion-charged evaluations, coherent about a self and able to be communicated directly to others, play an essential part."

As Edelman (1988) reminds us, through language we may simultaneously experience primary and higher-order consciousness in interaction. The false belief task may well demonstrate the interaction of an initial, iconic form of representation and a subsequent symbolic form. We have argued that the origins of a representation of other minds may lie in processes of direct perception but the simultaneous representation of reality, within different representational media, may explain why children have difficulties, which have now been well documented, when reasoning about counterfactual states of affairs or about information not fully available to other minds.

ACKNOWLEDGEMENTS

An earlier version of this chapter was presented at a symposium on "Consciousness" at the Royal Society of Edinburgh, November 1992. Part of the argument developed in this chapter was previously outlined in my commentary, "Towards an ecology of mind," 1993, *Behavioral and Brain Sciences, 16*, p. 32. Cambridge University Press.

The research on joint visual attention cited by Butterworth and Grover and Franco and Butterworth was funded by the Economic and Social Research Council of Great Britain.

REFERENCES

Baldwin, J.M. (1905). *Dictionary of philosophy and psychology*. London: Macmillan.

Bartsch, K., & Wellman, H. (1989). Young children's attribution of action to beliefs and desires. *Child Development, 60*, 946–964.

Bateson, G. (1972a). *Steps to an ecology of mind*. San Francisco: Chandler Publishing Co.

Bateson, G. (1972b). Redundancy and coding. In G. Bateson, *Steps to an ecology of mind* (pp. 417–425). San Francisco: Chandler Publishing Co.

Bradshaw, D.L., Campos, J.J., & Klinnert, M.D. (1986). *Emotional expressions as determinants of infants' immediate and delayed responses to prohibition*. Paper presented at the International Conference on Infant Studies, Los Angeles.

Bushnell, I.W.R., Sai, F., & Mullin, J.T. (1989). Neonatal recognition of the mother's face. *British Journal of Developmental Psychology, 7*, 3–15.

Butterworth, G.E. (1981). Object permanence and identity in Piaget's theory of infant cognition. In G.E. Butterworth (Ed.), *Infancy and epistemology* (pp. 137–169). Brighton: Harvester.

Butterworth, G.E. (1992). Origins of self perception in infancy. *Psychological Inquiry, 3* (2), 103–111.

Butterworth, G.E., & Cochran, E. (1980). Towards a mechanism of joint visual attention in human infancy. *International Journal of Behavioural Development, 3*, 253–272.

Butterworth, G.E., & Grover, L. (1988). The origins of referential communication in human infancy. In L. Weiskrantz (Ed.), *Thought without language* (pp. 5–25). Oxford: Oxford University Press.

Butterworth, G.E., & Grover, L. (1989). Joint visual attention, manual pointing and pre-verbal communication in human infancy. In M. Jeannerod (Ed.), *Attention and performance XIII* (pp. 605–624). Hillsdale, NJ: Lawrence Erlbaum Associates Inc.

Butterworth, G.E., & Jarrett, N.L.M. (1991). What minds have in common is space: Spatial mechanisms serving joint visual attention in infancy. *British Journal of Developmental Psychology, 9*, 55–72.

Chisholm, R.M. (1991/1957). Intentional inexistence. Reprinted in D.M. Rosenthal, *The nature of mind* (pp. 297–303). New York: Oxford University Press.

Coulter, J. (1979). Transparency of mind: The availability of subjective phenomena. In J. Coulter (Ed.), *The social construction of mind*. London: Macmillan.

DeCaspar, A.J., & Fifer, W. (1980). Of human bonding: Newborns prefer their mothers' voices. *Science, 208*, 1174–1176.

Edelman, G.M. (1989). *The remembered present*. New York: Basic Books.

Fantz, R.L. (1956). Visual perception from birth as shown by pattern selectivity. *Annals of the New York Academy of Sciences, 118*, 793–814.

Field, T.M., Woodson, R., Greenberg, R., & Cohen, D. (1984). Discrimination and imitation of facial expressions in neonates. *Science, 218*, 179–181.

Franco, F., & Butterworth, G.E. (1991, April). *Infant pointing, prelinguistic reference and co-reference*. Paper presented at the Society for Research in Child Development meeting, Seattle, USA.

Franco, F., Perrucchini, P., & Butterworth, G.E. (1992, September). *Referential communication between babies*. Paper presented at the Vth European Conference on Developmental Psychology, Seville, Spain.

Gallup, G.G. Jr. (1970). Chimpanzees: Self recognition. *Science, 167*, 86–87.

Gallup, G.G. Jr. (1992). Levels limits and precursors to self recognition: Does ontogeny recapitulate phylogeny? *Psychological Inquiry, 3* (2), 117–118.

Gibson, J.J. (1964). The uses of proprioception and the detection of propriospecific information. In E. Reed & R. Jones (Eds.), *Reasons for realism: Selected essays of James J. Gibson* (pp. 164–170). Hillsdale NJ: Lawrence Erlbaum Associates Inc.

Gibson, J.J. (1966). *The senses considered as perceptual systems*. Boston: Houghton-Mifflin.

Grover, L. (1988). Comprehension of the manual pointing gesture in human infants. Unpublished PhD thesis, University of Southampton, UK.

Hannay, A. (1990). *Human consciousness*. London: Routledge.

Humphrey, N. (1992). *A history of the mind*. London: Chatto & Windus.

James, W. (1947/1912). *Essays in radical empiricism: A pluralistic universe*. London: Longman.

Kaitz, M., Meschulach-Sarfaty, O., & Auerbach, J. (1988). A re-examination of newborns' ability to imitate facial expressions. *Developmental Psychology, 24* (1), 3–7.

Kugiumutzakis, G. (1985). *The origin, development and function of early infant imitation*. Unpublished PhD thesis, Department of Psychology, University of Uppsala, Sweden.

Kugiumutzakis, G. (1992). Intersubjective vocal imitation in early mother-infant interaction. In J. Nadel and L. Camioni (Eds.), *New Perspectives in early communicative development*. London: Routledge.

Kuhl, P., & Meltzoff, A.N. (1982). The bimodal perception of speech in infancy. *Science, 218*, 1138–1141.

Kuhl, P., & Meltzoff, A.N. (1986). The intermodal representation of speech in infants. *Infant Behaviour and Development, 7*, 361–381.

Leekam, S. (1993). Children's understanding of mind. In M. Bennett (Ed.), *The child as psychologist* (pp. 26–51). Hemel Hempstead: Harvester.

MacFarlane, A. (1975). Olfaction in the development of social preferences in the human neonate. *Ciba Foundation Symposium, 33* (pp. 103–113). Amsterdam: Elsevier.

Maratos, O. (1973). *The origin and development of imitation during the first 6 months of life.* Unpublished PhD thesis, University of Geneva, Switzerland.

Meltzoff, A.N. (1988). Infant imitation and memory: Nine-month-olds in immediate and deferred tests. *Child Development, 59,* 217–225.

Meltzoff, A., & Borton, R.W. (1979). Intermodal matching by human neonates. *Nature, 282,* 403–404.

Meltzoff, A.N., & Moore, M.K. (1977). Imitation of facial and manual gestures by human neonates. *Science, 198,* 75–78.

Moses, L.J., & Flavell, J.H. (1990). Inferring false beliefs from actions and reactions. *Child Development, 61,* 929–945.

Piaget, J. (1954). *The construction of reality in the child.* New York: Basic Books.

Piaget, J. (1962). *Play dreams and imitation in the child.* New York: Norton.

Premack, D.G., & Woodruff, G. (1978). Does the chimpanzee have a theory of mind? *Behavioral and Brain Sciences, 1,* 515–526.

Reissland, N. (1988). Neonatal imitation in the first hour of life: Observations in rural Nepal. *Developmental Psychology, 24,* 464–469.

Sherrington, C.S. (1906). On the proprioceptive system, especially in its reflex aspect. *Brain, 29,* 467–482.

Sperry, R., & Trevarthen, C. (1990, October). *Abstract: Turnabout on consciousness: A new concept of mental causation.* Paper presented at a meeting on Molecules and the Mind: The mind–body problem in epistemology and in the history of science. Cortina-Ulisse European Award (27th Edition) with Giorgio-Cini Foundation and the Sigma-Tau Foundation, Venice.

Trevarthen, C. (1990, October). *Consciousness in infancy: Its origins, motives and causal potency.* Paper presented at a meeting on Molecules and the Mind: The mind–body problem in epistemology and in the history of science. Cortina-Ulisse European Award (27th Edition) with Giorgia-Cini Foundation and the Sigma-Tau Foundation, Venice.

Trevarthen, C. (1992). The functions of emotions in early infant communication and development. In J. Nadel & L. Camioni (Eds.), *New perspectives in early communicative development.* London: Routledge.

Vinter, A. (1986). The role of movement in eliciting early imitation. *Child Development, 57,* 66–71.

Wimmer, J., & Perner, J. (1983). Beliefs about beliefs: Representation and constraining function of wrong beliefs in young children's understanding of deception. *Cognition, 13,* 103–128.

7

Early Understanding of Referential Intent and Attentional Focus: Evidence from Language and Emotion

Dare A. Baldwin and Louis J. Moses
University of Oregon, Eugene, USA

INTRODUCTION

Communication among adults is grounded in a theory of mind. As Grice (1957) and others (e.g. Clark & Marshall, 1981; Rommetveit, 1979) have made clear, we cannot make sense of communicative interactions without presupposing that the interlocutors possess mutual knowledge of relevant beliefs and intentions. In the case of children, recent research indicates that a rudimentary theory of mind is well in place by the early preschool years, as are a rich array of communicative skills (Moses & Chandler, 1992; Perner, 1991; Wellman, 1990). The present volume is centrally concerned with the origins of a theory of mind. One way in which we might profitably search for these origins is to examine the path of communicative development as a potential window on early understanding of the mental realm. Communicative development is a particularly rich arena for examining theory of mind development. Mature communicative skills depend on, and thus index, theory of mind abilities. Further, as communicative competence increases, children gain access to increasingly powerful sources of information about the mind. In this way communicative development not only reflects advances in mentalistic understanding, but also makes possible further enrichments in children's theories of mind.

In what follows we explore a variety of links between children's early communicative advances and their emerging theory of mind. We begin by describing the major communicative milestones of the infancy period. Next,

133

we sample the views of several authors with respect to what these early communicative achievements might indicate about infants' theory of mind and, in so doing, we find marked disagreement: For some, infants' communicative competence is taken as a clear indicator of an initial theory of mind, whereas for others more frugal, reductive interpretations of this competence seem preferable. We then describe our own programme of research, which is in part designed to help clarify the nature of the theory of mind abilities underlying early communicative skills. Two lines of research, one on language learning and the other on understanding of emotional signals, suggest that by 18 months of age, and possibly earlier, infants' communicative abilities are mediated by important insights into the nature of mental life, wherein other people are seen as psychological beings capable of thoughts, feelings, and intentions concerning what is taking place in the surrounding environment. In particular, by the middle of the second year, infants understand that other people's attentional cues (e.g. line-of-regard, gestures, and so on) reflect their *mental* focus and referential *intentions*. We end by considering more generally some of the interactive links between theory of mind and communicative development.

MILESTONES OF EARLY COMMUNICATIVE DEVELOPMENT

From the moment of birth infants are drawn into the circle of human interaction and are active participants in the social flow. Reflexive cries fortuitously summon adults when infants are distressed, and preferences for looking at detailed, dynamic, high-contrast visual stimuli lead infants to gaze intensely and persistently at others' faces (Banks & Salapatek, 1983; Haith, 1980; C. Nelson & Horowitz, 1987), a propensity adults find endearing and which promotes further interaction. Between two and three months of age infants begin to respond systematically to others' smiles with smiles of their own, a response that also serves to maintain and enhance the quality of interaction for both participants. They can discriminate facial expressions (e.g. happy from sad; C. Nelson, 1987), and by about four to seven months they have begun to abstract the invariance of facial expression across physically different instantiations, noting, for instance, the similarity of happy expressions even when they appear on different individuals' faces (Caron, Caron, & Myers, 1982; Ludemann & C. Nelson, 1988).

Around this age, infants also show an emerging interest in other sorts of communicative signals. For example, young infants will sometimes follow their mother's line-of-regard if they happen to notice that she is looking elsewhere (Scaife & Bruner, 1975; see also Butterworth, this volume), and they will also follow her pointing gestures to nearby objects (e.g. Murphy & Messer, 1977). Shortly after this—sometime between 8 and 12 months—

infants begin to comprehend a few individual words; for instance, they will look toward the correct object when a label such as "bottle" or "dog" is uttered by an adult (e.g. Oviatt, 1985). At about this same age "social referencing" is first observed: Infants make use of an adult's emotional signals—facial expression and/or vocal intonation—to guide their behaviour with respect to newly encountered events (e.g. Campos, 1983; Feinman, 1982; Feinman, Roberts, Hsieh, Sawyer, & Swanson, 1992; Sorce, Emde, Campos, & Klinnert, 1985).

Early in the second year infants begin to produce increasingly refined and conventionalised signals of their own. Points and showing gestures are now evident (Leung & Rheingold, 1981; Murphy, 1978), and by 14 months infants have been observed to check their partner's gaze direction after pointing, as if to determine whether their point has successfully effected the appropriate change in the other's attentional focus (Bretherton et al., 1981). At this time infants are often producing a few recognisable words as well as conventionalised gestures, such as holding their arms up high to indicate a wish to be picked up (Bates, Benigni, Bretherton, Camaioni, & Volterra, 1979; Bretherton, et al., 1981; Harding & Golinkoff, 1979). This is also a period of increased interest in engaging with others in co-operative enterprises. For example, Bakeman and Adamson (1984) found a marked increase between 15 and 18 months in the amount of time infants spend with others in joint focus concerning an object or external event.

As infants approach their second birthday, their communicative signals show a marked degree of sophistication. In the gestural realm they now show an ability to accommodate to the needs of their partner—for example, they will orient an object so as to take into account the other's line-of-sight (Lempers, Flavell, & Flavell, 1977). In addition, when an adult fails to respond appropriately to a gesture they will reproduce the gesture, and if this is not successful they will substitute other gestures as if to clarify their communicative intention (Bates, 1979; Golinkoff, 1986). In the language domain, learning begins to accelerate, although great strides have already been made. Infants between 18 and 24 months typically understand hundreds of words (Baldwin, 1991; Benedict, 1979), comprehend many multi-word sentences (Chapman, 1981; Hirsh-Pasek & Golinkoff, 1991), tend to be producing about a hundred words (Baldwin, 1991), and have begun to construct multi-word combinations of their own (K. Nelson, 1973).

IMPLICATIONS FOR INFANTS' THEORY OF MIND

We thus see the gradual emergence of a rich array of communicative skills in the first two years of life. However, although there is considerable agreement on when these various skills are acquired, it is much less clear what implications they have for how we should characterise infants' understanding of mental life. A broad spectrum of views can be found, many of them differing considerably over how richly the phenomena should be interpreted (Baron-Cohen, 1991; 1993; Baron-Cohen & Ring, this volume; Bretherton, 1991; Butterworth, 1991; this volume; Butterworth & Jarrett, 1991; Hobson, this volume; Leslie & Happé, 1989; Perner, 1991; Tomasello, Kruger, & Ratner, 1993; Wellman, 1993).

Toward one end of this spectrum are those who suggest that the communicative abilities of 9- to 12-month-old infants already presuppose some insight into the minds of others. Baron-Cohen (1991; 1993; Baron-Cohen & Ring, this volume), for example, argues that young infants' communicative behaviours rest on a primitive, but nonetheless genuinely mentalistic, understanding of other people's goals and focus of attention: Infants have what he calls an "attention-goal psychology" that will later blossom into a fully fledged "belief-desire psychology." In particular, Baron-Cohen believes that gaze monitoring, comprehension and production of proto-declarative points (points suggesting a desire to comment on, rather than obtain, an object of interest), and social referencing all indicate that infants comprehend another's focus of attention in terms of simple underlying mental states. That is, infants' ability to interpret focus of attention in these contexts suggests an understanding that the other is *interested* in some external object or event (in the case of gaze or point following) or has either a positive or negative evaluation of it (in the case of social referencing). Baron-Cohen bolsters his argument that these early-appearing competencies constitute the origins of a theory of mind by noting their absence in autistic children, a population for which there is mounting evidence of a range of other theory of mind impairments (Baron-Cohen, Tager-Flusberg, & Cohen, 1993). In a similar vein Wellman (1993), invoking much the same evidence, argues that one-year-olds possess a rudimentary understanding of the internal, subjective, and experiential nature of the psychological lives of others. In particular, he argues that infants of this early age already interpret others as intentional beings having subjective desires, perceptions, and emotions that are directed at things in the outside world.

At the other end of the spectrum are those who remain sceptical concerning whether a genuine theory of mind underlies infants' otherwise impressive communicative achievements. Butterworth (1991; Butterworth & Jarrett, 1991; see also Butterworth, this volume), for example, in discussing infants' ability to locate the target of an adult's gaze, argues that it is not necessary to attribute an abstract theory of mind on the basis of such abilities. Instead he proposes that infants may simply understand that changes in another's line of regard are good predictors of where an object might be located. For somewhat different reasons, Perner (1991) draws similar conclusions in discussing infants' gaze monitoring, pointing, and social referencing. He suggests, for example, that when infants point to a desired object and then check their mother's gaze to see if she has following the point, they need not understand the mentalistic aspects of her focus of attention but rather they may have simply figured out that appropriate looking on her part leads her to act in the right kind of way (e.g. to bring a desired object to the infant). Moreover, Perner argues, even cases of proto-declarative pointing—in which infants are clearly not pointing in order to obtain an object—do not amount to compelling evidence that infants are making a mentalistic interpretation of their mother's attentional focus. In such cases, he suggests, they may not be trying to manipulate her attention in order to produce a shared psychological experience but instead they may simply enjoy mastery over her eyes. Finally, with respect to social referencing, Perner points out that the mother's emotional expression might influence infants' behaviour without their understanding the mental experience underlying that expression. Instead of comprehending the psychological meaning of her emotional display, young infants may only understand what Perner calls its "environmental meaning." That is, they might merely have noticed the environmental correlation between the emotional expression and whether or not an object or event is threatening: They might just be following the rule (Perner, 1991, p. 128) that "when you see something dubious and your mother is watching you and shows a fearful face, then avoid that object or area." In sum, Perner suggests that early communicative abilities do not clarify whether infants understand the mental states of their communicative partners. He argues that other sources of evidence are required to illuminate early developments in theory of mind.

This brief sampling of opinion clearly indicates that there is very little agreement on how to interpret infants' early communicative competence. The existing evidence does not effectively discriminate between rich and lean interpretations of the kind we have just sketched. In view of this we have carried out several studies designed in part to determine just how sophisticated infants' communicative abilities might be and, in particular, to help decide between these alternative readings of the evidence. The logic of the studies has been to place infants in settings that would lead them to interpret communicative acts either accurately or inaccurately depending on whether they possessed insight into the mental lives of others. This approach has been taken in two domains: One of us has explored these issues extensively in the domain of language learning (Baldwin, 1991; 1993a; 1993b; in press), and we are now jointly pursuing a parallel set of studies in the domain of early emotional understanding (e.g. Baldwin, Moses, & Tidball, in preparation).

LANGUAGE LEARNING

As mentioned earlier, infants begin to comprehend a few individual words as early as 10–12 months, and by 18 months their comprehension vocabularies typically include hundreds of words. It has been argued by some that word learning during infancy proceeds primarily via simple associative mechanisms (e.g. Whitehurst, Kedesdy, & White, 1982). That is, new words may be acquired because over time infants register associative links between those words and the things with which the words correlate in their own experience. This process could be facilitated by the fact that parents often provide words at a time when infants happen to be focused on the object, event, or property to which the adult is referring (e.g. Collis, 1977; Harris, Jones, & Grant, 1983).

To the extent that such associative processes drive word learning, they would represent a surface-level analysis on the infants' part of others' communicative behaviour. Infants would simply note the presence of temporal contiguity between adult utterances and objects or events in the world, and recall the associations formed thereby; that is, they would not be undertaking any deeper analysis of *why* the adult happens to utter a word when a particular event occurs or a particular object is presented. If this is indeed a fair characterisation of how early word learning proceeds, then we would expect infants to make certain characteristic errors. In particular, they would tend to link a word with a given object or event any time those two things co-occurred in their experience, even when this co-occurrence was purely coincidental. For example, if an adult happened to utter an object label when infants were focused on something other than the correct thing—an instance of what we will call 'discrepant labelling"—infants would mistakenly link that label with whatever they themselves happened to be focused upon.

On the other hand, it may be that infants seldom fall prey to such mapping errors because they engage in a more sophisticated analysis of adults' utterances that helps to buffer them from the potential pitfalls of discrepant labelling. Infants may appreciate that people (1) utter words because they *intend* to refer to things or to talk about things, and (2) emit *attentional* cues as to the target of their reference—cues such as line-of-regard and gestures (e.g. showing, pointing, manipulating). If so, infants could then actively consult cues that speakers supply concerning the intended referents of their utterances. In a case of discrepant labelling, an active strategy to consult others' cues to reference would enable infants to avoid mapping errors, given that in speech to children speakers typically supply a rich and redundant set of cues regarding their intended reference (e.g. Kaye, 1977; Messer, 1978).

Making Sense of Discrepant Labelling

Observing how infants respond when discrepant labelling occurs is thus an ideal way to investigate whether they spontaneously initiate a deeper, mentalistic analysis of the speaker's reference. This is precisely what was done in two recent studies (Baldwin, 1991; 1993a). In this research, infants were shown two novel objects and heard a novel label applied four times to one of these objects under two different training circumstances: follow-in labelling (an adult looked at and labelled the toy of infants' focus) versus discrepant labelling (an adult looked at and labelled a different toy from the one upon which infants were focused). Later, infants were again shown the same two novel objects and were asked comprehension questions regarding the novel label (e.g. "Where is the *toma?*").

In the Baldwin (1993a) study, infants of 3 different ages participated: 14–15 months, 16–17 months, and 18–19 months. One finding was that infants across the 14–19 months span showed signs of noticing the discrepancy in focus that occurred between themselves and the experimenter in the discrepant labelling condition: In response to hearing the novel label during discrepant focus, infants were more likely to look at the experimenter's face and/or to look away from their own toy toward the other toy when discrepant labelling occurred relative to when the label was produced in a follow-in context. Apparently, then, even infants as young as 14 months actively monitor and follow another's attentional cues when language is provided.

However, such looking patterns alone do not clarify whether infants actually used the information they collected regarding the speaker's focus to guide their interpretation of the novel label. Of greatest interest is how infants interpreted the novel label in the two conditions as gauged by their response to the subsequent comprehension questions. First, it is important to consider how they performed on comprehension questions after follow-in labelling, because this provides a baseline estimate of their ability to establish a new word–object mapping in the experimental situation. In the two older age groups, infants selected the correct toy at high levels in response to comprehension questions after the follow-in condition training (68% [SD = 18] and 77% [SD = 21], on average, for the 16–17-month-olds and 18–19-month-olds, respectively), indicating that they had correctly linked the novel label with the appropriate referent. Infants in the youngest age group, however, were unsystematic in their responses (52% correct [SD = 31]). They appeared to be unable to establish stable word–object mappings in the experimental situation, perhaps because four exposures to the novel label was insufficient at this age.

Turning next to infants' comprehension performance following discrepant labelling, the question of interest is whether they would be led by a superficial analysis to make a mapping error, and hence to select the toy they themselves had focused on at the time of labelling, or whether they would select correctly the object that the speaker focused on at that time. Here again, age differences emerged. The 18–19-month-olds selected the correct referent at greater than chance levels (74% [SD = 3] on average), indicating that they had analysed the speaker's cues to determine the target of her utterance. However, infants in the 2 younger age groups (14–15-month-olds and 16–17-month olds) were unsystematic in their responses to the comprehension questions (59% correct [SD = 23] and 49% correct [SD = 37], respectively. In one sense, neither of these younger groups could be said to have made mapping errors. However, with the youngest group no mappings of *any* kind were established: Recall that infants in this age group even responded unsystematically to comprehension questions after follow-in labelling. Thus, little can be inferred about their ability to avoid errors from such random performance. In contrast, the 16–17-month-olds systematically selected the correct toy after follow-in labelling, and showed chance level responding only after discrepant labelling. This suggests that during discrepant labelling they had noticed the discrepancy between their own and the speaker's focus, and realised that the speaker was not referring to the toy of their own focus. Hence they avoided a mapping error they otherwise would have made had they relied purely on temporal contiguity. Yet, though they avoided errors, they seemed unable to identify the correct target of the speaker's utterance, a problem posing no difficulty for infants only slightly older.

An important control was included in this study to ensure that the results indeed tapped infants' use of others' attentional cues to guide their interpretation of new words: An additional group of infants in the study received the same training circumstances that were described earlier (follow-in vs. discrepant labelling), but instead of later being asked comprehension questions concerning the novel toys, they were asked preference-control questions (e.g. "Where is your favourite one?" or "Point to the one you like."). Since the novel label did not appear in the preference-control questions, infants were essentially free to select whichever toy they preferred (whether or not they understood the specific content of these questions). Thus the preference-control questions clarify whether the training circumstances led infants simply to prefer a particular toy. A preference on infants' part for the toy of their own focus after follow-in labelling but for the experimenter's toy after discrepant labelling would raise the possibility that the comprehension findings might reduce to simple preferential responding and hence be uninformative about word-learning. As it turned out, however, infants of all ages showed random responding to preference-control questions. This is in marked contrast to the systematic performance of the older age groups in response to comprehension questions, indicating that the comprehension findings truly reflected their use of attentional cues to interpret the novel labels.

In sum, then, when infants aged 16 months and up were faced with discrepant labelling they showed no sign of falling into mapping errors, indicating that they spontaneously initiated an analysis of the speaker's intended reference. Infants of 18–19 months provided especially clear-cut evidence that they had performed such an analysis successfully. Even though they had been looking at a different object when a novel label was uttered, they successfully linked that label with the appropriate referent, a referent which could only have been located through consulting the speaker's attentional cues.

One question raised by these findings is precisely what kind of analysis enabled infants to avoid mapping errors during discrepant labelling. As described earlier, a mentalistic analysis is one possibility: Understanding that people have *intentions* to refer, infants consult behavioural clues to that intent (e.g. line-of-regard, voice direction, body posture, etc.) and use these clues to help them in interpreting the new word. An intermediate possibility should also be considered, however. Perhaps infants simply orient to the speaker when sounds are uttered, and follow his or her line-of-regard or gestures without knowing why. These clues could merely serve to enhance the salience of the correct referent. In other words, infants may simply link the label to whichever object happens to be most salient, with line-of-regard and gestures being merely one way to enhance object salience. However, findings from two more recent studies (Baldwin, 1993b) rule out this intermediate possibility.

Distinguishing Referential from Non-referential Actions

The underlying logic of these studies was as follows. In a first study, infants heard a new label that was accompanied by *referential* action toward a novel toy. Then in a second study a different group of infants heard the novel label, but its presentation was this time accompanied by a salient *nonreferential* action. At issue, then, was whether infants would link the new label with the relevant object in the context of referential action, but inhibit such a link in the context of nonreferential action, despite the fact that both types of action enhanced the salience of the object involved.

In the first of these studies, in order to demonstrate that infants actually used the speaker's referential action to guide a new word–object mapping, it was necessary to rule out the possibility that mechanisms of association, such as temporal contiguity, were the source of infants' mappings. Although in the study described earlier infants did not rely on temporal contiguity to guide mappings, the robustness of this ability remained in question because temporal contiguity was only weakly instantiated. The present study was therefore designed to make temporal contiguity compete more strongly with the attentional cues available in referential action. Sixteen infants of 19–20 months participated in either of 2 conditions. In the conflict condition infants played with two novel objects that were then hidden in opaque containers (they did not know which object was in which container). The experimenter then raised the lid of one container, peered in, and produced a novel label (e.g. "It's a *modi*. A *modi*. There's a *modi* in here."). Next, she turned to the other container, extracted the toy that had not been labelled, and handed it to infants. At least ten seconds later, she extracted the toy that had been labelled from its container and offered it to infants. Thus, immediately after hearing the label infants viewed an incorrect object (the first toy), and only after an interval of ten or more seconds did they see the correct object (the second toy). After infants had finished playing with the two toys, their comprehension of the new label was tested: They were shown the two toys and asked questions such as "Where is the *modi*?" The issue of interest was whether infants would make use of the speaker's referential cues (e.g. her action of raising the lid and peering into the container during labelling) to guide any mapping that they established, in which case they should select the second toy. The other possibility was that temporal contiguity would determine the mapping, in which case infants should select the first toy. As it turned out, infants selected the second toy—the toy specified by referential cues—at greater than chance levels (67% [SD = 11.5]) when answering the comprehension questions.

To rule out the possibility that these accurate selections were due to a simple preference for the second toy over the first toy, another condition was included—the coincide condition. Infants in this condition received the identical training as infants in the conflict condition, except that they were immediately shown the toy the experimenter had labelled, and only ten seconds later were they shown the other toy. Hence, in the coincide condition, the first toy was now the appropriate toy to select in response to comprehension questions, and infants did indeed show an above-chance tendency to select the first toy (70% [SD = 14.9]). Clearly, then, a simple bias in favour of the second toy could not have been the basis for infants' selection patterns in the conflict condition. Finally, an additional control for preferential-responding, like that used in the earlier study (i.e. a further group of 16 infants received the same training but were asked preference questions instead of comprehension questions), clarified that these findings reflect word-learning rather than simple toy preferences on infants' part.

Taken together, then, these findings indicate that infants relied on the speaker's referential action, despite conflicting information from temporal contiguity, to direct the new word–object mappings they established. Perhaps, however, as described earlier, infants used the referential action only because it enhanced the salience of one object relative to the other, not because they understood that the speaker's action reflected her referential intent. To test this possibility, in a second study 16 infants of 19–20 months heard new labels in either a coincide or conflict condition in which the speaker provided a *nonreferential* action toward one container at the time of labelling. The training procedure in these two conditions was virtually identical to that in the first study, except that the experimenter manipulated the lid of one container *while looking in infants' direction* and saying "I'll show you a *modi*. Want to see a *modi*? A *modi*." This action, although not referential, was designed to make one container more salient than the other at the time of labelling. If infants establish new mappings simply on the basis of salience, then their pattern of responses to comprehension questions in this study should parallel that obtained in the first study—they should select the second toy in the conflict condition and the first toy in the coincide condition. However, this was not what occurred. Instead, infants responded unsystematically, suggesting that they recognised that the experimenter had not specified a clear referent for her utterance. As a manipulation check, infants' looking times for each of the containers were measured during the training phase to ascertain whether the nonreferential actions in the second study increased the salience of the container to the same degree as the referential actions in the first study had done. In both studies infants looked significantly longer at the container toward which the experimenter's action was directed than at the other container, and no significant differences emerged between the looking times across the two studies. Hence, although a non-referential action did in fact increase the salience of one container during labelling, this did not lead infants to link the new label with the object residing in that container. It is likely, then, that the mappings infants established in the first study were the result of an understanding of referential cues rather than mere salience effects. It is also noteworthy that in the second study infants failed to link the new labels with any object in a stable way, despite the fact that both salience and temporal contiguity were available to drive such mappings. These findings suggest that for infants as young as 19 months, as for adults, neither enhanced salience nor temporal contiguity is sufficient to justify a new word-object link. Infants seem to require clear-cut signs of referential intent before establishing a new word–object mapping. This is not to say that salience and temporal contiguity have no impact on word-learning; it is just that unambiguous signs of referential intent seem to be the crucial trigger for infants to initiate a new mapping.

Although these studies demonstrate that infants can distinguish referential from non-referential acts by at least 19 months, the precise basis on which they make this distinction is not yet clear. They could have used any combination of several sources of evidence concerning the speaker's referential intent. For example, in addition to differences on the action plane (i.e. line-of-regard plus contact with the container vs. contact alone), lexical and syntactic differences between the two studies in the carrier phrases within which labels were embedded may themselves have altered the likelihood that infants would infer referential intent. Whether infants of the age considered here possess the requisite lexical and syntactic knowledge to detect such subtle differences is currently unknown. In any case, what is important for present purposes is that infants are capable of distinguishing referential from nonreferential acts in at least some cases where multiple and redundant cues support this distinction.

All in all, the various studies described here provide the best evidence yet available that older infants are actually performing a mentalistic analysis of others' communicative behaviour. In the everyday world, surface effects like temporal contiguity and salience are often a consequence of infants' responsiveness to others' referential actions, but our findings clarify that these superficial contingencies are not the basis on which infants establish new mappings. That is, because infants follow others' attentional cues, they may often see the correct object first after hearing a new label, or find the correct object especially salient during labelling, yet they seem to regard such consequences as inessential to word mappings. Rather, they apparently draw inferences about others' intentions—specifically, their referential intentions—from close behavioural observation. It is these inferences that evidently serve as the impetus for establishing new word–object links.

INTERPRETING EMOTIONAL SIGNALS

Another context in which a mentalistic analysis of others' behaviour would serve infants well is the social-emotional domain. Emotions, like words, have an intentional, referential quality. They tend to be *about* things: One usually feels sad, ecstatic, disgusted, or fearful about something, be it an object, event, action, or outcome. Accurately interpreting others' emotional displays thus depends critically on both understanding this "aboutness" relation and being able to identify the relevant thing in any given instance. Attentional cues such as line-of-regard and ostensive gestures (e.g. showing, pointing, manipulating) can supply useful information regarding the target of others' emotional signals, just as they do in the language domain with respect to the target of others' utterances. An appreciation of the relevance of such attentional cues for guiding the interpretation of emotional displays would help infants to avoid certain kinds of misattributions. The problem here is analogous to that posed by discrepant labelling in the word-learning domain: In some cases infants may be focused on something other than the thing toward which another individual's affect is directed. If infants lack an ability to seek and utilise attentional cues to determine the target of the other's affect, temporal contiguity between the emotional expression and the object or event they are focusing on would lead them to link that affect with the wrong thing. If, however, infants appreciate the relevance that attentional cues have for interpreting others' emotional signals, such errors can be avoided. Again, then, under circumstances of discrepant focus, a superficial analysis of others' emotional signals would lead infants to a quite different pattern of mappings than would a mentalistic analysis.

As mentioned earlier, evidence concerning early social referencing is often taken as suggesting that even young infants are capable of a mentalistic analysis of others' affective displays. The social referencing phenomenon is this: When confronted with an unfamiliar object or person, infants of only 10–12 months have been seen to (1) glance toward a parent, and (2) subsequently behave toward the new object or person in accord with the affect that the parent displays (e.g. Feinman, 1982; Sorce et al., 1985). Based on such observations, many researchers have concluded that infants of this age spontaneously seek emotional information from the parent to help in resolving their uncertainty regarding the new object confronting them (e.g. Bretherton, 1992; Campos, 1983). Although several aspects of this interpretation have recently come under scrutiny (e.g. Baldwin & Moses, 1994; Feinman et al., 1992; Gunnar & Stone, 1984; Harris, 1989; Hornik, Risenhoover, & Gunnar, 1987; Mumme, 1993), of particular interest in the present context is whether infants' social referencing is informed by an appreciation of the significance of the other's attentional focus. Put another way, do infants recognise that the parent's affective display concerns a specific external thing, and can they actively consult attentional cues to locate the relevant thing even when a discrepancy of focus occurs?

An answer to at least the first part of this question is already available through work by Hornik et al. (1987) and Walden and Ogan (1988). In the Hornik et al. study, for example, infants were shown a novel toy toward which the parent displayed positive, negative, or neutral affect. Infants then had the opportunity to play with the toy in a room littered with other toys. Hornik et al. found that infants' behaviour toward the target toy was influenced by the quality of parental affect, whereas their behaviour toward the other toys was unaffected. This selective effect of parental emotional signals on infants' toy play persisted over time, even though parents displayed only neutral affect at the time of later assessment. It appears, then, that parental affect guides infants' behaviour in a specific rather than a global fashion, and that this effect is maintained for some time.

What has remained unclear, however, is whether infants appreciate the relevance of the parent's attentional focus to the interpretation of their affective displays. The Hornik et al. research was not directed at answering this question, and in their study infants were almost certainly already focused upon the target object when the parent provided affective information. Hence infants could simply apply parental affect to the particular object with which they were presently engaged without any need to check the parent's attentional focus. The critical issue, however, concerns infants' responses when there is a discrepancy of focus at the time of emotional signalling.

We are currently exploring this issue (Baldwin et al., in preparation). In a recently completed study, 32 infants (half 12–13 months, the other half 18–19 months) were shown 4 pairs of toys in succession, each pair in a different experimental condition. The toys included in the study were selected to be ambiguous to infants of 12–18 months, in the sense that they would be uncertain as to whether they should handle the toys or not. For example, one pair of toys included a fur-coated black plastic spider and a foam crescent-moon face displaying a dastardly expression. Toys within a pair were chosen so as to be easily distinguishable yet roughly balanced in salience. A standard procedure was followed across all four conditions: One toy in a given pair was pushed forward within infants' reach, and as they focused on that toy and initiated a reach, the experimenter supplied some affective information—positive in valence in two of the conditions (saying, for example, "Oh! Nice!" with exaggerated intonation), and of negative valence in the other two conditions (e.g. "Iiuu! Yecch!"). After producing the affect, the experimenter placed the toys side-by-side, equidistant from infants and within their reach. Infants were then allowed to play with the toys for up to two minutes. In one of the two conditions in which the experimenter produced positive affect, she looked toward the toy of infants' focus at the time of displaying affect (the *joint positive* condition), whereas in the other positive affect condition she looked toward the other toy—the toy with which infants were *not* currently engaged (the *discrepant positive* condition). The two negative affect conditions differed in precisely the same way—in one case, negative affect was supplied during joint focus (the *joint negative* condition); in the other case during discrepant focus (the *discrepant negative* condition).

This design enabled several questions to be addressed. A first question was whether infants would show any signs of having noticed discrepancies between their own and the experimenter's focus. If so, they might be more likely to glance toward the experimenter's face and/or the other toy in the discrepant focus conditions than in the joint focus conditions. Of even greater interest is how infants would respond to the toys following the experimenter's display of affect. If they fail to recognise the significance of the experimenter's attentional focus, then it is likely that they would link her affect with the toy on which they were focused at the time the affect was produced (the child's toy), regardless of whether the experimenter was focused on that toy when producing the affect (joint focus) or not (discrepant focus). Hence in both positive affect conditions they would respond positively toward that toy (contacting it quickly, manipulating it freely and at length, and showing positive affect toward it), whereas in both negative affect conditions they would respond negatively to that toy (being reluctant to contact it, treating it gingerly, manipulating it for a shorter period, and displaying negative affect toward it). In other words, infants would show an ability to distinguish between and be differentially guided by positive versus negative affect, yet no ability to appreciate the significance of joint versus discrepant focus. A different pattern would be expected if infants note and understand the importance of the experimenter's attentional focus: Their response to the experimenter's emotional display should be directed toward the toy of the experimenter's focus, rather than toward the toy of their own focus.

From videotapes, coders blind to condition judged whether, in response to the experimenter's emotional display, infants checked the experimenter's face and/or looked away from the toy of their own focus toward the other toy. These observations revealed that infants of both age groups were more likely to check the experimenter's face in response to a display of negative affect relative to positive affect, but no significant difference occurred for such checking during discrepant focus relative to joint focus. However, at both ages affect that occurred during discrepant focus elicited more looks away from infants' own toy toward the other toy than did affect displayed in a context of joint focus. These looking data suggest that negative affect led infants to be especially vigilant (see Mumme, 1993, for a related finding), and that infants across the 12- to 19-months span noticed when a discrepancy in focus occurred.

To ascertain whether infants were not only alert to such discrepancies, but also appreciated their significance for interpreting the experimenter's emotional signalling, a different set of blind coders was asked to judge the affective quality of infants' response to each of the toys in a pair on a five-point scale (ranging from extremely negative to extremely positive) both before (baseline estimate) and after the experimenter's affective display. We found that infants in both age groups were influenced by the quality of the affective display: They reacted more positively when the experimenter had displayed pleasure than when she had displayed disgust. Moreover, we found evidence that infants' reactions were appropriately influenced by the experimenter's attentional cues. That is, they reacted more positively to the toy of the experimenter's focus when the experimenter had signalled pleasure than when she had signalled disgust, and they did so not only in the joint focus condition but also in the critical discrepant focus condition, where the experimenter's focus conflicted with their own. These effects held up over and above infants' baseline affective response to the toys involved, hence clarifying that the results were not simply due to perseverance of infants' initial reactions to the toys, but indeed reflected the influence of the experimenter's emotional display.

In addition, however, some inappropriate generalisation occurred. That is, not only were infants influenced by the affect with respect to the toy of the experimenter's focus, they also tended to generalise their responses to the toy she had ignored (i.e. the other toy in the joint focus conditions and their own toy in the discrepant focus conditions). On the face of it, this generalisation effect might seem to call into question whether infants' emotional reactions were influenced at all by the experimenter's attentional cues. Perhaps the experimenter's affect simply had a global impact on infants, inducing either positive or negative mood and leading them to respond to both toys in accord with this mood. It is important to note, however, that infants' appropriate reactions to the toy of the experimenter's focus could not simply be the result of global responding or generalisation, because the effects held up for that toy even when infants' reactions to the other toy were partialled out. In other words, infants showed specificity in their reactions to the toys over and above generalisation: Their reactions to the toy of the experimenter's focus were more strongly influenced by the affect than were their reactions to the other toy.

These findings are noteworthy on several counts. This is the first evidence to date that infants of 12 months and older not only notice that another's attention is discrepant from their own, but also use another's emotional signals *in reference to* the object of that individual's focus. By this age, then, infants are capable of avoiding errors in the interpretation of others' emotions that would otherwise occur under circumstances of discrepant focus. The strength of their ability to do this, however, remains in question because in our study they also tended to generalise their emotional reactions to the other toy. To the extent that they do this in naturalistic circumstances, they would in fact make some errors in interpreting the target of other's emotions.

In fairness to our infants we should point out that a number of factors in the study may have created uncertainty in infants' minds as to whether just one rather than both toys was the target of the experimenter's affect. It is possible that the cues to both affect and attentional focus may not have been strong enough or clear enough in this study for infants to avoid overgeneralising. In addition, certain pragmatic aspects of the task may have actively misled infants to generalise to both toys. For example, although the experimenter displayed affect toward just one of the toys, she then subsequently gave infants both toys. This impartial approach on the experimenter's part may have led infants to be uncertain about the degree of specificity that should be assigned to her affect. For example, infants may have felt (with some justification) that, in the negative affect conditions, if she had been genuinely disgusted with the toy in question she would not have given it to them at all. Similarly, in the positive affect conditions, they may have felt that if she was only pleased with one of the toys she would not have given the other toy to them as well. We are currently designing a study that will circumvent these pragmatic problems. In this new study, the experimenter will not give the toys to infants but rather she and the infant will enter a setting in which the toys are already present. Moreover, stronger, more clear-cut cues to affect and attention focus will be provided. The experimenter will signal her affect not only via speech and facial expression but through action as well (in the positive affect conditions she will reach for and contact a toy whereas, in the negative affect conditions, she will reach for and then retract her hand from a toy). Finally, cues to her attentional focus will be strengthened by having her position be such that her back is toward one toy while she directs affect toward the other toy. If infants genuinely understand the relation between attentional focus and the intentionality of emotion then, under these enhanced conditions, even our 12-month-olds should again rely on attentional cues in reacting to the toys and, further, they should now be much less likely to generalise their reactions to the other toy.

CONCLUSIONS

Our findings indicate that when an adult utters a label or displays an emotion infants take pains to discover the intended referent of that label or emotion, and are aided in this process of discovery by skilful use of the adult's attentional cues. In the domain of language the relevant abilities were clearly present by 18 months of age and in the domain of emotion suggestive evidence emerged that they may be available as early as 12 months of age. In both domains infants were solving a complex problem of social co-ordination in a strikingly non-egocentric fashion. Not only did they need to notice a discrepancy between their own attentional focus and that of the adult, but they also needed to set aside the object of their own current focus, locate the target of the adult's attentional cues, and then infer that the adult's label or emotion related to this target.

These findings bring us back to the controversy raised at the beginning of this chapter concerning the appropriate interpretation of infants' early communicative abilities. The findings are more consistent with the rich interpretation of these abilities (Baron-Cohen, 1993; Wellman, 1993) than with the lean interpretation (Butterworth, 1991; Perner, 1991). The data are especially strong for the older infants in our studies. We would argue that by 18 months of age infants may grasp something about the mental states that cause people to direct their attention to one object rather than another, as evidenced in our studies by their steady reliance on attentional information as the preferred guide to interpreting others' utterances and emotional displays. Infants of this age do indeed operate with something like Baron-Cohen's "attention-goal psychology." They understand that when another person is labelling or reacting emotionally to an object, that person is not simply physically oriented to the object but rather is attending to it in the sense of being psychologically engaged with it, where that engagement might take the form of being interested in or thinking about the object, or being happy or disgusted with it. In addition, infants understand that coming to the correct interpretation of the goals underlying another's communicative act, be it linguistic or emotional, involves determining that individual's referential intent.

Our interpretation of infants' abilities at this age receives further support when we consider the developmental timetable of other theory of mind abilities. That is, a slough of abilities related to theory of mind begin to emerge or is strongly consolidated in the middle of the second year. For example, around this age important developments take place in areas as diverse as pretence (Leslie, 1988), self-recognition (Lewis & Brooks-Gunn, 1979), imitation (Asendorpf & Baudonnière, 1993; Meltzoff & Gopnik, 1993), empathy (Zahn-Waxler & Radke-Yarrow, 1982), and internal state language (Bretherton, 1991), suggesting that infants may have already achieved some general conceptual insight into the minds of others.

At younger ages these other abilities have yet to emerge in a sophisticated form and our own data are also less compelling. Our conclusions for younger infants are thus only tentative at this point. In the linguistic realm infants in our youngest age group (14–15-month-olds) were unable to establish word–object mappings in either the follow-in or discrepant labelling situations. Because these infants failed to establish mappings even under conditions of joint focus, we simply do not know whether they appreciate the significance of attentional focus for interpreting language. It is possible, however, that they do have an understanding of attentional focus but that their failure arose because of the processing demands imposed by what, for very young infants, may have been a complex and confusing situation. Our findings in the emotional realm provide some support for this hypothesis. In the emotional domain somewhat younger infants (12–13 months of age) were able to rely on attentional cues in reacting appropriately to the target of another person's affect. Hence there is at least preliminary evidence that, by the beginning of the second year, infants have a dawning appreciation of the mentalistic significance of attentional information as an index of the other's psychological engagement and referential intentions. Before strong conclusions can be drawn, however, we will need to carry out a study, such as that described earlier, designed to replicate and extend our finding that 12-month-olds show specificity in their use of attentional cues to interpret another's affect.

In response to our account of infants' behaviour in these various studies, it might be argued that a reductive interpretation is still possible. That is, perhaps a way could be found to redescribe the abilities displayed by these infants that would not require conceding them any real insight into the minds of others. However, we find it hard to imagine what a compelling reductive account would look like. It is true that when phenomenona like gaze following are taken alone, low-level interpretations have some plausibility: Infants might simply note an environmental correlation between direction of gaze and interesting sights that lie in that direction (Butterworth, 1991). It is more difficult, however, to come up with a *simple* associative account that would explain the range of skills infants displayed in the studies we have presented. For example, Perner's reductive interpretation of social referencing as simple rule-following cannot account for the performance of our infants. He suggests that infants might simply relate an adult's fearful expression to whatever they find dubious in the immediate environment and hence avoid that thing. In our study, however, more than one dubious object was present and yet infants successfully consulted the adult's attentional focus to disambiguate the target of her affect. Clearly, such discriminating use of attentional cues to clarify referential intent goes well beyond blind application of a simple associative rule. In this regard we find infants' ability in the language domain equally telling. Recall that older infants were able to override salient, nonreferential actions and very strong associative cues like temporal contiguity in establishing new word mappings. Instead they consistently relied on attentional cues and referential action as their preferred guide to such mappings. It is surely unlikely that infants would isolate, and interpret non-mentalistically, just those cues—namely, the cues with genuine referential import—for which adults have a mentalistic interpretation.

In sum, our findings suggest that between 12 and 18 months of age a fledgling understanding of attention as something like a psychological spotlight that can be intentionally directed at external objects and events has begun to emerge. A remaining question concerns *how* infants might traverse the conceptual distance from this early understanding regarding attentional focus and referential intent to the more explicit conception of others as thinking beings that is seen in children just a few years older. This richer understanding of thinking includes, for example, an appreciation of the distinction between mental entities like thoughts and the external referents of those thoughts (Estes, Wellman, & Woolley, 1989), and of the distinction between the process of thinking and related processes like perceiving, talking and acting upon (Flavell, Green, & Flavell, in press). Another important aspect is the knowledge that people can think about or focus attention upon things that are not physically present. In the studies we have described the conception of attention that infants revealed was always of attention to some currently available object. How infants extend this conception to include the possibility that attention may be focused on things not present in the immediate surround is unknown. However, we would speculate that one of the most influential factors in this regard might be the development of language itself. With the help of the referential abilities demonstrated in this research, infants have typically acquired a respectable comprehension vocabulary by the middle of their second year. Having fixed the reference of a sizeable number of terms, they are in a position to make some interesting observations about others' use of language. Language is a uniquely powerful medium for communicating about things that are spatially or temporally distant, and we utilise it heavily for this purpose. Infants will thus have many opportunities to note that people sometimes utter words when no potential referent is in view; for example, people talk about the family dog when the dog is outside or in another room. Without an understanding that attention and thinking can take place in the absence of tangible referents, such utterances would surely be difficult to fathom. In order to make sense of such anomalies, infants would be pushed toward inferring that what a person is thinking about, and the language which sometimes accompanies such thoughts, often goes well beyond the bounds of the immediate perceptual neighbourhood. In this way infants' budding linguistic knowledge might provide an especially strong impetus to construct a more powerful theory of mind (see Robinson, this volume, for an analogous suggestion with respect to later developments). At this point little is known about when infants begin to comprehend another person's references to absent objects but, given the findings from our language studies, such an understanding might be expected to develop from the middle of the second year. In this regard, there is at least some data from children's productions that is consistent with this hypothesis (Sachs, 1983). A final speculation with respect to the relation between language and theory of mind concerns species differences in mental state attribution. The fact that language seems to be a specialised skill that is largely unique to the human species may be at least some part of the explanation for why we eventually construct altogether richer theories of mental life than do even our closest phylogenetic relatives, the great apes.

The referential skills displayed by infants in our studies may also lay the groundwork for an awareness of the knowledge–ignorance distinction that develops more fully in the preschool period (e.g. Pillow, 1989; Pratt & Bryant, 1990). That is, infants with such skills will have plenty of opportunities to realise that, in situations like those they faced in our studies, they are ignorant while others are knowledgeable (i.e. others may know the name for a novel object and they may also know whether it is dangerous or safe). If infants are able to take advantage of these opportunities, we should expect to see them beginning actively to seek out and consult other people as potential sources of information about the world. Unfortunately, we currently know very little about just how sophisticated infants' social information-gathering abilities really are

(Baldwin & Moses, 1994). The fact that infants in our studies consulted attentional cues when the adult produced an utterance or emotional display does not clarify whether they actively *sought* such linguistic or emotional information. In other words, infants might be skilled at interpreting messages that are provided and yet not be capable of conceptualising the *possibility* of linguistic or emotional information before it is supplied.

Finally, the research we have presented here illustrates not only that communicative development opens a window on infants' developing theories of mind but that infants' growing awareness of mental life has profound implications for early learning. To the extent that infants fail to recognise the significance of others' attentional focus and how it reflects referential intent, knowledge acquisition will be greatly compromised in the flux of daily interaction. Errors of interpretation will occur and these will slow the path of acquisition. The skill that infants in the second year display in this arena thus helps to explain the phenomenal pace at which knowledge is acquired at this age. Because infants themselves play an important role in locating the target of others' linguistic and emotional messages, they not only avoid many potential pitfalls, but their opportunities for learning are also greatly expanded.

ACKNOWLEDGEMENTS

The research reported in this chapter was supported in part by grants from the Natural Sciences and Engineering Research Council of Canada and the Social Sciences and Humanities Research Council of Canada to the first author, and by an Izaak Walton Killam Memorial Postdoctoral Fellowship to the second author.

REFERENCES

Asendorpf, J.B., & Baudonnière, P. (1993). Self-awareness and other-awareness: Mirror self-recognition and synchronic imitation among unfamiliar peers. *Development Psychology*, 29, 88–95.

Bakeman, M., & Adamson, L.B. (1984). Co-ordinating attention to people and objects in mother–infant and peer–infant interaction. *Child Development*, 55, 1278–1289.

Baldwin, D.A. (1991). Infants' contribution to the achievement of joint reference. *Child Development*, 63, 875–890.

Baldwin, D.A. (1993a). Infants' ability to consult the speaker for clues to word reference. *Journal of Child Language*, 20, 395–418.

Baldwin, D.A. (1993b). Early referential understanding: Infants' ability to recognise referential acts for what they are. *Developmental Psychology*, 29, 832–843.

Baldwin, D.A. (in press). Understanding the link between joint attention and language. In C. Moore & P. Dunham (Eds.), *Joint attention: Its origins and role in development*. Hillsdale, NJ: Lawrence Erlbaum Associates Inc.

Baldwin, D.A., & Moses, L.J. (1994). *The ontogeny of social information-seeking*. Unpublished manuscript, University of Oregon, USA.

Baldwin, D.A., Moses, L.J., & Tidball, G. (in preparation). *Social referencing versus social receptiveness: Infants' use of others' attentional cues to clarify the reference of emotional displays.*

Banks, M.S., & Salapatek, P. (1983). Infant visual perception. In M.M. Haith & J.J. Campos (Eds.), *Handbook of child psychology: Vol. 2. Infancy and developmental psychobiology.* New York: Wiley.

Baron-Cohen, S. (1991). Precursors to a theory of mind: Understanding attention in others. In A. Whiten (Ed.), *Natural theories of mind: Evolution, development, and simulation of everyday mind-reading* (pp. 233–251). Oxford: Basil Blackwell.

Baron-Cohen, S. (1993). From attention-goal psychology to belief-desire psychology: The development of a theory of mind, and its dysfunction. In S. Baron-Cohen, H. Tager-Flusberg, & D. Cohen (Eds.), *Understanding other minds: Perspectives from autism* (pp. 59–82). Oxford: Oxford University Press.

Baron-Cohen, S., Tager-Flusberg, H., & Cohen, D. (1993). *Understanding other minds: Perspectives from autism.* Oxford: Oxford University Press.

Bates, E. (1979). Intentions, conventions, and symbols. In E. Bates, L. Benigni, I. Bretherton, L. Camaioni, & V. Volterra (Eds.), *The emergence of symbols: Cognition and communication in infancy.* New York: Academic Press.

Bates, E., Benigni, L., Bretherton, I., Camaioni, L., & Volterra, V. (Eds.) (1979). *The emergence of symbols: Cognition and communication in infancy.* New York: Academic Press.

Benedict, H. (1979). Early lexical development: Comprehension and production. *Journal of Child Language, 6,* 183–200.

Bretherton, I. (1991). Intentional communication and the development of an understanding of mind. In D. Frye & C. Moore (Eds.), *Children's theories of mind: Mental states and social understanding.* (pp. 49–75). Hillsdale, NJ: Lawrence Erlbaum Associates Inc.

Bretherton, I. (1992). Social referencing, intentional communication, and the interfacing of minds in infancy. In S. Feinman (Ed.), *Social referencing and the social construction of reality in infancy.* (pp. 57–77). New York: Plenum Press.

Bretherton, I., Bates, E., McNew, S., Shore, C., Williamson, F., & Beeghly-Smith, M. (1981). Comprehension and production of symbols in infancy: An experimental study. *Developmental Psychology, 18,* 906–921.

Butterworth, G. (1991). The ontogeny and phylogeny of joint visual attention. In A. Whiten (Ed.), *Natural theories of mind: Evolution, development, and simulation of everyday mind-reading* (pp. 223–232). Oxford: Basil Blackwell.

Butterworth, G., & Jarrett, N. (1991). What minds have in common is space: Spatial mechanisms serving joint visual attention in infancy. *British Journal of Developmental Psychology, 9,* 55–72.

Campos, J.J. (1983). The importance of affective communication in social referencing: A commentary on Feinman. *Merrill-Palmer Quarterly, 29,* 83–87.

Caron, R.F., Caron, A.J., & Meyers, R.S. (1982). Do infants see emotional expressions in static faces? *Child Development, 56,* 1552–1560.

Chapman, R.S. (1981). Cognitive development and language comprehension in 10- to 20-month-olds. In R.E. Stark (Ed.), *Language behavior in infancy and early childhood.* New York: Elsevier North-Holland.

Clark, H.H., & Marshall, C.R. (1981). Definite reference and mutual knowledge. In A.K. Joshi, B.L. Weber, & I.A. Sag (Eds.), *Elements of discourse understanding* (pp. 10–63). Cambridge: Cambridge University Press.

Collis, G.M. (1977). Visual co-ordination and maternal speech. In H.R. Schaffer (Ed.), *Studies in mother–infant interaction* (pp. 355–375). London: Academic Press.

Estes, D., Wellman, H.M., & Woolley, J.D. (1989). Children's understanding of mental phenomena. In H. Reese (Ed.), *Advances in child development and behavior, Vol. 22* (pp. 41–87). New York: Academic Press.

Feinman, S. (1982). Social referencing in infancy. *Merrill-Palmer Quarterly*, *28*, 445–470.

Feinman, S., Roberts, D., Hsieh, K., Sawyer, D., & Swanson, D. (1992). A critical review of social referencing in infancy. In S. Feinman (Ed.), *Social referencing and the social construction of reality in infancy* (pp. 15–54). New York: Plenum Press.

Flavell, J.H., Green, F.L., & Flavell, E.R. (in press). Young children's knowledge about thinking. *Monographs of the Society for Research on Child Development.*

Golinkoff, R.M. (1986). "I beg your pardon?": The preverbal negotiation of failed messages. *Journal of Child Language*, *13*, 455–476.

Grice, H.P. (1957). Meaning. *Philosophical Review*, *66*, 377–388.

Gunnar, M.R., & Stone, C. (1984). The effects of positive maternal affect on infant responses to pleasant, ambiguous, and fear-provoking toys, *Child Development*, *55*, 1231–1236.

Haith, M.M. (1980). *Rules that babies look by*. Hillsdale, NJ: Lawrence Erlbaum Associates Inc.

Harding, C.G., & Golinkoff, R.M. (1979). The origins of intentional vocalizations in prelinguistic infants. *Child Development*, *50*, 33–40.

Harris, M., Jones, D., & Grant, J. (1983). The nonverbal context of mothers' speech to infants. *First Language*, *4*, 21–30.

Harris, P.L. (1989). *Children and emotion*. Oxford: Basil Blackwell.

Hirsh-Pasek, K., & Golinkoff, R.M. (1991). Language comprehension: A look at some old themes. In N.A. Krasnegor, D.M. Rumbaugh, R.L. Schiefelbusch, & M. Studdert-Kennedy (Eds.), *Biological and behavioral determinants of language development* (pp. 301–320). Hillsdale, NJ: Lawrence Erlbaum Associates Inc.

Hornik, R., Risenhoover, N., & Gunnar, M. (1987). The effects of maternal positive, neutral, and negative affective communications on infant responses to new toys. *Child Development*, *58*, 937–944.

Kaye, K. (1977). Infants' effects upon their mothers' teaching strategies. In J.C. Glidewell (Ed.), *The social context of learning and development*. New York: Gardner Press.

Lempers, J.D., Flavell, E.R., & Flavell, J.H. (1977). The development in very young children of tacit knowledge concerning visual perception. *Genetic Psychology Monographs*, *95*, 3–53.

Leslie, A.M. (1988). Some implications of pretense for mechanisms underlying the child's theory of mind. In J.W. Astington, P.L. Harris, & D.R. Olson (Eds.), *Developing theories of mind* (pp. 19–46). New York: Cambridge University Press.

Leslie, A.M., & Happé, F. (1989). Autism and ostensive communication: The relevance of metarepresentation. *Development and Psychopathology*, *1*, 205–212.

Leung, E.H., & Rheingold, H.L. (1981). Development of pointing as a social gesture. *Developmental Psychology*, *17*, 215–220.

Lewis, M., & Brooks-Gunn, J. (1979). *Social cognition and the acquisition of self*. New York: Plenum Press.

Ludemann, P.M., & Nelson, C.A. (1988). Categorical representation of facial expression by 7-month-old infants. *Developmental Psychology*, *24*, 492–501.

Meltzoff, A.N., & Gopnik, A. (1993). The role of imitation in understanding persons and developing a theory of mind. In S. Baron-Cohen, H. Tager-Flusberg, & D. Cohen (Eds.), *Understanding other minds: Perspectives from autism* (pp. 335–366). Oxford: Oxford University Press.

Messer, D.J. (1978). The integration of mothers' referential speech with joint play. *Child Development*, *49*, 781–787.

Moses, L.J., & Chandler, M.J. (1992). Traveller's guide to children's theories of mind. *Psychological Inquiry*, *3*, 286–301.

Mumme, D.L. (1993). *Rethinking social referencing: The influence of facial and vocal affect on infant behavior*. Unpublished doctoral dissertation, Stanford University, Stanford, CA.

Murphy, C.M. (1978). Pointing in the context of a shared activity. *Child Development*, *49*, 371–380.

Murphy, C.M., & Messer, D.J. (1977). Mothers, infants, and pointing: A study of gesture. In H.R. Schaffer (Ed.), *Studies in mother–infant interaction* (pp. 325–354). New York: Academic Press.

Nelson, C.A. (1987). The recognition of facial expressions in the first two years of life: Mechanisms of development. *Child Development, 58,* 889–909.

Nelson, C.A., & Horowitz, F.D. (1987). Visual motion perception in infancy: A review and synthesis. In P. Salapatek & L. Cohen (Eds.), *Handbook of infant perception: Vol. 2. From perception to cognition.* New York: Academic Press.

Nelson, K. (1973). Structure and strategy in learning to talk. *Monographs of the Society for Research in Child Development, 38* (Serial No. 149).

Oviatt, S.L. (1985). Tracing developmental change in language comprehension before twelve months of age. *Papers and Reports on Child Language Development, 24,* 87–94.

Perner, J. (1991). *Understanding the representational mind.* Cambridge, Mass.: MIT Press.

Pillow, B.H. (1989). Early understanding of perception as a source of knowledge. *Journal of Experimental Child Psychology, 47,* 116–129.

Pratt, C., & Bryant, P. (1990). Young children understand that looking leads to knowing (so long as they are looking into a single barrel). *Child Development, 61,* 973–982.

Rommetveit, R. (1979). On the architecture of intersubjectivity. In R. Rommetveit & R.M. Blakar (Eds.), *Studies of language, thought, and verbal communication* (pp. 93–107). New York: Academic Press.

Sachs, J. (1983). Talking about there and then: The emergence of displaced reference in parent–child discourse. In K.E. Nelson (Ed.), *Children's language, Vol. IV* (pp. 1–28). Hillsdale, NJ: Lawrence Erlbaum Associates Inc.

Scaife, M., & Bruner, J. (1975). The capacity for joint visual attention in the infant. *Nature, 253,* 265–266.

Sorce, J., Emde, R.N., Campos, J.J., & Klinnert, M. (1985). Maternal emotional signalling: Its effect on the visual cliff behavior of one-year-olds. *Developmental Psychology, 21,* 195–200.

Tomasello, M., Kruger, A.C., & Ratner, H.H. (1993). Cultural learning. *Behavioral and Brain Sciences, 16,* 495–552.

Walden, T.A., & Ogan, T.A. (1988). The development of social referencing. *Child Development, 59,* 1230–1240.

Wellman, H.M. (1990). *A child's theory of mind.* Cambridge, Mass.: MIT Press.

Wellman, H.M. (1993). Early understanding of mind: The normal case. In S. Baron-Cohen, H. Tager-Flusberg, & D. Cohen (Eds.), *Understanding other minds: Perspectives from autism* (pp. 10–39). Oxford: Oxford University Press.

Whitehurst, G.J., Kedesdy, J., & White, T.G. (1982). A functional analysis of meaning. In S.A. Kuczaj, II (Ed.), *Language development: Vol. 1 Syntax and semantics* (pp. 397–427). Hillsdale, NJ: Lawrence Erlbaum Associates Inc.

Zahn-Waxler, C., & Radke-Yarrow, M. (1982). The development of altruism: Alternative research strategies. In N. Eisenberg-Berg (Ed.), *The development of prosocial behavior.* New York: Academic Press.

8

Changing Your Views: How Understanding Visual Perception Can Lead to a New Theory of the Mind

Alison Gopnik and Virginia Slaughter
University of California at Berkeley, USA

Andrew Meltzoff
University of Washington, Seattle, USA

INTRODUCTION

There is an unfortunate syndrome loose in developmental psychology: Call it "neurotic task fixation." Those of us interested in children's developing understanding of the mind have begun to notice the first symptoms of this disease with queasy anxiety. The task in question is, of course, the Wimmer and Perner (1983) false belief task. This chapter and, we hope, this volume is, in part, an attempt to stop the disease before it kills an interesting field yet again. The question should not be "Can three-year-olds do false belief?" Instead, we should ask what aspects of an understanding of belief develop in what ways and in what order, and how these changes are related to one another. How is three-year-olds' early knowledge of the mind related to their later knowledge? How do precursors lead to the things they precurse?

We have argued that the development of theories of mind involves a genuine conceptual change, or better, a series of genuine conceptual changes. In our formulation, we articulate this as a series of theories each replacing a previous theory (Gopnik & Wellman, 1992). In particular, we and others have proposed a theory change from an early nonrepresentational theory of the mind, with perceptions and desires as the central explanatory concepts, to a later representational theory with propositional contents as central explanatory concepts (Gopnik & Wellman, 1992; Perner, 1991; Wellman, 1990). On the basis of this formulation, we might also make predictions about the origins of an understanding of representation and about where the earliest precursors to the representational theory are likely to be found.

If this "theory theory" formulation is correct we might expect, indeed we would predict, that the earlier nonrepresentational view of the mind would provide a basis for the later account. The most distinctive feature of a theory account is precisely this systematic relation between earlier and later theories. We would not expect the understanding of false belief, for example, simply to emerge fully fledged when children turn four, with no consistent conceptual relation to earlier accounts, and with no transitional period. In fact, such a developmental pattern would be more consistent with a maturational explanation than with the theory theory. The theory theory predicts that the new theory arises through some combination of relations between the conceptual structures of the old theory and new evidence. What might such structures and such evidence be?

In this chapter we will primarily consider the question of the way that the new representational theory of mind has its roots in the earlier nonrepresentational theory, and also briefly consider the kinds of evidence that might lead to changes in the theory. In both cases we will focus on the ways that an early understanding of perception might serve as a model for the later understanding of belief. We will also present evidence that suggests that children show a better understanding of perceptual misrepresentation than of false belief, and that training children on perceptual tasks can accelerate their understanding of false belief.

There is already evidence that very young children, as young as two-and-a-half years old, have a good understanding of certain aspects of mental life, particularly (1) pretence, (2) desire, and (3) perception. Understanding all three of these types of mental states might be likely precursors to the understanding of belief:

1. Pretence is a likely candidate because, like false belief, it involves acting on a false proposition (Leslie, 1987; see also discussion in Harris, Lillard, & Perner, this volume). Unlike beliefs, however, pretences fail to make reference to the real world. Even two-year-olds pretend and show signs of understanding pretend states (Harris & Kavanaugh, 1993) and, in at least one experiment (Flavell, Flavell, & Green, 1987), a pretence-reality task proved to be substantially easier than a parallel appearance-reality task.

2. Understanding desire is also a likely precursor to understanding belief because in adult folk psychology desires, no less than beliefs, are intentional states. Moreover, most commonsense (and philosophical) theories of action see actions as the results of desires and beliefs. The "practical syllogism" (if a person desires x and believes y will lead to x, he will do y) is the first law of folk psychology. Two-and-a-half and

three-year-olds show an excellent grasp of the fact that desires may not be fulfilled, that different people may have different desires, and that unfulfilled desires lead to disappointment. They can predict actions by referring to actors' desires and they explain actions in terms of the desires of actors (Astington & Gopnik, 1991; Wellman, 1990; Wellman & Woolley, 1990; Yuill, 1984).

Several studies suggest that placing misrepresentation tasks in the context of earlier desire understanding may also improve performance. In particular, Flavell, Flavell, Green and Moses (1990) found that children were better able to solve a task involving conflicting values, more closely related to desires, than conflicting beliefs. Thus children were better at understanding that Ellie might think that a cookie was yucky whereas they thought it was yummy than at understanding false beliefs. Similarly, Gopnik & Slaughter (1991) found that children were better able to understand changes in their representation of the desirability of objects, than changes in their beliefs. Moses (in press) found that children were better able to understand a misrepresentation task when it was phrased in terms of intentions to act. In all these cases 3-year-olds' performance was not at ceiling, with around 30–40% of children making errors, but it was significantly better than their performance on false belief tasks.

3. A third area of early conceptual understanding, perception, might also serve as an important precursor to understanding belief. Visual perception shares more features with belief than any other mental state. Unlike pretences, visual perceptions make reference to the external world. Unlike desires, they have a mind-to-world direction of fit; the child changes his mind to fit the world, rather than changing the world to fit his mind (see Searle, 1983). Moreover, like beliefs, perceptions are representational states, and so may lead to misrepresentation, in a way that is not true of desire or pretence. You can have an inaccurate or false perception, but you cannot have an inaccurate or false pretence or desire. Much of our adult language about belief inherits perceptual metaphors. We "see the light" or we "change our views." Could children model their understanding of belief on their earlier understanding of visual perception? Could an earlier understanding of perception lead to an understanding of belief by some process of cognitive bootstrapping?

During the recent "theory of mind" boom children's understanding of perception has been less well investigated than their understanding of other mental states. This is a little ironic, since a series of ground-breaking studies on perceptual perspective taking by Flavell and his colleagues were actually among the earliest studies of theory of mind (Flavell, Everett, Croft, & Flavell, 1981; Lempers, Flavell, & Flavell, 1977; Masangkay et al., 1974). For the field as well as for the children, understanding visual perception may have served as a precursor for understanding belief. There is, however, at least some information about the understanding of perception that can be gleaned from these earlier studies and from the current literature.

THE DEVELOPMENT OF AN UNDERSTANDING OF VISUAL PERCEPTION

Infancy

There is a substantial body of evidence that suggests that a first understanding of visual perception may have its roots even in infancy. Even very young infants pay special attention to eyes (Haith, Bergman, & Moore, 1977; Maurer & Barrera, 1981). A number of writers have pointed out the significance of joint attention and social referencing behaviours, which emerge between about nine months and a year, for an understanding of the mind (Baron-Cohen, 1991; Butterworth, 1991; Wellman, 1993). At about this age infants develop the ability to follow the point or gaze of another person towards an object (Butterworth, 1991; Scaife & Bruner, 1975). They begin to use pointing to get someone else to look at an object (Bruner, 1983; Butterworth, 1991). They also draw attention to objects in order to discover another person's attitude towards them. Faced with an ambiguous situation, such as a visual cliff, infants look to their mother's face for information, and may draw her gaze to the objects in question (Campos & Sternberg, 1980).

These behaviours imply a primitive but genuine understanding of visual perception. These infants seem to know that the direction of the eyes, or perhaps just the direction of the head and body, indicates something about the person's knowledge of an object. There seems to be some connection in these children's minds between the visual display of another person's head and eyes, and the phenomenological experience of vision. As a number of writers have also pointed out, this sort of understanding of vision is also significant since it implies not only an understanding that people see, but also an understanding of the relation between people's vision and the external world. It implies a primitive understanding of a kind of reference. These joint attention behaviours are strikingly absent in children with autism (Baron-Cohen, 1991).

It is worth noting that, although these behaviours are referred to as joint attention behaviours, they actually imply simply an understanding of joint perception. In other words, the behaviours clearly suggest that children know that a particular set of bodily orientations are necessary in order to see. It is not so clear that they distinguish at this stage between seeing and attending. This is important, for example, because of Baron-Cohen's (Baron-Cohen & Cross, 1992; Baron-Cohen & Ring, this volume) argument that these behaviours imply some early understanding of propositional attitudes. If the behaviours really did involve an understanding of attention, this argument might go through. It is not so clear, however, that simply attributing vision to another person need involve the attribution of a propositional attitude.

It is interesting to speculate about the origins of these abilities. Baron-Cohen and Cross (1992) and Baron-Cohen and Ring (this volume) suggest that they are the result of a specific innate eye-direction detection module, and this may be correct. However, they might also have their origins in particular kinds of experiences in infancy. We have suggested elsewhere that mutual imitation may be a particularly potent source of information about the mind (Meltzoff & Gopnik, 1993). In imitation the infant maps an internal set of sensations, particularly kinaesthetic sensations, onto the behaviour of another person. For example, the infant maps the felt sensation of his own tongue onto the visually perceived tongue protrusion of another person. We have argued that this initial understanding of the fact that the infant's felt body is like the seen body of another person might serve as a framework for the later assumption that the infant's mind and the mind of another person are also similar.

Visual perception, like kinaesthetic sensation, is a particularly interesting intermediate case between understanding bodies and understanding minds. A wide array of bodily changes will result in consistently different visual perceptions. Closing your eyes will result in temporary darkness, moving your head dramatically to one side will cause your visual field to shift, and so on. The capacity for joint attention seems to presuppose a mapping from these bodily states (the position of the head and eyes, the fact that the eyes are open, etc.) onto the phenomenal experience of perceiving an object.

Neonates have been shown to imitate adult head-turns and may imitate eye blinks (Meltzoff & Moore, 1989). Normal one-year-olds will imitate eye closing. In order to do this children must see a correspondence between their own kinaesthetically registered experience of eye and head movement and the visual appearance of the eye and head movements of others. But their own experience, in addition to including kinaesthetic information about their movements, also includes their experience of the changes in visual perception that result from those movements. Thus imitative games might provide a tutorial in the further correspondence between bodily gesture and experience. I turn my head and see the object in the corner; I close my eyes and it disappears. Mom performs what I know is the same gesture, ergo, she must have the same phenomenal experience.

This account involves a powerful innate mechanism, of course, but it is a much more general mechanism than a specialised eye-detection module. On this view the infant innately detects the correspondence of his own kinaesthetically perceived body movements and those of others. The infant then generalises this discovery, and assumes that like body movements will be accompanied by like phenomenology, including both kinaesthetic sensations and visual ones. Early imitative abilities, and especially joint imitative activities and games, might help to establish the basic premise of joint attention: When you and I look in the same direction, we see the same thing.

An understanding of visual perception may also be implicated in the development of high-level object-permanence abilities at 15–21 months. Such abilities are commonly seen exclusively as part of the child's developing understanding of the physical world. But understanding object-permanence also involves knowing the relation between an object's physical location and its perceptual appearance. The job in an object-permanence problem is to predict where you need to look to find an object when you don't currently see it. It has as much to do with your perceptual relation to the object as with the object's physical characteristics. One way of thinking of the highest-level object-permanence abilities is to say that the child discovers that all (or almost all) disappearances are due to changes in the spatial relation between the child's eyes and the hidden object (see Gopnik, 1984, for further discussion).

The idea that these object-permanence developments reflect a more sophisticated understanding of visual perception is bolstered by data from children's spontaneous speech. Eighteen-month-olds talk about visual perception in their very earliest language. "Disappearance" words, such as "gone", are consistently among the very first words to appear (Bloom, 1973; Gopnik, 1982; 1984). These words encode the fact that the child cannot see an object, although she believes that the object continues to exist. They pick out a particular distinctive perceptual relation between the child and the world: Objects are out there but I can't see them. They do not refer to a particular state of the world itself. These words have consistently been found to be closely and specifically related to the development of high-level object-permanence abilities (Gopnik & Meltzoff, 1984; 1986; Tomasello & Farrar, 1984; 1986). Similarly, two-year-olds use perceptual terms like "see" appropriately and frequently in their spontaneous speech (Bretherton & Beeghly, 1982).

We might see the achievements of infancy as two-fold. First, at around nine months, the child understands that her visual perception may be shared by others (as in joint attention and social referencing). She understands that she and Mom see the same thing. Second, at around 18 months, the child comes to understand something quite general about the reasons why she may fail to perceive an object, even when it exists (as in object-permanence). The child understands that she may not see something from her current point of view.

Eighteen Months to Three Years

These two conceptual achievements of infancy can be combined in complicated ways: I can see something that you don't, you can see something that I don't. There is some interesting evidence that suggests that children only begin to understand these more complex relations later in their development. In their very early spontaneous speech, 18-month-old children will only use "gone" when they themselves fail to see an object. They don't use "gone" to describe the case where they see an object and the other doesn't, although they may use it when an object is invisible to them, but fully visible to another person (Gopnik, 1984). "Gone" seems to encode a very egocentric notion of disappearance. (It is interesting that it is almost impossible to think of a single adult mental state word that also has this character, that is that only refers to the speaker's own experience.) By the time children are using other mental states words productively, for example, by the time two- and three-year-olds use "look" and "see," the words are generalised to refer to the experience of others as well as the child's own experience.

Lempers et al. (1977) report some fascinating evidence along similar lines. In their studies, very young two-year-olds failed to reproduce situations in which their visual perceptions were discrepant with those of others. When they were asked to show Mommy a picture at the bottom of a long tube, for example, some switched the tube back and forth between themselves and their mother. Similarly, children who were asked to hide an object from their parent behind a screen sometimes produced the egocentric response of hiding the object on the far side of the screen. In studies currently underway in our lab, we have observed similar errors in 18–24-month-olds. One 24-month-old showed an interesting transitional behaviour; she was asked to hide a picture from her mother by turning it so that it faced the child. The child turned the picture back and forth several times, finally settled on the correct perspective (visible to her and invisible to the other) and then walked over to the other side of the table to check that the picture was indeed invisible from that perspective. Initially, very young children may overgeneralise the "social referencing' discovery, and have difficulty in understanding that their vision may not be shared by others.

By two-and-a-half, however, children do seem to understand these aspects of visual perception firmly. That is, they explicitly understand that an object may be visible to them but invisible to another, or vice-versa. Flavell has referred to this phenomenon as "level-1" visual perspective taking (Flavell et al., 1981). Children show a similarly advanced understanding of other perceptual modalities such as hearing and touch (Yaniv & Shatz, 1988). Three-year-old children also are near ceiling in understanding that they may now see an object that they did not see before and vice-versa. They understand "level-1" changes in their own visual perspectives (Gopnik & Slaughter, 1991).

Visual-Perspective Taking After Three

The similarity between these "level-1" perceptual abilities and false belief abilities should be clear. In fact, false belief abilities are sometimes referred to as "conceptual perspective taking." In both cases the child must understand a discrepancy between his own mental state and the mental state of another and, more significantly, must also understand the discrepancy between the mental state and the reality. The object really is there, even though you can't see it.

However, there are also several different features that distinguish the false belief task from the level-1 perceptual perspective-taking task, which is clearly well-established long before any understanding of false belief. First, the question is phrased explicitly in perceptual terms; it asks what the child sees rather than what the child thinks. Similarly, the task itself is clearly perceptual in character; the change in belief is due to a change in point of view.

In addition, however, the task is a "level-1" task; that is, it requires an understanding that the other, or the past self, simply did or did not know about the object. It requires the child to distinguish between having some knowledge of an object and having no knowledge at all about it. Several theorists have proposed that this simpler understanding requires a different and simpler theory of mind than the understanding of the mind as a representational system; and that this theory is in place at age three. The earlier "level-1" theory has been described in terms of a "copy theory" (Gopnik & Wellman, 1992; Wellman, 1990), "Gibsonian theory" (Astington & Gopnik, 1991), "cognitive connections" (Flavell, 1988), or "situation" view (Perner, 1988; 1991) of belief understanding.

The false belief task, in contrast to the early perceptual tasks, is phrased in terms of "think," involves a nonperceptual context, and requires that the child understands that the other or the past self represented the object differently, not just that they failed to represent it at all. It requires what Flavell (Flavell et al., 1981) calls a "level-2" understanding and what others have referred to as a "representational model of the mind" (Flavell, 1988; Forguson & Gopnik, 1988; Perner, 1988). The child who solves these tasks must recognise not only that someone may fail to know something about the world, but also that they may actively misrepresent it. An old saying has it that "it ain't the things you don't know that hurt you, it's the things you do know that ain't so." The three-year-olds understand that they or others may not know things; they don't understand that they may know things that ain't so.

Which aspect of these tasks is responsible for the difference? Are the perceptual perspective-taking tasks simpler because they are level-1 tasks or because they are perceptual?

A number of tasks seem to fall in between the simple level-1 perceptual task and the false belief task in one way or another. These tasks also seem to be solved at around age three, after level-1 perspective-taking, but before false belief. Wellman and Bartsch (1988) found that three-year-olds, though not two-and-a-half-year-olds, could generally solve what they called a discrepant belief task. In this task, the "level-1" structure remained the same, and the perceptual nature of the task remained the same, but the question was phrased in terms of action (and by implication thought) rather than "seeing." In this task children were told that objects were in two locations (the drawer and the cupboard) but that a child (say Johnny) had only looked in one location. Children were able to predict that Johnny would only search for the objects where he had seen them. Structurally, this task is quite similar to the "level-1" perspective-taking task; the child must realise that another person only sees part of the world that the child herself sees. Moreover, the task also involves perceptual content. However, the question is phrased in terms of thinking rather than knowing. It is not clear whether the children's improved performance is due to their "level-1" understanding or their understanding of perception, in particular.

There are some suggestive hints in the literature that even "level-2" perception understanding, that is a genuine understanding of perceptual misrepresentation, might appear before false belief understanding. Flavell kept the perceptual situation and the phrasing in terms of "see," but changed the task to a "level-2" task; the children were asked about the appearance of an object behind a coloured screen (Flavell, 1978; Flavell et al., 1981; Masangkay et al., 1974). These tasks were more difficult than "level-1" tasks. They require understanding not just that I may see something you don't, but that the very nature of my perceptual representations may be different from yours. They are the converse of Wellman's discrepant belief task; they ask about what you see rather than what you think, but they require level-2 rather than level-1 understanding.

These "level-2" perception tasks have often been equated with false belief and appearance-reality tasks. Nevertheless, the data suggest that these tasks may in turn be simpler than these other tasks. In Flavell, Green, and Flavell (1986) there were high correlations between children's performance on a "level-2" perspective-taking task and on appearance-reality tasks. However, the absolute levels of performance on the visual task were higher than on the A–R task, and higher than typical false belief performance, with over half of the three-year-olds answering correctly. Gopnik and Slaughter (1991) found that children performed substantially better on a level-2 perceptual task asking about their own past perception in a similar "colour change" task, than on a belief change task. Similarly, Gopnik and Astington (1988) presented children with a false belief task, phrased in terms of thinking rather than seeing, but involving a clearly perceptual task context; in fact, the same "colour change" context in which Flavell had demonstrated level-2 perceptual understanding. Three-year-old children in that study performed best on the task that was phrased in this way, with nearly half the questions answered correctly.

PERCEPTION AS A MODEL FOR BELIEF

All these hints in the literature suggest that children might understand perceptual misrepresentation, either problems phrased in terms of what the child sees, or simply problems that have a plainly perceptual content, some time before they understand false belief. In fact, children might use perceptual misrepresentation as a model for false belief.

How might this take place? We could draw an analogy to other processes of theory change in science, in which the theorist may draw on similarities between the previous theory and the current one. Often the central idea of a new theory is formulated before the fully fledged theory is developed, but is only used in a limited context. Expanding that idea and applying it very generally may be part of the conceptual change that leads to the new theory. We have used the example of Tycho Brahe's theory of planetary motion to illustrate this (Gopnik & Wellman, 1992). In Brahe's theory the rest of the planets go around the sun, which in turn goes around the earth. The crucial idea of Kepler's later theory, heliocentrism, appears, but only in a limited way. Similarly, Darwin's selection theory depends on ideas that were widely accepted to explain changes in domesticated animals that resulted from breeding. At least part of Galileo's achievement was to take principles that explained terrestrial movement in a relatively well-understood way and apply them to the movement of the planets.

Similarly, children might take the aspects of their earlier understanding of the mind that are well understood, particularly visual perception, and first formulate an understanding of misrepresentation in that limited context. Later, the idea would be available to be much more widely applied to all cases of belief. In effect, we might imagine the three-year-old psychologist saying "Oh I get it, these weird belief things are like supercharged perceptions. I know my view of things can change, I guess my views about them can change too."

UNDERSTANDING PERCEPTUAL
MISREPRESENTATION: NEW DATA

In a series of experiments, we have explored children's understanding of perceptual misrepresentation. In these experiments we have phrased the questions both in terms of perception and in terms of thought, we have posed both "level-1" and "level-2" problems, and we have used a variety of perceptual contexts. We have also asked children about changes both in their own representations and the representations of others.

This last question is extremely important for theoretical reasons. If children are introspecting their own mental states directly, and then using this knowledge as a basis for their generalisations to the states of others, we would expect them to report their own beliefs more accurately than they infer the beliefs of others. On the other hand, if understanding the self and the other develop in parallel, then we might infer that children are using a more general theory of mind to make inferences about both their own mental states and those of others (Gopnik & Wellman, 1992; Gopnik, 1993).

Gopnik and Astington (1988) had found that children's understanding of their own past states was actually somewhat worse than their understanding of the states of others. Both Wimmer and Hartl (1991) and Moore, Pure, and Furrow (1990) found no difference. Gopnik and Slaughter (1991) also found advanced levels of performance on desire and perception tasks for the self task that were similar to the levels reported by Flavell on "other" tasks. Again, however, there has been no systematic comparison of these conditions for the same children. A systematic pattern in which easy tasks were easy both for self and other, and difficult tasks were difficult both for self and other, would provide particularly convincing evidence that the two types of knowledge develop in parallel.

Experiment 1

In the first experiment we tested 14 children from preschools in the Berkeley area. Children's ages ranged from 3:2 to 3:11, with a mean of 3:7. The children were given two perception tasks, both involving a table with two chairs on either side, one blue and one brown, and a free-standing screen in the middle. In each case the child entered the room and immediately sat on the blue chair, on one side of the screen. The experimenter asked the child to identify what was on the table, and then asked the child to move to the other chair and again identify what was on the table. The experimenter then called in a confederate adult, Mamie, who sat in the original blue chair facing the child, and then the experimenter asked the child the test questions.

In the level-1 task the screen on the table was opaque and two different objects were on either side of it, a spoon on one side and a cup on the other. Thus children saw only one object and then the other, and Mamie similarly saw only one object. Children were asked "What do you see?" when they sat on the blue chair and "Now what do you see?" when they moved to the brown chair. For the "see" question the children were asked "What did you/ Mamie see on the table when you/she were over there, on the blue chair? Did you see a cup or did you see a spoon?." This is equivalent to the "level-1" perceptual perspective-taking task. For the "think" question children were asked "What did you/Mamie think was on the table, when you/she were over there on the blue chair? Did you think there was just a spoon, or also a cup?" This question is analogous to the Wellman and Bartsch "discrepant belief" question.

In the level-2 task the screen was cut out of coloured red translucent plastic. A free-standing green paper cut-out of a cat was placed on the far side of the screen. The result was a cat that looked black when it was first viewed and then turned out to be green when the speaker's visual perspective was changed. This condition was similar to Flavell's "level-2" perspective-taking task. As in the previous experiment, children were asked "How does the cat look to you? Does it look green or does it look black?" and then "Now how does the cat look to you...?" For the "see" question they were asked "How did the cat look to you/Mamie when you were over there, on the blue chair? Did it look like a green cat or did it look like a black cat?" For the think question they were asked "What did you/Mamie think was on the table when you/she were over there, on the blue chair? A green cat or a black cat?"

Children were also given a standard "Smarties and pencils" "deceptive box" false belief task. Children were shown a closed candy box that was then opened to reveal pencils. Children were asked "What do you think is inside this box?" both before and after they opened the box, to ensure that their belief had indeed changed. Mamie entered the room, and saw the closed box. Children were then asked "When you/Mamie first saw the box, all closed up like this, what did you/she think was inside it? Did you/she think there were candies inside or did you/she think there were pencils inside?"

At the beginning of each testing session, children were given two control tasks to ensure that they understood the questions, and could remember the past events. In the perception control task, children sat in the blue chair and saw one object on the table, then they moved to the other side of the table and the experimenter removed the original object and replaced it with another object. As in the perception task, children were asked to report what was on the table before and after they moved chairs. Then children were asked "What was on the table when you were over there on the blue chair?" In the belief control task, children were shown a box with one content, the content was removed, and another content was placed in the box. Again children were asked to report what was in the box, both before and after the change. The children were then asked "When you first saw the box, all closed up like this, what was inside it?" Children were only included in the study if they answered both these questions correctly.

Table 8.1 shows the results. There was no overall difference between performance on the self and other questions, with 67% of the self questions

TABLE 8.1
Number and Percent Correct Responses to Perception and Belief Questions in
Experiment 1 ($n=14$)

	Level-1 See	Level-2 See	Level-1 Think	Level-2 Think	Belief
Self	12	12	12	13	3
Other	13	9	12	9	1
% Correct	89	75	85	78	14.2

correctly answered, and 65% of the other questions correctly answered. There were also no significant differences on each individual task. We therefore combined the two answers to give children a single score: 0, 1 or 2.

Children performed significantly better on the perception tasks, including both "see" and "think" tasks and level-1 and level-2 tasks, than on the belief task (for level-1 see vs. belief, t = 8.64, $P < 0.001$; for level-1 think vs. belief, t = 5.70, $P < 0.001$; for level-2 see vs. belief, t = 4.43, $P < 0.001$; for level-2 think vs. belief, t = 6.62, $P < 0.001$). Moreover, the absolute level of performance on the perception tasks, with around 70–80% of the questions answered correctly, is also considerably higher than the usual false belief performance. There were no significant differences among the perception tasks. However, as we might expect from the earlier literature, the level-1 "see" task did show the highest performance, with 89% correct, near ceiling.

The results of this first experiment did indeed appear to support a difference between perceptual and nonperceptual tasks. In particular they replicated, in a single experiment, the pattern of results garnered from the previous literature. As in Wellman and Bartsch, the level-1 think task for the other proved simpler than the false belief task. Notably this was also true for the question about the child's own beliefs, which had not previously been tested. As in Flavell et al. (1981) and Gopnik & Slaughter (1991), level-1 perceptual perspective taking was near ceiling, and easier than false belief. The novel and surprising finding, however, was that the level-2 perceptual misrepresentation tasks, both using "looks like" and "think," were also easier than the false belief tasks.

However, some points of difficulty arose. First, the fact that the children received the "see" questions as well as the "think" questions about the same materials may itself have improved their performance on the "think" questions. In other words, asking children to say explicitly what they saw may have influenced their reports of what they thought. This would itself suggest, of course, that children may be using perception as a model for belief.

Second, there were slight differences in the form and procedure for the belief and perception questions. In two previous experiments (Lewis & Osborne, 1990; Siegal & Beattie, 1991), using a particular form of question improved false belief performance. In other studies, however, changes in form, including the use of the particular form in the Lewis and Osborne study, had no effect on performance (Gopnik & Astington, 1988; Hala, 1991; Moore et al., 1990; Robinson & Mitchell, 1992). In Experiment 1, the control tasks ensured that all the children understood the question form. Nevertheless, this possibility seemed worth controlling for.

Finally, in a number of cases, apparently improvements in performance in one study have failed to emerge in further experiments (see earlier; also Hala, Chandler, & Fritz, 1991 vs. Sodian, Taylor, Harris, & Perner, 1991; Robinson & Mitchell, 1992 vs. Robinson & Mitchell, in press). This suggests that sampling variation may sometimes lead to misleading differences in performance on variations of the task. It seemed particularly important, therefore, to replicate any such finding with an additional sample of children and different materials and questions.

Experiment 2

We tested an additional 12 3-year-olds from a local daycare centre in Berkeley. Ages ranged from 3:1–4:3, with a mean of 3:8. Children received the level-1 and level-2 perception tasks and the belief task exactly as in Experiment 1. They also received the two control tasks. In this experiment, however, children were not asked explicitly to state what they saw or thought before and after the change, as in Experiment 1. This helped ensure that the children had not discussed what they saw at the time that they answered the "think" question. Moreover, they were not asked "see" and "think" questions about the same materials, and they were not asked the level-1 "see" question, the easiest question, at all. Instead, they were only asked "think" questions about the table and the cat, and they received an entirely different level-2 "see" task, more closely analogous to the "belief" task. In this task, children were shown a stick immersed in water so that it appeared to be bent. The stick was removed from the water so that children could see it was straight. The stick was then returned to the glass, and an adult, Craig, entered the room. The children were asked "When Craig/you first saw this stick, in this glass here, how did the stick look to him/you? Did it look like a straight stick or did it look like a broken stick?" Thus the question was phrased in the same way as the belief question, and involved a similar sequence of events. In other respects the procedures were identical to the previous experiment.

Results are shown in Table 8.2. As in the previous experiments, there were no significant differences between performance on the "self" and

TABLE 8.2
Number and Percent Correct Responses to Perception and Belief
Questions in Experiment 2 (*n*=12)

	Level-2 See	Level-1 Think	Level-2 Think	Belief
Self	8	7	9	1
Other	7	9	10	0
% Correct	62	66	79	4.1

"other" questions on any of tasks. The general levels of performance on the perception tasks were somewhat lower in this experiment, with 66% of the level-1 questions correct and 79% of the level-2 questions correct. This suggests that the explicit use of the "see" question in Experiment 1 may have had a facilitatory effect, though the difference did not reach significance. Even without an explicit "see" question, however, the levels of performance on the perception tasks were still higher than those in previous studies using the false belief task. Moreover, as in the previous experiment, the children's actual performance on the perception tasks was consistently better than on the belief task (for level-1 think, t = 7.33, $P < 0.001$; for level-2 think, t = 9.94, $P < 0.001$). The new level-2 "see" task with the stick, which used exactly the same phrasing as the belief task and involved a similar sequence of events, also proved to be easier than the belief task. Correct answers were given to 62% of the questions in this task, and performance was significantly higher than in the belief task (t = 4.91, $P < 0.0005$).

The previous experiment suggested that children performed better on perception tasks than belief tasks, even when they were not asked "see" questions about them, and even when they were not asked the easiest level-1 "see" question. It was still possible, however, that the fact that children also received a separate level-2 "see" task influenced their performance on the level-2 "think" task. Moreover, we wanted to investigate yet another question form, and to ensure that the question form was identical in the perception and belief tasks. We had already done this in Experiment 2 for the level-2 "see" task; in this experiment we constructed a similar question for the level-2 "think" task.

Experiment 3

We tested 18 children recruited from local preschools. Ages ranged from 3:1 to 4:3, with a mean of 3:7. The "other" questions were asked about a small stuffed Snoopy puppet, which was placed on the correct chair. Only "think" questions were asked, ensuring that the children were not drawing the analogy to the "see" questions explicitly. As in Experiment 1, children were asked to state explicitly what they thought before and after the change. They were asked "What do you think is in the box?", "What do you think is on the table?", and "What colour do you think the cat is?" The belief question was "When you/Snoopy first saw the box, what did you/he think was inside it then? Did you/he think there were candies inside or pencils inside?" The level-1 perception question was "When you/Snoopy first saw the table, what did you/he think was on it then? Did you/he think there was just a spoon on the table or also an apple?" The level-2 question was "When you/Snoopy first saw the cat, what colour did you think it was then? Did you think it was green or black?" A similar form was used for the control questions.

Table 8.3 shows the results. These children performed better on the false belief task, with 47% of the questions correctly answered. Performance on the level-1 and level-2 "think" tasks was almost identical to the performance in the previous study, with 63% and 77% correct, in spite of the wording change. As in the previous study, the crucial level-2 think question was significantly easier than the belief question (t = 2.01; $P < 0.05$). The level-1 think question (analogous to the Wellman discrepant belief task) also showed improved performance compared to false belief, although this difference failed to reach significance. Importantly, this was true even though the three questions were virtually identical. Finally, as in the previous experiments, there was no significant difference between level-1 and level-2 versions of the "think" question.

The larger N and improved false-belief performance in this study also allowed us to look at the younger and older children separately. Some earlier studies found that the false belief task was most difficult for the younger three-year-olds. This was also the case in the current study. The 9 children under 3:6 only answered 33% of the false belief questions correctly, whereas they answered 66% of the level-1 perception questions and 72% of the level-2 perception questions correctly. The contrast between perception and belief was most striking for these younger children (t = 3.95, $P < 0.01$ for level-1 vs. belief; t = 4.72, $P < 0.01$ for level-2 vs. belief).

TABLE 8.3
Number and Percent Correct Responses to Perception and
Belief Questions in Experiment 3 (n=18)

	Level-1 Think	Level-2 Think	Belief
Self	12	14	10
Other	11	14	7
% Correct	63	77	47

As in the previous study, there were no significant differences between performance on the "self" and "other" questions. Moreover, the larger N in this experiment allowed us to test whether there was a positive association between answers on the "self" and "other" questions. Did children who answered one of these questions correctly also answer the other correctly? We can use the statistic phi to evaluate the association of two dichotomous variables. The phi values for the relation between self and other performance were 0.71 ($P < 0.01$ by Fisher's exact test), 0.68 ($P < 0.05$ by Fisher's exact test), and 0.41 ($P = 0.10$) for performance on the belief, level-2 think and level-1 think questions respectively.

This set of experiments suggested that children were better able to understand perceptual misrepresentation than false belief. Children were particularly competent when the perceptual nature of the task was made explicit (by saying "see" or "looks like") but they also showed improved understanding even when the tasks were phrased in terms of "think," in other words when the test question was identical to the classic false belief question. The actual levels of performance were strikingly similar to the levels on desire tasks in earlier experiments, with about 60–75% correct. This suggests that children may initially understand misrepresentation in the context of desire and perception and only later extend that understanding to belief.

INDUCING CONCEPTUAL CHANGE: A TRAINING STUDY

These experiments, however, only address half of the story. We have hypothesised both that the earlier theory may provide a basis for the new theory, and that new evidence causes the earlier theory to be restructured (Gopnik & Wellman, 1992). If understanding perceptual misrepresentation really contributes to the later understanding of false belief, then letting children experience the similarities between these two areas of understanding might help to accelerate conceptual change. Giving children information or experience with perceptual misrepresentation should improve their performance on false belief tasks.

Moreover, more generally on the theory theory, conceptual change should be a consequence of the accumulation of relevant counter-evidence to the theory. We have suggested that there might be three stages in theory change (Gopnik & Wellman, 1992). In the first stage, children might simply ignore countervailing evidence. There is substantial evidence to support this claim in the literature on false belief. In particular, Moses and Flavell (1990) found that explicitly presenting children with negative feedback, in the course of the false belief experiment itself, had no effect on their answers. Similarly, children who explicitly express their earlier belief in the representational change task may say that they actually said, as well as thought, that there were pencils in the box (Wimmer & Hartl, 1991).

In a second phase, children might take into account counter-evidence but only when they were forced to by the experimenter. Bartsch and Wellman (1989) found that some children who were forced to explain counter-evidence to the false belief task invoked false belief though they did not use the concept predictively. Similarly, Mitchell and Lacohée (1991) found that reminding children of a past explicit action they had performed (choosing a picture of Smarties), which contradicted the theory, improved performance on a representational change task.

Presumably, at some point these explanations are not only applied in the specific context of the falsification but are much more generally applied to all cases of false belief. This last phase was what we were interested in in the last experiment. It is not too surprising that children can be induced to give the right answer in the task itself by a combination of feedback and cues; actually it is more surprising that children resist such feedback. The question is whether such counter-evidence might have a longer-lasting effect on their understanding of the task. Therefore we provided feedback in the tasks but only tested its effects days or weeks after the training was accomplished, and on a different task. Moreover, if the theory theory is correct, training the children on related tasks—tasks that do not explicitly concern false belief but call on the representational theory in similar ways—should also accelerate false belief understanding.

We have gathered such data in a training study. Three-year-old children were pretested on a standard "deceptive box" false belief task (candles in a crayon box), both for self and the other. Only children who passed a control task and yet failed the belief task were included in the study. Three groups of children, with ten children in each group, were randomly assigned to one of three training conditions. In each condition the children were visited twice in the course of the two weeks following the pretesting visit. In the control condition children were given a conservation of number task on each visit. The tasks were designed to be very similar in overall length and structure to the false belief tasks. In each case children saw an array of objects and were asked, "Which line has more?" The array was rearranged and children were asked "Now which line has more?" Children received feedback on their responses, being told "Yes, this line had more" or "No, the other line had more."

In the belief training condition children received different false belief tasks with different materials on each visit. In one task children saw golf balls, which turned out really to be soap. In the second task children turned the pages of a book. On each page of the book a small cut-out hole in the black overlay revealed the ears of an animal; the whole animal was visible when the overlay was turned. On the last page, the object underneath the overlay turned out to be a flower, and the "ears" turned out to be petals (see Gopnik & Astington, 1988). In each case children were asked "What did you/Snoopy think these were? Ears/golf balls or petals/soap?" They received positive and negative feedback about their responses. The experimenter corrected the child's "self" response, "No, you thought they were golf balls" and the Snoopy puppet corrected the "other" response, "No, I thought they were golf balls."

In the third condition, the most interesting one from our current perspective, children in the intervening sessions received a perception task and a desire task, both designed to tap an understanding of misrepresentation. The perception task was the level-2 "cat" task, phrased in terms of "see." In the desire task children were seen at snack time and were asked "Do you want an apple slice?" Then they were fed apple slices until they were no longer hungry. They were asked "Did you want an apple slice?" and told "Snoopy hasn't had a snack, does he want an apple slice?" (see Gopnik & Slaughter, 1991). Just as in the belief tasks, the children received differential feedback about their responses from Snoopy or the experimenter.

Finally, in a post-test session exactly two weeks after the original test, children received yet another false belief task. This time the task involved a band-aid box with a small book inside. The task was administered in exactly the same way for all three groups of children and in exactly the same way as in the original pretest.

Table 8.4 shows the results. Children in the belief and perception/desire conditions performed significantly better on the post-test than those in the control condition, both for self and other. This is particularly striking, since the perception and desire tasks did not explicitly mention the word "think" or raise the false belief problem at all.

CONCLUSION: DEVELOPING THEORIES OF MIND REALLY DO DEVELOP

The results we report here suggest an (at least) four-stage process in children's developing theory of mind. (In fact, other data suggest even earlier developments in infancy and toddlerhood.)

TABLE 8.4
Number and Percent Correct Responses in a False Belief
Post-test in Three Training Conditions ($n=11$)

	Control	Belief	Perception/Desire
Self	3	7	5
Other	0	5	4
% Correct	13.6	54	40.9

1. In the earliest phase, before two-and-a-half, children begin to develop a foundational, if sometimes egocentric, nonrepresentational understanding of perception, as revealed in their joint attention, social referencing, and object-permanence abilities.

2. At two-and-a-half or so, children show a firm understanding of nonrepresentational states such as perception and desire. These children can solve simple desire tasks (Astington & Gopnik, 1991; Wellman & Woolley, 1990) and level-1 perspective-taking tasks. They cannot yet understand more complex tasks such as discrepant belief tasks (Wellman & Bartsch, 1988) or level-2 perception tasks (Flavell et al., 1981).

3. At around age three, children begin to show more competence on these tasks. They begin to show a better understanding of representational aspects of desire, as in the Flavell et al. (1990) values task and our desire change task (Gopnik & Slaughter, 1991). They also begin to show an understanding of level-1 perception, even when the question is phrased in terms of belief, as in the discrepant belief task, and of level-2 perspective-taking, that is perceptual misrepresentation, as in the tasks described here. Children's performance on all these tasks is not at ceiling, but more than half of the time they answer these questions correctly. Moreover, at least some of the time, they can invoke preliminary accounts of misrepresentation if they are confronted by direct counter-evidence (Bartsch & Wellman, 1989; Mitchell & Lacohée, 1991). All of these abilities are interesting conceptual precursors to the fully fledged representational theory of belief, which emerges at around age four. Pieces of the later theory—the very idea of belief, and the idea of perceptual misrepresentation and change and diversity of values—start to appear.

4. Finally, we suggest, at around age four, the force of the accumulating counter-evidence to the earlier theory leads the child to generalise the notion of misrepresentation from perceptual contexts, and to develop a general, predictive, and widely applicable notion of false belief.

This account makes sense of a variety of pieces of evidence about early false-belief-like understanding. It seems to us to do so considerably more coherently than alternative "information-processing" accounts. These accounts propose that the central representational model of the mind is in place at age three or earlier but that various more superficial information-processing and task difficulties mask that competence (Fodor, 1992; Lewis & Osborne, 1990; Siegal & Beattie, 1991). Unfortunately, the issue has become focused on the single question of whether or not children can "do better" on false belief tasks; the neurotic task-fixation we referred to earlier. Such improved performance, by itself, tells us little of interest. In particular, it does not tell us that an information-processing account is correct. The question is, why are there these differences in the performance? Do they reflect the performance demands of the tasks or their conceptual content?

In fact, to confirm one or the other account we would need to look at a wider pattern of evidence. If the information-processing account is correct we would want evidence that a range of tasks with similar information-processing demands, but widely different conceptual content, were similarly difficult for three-year-olds and easy for four-year-olds. For example, three-year-old children might always have difficulty answering questions phrased in a particular way. Similarly, we would want evidence that systematically varying information-processing complexity, in predictable ways, had effects on the developmental pattern. In contrast, on the theory theory account, tasks with very different information-processing demands, involving different materials, questions, etc., but with similar conceptual content, would be expected to develop in concert. Variations in conceptual content, with similar or even identical task demands, might lead to different patterns of development.

In terms of the three- to four-year-old shift, the pattern of results is more congruent with the second picture than the first. The results of the current study, as well as many other results in the literature, suggest that three-year-old children have little difficulty dealing with questions and tasks identical to the false belief task when the conceptual content of those tasks doesn't require an understanding of representation. This is dramatically true for the myriad control tasks that are standardly used in testing false belief. Indeed, the very logic of these tasks is to control for information-processing factors.

It is also true for the intermediate perception and desire tasks. Children in our studies, as well as in Wellman and Bartsch (1988) and Flavell et al. (1990), could answer questions literally identical to the false belief question, in tasks of indistinguishable performance complexity, when they concerned perception, level-1 understanding, or desire. These findings by themselves suggest that it would be difficult to identify a general information-processing difficulty, present at age three but not at age four, that could explain these developments. Why would these difficulties not apply to the control tasks, or to the intermediate tasks? In fact, no coherent account along these lines has ever been proposed, nor have there been any studies that showed that non-theory-of-mind tasks, with similar task demands, developed in close concert with false belief.

In contrast, there are now a number of studies suggesting that tasks with similar conceptual content, but very different information-processing demands—particularly tasks involving a representational understanding of belief—do develop in concert with false belief. These include not only the false belief and representational change tasks, but other tasks such as appearance-reality tasks (Flavell et al., 1986), tasks measuring children's understanding of the sources of their beliefs (Gopnik & Graf, 1988; O'Neill

& Gopnik, 1991; O'Neill, Astington, & Flavell, 1992), and subjective probability tasks (Moore et al., 1990), as well as analyses of the child's spontaneous speech (Wellman, 1990). All these measures suggest significant changes between ages three and four. Moreover, in several studies there have been significant and high correlations between performance on many of these measures, even with age controlled (Flavell et al., 1986; Gopnik & Astington, 1988; Moore et al., 1990).

The complementary alternative side of this pattern is also beginning to emerge. Evidence that information-processing changes by themselves cause differences in performance is thin on the ground and these results are typically fragile, weak, and variable from study to study. In contrast, changing conceptual content can have robust effects on tasks that are otherwise very similar to the false belief task. The Wellman & Bartsch (1988) discrepant belief task, confirmed here, is a striking example of this. So is the children's ceiling performance on pretence, imagery, and level-1 perception tasks, in contrast to their intermediate performance on desire, intention, and perception tasks that call on representational understanding, and their poor performance on tasks that involve a representational understanding of belief (Gopnik & Slaughter, 1991). Similarly, forcing children to confront counterevidence to their particular theory seems to induce changes in understanding, as seen in Bartsch and Wellman (1989), Mitchell and Lacohée (1991), and in our current training study. This is a result more congruent with the theory theory than with information-processing theories.

The results we report here, along with other results in the literature, suggest a truly developmental account of developing theories of mind. Understanding is not simply something that emerges fully blown from the child's head, like Athena from the head of Zeus, and then, also rather like Athena, wraps itself in the fogs and disguises of performance constraints. Instead understanding is a process, something painfully earned and constructed. Children move from confident ignorance at two-and-a-half to the glimmers, false starts, and puzzles of the three-year-old and finally to the fully productive and explanatory model at age four. Lest this sound too triumphal, the new model will itself lead to new puzzles, contradictions, and false starts, such as the puzzle of understanding inference or second-order belief (Wimmer, Hogrefe, & Sodian, 1988; Perner, 1991). The children trying to understand our minds are, in this regard, very much in the same fix as the psychologists trying to understand theirs.

REFERENCES

Astington, J.W., & Gopnik, A. (1991). Developing understanding of desire and intention. In A. Whiten (Ed.), *Natural theories of mind: Evolution, development and simulation of everyday mindreading* (pp. 39–50). Oxford: Blackwell.
Baron-Cohen, S. (1991). Precursors to a theory of mind: Understanding attention in others. In

A. Whiten (Ed.), *Natural theories of mind: Evolution, development and simulation of everyday mindreading* (pp. 233–251). Oxford: Basil Blackwell.

Baron-Cohen, S., & Cross, P. (1992). Reading the eyes: Evidence for the role of perception in the development of a theory of mind. *Mind and Language, 6,* 166–180.

Bartsch, K., & Wellman, H.M. (1989). Young children's attribution of action to beliefs and desires. *Child Development, 60* (4), 946–964.

Bloom, L. (1973). *One third at a time: The use of single word utterances before syntax.* The Hague: Mouton.

Bretherton, I., & Beeghly, M. (1982). Talking about internal states: The acquisition of an explicit theory of mind. *Developmental Psychology, 18,* 906–911.

Bruner, J. (1983). *Child's talk: Learning to use language.* New York: W.W. Norton.

Butterworth, G. (1991). The ontogeny and phylogeny of joint visual attention. In A. Whiten (Ed.), *Natural theories of mind: Evolution, development and simulation of everyday mindreading* (pp. 223–232). Oxford: Basil Blackwell.

Campos, J.J., & Sternberg, C.R. (1980). Perception, appraisal and emotion: The onset of social referencing. In M. Lamb & L. Sharrod (Ed.), *Infant social cognition* (pp. 273–311). Hillsdale, NJ: Lawrence Erlbaum Associates Inc.

Flavell, J.H. (1978). The development of knowledge about visual perception. In *Nebraska symposium on motivation 1977: Social cognitive development, 25* (pp. 43–76). Lincoln, Nebraska: University of Nebraska Press.

Flavell, J.H. (1988). The development of children's knowledge about the mind: From cognitive connections to mental representations. In J.W. Astington, P.L. Harris, & D.R. Olson (Eds.), *Developing theories of mind.* Cambridge, Mass.: Cambridge University Press.

Flavell, J.H., Everett, B.A., Croft, K., & Flavell, E.R. (1981). Young children's knowledge about visual perception: Further evidence for the Level 1–Level 2 distinction. *Developmental Psychology, 17,* 99–103.

Flavell, J.H., Flavell, E.R., & Green, F.L. (1987). Young children's knowledge about the apparent-real and pretend-real distinctions. *Developmental Psychology, 23* (6), 816–822.

Flavell, J.H., Flavell, E.R., Green, F.L., & Moses, L.J. (1990). Young children's understanding of fact beliefs versus value beliefs. *Child Development, 61* (4), 915–928.

Flavell, J.H., Green, F.L., & Flavell, E.R. (1986). Development of knowledge about the appearance-reality distinction. *Monographs of the Society for Research in Child Development, 51,* No. 1.

Fodor, J. (1992). A theory of the child's theory of mind. *Cognition, 44,* 283–296.

Forguson, L., & Gopnik, A. (1988). The ontogeny of common sense. In J.W. Astington, P.L. Harris, & D.R. Olson (Eds.), *Developing theories of mind* (pp. 226–243). Cambridge, Mass.: Cambridge University Press.

Gopnik, A. (1982). Words and plans: Early language and the development of intelligent action. *Journal of Child Language, 9,* 303–308.

Gopnik, A. (1984). The acquisition of "gone" and the development of the object concept. *Journal of Child Language, 11,* 273–292.

Gopnik, A. (1993). How we know our minds: The illusion of first-person knowledge of intentionality. *Behavioral and Brain Sciences, 16,* 1–14.

Gopnik, A., & Astington, J.W. (1988). Children's understanding of representational change and its relation to the understanding of false belief and the appearance-reality distinction. *Child Development, 59,* 26–37.

Gopnik, A., & Graf, P. (1988). Knowing how you know: Young children's ability to identify and remember the sources of their beliefs. *Child Development, 59,* 1366–1371.

Gopnik, A., & Meltzoff, A.N. (1984). Semantic and cognitive development in 15- to 21-month-old children. *Journal of Child Language, 11,* 495–513.

Gopnik, A., & Meltzoff, A.N. (1986). Relations between semantic and cognitive development in the one-word stage: The specificity hypothesis. *Child Development, 57*, 1040–1053.

Gopnik, A., & Slaughter, V. (1991). Children's understanding of changes in their mental states. *Child Development, 62*, 98–110.

Gopnik, A., & Wellman, H. (1992). Why the child's theory of mind really is a theory. *Mind and Language, 7* (1&2), 145–172.

Haith, M., Bergman, T., & Moore, M. (1977). Eye contact and face scanning in early infancy. *Science, 198*, 853–855.

Hala, S. (April, 1991). *The role of personal involvement in facilitating false belief understanding.* Paper presented at the Meeting of the Society for Research in Child Development, Seattle, Washington.

Hala, S., Chandler, M., & Fritz, A.S. (1991). Fledgling theories of mind: Deception as a marker of three-year-olds' understanding of false belief. *Child Development, 62*, 83–97.

Harris, P., & Kavanaugh, R. (1993). Young children's understanding of pretence. *Monographs of the Society for Research in Child Development.* Chicago: University of Chicago Press.

Lempers, J.D., Flavell, E.R., & Flavell, J.H. (1977). The development in very young children of tacit knowledge concerning visual perception. *Genetic Psychology Monographs, 95*, 3–53.

Leslie, A.M. (1987). Pretence and representation: The origins of "theory of mind." *Psychological Review, 94* (4), 412–426.

Lewis, C., & Osborne, A. (1990). Three-year-olds' problems with false-belief: Conceptual deficit or linguistic artifact? *Child Development, 61*, 1514–1519.

Masangkay, Z., McCluskey, K., McIntyre, C., Sims-Knight, J., Vaughan, B., & Flavell, J.H. (1974). The early development of inferences about the visual percepts of others. *Child Development, 45*, 357–366.

Maurer, D., & Barrera, M. (1981). Infants' perception of natural and distorted arrangements of a schematic face. *Child Development, 52*, 196–202.

Meltzoff, A.N., & Gopnik, A. (1993). The role of imitation in understanding persons and developing a theory of mind. In S. Baron-Cohen, H. Tager-Flusberg, & D. Cohen (Eds.), *Understanding other minds: Perspectives from autism* (pp. 335–366). Oxford: Oxford University Press.

Meltzoff, A.N., & Moore, M.K. (1989). Imitation in newborn infants: Exploring the range of gestures imitated and the underlying mechanisms. *Developmental Psychology, 25*, 954–962.

Mitchell, P., & Lacohée, H. (1991). Children's early understanding of false belief. *Cognition, 39* (2), 107–117.

Moore, C., Pure, K., & Furrow, D. (1990). Children's understanding and its relation to the development of a representational theory of mind. *Child Development, 61* (3), 722–730.

Moses, L.J. (in press). Young children's understanding of belief constraints on intention. *Cognitive Development.*

Moses, L.J., & Flavell, J.H. (1990). Inferring false beliefs from actions and reactions. *Child Development, 61* (4), 929–945.

O'Neill, D.K., Astington, J.W., & Flavell, J.H. (1992). Young children's understanding of the role that sensory experiences play in knowledge acquisition. *Child Development, 63* (2), 474–491.

O'Neill, D.K., & Gopnik, A. (1991). Young children's ability to identify the sources of their beliefs. *Developmental Psychology, 27* (3), 390–7.

Perner, J. (1988). Developing semantics for theories of mind: From propositional attitudes to mental representations. In J.W. Astington, P.L. Harris, & D.R. Olson (Eds.), *Developing theories of mind* (pp. 141–172). Cambridge: Cambridge University Press.

Perner, J. (1991). *Understanding the representational mind.* Cambridge, Mass.: Bradford Books/MIT Press.

Robinson, E.J., & Mitchell, P. (1992). Children's interpretation of messages from a speaker with a false belief. *Child Development, 63* (3), 639–652.

Robinson, E.J., & Mitchell, P. (in press). Young children's false-belief reasoning: Interpretation of messages versus the classic task. *Developmental Psychology.*

Scaife, M., & Bruner, J. (1975). The capacity for joint visual attention in the infant. *Nature, 253,* 265.

Searle, J.R. (1983). *Intentionality: An essay in the philosophy of mind.* Cambridge: Cambridge University Press.

Siegal, M., & Beattie, K. (1991). Where to look first for children's knowledge of false beliefs. *Cognition, 38,* 1–12.

Sodian, B., Taylor, C., Harris, P.L., & Perner, J. (1991). Early deception and the child's theory of mind: False trails and genuine markers. *Child Development, 62,* 468–483.

Tomasello, M., & Farrar, J. (1984). Cognitive bases of lexical development: Object permanence and relational words. *Journal of Child Language, 11,* 477–493.

Tomasello, M., & Farrar, J. (1986). Object-permanence and relational words: A lexical training study. *Journal of Child Language, 13,* 495–505.

Wellman, H.M. (1990). *The child's theory of mind.* Cambridge, Mass.: Bradford Books/MIT Press.

Wellman, H.M. (1993). Early understanding of mind: The normal case. In S. Baron-Cohen, H. Tager-Flusberg, & D. Cohen (Eds.), *Understanding other minds: Perspectives from autism.* Oxford: Oxford University Press.

Wellman, H.M., & Bartsch, K. (1988). Young children's reasoning about beliefs. *Cognition, 30,* 239–277.

Wellman, H.M., & Woolley, J.D. (1990). From simple desires to ordinary beliefs: The early development of everyday psychology. *Condition, 35* (3), 245–275.

Wimmer, H., & Hartl, M. (1991). Against the Cartesian view on mind: Young children's difficulty with own false beliefs. *British Journal of Developmental Psychology, 9,* 125–128.

Wimmer, H., Hogrefe, J.-G., & Sodian, B. (1988). A second stage in children's conception of mental life: Understanding sources of information. In J.W. Astington, P.L. Harris, & D.R. Olson (Eds.), *Developing theories of mind.* Cambridge: Cambridge University Press.

Wimmer, H., & Perner, J. (1983). Beliefs about beliefs: Representation and constraining function of wrong beliefs in young children's understanding of deception. *Cognition, 13,* 103–108.

Yaniv, I., & Shatz, M. 91988). Children's understanding of perceptibility. In J.W. Astington, P.L. Harris, & D.R. Olson (Eds.), *Developing theories of mind.* New York: Cambridge University Press.

Yuill, N. (1984). Young children's coordination of motive and outcome in judgements of satisfaction and morality. *British Journal of Developmental Psychology, 2,* 73–81.

9
A Model of the Mindreading System: Neuropsychological and Neurobiological Perspectives

Simon Baron-Cohen
Institute of Psychiatry, University of London, UK

Howard Ring
Institute of Neurology, University of London, UK

INTRODUCTION

There is mounting evidence that ToMM (the Theory of Mind Mechanism) may be a modular system (Baron-Cohen, 1992; Leslie, 1991; Leslie & Roth, 1993). ToMM is the name Leslie gives to the system underpinning our everyday theory of mind. ToMM's modularity rests on two arguments:

1. Children with autism are impaired in their understanding of epistemic mental states (such as beliefs: Baron-Cohen, Leslie, & Frith, 1985; Perner, Frith, Leslie, & Leekam, 1989), but are unimpaired in their understanding of nonmental representations (such as photographs, drawings, maps, and models: Charman & Baron-Cohen, 1992; 1993; Leekam & Perner, 1991; Leslie & Thaiss, 1992); and

2. Understanding mental states requires the processing of a special kind of representation. Leslie and Roth (1993) call these *M-Representations*[1], and suggest they have the following structure[2]:

[Agent-Attitude-"Proposition"].

---

[1] They adopt this term in order to avoid the confusions arising from the earlier term 'metarepresentations' (Perner, 1993).

[2] In recent writings, Leslie suggests M-Representations have a 4th term, to express an anchor in reality (e.g. see Leslie, German, & Happé, 1993).

Examples of what could fill these three slots are:

[John-thinks-"The money is in the biscuit tin"], or
[Mary-believes-"The moon is made of green cheese"].

In these examples, the whole M-Representation can be true even if the proposition is false (i.e. even if the money is not in the biscuit tin, or if the moon is not made of green cheese). For example, the M-Representation can be true if John indeed *thinks* the money is in the biscuit tin, or if Mary really *believes* the moon is made of green cheese. The usefulness of M-Representations is that they allow prediction of an Agent's future action. For example, they lead us to predict that John will go to the biscuit tin if he wants the money. M-Representation also allow one to make sense of an Agent's behaviour. For example, they help make sense of why John looks disappointed when he opens the biscuit tin.

The evidence from autism, showing that such children have specific difficulties in predicting an Agent's behaviour on the basis of beliefs and other mental states, in combination with Leslie's account of ToMM's unique class representations, satisfy two criteria for a system to be modular: the possibility of neural dissociation, and the existence of specific, dedicated representations (Fodor, 1983; Jackendoff, 1987).

According to Leslie (1987), ToMM comes on line in the middle of the second year of life, and its arrival is marked by the production and comprehension of pretence. Building on Leslie's model, Baron-Cohen (in press a; in press b) argues for the existence of three developmentally earlier modules:

1. ID (the Intentionality Detector),
2. EDD (the Eye-Direction Detector), and
3. SAM (the Shared Attention Mechanism).

As will be explained, SAM is held to play a crucial role in triggering ToMM to function. In this chapter, we begin by briefly summarising the neuropsychology of these mechanisms. We then shift levels to consider the possible neurobiology of these mechanisms. In doing this, we seek to integrate Baron-Cohen's (in press a; in press b) psychological theory with Brothers' (1990) neurobiology theory.

THE NEUROPSYCHOLOGY OF THE MINDREADING SYSTEM

Figure 9.1 shows the four postulated components in the Mindreading System[3]. Here, we review each of the four mechanisms in turn.

---

[3] Further details of each of them can be found elsewhere (Baron-Cohen, in press a; in press b).

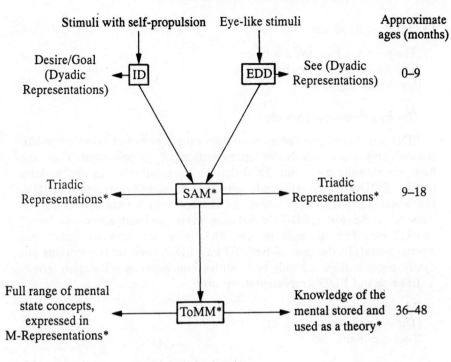

FIG. 9.1 The four components of the Mindreading System (adapted from Baron-Cohen, in press a).

The Intentionality Detector

ID is a primitive perceptual mechanism that is amodal, and that interprets self-propelling stimuli in terms of that stimulus' goal or desire. That is, it reads directional stimuli as volitional. In this system, "goal" is defined as the target of an action, and "desire" is defined as a movement towards or away from a target. ID is very similar to Premack's (1990) notion of a module that is hand-wired into our visual system to detect intentionality—though in the case of ID, the mental states of goal and desire are read into a wide range of stimuli with *direction* (a touch, a push, a jump, a shout, any movement that occurs without an apparent external cause, etc). ID builds *dyadic* representations of behaviour, of the form:

[Agent–Relation–Object], or
[Agent–Relation–Self], or
[Self–Relation–Object], or
[Self–Relation–Agent].

Examples of these are:

[The man-has goal-the door], or
[The mouse-wants-the cheese],
[I-want-the cup].

The Eye-direction Detector

EDD is a system that functions to detect the presence of eyes (or eye-like stimuli), and then builds dyadic representations of eye behaviour. These are built, for example, every time EDD detects that another's eyes are "looking at me." EDD's dyadic representations have an identical structure to ID's, but whereas for ID the Relation slot is filled with a term like "goal" or "desire," in the case of EDD the Relation slot is filled with a term like "see," "look," etc. That is, eyes or eye-like stimuli are read as visual and informational. In the case of both ID and EDD, their representations are dyadic because there are only two entities, connected by a Relation term.

Examples of EDD's representations are:

[Mother-sees-me], or
[The cat-sees-the mouse], or
[I-see-the man].

The Shared Attention Mechanism

SAM is a mechanism that functions to check if you and another organism are attending to the same object. To do this, SAM builds *triadic* representations[4]. These are more complex than dyadic representations. They have a structure that is expressed by something like the following:

[Agent–Relation–(Self–Relation–Object)], or
[Self–Relation–(Agent–Relation–Object)].

Examples are:

[Mother-sees-(I-see-the car)], or
[I-see-(Mother-looking at-the door)].

What makes these representations triadic is the inclusion of an embedded dyadic representation (e.g. [Self-Relation-Object] or [Agent-Relation-Object]). This is required in order for the triadic representation to specify that both Self and Agent are looking at the *same* object, and that one or

---

[4] The distinction between dyadic and triadic relations stems from Bakeman and Adamson (1984). They are also key distinctions that Gomez (1991) draws. Hobson (this volume) brings out the importance of such relations in talking about the "triangle." In Baron-Cohen's (in press a; in press b) theory, these terms describe types of *representation*.

both of the Agents has detected this. Perhaps a more accurate way of expressing this is via the diagram in Fig. 9.2.

SAM is a central mechanism that depends on ID and EDD for its input. That is, it can only build triadic representations out of dyadic ones. Because these are more easily constructed out of EDD's dyadic representations, EDD and SAM are held to have a privileged relationship: EDD sends its output to SAM, as is shown in Fig. 9.1.

SAM can do a few more things. First, it connects ID to EDD. This means that in the triadic representations that SAM builds, the Relation slot can be filled by either visual terms ("see," "look," etc.) or volitional terms ("goal," "desire," etc.). This allows SAM to read eye-direction in terms of an Agent's goals and desires. Secondly, SAM passes its triadic representations to the fourth of the components in the Mindreading System, ToMM. This is held to be necessary to trigger ToMM to function (Baron-Cohen, 1989; 1991a; 1993; in press a; in press b).

The Theory of Mind Mechanism

As briefly mentioned in the Introduction to this chapter, we follow Leslie's description of this component. That is, ToMM is held to represent something like M-Representations, employing the full range of mental state concepts in the Attitude slot. These include the epistemic states (believe,

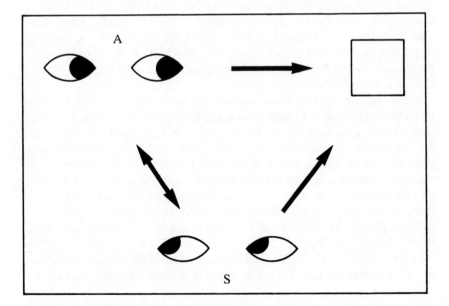

FIG. 9.2   A triadic representation (adapted from Baron-Cohen, in press a). S = Self, and A = Agent.

think, know, pretend, imagine, dream, etc.). ToMM's second function is to organise mental state knowledge into a useful and coherent theory of action, such that it becomes both explanatory and predictive (Premack & Woodruff, 1978; Wellman, 1990).

So much for the background. What of the neuropsychology of these four mechanisms? Here, we examine both the normal developmental timetable of these four mechanisms, and the possible dissociability between them in cases where development goes wrong. Specifically, we focus on two kinds of pathology: autism, and congenital blindness[5].

Normal Development

ID is probably functional from early in infancy (Premack, 1990). Rather than infants operating like behaviourists at any point in development, they probably read movement in terms of goal-directed action from the outset. Certainly, by the time they speak they refer to goal-directed action and desires (Wellman, 1990).

EDD is clearly functioning in infancy, as shown by infants' selective attention to other people's eyes (Maurer & Barrera, 1981). This selective attention to the eyes appears to have a long evolutionary heritage: From the reptiles, to the birds, to the primates one can find selective attention to the eyes of another organism (Baron-Cohen, in press a; in press b). The fact that human infants smile when they receive eye-contact (Wolff, 1963) is evidence that they can detect when "eyes are directed at me." Certainly by preschool age, when they can be tested verbally, they have no difficulty in correctly responding to the test question "Which one is looking at you?" when presented with pairs of photographs of faces like those in Fig. 9.3 (Baron-Cohen & Cross, 1992).

SAM is held to come on line slightly later than the two previous mechanisms: around 8–12 months of age. The clearest expressions of this are spontaneous gaze-monitoring (Butterworth, 1991; Scaife & Bruner, 1975) and spontaneous gaze-directing behaviours such as protodeclarative pointing (Bates, Camaioni, & Volterra, 1975). In both phenomena, the infant alternates his or her own gaze back and forth between the adult's eyes and the object to which they are both attending, or at which the infant is directing the adult's gaze (Baron-Cohen, 1989; 1991a; Gomez, 1991).

Regarding SAM's function of inferring goal from eye-direction, Phillips, Baron-Cohen, and Rutter (1992) investigated this with normal toddlers ranging from 9–18 months. The child was presented either with an ambiguous or an unambiguous action. One ambiguous action comprised *blocking* the

---

[5] We follow Hobson (1990) in drawing this comparison, though we use it to emphasise the differential dissociation of the four components of the Mindreading System.

FIG. 9.3   "Which one is looking at you?" (from Baron-Cohen & Cross, 1992, reproduced with permission).

child's hands during manual activity, by the adult cupping her hands over the child's. A second ambiguous action comprised offering an object to the child, but then at the last minute *teasingly* withdrawing it, just as the child began to reach for it. The unambiguous action simply comprised *giving* or presenting an object to the child. Phillips et al. found that, on at least half of the trials, 100% of the infants responded to the ambiguous actions by instantly looking at the adult's eyes (within the first 5 seconds after the tease or the block), whereas only 39% of them did so following the unambiguous action, using the same criteria. This suggests that under conditions in which the goal of an action is uncertain, the first place young children (and indeed adults) look for information to disambiguate the goal is the eyes.

A further study demonstrated that it is indeed eye-*direction* that children use to infer the mental state of goal (Baron-Cohen, Campbell, et al., 1993). Since this paradigm was verbal, young three-year-olds were tested. The child was asked "Which chocolate will Charlie take?" after being shown a display of four sweets and a cartoon character (Charlie's face) looking at one of these (see Fig. 9.4). Subjects tended to pick the one Charlie was *looking at* as the goal of his next action, and this was statistically significant. Regarding evidence for SAM's function of inferring desire from eye-direction, Baron-Cohen, Campbell, et al. (1993) also presented normal three- to four-year-olds with the display of the four sweets, with Charlie's eyes pointing towards one of the four sweets, randomly selected (as in Fig. 9.4), and asked the

FIG. 9.4   The Four Sweets Display (adapted from Baron-Cohen, Campbell et al., 1993).

subject "Which one does Charlie *want*?" Children of this age had no difficulty at all in inferring Charlie's desire from his eye-direction.

ToMM, as Leslie (1987) suggests, probably makes its first appearance with pretence, around 18–24 months of age. By 3 years of age, preschoolers are able to understand aspects of what people know (Pratt & Bryant, 1990), and by 4 years of age they can distinguish true and false beliefs (Wimmer & Perner, 1983). Their mental-state knowledge is also highly organised into a coherent "theory" which the child uses for both explanation and prediction of behaviour (Wellman, 1990).

Autism

Both ID and EDD appear to be intact in children with autism. Evidence for these claims includes the following: Such children use words referring to goal-directed action and desire in their spontaneous speech (Baron-Cohen, Leslie, & Frith, 1986; Tager-Flusberg, 1993), they can predict emotions on the basis of a person's desire (Baron-Cohen, 1991b), and they can detect when the eyes of another person are directed at them (Baron-Cohen, Campbell, et al., 1993). However, SAM appears to be impaired in autism. Key evidence for this is that they show little if any spontaneous gaze monitoring (Leekam et al., 1993; Sigman, Mundy, Ungerer, & Sherman, 1986) or spontaneous protodeclarative pointing to direct another's gaze to share interest in something, as an end in itself (Baron-Cohen, 1989).

If SAM is impaired in autism, then children with autism should also have difficulties in reading eye-direction in terms of mental states such as goal and desire. There is some evidence that supports this prediction. Phillips et al. (1992) tested very young children with autism for their ability to use eye-direction to detect a person's goals, using the ambiguous and unambiguous actions described earlier. However, these children did not use eye-contact to disambiguate the ambiguous actions, looking as little in both conditions (less than 11% looking, in each). Baron-Cohen, Campbell, et al. (1993) went on to test children with autism to see if, on the Four Sweets Task, they were able to use eye-direction to infer the mental states of want and goal. They found significant impairments in the use of eye-direction in inferring both of these.

Autism and Congenital Blindness

SAM and ToMM, as so far described, are independent systems with a special relationship: ToMM is activated by taking SAM's triadic representations as input. This is a testable claim about a certain kind of precursor relationship[6] between the two systems in development. The claim is that SAM is a necessary (though not sufficient) condition for the development of ToMM. Note, though, that although SAM usually builds triadic representations using EDD's dyadic representations, this need not be the case. For example, since children with congenital blindness lack EDD, SAM must be restricted to building triadic representations specifying joint-attention via touch or audition (e.g. [Mother-touches-(I-touch-the apple)]). So, in their case, SAM must be building triadic representations using ID's dyadic representations. These kind of triadic representations are likely to be considerably more difficult to build than those derived from EDD.

To summarise, the key claims can be elaborated as follows:

1. SAM's triadic representations are necessary to trigger ToMM's development.
2. SAM exploits EDD as the system of choice for building triadic representations.

---

[6] Gopnik, Slaughter, and Meltzoff (this volume) also pursue the argument that understanding perception is a precursor for understanding belief, though for them this is couched in terms of theory-change. Butterworth (this volume) similarly argues that joint-attention is one of the important routes towards an understanding of mind in the developing child. Our account is compatible with both of these accounts, but as the reader will gather, ours is both a modular and a neurobiological thesis.

3. In most cases of autism, SAM is impaired whilst EDD is not.
4. In congenital blindness, EDD is impaired but SAM is not.

Regarding (2), this is not only because joint attention can be established on distal objects more easily via vision than it can via touch or audition, but also because eye-direction is a more reliable source of information about a person's goals, interest, etc., than is (say) body-orientation. Hence the assumption that EDD and SAM have been prioritised in evolution for solving the problem of detecting a person's mental states of attention, desire, and goal (Baron-Cohen, in press a; in press b).

Given the evidence presented earlier, that most children with autism fail to develop a fully functioning SAM, it follows from the theory outlined here that in these children this would have the knock-on effect of not activating ToMM. In principle, however, the theory predicts two subgroups of autism:

Subgroup 1.   Both SAM and ToMM are impaired, as explained by the knock-on hypothesis. There is considerable evidence suggesting that many subjects with autism fall into this group (see Baron-Cohen, 1993, for a review)[7].

Subgroup 2.   SAM is intact, whereas ToMM is impaired in its own right. This group remains to be properly investigated. One possibility is that this group corresponds to those children with autism who are reported to have a period of normal development up to the age of 18 months (Derek Ricks, personal communication, 1985; Volkmar & Cohen, 1989), and then show clear signs of autism.

Finally it follows from this theory that in children with congenital blindness, since SAM is intact, ToMM should also develop, although a slight delay in this would not be surprising given the need for SAM to use ID instead of EDD. Here too, we await the relevant tests of ToMM in children with congenital blindness.

THE NEUROBIOLOGY OF THE MINDREADING SYSTEM

In this section we present a neurobiological model. This model is of necessity speculative, as many pieces of the jigsaw are not yet in place. However, we feel that there are enough clues to begin to sketch the model. Our model is based on an integration of our work (Baron-Cohen, in press a; in press b;

---

[7] Consistent with this, absence of joint attention and pretend play is one predictor of autism at 18 months of age (Baron-Cohen, Allen, & Gillberg, 1992).

Baron-Cohen, Ring, et al., 1993) with that of Brothers (Brothers, 1990; Brothers & Ring, 1992). The model proposes:

1. that the superior temporal sulcus (STS) is responsible for EDD's functions;
2. that since SAM uses EDD, the STS may be responsible for aspects of SAM too;
3. that the orbito-frontal cortex (OFC) is responsible for some of ToMM's functions;
4. that the amygdala may be involved in several components of the Mindreading System; and
5. that these three brain areas form a circuit via important neural interconnections.

These three brain regions are shown in Fig. 9.5. Frith (1992) proposes a similar model, also based on Brothers (1990). We turn to consider the evidence for these assumptions.

The STS: The Seat of EDD and SAM?

Specific "face" cells were identified by Bruce, Desimone, and Gross (1981) and Perrett, Rolls, and Caan (1982) in the STS. Later studies demonstrated the role of specific cells which respond selectively to *individual* familiar faces (Bayliss, Rolls, & Leonard, 1985; Desimone, Albright, Gross, & Bruce, 1984; Kendrick & Baldwin, 1987; Perrett et al., 1984; Yamane, Kaji, & Kawano, 1988), and to the orientation of the head (Perrett et al., 1985). Perrett's group found that some cell types respond selectively to the left profile, others to the back of the head, etc.

Other studies have found that specific cells respond selectively to direction of gaze (Perrett et al., 1985; 1990). For example, Fig. 9.6 shows significantly more excitation from a cell in the STS of an observer when looking at eyes which are directed forward. (Other cells in the STS show the opposite pattern.) Perrett et al. (1985) found that 64% of cells in the STS responsive to the face or profile views of the head are also selective for the direction of gaze. Other evidence consistent with the notion of the STS being the brain basis of EDD comes from neuropsychology: Lesions in the STS produce an impairment in the ability to discriminate gaze direction by monkeys (Campbell et al., 1990), and by some patients with prosopagnosia (Campbell et al., 1990; Heywood & Cowey, 1991; Perrett et al., 1990). Perrett and his colleagues, in their most recent publications (Perrett et al., 1990; 1991), refer to the cells which respond to gaze-direction as cells responsive to the state of *attention* of the other individual, and which have the primary function of detecting if another individual is "looking at me" or not. In our model, such

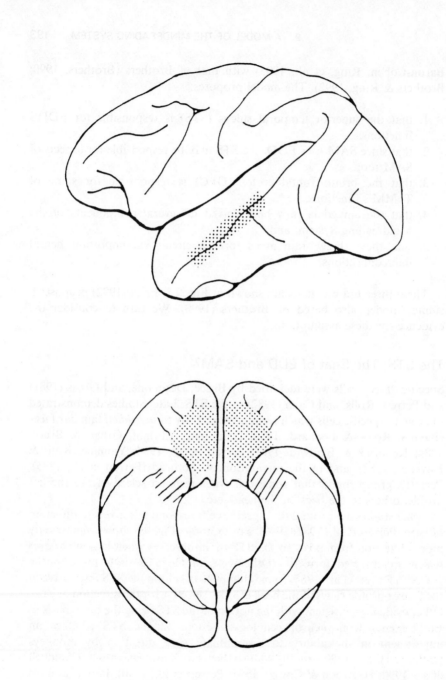

FIG. 9.5 The orbito-frontal cortex (OFC: lower illustration: basal view) and the superior temporal sulcus (STS: upper illustration: lateral view) in the macaque brain. The shaded regions show medial portions of the amygdala (from Brothers, 1990, reproduced with permission).

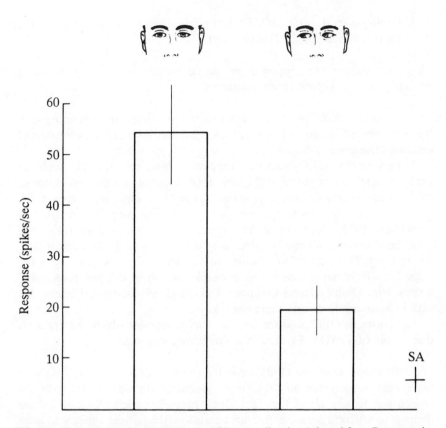

FIG. 9.6 Responsivity of cell M047 in the STS to eye-direction (adapted from Perrett et al., 1990, reproduced with permission).

cell assemblies serve EDD, and we speculate that since SAM works so closely with EDD, such cell assemblies in the STS may serve aspects of SAM's functioning as well. SAM's link with ToMM, however, requires the connection from STS to OFC. OFC receives direct inputs from rostral temporal cortices, including the depths of the STS (Barbas, 1988).

The OFC and ToMM

Damasio (1984) argues that the prefrontal region can be divided into three distinct functional sectors:

1. Superior mesial cortex (SMC: Brodmann Areas 6 and 24);
2. Dorsolateral cortex (DLC: Brodmann Areas, 4, 6, 8–11, and 43–47); and

3. Orbito-frontal cortex (OFC: Brodmann Areas 10–14, lying on the ventral surface of the frontal lobe).

These distinctions are proposed on the basis that lesions in these three regions produce very different symptoms:

1. Lesions in SMC produce a lack of drive or interest in interacting with the environment, social or nonsocial; and abnormalities in the expression of emotion (Damasio, 1984).

2. Lesions in DLC produce executive function deficits, such as perseveration and impulsivity (Milner, 1964; Shallice, 1988). For example, DLC lesions in juvenile monkeys impair the delayed response, whereas OFC lesions in juvenile monkeys produce no lasting impairment in this (Goldman, 1971; Goldman & Alexander, 1977). This suggests OFC and DLC have separate functions. OFC and DLC also have distinct anatomical connectivity (Fuster, 1989). Additional evidence for the role of DLC (especially Brodmann area 9: the principle sulcus) in delayed responding comes from Diamond and Goldman-Rakic's (1989) study of Piaget's AB task in human infants and rhesus monkeys.

3. Lesions in OFC produce *loss of social judgement* which, we argue, is due to loss of ToMM. Evidence for this is reviewed next.

Eslinger and Damasio (1985) reported the case of a patient (EVR) who underwent surgery for an OFC meningioma at the age of 35, with the consequent loss of all of the right OFC, part of the left OFC, and some damage to adjacent areas. Before his operation, the patient appears to have been socially normal: He held a senior position in a firm of accountants, was active in the local church, was married, and was a father of two. After his surgery, his family reported that he began to make decisions that suggested he had lost his social judgement: He went into business with a man of questionable reputation, against the advice of his friends and family; he then invested all of his savings into the new partnership, only (predictably to everyone else) to end up bankrupt. Similar difficulties led to a breakdown in his marriage. He married again, but this second marriage ended after just two years, again, quite predictably to everyone else.

Eslinger and Damasio's comment on EVR's decline is that his social judgement had become markedly impaired[8]. They describe him (1985, p.

---

[8] Of interest, he has also become markedly obsessional (e.g. refusing to part with useless possessions such as old telephone directories, taking two hours to wash and shave in the morning) and unable to form plans (taking several hours to decide which restaurant to go to, etc.). The interest of this association stems from the co-association of social impairment and "obsessional" behaviour in autism.

1737) as a case of "acquired sociopathy," to convey how post-operatively EVR had lost (1985, p. 1739) his "social sense." They note the similarity with Ackerley and Benton's (1948) case (JP) of a "primary social defect" following early, bilateral prefrontal lobe atrophy damage. Damasio, Tranel, and Damasio (1990) report another case with a similar social deficit from OFC lesions.

Although these neurological cases constitute at least suggestive hints for OFC involvement in ToMM, Price, Daffner, Stowe, and Mesulam (1990) report the only explicit test of a theory of mind deficit in two patients with acquired early frontal damage (at birth in one case, and at age four in the other). Both of their patients showed poor empathy in their social behaviour, and failed (what would today be seen as) a theory of mind test (a test of Flavell et al.'s, 1968). Further converging evidence comes from Kaczmarek (1984), who reported that damage to OFC produces more disturbance to narrative or discourse skills than does damage to DLC. This was mirrored in a report by Alexander, Benson, and Stuss (1989). Since discourse/pragmatic skills depend on ToMM (Baron-Cohen, 1988a; 1988b; Happé, 1993; Tager-Flusberg, 1993), this evidence is consistent with the OFC theory of ToMM.

On the basis of these strong clues for OFC involvement in ToMM, Baron-Cohen, Ring, et al. (in press) carried out a neuroimaging study of ToMM with normal adult subjects, using SPECT (Single Photon Emission Computed Tomography). Subjects were asked to detect the mental state terms in a word list that was played through headphones. We predicted significant OFC activation. A significant increase in cerebral blood flow in the right OFC was indeed found during this task, relative to a control (non-ToMM) task. No specific increase in activation occurred in an adjacent frontal lobe region (right frontal polar). To the extent that this mental state term detection task taps ToMM, this implies that at least some functions of ToMM require the right OFC.

Of the major three prefrontal regions (OFC, SMC, and DLC), OFC is the richest region in terms of limbic system connectivity (Damasio, 1984). The connections come from, among other centres, the amygdala (Nauta, 1962; 1964). Extending Brothers' (1990) model once again, we turn next to consider the role of the amygdala in a possible ToMM circuit.

The Amygdala: The Seat of ToMM's Affective Function?

The STS projects to the lateral nucleus of the amygdala (Aggleton, Burton, & Passingham, 1980). The OFC receives significant inputs from the medial structures of the amygdala (Aggleton, 1985; Amaral & Price, 1984; Porrino, Crane, & Goldman-Rakic, 1982; Van Hoesen, 1981). These observations suggest an *STS-amygdala-OFC circuit* (Brothers, 1990). Like the STS, both the medial and lateral nuclei of the amygdala also have face-sensitive cells (Leonard, Rolls, Wilson, & Bayliss, 1985; Nakamura, Mikami, & Kubota, 1992). Since face-responsive units in the amygdala fire at a longer latency than do those in the STS, it is thought that they probably occur "downstream" from the STS (Leonard et al., 1985). Furthermore, like the STS, the amygdala also has cells sensitive to aspects of facial expression and gaze direction (Brothers, Ring, & Kling, 1990). Lesions in the amygdala alone can produce the Kluver-Bucy syndrome[9] (Schreiner & Kling, 1953). More recent accounts of the effects of amygdalectomy (Kling & Brothers, 1992) include not only social isolation, but also difficulties in social perception (e.g. an inability to respond selectively to different social ranks such as enemies versus friends; Kling, Lancaster, & Benitone, 1970), and a failure to attach emotional significance to sensory stimuli. The precise relationship between ToMM and the amygdala remains to be investigated, but certainly it seems plausible, on the basis of both its connectivity (to OFC and STS) and its importance in social and emotional perception, that it plays a role in supporting EDD, SAM, and ToMM.

The Relationship Between ToMM and Executive Function

We have already mentioned that OFC is implicated in ToMM, whereas DLC is implicated in executive function (planning and response inhibition). Additional evidence that ToMM and executive function are neurally very close to each other comes from other studies. First, children with autism show an impairment in both ToMM and executive function (Hughes & Russell, 1993; Ozonoff, Pennington, & Rogers, 1991; Prior & Hoffman, 1990; Rumsey & Hamburger, 1988). Secondly, measures of empathy and "cognitive flexibility" (an executive function index) tend to correlate in adults with acquired cerebral lesions (Grattan, Bloomer, Archambault, & Eslinger, 1990). For example, both EVR (Eslinger & Damasio, 1985) and JP (Ackerley & Benton, 1948) showed the association of loss of social sense and lack of cognitive flexibility. Grattan and Eslinger (1991) review a range of other similar cases. Such studies are consistent with the notion that the frontal lobes can be "fractionated" (Grattan & Eslinger, 1991, p. 299) and may possess modularity (Damasio, 1984; Pribam, 1987). However, since not

---

[9] In Kluver and Bucy's (1939) description of this syndrome, the symptoms occurred following bilateral removal of the temporal lobes in monkeys, and included (a) loss of the ability to discriminate animate and inanimate objects: (b) excessive oral exploration of objects; (c) a tendency to react to every visual stimulus; (d) a failure to vocalise towards other monkeys; (e) unusual movements; (f) changes in, or complete absence of, emotional reactions; and (g) hypersexuality.

all patients with executive function impairments have a ToMM impairment, it is possible that ToMM and the executive function are connected, but independent, systems. Anatomical connections from OFC to DLC have been demonstrated by Van Hoesen, Pandya, and Butters (1975). See also Ozonoff et al. (1991) for a discussion of the different possible relationships between ToMM and executive function.

The Neurobiology of Autism and the Mindreading System

We now wish to clarify the circuit-based model of the Mindreading System discussed earlier. To reiterate, Brothers (1990) proposed that a major neural circuit exists, linking OFC, STS, and the amygdala. We extend this idea as follows: first, the Mindreading System may be distributed across all three centres. Second, we propose that lesions in any one of these three centres, *or* in any one of the three connections between these three centres, could produce autism; and that the different subgroups of autism we discussed earlier would be determined by where in the circuit the lesion was.

Our theory of autism is most closely related to Frith's (1992), which itself is based on Brothers (1990); however, we elaborate this to incorporate the theory of four components of the Mindreading System. Our theory is also related to Damasio and Maurer's (1978), which also postulates damage to a frontal-temporal area, though in their case this is relatively wide (incorporating the supplementary motor area, cingulate gyrus, entorrhinal area, perirhinal area, parahippocampal gyrus, and subicular and presubicular regions). Our model is more specific than this, in focusing on the OFC and STS components. It is unclear as yet what the relationship is between our theory and those of Bachevalier (1991) and DeLong (1992), both of which propose an amygdalo-hippocampal dysfunction.

At present, although there are few consistent findings in the neurobiology of autism (Bailey, 1993; Bishop, 1992), there are some neuroimaging studies that are compatible with frontal lobe dysfunction in this group. For example, Piven et al. (1990) reported evidence of abnormal neuronal migration in the frontal lobes of three subjects with autism. Such abnormalities would be consistent with either executive function deficits (from a DLC lesion) or theory of mind impairments (from an OFC lesion), or both, as Ozonoff (in press) points out. Horwitz, Rumsey, Grady, and Rapoport's (1988) PET study found significantly lower correlations of metabolic activity between frontal and parietal regions in subjects with autism. Ozonoff speculates that this might reflect an abnormality in integrating the processing between these two lobes, hinting that frontal lesions might be leading to a relative over-reliance on parietal processing. L'Hermitte (1984) suggests that the frontal lobes may exert an inhibiting control over the parietal lobes[10]. If this is correct, then Horwitz et al.'s results might indicate a dysfunction in this frontal inhibitory control over the parietal lobes. Further studies of this kind are needed.

There are also some studies that are compatible with a temporal lobe dysfunction in autism. Thus, EEG abnormalities from the temporal lobes have been reported (DeLong, 1978; Hauser, DeLong, & Rosman, 1975), as has enlargement of the temporal horn of the lateral ventricles (Hauser et al., 1975). Hetzler and Griffin (1981) give a good review of the arguments for temporal lobe involvement in autism, in particular noting some of the overlap between autism and the Kluver-Bucy syndrome, which as mentioned earlier can be produced by bilateral removal of the temporal lobes (Kluver & Bucy, 1939; see footnote 9). Finally, there are some studies that are compatible with an amygdala lesion in autism (Bauman & Kemper, 1985; 1988).

If autism was produced by an OFC lesion, what would one expect to see? The symptoms associated with OFC lesions consist of the following:

1. Impaired social judgement (in humans: Eslinger & Damasio, 1985).
2. Utilisation behaviour (in humans: L'Hermitte, 1984).
3. Pragmatic/discourse breakdown (in humans, of course: Kaczmarek, 1984).
4. Diminished aggression (in humans: Mateer & Williams, 1991)
5. Increased indifference (in monkeys: Meyer, 1972).
6. Decreased appreciation for dangerous situations (in humans: Case JB[11]: Mateer & Williams, 1991).
7. Hyper-olfactory exploration (in monkeys: Thorpe, Rolls, & Maddison, 1983).
8. Diminished response to pain (in humans: Goldman-Rakic, 1987).
9. Excessive activity (in monkeys: Ferrier, 1886).

All of these nine features are commonly seen in autism. In addition, damage to frontal regions adjacent to OFC would risk producing deficits in Broca's area (language production) and in DLC (executive function). An OFC lesion thus provides one way of accounting for the association between these impairments and ToMM deficits in autism.

---

[10] L'Hermitte suggests that loss of this inhibitory control may account for "utilisation behaviour" (the tendency to pick up and use objects, even when this is inappropriate). L'Hermitte reports this behaviour in some of his patients with frontal damage, and interestingly this behaviour has also been reported in children with autism (Fox & Tallis, in press).

[11] Note that JB not only received OFC damage, but also temporal damage. It is therefore unclear if this symptom is unique to the OFC syndrome.

Similarly, if autism was produced by a dysfunction in the amygdala, what would one expect to see? The effects of amygdalectomy were reviewed earlier, but are elaborated here:

1. Abnormalities in social perception (Kling et al., 1970).
2. Failure to attach emotional significance to stimuli (Kluver & Bucy, 1939; Weiskrantz, 1956).
3. Diminution in aggression and fear (Kling & Brothers, 1992).
4. Decrease in affiliative behaviour (Kling & Brothers, 1992).

Again, all of these four features are commonly seen in autism.

Finally, if the lesion was in the STS, this would not only impair EDD (and thus SAM), which are postulated to require the STS, but depending on the extent of temporal lobe damage, could risk receptive language (Wernicke's) areas being impaired. Again, this provides a possible account for the association between autism and language disorder. The pragmatics of language, as was mentioned earlier, are likely to be independent of Wernicke's area, and to require OFC involvement (Kaczmarek, 1984).

CONCLUSIONS

In this chapter we have elaborated the theory of the Mindreading System (Baron-Cohen, in press a; in press b) by focusing on both the neuropsychological and the neurobiological level. In particular, we have elaborated Brothers' (1990) model of the "social brain" to suggest that EDD, SAM, and ToMM lie in a three-node circuit between the STS, the OFC, and the amygdala, and that if this circuit is broken at any point, autism can be produced. We have not speculated about any possible localisation of ID, as there are currently no clues as to where this might be found. However, we have equated the neurobiological connections between the STS and the OFC with the psychological relation between EDD, SAM, and ToMM. The evidence for these claims has been summarised, though it is noted that many empirical gaps remain to be filled. Nevertheless, we hope that our model suggests new directions for research: It contains a number of testable predictions about the precursor status of SAM in triggering ToMM, and the proposed sites of neural dysfunction in autism.

ACKNOWLEDGEMENTS

We are indebted to Leslie Brothers, who helped us think through the neurobiological ideas in this paper, and guided us through the literature. Peter Mitchell and Charlie Lewis also gave us excellent editorial advice. The authors were supported by the Medical Research Council, the Mental Health Foundation, the Nuffield Foundation, and the Raymond Way Trust during the preparation of this work.

In Figure 9.4: KitKat, Smarties, and Polo are all registered trademarks, © Société des Produits Nestlé S.A.; and MilkyWay is a registered trademark, © Mars.

REFERENCES

Ackerley, S., & Benton, A. (1948). Report of a case of bilateral frontal lobe defect. *Association for Research in Nervous and Mental Diseases, 27,* 479–504.

Aggleton, J. (1985). A description of intra-amygdaloid connections in old world monkeys. *Experimental Brain Research, 57,* 390–399.

Aggleton, J., Burton, M., & Passingham, R. (1980). Cortical and subcortical afferents to the amygdala of the rhesus monkey (Macaca Mulatta). *Brain Research, 190,* 347–368.

Alexander, M., Benson, D., & Stuss, D. (1989). Frontal lobes and language. *Brain and Language, 37,* 656–659.

Amaral, D., & Price, J. (1984). Amygdalo-cortical projections in the monkey (Macaca fascicularis). *Journal of Comparative Neurology, 230,* 465–496.

Bachevalier, J. (1991). An animal model for childhood autism. In C. Tamminga & S. Schulz (Eds.), *Advances in neuropsychiatry and psychopharmacology, Vol. 1: Schizophrenia Research.* New York: Raven Press.

Bailey, A. (1993). The biology of autism. Editorial. *Psychological Medicine, 23,* 7–11.

Bakeman, R., & Adamson, L. (1984). Coordinating attention to people and objects in mother–infant and peer–infant interaction. *Child Development, 55,* 1278–1289.

Barbas, H. (1988). Anatomic organization of basoventral and mediodorsal visual recipient prefrontal regions in the rhesus monkey. *Journal of Comparative Neurology, 276,* 313–342.

Baron-Cohen, S. (1988a). Social and pragmatic deficits in autism: Cognitive or affective? *Journal of Autism and Developmental Disorders, 18,* 379–402.

Baron-Cohen, S. (1988b). Without a theory of mind one cannot participate in a conversation. *Cognition, 29,* 83–84.

Baron-Cohen, S. (1989). Perceptual role-taking and protodeclarative pointing in autism. *British Journal of Developmental Psychology, 7,* 113–127.

Baron-Cohen, S. (1991a). Precursors to a theory of mind: Understanding attention in others. In A. Whiten (Ed.), *Natural theories of mind.* Oxford: Basil Blackwell.

Baron-Cohen, S. (1991b). Do people with autism understand what causes emotion? *Child Development, 62,* 385–395.

Baron-Cohen, S. (1992). On modularity and development in autism: A reply to Burack. *Journal of Child Psychology and Psychiatry, 33,* 623–629.

Baron-Cohen, S. (1993). From attention-goal psychology to belief-desire psychology: The development of a theory of mind, and its dysfunction. In S. Baron-Cohen, H. Tager-Flusberg, & D.J. Cohen (Eds.), *Understanding other minds: Perspectives from autism.* Oxford: Oxford University Press.

Baron-Cohen, S. (in press a). How to build a baby that can read minds: Cognitive mechanisms in mindreading. *Current Psychology of Cognition/Cahiers de Psychologie Cognitive.*

Baron-Cohen, S. (in press b). *EDD and SAM:* Two cases for evolutionary psychology. In C. Moore & P. Dunham. (Eds.), *The role of joint attention in development.* Hillsdale, NJ: Lawrence Erlbaum Associates Inc.

Baron-Cohen, S., Allen, J., & Gillberg, C. (1992). Can autism be detected at 18 months? The needle, the haystack, and the CHAT. *British Journal of Psychiatry, 161,* 839–843.

Baron-Cohen, S., Campbell, R., Karmiloff-Smith, A., Grant, J., & Walker, J. (1993). *Are children with autism blind to the mentalistic significance of the eyes?* Unpublished manuscript, Institute of Psychiatry, University of London.

Baron-Cohen, S., & Cross, P. (1992). Reading the eyes: Evidence for the role of perception in the development of a theory of mind. *Mind and Language, 6,* 166–180.

Baron-Cohen, S., Leslie, A.M., & Frith, U. (1985). Does the autistic child have a "theory of mind?" *Cognition, 21,* 37–46.

Baron-Cohen, S., Leslie, A.M., & Frith, U. (1986). Mechanical, behavioural and Intentional understanding of picture stories in autistic children. *British Journal of Developmental Psychology, 4,* 113–125.

Baron-Cohen, S., Ring, H., Moriarty, J., Shmitz, P., Costa, D., & Ell, P. (in press). *Recognition of mental state terms: A clinical study of autism, and a functional neuroimaging study of normal adults. British Journal of Psychiatry.*

Baron-Cohen, S., Tager-Flusberg, H., & Cohen, D.J. (Eds.). (1993). *Understanding other minds: Perspectives from autism.* Oxford: Oxford University Press.

Bates, E., Camaioni, L., & Volterra, L. (1975). The acquisition of performatives prior to speech. *Merrill-Palmer Quarterly, 21,* 205–226.

Bauman, M., & Kemper, T. (1985). Histoanatomic observation of the brain in early infantile autism. *Neurology, 35,* 866–874.

Bauman, M., & Kemper, T. (1988). Limbic and cerebellar abnormalities: Consistent findings in infantile autism. *Journal of Neuropathology and Experimental Neurology, 47,* 369.

Bayliss, G., Rolls, E., & Leonard, C. (1985). Selectivity between faces in the responses of a population of neurons in the cortex in the superior temporal sulcus of the monkey. *Brain Research, 342,* 91–102.

Bishop, D. (1992). Autism and frontal-limbic functions. *Journal of Child Psychology and Psychiatry, 34,* 279–294.

Brothers, L. (1990). The social brain: A project for integrating primate behaviour and neurophysiology in a new domain. *Concepts in Neuroscience, 1,* 27–51.

Brothers, L., & Ring, B. (1992). A neuroethological framework for the representation of minds. *Journal of Cognitive Neuroscience, 4,* 107–118.

Brothers, L., Ring, B., & Kling, A. (1990). Responses of neurons in the macaque amygdala to complex social stimuli. *Behavioural Brain Research, 41,* 199–213.

Bruce, C., Desimone, R., & Gross, C. (1981). Visual properties of neurones in a polysensory area in superior temporal sulcus of the macaque. *Journal of Neurophysiology, 46,* 369–384.

Butterworth, G. (1991). The ontogeny and phylogeny of joint visual attention. In A. Whiten (Ed.), *Natural theories of mind.* Oxford: Basil Blackwell.

Campbell, R., Heywood, C., Cowey, A., Regard, M., & Landis, T. (1990). Sensitivity to eye gaze in prosopagnosic patients and monkeys with superior temporal sulcus ablation. *Neuropsychologia, 28,* 1123–1142.

Charman, T., & Baron-Cohen, S. (1992). Understanding beliefs and drawings: A further test of the metarepresentation theory of autism. *Journal of Child Psychology and Psychiatry, 33,* 1105–1112.

Charman, T., & Baron-Cohen, S. (1993). *Understanding photos, models, and beliefs: A further test of the modularity thesis of theory of mind.* Unpublished manuscript, University College, London.

Damasio, A. (1984). The frontal lobes. In K. Heilman & E. Valenstein (Eds.), *Clinical neuropsychology* (Revised). New York: Oxford University Press.

Damasio, A., & Maurer, R. (1978). A neurologic model for childhood autism. *Archives of Neurology, 35,* 777–786.

Damasio, A., Tranel, D., & Damasio, H. (1990). Individuals with sociopathic behaviour caused by frontal lobe damage fail to respond autonomically to socially charged stimuli. *Behavioural Brain Research, 14,* 81–94.

DeLong, G. (1978). A neuropsychologic interpretation of infantile autism. In M. Rutter & E. Schopler (Eds.), *Autism: A reappraisal of concepts and treatment.* New York: Plenum Press.

DeLong, G. (1992). Autism, amnesia, hippocampus, and learning. *Neurobehavioural Review, 16,* 63–70.

Desimone, R., Albright, T., Gross, C., & Bruce, C. (1984). Stimulus selective properties of inferior temporal neurons in the macaque. *Journal of Neuroscience, 8*, 2051–2062.

Diamond, A., & Goldman-Rakic, P. (1989). Comparison of human infants and rhesus monkeys on Piaget's AB̄ task: Evidence for dependence on dorsolateral prefrontal cortex. *Experimental Brain Research, 74*, 24–40.

Eslinger, P., & Damasio, A. (1985). Severe disturbance of higher cognition after bilateral frontal lobe ablation: Patient EVR. *Neurology, 35*, 1731–1741.

Ferrier, D. (1886). *Functions of the brain* (2nd edn.). London: Smith & Elder.

Flavell, J., Botkin, P., Fry, C., Wright, T., & Jarvis, P. (1968). *The development of role-taking and communication in children.* New York: Wiley.

Fodor, J. (1983). *The modularity of mind: An essay on faculty psychology.* Cambridge, Mass.: MIT Press.

Fox, N., & Tallis, F. (in press). Utilization behaviour in adults with autism: A preliminary investigation of frontal lobe functioning. *Journal of Clinical and Experimental Neuropsychology.*

Frith, C. (1992). *The cognitive neuropsychology of schizophrenia.* Hove: Lawrence Erlbaum Associates Ltd.

Fuster, J. (1989). *The prefrontal cortex: Anatomy, physiology, and neuropsychology of the frontal lobe.* New York: Raven Press.

Goldman, P. (1971). Functional development of the prefrontal cortex in early life and the problem of neuronal plasticity. *Experimental Neurology, 32*, 366–387.

Goldman, P., & Alexander, G. (1977). Maturation of prefrontal cortex in the monkey revealed by local reversible cryogenic depression. *Nature, 267*, 613–615.

Goldman-Rakic, P. (1987). Circuitry of primate prefrontal cortex and regulation of behaviour by representational memory. In V. Mountcastle, F. Plum, & S. Geiger (Eds.), *Handbook of physiology: Section 1: Nervous system: Part 1.* Bethesda, Maryland: American Physiological Society.

Gomez, J.C. (1991). Primates' reading of other minds. In A. Whiten (Ed.), *Natural theories of mind.* Oxford: Basil Blackwell.

Grattan, L., Bloomer, R., Archambault, F., & Eslinger, P. (1990). Cognitive and neural underpinnings of empathy. *The Clinical Neuropsychologist, 4*, 279.

Grattan, L., & Eslinger, P. (1991). Frontal lobe damage in children and adults: A comparative review. *Developmental Neuropsychology, 7*, 283–326.

Gross, C., Rocha-Miranda, C., & Bender, D. (1972). Visual properties of neurons in the inferotemporal cortex of the macaque. *Journal of Neurophysiology, 35*, 96–111.

Happé, F. (1993). Communicative competence and theory of mind: a test of relevance theory. *Cognition, 48*, 101–119.

Hauser, S., DeLong, G., & Rosman, N. (1975). Pneumographic findings in the infantile autism syndrome. *Brain, 98*, 667–688.

Hetzler, B., & Griffin, J. (1981). Infantile autism and the temporal lobe of the brain. *Journal of Autism and Developmental Disorders, 9*, 153–157.

Heywood, C., & Cowey, A. (1991). The role of the "face cell" area in the discrimination and recognition of faces in monkeys. *Philosophical Transactions of the Royal Society of London: Series B, 335*, 31–38.

Hobson, R.P. (1990). On acquiring knowledge about people and the capacity to pretend: Response to Leslie (1987). *Psychological Review, 97*, 114–121.

Horwitz, B., Rumsey, J., Grady, C., & Rapoport, S. (1988). The cerebral metabolic landscape in autism: Intercorrelations of regional glucose utilization. *Archives of Neurology, 45*, 749–755.

Hughes, C., & Russell, J. (1993). Autistic children's difficulty with mental disengagement from an object: Its implications for theories of autism. *Developmental Psychology, 29*, 498–510.

Jackendoff, R. (1987). *Consciousness and the computational mind.* Cambridge, Mass.: MIT Press/Bradford Books.

Kaczmarek, B. (1984). Neurolinguistic analysis of verbal utterances in patients with focal lesions of frontal lobes. *Brain and Language, 21*, 52–58.

Kendrick, K., & Baldwin, B. (1987). Cells in the temporal cortex of conscious sheep can respond preferably to the sight of faces. *Science, 236*, 448–450.

Kling, A., & Brothers, L. (1992). The amygdala and social behavior. In J. Aggleton (Ed.), *Neurobiological aspects of emotion, memory, and mental dysfunction*. New York: Wiley-Liss Inc.

Kling, A., Lancaster, J., & Benitone, J. (1970). Amygdalectomy in the free ranging vervet. *Journal of Psychiatric Research, 7*, 191–199.

Kluver, H., & Bucy, P. (1939). Preliminary analysis of function of the temporal lobe in monkeys. *Archives of Neurology, 42*, 979–1000.

Langdell, T. (1978). Recognition of faces: An approach to the study of autism. *Journal of Child Psychology and Psychiatry, 19*, 225–238.

Leekam, S., Baron-Cohen, S., Perrett, D., Milders, M., & Brown, S. (1993). Eye-direction detection: A disassociation of geometric and joint attention skills in autism. Unpublished manuscript, Institute of Applied and Social Psychology, University of Kent, Canterbury.

Leekam, S., & Perner, J. (1991). Does the autistic child have a metarepresentational deficit? *Cognition, 40*, 203–218.

Lempers, J., Flavell, E., & Flavell, J. (1977). The development in very young children of tacit knowledge concerning visual perception. *Genetic Psychology Monographs, 95*, 3–53.

Leonard, C., Rolls, E., Wilson, F., & Bayliss, G. (1985). Neurons in the amygdala of the monkey with responses selective for faces. *Behaviour and Brain Research, 15*, 159–176.

Leslie, A.M. (1987). Pretence and representation: The origins of "theory of mind." *Psychological Review, 94*, 412–426.

Leslie, A. (1991). The theory of mind impairment in autism: Evidence for a modular mechanism of development? In A. Whiten (Ed.), *Natural theories of mind*. Oxford: Basil Blackwell.

Leslie, A., German, T., & Happé, F. (1993). Even a theory-theory needs information processing: ToMM, an alternative theory-theory of the child's theory of mind. *Behavioral and Brain Sciences, 16*, 56–57.

Leslie, A., & Roth, D. (1993). What autism teaches us about metarepresentation. In S. Baron-Cohen, H. Tager-Flusberg, & D.J. Cohen (Eds.), *Understanding other minds: Perspectives from autism*. Oxford: Oxford University Press.

Leslie, A., & Thaiss, L. (1992). Domain specificity in conceptual development: Neuropsychological evidence from autism. *Cognition, 43*, 225–251.

L'Hermitte, F. (1984). "Utilisation behaviour" and its relation to lesions of the frontal lobes. *Brain, 106*, 237–255.

Mateer, C., & Williams, D. (1991). Effects of frontal lobe injury in childhood. *Developmental Neuropsychology, 7*, 359–376.

Maurer, D., & Barrera, M. (1981). Infants' perception of natural and distorted arrangements of a schematic face. *Child Development, 52*, 196–202.

Maurer, R., & Damasio, A. (1982). Childhood autism from the point of view of behavioural neurology. *Journal of Autism and Developmental Disorders, 12*, 195–205.

Meyer, D. (1972). Some features of the dorsolateral frontal and inferotemporal syndromes in monkeys. *Acta Neurobiologica Experimenta, 32*, 235–260.

Milner, B. (1964). Some effects of frontal lobectomy in man. In J. Warren & K. Akert (Eds.), *The frontal granula cortex and behaviour*. New York: McGraw-Hill.

Nakamura, K., Mikami, A., & Kubota, K. (1992). Activity of single neurons in the monkey amygdala during performance of a visual discrimination task. *Journal of Neurophysiology, 67*, 1447–1463.

Nauta, W. (1962). Neural associations of the amygdaloid complex in the monkey. *Brain, 85*, 505–520.

Nauta, W. (1964). Some efferent connections of the prefrontal cortex in the monkey. In J. Warren & K. Akert (Eds.), *The frontal granula cortex and behavior*. New York: McGraw-Hill.

Ozonoff, S. (in press). Executive functions in autism. In E. Schopler & G. Mesibov (Eds.), *Learning and cognition in autism*. New York: Plenum Press.

Ozonoff, S., Pennington, B., & Rogers, S. (1991). Executive function deficits in high-functioning autistic individuals: Relationship to theory of mind. *Journal of Child Psychology and Psychiatry, 32*, 1081–1105.

Perner, J. (1993). The theory of mind deficit in autism: Rethinking the metarepresentation theory. In S. Baron-Cohen, H. Tager-Flusberg, & D.J. Cohen (Eds.), *Understanding other minds: Perspectives from autism*. Oxford: Oxford University Press.

Perner, J., Frith, U., Leslie, A.M., & Leekam, S. (1989). Exploration of the autistic child's theory of mind: Knowledge, belief, and communication. *Child Development, 60*, 689–700.

Perrett, D., Harries, M., Mistlin, A., Hietanen, J., Benson, P., Bevan, R., Thomas, S., Oram, M., Ortega, J., & Brierley, K. (1990). Social signals analysed at the single cell level: Someone is looking at me, something touched me, something moved! *International Journal of Comparative Psychology, 4*, 25–55.

Perrett, D., & Mistlin, A. (1990). Perception of facial characteristics by monkeys. In W. Stebbins & M. Berkley (Eds.), *Comparative perception, Vol II: Complex signals*. New York: John Wiley & Son.

Perrett, D., Oram, M., Harries, M., Bevan, R., Hietanen, J., Benson, P., & Thomas, S. (1991). Viewer-centred and object-centred codings of heads in the macaque temporal cortex. *Experimental Brain Research, 86*, 159–173.

Perrett, D., Rolls, E., & Caan, W. (1982). Visual neurones responsive to faces in the monkey temporal cortex. *Experimental Brain Research, 47*, 329–342.

Perrett, D., Smith, P., Potter, D., Mistlin, A., Head, A., Milner, A., & Jeeves, M. (1984). Neurones responsive to faces in the temporal cortex: Studies of functional organization, sensitivity to identity, and relation to perception. *Human Neurobiology, 3*, 197–208.

Perrett, D., Smith, P., Potter, D., Mistlin, A., Head, A., Milner, A., & Jeeves, M. (1985). Visual cells in the temporal cortex sensitive to face view and gaze direction. *Proceedings of the Royal Society of London, B223*, 293–317.

Phillips, W., Baron-Cohen, S., & Rutter, M. (1992). The role of eye-contact in goal detection: Evidence from normal infants, and children with mental handicap or autism. *Development and Psychopathology, 4*, 375–383.

Piven, J., Berthier, M., Starkstein, S., Nehme, E., Pearlson, G., & Folstein, S. (1990). Magnetic resonance imaging evidence for a defect of cerebral cortical development in autism. *American Journal of Psychiatry, 147*, 737–739.

Porrino, L., Crane, A., & Goldman-Rakic, P. (1982). Direct and indirect pathways from the amygdala to the frontal lobe in rhesus monkeys. *Journal of Comparative Neurology, 198*, 121–136.

Pratt, C., & Bryant, P. (1990). Young children understand that looking leads to knowing (so long as they are looking into a single barrel). *Child Development, 61*, 973–983.

Premack, D. (1990). Do infants have a theory of self-propelled objects? *Cognition, 36*, 1–16.

Premack, D., & Woodruff, G. (1978). Does the chimpanzee have a "theory of mind?" *Behaviour and Brain Sciences, 4*, 515–526.

Pribam, K. (1987). The subdivisions of the frontal cortex revisited. In E. Perceman (Ed.), *The frontal lobes revisited*. New York: IRBN Press.

Price, B., Daffner, K., Stowe, R., & Mesulam, M. (1990). The compartmental learning disabilities of early frontal lobe damage. *Brain, 113*, 1383–1393.

Prior, M., & Hoffman, W. (1990). Brief report: Neuropsychological testing of autistic children through an exploration with frontal lobe tests. *Journal of Autism and Developmental Disorders, 20*, 581–590.

Rumsey, J., & Hamburger, S. (1988). Neuropsychological findings in high functioning men with infantile autism, residual state. *Journal of Clinical and Experimental Neuropsychology*, *10*, 201–221.

Scaife, M., & Bruner, J. (1975). The capacity for joint visual attention in the human infant. *Nature*, *253*, 265.

Schreiner, L., & Kling, A. (1953). Behavioural changes following rhinencephalitic injury in the cat. *Journal of Neurophysiology*, *16*, 643–659.

Shallice, T. (1988). *From neuropsychology to mental structure*. Cambridge: Cambridge University Press.

Sigman, M., Mundy, P., Ungerer, J., & Sherman, T. (1986). Social interactions of autistic, mentally retarded, and normal children and their caregivers. *Journal of Child Psychology and Psychiatry*, *27*, 647–656.

Sorce, J., Emde, R., Campos, J., & Klinnert, M. (1985). Maternal emotional signalling: Its effect on the visual cliff behaviour of one-year-olds. *Developmental Psychology*, *21*, 195–200.

Tager-Flusberg, H. (1993). What language reveals about the understanding of minds in children with autism. In S. Baron-Cohen, H. Tager-Flusberg, & D.J. Cohen (Eds.), *Understanding other minds: Perspectives from autism*. Oxford: Oxford University Press.

Tan, J., & Harris, P. (1991). Autistic children understand seeing and wanting. *Development and Psychopathology*, *3*, 163–174.

Tantam, D. (1992). Characterizing the fundamental social handicap in autism. *Acta Paedopsychiatrica*, *55*, 83–91.

Thorpe, S., Rolls, E., & Maddison, S. (1983). The orbito-frontal cortex: Neuronal activity in the behaving monkey. *Experimental Brain Research*, *49*, 93–115.

Van Hoesen, G. (1981). The differential distribution, diversity, and sprouting of cortical projections to the amygdala in the rhesus monkey. In Y. Ben-Ari (Ed.), *The amygdaloid complex*. Amsterdam: Elsevier.

Van Hoesen, G., Pandya, D., & Butters, N. (1975). Some connections of the entorhinal (area 28) and perirhinal (area 37) cortices of the rhesus monkey, II. Frontal lobe afferants. *Brain Research*, *95*, 25–38.

Volkmar, F., & Cohen, D. (1989). Disintegrative disorder or "late onset" autism? *Journal of Child Psychology and Psychiatry*, *30*, 717–724.

Volkmar, F.R., Sparrow, S., Rende, R.D., & Cohen, D.J. (1989). Facial perception in autism. *Journal of Child Psychology and Psychiatry*, *30*, 591–598.

Wellman, H. (1990). *Children's theories of mind*. Cambridge, Mass: Bradford Books/MIT Press.

Weiskrantz, L. (1956). Behavioural changes associated with ablation of the amygdaloid complex in monkeys. *Journal of Comparative Physiology and Psychology*, *4*, 381–391.

Wimmer, H., & Perner, J. (1983). Beliefs about beliefs: Representation and constraining function of wrong beliefs in young children's understanding of deception. *Cognition*, *13*, 103–128.

Wolff, P. (1963). Observations on the early development of smiling. In B. Foss (Ed.), *Determinants of infant behaviour, Vol. 2*. New York: Wiley.

Yamane, S., Kaji, S., & Kawano, K. (1988). What facial features activate face neurons in the inferotemporal cortex of the monkey: *Experimental Brain Research*, *73*, 209–214.

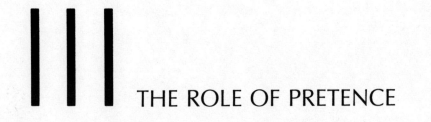

THE ROLE OF PRETENCE

10 Making Sense of Pretence

Angeline Lillard
University of San Francisco, USA

INTRODUCTION

Several of the major accounts of how children develop an understanding of the mind assign some sort of special role to pretence. For example, in Harris's simulation account (1991; this volume), the child learns about other people's mental states by using a capacity that is also exercised in pretend play: The capacity to simulate nonexistent situations. In Leslie's (1987; 1988) computational model, the same cognitive architecture that is used in pretend play is also used in understanding others' mental states. Perner, Baker, and Hutton (this volume) maintain that pretence and belief understanding arise from a single concept, which they term "prelief." Others (Flavell, 1988; Fodor, 1992; Forguson & Gopnik, 1988) have written that children have an early understanding of mental representation in the domain of pretence. (Flavell has since retracted this claim.)

Some recent research supports the idea that pretence and understanding the mind might be linked. These reports indicate that children who engage in more joint pretend play (Jenkins & Astington, 1993) or role enactment (Dunn, 1993), or who have a higher fantasy predisposition (Taylor, Gerow, & Carlson, 1993) perform at a higher level than do other children on theory of mind tasks.

In my recent work I have set out to explore just what the relationship between understanding the mind and pretence might be (Lillard, 1991; 1993a; 1993b). In this chapter I elaborate on what is involved in the mental

211

state of pretence, and hence what a child must know about pretence in order to be said to truly understand it. I then discuss research pertinent to this understanding, focusing in particular on others' reports concerning children's ability to maintain a real–pretend boundary, and on two of my recent studies of children's understanding of the mental representations underlying pretence. I conclude by describing current and planned research investigating other aspects of children's understanding of pretence.

DEFINING PRETENCE

What exactly is involved in pretence? Pretence involves stretching one "reality" over another, or (Austin, 1979, p. 260) holding "one thing in front of another in order to protect or conceal or disguise it." There are six features that could be considered necessary for pretence. These features are described next, followed by an example illustrating each.

First, in an act of pretence there is always a pretender—an animate, mindful being who does the pretending. Lamps, trees, and clumps of soil do not pretend. Second, there must be some real situation with which the pretence contrasts. A minor technicality here is that the pretence might not *actually* differ from reality, but the pretender generally must *think* it does. One would not pretend George was at the door if one knew he really was at the door. However, lacking the knowledge that he was truly there, one might pretend he was. (A bizarre coincidence would then be brought to light when one opened the door!) A further technicality regarding this second feature is that at some points the pretence and the reality might coincide, and (unlike the case mentioned as a first technicality) the pretender might be fully aware of their coinciding. Leslie (1987) pointed out that a child can pretend a cup is full of water, and then pour the pretend water out, at which point we would say the child is pretending the empty cup is empty. Note, however, that in this example the cup is empty *in contrast to* its prior state of being full. The pretend-empty-cup exists on a different plane to the real one, and it has an independent history and network of associations (to tea, for example). In sum, although at times a given element of the pretence world might happen to coincide with the real world, the elements do exist on two different planes—a pretence plane and a real plane—and in this sense they are distinctly different elements. These technicalities aside, in general, pretence does not match reality.

The third defining feature of pretence is mental representation. The pretender holds a mental representation of the pretence scenario in his or her mind. For example, the pretender mentally represents tea in the empty cup, then tea spilling from the cup, and then the consequences of its having spilled. The fourth feature of pretence is that the pretence representation is projected onto the reality, such that they exist within the same space and time. One pretends that one thing is another, or that one situation is another situation. Sometimes, of course, the reality is that there is nothing there. These are cases of imaginary entities pretence.

This projection of the pretence representation onto reality implies the fifth and sixth features, which also concern the pretender's mental state. The fifth feature is awareness. The pretender is aware of the reality, the representation, and the fact that the representation is projected onto the reality. Without such awareness, one would merely be mistaken, rather than pretending. Note that one might not necessarily be aware of the representation *as* a representation (Perner, 1991). A girl who is pretending a block is a cookie probably sees herself as simply play eating a pretend cookie, and does not focus on the mental representation as such. However, she is aware that she is dealing with a pretend cookie, and hence is aware of the pretence representation ("cookie") even if she is not aware of it *as* a representation. The sixth feature of pretence is intention. Pretence involves intention because the projection of the pretence representation onto reality is done on purpose. The pretender tries to enact the pretence scenario, or tries to see and treat the real object as the pretend one. In contrast, when a patient in psychoanalysis unintentionally projects his mental representation of his mother onto the analyst, we do not say he is pretending the analyst is his mother. Pretence involves conscious, intended projections of mentally represented scenarios onto real ones.

As an example, take a boy pretending that a stick is a horse. The boy is of course the pretender, and the reality is the stick. The boy represents a horse, rather than a stick (although he still represents a stick at some level). He represents the horse right where the stick is, in fact projecting the horse representation on to the stick. The top of the stick is represented as the horse's head, the bottom as the legs, and so on. In addition, the pretender is aware of several aspects of the process: He knows the item is a stick (or at the very least he knows that it is not a horse), he knows what a horse is, and he knows that he is conceptualising the stick as a horse. If he were not aware of all this we would simply say he was mistaken about sticks or horses or both. Finally, the boy is projecting the horse representation onto the stick intentionally.

These six features are necessary to pretence. However, there are two other features that frequently accompany pretence, particularly when pretence is performed for young children. These could be said to be characteristic of pretence, in Keil's (1989) sense. The first of these is a nonserious emotional tone. Although pretence can be serious business and sometimes seems truly to frighten children, it is often a silly, fun activity. How exactly this "emotional tone" is conveyed is uncertain, but facial expression and vocal intonation (see Dias & Harris, 1990) seem to be likely candidates. The second characteristic feature is activity. (Throughout this discussion, activity is used to denote corporal and not mental activity.) Informal interviews suggest that adults vary in their estimation of whether pretending *requires* activity (but see Fein, 1981). Whereas some adults feel that pretending always involves bodily movement, others think that even immobile daydreaming is a kind of pretence. In the present analysis, the action component of pretence is one of potentiality: One does not have to move, but were one to move, one would do so in accord with the pretence. However, there are two cases in which bodily activity is central to pretence. First, pretending to perform an action requires some sort of movement to mime the action that one is pretending to perform. It is for this reason, as Austin (1979) points out, that one cannot pretend to bend one's trunk: The only way to mime such an action would be to do it. The second case is that of pretending for an audience (as in deception or play-acting). Such pretence requires an external manifestation of what is being pretended. The content of the pretence must be communicated, be it via actions, static appearances, or a Greek chorus. But aside from these two special cases, one can pretend without any action or other externally readable manifestation of what is being pretended.

To summarise, pretence entails six defining features: (1) a pretender, (2) a reality, and (3) a mental representation that is (4) projected onto reality, with (5) awareness and (6) intention on the part of that pretender. Pretence is also linked with two commonly co-occurring features; a nonserious emotional tone and action. This analysis of pretence points out several "developables" in children's understanding of the mental state of pretence. In the following discussion I address three of these. First, I review the literature on children's understanding of the fact that the real situation is not the represented one, and children's ability to negotiate what is often referred to as the "real–pretend boundary." Next, I present two experiments addressing children's understanding of the fact that mental representation undergirds pretence. The second of these experiments also touches on the fourth feature: That the pretence representation is project onto reality. Finally I discuss other possible developments in understanding the mental state of pretence.

THE REAL–PRETEND BOUNDARY

Bateson (1955/1972, p. 180), in writing about play in animals, discussed the paradox inherent in pretend play: "Expanded, the statement 'This is play' looks something like this: 'These actions in which we now engage do not denote what those actions *for which they stand* would denote' (emphasis his)". The word "not" is at the crux: The behaviour is not serious, the playful nip is not a bite, and the real object is not the pretend object. To be truly engaged in pretence, the pretender must be aware of this paradox. For example, if one is trying to eat a block because one *believes* it's a cookie, then one is not pretending; rather, one is mistaken. On the other hand, if one enacts the same eating behaviour knowing full well that what one is acting on is in fact a block, then one is pretending. To be truly pretending, one must grasp the situation on two levels: both as the real situation (the block) and as the pretend situation (the cookie).

Furthermore, the real and pretend situations are kept distinct in pretence. There are two clearly separate worlds, one layered over and projected onto the other. The pretend world is not expected to seep into the real world (e.g. one does not expect the block to become a real cookie in real life). Nor is the real world expected to adopt features of the pretend one (e.g. when one buys a bag of blocks, one does not expect it to contain cookies). Keeping these two worlds separate is referred to as maintaining the real–pretend boundary, and such maintenance is essential to pretence. If the pretend world and the real world are not clearly differentiated, the paradox is not understood, and the pretender is not actually pretending. Likewise, if the two worlds were not kept separate by an outside observer then that observer would not have a clear understanding of the fact that the pretender was engaged in pretence. Many developmental psychologists believe that young children do not maintain a solid real–pretend boundary. Bretherton, for example (1989, p. 390), has asserted that the toddler's boundary "tends to be diffuse." If this is true, then children do not really understand pretending. Pretending entails knowingly projecting a pretence representation that is thought to be different from reality onto that reality.

There are three ways in which the real–pretend barrier could be lacking. One is that the barrier does not exist, and children assume that the pretend world and the real world are one. This does not seem likely, for two reasons. One reason that it does not seem likely is that if children had no awareness of the separateness of real and pretend worlds, then they should not issue the metacommunicative signs of pretence (such as "knowing" smiles and exaggerated gestures) (Bateson, 1955/1972; Bretherton, 1984a; 1984b; Garvey, 1990) more frequently in pretend situations than in other situations. Although the exact frequency with which children emit these signs in various situations has not been studied, they do seem to know to produce them in pretence situations as early as 18 months (Piaget, 1962; see also Verba, 1993), and they do not seem to emit them erroneously at inappropriate moments.

A second reason to expect that children have at least a basic understanding of the real–pretend boundary is that if they did not, then their understanding of the real world would be abused by pretence (Leslie, 1987). For example, a child who watched an adult pretend a banana was a telephone would become confused about the true properties or functions of bananas. Although such reality confusion does appear to occur with fantasies that parents want children to believe are real, like Santa Claus, it does not appear to happen in other cases, when parents are not trying to dupe their children. The fact that children do not seem to have great confusion about reality after every instance in which it has been supplanted by pretence suggests that young children have some understanding of a real–pretend boundary.

There is some experimental support for a basic awareness of the separateness of the real and pretend worlds. For example, Wellman and Estes (1986) showed that children differentiate real and pretend entities in that children understand that only real entities can be acted on physically. Wellman and Estes presented children with two pictures, one of a boy whom they described as having a cookie, and one of a boy whom they described as pretending he had a cookie. Children were asked questions like which boy could touch the cookie and which boy could eat the cookie. Even three-year-olds differentiated between the two boys, apparently understanding that real but not imagined objects can be manipulated physically (see also Estes, Wellman, & Woolley, 1989). Furthermore, Harris and his colleagues (1991) have shown that three-year-olds can distinguish reality from fantasy even when asked to imagine a monster that is chasing them, in that they know that the monster is not real, and that others cannot see the monster. Finally, Morison and Gardner (1978) found kindergarteners were correct 70% of the time on tasks requiring them to sort pictures of real versus fantasy characters (such as dogs versus mermaids). These studies all indicate that young children have the ability to distinguish real entitles from pretend ones, and thereby imply that by three or four years of age children do not completely lack a real–pretend boundary.

The second way that the real–pretend boundary might be diffuse is that the boundary might be generally present but penetrable, like a semi-permeable membrane (Kuersten, 1991, expresses a similar idea). Certain real-world features could seep across the membrane into the pretend world and/or vice-versa. Regarding the first option, real life certainly does surface in the pretend world. Children's real-world knowledge (scripts, language, and so on) is often the basis for their play (see Bretherton, 1984a; Nelson & Seidman, 1984). However, use of real-world knowledge does not necessarily indicate a lack of boundary; it could merely reflect that knowledge from one domain is applied in another domain. As an example of this transfer, Bretherton and her colleagues have found that securely attached children differ from insecurely attached children in how they represent family relations in doll play (Bretherton, Prentiss, & Ridgeway, 1990; Bretherton, Ridgeway, & Cassidy, 1990). Similarly, Schwartzman (1978) found that more popular children tend to take higher status positions in pretend play than do less popular children, indicating that the social hierarchy children establish outside of the play frame is reflected within it as well. Although this is very interesting in itself, and provides experimental validation for clinical psychologists' use of play to reveal children's representations of the world (Erikson, 1950; Freud, 1959; Peller, 1952), it only demonstrates that children represent relations in play as they represent them in real life, which is how they know them to be. It is natural that play reflects children's psychological structures, since those very structures create the play. The fact that pretend play reflects real-world knowledge speaks only of the fact that it is a subset of children's behaviour, not that children do not differentiate what is real from what is pretend. Therefore real life seeping into pretend play is not necessarily a concern for the real–pretend boundary.

The reverse of this sort of real–pretend boundary breakdown is that pretend-world features could seep across the semi-permeable membrane into the real world. If this were the case, then children, although operating in the real world, might expect pretend-world features to surface. For example, they might expect that if, in the pretend world, a block was a cookie, then in real life that which is called a "cookie" should actually be a block. Although it has not been directly studied, the available reports suggests no such confusion.

Hence it does not appear that children routinely suffer from the first two forms of real–pretend boundary breakdown—a general inability to discriminate the real and the pretend, and having pretend-world elements seep into the real world. A third type of real–pretend boundary breakdown is confusion about the reality status of particular real- or pretend-world elements. One might, for example, be confused as to whether the real was actually pretend, or as to whether the pretend was actually real.

Wondering whether what is real is actually pretend occurs when one suspects (but is not actually faced with) deception. One might wonder whether a child was just pretending to be hurt; if the child truly was hurt, then one would have been wondering if what was truly real pain was actually feigned. A recent study by Samuels and Taylor (1992) provides evidence relevant to whether children sometimes think that what is real is actually pretend. They showed some children scary pictures and showed others emotionally neutral pictures; for each group, half of the pictures depicted impossible (fantasy) events and half depicted possible events. Children were asked whether the event in the picture could really happen. The group that saw pictures of frightening events performed worse than the group that saw neutral events, because they claimed that real and scary events (the example given is a policeman talking to a child) could not really happen. In other words, they claimed that what was real was actually pretence. As the authors suggest, such claims might be due to a self-protection mechanism, whereby denial helps the child to mitigate negative feelings because it involves disavowing the reality of their source (see also Golomb & Kuersten, 1992). In this sense, then, children might suffer from a real–pretend boundary breakdown, in that they misjudge the real as pretend when the real event is frightening. Note that it is possible in such cases that the boundary is still firmly in place, and that children are simply moving certain events, which they find difficult to cope with in the real world, over to the pretence side of the boundary. The extent to which this really constitutes a loss of the real–pretend boundary is therefore questionable. (For further discussion of denial and self-deception, see Mitchell, 1993.)

Samuels and Taylor's (1992) study indicates that in *non*emotional situations children do not have trouble differentiating between real and pretend. This finding is corroborated by Johnson and Harris (in press). They asked children to judge whether certain events (like having a toy move across the floor by itself or by being transferred by a person's hand) were performed by a magic fairy or a real boy (Experiment 2). Three-year-olds were quite good at making these judgements, claiming that the fairy was behind the magical events but that the real boy was responsible for the real events. In other words, children appeared to see the real event as something that would be done by a real person, and hence they did not mistake the real for pretend. In sum, it appears that children do not have a general problem with mistaking the real for pretend, although they do sometimes deny the reality status of frightening events.

The other way this type of breakdown in the real–pretend boundary could be manifested is that, while in the pretend world, children could become confused and think that what they are pretending is in fact really happening. This species of breakdown has been the focus of several reports in the literature. These reports can be divided into emotional and nonemotional events; for each, there are both anecdotal and experimental reports of children thinking that what is being pretended is in fact really happening.

Two anecdotal reports from a situation that does not appear to be emotionally charged are sometimes cited as evidence for an insufficient real–pretend boundary. Both are reported by DeLoache and Plaetzer (1985), and come from their observations of children playing tea with their mothers. They noted that a 15-month-old peered into a cup of pretend tea as if to look for real tea, and that a 30-month-old apparently looked for pretend spilled tea to wipe up. In these cases, however, the children gave no definitive evidence (like verbal report of their intentions) of losing the real–pretend boundary. The first child might have been looking to see if anything *was* in the cup, or might have been looking there as part of the pretence, and the second child might have been pretending he did not know where the pretend spilled tea was. These two nonemotional observations are not clearly interpretable.

Better evidence on this issue comes from experimental work involving nonemotional situations. Johnson and Harris (in press, Experiment 3) asked

3-, 5-, and 7-year-olds to imagine that either an ice cream cone or a fairy was in one box, and not to imagine anything about a second box. After the child was led through an imagination procedure, the experimenter asked, "Is there really some ice cream in the box, or are you just pretending that there's some ice cream?" The experimenter then observed whether the children, when left alone in the room with the boxes, peeked inside the boxes, and if so, how long it took them to do so for each box. After two minutes the experimenter returned, and asked children whether they had peeked, and whether they had thought the imagined object might really have been inside the box.

There were two main findings relevant to the question of whether children lose the real–pretend boundary in such circumstances and think the pretence (or imagined) event is real. First, in response to the initial question, very few of the children (16–19%) incorrectly stated that the imagined object was truly inside. This might suggest some confusion among a minority of children. Woolley and Wellman (1993), using a similar method, found about this percentage of such errors (they term them "true fiction errors") in older 3-year-olds but more of such errors (57%) among younger 3-year-olds. Perhaps this higher failure rate was due to their test question not including the alternative "just pretending," or perhaps it was due to asking the reality question after a series of imagination questions. In later work Woolley (1993, Study 2) asked the reality question first and children did not make this error.

The second finding of interest in Johnson and Harris's (in press) study was that children peeked into the imagined-about box sooner and more frequently than they peeked into the other box. This effect was especially marked in 3-year-olds. Johnson and Harris suggest that the imagined event could be more cognitively available for some children, and that availability, coupled with a tendency to embrace magical thinking, might lead children to consider that the imagined entity might somehow have got into the box. Another possibility is that children who are generally more curious are especially curious about things that they imagine about, and their curiosity leads them to explore those things. Having explored the boxes, children then answered that they thought the pretend object might be in the box in order to provide an explanation for why they had opened the box. In either case, children do not seem to have lost the real–pretend boundary in these nonemotional situations.

There are several emotional anecdotal reports. Scarlett and Wolf (1979) describe how, when an adult animated a small toy alligator in a threatening manner, a child retreated to her mother's lap, apparently afraid. Garvey and Berndt (1975) mention a child who refused to pretend that a monster is coming, reasoning, "Because it's too scary, that's why." Fein (1985) tells of a child chasing her father with a pretend knife. When a co-player commented, "She picked up a knife. Was trying to kill her dad," the child stopped short and said, "No, I did not. I just maked a play one," as if concerned that others might take the pretend world for real. (This example could also be taken as counter-evidence for the claim, since it explicitly shows awareness of the boundary.)

In addition to these anecdotal reports, there are also experimental emotional examples of an apparent breakdown in the real–pretend boundary. Harris and his colleagues (Harris et al., 1991) found that although 4- to 6-year-olds said that pretend entities, like monsters, were not real, they acted as though they were. For example, they were more apt to approach a box that they had pretended contained a puppy than a box that they had pretended contained a monster. These reports suggest that in emotional situations young children are perhaps not entirely confident that what is being pretended is quarantined from the real world when the pretence is frightening.

There are several possible explanations for the apparent confusion children have about the real–pretend boundary in emotional situations. Taylor (personal communication, September, 1990; see also Harris et al., 1991) has proposed that children may use their emotions as a cue to reality. When they feel fear, they may assume there really is something around of which to be fearful. Although not exactly analogous, this is reminiscent of Schachter and Singer's (1962) claim that emotional arousal leads to cognitive assessment. In their case, the assessment mainly concerned how to label the arousal (fear, love, etc.), but also had implications for what caused the arousal. If we assume the child has labelled the emotion as fear, then the child must access what is causing the fear, and the obvious choice is the monster.

Alternatively, Harris et al. (1991) suggested that children know the difference between pretence and reality, but they think that pretend entities can "transmigrate" from the pretend world into the real one, perhaps in the manner of Casper the Friendly Ghost. However, the follow-up study by Johnson and Harris (in press, Experiment 3) provided little evidence for such confusion.

Another possibility hinges on the fact that most of these episodes of apparent real–pretend boundary breakdown occur in emotionally charged situations. Bretherton (1989) and Bateson (1955/1972) point out that even adults do not completely cordon off fantasy from reality, especially when the fantasy arouses emotion, in that we really feel the emotion that the fictional situation elicited. For example, we feel fear in scary movies, despite being absolutely certain that they are just movies. These effects can even persist for some time. Watching the movie *Psycho*, in which a person is killed in a shower, can leave one feeling a bit nervous the next few times one is in a shower. What we see in the fictional world therefore influences what we expect in the real world. However, this does not mean that we think that the fictional event really happened in real life. A study by Rozin, Millman, and Nemeroff (1986) with adult subjects demonstrates how, even for adults, what we clearly know to be true about something does not always dictate our behaviour towards it. Subjects were shown two bottles, and sugar was poured into each. Then subjects were told to place a "sodium cyanide" label on one bottle and a "sugar" label on the other. Later, despite knowing that they had made an arbitrary choice of bottles, and that both really contained the same thing, subjects were reluctant to eat from the bottle labelled "sodium cyanide." Hence the presence of a label had similar effects as imagining (Woolley & Wellman, 1993, make the same point. See also Lillard, 1990). We see the same phenomena after strong dreams: If we dream something happened, we sometimes feel like it happened, and those feelings can drive our behaviour, even though we know the dream was not real. The cause of one's behaviour in such cases might in part be due to increased incognitive availability (Johnson & Harris, in press), but the more important cause might be the emotional aftermath of the imagined situation.

In sum, knowledge about what is real does not always insulate the emotional system from the power of suggestion (see Walton, 1990, for a discussion of emotional participation in make-believe). However, adults feeling fearful, and occasionally desiring to leave the theatre, does not constitute their lacking a reality–fiction boundary. Just as some children prefer not to play monster because it's too scary, some adults prefer to avoid horror films. Reports of young children having difficulty with the real–pretend boundary are rare[1]. Most of the examples are anecdotal, and may be the exceptions rather than the rule. Most of the experimental examples were collected in emotionally charged situations, in which the child's behaviour may stem from the fear itself rather than from uncertainty about reality. Indeed, children must be fairly good at maintaining a real–pretend boundary or they would be sorely confused about real-world relations (Leslie, 1987). Every instance of watching an adult pretend an x was a y would result in a misrepresentation of x's identity and/or function. Hence, at least by three years of age children appear to have a good grasp of the fact that the pretend world is separate and different from the real world, and that the pretend representation is different from reality. Emotional arousal appears to throw this judgement off somewhat, but this is an apparent rather than a real problem, possibly caused by children's desire to exit the fear-evoking situation.

---

[1] DiLalla and Watson (1988) maintain that another form of breakdown of the real-pretend boundary occurs when children slip out of and abandon a given pretence. However, this could also simply demonstrate lack of interest in pretence. In any case, a follow-up study by Golomb and Kuersten (1992), using a modified procedure, found better performance among three-year-olds on a task very similar to that used by DiLalla and Watson (1980).

UNDERSTANDING PRETENCE REPRESENTATIONS

The preceding section concerned children's understanding that in pretence there is a pretend situation contrasting with, and clearly separate from, the real situation. This section deals with children's understanding of another of the defining features of pretence described earlier: When do children understand that pretence is based on mental representation? Pretence is of special interest to theorists in this area because of its similarity to false belief. Pretence is similar to false belief in that actions stemming from both mental states (Harris & Kavanaugh, 1993, p. 1) "are directed at situations that do not actually obtain." In both cases, someone is mentally representing something that is in fact not true. The primary means for probing children's understanding of false belief is the now classic false belief task, originally reported by Wimmer and Perner (1983). For example, in the deceptive box version of a false belief task, children are shown a band-aid box that contains a cow, and are asked what someone who has never seen inside the box before would think was inside. Children under age four tend to fail such tasks, by persistently claiming that anyone and everyone would think the box contained a cow even if they had never looked inside the box. Young children's failing such tasks is thought to be caused by their not understanding that the mind represents the world (Flavell, Green, & Flavell, 1990; Forguson & Gopnik, 1988; Perner, 1991). To understand mental representation is to understand that the mind uses internal symbols that stand for and yet are largely independent of objects, events, and situations in the real world. The child needs to understand that a person would mentally represent the band-aid box as containing band-aids, even though it actually contains a cow. Young children's failure to understand mental representation is thought to explain their difficulty not only on false belief tasks but on several other types of tasks as well, such as appearance-reality, visual perspective-taking, and conceptual perspective-taking tasks. These tasks will involve understanding that the same object or situation can be construed or mentally represented in more than one way (Flavell, 1988; Flavell et al., 1990; Gopnik & Astington, 1988; Perner, 1991; Taylor, 1988).

However, pretend play seems to be in strict opposition to this hypothesis, since in pretence one routinely bears two different representations of a situation in mind—the real situation, and the pretend one (see Lillard, 1993b, for discussion). The fact that children pretend, and appear to understand pretence in others, as early as 18 months of age, would seem to indicate that they do understand mental representation at least in pretence contexts (Flavell, 1988; Forguson, 1989; Siegler, 1991). As suggestive evidence for the claim that pretence and false belief understanding are supported by a single ability, it has been noted that children with autism both tend to fail false belief tasks and do not engage in spontaneous pretence play (Baron-Cohen, 1987; 1991; Leslie, 1991).

In several recent experiments I have addressed the question of whether young children have an advanced understanding of mental representation as part of their conceptualisation of pretence. Two of these experiments (Lillard, 1993a, Experiments 3 and 4) are discussed next. Both experiments pit the possibility that young children understand that pretence requires mental representation against the alternative possibility that children have a simpler, nonrepresentational conceptualisation of pretence as action.

One experiment tested this indirectly, by presenting children with protagonists who did not know about and therefore could not mentally represent some crucial aspect of an animal. Four- and five-year-olds were shown a troll and were told, for example, "This is Moe, and he's from the Land of the Trolls. Moe's hopping around, kind of like a rabbit hops. Moe doesn't know that rabbits hop like that; he doesn't know anything about rabbits. But he is hopping like a rabbit." To ensure that children had correctly heard the premises, they were asked two control questions: "Does he know that rabbits hop?" and "Is he hopping like a rabbit?" Then children were asked, "Would you say he's pretending to be a rabbit, or he's not pretending to be a rabbit?" In effect, then, children were asked whether mental representation or action was the more important factor to consider in judging whether a character was engaging in pretence. Each child received four such tasks, and after the fourth they were administered a standard false belief task. For this task, they were shown a band-aid box and were asked, "Do you know what's in here?" After they responded, "Band-aids," the experimenter said, "Let's look," and opened the box, which contained a cow. She showed the cow to the child, exclaiming, "Hey—there's a cow in here! Imagine that, a band-aid box with a cow inside!" Then the box was closed and children were asked. "If [a child in their class] came in here right now and saw this box, all closed up like this, what would she [or he] think was inside here?" The purpose of including this task was to ensure that the children were normal for their age with regard to a benchmark "theory of mind" test.

Most children answered all four pretend questions the same way: of 16 4-year-olds, 9 always said the troll was pretending, and 3 always said he was not pretending. Of 16 5-year-olds, 4 always said the troll was pretending, and 6 always said he was not pretending. If we set passing criteria at 3 tasks, only 37% of the 4-year-olds (6 of the 16) passed the pretend tasks; 5-year-olds performed somewhat better, with 68% (11 of the 16) passing (see Table 10.1). In other words, 4-year-olds tended to claim that even though Moe did not even know that rabbits hop, he was pretending to be a rabbit when he was hopping like one. This suggests that 4-year-olds might have a low-level,

TABLE 10.1
Experiment 1: Percentages (and Ns) of Children Passing False
Belief and Pretend Tasks

Pretend Tasks	False Belief Task		
	Fail	Pass	Total
4-year-olds ($n = 16$)			
Fail	13(2)	50(8)	63(10)
Pass	6(1)	31(5)	37(6)
Total	19(3)	81(13)	100(16)
5-year-olds ($n = 16$)			
Fail	19(3)	13(2)	32(5)
Pass	6(1)	62(10)	68(11)
Total	25(4)	75(12)	100(16)

nonrepresentational understanding of pretence as action. It seems that 5-year-olds might be beginning to grasp that, in order to pretend to be a rabbit by hopping, one would have to know that rabbits hop. However, the 5-year-olds' level of performance was not significantly higher than that of the 4-year-olds on the pretend tasks, and so the possibility of a developmental advance occurring between these ages is speculative. The children were not simply delayed with regard to mental state understanding, because 13 of the 16 4-year-olds and 12 of the 16 5-year-olds passed the false belief task. Indeed, significantly more children ($n = 10$) failed the pretend tasks but passed the false belief task than showed the reverse pattern ($n = 2$, $P < 0.05$, binomial distribution). At the very least, this result indicates that this sample of children was not simply slow to acquire theory-of-mind-related knowledge. It might also indicate that children understand mental representation in the domain of belief even earlier than they understand it in the domain of pretence.

These results were pursued further in a second experiment. This experiment addressed the possibility that children might have been confused by the troll (perhaps trolls are always pretending), as well as the possibility that they might be prone to answer any question about pretence in the affirmative. It also attempted more directly to address the contention that the four-year-olds' poor performance in the first experiment was due to their not understanding pretence as based on mental representation. In a sense, the causal chain in the first experiment went from knowledge (knowing that rabbits hop) to mental representation (being able to represent a hopping rabbit) to pretence (projecting a hopping-rabbit representation onto one's own hopping). Perhaps children's confusion stemmed *not* from failing to understand the link between the latter two components (mental representation and pretence) but rather from a difficulty with the link between the former two (knowledge about rabbit behaviour and having a mental representation of a hopping rabbit). To circumvent this problem, in the second experiment mental representational information was more directly specified. Four-year-olds were presented with photographs of other children, who were variously described as thinking (or not thinking) about being a rabbit, and hopping (or not hopping) like a rabbit hops. They were asked to tell Wolfie, a dog puppet who was particularly ignorant about pretending, if the children were pretending or not. Along with providing a more direct test of understanding the mental representational component of pretence than was provided by the first experiment, this method also avoided the problem of children possibly answering incorrectly in the earlier experiment because they were swayed by the presence of a salient action (since in this experiment still photographs of children's faces were used).

Two training trials were presented in which the child in the photo was described either as both thinking about being a lion and growling like a lion, and therefore as pretending to be a lion, or as not thinking about being a monkey and not swinging like a monkey, and therefore as not pretending to be a monkey. Following training, 12 test trials were presented. Four of these were controls of the type used in training, in which the child was described as both thinking about being and hopping like a rabbit (for example) or as not thinking about being and not hopping like a rabbit. Four were test trials, in which the child was described as hopping like a rabbit, but not thinking about being a rabbit. The remaining trials were ambiguous with regard to pretence: the child was thinking about being a rabbit, but was not hopping like one. As in the first experiment, children were consistent in their responses to a given type of task: 19 of the 24 children responded in the same way to all 4 test tasks; the remaining 5 responded in the same way to 3 of the 4. In addition, most of those responses indicated a nonrepresentational understanding of pretence: of the 24 4-year-olds, 15 (or 63%) claimed on at least 3 or 4 trials that the protagonist was pretending to be an x when the action was consistent with that pretence but the mental state was not; only 9 made the opposite claim, that the child was not pretending in such circumstances (see Table 10.2).

Because all the children passed the control trials, we know that they were not simply biased to answer yes to any question concerning pretence. In fact, nine children who claimed the protagonist was pretending on all four test trials also claimed the protagonist was not pretending on all four ambiguous trials. In other words, they claimed the protagonist was pretending whenever and only when an action was designed, regardless of the protagonist's mental state. Only two children, on the other hand, relied solely on mental state information, and claimed that the protagonist was pretending whenever and only when the mental state was compatible with pretence, regardless of action.

TABLE 10.2
Experiment 2: Percentages (and Ns) of 4-year-olds Claiming
Protagonist is Pretending or Not Pretending for 4 Conditions in
Experiment

Condition		Child's Judgement	
Action	Mental State	Pretending	Not Pretending
+	+	100(24)	0(0)
+	−	63(15)	38(9)
−	+	25(6)	75(18)
−	−	0(0)	100(24)

These experiments indicate that children do not understand that pretending is based on mental representation, and they suggest instead that children's earliest understanding of pretence might be as acting-as-if. This result runs counter to the notion that the mental representational underpinning of pretence is understood early. It is surprising because it seems reasonable to assume that children's understanding of pretence does entail understanding mental representation—that in watching someone pretend a sand pie was a cherry pie, children understand the person to be mentally representing cherry pie. Another reason it is surprising is that pretence seems to be an area of early proficiency. For example, children do better on syllogistic reasoning tasks when they are put in a pretend context (Dias & Harris, 1990). And finally, it is surprising because it has been thought, even by those who believe that children under four years of age do not understand representation, that once representation is understood in the domain of belief it should be understood across the board (see Zaitchik, 1990). In contrast, even children who passed the false belief task tended to fail the pretend tasks in the first experiment; had such a task been administered in the second experiment, those four-year-olds probably would have passed it as well, since four-year-olds generally do pass such tasks (see also Lillard, 1993a, Experiments 1 and 2).

These studies suggest that there is a décàlage in understanding mental representation, such that children understand it with regard to some mental states before others. Children might learn gradually about mental representation, first in domains that they really could not otherwise understand, like false belief. When children first learn about pretence, they do not yet understand mental representation, and therefore they understand it nonrepresentationally, as acting-as-if. Because adults usually act out their pretence when they pretend with young children, this understanding is perfectly useful and does not cause any disequilibrium.

Around age four, children begin to understand mental representation. However, because they have a useful understanding of pretence as acting-as-if, they do not revise their concept of pretence to include mental representation for a year or more.

A pertinent question to raise here is what might motivate children's understanding of pretence to change from an activity-based understanding to a mental representational one. Fisher, Gleitman, and Gleitman (1991) recently put forth the hypothesis that semantic advances may be led by syntactic insights (see also Landau & Gleitman, 1985). They present evidence of some parallels between structural and semantic properties of verbs, and posit that syntax might sometimes bootstrap children's semantics. Most verbs pertaining to cognition and perception, for example, are used in "sentence complement frames": "He _____ that _____." Extrapolating from their hypothesis, one might say that during the fourth and fifth years children learn that mental verbs have a certain syntax, and, because *pretend* shares this syntax, children eventually come to view it as a mental verb rather than as an action verb. This insight would cause them to revise their concept of pretence to include mental representation.

OTHER STEPS IN ACHIEVING AN UNDERSTANDING OF PRETENCE

The foregoing discussion concerned three aspects of preschool children's understanding of pretence. First, the ability to negotiate the real–pretend boundary implies understanding that pretence involves some reality that is different from the pretence (the second component in the definition given earlier). The experiments addressed two other components of understanding pretence. They both addressed the third component: that pretence is based on mental representation. To some degree the second experiment also addressed the fourth feature: that the mental representation is intentionally projected onto reality. One must be thinking about being a rabbit and about how to make one's own motions match one's idea of how rabbits hop in order to be pretending to be a rabbit by hopping. The experiments indicate that preschoolers do not understand these two features of pretence. There is certainly much more to be understood about how and when children understand pretence—more concerning these features as well as more concerning several aspects of the other three necessary features. Regarding these three features, when do children first identify some acts as pretence acts rather than real ones? When do they first construe an adult mimicking eating as pretending to eat? And when do children understand that mental representation is not only necessary to pretence but that it is also sufficient, such that one can pretend in the absence of any actions at all? In addition, there are also several unresolved questions concerning the other three features of pretence discussed earlier.

One such question is when children understand that pretence necessarily involves a pretender—an animate, mindful being who puts up the pretence. Pretence is the province of animates. Trees in the dark are not pretending to be monsters, and chairs with sheets thrown over them are not pretending to be ghosts. On the other hand, precisely what types of animates we might attribute pretence to is open to question. For example, is the plover pretending to have a broken wing when it leads predators away from its young? Whether it is pretending hinges on what sort of mind one is willing to attribute to the plover (if any). Is the plover representing its wing as broken, or, at the other extreme, is it simply carrying out a behaviour that it is genetically programmed to carry out in the face of predators near its progeny? Is the cat who bats a spool of thread around pretending the spool is a mouse? Whether other species engage in pretence is uncertain (see Byrne & Whiten, 1991, and Mitchell, 1993, for discussion). Regardless, there is agreement that living human beings pretend, and that nonliving objects do not. The fact that pretence is something that only animals do, and that inanimates do not do, might be one of the first things young children understand about pretence. Since children seem to understand animacy fairly early (Gelman, Spelke, & Meck, 1983; Poulin-DuBois & Shultz, 1988), and begin to engage in pretence around 18 months of age, it seems they have the necessary information to understand that only animates pretend quite early. Alternatively, however, children might think of pretence in other ways. For example, they might first think of it as pure physical movement. For example, if pretending to be a log is the equivalent of the physical behaviour of rolling, then a pencil rolling down an incline would be thought of as pretending to be a log. Perhaps young children think of pretence as any external manifestation, so that a lamp with a sheet tossed over it would be thought of as pretending to be a ghost. Hence one question for future research is when children understand that pretence is the province of animate, mindful beings.

Another question concerns components five and six of the features of pretence outlined earlier. When do children realise that people who are engaged in pretence are actively trying to enact the pretence—that they are aware of what they are doing, and that they are doing it intentionally? As stated earlier, pretence actions carried out in the absence of intention are not pretence. If I hop because the tarmac is burning my feet, I am certainly not pretending to be a rabbit. I must be hopping with the intention to hop like a rabbit.

Discussion of intention is often fraught with confusion because *intention* has several closely related but different meanings: Intentionality meaning "aboutness" (as used in the philosophy of mind literature, see Searle, 1983), intention as a plan (characterising the mind, in Bratman's, 1987, terms), and intentionally in the sense of having done something on purpose (characterising an action, according to Bratman). Pretence entails intention in all three senses, but the focus here is on the latter two. Understanding intention as a plan requires that one understand mental representation, because the very nature of a plan is that it is a representation of some future state of affairs and how to bring it about. However, understanding intention in the sense of doing something on purpose does not require understanding mental representation (see Astington, 1991). One can understand that Bill kicked the ball on purpose without seeing Bill as mentally representing himself kicking the ball before he kicked it. One can understand "on purpose" as having an attitude of conviction. One could think of these two species of intention in temporal terms, with the planning sense being "intention in the future" and the on purpose sense being "intention in the present" (see Bratman, 1987).

How does intention figure in pretence? Intention in the future or the planning sense is involved when a group of children decide play house, and they plan out who will play what character, where the house is, and so on, prior to beginning the pretence. The plans are mental representations of the future state of affairs, and they drive the pretence. Intention in the present or on purpose sense is seen when the children actually enact those characters. For example, when a boy who is pretending to be the baby mimics crying, he does so on purpose, intentionally enacting the behaviours he associates with babies. He might not have explicitly planned to cry beforehand, but he does cry on purpose.

When do children *understand* that pretence involves intention? Because intention in the planning sense rests on understand mental representation, it is probably a later acquisition: The experiments described earlier indicate that the mental representational underpinnings of pretence (such as knowing and thinking about the pretend object) are not understood until at least the sixth year. But understanding intention as doing something on purpose might be acquired prior to understanding mental representation, and might be part of younger children's conceptualisation of pretence.

Children appear to have an early nonrepresentational understanding of intention in the sense of doing something on purpose. Shultz (1980), for example, has shown that three-year-olds discriminate between intended and unintended actions. Children might also have an early grasp of the fact that pretence actions are done on purpose. There are several facets to such an understanding. First, if some other purpose for doing something has been specified, children might understand that the activity is not pretence. For example, if a girl is jumping up and down because she is trying to see inside a high window, children might understand that she is not pretending to be a kangaroo. Second, if someone is doing something inadvertently, children might understand that the person is not pretending. For example, if someone accidentally trips, children might understand that the person was not pretending to have a limp. Third, since one cannot intend two contrary things at once (Bratman, 1987), children might understand early on that one who is pretending to be a rabbit is not simultaneously pretending to be a kangaroo. Fourth, children might understand that a change in intention accompanies a change in pretence or from pretence to not pretence. For example, a little girl wearing a tiger suit at a birthday party, who was earlier growling on all fours, and is later crying and asking to go home, is probably no longer pretending to be a tiger at the second point, even if she is still wearing the tiger suit. In order to be pretending, one must be purposefully evoking a certain situation.

A further issue regarding children's understanding of pretence is the extent to which children regard it as a mental state at all, as opposed to pure physical behaviour. Although the experiments described earlier suggest they conceptualise it more as an action than as a mental representational state, there are several degrees of mentalness, in between these two poles, at which children might put pretence. For example, do young children categorise pretence with other mental states or with behaviours? Johnson and Wellman (1982) found that over the preschool years, children increasingly distinguish a category of mental processes that is distinct from overt behaviour in that children think the former but not the latter require a brain. By five years of age, most children understand that the brain is needed to think, dream, and remember, but they do not yet realise that the brain is needed to walk or to tell a story. Pretence is an unusual mental state in that, unlike thinking or remembering, it is frequently accompanied by actions. As stated earlier, children might at first equate pretending with external actions (and other manifestations) and not attend to the fact that it is a mental activity. Given that young children do not seem to understand that the brain is used for actions, but do seem to understand that it is used for mental processes, Johnson and Wellman's method applied to pretence could provide indirect evidence as to whether children conceptualise pretence as a mental state or as an activity. In ongoing work we are presenting three-to five-year-olds with pictures of other children who we describe according to mental states or activities, for example, as thinking, pretending, or swimming. For each, we ask if a brain is needed for the activity. We are interested in whether children will cluster pretence with mental states or activities. If they cluster it with the mental states by claiming that all these states require a brain, this will suggest that they have at least some inkling that pretence is mental rather than purely physical. If this is the case, then in further work we plan to add propositions to the verbs (thinking about a fish, pretending to be a fish, swimming like a fish), to see whether children's judgements change under such circumstances. It might be that when children can easily envision an activity that would portray a pretence, they abandon whatever notion they might have of pretending as a mental process.

SUMMARY

This chapter began with a working definition of the mental state of pretence and then discussed children's understanding of several components of pretence. A review of literature on children's ability to negotiate the real–pretend boundary suggests that at least by about three years of age, most children in most circumstances appear to have a clear sense that reality and pretence are separate and different. In emotional situations, children's judgements on these issues can waver, but such uncertainty is better explained as their response to fright than as true confusion about reality. However, despite their apparent understanding that pretence and reality are different, children seem not to understand a crucial aspect of pretence until at least the sixth year: that pretence is based on mental representations. Rather, young children appear to conceptualise pretence as acting-as-if at least when actions and mental states are discrepant. Ongoing and future work will address several other aspects of the early understanding of pretence, such as its being the province of animates, being done on purpose, and belonging to a category of mental states rather than behaviours.

ACKNOWLEDGEMENTS

The research described in this chapter was supported in part by NIH Training Grant IT32MH19114-01, a Stanford University Fellowship, a University of San Francisco Faculty Development Grant, and NIMH Grant 40687 to John H. Flavell. Paul Harris made helpful comments on an earlier draft.

REFERENCES

Astington, J.W. (1991). Intention in the child's theory of mind. In C. Moore & D. Frye (Eds.), *Children's theories of mind*, (pp. 157–172). Hillsdale, NJ: Lawrence Erlbaum Associates Inc.

Austin, J.L. (1979). Pretending. In J.O. Urmson & G.J. Warnock (Eds.), *Philosophical papers*, (pp. 253–271). Oxford: Oxford University Press.

Baron-Cohen, S. (1987). Autism and symbolic play. *British Journal of Developmental Psychology, 5*, 139–148.

Baron-Cohen, S. (1991). The development of a theory of mind in people with autism: Deviance or delay? *Pervasive Developmental Disorders, 14*, 33–51.

Bateson, G.A. (1955/1972). A theory of play and fantasy. In G.A. Bateson (Ed.), *Steps to an ecology of mind* (pp. 39–51) (reprinted from American Psychiatric Association Research Reports, 1955, II). New York: Chandler.

Bratman, M.E. (1987). *Intentions, plans, and practical reasons*. Cambridge, Mass.: Harvard University Press.

Bretherton, I. (1984a). Representing the social world in symbolic play: Reality and fantasy. In I. Bretherton (Ed.), *Symbolic play: The development of social understanding* (pp. 3–41). New York: Academic Press.

Bretherton, I. (1984b). *Symbolic play: The development of social understanding.* New York: Academic Press.

Bretherton, I. (1989). Pretence: The form and function of make-believe play. *Developmental Review, 9,* 383–401.

Bretherton, I., Prentiss, C., & Ridgeway, D. (1990). Family relationships as represented in a story completion task at 37 and 54 months. In I. Bretherton & M. Watson (Eds.), *Perspectives on the family* (pp. 85–105). San Francisco: Jossey-Bass.

Bretherton, I., Ridgeway, D., & Cassidy, J. (1990). Assessing internal working models of the attachment relationship: An attachment story completion task for three-year-olds. In M. Greenberg, D. Cicchetti, & E.M. Cummings (Eds.), *Attachment during the preschool years: Theory, research, and intervention* (pp. 273–308). Chicago: University of Chicago Press.

Byrne, R.W., & Whiten, A. (1991). Computation and mindreading in primate tactical deception. In A. Whiten (Ed.), *Natural theories of mind* (pp. 127–141). Oxford: Basil Blackwell.

DeLoache, J.S., & Plaetzer, B. (1985). *Tea for two: Joint mother–child symbolic play.* Paper presented at the Biennial Meeting for the Society for Research in Child Development, Toronto.

Dias, M.G., & Harris, P.L. (1990). The influence of the imagination on reasoning by young children. *British Journal of Developmental Psychology, 8,* 305–318.

DiLalla, L.F., & Watson, M.W. (1988). Differentiation of fantasy and reality: Preschoolers' reactions to interruptions in their play. *Developmental Psychology, 24,* 286–291.

Dunn, J. (1993). *Children's understanding of "other minds": Antecedents and later correlates in interaction with family and friends.* Paper presented a Symposium conducted at the Biennial Meeting of the Society for Research in Child Development, New Orleans, Louisiana.

Erikson, E.H. (1950). *Childhood and society.* New York: Norton.

Estes, D., Wellman, H.M., & Woolley, J.D. (1989). Children's understanding of mental phenomena. In H. Reese (Ed.), *Advances in child development and behavior* (pp. 41–87). San Diego: Academic Press.

Fein, G.G. (1981). Pretend play in childhood: An integrative review. *Child Development, 52,* 1095–1118.

Fein, G.G. (1985). The affective psychology of play. In A.W. Gottfried & C.C. Brown (Eds.), *Play interactions: The contribution of play material and parental involvement to children's development* (pp. 31–49). Lexington, Mass.: Lexington Books.

Fisher, C., Gleitman, H., & Gleitman, L.R. (1991). On the semantic content of subcategorization frames. *Cognitive Psychology, 23,* 331–392.

Flavell, J.H. (1988). The development of children's knowledge about the mind: From cognitive connections to mental representations. In J.W. Astington, P.L. Harris, & D.R. Olson (Eds.), *Developing theories of mind* (pp. 244–271). Cambridge: Cambridge University Press.

Flavell, J.H., Green, F.L., & Flavell, E.R. (1990). Developmental changes in young children's knowledge about the mind. *Cognitive Development, 5,* 1–27.

Fodor, J.A. (1992). A theory of the child's theory of mind. *Cognition, 44,* 283–296.

Forguson, L., & Gopnik, A. (1988). The ontogeny of common sense. In J.W. Astington, P.L. Harris, & D.R. Olson (Eds.), *Developing theories of mind* (pp. 226–243). New York: Cambridge University Press.

Forguson, L. (1989). *Common sense.* London: Routledge.

Freud, S. (1959). Creative writers and daydreaming. In J. Stackey (Ed.), *The standard edition of the complete psychological works of Sigmund Freud.* London: Hogarth.

Garvey, C. (1990). *Play.* Cambridge, Mass.: Harvard University Press.

Garvey, C., & Berndt, R. (1975). *Organization in pretend play.* Paper presented at the Annual Convention of the American Psychological Association, Chicago.

Gelman, R., Spelke, E.S., & Meck, E. (1983). What preschoolers know about animate and inanimate objects. In D. Rogers & J. Sloboda (Eds.), *The acquisition of symbolic skills* (pp. 297–326). Plenum: New York.

Golomb, C., & Kuersten, R. (1992). *On the transition from pretence play to reality: What are the rules of the game?* Paper presented at the Annual Convention of the American Psychological Association, Washington, DC.

Gopnik, A., & Astington, J.W. (1988). Children's understanding of representational change and its relation to the understanding of false belief and the appearance-reality distinction. *Child Development, 59,* 26–37.

Harris, P.L. (1991). The work of the imagination. In A. Whiten (Ed.), *Natural theories of mind* (pp. 283–304). Oxford: Basil Blackwell.

Harris, P.L., Brown, E., Marriott, C., Whittall, S., & Harmer, S. (1991). Monsters, ghosts, and witches: Testing the limits of the fantasy–reality distinction in young children. *British Journal of Developmental Psychology, 9,* 105–124.

Harris, P.L., & Kavanaugh, R.D. (1993). Young children's understanding of pretence. *Monographs of the Society for Research in Child Development, 58* (1, Serial No. 231).

Jenkins, J.M., Astington, J.W. (1993). *Cognitive, linguistic, and social factors associated with theory of mind development in young children.* Paper presented at Symposium conducted at the Biennial Meeting of the Society for Research in Child Development, New Orleans, Louisiana.

Johnson, C., & Harris, P.L. (in press). Magic: Special but not excluded. *British Journal of Developmental Psychology.*

Johnson, C.N., & Wellman, H.M. (1982). Children's developing conceptions of the mind and the brain. *Child Development, 52,* 222–234.

Keil, F.C. (1989). *Concepts, kinds, and cognitive development.* Cambridge, Mass.: MIT Press.

Kuersten, R. (1991). *Boundaries of fantasy and reality in the pretence play of preschool children.* Unpublished Honours thesis, University of Massachusetts, Boston.

Landau, B., & Gleitman, L.R. (1985). *Language and experience: Evidence from the blind child.* Cambridge: Cambridge University Press.

Leslie, A.M. (1987). Pretence and representation: The origins of "theory of mind." *Psychological Review, 94,* 412–426.

Leslie, A.M. (1988). Some implications of pretence for mechanisms underlying the child's theory of mind. In J.W. Astington, P.L. Harris, & D.R. Olson (Eds.), *Developing theories of mind* (pp. 19–46). New York: Cambridge University Press.

Leslie, A.M. (1991). The theory of mind impairment in autism: Evidence for a modular mechanism of development? In A. Whiten (Ed.), *Natural theories of mind* (pp. 63–78). Oxford: Basil Blackwell.

Lillard, A.S. (1990). *Pretend play: Zone of proximal development or fool's gold?* Unpublished manuscript, Stanford University.

Lillard, A.S. (1991). *Young children's conceptualization of pretend.* Unpublished Doctoral dissertation, Stanford University.

Lillard, A.S. (1993a). Young children's conceptualization of pretense: Action or mental representational state? *Child Development, 64,* 372–386.

Lillard, A.S. (1993b). Pretend play skills and the child's theory of mind. *Child Development, 64,* 348–371.

Mitchell, R.W. (1993). Animals as liars: The human face of nonhuman duplicity. In M. Lewis, & C. Saarni (Eds.), *Lying and deception in everyday life* (pp. 59–89). New York: Guilford.

Morison, P., & Gardner, H. (1978). Dragons and dinosaurs: The child's capacity to differentiate fantasy from reality. *Child Development, 49,* 642–648.

Nelson, K., & Seidman, S. (1984). Playing with scripts. In I. Bretherton (Ed.), *Symbolic play* (pp. 45–72). London: Academic Press.

Peller, L.E. (1952). Models of children's play. *Mental Hygiene, 36*, 66–83.

Perner, J. (1991). *Understanding the representational mind.* Cambridge, Mass.: MIT Press.

Piaget, J. (1962). *Play, dreams, and imitation in childhood.* New York: Norton.

Poulin-DuBois, D., & Shultz, T.R. (1988). The development of the understanding of human behavior: From agency to intentionality. In J.W. Astington, P.L. Harris, & D.R. Olson (Eds.), *Developing theories of mind* (pp. 109–125). Cambridge: Cambridge University Press.

Rozin, P., Millman, L., & Nemeroff, C. (1986). Operation of the laws of sympathetic magic in disgust and other domains. *Journal of Personality and Social Psychology, 50*, 703–712.

Samuels, A., & Taylor, M. (1992). *Children's ability to distinguish fantasy events from real-life events.* Unpublished manuscript, University of California at Santa Cruz.

Scarlett, W.G., & Wolf, D. (1979). When it's only make-believe: The construction of a boundary between fantasy and reality. In E. Winner & H. Gardner (Eds.), *Fact, fiction, and fantasy in childhood* (pp. 29–40). San Francisco: Jossey-Bass.

Schacter, S., & Singer, J. (1962). Cognitive, social, and physiological determinants of emotional state. *Psychological Review, 69*, 379–399.

Schwartzman, H.B. (1978). *Transformations: The anthropology of children's play.* New York: Plenum.

Searle, J.R. (1983). *Intentionality.* Cambridge: Cambridge University Press.

Schultz, T.R. (1980). Development of the concept of intention. In W.A. Collins (Ed.), *Development of cognitive affect and social relations. The Minnesota Symposium on Child Psychology* (pp. 131–164). Hillsdale, NJ: Lawrence Erlbaum Associates Inc.

Siegler, R.S. (1991). *Children's thinking.* Englewood Cliffs, NJ: Prentice-Hall.

Taylor, M. (1988). The development of children's understanding of the seeing–knowing distinction. In J.W. Astington, P.L. Harris, & D.R. Olson (Eds.), *Developing theories of mind* (pp. 207–225). Cambridge: Cambridge University Press.

Taylor, M., Gerow, L.E., & Carlson, S.M. (1993). *The relationship between individual differences in fantasy and theory of mind.* Paper presented at a Symposium conducted at the Biennial Meeting of the Society for Research in Child Development, New Orleans, Louisiana.

Verba, M. (1993). Construction and sharing of meanings in pretend play among young children. In M. Stambak & H. Sinclair (Eds.), *Pretend play among three-year-olds* (pp. 1–30). Hillsdale, NJ: Lawrence Erlbaum Associates Inc.

Walton, K.L. (1990). *Mimesis as make-believe.* Cambridge, Mass.: Harvard University Press.

Wellman, H.M., & Estes, D. (1986). Early understanding of mental entities: A re-examination of childhood realism. *Child Development, 57*, 910–923.

Wimmer, H., & Perner, J. (1983). Beliefs about beliefs: Representation and constraining function of wrong beliefs in young children's understanding of deception. *Cognition, 13*, 103–128.

Woolley, J.D. (1993). *Young children's understanding of fictional versus epistemic mental representations: Imagination and belief.* Unpublished manuscript, University of Texas, Austin.

Woolley, J.D., & Wellman, H.M. (1993). Origin and truth: Young children's understanding of imaginary mental representations. *Child Development, 64*, 1–17.

Zaitchik, D. (1990). When representations conflict with reality: The preschooler's problem with false beliefs and "false" photographs. *Cognition, 35*, 41–68.

11 Understanding Pretence

Paul L. Harris
University of Oxford, UK

INTRODUCTION

Early pretend play has long been seen, following Piaget's inspiration, as part of the child's emerging symbolic capacity—a symbolic activity that involves three-dimensional props and miming gestures rather than arbitrary signifiers such as words. More recently, the emergence of pretend play in the second and third year of life has taken on a new theoretical significance. There are, I think, two reasons for this. First, it is tempting to argue that a child who is engaged in pretend play, especially a child who is watching a play partner produce a pretend action, must be engaged in some kind of psychological attribution in order to make sense of what the partner is doing.

Consider, for example, a piece of pretence that we might enact for a two-year-old. We take a cardboard box and make twiddling movements at one end of it. We extend a finger into the empty box, and say "Too hot!" We twiddle some more and then lift a Teddy bear and seat him in the box. We rub his back vigorously, and then lift him out. We take a piece of paper and swaddle him in it, unwrap him, and pronounce him: "All dry, now!" What is a two-year-old to make of an adult who carries out this sequence of actions and utterances. Why twiddle with thin air? What is supposed to be "too hot"? And why does wrapping an already dry bear in some paper make him "dry now"?

One answer to these questions is to say that the various explanatory gaps can be filled as soon as the two-year-old realises what is going on in the

235

adult's mind: The adult who twiddles with thin air is mentally turning on the hot water tap. The adult who says: "Too hot!" is referring to the water in their mind's eye rather than any real water. The two-year-old who makes these psychological attributions can make sense of the adult's pretend actions and remarks: The two-year-old who registers the adult's movements and remarks without making such attributions will be mystified. Evidence that two-year-olds understand the pretend gestures and utterances of their play partner would, according to this account, be a demonstration of the early emergence of the child's theory of mind. Although most current theoretical claims about the child's so-called theory have focused on the transition between three and four years, evidence from pretend play would imply that critical building blocks for a fully fledged theory are in place before any such alleged transition.

An alternative account—which I shall propose—is that children do make sense of an adult's pretend actions and utterances but they do so without any assumptions about the mental life of the adult. I shall argue that pretending is seen by two-year-olds as a special form of activity, rather than a special type of inner mental state. It is an activity that is directed at objects and situations that are make-believe—for example "twiddling" can be directed at make-believe taps, that can, in turn, produce make-believe water. Two-year-olds can understand actions and utterances that are directed at make-believe entities without any understanding of the mental machinery involved in the manufacture of those entities.

The second reason for current interest in pretend play stems from research on children with autism. It has long been known that such children are impoverished in their spontaneous pretend play (Harris, 1993; Wing & Gould, 1979). More recently, it has been claimed that they are deficient in solving certain standard theory-of-mind tasks: the first-order (Baron-Cohen, Leslie, & Frith, 1985) and particularly the second-order false belief task (Baron-Cohen, 1989; Ozonoff, Pennington, & Rogers, 1991). Linking these two problems together, Leslie (1987) has suggested that children with autism lack an ability to understand mental attitudes: the attitude of *pretend* in the case of pretend play, and the attitude of *belief* in the case of first- and second-order belief tasks. I shall argue instead that children with autism have particular difficulties in tasks that require the selection—or comprehension—of an action that is guided by a hypothetical outcome, rather than the existing stimulus array. This difficulty reveals itself in their stereotyped play, their problems on false belief tasks, and their poor performance on so-called planning tasks.

Before turning to these theoretical issues, however, we first need some empirical evidence showing what two-year-olds do understand when an adult acts out a pretend sequence. Because Piaget concentrated on the production of pretence and because subsequent investigation has followed his lead, we know very little about young children's understanding of pretence. I shall describe a series of experiments in which we have examined this issue. With one exception, all the experiments included a group of young 2-year-olds with an average age of approximately 28 months. In the initial set of experiments, we compared these young 2-year-olds to children below 2 years with an average age of approximately 21 months. In the final set of experiments, we compared them to older 2-year-olds with an average age of 33–34 months.

Most of the children were recruited and tested in their preschool or playgroup by a female experimenter. In each experiment, children were invited to join in with, or describe, a pretend episode enacted by the experimenter; the episode involved toy animals and puppets in order to capture the child's interest. We examined four inter-related issues: children's understanding of make-believe stipulations; their ability to select an action in accordance with such a stipulation; their understanding of make-believe transformations; and their ability to offer a description of that transformation. I take up each of these four issues in turn.

UNDERSTANDING MAKE-BELIEVE STIPULATIONS

When an adult acts out a piece of pretence in front of a child, the existence of various make-believe entities is "stipulated." Either through an utterance or a gesture, the adult acts as if particular objects or substances are present when they really are not. For example, returning to the episode described earlier, when the adult twiddles with thin air, he or she is effectively stipulating the presence of make-believe taps. Unless the child grasps this stipulation, the adult's action will be opaque. Similarly, when the adult says, "Too hot!," they are stipulating the make-believe temperature of the water, and in so doing presupposing, of course, the existence of the water that was generated by the prior twiddling.

Our initial experiment was aimed at finding out whether children can grasp a simple stipulation. From observation of free play between mothers and toddlers, it is clear that mothers often produce such stipulations in the presence of a supportive cue (Kavanaugh & Harris, 1991). For example, a make-believe substance is often stipulated in the context of a familiar container for that substance: A mother might hand the child an empty cup, saying, "Here's your tea." We exploited this association in our experiment (Harris & Kavanaugh, 1993, Experiment 1). Children were first involved in a warm-up phase, in which the experimenter "poured" pretend milk from a milk carton into a glass, and children were encouraged to feed a toy elephant with it. In the test phase, they were given two sets of props. On one side, we placed a cup and an empty teapot, and on the other side an empty cereal box, a bowl, and a spoon. The experimenter then introduced four different toy animals, one after the other. As each animal was introduced, the experimenter told the child what make-believe substance the animal wanted. For example, she might say: "Here's the cow. The cow wants some tea. You give the cow some tea." or "Here's the pig. The pig wants some cereal. You give the pig some cereal." Children were then scored for their selection between the two sets of props. In the case of an animal who wanted tea, they were given credit for both "pouring" make-believe tea from the empty teapot into the cup, and "feeding" the animal by lifting the cup to its mouth. In the case of an animal who wanted cereal, they were given credit for "pouring" make-believe cereal from the empty box, and for "feeding" the animal by lifting the bowl or spoon to the animal's mouth. Pretend actions of "pouring" and "feeding" with the incorrect props were not given credit. Figure 11.1 shows the proportion of trials on which children gained credit by acting on the correct prop. Young 2-year-olds (mean = 27 months) were very accurate for both "pouring" and "feeding." Children below 2 years (mean = 22 months) often omitted the "pouring" but they were quite accurate in "feeding."

This exploratory study shows that two-year-olds—and indeed, children below two years—can make sense of a make-believe stipulation. They took the experimenter's references to "tea" and "cereal" to refer to make-believe entities, and they acted in an appropriate fashion vis-à-vis those make-

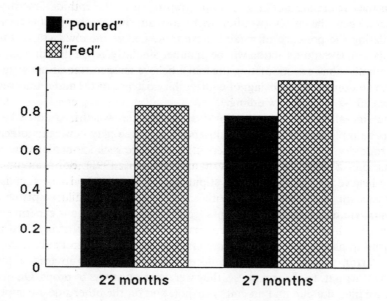

FIG. 11.1   Proportion of trials on which children "poured" and "fed" with the correct props.

believe entities. Children were not puzzled by the absence of any real tea or real cereal, and they were not prompted by the mere presence of the props to produce a familiar pretend script: They chose accurately between the two sets of props, depending on the experimenter's request to offer a particular make-believe substance.

In the next study (Harris & Kavanaugh, 1993, Experiment 2), we showed that children can extend these stipulations from one prop to another similar prop in a categorical fashion. Walton (1990) makes the important conceptual point that make-believe truths are not necessarily represented in the mind of the players. This point applies with obvious force to a set of similar props belonging to the same category. Consider two boys who have agreed that they will pretend to be hunters. In the course of their expedition, they stipulate that tree stumps are to count as bears. As they tip-toe through the forest, there will be many as yet undiscovered bears. In fact, even though they do not yet know it, there is a tree-stump hidden in the thicket that they are approaching at this very moment. The first one to spot this tree-stump can be sure that it is a "bear," even though neither he nor his partner have represented it as such until now. Indeed, as they will probably acknowledge, it has been hiding in the thicket all along, waiting to pounce on them! This example makes clear how far make-believe truths extend beyond any specific stipulation by an individual players: Make-believe truths can exist "out there," awaiting discovery or acknowledgement by individual players.

Do young children make similar extrapolations? To test this possibility, children first participated in a warm-up phase in which they watched the experimenter feed an animal with some "banana" (a yellow brick); they were also handed a yellow brick and encouraged to "give the monkey some more banana." Similarly, they watched while the experimenter fed the horse some cake (a red brick); again, they were given a red brick and encouraged to give him some more cake. In the test phase, new animals were introduced, and the child was asked to feed each animal its preferred food, either "cake" or "banana." A pile of yellow bricks and a pile of red bricks were available on either side of the child. As Fig. 11.2 shows, young 2-year-olds (mean = 28 months) realised that these hitherto unused and unstipulated bricks could also count as "banana" and "cake" respectively, and they chose appropriately between the 2 piles in feeding the animal. Children below 2 years (mean = 21 months) were less systematic.

Taken together, these first two experiments show that around their second birthday, children can understand an adult's make-believe stipulations. They realise that such stipulations apply to imaginary substances such as tea or cereal as shown in Experiment 1, to specific props as in the introductory phase of Experiment 2, and finally to hitherto unused and unstipulated props, as in the test phase of Experiment 2.

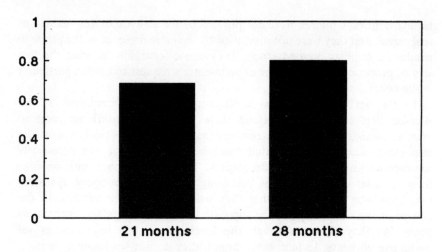

FIG. 11.2   Proportion of trials on which children selected from correct pile of unused props.

SELECTING A PRETEND ACTION

In the two experiments just described, children needed only to choose appropriately between the sets of props that were available. The particular pretend action that they produced was one that they had carried out in the warm-up phase, or they had seen the experimenter produce. However, if children understand a make-believe stipulation, they ought to be able to produce a new pretend response that is appropriately tailored to the make-believe stipulation that their partner has provided. This kind of productivity is very important for joint play because it enables one partner to comply with, yet also elaborate on, the stipulations introduced by the other partner.

To investigate children's productivity, we carried out two studies. In each study, the experimenter enacted—with the help of Teddy, a glove puppet—two familiar routines such as getting ready for bed or having dinner (Harris & Kavanaugh, 1993, Experiments 3 and 4). Within each of the two scripts, three props were introduced one at a time. As they were introduced, the experimenter stipulated their make-believe identity, and asked the child to show what Teddy would do with the prop in question. For example, in the course of the bedtime script the experimenter might say: "Teddy is having a bath. This is Teddy's soap (offering the child a yellow block). Show me what Teddy does with his soap." Children's flexibility in using the props was checked by asking them to use each prop twice—once within each of the two scripts. For example, when the yellow block appeared in the dinner script the experimenter said: "Teddy is having his dinner. This is Teddy's sandwich (offering the child a yellow block). Show me what Teddy does with his sandwich." Children were scored for the frequency with which they produced so called dual-responses: An appropriate pretend response to the prop in each of its make-believe identities. For example, children were credited with a dual response to the yellow block if they "washed" Teddy with it when it was soap but "fed" it to him when it was a sandwich.

Figure 11.3 shows the proportion of dual responses that young 2-year-olds (mean = 28 months) and children below 2 years (mean = 21–22 months) successfully produced in each of 2 studies. The design of the two studies was similar except that in the first study, the experimenter mentioned an action word appropriate to the prop's make-believe identity (e.g. "wash," "eat") whereas in the second these clues were omitted, and the more general phrase—"Show me what Teddy does"—was used instead. Two-year-olds performed well in each experiment. Even in the second study where they were given no clues—other than the make-believe identity of the prop and the ongoing routine—they were able to produce dual responses almost half the time.

We checked to see how often children showed interference between scripts—for example, treating the yellow block in accord with its prior identity (soap) rather than its current identity (sandwich). Such intrusion errors were extremely rare. Almost 90% of children's errors consisted in acting on the prop in a literal manner, rather than in an inappropriate pretend fashion. Thus, children not only understand make-believe

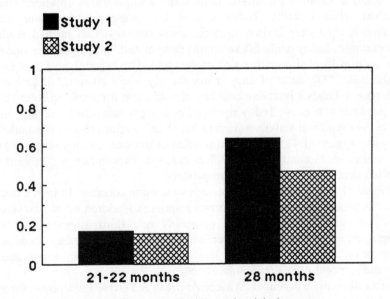

FIG. 11.3   Proportion of trials on which children produced dual responses.

stipulations, they also appreciate that a given make-believe identity is tied to the ongoing, pretend episode. A prior stipulation ceases once a new episode is begun and a new identity is assigned.

UNDERSTANDING MAKE-BELIEVE TRANSFORMATIONS

Consider, once again, the illustrative episode described in the introduction. At the start of the episode, the adult turns on make-believe taps. A child who understands this action should be able to infer that the bath will be filled with water. In its turn, this inference allows the child to appreciate that Teddy is made "wet" when he is placed in the make-believe water. This inference, in its turn, allows the child to understand why it is appropriate to wrap Teddy in a "towel" that can make him dry again.

We have conducted a series of experiments to find out whether two-year-olds understand these successive make-believe transformations. Such transformations were either simple or more complex. In the simple case, there was a single pretend transformation. For example, make-believe liquid was "poured" so as to "fill" a container. In the more complex case, two successive pretend transformations were carried out with the second undoing the change brought about by the first—for example, liquid was first "poured" into a container but then "poured" out again, leaving the container empty.

In our first study of this type (Harris & Kavanaugh, 1993, Experiment 5), we looked at children's ability to understand a single transformation: They watched while naughty Teddy carried out some misdemeanour and afterwards they were invited to make good the mess that he had made. For example, Teddy might lift an (empty) teapot and "pour" tea over one of two toy pigs located on either side of the child. The experimenter then said to the child: "Oh dear!" Can you dry the pig who's all wet?" If children understood Teddy's intervention, they should have been able to infer that the pig directly beneath Teddy's pretend pouring would now be all wet, and direct their remedial activity at him rather than his relatively dry companion opposite. Figure 11.4 shows the proportion of trials on which young 2-year-olds (mean = 28 months) and children below 2 years (mean = 20 months) directed their remedial action appropriately.

Figure 11.4 shows that two-year-olds were quite accurate. In fact, a clear majority produced at least three correct responses. Children below two years were less accurate overall: Approximately one third appeared not to understand what the experimenter wanted of them since they made no response on any of the four trials. However, those children below two years who did respond were predominantly correct.

In a follow-up experiment (Walker-Andrews & Harris, 1993), two-, three-, and four-year-olds watched episodes that included either a simple or a

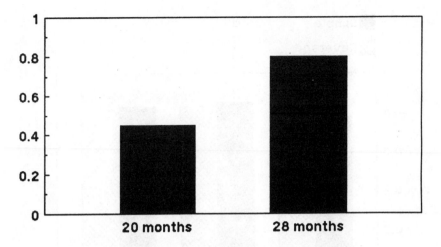

FIG. 11.4   Proportion of trials on which children directed their remedial action correctly.

reversed transformation. For example, in a simple transformation episode, pretend cereal might be "poured" into one of two bowls, and children were invited to give the doll her cereal. To gain credit, they needed to "feed" the doll from the bowl containing make-believe cereal. In a reversed transformation episode, cereal was poured into each bowl, the experimenter pretended to eat the cereal in one, and then invited the child to give the doll her cereal. As before, they needed to select the bowl containing make-believe cereal to receive credit, but to choose accurately they had to recognise that the initial transformation of one bowl (i.e. its being filled with cereal) had been subsequently reversed by the experimenter, who had eaten its make-believe contents.

Figure 11.5 shows that all three age groups, including the two-year-olds, did very well on the simple transformations—as we might expect from the results of the preceding experiment. Children were also quite accurate on the reversed transformations, although the two-year-olds were less accurate than the two older groups. Nevertheless, the majority of responses in all three age groups was correct. This overall pattern is important because it might be argued that children adopted a response heuristic of acting on the prop last approached by the experimenter. This strategy would have led to systematic error in the reversed transformations because the prop last approached by the experimenter was precisely the one that children should ignore. Because children were mostly correct, we may rule out this response heuristic.

Summarising across these two experiments, it is clear that two-year-olds are adroit at working out the consequence of a pretend transformation:

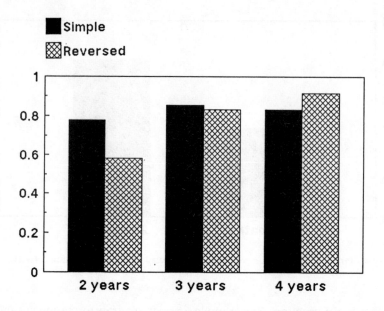

FIG. 11.5 Proportion of trials on which children were correct for simple and reversed transformations.

They realise that a make-believe substance can be transferred from one place to another with consequences for the final location. At that new location, it can be subjected to various additional transformations. It can be wiped up, or eaten, or fed to someone else. Even though such pretend transformations obviously produce no visible consequences—one cannot see make-believe tea spilled on the back of a toy pig, or make-believe cereal in a bowl—they could imagine those consequences and act appropriately.

One final point is worth underlining. To respond appropriately to the experimenter's request, children not only had to understand the make-believe transformations that had been effected; they also needed to understand the experimenter's verbal references to the make-believe outcomes that those pretend actions had engendered. For example, they had to understand that when the experimenter referred to the pig who was "all wet", she meant the pig who was make-believe wet, not literally wet; similarly, when they were invited to feed the doll some cereal, they needed to realise that the experimenter was referring to make-believe cereal in one of the bowls, and not to genuine cereal. Children's correct responses showed that they understood these nonliteral remarks by the experimenter. We wondered if children could produce such nonliteral statements themselves—an issue examined in the next section.

DESCRIBING MAKE-BELIEVE TRANSFORMATIONS

To study children's ability to produce descriptions of a make-believe episode, we adopted the following technique. Children watched while a glove puppet carried out various pieces of pretend mischief. In one study (Harris & Kavanaugh, 1993, Experiment 6), a single pretend transformation was involved. For example, naughty Teddy might pour pretend tea from an (empty) teapot over the head of a toy monkey, or he might squeeze pretend toothpaste from a (closed) toothpaste tube onto the ear of a toy rabbit. In a second and third study (Harris, Kavanaugh, & Meredith, in press, Experiments 1 and 2), two successive transformations were involved. For example, naughty Duck might first pour pretend milk from a milk carton—or pretend talcum powder from a talcum powder tin—into a matchbox tray, and then lift the tray and pour the pretend contents over the toy monkey. After each episode, children were asked a series of questions about what Teddy or Duck had done to their victims—what substance had been put or poured on the victim and what had happened to the victim as a result.

Figure 11.6 shows the proportion of trials on which younger 2-year-olds (means = 28–31 months) and older 2-year-olds (means = 34–36 months) correctly identified the pretend substance that had been poured onto the victim in each of the 3 studies. Younger and older 2-year-olds alike were

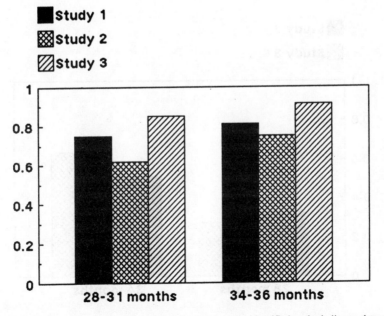

FIG. 11.6 Proportion of trials on which children correctly identified make-believe substance.

quite accurate in each study. Whether the substance was poured directly from an associated container (e.g. pretend milk from a milk carton) or first into a neutral container (e.g. a matchbox tray) and thence over the victim, children accurately named the substance.

In studies 1 and 3 of this series, we also asked children to say what had happened to the victim by posing an open-ended question: "Teddy (Duck) made the monkey all..." Children produced a variety of appropriate descriptions using standard or unconventional adjectives. For example, the tea-stained victim was variously described as "dirty," "black," "wet," "soggy," "grubby," "soaky," or teaey." The talcum-covered victim was described as "powdery," "covered in powder," or "white." Figure 11.7 shows the proportion of trials on which children in each age group produced an appropriate adjective, whether standard or unconventional, across the three studies. This question was clearly more taxing than the initial question about the make-believe substance. Nevertheless, the majority of younger children were successful on at least one episode (out of four) and older children on at least two.

The results support two conclusions. First, two-year-olds can not only understand a partner's reference to a make-believe substance and its effects as described earlier, they can also produce such references themselves. Second, the results reinforce the earlier claim, that children can understand

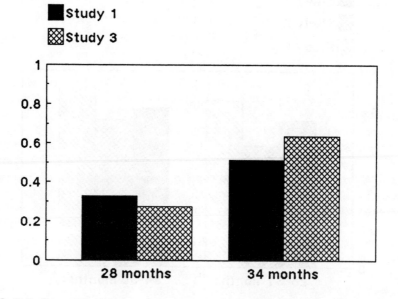

FIG. 11.7   Proportion of trials on which children correctly described make-believe outcome.

make-believe transformations. Were they unable to do so, they could not produce an appropriate make-believe description of the substance and its impact on the victim.

We also presented children with episodes that incorporated substitute props. Appropriate pretend references to such props are especially interesting because they require the temporary suspension of a standard term of reference (e.g. "brick") and its replacement by a term for the object that the prop represents (e.g. "ice-cream"). We asked whether children would be capable of such suspension and replacement. In each of two experiments, younger 2-year-olds (mean = 28 months) and older 2-year-olds (mean = 33 months) watched while the experimenter stipulated the identity of a prop. For example, the experimenter might say: "The monkey likes to eat ice-cream. Let's give him some ice-cream" whilst placing a wooden brick into a container. Teddy then abruptly intervened in his customary, insubordinate fashion. In an initial study, he poured a make-believe substance onto the prop, for example make-believe liquid from a bottle (Harris & Kavanaugh, 1993, Experiment 7). In a second study, he lifted the monkey and sat it on the prop (Harris et al., in press, Experiment 3). Children were asked to say what Teddy had done. In particular, they were asked to say what Teddy had put the substance or the toy animal onto—they could reply by referring either to the prop's actual identity (e.g. "onto the brick") or to the prop's temporary, pretend identity (e.g. "onto the ice-cream").

As Fig. 11.8 shows, children in both experiments were quite accurate in referring to the prop in terms of its pretend identity. Errors mostly consisted of a failure to respond altogether rather than a reference to the prop's actual identity. This was not because children did not know the actual identity of the prop. They had already identified it accurately in a pre-test.

UNDERSTANDING PRETENCE

In the introduction, I suggested that pretending is recognised as a special form of activity by young children but not as a special type of mental state. I now describe a theoretical model that spells out this claim. Consider a child who watches an adult pick up an empty teapot, tilt it in a pouring motion, pick up the empty cup positioned directly beneath it, and then lift the cup to the lips, making drinking noises. Such a sequence of actions is highly familiar in part: Tea is usually poured and drunk in exactly that fashion. The crucial missing ingredient is, of course, the tea itself: None emerges from the spout of the teapot, and none can be seen in the cup from which the adult drinks. I propose that when children observe a familiar sequence of actions carried out in the absence of critical accompaniments to that sequence, they engage in two interpretive acts. First, they perceive that the

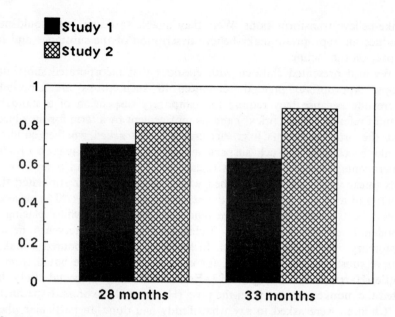

FIG. 11.8 Proportion of trials on which children identified prop in terms of its pretend identity.

adult is engaged in a special or deviant form of activity. Thus, when they observe an adult produce a familiar gesture of lifting and tilting a container—but with the notable absence of the standard consequences, namely the pouring of actual liquid—they perceive the adult to be engaged in nonstandard pouring.

Second, they process the action in a constructive fashion, whereby missing components of the sequences are restored in the child's imagination: The child actually sees the adult tilting an empty teapot, but imagines her to be pouring make-believe tea. The output of such constructive processing is stored as part of the child's representation of the nonstandard pouring action. Thus, following the adult's pretend action, the child notes and remembers that make-believe tea can be poured from the teapot. Such information is not stored as general, factual information, however, but as part of a representation of the current play episode. Thus, the child remembers that make-believe tea can be poured from the teapot in the current context, but draws no conclusion about there being make-believe tea in the pot outside of that context.

The example that I have used is one involving a familiar practical action of pouring liquid. It is clear, however, that children apply the same stance to other types of nonstandard action. Consider an adult who points to an empty cup, saying as she does so: "This is your tea." The adult's act of referring is nonstandard because the customary referent of such an act is plainly absent. Here too, then, we may assume that the child engages in two interpretative acts. First, the act of referring is perceived as deviant but, second, the child constructively fills in the missing components to the standard act. Thus, the child imagines make-believe tea in the cup, and regards the adult as referring to make-believe tea.

In sum, the child treats actions by a play partner, be they practical acts or communicative acts, as deviant. Nevertheless, the child restores such deviant acts to normality by filling in the missing components in their imagination. Such restorations are not, however, like perceptual illusions. The child does not misperceive what has actually happened. Rather, the child supplements what has happened with suppositions that specify the presence or availability of make-believe entities.

We can now apply this model to the various findings described earlier. The model offers a straightforward explanation for children's reaction to make-believe stipulations. Such stipulations were made by the adult in the course of a deviant action or remark: For example, the adult asked children to give an animal some tea, when only an empty teapot was available. Alternatively, the adult handed an animal a yellow brick, while simultaneously explaining that the animal liked bananas. Children interpret such stipulations by introducing make-believe assumptions into the ongoing episode: they pretend that the teapot contains tea, and pour from it in a pretend fashion. Alternatively, they pretend that yellow bricks are bananas and feed them to animals who like bananas.

Why do these make-believe assumptions not distort the child's subsequent construal of reality, creating what Leslie (1987) has called "representational abuse?" According to the proposed model, the assumptions are stored in relation to the ongoing pretend episode. As soon as the game is over, or indeed as soon as a new play episode is initiated by the adult, the make-believe assumptions made during an earlier episode fall into disuse. This claim is borne out by children's flexibility in selecting a pretend response, as described earlier: Children were able to produce so-called dual-responses. They could treat a block as a piece of soap when Teddy was getting ready for bed, and then, a minute or so later, as a sandwich when Teddy was eating his dinner. Intrusion errors, in which the child carried over a prop's identity from an earlier episode into a subsequent episode, were extremely rare.

We need two further assumptions to explain the remaining results. First, constructive processing is constrained by the child's causal knowledge of actions and their impact in the real world. More specifically, when faced with an action that has been perceived as deviant, the child fills in, from his or her pool of causal knowledge, any missing preconditions or consequences—treating them as make-believe preconditions and consequences. Thus, pursuing the earlier example, when faced with an act of pretend pouring, the child stores, as part of its constructive make-believe representation of that act, the standard precondition for an act of pouring—that there is make-believe liquid in the container. Similarly, the child stores the standard consequence—that make-believe liquid will emerge from the container.

This assumption implies that make-believe entities such as imaginary tea retain the causal properties of their real-world equivalents. Make-believe tea, like real tea, can be "poured" if the container that holds it is tilted or inverted; once "poured," it will fall to a surface beneath, and make it "wet." Children's reactions to make-believe transformations show that they grasp such make-believe implications: They "dried" the pig on which Teddy had "poured" make-believe tea, and they "fed" a doll from the bowl into which make-believe cereal had been "poured."

The second assumption is that, when children are asked to describe an act of pretence, they do not base their description on any literal representation of what they have actually seen during the pretend episode. For example, when asked what naughty Teddy has done, they do not say that he lifted a teapot and waved it in the air. Instead, they base their description on the enriched representation that they have constructed in their imagination. They say that Teddy "poured tea" from the teapot, and they can go on to describe the surface underneath as "wet."

UNDERSTANDING PRETENCE AND THE MIND

We may now return to the theoretical issues raised at the beginning of this chapter. To the extent that two-year-olds understand a pretend episode and can describe it appropriately, should we credit them with an ability to grasp the mental attitude of their play partner? The model that I have proposed eschews any such claim. I argued instead that the two-year-old notices that a play partner is engaged in a special form of activity, one in which gestures and remarks are directed at imaginary or substitute entities. To make sense of a play partner's behaviour, it is important that the child construct—in parallel with their partner—a make-believe world containing pretend tea, pretend ice-cream, and so forth. In so doing, they do not need to conceive of the imaginative processes that underlie their partner's pretend performance, merely to conceive of the same pretend entities as their partner.

The irrelevance of the partner's mental processes can be illustrated if we consider another genre of imaginative activity that two-year-olds enjoy: Being told a story from a picture book. To understand the story, children need to accept the stipulated existence of various make-believe entities—the main protagonist, the hollow tree where he lives—and they need to understand the causal connections between successive pictures. The pictures and words that make up the story provide a set of prompts for the child's imagination, just as the gestures and remarks of a play partner provide a set of prompts in the course of pretend play. We do not expect the child who follows and enjoys the story to have any appreciation of the mental processes of the author of the story, or even its current narrator. As in pretend play, the critical requirement is simply that the child construct the stipulated make-believe world in their imagination.

One possible objection to this analogy between understanding a story in a picture book and understanding pretence is that the adult's role in the two activities is different. In the case of the picture book, the adult showing it to the child does not create the make-believe episode, but simply narrates it. In the case of pretend play, however, the adult is not a narrator, but a co-author in the construction of the make-believe situation. However, this is a sophisticated distinction that the child can ignore. Indeed, my claim is precisely that the two-year-old can ignore the mental processes that lie behind the generation of a piece of pretence, and simply treat a narrator or a play partner as someone who enters into the same make-believe situation as themselves.

Young children's focus on pretending as a special activity rather than a mental process is illustrated in recent research by Lillard (1993; this volume). Children were told about two characters who were both producing what appeared to be a pretend action of flying, by waving their arms up and down. Four- and five-year olds were inclined to judge that both characters were pretending to be a bird, even if they were explicitly told that one of them knew nothing about birds. More generally, the necessary role of mental processes in various routine activities such as walking and talking is not systematically acknowledged even among school-aged children (Johnson & Wellman, 1982).

Granted that two-year-olds understand pretence as a special form of activity—one directed at make-believe entities with make-believe outcomes—how should we characterise the four-year-old by comparison? In particular, why is the two-year-old able to understand pretence but not false beliefs, whereas the four-year-old understands both? One possible answer is that the two-year-old understands the existence of hypothetical or make-believe situations. The four-year-old understands in addition that a representation, such as a belief, can be taken to refer reality even though it actually represents a hypothetical or nonexistent situation. According to this view, the major breakthrough between two and four years is an understanding of the way that such a misrepresentation may be taken as an accurate representation of reality by a false believer (Perner, 1991; this volume).

I also think that there is an important, qualitative change taking place but I would characterise it differently. Two-year-olds think of pretence as a special, nonstandard action because it is aimed at situations that do not exist[1]. False beliefs, and the mistaken actions and utterances to which they lead, are also aimed at situations that do not exist. For example, in the unexpected transfer task the false believer guides his or her search in terms of a situation that does not obtain, though it may have done at some earlier point. Why then is it relatively easy for the two-year-old to make sense of a pretend action, but not a false belief?

A critical difference between the two is that the false believer mistakenly thinks that the nonexistent situation (that figures in his or her mistaken belief) does actually obtain. Not finding actual chocolate where it is expected to be, the false believer does not "eat" pretend chocolate instead, but is puzzled or looks elsewhere. Thus, a paradoxical feature of false beliefs, and the actions, remarks and expectations to which they give rise, is that they are mistakenly taken to be well-founded even though, to an informed observer, they patently are not.

This means that the mental adjustment—or simulation process, as I have called it elsewhere (Harris, 1991)—is different in the two cases. To join in with and make sense of another person's pretence it is enough for the child to conjure up the make-believe situation that is presupposed or created by a play partner. There is no need for the child to make any adjustment for the way that the partner conceives of that situation. The child can continue to regard the situation as purely make-believe and join in with their play partner appropriately.

The mental adjustment required for understanding another person's false belief is more complicated. One critical step is to imagine the hypothetical situation that the false believer takes to be true. Yet that is insufficient. It is also vital that the child take into account the false believer's attitude, which is of course different from the child's. The child needs to set aside its own disbelief, and temporarily adopt the same believing attitude as the false believer. According to this view, the major breakthrough between two and four years is not a discovery about the nature of representation, but an ability to share temporarily the stance that someone may take to the counterfactual. Whereas two-year-olds appreciate that someone may act as if a nonexistent situation were the case, four-year-olds appreciate that someone may believe that such a situation is the case.

---

[1] Strictly speaking, pretence can be aimed at situations that happen to exist. For example, two children who play at being sisters may happen to be sisters (Vygotsky, 1962). Likewise, a child who pretends that a cup is empty (having "drunk" all the pretend tea inside it) may happen to use an objectively empty cup (Walker-Andrews & Harris, 1993). Even in cases such as these, however, the make-believe situation and the real situation, although coincidentally similar, are conceptually different. In play, the sisters may display a sisterly affection that is rare in their actual sisterhood, and the cup that is now make-believe empty (unlike the real cup) is ready for the washing-up bowl.

We can unpack this claim in more detail, as follows. In the case of action based on either pretence or false belief, the real situation is not the sole basis for action; action is directed at an alternative, hypothetical situation. The relationship between the actual situation and the alternative situation differs, however, for pretence as compared with false belief. In the case of pretence, the actor may exploit a feature of the actual situation (e.g. the availability of a cup), but imagine a supplement to that actual situation (e.g. the presence of make-believe liquid in the cup). Thus, the actual situation may serve as a prop to, but fall short of, the alternative pretend situation.

Consider now the case of false belief. The actor thinks that an object is in one place when it is actually in another. As in pretence, the actor may act on an empty locus, but act as if it were not empty but contained something that could be retrieved. So far, there is no difference between a pretend action and an action based on a false belief. However, in the case of false belief, there also exists—unknown to the actor—a locus or entity that fully matches the actor's target. For example, although the false believer searches as if A contained chocolate, when it does not, an alternative location B actually does contain chocolate but is ignored. The false-believer's action is therefore anomalous. There is a portion of reality that would be fully appropriate for his or her action, yet the actor searches elsewhere. This helps to explain why a simulation of the false believer is more demanding than a simulation of a pretend partner. In the case of false belief, the actual situation is a plausible competitor to the hypothetical situation; in the case of pretence, the actual situation typically falls short of the hypothetical situation. More generally, a simulation of the false believer requires an appreciation of his or her commitment to the hypothetical situation versus the actual situation.

AUTISM

The difficulties displayed by children with autism remind us that, despite the important change that takes place between two and four years, there is also some continuity. Children with autism are impoverished in their spontaneous pretend play, and frequently inaccurate in diagnosing false beliefs. An adequate developmental model should explain this link.

Leslie (1987) has claimed that there is a continuity between pretending and believing because each calls for the diagnosis of a mental attitude, namely the attitude of pretence or belief. I have argued against the claim that two-year-olds need to understand mental attitudes to join in appropriately with pretend play. An implication of this claim is that the limited pretend play of children with autism is not likely to be caused by any deficiency in diagnosing mental attitudes.

Acceptance of this conclusion means that we must seek a different explanation for the difficulties that such children have with pretence and false belief. An answer emerges if we re-examine the argument set out here: I claimed that participation in pretend play requires the ability to imagine a nonexistent situation rather than the actual situation, and to select acts in accordance with that nonexistent situation; participation in pretend play does not require any diagnosis of the partner's state of mind. The understanding of another person's false belief requires that same ability to entertain a nonexistent situation, combined with a capacity to set aside one's current disbelief in that situation and to recognise the other's commitment to it. Thus, each task requires the ability to entertain a nonexistent situation and to select a response that fits it as opposed to the actual situation. A plausible hypothesis, therefore, is that the difficulties displayed by children with autism, both in pretend play and on false belief tasks, reflect a deficit in entertaining a hypothetical but nonexistent situation (Harris, 1993).

Such a deficit ought to manifest itself outside of the standard set of tasks used in research on the child's theory of mind. Recent evidence provides support for that claim. Ozonoff et al. (1991) tested children with autism on a battery of tasks. They found that a second-order false belief task (which called for an understanding of one story character's belief about another character's belief) was good at discriminating between the children with autism and control groups. Equally good, however, was the Tower of Hanoi Task. In this task, subjects reconstruct a conical tower by stacking discs of varying size onto a peg. Accurate reconstruction requires that children work out in advance the sequence of moves that will enable them to put the discs on the peg from largest to smallest without violating a general rule that a larger disc may not be placed on top of a smaller disc. Good performance obviously requires the child to imagine a hypothetical move, and before executing it, to evaluate the subsequent moves that it will permit. A child who tackles the task simply by selecting a legal move for the current array may end up in a position that permits no further legal progress.

Hughes and Russell (1993) provide further evidence that children with autism have difficulties on tasks that cannot be readily construed as theory of mind tasks. In an earlier study (Russell, Mauthner, Sharpe, & Tidswell, 1991), children could gain some chocolate if they fooled an opponent by pointing at an empty box rather than at a box holding chocolate. Children with autism had difficulty in indicating the empty box—they repeatedly pointed at the box containing the chocolate, and thereby lost it to their opponent. At first sight, these results might be explained by arguing that children with autism find it difficult to deceive an opponent, because deception presupposes an understanding of false belief. However, their difficulties persisted in a follow-up study, when the element of deception was eliminated by removing the opponent. Children with autism also had difficulty in solving a detour box problem: A direct reach into the box for a marble visible inside it triggered a trap-door, and rendered the marble unobtainable. On the other hand, throwing a switch to one side of the box disabled the trap-door mechanism and permitted a direct reach. Children with autism had great difficulty in suppressing an immediate direct reach, by first throwing the switch.

The results for both of these tasks fit the hypothesis proposed earlier. Indicating an empty box is clearly anomalous whether an opponent is present or not, but it makes sense if one conjures up a hypothetical but nonexistent situation, for example by pretending that the empty box holds or dispenses chocolate, and then indicating that make-believe content of the empty box. If the earlier hypothesis is correct, children with autism would be incapable of this as-if strategy. Similarly, in the detour task, they also need to envisage a hypothetical interim situation, one that does not obtain at the outset of a trial but can be created, namely a disablement of the trap-door. With that hypothetical situation in mind as an interim goal, the strategy of first throwing the switch, and then reaching directly, makes sense. If that situation cannot be brought to mind and used as a guide for action, then more obvious responses—such as a direct reach that triggers the trap-door—will persist.

To conclude this section, we may step back to consider the optimal research strategy for understanding autism. The influential hypothesis, that children with this syndrome are deficient in their understanding of mind, has led to a systematic empirical search. We now know that they have special difficulties with pretend play, with false beliefs, and with joint attention. In addition, considerable theoretical effort has been devoted to the relations among these specific difficulties. Such concentration of effort has its costs, however. By focusing on tasks that are assumed to reflect various aspects of a theory of mind, the potential difficulties that children with autism might have outside of that domain have been neglected. The hypothesis that I have outlined predicts that such difficulties exist. For example, it predicts that children with autism will find it difficult to reason from contrary-to-fact premises. It predicts that they will also have special difficulties with past and future hypothetical utterances—a facility that emerges in normal children at around three to five years of age (Kuczaj & Daly, 1979). Whatever the fate of these specific predictions, the key point is that the success of the theory-of-mind hypothesis should not blinker us to its possible limits: We shall not detect those limits by testing autistic children exclusively on tasks that fall within its ambit.

THE BASIS OF PRETENDING: A SPECULATION

From a biological point of view, the capacity for pretence seems anomalous. Why does the human species have the ability to produce or understand a pretend action such as pouring or drinking make-believe liquid? A creature who devoted much time to gathering make-believe berries, or hunting make-believe animals, would seem destined for extinction. On the other hand, it is unlikely that pretending is a culturally induced activity. The stable timing of its onset in different cultures strongly suggests a neuropsychological timetable and a biological basis.

My speculation is that the production and comprehension of pretence is a by-product of our competence at producing and interpreting "serious" goal-directed action. A great deal of human action involves a sequence of motor movements aimed at a future goal. We lie down and close our eyes in order to go to sleep. We rub our hands with water and soap in order to wash them clean. We pour liquid into a container, and lift it to our mouth in order to drink it. The execution of such actions is regulated by planning and goal-seeking; the actions are not normally triggered by the availability or visibility of the props that might be incorporated into the action-sequence. For example, we lie down when we want to go to sleep, not when we notice a bed in the immediate vicinity. Washing and eating are not normally triggered—except in cases of pathology—by the mere availability of soap and water, or food.

Pretend activities typically mimic the motor gestures of goal-directed actions. We can pretend to sleep by lying down and closing our eyes. We can pretend to wash our hands by rubbing them together. Notice that we cannot pretend to engage in an action that is an end in itself. As Austin (1979) pointed out, we cannot pretend to bend our trunk because in the very act of miming the action, we successfully do it. Thus, pretending consists of reproducing the motor activities that occur en route to a goal without following through to the goal itself; an act of pretence should not attain the goal itself because then it ceases to be pretending.

This analysis suggests that pretend actions are organised in the same way as goal-directed actions without fully duplicating them. Genuine goal-directed action is set in motion by the activation of a goal; the various motor acts along the way are monitored for their success in bringing that goal closer. In the case of pretending, the same goal-directed sequence of actions is set in motion but attainment of the goal is set to one side. Since goal-attainment is not critical, the actor can perform the standard actions associated with goal-attainment but in the absence of the props and external way-stations that would enable and mark progress toward the goal. For example, pretend washing can be executed without soap and water and without any change in the state of the hands. Pretend drinking can be enacted with an empty teapot and an empty cup, or even with mouth movements and sounds.

Piaget's (1951) description of the emergence of pretending fits this analysis quite well. By the end of the first year, children have a repertoire of well-organised, goal-directed actions. In the course of the second year, they begin to re-enact those goal-directed actions, but in the absence of the props and context that would allow an attainment of the goal in question. For example, Piaget describes Jacqueline at 15 months re-enacting, outside of its normal context, a detailed motor sequence normally executed before going to sleep: she seizes a cloth that resembles her pillow with her right hand, sucks the thumb of that same hand, lies down on her side, and closes her eyes repeatedly; at 18 months, she re-enacts washing: she says "avon" (savon = soap), rubs her hands together, and pretends to wash them without any water (Piaget, 1951, observation 64a).

Recent observational studies of the earliest signs of pretend play also fit the proposal. Playful acts with some of the features of pretence can be seen toward the end of the first year. Thus, infants will proffer an object or food to an adult but teasingly withdraw it at the last moment (Reddy, 1991). Here, we see in embryonic form the same pattern that is extended and elaborated in the second year: The infant engages in a familiar, goal-directed sequence but deliberately stops short of the standard terminus for that sequence. Thus, the infant holds out an object or a spoonful of food, but omits to hand over the object or let the food be eaten. In the course of the second year, similar behaviours are produced but with the terminus suspended in an even more radical fashion. For example, Lucienne at 19 months pretends to drink out of a box and then holds it to the mouths of all who are present (Piaget, 1951, observation 65).

Lucienne's invitation to other people to engage in the same act of pretence as herself leads us to a consideration of pretence comprehension. My analysis of comprehension is complimentary to that just proposed for production. Specifically, because a great deal of human action involves motor sequences aimed at a goal, it is useful for children to gloss other people's actions in terms of the goals to which they are directed. To take a concrete example, when children watch another person lift food to his or her mouth, they can focus on the movement as such—the displacement of the hand and the transport of the food. Alternatively, they can interpret the action in terms of the goal that it is meant to attain, namely eating. Similarly, when children watch someone tilt a carton or teapot above an empty container, they can either focus on the movement of the hand and the container, or they can interpret the action in terms of the goal that it is aimed at, namely pouring liquid.

To the extent that children can interpret other people's movements as aimed at a goal, their ability to interpret pretend actions appropriately becomes explicable. The same motor movements are executed, sometimes in an exaggerated fashion. The task, therefore, is to gloss these movements in terms of their make-believe goal. In so far as "serious" actions involve motor movements that are executed ahead of goal-attainment (we lie down before we sleep; we tip a carton before liquid emerges), the difference between "serious" actions and pretend actions is less acute than it might first appear. In each case, the motor sequence needs to be interpreted by an observer in the absence of concurrent information about goal attainment, but with anticipation of the to-be-attained goal.

The implication of this analysis is that children's understanding of pretence by other people is a by-product of the interpretive activity that they bring to the understanding of ordinary, "serious" human action. In the case of pretend actions, as well as serious actions, they must invoke—in their imagination—the goals and potential outcomes of their partner's current movements. By characterising pretence as a by-product, I do not mean to under-estimate its potential. Gould and Vrba (1982) point out that evolution offers many examples of "exaptations:" Features that initially serve one function, but are then refined in the service of a new function that may be quite different. For example, feathers initially served as an insulation device before being selected for flight. You never know where a by-product might get you.

ACKNOWLEDGEMENTS

This chapter was partially written while the author was a Fellow at the Centre for Advanced Study in the Behavioural Sciences. I am grateful for financial support to the John D. and Catherine T. MacArthur Foundation (#890078) and to the ESRC, United Kingdom (R000 23 3543). I thank Angeline Lillard, Josef Perner, and members of the Stanford "Pretense and Imagination" seminar for helpful discussion.

REFERENCES

Austin, J.L. (1979). Pretending. In J.O. Urmson & G.J. Warnock (Eds.), *Philosophical papers*. Oxford: Oxford University Press.

Baron-Cohen, S. (1989). The autistic child's theory of mind: A case of specific developmental delay. *Journal of Child Psychology and Psychiatry, 30,* 285–297.

Baron-Cohen, S., Leslie, A.M., & Frith, U. (1985). Does the autistic child have a theory of mind? *Cognition, 21,* 37–46.

Gould, S.J., & Vrba, E.S. (1982). Exaptation—a missing term in the science of form. *Paleobiology, 8,* 4–15.

Harris, P.L. (1991). The work of the imagination. In A. Whiten (Ed.), *Natural theories of mind* (pp. 283–304). Oxford: Blackwell.

Harris, P.L. (1993). Pretending and planning. In S. Baron-Cohen, H. Tager-Flusberg, & D.J. Cohen (Eds.), *Understanding other minds: Perspective from autism* (pp. 228–246). Oxford: Oxford University Press.

Harris, P.L., & Kavanaugh, R.D. (1993). Young children's understanding of pretense. *Society for Research in Child Development Monographs.* Serial No. 231.

Harris, P.L., Kavanaugh, R.D., & Meredith, M. (in press). Young children's comprehension of pretend episodes: The integration of successive actions. *Child Development.*

Hughes, C., & Russell, J. (1993). Autistic children's difficulty with mental disengagement from an object: Its implications for theories of autism. *Developmental Psychology, 29,* 498–510.

Johnson, C.N., & Wellman, H.M. (1982). Children's developing conceptions of the mind and brain. *Child Development, 53*, 222–234.

Kavanaugh, R., & Harris, P.L. (1991). Comprehension and production of pretend language by two-year-olds. Paper presented at the annual meeting of the Developmental Section, British Psychological Society, Cambridge, September.

Kuczaj, S.A, II, & Daly, M.J. (1979). The development of hypothetical reference in the speech of young children. *Journal of Child Language, 6*, 563–579.

Leslie, A.M. (1987). Pretense and representation: The origins of "theory of mind". *Psychological Review, 94*, 412–426.

Lillard, A. (1993). Young children's conceptualization of pretense: Action or mental representational state? *Child Development, 64*, 372–386.

Ozonoff, S., Pennington, B.F., & Rogers, S.J. (1991). Executive function deficits in high-functioning autistic individuals: Relationship to theory of mind. *Journal of Child Psychology and Psychiatry, 32*, 1081–1105.

Perner, J. (1991). *Understanding the representational mind*. Cambridge, Mass.: Bradford/MIT.

Piaget, J. (1951). *Play, dreams and imitation*. London: Heinemann.

Reddy, V. (1991). Playing with other's expectations: Teasing and mucking about in the first year. In A. Whiten (Ed.), *Natural theories of mind*. Oxford: Blackwell.

Russell, J., Mauthner, N., Sharpe, S., & Tidswell, T. (1991). The "windows" task as a measure of strategic deception in preschoolers and autistic subjects. *British Journal of Development Psychology, 9*, 331–349.

Vygotsky, L.S. (1962). Play and its role in the mental development of the child. *Soviet Psychology, 12*, 62–76.

Walker-Andrews, A., & Harris, P.L. (1993). Young children's comprehension of pretend causal sequences. *Developmental Psychology, 29*, 915–921.

Walton, K.L. (1990). *Mimesis as make-believe*. Cambridge, Mass.: Harvard University Press.

Wing, L., & Gould, J. (1979). Severe impairments and associated abnormalities in children: Epidemiology and classification. *Journal of Autism and Developmental Disorders, 9*, 11–29.

12
Prelief: The Conceptual Origins of Belief and Pretence

Josef Perner, Sarah Baker, and Deborah Hutton
University of Sussex, Brighton, UK

INTRODUCTION

There is an old problem for theories about how children develop their understanding of the mind that has provided much inspiration for the field. The puzzle is, why children are able to understand pretence considerably earlier (in their second year) than false belief (in their fourth or fifth year), and this creates difficulties for some theorists for at least two reasons. One is that pretence and false belief are based on very similar mental representation abilities, which makes it difficult to explain why they should develop at such different ages (Forguson & Gopnik, 1988; Leslie, 1988; Perner, 1988; Wimmer, Hogrefe, & Sodian, 1988). The other reason is that pretence and belief are conceptually related in such a way that some theorists concluded that one could not pretend without understanding that one is not falsely believing something (e.g. Fodor, 1992).

We attempt to solve these problems through a careful analysis of how much children have to understand about their own activity so that their activity can be classified as a genuine act of pretence. This analysis shows that children must be acting according to a fictitious scenario (or acting-as-if a proposition P were true) and be aware that the scenario is not real (the proposition P is false). However, children need not be aware of the fact that their acting is a case of pretence rather than false belief. In fact, our claim is that young children cannot distinguish these two mental states—at least not in their defining characteristics—and view all acting-as-if (be it pretence or

261

mistaken action) as based on a compound state of pretence and belief, which we term "prelief."

To understand the difference between belief and pretence the child must not only represent the truth of a proposition but also that different people can attach different truth values to one and the same proposition. This representational ability also underlies children's mastery of the traditional false belief tasks.

After a more extensive discussion and sharpening of our conceptual analysis we present data showing that children do, indeed, not differentiate between belief and pretence until they solve the typical false belief task around the age of four or four-and-a-half years. We then discuss the implication of our empirical findings and conceptual analysis for some discrepant results on variations of the false belief paradigm, for related research on children's memory for their own beliefs, and on their ability to understand reflection as a prerequisite for pretence.

BELIEF AND PRETENCE

Sometime in the second year of life those playful activities emerge that go by many names, like "pretend play," "make-believe," "acting-as-if," "symbolic play," "imaginative play," or "fantasy play." Piaget (1945/1962, p. 96) gives an example of his daughter Jacqueline at one year and three months, amid laughter and saying "no-no," treating a piece of cloth like her pillow.

The different labels that have been given to this kind of play suggest different interpretations of the observed behaviour. Chief among them is Piaget's view that the pretend activity and object symbolise something else, e.g. Jacqueline, in this example, uses the piece of cloth to symbolise her pillow. The other main theoretical position is that children act-as-if, i.e. Jacqueline acts as if the cloth were her pillow. This interpretation of pretence is in line with Leslie's (1987) decoupling theory of pretence and with Harris's (1991) idea of pretence as an early sign of hypothetical reasoning. Perner (1991) emphasised that Piaget's "symbolic" view of pretence and the "acting-as-if" view are quite distinct theoretical positions (for a supportive view see Lillard, in press a).

Observing a child acting-as-if something were the case does, of course, not establish that the child is pretending. Figure 12.1 shows why. All meaningful action is action that makes sense in a certain situation, i.e. when a certain proposition P is true (e.g. putting one's head on an object and closing one's eyes usually makes sense only if the proposition "this object is a pillow" is true). Actions can be classified into those that are *reality adequate* (that makes sense in the world as it is, for short: *Acting-as-is*) and those that are *reality inadequate* and, therefore, make no sense but would make sense if reality were different: i.e. *acting-as-if* P were true.

However, as Fig. 12.1 shows, not every acting-as-if can count as pretence. There are also mistaken actions. For instance, Jacqueline might simply mistake the piece of cloth for her pillow. She would thus act-as-if the cloth were her pillow, yet this would not count as pretence but as a simple mistake. For her action to quality as pretend play Jacqueline must have some awareness of what she is doing.

What Jacqueline must be aware of so that her action can count as pretend play is critical. Obviously, she must mentally represent that she is acting according to P (the piece of cloth is her pillow) and realise that P is false (the cloth is not really a pillow) or else her behaviour could not be distinguished from a simple mistake. It is for this reason that Piaget emphasised in his report on Jacqueline's first pretence that her action was accompanied by laughter and a "no-no." For, without these signs of self-reflective awareness, we could not be sure whether Jacqueline had just misidentified the piece of cloth as a kind of pillow or whether she was pretending it was her pillow.

The critical point here is that we require Jacqueline to be aware only of P being false (first distinction in Fig. 12.1) but not that she be aware that she is pretending, as opposed to making a mistake. In other words, Jacqueline has, as it were, to say to herself: "Look, I am acting as if this object were my pillow, but it really isn't my pillow, it's just a piece of cloth," but she need *not* say to herself. "I am just pretending that this is a pillow, I don't really think it is a pillow." Hence, *pace* Fodor (1992), Jacqueline can be pretending without a concept of false belief.

Piaget's observation of Jacqueline's pretence is one of the early signs of pretend activity. But soon, at the end of the second year and into the third

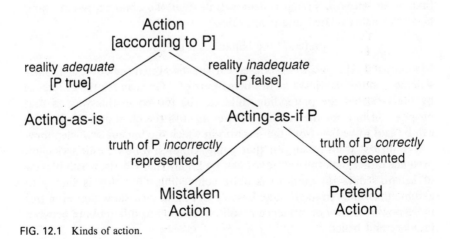

FIG. 12.1   Kinds of action.

year, this kind of activity starts to flourish and becomes an indicator of *counterfactual reasoning* ability that can be studied under experimental conditions (Harris, this volume). In the natural environment it blossoms particularly strongly in *joint pretence* with siblings (e.g. Dunn & Dale, 1984). In the fourth year children can keep track of different people pursuing different pretend scenarios, as a study by Freeman, Lewis, Smith, and Kelly (1992b) on *diversity of pretence* illustrates. When pretending that balls of clay are plums, which are made into plum cake, three-year-olds understand that if a friend entertains the proposition that the balls of clay are apples then the pretend case in the end will be an apple cake for the friend but a plum cake for themselves.

What all these intricate pretend abilities indicate is great sophistication in counterfactual reasoning. Children can keep track not only of a false proposition in relation to the real world but also of different false propositions. But even diversity of pretence does not require the child to distinguish pretend actions from mistakes, or pretence from false beliefs.

In fact there are two different ways in which the child might conceptualise pretence at this level of sophistication without being able to differentiate pretence from belief. One way is to understand the pretending person to be simply *part of* the pretend scenario, which means that the person is prone to act according to this scenario. There is no essential difference between the pretending person and the objects used for pretence. They all just act or are made to behave according to the assumed scenario. So when Rachel pretends that the balls of clay are plums then all that means is that Rachel is part of that "plum" scenario as much as the ball of clay is part of that scenario. Lillard (this volume) and Harris (this volume) favour such a view of early pretence.

Leslie (1987), in contrast, takes a different view. He suggests that even the first occurrences of pretence demonstrate that the child represents him/herself as being related to a proposition:

I pretend "the banana is a telephone."

In contrast to the position espoused earlier, the pretend relation in Leslie's scheme is more than just one of "being-part-of." One can see the difference by the fact that the pretending child can be related in this way to that proposition but not the banana. However, both the child and the banana can be said to be "part-of" the scenario in which the banana is a telephone.

We do not want to suggest that young children follow Leslie's view on pretence rather than the one advocated by Lillard and Harris, which in view of Lillard's data (in press b) is quite compelling. Our ploy is simply to assume that children might take Leslie's view, and then show that even this more powerful view on pretence is still not enough to differentiate between pretence and belief.

One thing to notice is that, if we follow Leslie's suggestion, then we need to conclude that the young children see pretence as a *mental* relation. This follows because the pretend relation relates the person to a nonexisting state of affairs. Since a relationship to a nonexisting state of affairs cannot be a physical relationship it must be a mental relationship by Brentano's (1874/ 1970) criterion of the mental. We called this mental attitude "prelief," because it is the undifferentiated state of pretence and belief. If pretence is the mental state that underlies pretend acting-as-if, and if false belief underlies mistaken acting-as-if, then *prelief* is the mental state that underlies acting-as-if without differentiation as to whether the acting-as-if is a case of pretence or a mistake.

So, to describe a person as *prelieving* a proposition P (which tends typically to be false) captures that the person has a certain attitude towards the proposition P that is similar to the attitude held when described as either pretending or (falsely) believing that P (in particular that it predisposes the person to act according to P). However, whatever makes for the difference between pretending and believing is not part of *prelieving*.

One way of explicating the difference between pretence and false belief is that they are not just relations to false propositions but also attitudes towards the truth value of that proposition. The difference is that a person who is pretending P does not take P subjectively as true, whereas a person who falsely believes P does exactly this. Perner (1988) has argued that it is the fact that different people may attach different truth values to the same proposition that makes the false belief task so difficult for young children. Let us see why.

FALSE BELIEF TASKS

In the paradigm used by Wimmer and Perner (1983), a story character Maxi puts some chocolate into a cupboard; in his absence the chocolate is unexpectedly transferred to another cupboard. The child's task is to predict where Maxi will look for his chocolate on his return. This ought to be an easy task, since all it requires is a prediction that Maxi will act-as-if the chocolate were still in the cupboard where he put it. Why is this prediction so difficult for two- and even three-year old children, who are so proficient in making such as-if predictions in the context of intricate pretend games? Their difficulty cannot be, as some theorists have put it (e.g. Flavell, 1988), that they cannot represent something (e.g. the location of the object) as being different from what it really is, since they can do that in their pretend games.

The difficulty in the false belief task is that there is no clue that the story character is to act-as-if. If anything, the opposite impression is conveyed, since Maxi *really* wants his chocolate. Why should he act-as-if it were still in its old place ("puzzle of false belief," Perner, 1988, p. 157)? A new understanding of why people act-as-if is required, namely an understanding of the critical difference between pretence and false belief. *Prelief* will not do any more.

This analysis of the false belief task also highlights the important methodological point that it assesses understanding of belief (as opposed to *prelief*) only because there is no suggestion in the test story that the character *prelieves* P (the chocolate is still in its old location) and therefore is predisposed to act-as-if P. This may not be so clear in some variations of the original false belief test, in which the protagonist is associated explicitly with the false proposition P.

For instance, Wellman and Bartsch (1988) read children short vignettes in which the protagonist's belief was explicitly stated (e.g. "Jane wants to find her kitten. Jane's kitten is in the playroom. Jane thinks her kitten is in the kitchen. Where will Jane look for her kitten?"). The impression that this is a test of false belief understanding stems from the use of the word "think," which we naturally read as Jane *believing* her kitten is in the kitchen. But correct responses do not guarantee that children make this interpretation and understand what a belief is. They might not have a concept of *belief*, but map the word "think" (as much as they would "pretend") onto their concept *prelief*.

Admittedly the story becomes somewhat ambiguous. On the one hand, if Jane *prelieves* that her kitten is in the kitchen, then she might act-as-if the kitten were there. On the other hand, Jane wants to (really) find the kitten, and so might look in the playroom, where it really is. So, from the young child's point of view the story provides no clear answer to the test question, and that is perhaps why most three- and even four-year-olds opt to say that Jane will look in the playroom. In other versions of that vignette, the kitten's real location is not specified and, not surprisingly, even most three-year-olds opt for the kitchen. Of course, we cannot be sure that that is the reason, but the point is that, because the vignettes explicitly relate Jane with the word "think" to the proposition "the kitten is in the kitchen," it becomes impossible to conclude that children who say that she will look for the kitten in the kitchen understand *belief* (rather than *prelief*)[1].

A similar interpretation problem is created by Bartsch and Wellman's (1989) explanation paradigm. Children were shown that the band-aids had been moved from the typical band-aid box to an unmarked location. In the

---

[1] The same argument applies to the *simplified false belief task* in a recent study by Sheffield, Sosa, and Hudson (1993), where children, who knew that both boxes were empty, were told that the protagonist thought his lost object was in one of the boxes indicated. When asked where the protagonist will look for his object, more than 80% of 2½- and 3½-year-old children answered with the indicated location.

(traditional) *prediction task* the story protagonist hurt himself and children had to predict in which box he would look for a band-aid. In the *explanation task* children were shown that the protagonist was looking for band-aids in the empty band-aid box and they were asked why the protagonist was looking there.

Some children gave a very sophisticated response: "He didn't know there weren't any bandaids in there" (Bartsch & Wellman, 1989, Table 2), but these children were few in number and certainly not more than those who could do the prediction task anyway. Some of the other children spontaneously used the word "think" (he thinks there are band-aids in there), but most said nothing. In that case they were asked directly "What does the protagonist think?" With this prompt a substantial additional number of children volunteered something like "band-aids in there."

What we want to highlight for present purposes is a methodological problem of interpreting these responses. What these responses certainly do show is that children at this age can infer from an evidently reality-inadequate action a hypothetical scenario (false proposition) under which the observed action would make sense (P = the *band-aids are in the band-aid box*). But one cannot conclude that children understand the protagonist's attitude towards this proposition as one of *belief* rather than *prelief*. Their use of the word "think" in their explanation is no guarantee for that, since they may map that word onto the concept of *prelief* rather than *belief*.

Children's ability to go beyond *prelief* was tested in our two experiments by asking them to distinguish between "think" and "pretend."

Experiment 1

We assessed children's ability to differentiate between pretence and belief using a variation of Bartsch and Wellman's explanation paradigm. For instance, a story character acted-as-if feeding the rabbit in the box when the box was actually empty. Children were explicitly asked whether the protagonist acted as he did because he was *pretending* that there was a rabbit in the box or because he *really thought* the rabbit was in the box. In one story, where the protagonist knew that the box was empty, the correct answer was that he had been pretending, whereas in the other story, where the protagonist had not witnessed the rabbit being removed, he mistakenly thought the rabbit was still in it. As a check on whether children were able to understand the forced-choice questions, they were also told a reality version, in which the rabbit was actually in the box and the protagonist knew it. It was thought that, since the protagonist's action was really adequate, they would reject the "pretend" option and opt for "really thought."

Children were also tested on two traditional false belief tasks, to see whether the ability to differentiate between belief and pretence in an explanation paradigm emerges earlier or at the same time as the ability to predict false belief based action.

Method

Subjects.   Thirty-four children from a nursery in Ewell, Surrey and from a nursery in Brighton, Sussex participated in this study. There were 3 age groups, with 13 children between ages 3 years and 2 months (3:2) and 3:4 (median age = 3:3, 5 boys and 8 girls), 13 children between 3:6 and 3:10 (median age = 3:8, 8 boys and 5 girls), and 8 children between 4:1 and 4:4 (median = 4:2, 4 boys and 4 girls).

Procedure and Materials.   The child was seated at a small table facing the experimenter in a small side room off the main nursery. Each child was told three stories: first the doll, then the rabbit, and lastly the curtain story. Each child had one story in its think-, another in its pretend-, and the third story in its reality-version. The assignment of version to story was randomised. At the end each child was tested on two false belief tests in random order. The experimenter enacted each story and the false belief tests on the small table with suitable accessories.

In the *think-version* of the doll-story, children were shown a naked cardboard cut-out doll with a penis, which they all recognised as a boy. The child was then told that the boy was going to be dressed up as a girl to play a trick on Jessica, another doll. The boy was then dressed in a hat and dress, at which point Jessica appeared. Jessica went up to the boy and said, "What a pretty doll! Let's call her Sally!" The child is then asked the TEST QUESTION: "Did Jessica really think it was a girl or did she just pretend?," to which the correct answer would be "really thought," since Jessica had no way of knowing that it was actually a boy.

In the *pretend-version* Jessica was present from the beginning, and thus saw the boy being dressed up as a girl. The correct answer to the test question would, therefore, be "just pretended," since Jessica was aware that the doll was a boy.

The *reality-version* was like the pretend-version except that the doll was actually a girl and the correct answer would be "really thought it was a girl" since it was a girl and Jessica knew it.

In the rabbit story, a doll fed the rabbit in a box either *thinking* the rabbit was in there when it had—unbeknownst to the doll—been removed, or *pretending* the rabbit was in there when the doll knew the rabbit had been removed, or *knowing* that the rabbit was indeed in there.

In the curtain story a doll, angry with her friend, was hitting the curtain either *thinking* her friend was behind it, or *pretending* the friend was behind it, or *knowing* that the friend was actually behind it.

In one of the two false belief tests the unexpected transfer paradigm was employed (Wimmer & Perner, 1983), in which a doll called Penny puts her favourite pencil in one of two boxes. While she is looking for some paper Susan comes in to play a trick on Penny and hides the pencil in the other box and then runs away. When Penny returns, looking for her pencil, subjects are asked: "Where will Penny look for her pencil?"

The other false belief task employed the deceptive container paradigm (Perner, Leekam, & Wimmer, 1987). Children were shown a well-known sweets container and asked what they thought was in that box, to which all children replied "sweets." The box was then opened and, instead of sweets, five coloured paper-clips emerged. The clips were put back into the box, the box closed, and the child was asked: "When I call your friend (name of next child waiting to be tested) in and ask him/her what is in this box, what will he/she say is in it?"

Results

Inspection of the data revealed no significant difference in proportion of correct responses between the three story themes (doll, rabbit, and curtain story).

The dark bars in Fig. 12.2 show the proportion of children at different ages who differentiated correctly between thinking and pretending in the belief- and in the pretence-condition. There is a clear developmental onset at the age of four years for this particular sample of children. Hardly any of even the older three-year-olds differentiated correctly, whereas practically all four-year-olds did so: Fisher's test: $P < 0.001$.

Performance on the two belief tasks, which require prediction of a reality-inadequate action, is, if anything, slightly better. The hatched bars in Fig. 12.1 give the proportion of children who answered test questions in both tasks correctly. The difference is not significant on this criterion (Binomial test: $n = 9$, $x = 3$, $P = 0.25$), but there is a statistically significant correlation between the belief tasks and the pretend-think tasks: $\Phi = 0.44$, $\chi^2 (1, n = 34) = 6.38$.

On the more lenient criterion of giving at least one correct answer in the two belief tasks, significantly more subjects understood belief than could differentiate between thinking and pretending (McNemar's $\chi^2 [1, n = 13] = 4.08$, $P < 0.05$). This result demonstrates that children do not find explanation easier that prediction of a mistaken act, if we require that their explanation should differentiate between mistakes and pretence.

One objection to this conclusion might be that our test paradigm for assessing the ability to differentiate between pretending and thinking is simply too demanding for the younger children. To test for this possibility we had introduced the reality condition. Table 12.1 gives a detailed analysis

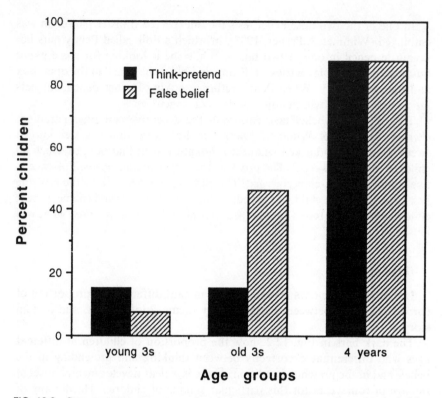

FIG. 12.2   Correct answers to test questions in belief and pretence stories and in both false belief tasks of Experiment 1.

of all response patterns across the three conditions. It shows that many three-year-olds also failed this condition by saying "pretended the rabbit was in the box," when in fact the person knew that it really was in the box (lower two panels in Table 12.1). However, there was also a substantial number of three- and all four-year-olds who rejected the think-pretend question as not applicable in the reality version of the stories. Their rejection indicates that these children were able to understand the think-pretend question. Even if we restrict our analysis of the ability to differentiate between thinking and pretending to these children, the developmental conclusions do not change but become even more pronounced, as shown in Fig. 12.3.

Again, there is a massive increase in correct differentiations between three and four years of age (Fisher's test: $P < 0.001$). Also these children are not better at explaining reality-inadequate actions than at predicting such action (if anything they are worse) as shown by their ability to make correct

TABLE 12.1
Frequency of Response Patterns

Story Version			Age Group			Main Patterns
Real	Pretend	Think	Young 3	Old 3	4 Years	
Correct in reality condition and correct on pretend-think						8
T	P	T	1	0	0	
r	P	T	0	0	7	
Correct in reality condition and incorrect on pretend-think						13
r	T	P	3	0	0	
r	P	P	3	5	1	
r	T	T	0	1	0	
Incorrect in reality condition and incorrect on pretend-think						10
P	T	P	1	0	0	
P	P	P	4	4	0	
P	T	T	0	1	0	
Incorrect in reality condition but correct on pretend-think						3
P	P	T	1	2	0	

"T" indicates a "think" and "P" a "pretend" response, and "r" indicates rejection of the test question.

predictions on both false belief tests. This difference is not significant (Binomial test: n = 5, x = 1, P = 0.19) but there is a significant correlation between belief tests and the think-pretend stories: Φ = 0.55 (Fisher's test: P < 0.05).

In Experiment 2 we replicated the developmental course of the ability to differentiate thinking from believing on a new sample of children and to obtain more direct evidence for young children's ability to differentiate between knowing and pretending.

Experiment 2

Instead of telling stories, children observed a real person in corresponding situations to the belief and the pretence story pair of Experiment 1, in which forced response choices between thinking and pretending were given. The reality condition was replaced by a knowledge and pretence pair of conditions, in which a forced choice between knowing and pretending was offered. The additional pretence condition was to control for the possibility

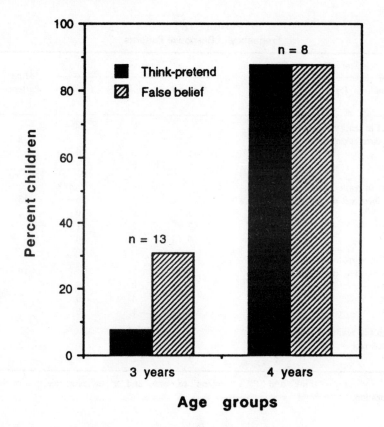

FIG. 12.3 Correct answers to test questions in belief and pretence stories and in both false belief tasks by children with correct responses in reality story.

that children display a mere preference for answering with "know" in the knowledge condition.

In sum, there were two pairs of conditions, one pair consisting of a belief and a pretence condition, both with a think-pretend question at the end, and the other pair consisting of a reality and a pretence condition, both with a know-pretence at the end.

Method

Subjects.   Thirty-six children from a nursery and reception class in a school in Brighton participated in this study. There were 12 "old 3-year-olds" (8 girls and 4 boys aged 3:4 to 4:0); 12 "young 4s" (8 girls and 4 boys aged 4:0 to 4:5); and 12 "old 4s" (6 girls and 6 boys between 4:6 and 5:2).

Procedure and Materials. The themes of the doll story and the rabbit story of Experiment 1 were adopted for this experiment. However, instead of a story, a brief interaction with another person other than the experimenter took place. For instance, in the *belief condition* of the rabbit scenario, the child and the other person were shown a box with a soft toy rabbit in it. The other person then was sent out to fetch a carrot for the rabbit. In the person's absence child and experimenter agreed to play a trick on the other person and let the rabbit go for a walk (and hide it in the experimenter's bag). The other person on his return brought a carrot with him, which he put into the hole in the top of the box, and said, "Here, little rabbit, is your carrot." It was then revealed to the person that the rabbit had run away, and the child was asked the TEST QUESTION: "Why did he put the carrot in the box, because he thought that the rabbit was really in there or because he was just pretending?"

In the *pretence condition*, the other person was still present when the rabbit "took a walk," and in the *knowledge condition* the rabbit remained in its box. The same three conditions were possible with the *doll scenario*. In the belief condition the other person did not see the boy doll being dressed up as a girl and therefore, when asked to name the doll, suggested Mary. In the pretence condition the other person was there when the doll was dressed and, therefore, knew that it was a boy dressed up as a girl but suggested Mary as a name to play along with the dressing-up game. In the knowledge condition the doll was a girl dressed as such.

Each child was seen on two different occasions. On one occasion the child was told the knowledge version of one scenario and the pretence version of the other scenario, and on the other occasion the pretence version of the first scenario and the belief version of the second scenarios. The assignment of version to scenario was counterbalanced.

On the occasion when the knowledge and pretence version were used, the test question for both conditions offered a choice between "know" and "pretend", e.g. "Did he put the carrot in the box because he really knew the rabbit was in there or because he was just pretending?" When the belief and the pretence version were used the test question offered the choice between "think" and "pretend."

Results

Inspection of the data showed no systematic effects of presentation order of the four tasks.

Figure 12.4 shows the percentage of children who gave correct "think"-"pretend" answers to the belief-pretence story pair, and correct "know"-"pretend" answers to the knowledge-pretence story pair. The dark bars show that, as in Experiment 1, there was a sharp developmental

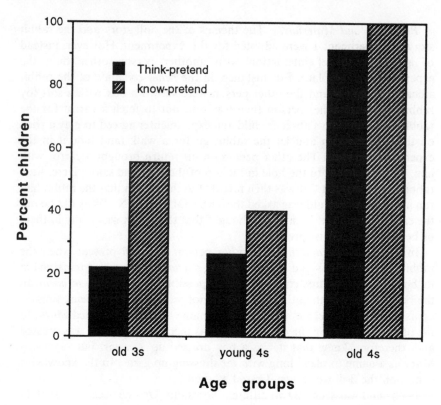

FIG. 12.4   Correct answers to test questions in each pair of tasks of Experiment 2.

change in children's ability to differentiate belief from pretence. The change occurred at around four-and-a-half years (Fisher's test: $P < 0.01$), which is about half a year later than for the sample tested in Experiment 1 (about four years).

The light bars show that the younger children also had noticeable problems with the know-pretend distinction. Nevertheless their difficulties were somewhat less serious than with belief and pretence. To test the statistical significance of this difference we assigned $+1$ for a correct response pattern (i.e. "know"-"pretend" for the knowledge-pretence task pair, and "think"-"pretend" for the belief-pretence pair), -1 for the opposite responses (i.e. "pretend"-"know", and "pretend"-"think") and 0 otherwise (i.e. "pretend"-"pretend," "think"-"think," and "know"-"know" responses). We then subtracted the score for the belief-pretence distinction from that for the knowledge-pretence distinction. There were 11 children with a positive difference score (indicating more correct responses on know-pretend than on think-pretend) and only 3 with a negative difference score (Sign test: x = 3, n = 14, P = 0.029).

To confirm the younger children's specific difficulty with the belief-pretence distinction we selected only those children who gave correct answers to the know-pretend questions. This leaves only 11 children in the younger 2 age groups. Of these 11 children only 3 gave correct answers to the think-pretend questions, which is significantly fewer than in the oldest group (Fisher's test: P < 0.01).

Discussion

Both our experiments demonstrated that children cannot differentiate between pretence and false belief in their explanation of reality-inadequate actions (acting-as-if P) before the age of four years, and more importantly, not before they can predict false belief based action as measured in the traditional false belief paradigm. This confirms the results from our conceptual analysis that pretending, which children can do long before their fourth birthday, does not require a clear differentiation between belief and pretence. It only requires a clear differentiation between reality-adequate (acting-as-is) and reality-inadequate action (acting-as-if P).

Our results also showed that children can distinguish between the mental states underlying acting-as-is (knowledge) and those underlying acting-as-if (pretence) before they can differentiate between belief and pretence. Unfortunately this difference did not come out as clearly as one would have wished because children had a strong preference to opt for "pretend" even in the knowledge condition (reality story).

We thought that this distinction ought to be easy for children because they can make the distinction between *know P* and *pretend P* on the basis of whether P is true or not, which as early pretence and rejection of false statements by the age of two years show (Antes, 1991; McNeil & McNeil, 1968; Pea, 1980). However, it seems that children may not be familiar with the factivity implicatures of verbs like "know," as a study by Moore, Bryant, and Furrow (1989) indicates. Only four-year-olds, but not three-year-olds, understood that when one person was described as *knowing* and another person as *thinking* where an object was, that one should look where the person described as knowing had said it was. The reason why our three-year-olds were not as hopeless as Moore et al.'s study suggests may be that the contrast between know and pretend is clearer than the one between know and think, since "think" can be used with true propositions, whereas "pretend" is used almost exclusively with false propositions.

However, in some ways our test material and scenarios were not optimally chosen for this purpose, since even the knowledge condition was based on pretence, i.e. it involved a pretend rabbit, not a real one, and it involved a boy doll, not a real boy. Hence the overall pretend character of the test situation may have elicited this strong tendency to answer in terms of "pretend" in all conditions. Nevertheless, the finding that this tendency was easier to overcome in the knowledge conditions (reality stories) than in the belief conditions shows that the differentiation between belief and pretence does pose a specific problem for children up to four years of age.

Our explanation for this difficulty is that young children cannot differentiate between belief and pretence but see every as-if action as based on an undifferentiated mental state of *prelief*[2]. We now discuss how other findings in the literature can be explained with this hypothesis.

ACCOUNTING FOR OTHER FINDINGS WITH PRELIEF

The *prelief* hypothesis can be used to make sense of an attempt by Moses and Flavell (1990) to replicate Bartsch and Wellman's findings. These authors did replicate a small effect of explanation (25% correct in "action" and 34% correct in "surprise" condition) over prediction (12% correct in "perception" condition) in their first experiment (their Table 1). Also, in their second experiment, they found that 3-year-olds gave 47% correct answers to what Mary thought was in the empty band-aid box, where she was looking for band-aids and was surprised that there weren't any. However, there was an additional surprising finding. When asked what Mary now thought, after she had discovered the box empty (and by then knew that the box didn't have band-aids), almost as many said Mary still thought band-aids were in it (41%) as before. This result does not make sense if the questions, "What did/does Mary think is in the box?" tap children's understanding of belief, because they should realise that, after opening the box, Mary would know what it contained. But these results do make sense on the assumption that the children interpret Mary's looking in the empty box (acting-as-if it contained band-aids) as a sign of *prelief* (Mary *prelieves* the box contains band-aids) and she *prelieves* this before acting (from our view: as a belief) and after acting (we would have to say: as a thought or pretence).

Another result that can be explained by recourse to *prelief* is one by Roth and Leslie (1991). In their second experiment children were shown a monkey, who watched with them an enacted story with two characters, Rina and Yosi. In the story, Rina hides Yosi's chocolate while he is looking for

---

[2] Our claim should be formulated more precisely as: Young children cannot differentiate between belief and pretence *on essential grounds*. This is to leave open the possibility that children can see some difference between belief and pretence on the basis of *characteristic features* (e.g. pretence is more playful, nonserious than belief) but not *defining features* (Keil, 1989). The defining features that children are missing are that believers evaluate the proposition according to which they act as true, regardless of the proposition's real truth value, whereas pretenders evaluate the proposition's truth value accurately, i.e. typically as false.

their lost ball. On Yosi's return Rina tells him that the dog had taken the chocolate and that it was now over in the dog's kennel. Then children were asked three belief questions, one about the monkey and one about each of Rina and Yosi. Surprisingly, almost all (85%) 3-year-olds (2:9 to 4:0) gave correct answers to the question about Yosi's false belief, namely that he thought the chocolate was in the kennel, and 89% also correctly answered that the observing monkey thought it was where Rina actually put it. However, when asked about where Rina thought it was, all three-year-olds who were asked this question (it was put to only half of all children) answered wrongly that she too thought it was in the kennel. None of the five-year-olds committed this error.

This pattern of results can be explained nicely by the assumption that three-year-olds, unable to understand belief, assimilate the story characters' beliefs to their concept of *prelief*. Rina's storing away of the chocolate in a box and then making up an interesting story about the dog having taken the chocolate to the kennel may have acted as a strong invitation to pretend play, i.e. acting as if the chocolate were in the kennel. The underlying mental state is conceived of as *prelief*, i.e. the involved actors *prelieve* the chocolate is in the kennel. Hence, when asked where Rina and Yosi "think" (*prelieve*) the chocolate is, children answer "in the kennel." The monkey, however, like themselves, is not part of the scene and hence not part of the joint pretence between Rina and Yosi. Consequently, he does not *prelieve* the chocolate is in the kennel but thinks (knows) that it is in the box[3].

---

[3] Recent findings by Sullivan and Winner (1993) can be explained along these lines. Children give more correct answers to false belief questions when embedded in a game of trickery. It is not inconceivable that children understand trickery as trying to get a person to act according to a false proposition. So when the typical content of a crayons box is conspiratorially removed and replaced by some red string then children may just get the idea that the tricked character will *prelieve* that the original content is still in the box. Winner and Sullivan (1993) may have further reinforced that impression by giving a warm-up demonstration that a person will say "cereal" when asked about the contents of a cereal box even when, as they revealed, it contains rubber rings.

Another relevant finding by Winner and Sullivan (1993) is that children give more correct answers than on the traditional false belief test to the question who Little Red Riding Hood thinks is in the bed when they know it is the wolf and when they can see that he is dressed up in Grandmother's bonnet. It is quite possible that dressing up as Grandmother is interpreted as pretending to be Grandmother and, unable to understand the real deceptive nature of the wolf's act, children may assume that Little Red Riding Hood is in on the pretend act and "prelieves" that Grandmother is in the bed. This possibility is underlined by Peskin's (1993) research on children's understanding of deceptive stories. Although they appreciate the pretend aspect of such stories, they do not understand their deceptive nature.

More generally speaking, it has always been clear that "deceptive appearance tasks" of various sorts (e.g. Hogrefe et al.'s, 1986, and Perner, et al.'s, 1987, deceptive container tasks) are prone to false positives. Results from these tasks are only impressive when children fail to give correct answers to belief questions because correct answers are so strongly suggested by the deceptive appearance. So, when children can be induced to give more "correct" answers in these tasks, it remains unclear whether these responses reflect understanding of belief or just increases the suspected tendency of false positives.

This analysis is further substantiated by the finding that children with autism do not interpret Rina's misinformation as an invitation to pretend, because these children are known to be reluctant to engage in pretend play unless explicitly asked to do so (Lewis & Boucher, 1988). Children with autism are also known to have difficulty understanding false belief (Baron-Cohen, Leslie, & Frith, 1985). So the vast majority of them, when asked about Rina's and Yosi's belief, answered in terms of where the chocolate really was: in the box.

MEMORY FOR OWN BELIEF OR PRELIEF?

One of the more interesting claims in children's theory of mind is that children's difficulty in understanding belief in other people also extends to their own beliefs. Gopnik and Astington (1988) and Wimmer and Hartl (1991) found that when children are duped into thinking there are sweets in a typical sweets box and then discover that it contains something else, they find it as difficult to remember what they had originally believed was in the box as they find it to predict what another, naive person will wrongly believe. Subsequently Gopnik and Slaughter (1991) showed that children find it easier to remember their previous pretence (and other mental states) than their previous false belief. More recently, however, Mitchell & Lacohée (1991) showed that three-year-olds' difficulty with remembering belief can be remedied by letting them post a picture of the sweets they expect to find in the box into a posting box.

In the previous paragraph I have intentionally used the typical, very natural, but potentially misleading way of using words like "belief," "pretence," etc. We need to remember that *believing* is a relationship between a person and a proposition, e.g.:

I ——————believed————> there were candies in the box.

Now, when asked what my belief is I might answer with the propositional content of my belief: "there are candies in this box." However, that proposition in itself is not a belief, it is only one by virtue of being held by me as my belief. The memory paradigm, however, ensures only that children can retrieve the content of their belief without any guarantee that they also understand that they were holding this content as a *belief* (rather than a *prelief*).

In other words, how the paradigm works is that children are given a cue in terms of the word "think" (When I first showed you the box, what did you *think* was in it?) to help them retrieve the propositional content of their belief at that time. From the failure to retrieve that content it is concluded that children do not understand belief (Gopnik & Astington, 1988; Wimmer & Hartl, 1991) and from retrieval success it is concluded that they do understand belief (Mitchell & Lacohée, 1991). But this raises a by now familiar problem, namely that from children's sensible reaction to the word "think" we cannot easily conclude that they understand it as referring to *belief* rather than *prelief*.

Perhaps an analogy will help drive home this point. Let's assume one of the authors, whose knowledge of equestrian locomotion is not very sophisticated, is asked about where Silver Arrow has galloped. He doesn't know what the difference between gallop, canter, or trot is, but he does know that all three are terms for how horses move. Roughly speaking we could say he has only a concept of *cantrollop*, onto which the three words "canter," "trot," and "gallop" map. Nevertheless, he can give the correct answer to the question about where Silver Arrow galloped because he has seen him gallop to the home stables. Yet from the correctness of this answer we cannot conclude that he has a clear concept of *gallop*, as opposed to *cantrollop*.

So young children do notice their wrong statement "there are sweets in the box" and realise that it was wrong when discovering the box's real contents. However, the children do not encode the wrong proposition as being the content of a *belief* (as we would) but as the content of *prelief*. When later cued by the word "think" in the question "What did you *think* was in the box?" the children can use that cue to retrieve the counterfactual proposition that they have encoded as a *prelief*.

How successful children are in retrieving the contents of their *prelief* depends on various factors that usually affect memory retrieval. Here are some ideas that go some way in explaining available data.

1. If the proposition to be recalled conforms to an actual past state of affairs then it is *easy* to recall.

That explains why children in Gopnik and Slaughter's study (see further details in Gopnik, Slaughter, & Meltzoff, this volume) had little problem with the control condition (there was an apple in the box, now there is a truck inside) and the level-2 perception task (the turtle was lying on its back, now it's standing on its feet).

2. If the proposition to be remembered is emphasised at the time it is being entertained (as a belief, pretence, etc.) it is easier to remember later.

This explains the posting effect by Mitchell and Lacohée, where it is emphasised that a picture of sweets is posted to mark the event that *there are sweets in the box*[4]. It can also explain the very intriguing result reported by

---

[4] One should note that Robinson and Goold (1992) intended to test this hypothesis by using a "deeper processing task" in which they emphasised the expected kind of object, e.g. crayons, by asking questions like, "do you have crayons at home?," etc. However, it is not clear whether this leads to deeper processing or whether it actively distracts the child from encoding the proposition "crayons in the box," because it does not strengthen that proposition but creates new, potentially interfering propositions all containing the concept crayons.

Freeman, et al. (1992a; see Freeman, this volume) that the posting effect (when, e.g., an eggbox is shown) is stronger if a *picture* of the expected content (e.g. picture of an egg) is posted than if a *sample* egg is posted. Our explanation of this effect works on the principle that the memory effect of posting is stronger the closer the posting highlights the exact proposition to be remembered. Since the picture can be understood as showing the very egg expected in the box, it is closely related to the exact proposition believed, "*this* egg is in the box." In contrast, children at the age tested know that the sample egg which they post cannot be the same individual egg they expect to be in the box. Hence the sample egg is a less direct memory cue: "an object of the same type is in the box."

3. If, at the time of encoding, the proposition to be remembered is explicitly associated with the future memory cue, then it is easier to recall.

This explains why the picture condition in Investigation 2 by Robinson and Goold (1992) produced an even stronger effect than the Mitchell and Lacohée posting procedure. In that condition, Robinson and Goold engaged children in the following discourse: "Look at this picture on this box. What is it? [Child: crayons]. So what do you think is inside the box? [Child: crayons]." As one can see, the proposition that there are crayons in the box is explicitly associated at encoding with the word "think," which is later used as a retrieval cue.

It is also part of the explanation of why, in Gopnik and Slaughter's study, the propositional content of pretence and images (where children were explicitly instructed to "pretend" or "think about") and of desires, intentions, and perceptions (where children were explicitly asked what they "wanted," "were going to do," or "saw,") were easier to remember than that of belief, where no such explicit association with the later retrieval cue was provided.

4. If the future memory cue is used in the instruction to construct the propositional content, then the more intentional effort the construction process takes the better the memory of the content.

This can explain why in Gopnik and Slaughter's study the pretend and the image condition tended to lead to better recall than desire, intention, and false belief.

So we see that from children's performance on these tasks we cannot conclude much directly about their understanding of mental concepts. If their memory for the content of a particular state is bad we cannot conclude that their concept of that state is at fault, because some encoding or retrieval problem may prevent them from recalling the content of that state. Conversely, successful retrieval of the propositional content of a state does not tell us whether they have acquired the concept of that state because they may, for instance, retrieve the content of their belief but on the basis of having encoded it as a *prelief* rather than *as a belief*.

If we want to be sure children remember the proposition *as* the content of a particular mental state, we need to test their ability to differentiate that state from closely related ones. In pilot work we have used the method described in Experiment 2 on children's memory for the content of their own false beliefs and pretence and asked them to differentiate between belief and pretence. First impressions indicate that children find it at least as difficult to differentiate their own false beliefs from their pretence as they found it to differentiate between these states in another person in Experiments 1 and 2.

UNDERSTANDING SELF-REFLECTION AS A PREREQUISITE FOR PRETENCE

In the Introduction to this chapter we have been discussing the fact that, in order to be able to classify children's activities as being of a certain kind, it is often necessary for the children to have certain mental representations, which at some point amount to metacognitive insights into their own minds.

So, for instance, in order to describe children as acting according to a proposition P (top level of Fig. 12.1) it is necessary that they represent P. Otherwise it would not be an action but random behaviour. In contrast, the distinction between acting-as-is and acting-as-if P can be made if the observer represents whether P is true or false (Fig. 12.1, second level). However, to describe children who are acting-as-if P as "pretending that P," it is necessary that they themselves represent P as false and see themselves as acting according to P. As mentioned earlier, there are two ways in which children can represent themselves as acting according to a false proposition. They can understand it in terms of being part of the pretend scenario, in which case they are not necessarily different from the objects that are also part of this scenario (Harris, this volume; Lillard, this volume). Alternatively they can represent themselves as relating as pretenders to the false proposition, as Leslie (1987) suggested. In this case, they see themselves as relating to a nonexistent state of affairs, which by Brentano's (1874/1970) criteria cannot be a physical relationship and thus counts as a mental state. For lack of a better concept we named this mental state *prelief*, to indicate that it is a state that has the defining features shared by pretence and belief but lacks the defining features that differentiate belief from pretence. This insight on the child's part provides the objective basis for deciding whether children are pretending or making a mistake (Fig. 12.1, third level), but the children themselves need not be able to interpret their own activities in that light.

In order for children to understand their own activity as pretence (rather than merely as acting-as-if based on prelief) they have to represent their own attitude towards the truth of P, i.e. that they hold P as false and do not mistake it for true. Only at this level can they interpret their own as well as other people's acting-as-if as a case of genuine pretence. Only at this level does an understanding of pretence imply an understanding of belief, as Fodor (1992, p. 290) pointed out: "Pretending involves acting as though one believes that P is true when, in fact, one believes that P is false. It would thus seem to be impossible for a creature that lacks the concept of a belief *being* false."

However, *pace* Fodor, from the earlier inability to differentiate belief from pretence (at level 3 of Fig. 12.1) it does not follow that children would be incapable of differentiating acting-as-if from acting-as-is (Fig. 12.1, level 2) and therefore mistake what they pretend there is with what there really is, as Fodor (1992, p. 290, footnote 9) wrongly claims. "Presumably even young children know the difference between acting as if P *because one is pretending that* P and acting as if P *because one believes that* P. Only a demented creature would *really* try to make a phone call with a banana." This does not follow, because even without differentiating belief from pretence children still can differentiate using the banana as-if it were a telephone (because they know that it is not a telephone) from making a *real* phone call with a telephone (because they know that it is a real telephone). Only if they were incapable of this distinction would children who use a banana as a telephone be as demented as Fodor suggests.

What underlies the ability to differentiate pretence from false beliefs is the understanding that people do not just relate to propositions (prelief) but also to the truth values of propositions. If they attach the correct truth value to a false proposition then it is pretence; if they attach the wrong value of "true" to a false proposition then it is belief. Our experimental results suggest that this ability emerges at around four years of age.

Children's insight into the nature of pretence, however, does not stop here. Lillard (in press b, Experiment 3; see this volume) investigated children's appreciation that a person has to know what he is pretending for it to be a genuine case of pretence. She showed children the troll Moe and how he was hopping around like a rabbit, but that he doesn't know that rabbits hop like this. They were then asked whether Moe is pretending that he is a rabbit. This question was surprisingly difficult. Only 37% of 4- and 68% of 5-year-olds understood that if Moe doesn't know that rabbits hop then his hopping like a rabbit (acting as if he were a rabbit) cannot count as pretending to be a rabbit. Lillard's other two experiments, where Moe's ignorance was stated less explicitly (only in terms of Moe not knowing what a rabbit is) proved even more difficult: Less than 40% of 5-year-olds answered correctly.

These demonstrations of children's failure to understand that pretending to hop like a rabbit requires knowledge of the fact that rabbits hop fits naturally with the view that children's understanding of pretence is nonmental, as Lillard (this volume) and Harris (this volume) suggest. That is, children understand the pretender purely as acting according to the counterfactual situation of which he is a part.

Although this interpretation fits naturally, the data are still compatible with a minimally mentalistic view (along the lines of Leslie's, 1987, suggestion) that children represent pretence as a propositional attitude to a false proposition (nonexisting situation). Since a relationship to something nonexistent cannot be a physical relationship, it must be mental, unless one allows for other nonphysical relations beside mental ones.

Yet clearly these children are missing something about the mental nature of pretence, namely the fact that to be mentally related to a proposition one needs to have the conceptual means to express this proposition. It is not just pretence that requires this understanding but any other mental relation. One cannot *hate, hope, think, want,* etc. that your friend will hop like a rabbit at tonight's party without knowing what a rabbit is and what rabbits hop.

Perner (1991) suggested that this feature of mentality is grasped through construing mental states as representations and that the understanding of false belief is a reflection of such a representational view of the mind. Comparing our results with those of Lillard it seems that with the ability to distinguish pretence and false belief at about four or four-and-a-half years a representational view is at best starting and not yet firmly in place. It cannot be firmly in place because, as Lillard's data suggest, the understanding that a person who pretends to hop like a rabbit must represent (know) that rabbits hop is not formed until about five or even six years. One likely reason, as Lillard mentions, for why the representational view of mind takes a hold of pretence so late is that pretence has been dealt with so proficiently for some years on the basis of a nonmental view. So it may take some time for the newly emerging representational view to override this well-established nonmental view of pretend activities.

SUMMARY

We have argued that conceptual development of mental state terms like pretence and belief should be viewed as an unfolding of increasingly refined reflections. Children's reflection on the truth value of the proposition according to which they act establishes (for the observer) whether they engage in pretence or commit a mistake. Early pretence and explicit rejection of false statements shows that this ability is in place in the second year of life.

In order to pretend, children need not reflect on their attitude towards truth values, hence they need not to be able to classify action according to pretend or mistaken action. Their concepts of pretence and false belief remain undifferentiated within a more primitive concept of *prelief*[5]. In two experiments we demonstrated that the ability to differentiate between belief and pretence emerges at around four years and, in any case, it does not emerge before children can understand false belief in the traditional false belief tasks.

Our conceptual analysis and data thus solve the puzzle of why children can be such proficient pretend actors long before they can demonstrate an understanding of belief. We also used the assumption that young children's understanding of acting-as-if is based on an undifferentiated concept of *prelief* to explain children's apparently better performance on certain variations of the original false belief tasks and their concomitant problems with control questions in these tasks. Furthermore, our analysis highlighted interpretational problems in the important experimental paradigm that relies on children's memory for the content of their own mental states and suggests that a conceptual rethinking of these tasks is needed.

Finally we pointed out that the ability to distinguish pretence from belief is not the end of development in this respect. The links between pretence and other mental states still need to be worked out, like the understanding that pretending to act like a particular animal presupposes that the pretending person has to know that animal and that it engages in these actions.

ACKNOWLEDGEMENTS

The experimental evidence reported as Experiment 1 was part of Sarah Baker's third year BSc project (1990). These and other data were presented as a poster by Deborah Hutton at the Annual Meeting of the Developmental Section of the British Psychological Society at Cambridge University in September 1991. Collection of data was financially supported by grant G9026071N from the Medical Research Council.

REFERENCES

Antes, G. (1989). *Zur Entwicklung der Konstatierenden Negation in der Kindersprache.* Unpublished Doctoral dissertation, Institute of Psychology, University of Salzburg.
Baron-Cohen, S., Leslie, A.M., & Frith, U. (1985). Does the autistic child have a "theory of mind"? *Cognition, 21,* 37–46.

---

[5] On Henry Wellman's request we point out that understanding of the mind in terms of *prelief* is within the abilities of, as Perner (1991) referred to them, young *situation theorists.* Prelief can be understood as a relation to real or nonreal situations (true or false propositions). It is the distinction between belief and pretence that goes beyond this level of competence because it requires understanding that the people are not just related to situations (propositions) but can relate differently to a given situation (proposition) in terms of how this situation is evaluated as to its reality status (truth). Perner's suggestion is that this insight comes through understanding belief as a relation to a mental representation that can represent or misrepresent situations (propositions). A more detailed discussion of these issues can be found in Perner (1993).

Bartsch, K., & Wellman, H.M. (1989). Young children's attribution of action to beliefs and desires. *Child Development, 60,* 946–964.

Brentano, F. von (1874/1970). *Psychology from an empirical standpoint.* In O. Kraus (Ed.) (Translated by L.L. McAllister.). London: Routledge & Kegan Paul.

Dunn, J., & Dale, N. (1984). I a daddy: two-year-olds' collaboration in joint pretend with sibling and with mother. In I. Bretherton (Ed.), *Symbolic play,* (pp. 131–158). New York: Academic Press.

Flavell, J.H. (1988). The development of children's knowledge about the mind: From cognitive connections to mental representations. In J.W. Astington, P.L. Harris, & D.R. Olson (Eds.), *Developing theories of mind* (pp. 244–267). New York: Cambridge University Press.

Fodor, J.A. (1992). A theory of the child's theory of mind. *Cognition, 44,* 283–296.

Forguson, L., & Gopnik, A. (1988). The ontogeny of common sense. In J.W. Astington, P.L. Harris, & D.R. Olson (Eds.), *Developing theories of mind* (pp. 226–243). New York: Cambridge University Press.

Freeman, N.H., Lacohée, H., Lewis, C.N., & Coulton, S. (1992a). *A cue for representation apparently lost in childhood.* Unpublished manuscript, Department of Psychology, University of Bristol.

Freeman, N.H., Lewis, C.N., Smith, C., & Kelly, S. (1992b). *Facts and fictions in preschoolers' theory of mind: "Wrong pretence" and false belief.* Unpublished manuscript, Department of Psychology, University of Bristol.

Gopnik, A., & Astington, J.W. (1988). Children's understanding of representational change and its relation to the understanding of false belief and the appearance-reality distinction. *Child Development, 59,* 26–37.

Gopnik, A., & Slaughter, V. (1991). Young children's understanding of changes in their mental states. *Child Development, 62,* 98–110.

Harris, P.L. (1991). The work of the imagination. In A. Whiten (Ed.), *Natural theories of mind: The evolution, development and simulation of everyday mindreading* (ch. 19). Oxford: Basil Blackwell.

Hogrefe, G.J., Wimmer, H., & Perner, J. (1986). Ignorance versus false belief: A developmental lag in attribution of epistemic states. *Child Development, 57,* 567–582.

Keil, F.C. (1989). *Concepts, kinds, and cognitive development.* Cambridge, Mass.: MIT Press.

Leslie, A.M. (1987). Pretense and representation: The origins of "theory of mind." *Psychological Review, 94,* 412–426.

Leslie, A.M. (1988). Some implications of pretense for mechanisms underlying the child's theory of mind. In J.W. Astington, P.L. Harris, & D.R. Olson (Eds.), *Developing theories of mind* (pp. 19–46). New York: Cambridge University Press.

Lewis, V., & Boucher, J. (1988). Spontaneous, instructed and elicited play in relatively able autistic children. *British Journal of Developmental Psychology, 6,* 325–339.

Lillard, A.S. (in press a). Pretend play skills and the child's theory of mind. *Child Development.*

Lillard, A.S. (in press b). Young children's conceptualization of pretense: Action or mental representational state? *Child Development.*

McNeil, D., & McNeill, N. (1968). What does a child mean when he says "no"? In E.M. Zale (Ed.), *Language and language behavior.* New York: Appleton Century Crofts.

Mitchell, P., & Lacohée, H. (1991). Children's early understanding of false belief. *Cognition, 39,* 107–127.

Moore, C., Bryant, D., & Furrow, D. (1989). Mental terms and the development of certainty. *Child Development, 60,* 167–171.

Moses, L.J., & Flavell, J.H. (1990). Inferring false beliefs from actions and reactions. *Child Development, 61,* 929–945.

Pea, R.D. (1990). The development of negation in early child language. In D.R. Olson (Ed.), *The social foundations of language and thought: Essays in honour of Jerome S. Bruner* (pp. 156–186). New York: W.W. Norton.

Perner, J. (1988). Developing semantics for theories of mind: From propositional attitudes to mental representation. In J.W. Astington, P.L. Harris, & D.R. Olson (Eds.), *Developing theories of mind* (pp. 141–172). New York: Cambridge University Press.

Perner, J. (1991). *Understanding the representational mind.* Cambridge, Mass.: MIT Press/Bradford Books.

Perner, J. (1993). Fodor's and the child's theory of mind. Unpublished manuscript, Laboratory of Experimental Psychology, University of Sussex.

Perner, J., Leekam, S.R., & Wimmer, H. (1987). Three-year olds' difficulty with false belief: The case for a conceptual deficit. *British Journal of Developmental Psychology, 5,* 125–137.

Peskin, J. (1993, March). *When the purpose of pretence is deception: Preschoolers' understanding of intentional states.* Poster presented at the 60th Anniversary Meeting of the Society for Research in Child Development, New Orleans, Louisiana.

Piaget, J. (1945/1962). *Play, dreams, and imitation in childhood.* New York: W.W. Norton.

Robinson, E.J., & Goold, J. (1992). Young children's ability to report their own superseded beliefs: Facilitation via physical embodiment. Unpublished paper, School of Psychology, University of Birmingham.

Roth, D., & Leslie, A.M. (1991). The recognition of attitude conveyed by utterance: A study of preschool and autistic children. *British Journal of Developmental Psychology, 9,* 315–330.

Sheffield, E.G., Sosa, B.B., & Hudson, J.A. (1993). *Narrative complexity and two- and three-year-olds' understanding of false belief.* Paper presented at the 60th Anniversary Meeting of the Society for Research in Child Development, March, New Orleans, Louisiana.

Sullivan, K., & Winner, E. (1993). *Three-year-olds' understanding of mental states: The influence of trickery.* Unpublished manuscript. Department of Psychology, University of Massachusetts, Boston.

Wellman, H.M., and Bartsch, K. (1988). Young children's reasoning about beliefs. *Cognition, 30,* 239–277.

Wimmer, H., & Hartl, M. (1991). The Cartesian view and theory view of mind: Developmental evidence from understanding false belief in self and other. *British Journal of Developmental Psychology, 9,* 125–138.

Wimmer, H., Hogrefe, G.-J., & Perner, J. (1988). Children's understanding of informational access as source of knowledge. *Child Development, 59,* 386–396.

Wimmer, H., Hogrefe, G.-J., & Sodian, B. (1988). A second stage in children's conception of mental life: Understanding sources of information. In J.W. Astington, P.L. Harris, & D.R. Olson (Eds.), *Developing theories of mind* (pp. 173–192). New York: Cambridge University Press.

Wimmer, H., & Perner, J. (1983). Beliefs about beliefs: Representation and constraining function of wrong beliefs in young children's understanding of deception. *Cognition, 13,* 103–128.

Winner, E., & Sullivan, K. (1993). *Deception as a zone of proximal development for false belief understanding.* Poster presented at the 60th Anniversary Meeting of the Society for Research in Child Development, March, New Orleans, Louisiana.

13 Commentary: Triangulating Pretence and Belief

Paul L. Harris
Oxford University, UK

Angeline Lillard
University of San Francisco, USA

Josef Perner
University of Sussex, Brighton, UK

COMMENTARY

In this commentary, we identify three issues that arise in the comparison of pretence and belief, drawing attention to the ways that our positions diverge or converge.

Understanding the Relation Between the Pretender and the Make-believe Situation

A child who watches a play partner will see that partner engage in various "peculiar" actions and comments. The partner will "drink" from an empty cup, "feed" a lifeless doll, and call a piece of play-doh "cake." There are many different ways that the child might construe the relation between the partner and the make-believe situation that is implied by the partner's actions. Here, we consider four important possibilities.

1. The child might construe the partner as producing familiar and recognisable actions (e.g. hopping like a kangaroo; lifting a cup to the lips) or as orchestrating such actions via a prop (e.g. a doll is made to "eat" or a toy horse is made to "gallop") even though these actions fall short of the criteria for real or serious action: The actions (contrary to normal practice) involve substitute or imaginary entities or they are not carried through to the usual goal. These entities or goals would be imagined by the child without any judgement about the mental state of the partner. For example,

the child might appropriately imagine the partner as a kangaroo, or imagine tea inside the empty cup lifted by the partner, or imagine the doll eating or the toy horse galloping. Despite this appropriate imaginative activity on the part of the child, he or she could operate with no conception of the partner's mental state. This is particularly clear when the partner orchestrates an action via a prop: The child can simply focus on the action that is engaged in by the doll or toy (e.g. pretend feeding or galloping) and ignore the fact that the partner is directing that pretence, and has ultimate control over it. In short, according to this account, the child focuses on the actions that occur within the pretend situation, and only takes account of the partner insofar as he or she is part of the pretend situation. The child neglects the partner's orchestration of the make-believe scenario and the partner's mental relation toward that scenario.

2. The child might do all that is implied by (1) but also construe the partner as adopting a mental relation to the make-believe situation, as implied by Leslie's (1987) analysis of early pretence. For instance, a construal of pretence as a mental relation might be realising that the partner has control over the make-believe situation, and is deliberately creating it by his or her pretend actions. Since the partner's control over the pretend scenario is a relation with something that is not real, it is necessarily a mental relation. Thus, the child who understands this control relation must construe a pretending partner as engaged in a mental relation.

3. A still more extensive analysis of the partner would involve some conception of the representational process that underpins the mental attitude of pretence. For example, when a partner pretends to drink tea from a cup, the partner must mentally represent the pretend state of affairs ("cup contains tea"), which does not, of course, correspond to the actual state of affairs (the cup is actually empty). When watching a play partner "drink" pretend tea, a child might postulate that such a representational process is occurring in the mind of the partner and use it to make sense of the partner's mental state and resulting actions and comments.

4. Finally, irrespective of how the child conceives of the mental attitude of pretence (i.e. whether as described in (1), (2), or (3), the child may or may not have some conception of the relation between pretence and other mental states such as knowing and thinking. For example, the child may realise that if a partner is pretending that X is the case, then the partner must also (a) know something about X, and (b) think that X is true of the make-believe scenario.

In assessing the relative merits of (1), (2), and (3), none of us wish to argue for option (3). There is, at present, no evidence suggesting that two-year-olds understand the representational processes that underlie pretence. We agree, then, that the two-year-old probably adopts option (1) or (2). One of us (Harris) emphasises option (1) as a description of two-year-olds. Consistent with this parsimonious position is the fact that overt activity almost invariably accompanies the pretend play of toddlers. In addition, Lillard presents experiments in which children watch a troll and are offered two conflicting cues for interpreting the troll's behaviour: an action cue consistent with pretence (e.g. the troll hops like a rabbit) and a mental cue inconsistent with pretence (e.g. the troll is not thinking about being a rabbit). Most four-year-olds and many five-year-olds are guided by the action rather than the mental cue.

Perner also favours option (1), at least for two-year-olds, and possibly for three-year-olds. He emphasises, however, that even if we were to credit the three-year-olds with option (2), this would still not enable children of this age to differentiate pretence from false belief.

Lillard favours option (1) for two-year-olds. She also thinks that, by three years of age, children are beginning to work out the relations between pretence and other mental states (option [4]). Further, because she construes pretence as being composed of other mental processes rather than as simply related to them, Lillard also believes that option (2) characterises three-year-olds. However, she claims that until age five, despite having some inkling about these relations, children will bypass them completely in the face of an action that runs counter to an alleged mental state of thinking or knowing. In other words, although they see pretence as involving both actions and mental relations (of knowing or thinking), until age five they think that action is the more definitive component.

Freeman, Lewis, Smith, and Kelly (1992) have carried out a test that is pertinent to option (4). Both the child and Teddy pretend that there is a puppy in the box. Teddy leaves and the experimenter and the child then pretend that the puppy is hiding in another box. Most children under four years of age wrongly assume that Teddy will appreciate the new pretend situation on his return, whereas most children older than four years realise that he will not. Not surprisingly, the emergence of this insight is linked to success on a false belief task. Similar results have been obtained in ongoing research by Astington, Olson, Peskin, and Zelazo (personal communication). These findings leave open the possibility that children might have some understanding of the relation between pretence and other mental states when no false belief is involved.

Hickling, Wellman, and Gottfried (1993) are currently undertaking related experiments. Suppose a child and a partner are both pretending that a glass contains chocolate milk. The partner leaves the room, and the child then "empties" all the milk out of the glass. The partner then returns and the child is asked what the partner "thinks" is in the glass. A correct answer ("chocolate milk") will show that the child realises that when a partner engages in a distinctive pretence, that will affect his or her thoughts—it is not just a question of engaging in pretend actions. Thus, a person who is pretending that there is milk in a glass thinks that it is true that there is (make-believe) milk in the glass—and may continue to do so even when another partner pretends otherwise. Hickling et al. (1993) claim—notwithstanding the results of Freeman et al. (1992) and Astington et al. (1993)—that experiments with three-year-olds reveal that they do understand this aspect of pretence.

The Relation Between Understanding Pretence and Understanding False Belief

In many ways, acts of pretence and acts based on a false belief are quite similar. To borrow an example from Perner's chapter, someone might poke a carrot into an empty box because they mistakenly believe that a rabbit is in the box or because they are pretending that a rabbit is in the box. How and when do children go beyond the surface form of the action of poking the carrot (which may be equivalent in the two cases) and realise that pretend actions and actions based on false beliefs are different? The chapters focus on two different options.

1. The distinction between pretence and false belief calls for an appreciation of the differential commitment of the false believer and the pretend player. That differential commitment is understood through a more accurate simulation of the false believer (who mistakes the counterfactual situation for reality) as distinct from the pretend partner (who does not).

2. As in (1), it is assumed that the distinction between pretence and false belief calls for an appreciation of the different commitments that the false believer and the pretend player adopt to the nonveridical world within which they act. However, an understanding of that difference in commitment is attained not through a simulation process but by understanding that people can have different views on the truth value of a given proposition, in particular in the case of false belief, where they can construe a false proposition as being true.

Harris opts for (1). Both Harris and Perner acknowledge that children need to distinguish between the mental stance of the false believer, and the mental stance of the pretend partner, notwithstanding the surface similarity in their potential actions, and they deny that two-year-olds make that distinction in terms of the mental processes involved. However, unlike Perner, Harris does not claim that the eventual differentiation between pretence and false belief is based on an insight into the representational process. Instead, he emphasises the emergence of a new-found capacity for simulation. To engage in shared pretence, it is enough for the child to reproduce in his or her imagination the make-believe scenario entertained by a play partner. To understand a false believer, on the other hand, the child must, in addition, simulate the commitment that the false believer has to the counterfactual situation (i.e. mistaking it for the real situation), despite the child's knowledge that the counterfactual situation does not correspond to reality.

Perner is sceptical of the proposal that understanding of such a commitment on the part of the false believer can emerge through simulation. This claim (Gordon, 1986) is controversial even among simulation theorists (Goldman, 1989; Heal, 1993). Instead, Perner opts for (2), arguing that the distinction between pretence and false belief is understood at approximately four years of age, when the child develops the necessary conceptual means to distinguish between the actual truth value of a proposition and the truth value assigned to it by another person. He suggests that prior to that time children have no basis for understanding the essential difference between pretence and false belief. Rather, when they observe someone poking a carrot into an empty box, they attribute to that person an undifferentiated stance of "prelief." Specifically, they conclude that the person "prelieves" that there is a rabbit in the box. By four years a major conceptual advance has occurred: the child can (a) conceive of a mental representation as representation, and hence (b) distinguish what a mental state represents (its referent, e.g. the real state of affairs) and how it represents it as being (its sense). As a consequence, the child can (c) conceive of a false belief as a misrepresentation of reality (e.g. representing the real state of affairs as being different than it really is) and pretence as a correct representation of a nonreal state of affairs (e.g. representing the pretend scenario as is).

Harris and Perner agree, nonetheless, that a two-year-old might detect some characteristic (but nondefining) differences between a pretend action and an action based on false belief. Consider, once more, the carrot-poking incident. Someone who wrongly believes that there is a rabbit in the box, and is genuinely attempting to feed the rabbit, is likely to discover that the rabbit is missing and the carrot uneaten. They may comment on their mistake ("Where's the rabbit gone?") and then search for the rabbit. By contrast, someone who is pretending to feed a rabbit is likely to do so in the context of a game of pretend—they may embellish their pretend action by imitating the nibbling of a rabbit, and they will not be disconcerted by the absence of the rabbit or the fact that the carrot is uneaten. A child can therefore watch someone poking a carrot in the context of a longer action sequence: One consequence marks the carrot poking as unsuccessfully aimed at a goal in the real world (giving food to the real rabbit), and the other marks the action as successfully aimed at a goal in the make-believe world (giving food to the make-believe rabbit). Comments such as "Where is the rabbit?" do not fit the typical scenario of pretending to feed a rabbit in a box. Thus, children may be able to classify one correctly as based on "belief" and the other as based on "pretence," but not understand the defining difference between these two states. They distinguish these two forms of action simply in terms of whether their goals (feeding a real rabbit in the case of the false believer versus feeding a make-believe rabbit in the case of the pretend partner) are successfully realised. At present, it is an open question whether young children do make such a distinction.

Once the Child Understands False Belief, Does this Immediately Lead to an Understanding of Pretence in Representational Terms?

The chapters highlight two distinct options concerning this issue.

1. The distinction between false belief and pretence marks an important watershed. Once the representational process is understood it can be applied to each stance, clarifying the difference between them. This process of clarification may not be immediate—it may take months or even years—but it will involve an analysis of the ramifications of a representational theory of mind, as concurrently applied to both pretence and belief. Thus, according to this option, an understanding of the representational basis for false belief and pretence would proceed in tandem.

2. Although it is possible to argue that an understanding of representation is critical to an understanding of false belief, that insight may not have any repercussions for an understanding of pretence. Even if pretence is eventually understood in representational terms, that understanding may be acquired more slowly than in the case of belief.

Perner considers option (1) but ultimately favours (2). He emphasises that the child must eventually grasp that a pretend partner does not regard their current reality-inadequate representation as a veridical description. This insight flows from a wider insight into the nature of mental representation, particularly the distinction between the sense of a representation and its referent. However, he notes that children might not immediately apply such a representational theory to pretence, even when they have established one for false belief. The young child operates with a nonrepresentational account of pretence from an early age (from approximately 18 months upward) and may, for that reason, find it hard to abandon.

Lillard argues that the young child initially learns about pretence before having a concept of mental representation. For this reason, she argues children must understand pretence in terms of other concepts that they do understand, like action. In her account, children first come to understand mental representation as applied to belief. But because their incomplete understanding of pretence has served them adequately, they are not motivated to revise their understanding of pretence to include mental representation right away. She speculates that, over time, children might begin to recognise syntactic parallels between pretend and other propositional mental verbs like "think" and "know," and that recognition might lead them to see "pretend" as a mental verb.

In any case, she emphasises that further insights into the associations between pretence and other mental states are also needed for a full understanding of pretence. Children come to appreciate that a mental process must be active during the enactment of a pretence (e.g. to pretend to hop like a rabbit one must simultaneously be thinking about a rabbit). They also come to appreciate that pretend actions presuppose a background of beliefs (e.g. thoughts about a rabbit moving will be based on knowledge of how it moves). Finally, children should eventually appreciate that pretence may not immediately issue in any overt action. Thus, according to Lillard, an understanding of false belief is, at best, one step toward an understanding of pretence. Further steps are needed, and these may not have any close link to an understanding of the representational nature of mind.

REFERENCES

Freeman, N.H., Lewis, C.N., Smith, C., & Kelly, S. (1992). *Facts and fictions in preschoolers' theory of mind: "Wrong pretence" and false belief.* Unpublished manuscript, University of Bristol.

Goldman, A.I. (1989). Interpretation psychologized. *Mind and Language, 4*, 161–185.

Gordon, R.M. (1986). Folk psychology as simulation. *Mind and Language, 1*, 158–171.

Heal, J. (1993). How to think about thinking. In M. Davies & T. Stone (Eds.), *Mental Simulation: Philosophical and psychological studies.* Oxford: Blackwell.

Hickling, A.K., Wellman, H.M., & Gottfried, G.M. (1993). *Conceptualizing pretense: Early understanding of others' mental attitudes toward pretend happenings.* Unpublished paper, University of Michigan.

Leslie, A.M. (1987). Pretense and representation: The origins of "theory of mind." *Psychological Review, 94*, 412–426.

IV

THE ROLE OF
COMMUNICATION

14 Changing Minds and Changing Relationships

Judy Dunn
Pennsylvania State University, University Park, USA

INTRODUCTION

Our picture of what children understand of "other minds" has been transformed in the last few years by recent research—at least in terms of the general changes most children go through: the normative patterns of development. There is plenty of controversy, still, about the particular limitations that characterise very young children's understanding of other minds, and about the nature and timing of the cognitive changes that take place between two and five years (Frye & Moore, 1991; Perner, 1991; Wellman, 1990). However, there is general agreement that major developments take place as children reach their fifth year. What has been surprisingly little examined is the significance of such developments for children's real-life relationships. Interest in autism is the only domain in which the connections between understanding of other minds and children's social behaviour has been considered (see, for instance, Baron-Cohen, Tager-Flusberg, & Cohen, in press). Yet what we understand of others' inner states must profoundly influence the kind of relationships we have, and changes in children's understanding of the emotions, desires, and mental states of those with whom they have close relationships should surely have major significance for the *nature* of those relationships.

Why have these implications not been considered? On the one hand, those interested in children's theory of mind have been concerned chiefly with the design and execution of precise experiments to delineate the

297

limitations and capabilities of children of different ages. As other chapters in this volume make clear, the task demands and design of such experiments can greatly influence the success of children participating in such studies (see, for example, Lewis, this volume). On the other hand, those interested in young children's close relationships have primarily focused on the attachment quality of those relationships and, paradoxically, within an attachment framework, developmental changes in the nature of the relationship under scrutiny have not been of central interest. The assumption has been one of stability over time in the quality of children's relationships—whether secure or insecure—unless the child and others are under considerable stress (Vaughn, Egeland, Sroufe, & Waters, 1979). So the question of how children's close relationships are affected by, or in their turn influence, the striking changes in understanding of other minds that take place in the early years has hardly been raised, let alone studied systematically.

In this chapter, then, the issue that I want to consider is this: If we take a close look at children's interactions with those with whom they are intimately involved, over the period when there are these major changes in children's understanding of others and of self, we may gain illumination both on the nature and development of young children's understanding of others, and on the significance of these developments in understanding for their relationships. In an ongoing study we are currently examining a range of different aspects of young children's interactions and relationships with their mothers, siblings, and close friends, aspects that relate to their ability to understand the links between others' inner states and their actions. The domains under examination include the following: first, children's conversations about causality and inner states as cause and consequence of behaviour; second, children's management of conflict—including their propensity to take account of their antagonist's feelings, goals, or point of view; third, their engagement in joint shared fantasy play; fourth, their engagement in shared jokes and humorous exchanges with others; and fifth, their judgement and reasoning concerning moral issues involving other people. In this chapter the focus will be upon the first two of these domains—conversations about causality and the management of conflict; for each domain, the changes over the period from the end of the third year through the fourth year will be considered. In the final section of the chapter, changes in the other domains of children's relationships will be discussed briefly.

The findings examined come from a longitudinal study of second-born children observed at home with their mothers, siblings, and close friends (Dunn, Brown, Slomkowski, Tesla, & Youngblade, 1991). During the unstructured observations, conducted when the children were 33, 40 and 47 months, the children's conversations were tape-recorded and a narrative record of the people present, affect expressed, and details of conflict incidents and pretend play was kept by the observer. The transcripts of these family conversations formed the basis of the analysis of the children's causal discourse and their argument in conflict (for details of the sample and methods see Dunn et al., 1991).

CONVERSATIONS ABOUT CAUSALITY

From an early age, children take part in conversations about the causes of other people's behaviour. Bloom and her colleagues, in a classic study of children's early expressions of causality, showed that between two and three years of age the eight children they studied with their mothers were able to express causal relations between events and/or states, and were especially interested in causal relations that involved people's behaviour (Bloom & Capatides, 1987; Hood & Bloom, 1979). The particular aspects of social behaviour that the children discussed, and the pragmatic situations in which such causal conversations took place, were not differentiated in that study. In the research to be described here, issues both of content and pragmatics were examined; we wished to distinguish, for example, children's discussion of the causes and consequences of inner states from their comments on social practices or abilities. We also wished to examine the context and functions of children's early attempts to discuss the causes of people's behaviour (for details see Dunn & Brown, 1993). We focused specifically on changes in causal talk between 33 and 40 months of age—a relatively short developmental period but one in which the early stages of understanding "other minds" are already evident for some children (Dunn et al., 1991).

The first point to be noted is that children's causal talk to both their mothers and siblings increased markedly over this seven-month period. It nearly doubled in frequency, when expressed in terms of the time that the children spent together with the other family members (Dunn & Brown, 1993). The children engaged in more causal talk with their mothers than with their siblings as 33-month-olds; however, by 40 months this difference was not significant.

What was this increase in causal talk chiefly focused upon? We categorised the content of the conversations—the topics about which the children discussed causal relations, and to which they referred as reasons—according to whether they were concerned with behaviour/action, internal states, social practices, abilities or knowledge, or physical reality. Given the evidence that children are, by the end of the fourth year able to understand the causal relations between desires, beliefs, and behaviour (Wellman, 1990), our prediction was that discussion of causal relations concerned with internal states would increase over this period. The prediction was confirmed. When the children were 33 months old, their causal references were most frequently concerned with overt behaviour or action. Talk about internal states occurred only half as often. By 40 months, however, their causal talk centred on internal states, with a significant increase in such discussion over the 7 months. Specifically, the frequency of children's causal turns to their mothers that were concerned with internal states increased from an average of 0.78 turns per hour to an average of 2.27 per hour over the 7-month period (paired comparison ANOVA from the 2 time points, $F[1,48] = 6.07$, $P < 0.01$). The increase in children's causal turns concerning internal states in conversation with their siblings was similar, from an average of 0.34 to 1.79 turns per hour ($F[1,48] = 26.43$, $P < 0.01$). There was also a significant increase in their causal talk concerning social practices and rules, to both mother and sibling (paired comparison ANOVA $F[1,48] = 6.07$ and 5.58, both $P < 0.05$, for talk to mother and to sibling, respectively; for further details see Dunn & Brown, 1993).

The findings remind us, then, that children engage in causal discourse concerning inner states well before they are four years old (the age considered to be a "watershed" developmental stage in much discussion of children's understanding of other minds), and that they are *interested* in the links between inner states and action. The content of both mothers' and siblings' causal discourse also changed over this short period, in a parallel fashion. At 33 months, the most frequent content category for mothers' and for siblings' causal talk was behaviour and action, but by 40 months the frequency of both partners' talk about internal states had doubled. For mothers, the increase was from 2.97 turns to 6.70 turns per hour; for siblings it was from 1.15 to 3.35 turns per hour (paired comparison ANOVA for the 2 times points, $F[1,48] = 21.86$ for mothers, 5.06 for siblings, both significant at $P < 0.05$). In contrast to these findings for the causal discussion concerning internal states, for all family members the frequency of causal turns concerned with behaviour or action stayed about the same over these months.

We next examined the social context in which the children began to reflect on and discuss the causal relations between inner states and action. Studies of children's logical abilities have shown that, in the context of conversational discourse with an adult partner, children show powers of inference well beyond what they can do in more formal abstract tasks (Scholnick & Wing, 1992). We were interested in going beyond the general Vygotskyan notion—supported by such evidence—that it is in the context of interaction with a more mature member of the culture that children make developmental advances, towards clarifying the particular features of social exchanges that are associated with children's mature behaviour. Evidence from studies of preschool children (for example Miller, et al., 1991; Scholnick & Wing, 1991) and observations of children in their second and third year in family interaction (Dunn, 1988) have highlighted the developmental significance of those contexts in which children's immediate self-interest is at issue, including disputes (Stein & Miller, 1991). One possibility that we wished to examine was that, with the increased powers of reflection and metacognitive skills of the fourth and fifth years, children begin to talk more about causal relations and inner states when they are engaged in reflective discussion that is not immediately concerned with the satisfaction of their own urgent goals.

A number of different pragmatic contexts in which causal discussions took place were examined. These were categorised as follows. *Self-interest* included those exchanges in which the speaker was attempting to get his/her own immediate needs or goals met (e.g. "Put it there so I can get warm"). *Reflective-pretend* included discussion of causal relations not concerned with controlling others' behaviour or with the achievement of immediate goals, including reflective comments about past events, solo or shared pretend (e.g. commenting on a character in a story book: "He doesn't know where it is, 'cause he forgot"). *Shared positive* included friendly sharing of humour, verbal play, comforting, or assistance (e.g. child clowning with sibling: "We're poo-poo 'cause we got mud on us!"). The category *Control* included efforts to control or reinforce socially acceptable behaviour (e.g. "Don't do that or you'll break it and that'll make me sad!"). In addition we looked at whether the causal conversations took place in the context of a *dispute* between the conversational partners. The analyses of the children's causal discourse showed that at 33 months, in conversation with either mother or sibling, children were equally likely to talk about causal relations when trying to achieve their own immediate goals (*self-interest*), and when they were talking in a reflective or pretend context (*reflective-pretend*). The pattern changed, however, over the 7 months between the 33 and 40 months visits. By the later time point, the children were more likely to talk about causal relations in the *reflective-pretend* context than when they were trying to get their own immediate needs or goals met. This change presumably reflects the growing ability of the children to reflect; such conversations come to play a more prominent role in children's relationships over this period, a point that we return to later.

However, in addition to this spotlight on the growth of reflective discussion, the importance of disputes as a forum in which children begin to articulate causal relations was also confirmed. Included in the study was an analysis of individual differences in children's performance on tests of their understanding of others' feelings, and in a "false belief" assessment of their grasp of the links between beliefs and action (Bartsch & Wellman, 1989). This examination of individual differences showed first that the frequency with which children participated in causal discourse at 33 months was related to their success on the "false belief" task 7 months later, and second that children who frequently engaged in causal discourse in the context of a dispute with either their mothers or siblings were more successful in the assessments of their understanding of inner states made at 40 months. Both the topic and the context of the causal talk were linked to these later individual differences (Dunn & Brown, 1993). It must be emphasised that no conclusions about the causal significance of the children's participation in such disputes can be drawn from the correlational data. It is quite possible that the pattern of results reflects a continuity of child differences, with children who are mature in their understanding of causal relations engaging in more frequent disputes about causality, and performing better in the test situations too. But at the very least, we should take seriously the possibility that talk about causal relations in particular contexts does contribute to the growth of children's understanding of the links between inner states and action. One implication of these findings on individual differences is that, in considering the experiences that may contribute to the growth of children's understanding, we need to examine not just their participation in discourse concerning the question of why people behave the way they do, but also the use to which such causal talk is put—the pragmatics of the discourse. A parallel here would be the argument that Bruner (1990) made for the significance of "contexts of practice": that what people are *trying to do* may well influence the way that things are learned.

The comparison of children's causal discourse with their mothers and their siblings highlights a further point. There were no significant correlations across the dyads—child–mother and child–sibling—in causal talk, even though there was considerable stability over time and reciprocity within each dyad. Children in some families engaged in frequent causal talk about inner states with their mothers, but not their siblings, whereas in other families children engaged in such talk with their siblings but not their mothers. The development of this ability to reflect on and articulate the causal relations between inner states and action does not lead to *common* features of children's relationships with their mothers and their siblings. The new ability does not, it seems, transform both relationships, and is not necessarily evident in how a child interacts with mother *and* sibling. The implication of this lack of consistency is an issue we return to later.

ARGUMENTS IN CONFLICT

The second domain of social interaction to be considered concerns conflict. We were particularly interested in the development of the ability to take account of others' wishes and goals in argument during conflict. Clearly, if the growth of understanding other minds leads to an increased likelihood that children will appreciate the views of others, a great step forward will have been achieved in family relationships. Conflict episodes are extremely common within families with small children (our families averaged 11 disputes an hour between the 33-month-olds and their mothers, for instance), and are a potent source of stress for all. The examination of the developmental changes in children's conflict interactions is reported in detail elsewhere (e.g. Slomkowski & Dunn, 1992; Tesla & Dunn, 1992). For the present focus on the connections between changes in understanding and in social relationships, some key points from these analyses will simply be summarised; the evidence for change in children's use of reasoned argument, and in their attempts to take account of others' desires or goals, will be the chief concern.

There was a substantial increase over the period of 33 to 47 months in the proportion of conflicts in which children reasoned with their antagonists— as opposed to simply protesting in an unreasoned way. With their mothers, for example, children provided some reasoned argument in 36% of conflicts at 33 months on average, but this rose to 45% of conflicts at 47 months. However, this increase in the propensity to provide some reasoning, justification, or excuse in conflict with another was not used, primarily, to resolve conflict by taking into account the other's viewpoint or desires. We distinguished between reasoned argument that took account of the other's needs and desires in attempts to conciliate or negotiate, which we termed *other-oriented argument* (see also Kruger, 1992), from reasoned argument that was used explicitly in the service of the speaker's own self-interest (termed *self-oriented argument*). To illustrate the difference, consider the following 2 examples drawn from our observations when the children were 47 months:

Example 1: Two girls are dressing up as queens in the course of pretend play, and are in conflict over who should wear a crown. Then the child who is not in possession of the coveted crown says: "I should wear the crown. Because it matches my dress. It looks ugly on you."

Example 2: Two girls in a pretend game about royalty are in conflict over who should be the Queen. Finally one proposes a compromise: "I know—we'll *both* be Queens, OK?"

In the first example, the girl's argument—relatively sophisticated in its power to influence the other girl—was categorised as *self-oriented*. In the second example, the girl's comment was categorised as *other-oriented*.

Perhaps sadly, we found that the growth of children's ability to use reasoned argument between 33 and 47 months was reflected only in an increase in self-oriented argument, not in an increase in the proportion of conflict incidents in which children took explicit account of the other person's goals or desires in order to resolve conflict. This pattern of change was significant both for the children's conflicts with their mothers, and for those with their siblings. And perhaps even more sadly, our analysis of the partner's talk in these conflict incidents showed a parallel pattern. There was an increase between 33 and 47 months in the proportion of reasoned argument used by both mothers and siblings in their disputes with the children. However, there was actually a decrease in the proportion of reasoned argument used by mothers and siblings for conciliation and negotiation to resolve the conflict. The rapidly growing ability of children to understand others' feelings and goals was *not* reflected, that is, in increased harmony between the children and the other family members.

OTHER CHANGES IN CHILDREN'S RELATIONSHIPS

The children's growing ability to grasp how others think and feel was reflected in several other changes in their close relationships, in addition to the changes in their management of conflict, and their engagement in causal discourse. For example, the increase in the frequency and elaboration of their shared pretend play in their relationships with other children—whether siblings or friends—was especially striking. The ability to share a fantasy world with another person is clearly useful evidence for children's understanding of other minds (Leslie, 1987; 1988); indeed, we found that individual differences in children's engagement in joint pretend with others was correlated with their performance on "false belief" tasks (Youngblade & Dunn, submitted). In particular, the frequency with which children engaged in role enactment—taking on the role of another person—within the pretend play was correlated with their ability to explain another's actions in terms of his or her (false) beliefs in a test situation. These findings take on particular significance when we consider how important such play becomes in the close relationships of many children during their fourth and fifth years. As Gottman and Parker (1986) have argued, shared pretend play in early childhood is *the* core feature of friendships. The development of the ability to share the thoughts, feelings, and goals of pretend characters—evident in the role enactment and the (endless) discussion of how the pretend characters would or would not act—transforms, in an important sense, the quality of friendship between young children. As Howes and her colleagues (Howes, Unger, & Matheson, 1992, p. 133) have argued from their longitudinal studies of preschool children: "social pretend play becomes an opportunity to explore issues of intimacy and trust." Their data highlights the links between social pretend play, friendship, and self-disclosure. Further, it is evident that pretend play is a forum in which understanding of social roles and rules—and presumably other minds—is fostered (Garvey, 1977).

The ability to engage in such pretend play can also affect the quality of sibling relations importantly. Children become far more attractive playmates and companions to their older siblings when they are able to engage in pretend play. Partly for this reason, we find there is a notable increase in the time that children spent talking with and interacting with their siblings (expressed as a proportion of the time they were together) between 33 and 47 months—and a parallel decrease in the time they spent interacting with their mothers (Brown & Dunn, 1992). Siblings gain prominence as children's conversational partners over the fourth year. The conversational turns that the children directed to their siblings nearly doubled over this period, and their siblings were, by 47 months, far more likely to talk to them than they had been at 33 months.

This change is evident, for example, in the conversations children have about inner states with family members. By 47 months, the second-born children we studied engaged their older siblings in discussions concerning inner states as much as they had engaged their mothers at 33 months of age. And these conversations about inner states with siblings differed in many ways from the discourse concerning inner states in which children engaged with their mothers. Mothers of young children talk about the *child's* feelings most often in their conversations together (Brown & Dunn, 1991; 1992). Siblings, in contrast, draw attention to their own feelings most often.

The pragmatics of such conversations differ, too. Mother–child talk about inner states can be broadly described as "caretaking" in function: concerned with comforting the child's distress, enquiring about their desires, controlling their behaviour and explaining the child's own feelings. In contrast, siblings' talk about inner states was rarely in these contexts, but was likely to be in playful or humorous contexts, sharing jokes about disgusting objects, teasing, or drawing the child's attention to the sibling's own thoughts, desires, or needs. In conversations with a sibling, children are much more likely to be involved in discussion of *the other person's* inner states than they are in conversations with a parent. It is quite possible that these differences in the focus and pragmatics of talk about inner states make conversations with a sibling, together with the experiences of pretend play with siblings, of distinctive developmental importance in the growth of understanding other minds—an argument that fits with the evidence from Perner and his colleagues that children with siblings are more successful in "false belief" tests than children without siblings (Perner, Ruffman, & Leekam, in press).

Two other changes in children's relationships over this period are worth noting. One is that the *connectedness* of their communication with others increases—the degree to which a speaker relates to or takes account of the previous speaker's turn. Connectedness is a dimension of relationships that has received much attention in studies of adolescents (e.g. Cooper, Grotevant, & Condon, 1983), but it has rarely been considered in relation to young children. Yet it is apparent from our observational data that during the third and fourth years there are considerable increases in the connectedness of children's communication with their friends and siblings (Slomkowski & Dunn, submitted). This increased coherence of their communication with other children can plausibly be linked to their increasing appreciation of the other's goals and thoughts. And it is to be noted that, in our Pennsylvanian study, individual differences in the connectedness of children's communication with their friends as 47-month-olds were correlated with their performance on false belief tasks 7 months earlier (Dunn, 1993).

The second change is the increasing role that shared humour plays in many children's relationships with others over this period. Psychologists who study young children's relationships tend to focus primarily on the more negative aspects of insecurity, guilt, and anxiety. Yet to any observer of young children the key role that humour plays in their relationships stands out. As three and four year olds, they have a growing appreciation of *what other people will find funny*—and this too can be seen as reflecting a new understanding of other minds. As adults we would all agree that sharing amusement is a core feature of our intimate relationships—so too, with these young children, their growing understanding of others makes this key aspect of relationships more and more prominent. The frequency of jokes made by the children in our Pennsylvanian sample increased markedly between 33 and 47 months—from an average of 2.1 jokes per hour to 3.3 an hour—and the most notable increase was in jokes the children made about their own inadequacy (Woodworth, 1993). Moreover, both the children in this study and those in a separate study of children in Cambridge (McGhee, 1989) tended to make different jokes with their siblings from those they made to their mothers—and such distinctions again reveal that they were already aware of what this *particular* other person will find funny. Jokes with the sibling focused very often on the scatalogical, the disgusting, or the forbidden, whereas jokes to the mother were less often on such topics (Dunn, 1988; Woodworth, 1993). Here, too, we found that individual differences in very young children's use of humour in their family interactions were associated with differences in their performance on false belief tasks: Children who made frequent jokes were relatively successful on the false belief tasks, in comparison with the less humorous children (Woodworth, 1993).

DIFFERENCES ACROSS RELATIONSHIPS

The changes we have described in the nature of children's relationships can be linked to their growing grasp of the feelings and mental states of others, in commonsense terms and in terms of their association with performance on assessments of understanding. But it is important to underline that these developments are not reflected in uniform changes across an individual child's relationships. The child who demonstrates understanding of her best friend's goals and needs in conflict with explicit acknowledgment of those inner states, does not necessarily do so in conflict with her sibling or her mother. There are no significant correlations across social partner for the conflict management categories we have discussed. Similarly, there is little relation between the likelihood that children will engage in causal talk about inner states with their mothers and with their siblings. And the frequency and elaboration of shared pretend play with a sibling shows no systematic link with the pretend play engaged in with a friend or mother. The new social understanding that children reveal over the fourth year is not expressed uniformly across their relationships; whether and how children use their understanding of the other depends on the nature of the particular relationship at issue.

Two implications of this pattern of differences across relationships for the study of the development of children's "theory of mind" should be considered. The first is that the socio-emotional context in which children are interacting or *being tested* is profoundly important as an influence on the understanding that they express. The ability to "understand other minds" is not a capability that, once achieved, will be evident across contexts; rather, it will be subtly and not-so-subtly affected by what the child is trying to do in the social encounter, and how the child interprets what the other is trying to do. The lessons for those designing assessments of children's "understanding" are serious.

The second point is that the results—especially those on causal discourse—raise questions about the contexts in which children begin to make developmental advances in this understanding. The evidence on the importance of contexts in which children's self-interest is at issue could imply that children first begin to reflect on other minds in such settings of emotional significance. But is it possible that, as children develop powers of metacognition during the fourth year, these settings become less prominent as the contexts in which children make developmental advances? Clearly the issue is an important arena for the next steps in theory of mind research.

CONCLUSION

The study of children's interactions within their close relationships has raised a number of general issues for those interested in the development of children's understanding of other minds.

First, the evidence reminds us that children begin to be interested in and to understand the connections between inner states and behaviour far earlier than the conventional assessments of the understanding of false belief would suggest (see also Reddy, 1991).

Second, the findings show that the expression of understanding depends on the social context, and varies importantly across different relationships, for the same child. It is not simply that the understanding is *there* or *not yet there*. Rather, the emotional setting and what the child is trying to do are important considerations, and are likely to be so in experimental settings as well as in family interactions (see also Hala, 1991, for parallel findings).

Third, the evidence shows how the growth of understanding others is reflected in new dimensions of children's relationships, and these new dimensions are particularly significant in children's relationships with other children. The balance of relationships within the family changes as a consequence, and the importance of relationships outside the family becomes increasingly apparent. Relationships with other children may indeed have a particular significance for further developments in understanding other minds.

Fourth, the evidence shows that individual differences in understanding other minds are striking both within and across relationships, as they are in more formal assessments such as the false belief tests (Dunn et al., 1991). These individual differences have, until now, rarely been studied in theory of mind research; however, what little evidence we have indicates that the quality of family and peer relationships may well be implicated in their development. We cannot as yet draw conclusions about the direction of connections between differences in understanding and in relationships— indeed, it seems highly likely that such links are a two-way affair. But it is clear that these connections deserve further study.

ACKNOWLEDGEMENTS

The research described was supported by grants from NICHD (HD 23158), NIMH (MH 46535), and by the Medical Research Council of Great Britain.

REFERENCES

Baron-Cohen, S., Tager-Flusberg, H., & Cohen, D.J. (in press). *Understanding other minds: Perspectives on the theory of mind hypothesis of autism*. Oxford: Oxford University Press.

Bartsch, K., & Wellman, H. (1989). Young children's attribution of action to beliefs and desires. *Child Development, 60*, 946–964.

Bloom, L., & Capatides, J.B. (1987). Sources of meaning in the acquisition of complex syntax: The sample case of causality. *Journal of Experimental Child Psychology, 43*, 112–128.

Brown, J.R., & Dunn, J. (1991). "You can cry Mum": The social and developmental implications of talk about internal states. *British Journal of Developmental Psychology, 9*, 237–256.

Brown, J.R., & Dunn, J. (1992). Talk with your mother or your sibling? Developmental changes in early family conversations about feelings. *Child Development, 63*, 336–349.

Bruner, J. (1990). *Acts of meaning*. Cambridge, Mass.: Harvard University Press.

Cooper, C.R., Grotevant, H.D., & Condon, S.M. (1983). Individuality and connectedness in the family as a context for adolescent identity formation and role taking skill. In H.D.

Grotevant & C.R. Cooper (Eds.), *Adolescent development in the family* (pp. 43–59). San Francisco: Jossey-Bass.

Dunn, J. (1988). *The beginnings of social understanding*. Cambridge, Mass.: Harvard University Press.

Dunn, J. (1993, March). *Children's understanding of "other minds": Antecedents and later correlates in interaction with family and friends*. Paper presented at the Biennial Meetings of the Society for Research in Child Development, New Orleans.

Dunn, J., & Brown, J.R. (1993). Early conversations about causality: Content, pragmatics, and developmental change. *British Journal of Developmental Psychology, 11*, 107–123.

Dunn, J., Brown, J., Slomkowski, C., Tesla, C., & Youngblade, L. (1991). Young children's understanding of other people's feelings and beliefs: Individual differences and their antecedents. *Child Development, 62*, 1352–1366.

Frye, D., & Moore, C. (1991). *Children's theories of mind*. Hillsdale, NJ: Lawrence Erlbaum Associates Inc.

Garvey, C. (1977). *Play*. Cambridge, Mass.: Harvard University Press.

Gottman, J.M., & Parker, J.G. (1986). *Conversations of friends*. Cambridge: Cambridge University Press.

Hala, S. (1991, April). *The role of personal involvement in facilitating false belief understanding*. Paper presented at the Biennial Meeting of the Society for Research in Child Development, Seattle.

Hood, L., & Bloom, L. (1979). What, when, and how about why: A longitudinal study of early expressions of causality. *Monographs of the Society for Research in Child Development, 44* (6, Serial No. 181).

Howes, C., Unger, O., & Matheson, C.C. (1992). *The collaborative construction of pretend*. Albany: State University of New York Press.

Kruger, A.C. (1992). The effect of peer and adult-child transactive discussions on moral reasoning. *Merrill-Palmer Quarterly, 38*, 191–211.

Leslie, A.M. (1987). Pretense and representation: The origins of "theory of mind." *Psychological Review, 94*, 412–426.

Leslie, A.M. (1988). Some implications of pretense for mechanisms underlying the child's theory of mind. In J.W. Astington, P.L. Harris, & D.R. Olson (Eds.), *Developing theories of mind* (pp. 19–46). Cambridge: Cambridge University Press.

McGhee, S.A. (1989). *Humor and social interaction: A study of children's use and appreciation of humor in everyday situations*. Unpublished Master's thesis, Pennsylvania State University.

Miller, P.J., Mintz, J., Hoogstra, L., Fung, H., & Potts, R. (1991). The narrated self: Young children's construction of self in relation to others in conversational stories of personal experience. *Merrill-Palmer Quarterly, 38*, 45–67.

Perner, J. (1991). *Understanding the representational mind*. Cambridge: Cambridge University Press.

Perner, J., Ruffman, T., & Leekam, S. *Child Development. Theory of mind is contagious: You catch it from your sibs*, in press.

Reddy, V. (1991). Playing with others' expectations: Teasing and mucking about in the first year. In A. Whiten (Ed.), *Natural theories of mind: Evolution, development and simulation of everyday mindreading* (pp. 143–158). Oxford: Basil Blackwell.

Scholnick, E.K., & Wing, C.S. (1991). Speaking deductively: Preschoolers' use of *if* in conversation and in conditional inference. *Developmental Psychology, 27*, 249–258.

Scholnick, E.K., & Wing, C.S. (1992). Speaking deductively: Using conversation to trace the origins of conditional thought in children. *Merrill-Palmer Quarterly, 38*, 1–20.

Slomkowski, C., & Dunn, J. (1992). Arguments and relationships within the family: Differences in children's disputes with mother and sibling. *Developmental Psychology, 28*, 919–924.

Slomkowski, C., & Dunn, J. (submitted). *Connectedness in children's relationships with siblings and friends.*

Stein, N.J., & Miller, C.A. (1991). The process of thinking and reasoning in argumentative contexts: Evaluation of evidence and the resolution of conflict. In R. Glaser (Ed.), *Advances in instructional psychology.* Hillsdale, NJ: Lawrence Erlbaum Associates Inc.

Tesla, C., & Dunn, J. (1992). Getting along or getting your way. *Social Development, 1,* 107–121.

Vaughn, B., Egeland, B., Sroufe, L.A., & Waters, E. (1979). Individual differences in infant–mother attachment at twelve and eighteen months: Stability and change in families under stress. *Child Development, 50,* 971–975.

Wellman, H.M. (1990). *The child's theory of mind.* Cambridge, Mass.: Bradford Books.

Woodworth, S. (1993, March). *A funny thing about social cognition.* Presentation at the Biennial Meetings of the Society for Research in Child Development, New Orleans.

Youngblade, L., & Dunn, J. (submitted). *Individual differences in young children's pretend play with mother and sibling: Links to relationship quality and understanding of other people's feelings and beliefs.*

15

Theory of Mind and the Development of Social-linguistic Intelligence in Early Childhood

Marilyn Shatz
University of Michigan, Ann Arbor, USA

INTRODUCTION

How and when children acquire the ability to think about and take account of others' mental states, as well as their own, is a topic of much current interest to developmental psychologists. It is easy to see why: The ability influences almost every aspect of human social behaviour. To be a good conversationalist, to participate appropriately in a full range of social relationships, and to reason intelligently about behaviour, an individual must know something about others—how they are similar to and different from the self, what they are likely to know, and how they are likely to behave in various circumstances. Despite the fact that understandings of self and others grow and deepen over the years (e.g. Hickling, 1993), most research on the topic has dealt with the early development of a "theory of mind," focusing on whether young children recognise that others have internal states and which internal states children attribute to others (Woolley & Wellman, 1990). At present, what counts as a theory of mind (Gopnik & Wellman, 1994; Harris, 1994) and when children acquire it (Golinkoff, 1993; Shatz & O'Reilly, 1990; Shatz, 1994) are matters of some controversy.

There is little doubt that learning about others begins in infancy—even very young children acquire bits of knowledge that are ultimately integrated into the relatively sophisticated understanding of mind we see in older children. Yet, a basic understanding of mind, both in the self and others, is

311

only achieved after the conjoining of linguistic experience with early experiences of other humans. In other words, it depends on the development of social-linguistic intelligence, a capacity founded on the growing ability to understand and explain the behaviours of self and others in terms common to all members of one's discourse community. Children use two major tools to develop social-linguistic intelligence. First, in the course of social experience, young children compare themselves to others as they develop a sense of self. Second, as they acquire the language of their community, they begin to participate in conversations giving verbal expression to internal motivations, understandings, expectations, and justifications; they discover how internal states are made public, when they are to be taken into account, and the causal role they play in the society. Thus the toddler years, during which children acquire language, are a crucial time for the development of social-linguistic intelligence. Before this development, infants may have some of the building blocks, but they cannot truly be said to have achieved an understanding of "mind."

Two stories about my grandson, Ricky, offer dramatic illustrations of the progress made by toddlers in understanding the internal states and capacities of others. The first incident took place when Ricky was 17 months old. We were having a phone conversation, and Ricky, who was a one-word speaker at the time, said "house." I discovered later from his mother that he was trying to tell me he had been playing with his toy schoolhouse when I had called; but at that moment, I misunderstood him and started talking about his impending visit later that day to *my* house. Recognising we had no mutual focus, Ricky tried to correct the situation. He dropped the phone, went to the schoolhouse and dragged it over to the telephone. Apparently, he hoped its proximity to my voice would give me access to his intended referent.

The second incident occurred 17 months later, when Ricky was 34 months old. He had been visiting without his parents at my house for a 2-night stay. During the first night, there had been a bedwetting accident. I had responded by changing his sheets and pyjamas and putting him back to bed without discussion. Indeed, he had hardly awakened. The second night passed without incident, but in the morning, Ricky appeared at my bedside naked. When I asked where his pyjamas were, he replied "in the bathroom." I asked whether Ricky wanted to put on some underwear, but he refused. Sceptically, I asked whether he wanted to put his pyjamas back on. Ricky nodded yes. I retrieved the—to my surprise—dry pyjamas from the bathroom and began to dress him without comment. He volunteered, "You thought these were wet."

At 17 months, Ricky seemed able to recognise that we had not established a joint focus, but he had a very erroneous view of human perceptual capacities (to say nothing of the way telephones worked) and what it would take to establish mutuality. In contrast, at 34 months, not only did he understand that I lacked his knowledge of the condition of the pyjamas, but he could infer from my questions and our shared past experience of the earlier incident that I had a misconception or false belief about the state of the pyjamas, and he could tell me what he (correctly) thought I was thinking. Even at 17 months, Ricky had taken language as a way of establishing mutual focus; however, when it failed to achieve his intended goal, he was at a loss as to how to modify what he'd said with additional words. Instead, he relied on a proximity strategy, one I'd seen before in other circumstances (Shatz, 1994), namely, getting the object of desired mutual focus as close to the other person as possible and hoping for the best. Seventeen months later, he could put into words his thoughts about my thoughts.

How had Ricky moved from these early glimmers of understanding and misunderstanding about people to the rather sophisticated knowledge he displayed hardly a year and a half later? This chapter describes several aspects of that course, illustrating the changes in three areas of knowledge; knowledge of language, knowledge of self, and knowledge of others, which are central to the emergence of social-linguistic intelligence. As Fig. 15.1 illustrates, the three areas are not wholly independent domains. Knowledge

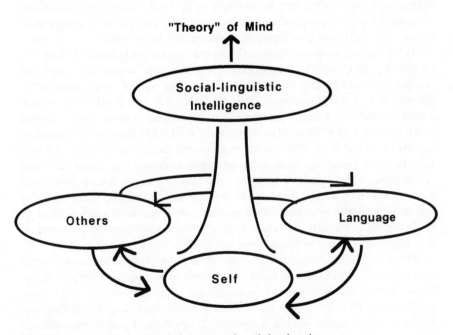

FIG. 15.1 A schematic for the relations among knowledge domains.

in one domain influences development in the others as the areas bootstrap each other via the child's use of language and comparison processes to learn more. From the gradual accrual of interrelated knowledge in these areas, social-linguistic intelligence emerges. It is this sort of intelligence that enables coherent, causal reasoning about the mind.

METHOD

The data for this chapter come from a larger project on the toddler years that combined the longitudinal study of a single child, Ricky, with a review of the research that has revealed many developmental achievements of the period from 15 to 36 months of age (Shatz, 1994). There are several advantages to such a method. The first three have to do with intensive longitudinal observations in the child's natural environment. For one, because the display of early competence in children so young can be hard to capture in short visits to the laboratory, the likelihood of finding evidence of early competence, however ephemeral or rare, is higher in a large data set collected in natural settings. For another, intensive study allows the researcher to witness how many small components of skills are acquired and practised on virtually a daily basis as competence is gained. Also, because researchers often focus on particular topics or areas of development, the relations between areas can be masked or ignored. Intensive longitudinal observation of a single child makes it more likely that the ways competence in one area influence development in others will be noticed.

Yet, there are disadvantages to the intensive case study method. There is, of course, the question of generality. How can one be sure that the child studied is paradigmatic of children at this age or that the processes of development the child evinces are typical? Here is where other research is extremely helpful. From both experimental and naturalistic studies, I was often able to find evidence that aspects of Ricky's behaviour are common among other toddlers. What was unique about the intensive study of Ricky was that he could be seen working simultaneously on many different components of knowledge and using what he knew in one area to help learn more in another. Ricky, then, can be seen as the whole child standing in for the many children who have been studied piecemeal with more limited or narrower foci, but whose data taken together corroborate the picture of development during the toddler years I present.

There is also the question of interpretability. Any single incident observed in the natural world is likely to be compatible with multiple interpretations. How, then, to decide on unique explanations? Here, the quantity and variety of observations helps. From more than 60 visits consisting of hundreds of hours of observation over a period of 21 months, I culled examples of behaviour that show capacities emerging and converging to bring Ricky to the point, just under age 3, where he could reason about others' misconceptions. My aim was not just to document in quantified terms the uses of words that might indicate an early "theory" of mind, but to capture the early behaviours—both linguistic and nonlinguistic—that would help identify precursors to or early manifestations of an understanding of mind.

Convergence and consistency of behaviours across multiple instances allow for the elimination of some candidates for interpretation and the promotion of others. Often it is impossible to arrive at a single best interpretation of one incident; instead, it is the sum total of the descriptions of Ricky's behaviour over time that leads to the proposal of the development of social-linguistic intelligence and the consequent early understanding of mind.

In what follows, I outline some of the component skills I saw Ricky acquiring during the 21 months of my observations, and I give some examples of the ways he used language and comparison to learn more about language, about himself, and about others. It is important to remember that what is reported here is only a sample of all the observations I made; for many of the behaviours there are multiple instances of similar character. Space limitations necessarily restrict the number of references to supporting literature. Also, the data are organised in two ways, more for expositional efficiency than on theoretical grounds. First, I describe 4 time periods, the first from 15 to 17 months, and the remaining 3 covering roughly 6 months each; 18 to 24 months, 25 to 30 months, and 31 to 36 months. No stage theory is implied by these divisions; the actual course of development was more seamless than that. Second, I discuss developments in the three areas of knowledge of self, others, and language somewhat separately, but this too is primarily for expositional purposes. Indeed, on several occasions, I show explicitly how the areas interrelate.

My case study subject, Ricky, was the first child of a stay-at-home mother with a bit more education than high school and a father who worked and went to college part time. One parent had an East-European family background while the other had Mexican-Irish origins. At the time he was studied, Ricky lived with his parents in an apartment on the outskirts of Detroit. A few months before the end of the study, he began a part-day programme at a local nursery school. I began to observe Ricky closely when he was 15 months old and to take extensive notes, audiotapes, and videotapes on a regular basis a few weeks later. I visited with Ricky on average about every 10 days, with no more than a 3-week hiatus during the 21 months of the study. Most visits lasted at least 3 hours, and all the notes from a single visit were turned into a computer record within a day of the visit. (See Shatz, 1994, for more methodological detail.) The study began when I saw Ricky emerging from infancy, starting to use language regularly to manage his social interactions and to learn more from others.

15 TO 17 MONTHS

Knowledge of Self and Others

By 15 months, Ricky had a sense of himself as an individual entity with a name. He loved to play hiding games, often initiating them and even making up new ones. However, his behaviours in various "Where's Ricky?" games suggested that "hiding" meant something like concealing one's own eyes from contact with others. Thus, he would initiate interactions in which he would cover his face with a dishtowel and then call "Where?" or he would run into the bathroom and do the same thing. The vocalisation was a cue to others that they were to respond "Where's Ricky?," following which he would gleefully uncover his face or come running out of the bathroom. He did not seem to have an inkling that he could behave in a way that would truly conceal his location from others, who clearly knew all along just "where" Ricky was. Whether this was because he believed lack of eye contact was sufficient for lack of knowledge or because he did not even consider what knowledge others might have—and how they got it—is unclear.

The incident described earlier, in which Ricky dragged the schoolhouse to the telephone in an attempt to repair my misunderstanding of the referent of his word "house," suggests that he did not understand much about the role of visual perception in knowledge acquisition or communication. Since he must have known he couldn't see me through the telephone, it is unlikely he thought I could see him. More likely, he hoped proximity to my voice would somehow convey the essence of the referent of "house." Other incidents, such as when he wanted to show a picture in a book to another person, confirmed that proximity and not line of sight seemed to be the factor that determined his placement of objects for others. This suggests that before 18 months he had no idea that visual perception was an avenue to knowledge. "Hiding" may have been no more than a game of limited or self-governed eye contact. (Also see Flavell, Shipstead, & Croft, 1978; Lempers, Flavell, & Flavell, 1977.) Nonetheless, his behaviour shows at least this much understanding: He was a different being from others, he could get others to respond to him by talking to them, talking was a way to establish mutual attention or focus, and he could do various things (albeit often ineffective things) to try to change others' responses when mutual focus was not established.

Knowledge of Language

Ricky's language reflected this level of understanding about self and others. Largely a one-word speaker at the time, he often used imitation to confirm mutual focus or attention. As other researchers have noted (Mayer &

Valian, 1977; McTear, 1978), imitation is a way to take a turn or establish or maintain a topic without having to do much linguistic or conceptual work. It functions especially well with interlocutors who frequently ask clarification and yes/no questions of children who are just starting to talk. Often, however, more than mutual focus is intended by the speaker, and then imitations do not work so well. Ricky would sometimes answer "juice" to questions like "Do you want milk or juice?" and then refuse to drink the juice, indicating he had not really understood the intent of the question.

Ricky showed that he had a sense of a separate self when, at less than 18 months, he began to differentiate his possessions from others' with appropriate personal pronouns. I misunderstood one day when as we played with toy cars, he said "urs." "Hurt?" I asked, "what hurts?" Here, too, he recognised a lack of mutual focus. Emphatically, he repeated "urs," as he held out a car toward me. Then I realised that he had been saying "yours." In response to my "Oh—'yours'," Ricky confirmed my realisation with a slightly improved pronunciation, "yurs."

In sum, prior to 18 months of age, Ricky's understandings of others can hardly be said to involve much of a notion of mind. His lack of understanding of perceptual capacities and internal states limited the complexity of his social games and the success of his attempts to establish joint focus. He had recognised, however, the power of speech, and used it frequently to initiate and maintain interaction with others, giving him more opportunities to learn more about them, himself, and language.

18 TO 24 MONTHS

Language Use

In the next six months, Ricky's growing language ability showed an increasingly rich sense of himself and of others. He revealed his view of adults as sources of assistance and information by saying "help" when he could not manage some desired physical action alone (such as opening a package) and asking "why" when he wanted adults to keep talking about something he didn't understand. He may not have understood "why" as a causal question; nonetheless, it was an effective tool for maintaining interaction with adults who talked in response and gave him more information.

He began to talk about himself in various ways, using descriptors that he had heard others use in their references to him. For example, one day he insistently corrected his grandfather who had called him a boy by saying "I a *man*." (this was based on his father's often telling him, "You're my main man."). Still, he was not above referring to himself plaintively as "baby boy" when he was trying to arouse his mother's compassion on an occasion when he had been taken from the company of the adults and put to bed. His attention to self was also revealed in his monitoring of his own language. He began to correct his pronunciations of words even in the absence of misunderstanding or direct feedback from a listener, saying, for example, "faiyers" and then "fowers" when he noticed some flowers. He must, then, have internalised a standard of pronunciations from others that he used to compare his own productions. (See Shatz & Ebeling, 1991, on children's self-corrections.)

Self-awareness

The process of comparing self to others was not limited to language. Elsewhere Ricky showed he was considering how he was alike and different from others—even other animals. One day at the zoo, he watched a giant Siberian tiger cleaning itself with a huge tongue; he fingered his own tongue and then made clear he wanted to see his mother's and my tongues. Ricky's mother verbalised Ricky's interest in our similarities, commenting on the fact that we all had tongues; she then turned our attention to the tiger's sleek tail, saying "Look at the tiger's long tail." At that, Ricky cast a surreptitious look over his shoulder, feeling his own bottom to check on whether he too had a tail. The zoo experience is a good example of how language worked in concert with the process of comparison to produce new knowledge for Ricky. Possibly he had never considered his tailedness status before; the use of language to draw his attention to the tiger's tail in the context of actions and talk about the commonalities of tongues led him to check as well for another body part.

Ricky's increased awareness of self extended to possessions. He was willing to share with other children, but only after he had touched his possessions and announced they were his. He often would label the objects in a room as his own or according to their owners, thereby simultaneously practising the language of possessive constructions and categorising objects with regard to his understanding of the rules governing possession rights. Not only did he assert himself over his possessions, but toward the end of this period, he began to delight in minor infractions of household rules and to see how far he could stretch the patience of the adults around him. For example, he ran headlong toward the street, despite calls to wait, only to stop abruptly just short of the curb.

Knowledge of Others

By 18 months, Ricky realised that proximity to others was inadequate for directing their visual attention, and he began to turn books to the proper orientation for other readers when he wanted them to attend to pictures in books. He was especially interested in eyes, taking pains to align dolls that were "driving" cars so that their eyes faced forward. Even more impressive than his new-found attention to visual perception was the evidence that he was beginning to recognise that others could have (or not have) knowledge and expectations. At 18 months, he began to make a point of showing me, on each of my visits to his house, some of his newest possessions, such as books and puzzles, that I could not have seen on the prior visit. This suggests he kept track of what I had and had not previously seen and that he thought he needed to show me the new things in order for me to know about them. Within six months, he was talking explicitly about his intentions and giving justifications for his behaviour, thereby suggesting that he believed others could not know his motives for action unless he told them. Sometimes, however, his justifications were not especially informative to his adult interlocutors because he frequently did not adjust his message to be truly useful to competent listeners who, as mature social beings, either had the necessary knowledge or could make appropriate inferences about the motives for his behaviours. Hence, on some occasions, his actual message was not communicatively appropriate although his goal of justification was.

Dunn (1988) has proposed that teasing by toddlers reveals their knowledge of others' emotional lives. Early attempts at teasing provided further evidence for Ricky's awareness of cognitive states in others. Leading me upstairs to his apartment as he regularly did, one day he turned as though to head down a second stairway. Then he stopped and looked at me mischievously, awaiting my reaction. He seemed to understand that he could affect *my* behaviour by violating my expectations about *his* behaviour. Also, he enjoyed violating expectations in pretend play with others, for example, pretending to put objects in expected places but actually placing them elsewhere. However, it is unlikely he intended to deceive others, because he made no serious attempt to conceal the objects' true locations from them. Indeed, evidence for truly deceptive behaviour has been hard to find in two-year-olds (Ruffman, Olson, Ash, & Keenan, 1993). It is more likely that Ricky simply took delight in the mutual awareness of violation of expectations.

Thus, the first real indications that Ricky went beyond the establishment of mutual focus to thinking about the mental states of others came from two sorts of behaviours. First, his acts of showing and justifying suggested that he was making judgements about others' ignorance or knowledge based on their direct, particularly visual, experience. Second, behaviours of teasing and pretence showed that he believed others had expectations of regular events or actions that he could violate. Clearly, he had begun to think about others' internal states, but he still had much to learn about what others actually knew, how they acquired knowledge, and how they made inferences.

The claim that Ricky had only fledgling understanding of mental states is corroborated by the fact that not all other people were treated alike. His mother held a special status: He used her as a general knowledge store, referring to her many of the questions others directed to him, and then passing her answers on to his interlocutors after modifying their form appropriately. For example, when asked, "What did you eat for lunch?" Ricky would turn to mother and ask "what?" Upon receiving her reply ("You had cottage cheese"), he would reply to his questioner, "I had cottage cheese." He attempted to do this even on occasions when she could not have known the answer to the question, and he should have known that she was ignorant.

This referral strategy had two advantages for additional knowledge acquisition: for one, he could easily take his turn in a conversation, thereby increasing the likelihood conversations would be extended and he would have more opportunities to use and learn from language; for another, he could gain more information about the things his mother could reasonably be expected to know and not know. Nonetheless, it revealed how difficult it was for him to anticipate the need to take account of her knowledge state and to integrate an assessment of it on a regular basis. It was easier simply to refer questions to her and see what would be forthcoming. In that sense, the strategy was reminiscent of the earlier proximity strategy for establishing a joint focus of attention. Still, Ricky had made progress toward a theory of mind; he was beginning to understand that people could know about, be ignorant of, or expect events in the world.

25 TO 30 MONTHS

Language Practice

The next six months brought much language play and practice with various speech registers, as Ricky tried out ways of talking that showed he was thinking about the different relations people could have with one another. The recognition that people differed in their ways of interacting with others showed he was comparing social roles and assessing his own behaviour vis-à-vis others. For example, he was more solicitous of me than of his grandfather, with whom he had a much more teasing, competitive relationship. In speech to dolls and animals, he tried out some of the dominant roles he ordinarily did not get a chance to take with the adults around him; he would be alternatively authoritative and nurturing with entities that didn't talk back. Thus, he seemed to understand that different social roles called for different kinds of language. He recognised also that language was an avenue to knowing others, and he practised imminent interactions, perhaps reassuring himself that conversational ritual would ease the dangers of the unknown. As we were on our way to a mall so that he could meet an impersonator of one of his favourite storybook characters, Babar the elephant, I heard him rehearsing in the back of the car. "Knock, knock. Babar opens the door. 'Hi, Babar.' 'Hi!' "

Not only did Ricky practise the social uses of language, but he exercised his budding repertoire of mental terms. He showed he understood the verb *think*, at least as a marker of probability, when he responded to his mother's use of it that way by a rephrasing with the word *maybe*. He was looking for some little dolls in a duffel bag when I asked his mother, "Are there toys in that bag?" She responded, "Yes, some little people, I think." Ricky added "And a pig, maybe." Starting out with *maybe* as an expression of uncertainty, he gradually moved to tagging "I think" onto his statements. In both cases, he overused the term when he first began to use it, as if to take every opportunity to try it out and see whether it worked. By the end of this period, he used *think* in ways that indicated he understood it to involve some sort of mental activity.

He used other mental terms too, like *know*, *guess*, and *hide*, but the ways he initially used them suggested that he had limited knowledge of their meaning. *Know* was at first found solely in responses that seemed to rely on the frozen phrase, "I don't know;" only at the end of the period was it used appropriately to indicate states of nonignorance. *Guess* and *hide* were used to initiate games with others (e.g. "I want you to guess his name" or "Let's hide"), but they did not seem to carry the presupposition that the guessers or the seekers would be ignorant of the relevant information. For example, he asked adults to guess names of objects pictured in books that they obviously knew. As with the earlier games of hiding, it seemed unimportant what others knew; instead, it was playing—or practising—the game itself that was of interest. The games and the language accompanying them had become more sophisticated; yet, true ignorance from the players was still not required. Again, it was unclear whether Ricky was misreading the knowledge states of others (maybe thinking that if they agreed to "guess," they could not know) or whether he was simply ignoring completely the issue of their state of knowledge. Increasingly, the games were taking on some of the features of more mature games, but still the practice of these skeletal games seemed to be a goal in and of itself; eventually more mature strategies for influencing others' knowledge states would be incorporated into these primitive formats to produce "genuine" hiding and guessing games. (See Bruner, 1972, on the role of play in development.)

Gaining Knowledge about Self and Others

It may have been too difficult for Ricky both to practise the language of game formats and to think about and evaluate others' knowledge states. In ordinary discourse he was better able to consider what others might know, especially relative to what he knew. He regularly exchanged information with other adults, asking them to provide more information and also offering more information when adults did not understand. For example, on the phone one day with him, I asked what sort of ornaments were on his Christmas tree. "What?" I asked when he responded with "yights and aminals." "Yights!" he said, "Binking yights—bink, bink, bink." (Blinking lights—blink, blink, blink.) No longer did he need to rely on a proximity strategy when mutual focus was lacking. He had both a better sense of how to reach his listener and broader linguistic competence to express himself.

He continued to compare himself with others, but now he could even do it via language. I told him one day, as we listened to a record, "Uncle Jay used to play that music on the piano." Although he had never heard his uncle play, he made an immediate comparison, "Ricky play the piano very bad." His increased language ability allowed him to use comparison processes indirectly, enhancing his ability to learn in the social sphere. Beginning to recognise that people could have different preferences as well as skills, he also would use his language to ask what things others liked to eat and drink.

In sum, Ricky's behaviours make it clear that he thought of himself and others as both alike and different. Both he and others had knowledge, skills, and preferences; but these could vary among people. Moreover, he recognised that these differences were topics of conversation. He was starting to acquire the language of mental life. He could not yet use it appropriately in all situations, but he had made real progress in talking as others around him did about what they thought, knew, and liked.

31 TO 36 MONTHS

Increasing Complexity in the Language of the Mind

The mental verb *think* can function in a variety of ways in an utterance; it can be used to express possibility, to modulate an assertion, to label mental activity, and to mark states of belief (Gelman & Shatz, 1977). Limited at first to interactional functions, the term gradually takes on meanings that refer more directly to mental states (Shatz, Wellman, & Silber, 1983). Although he started using *think* fairly early, Ricky followed this progression, too, with his most sophisticated use of the verb, to mark states of false belief, appearing last. As with other children, it was only in the second half of the third year of life that he began contrasting his prior state of belief with current knowledge or reality (Shatz et al., 1983). For example, he expressed surprise as he walked out into the night and saw a bright full moon, saying "I thought it was just a little, little slice." Soon after, he also began to make statements about others' belief states, even ones that did not match his own or the state of reality. His utterance about the dry pyjamas cited earlier, "You thought these were wet," is an example of this.

The close proximity in time between the emergence of contrastives having to do with Ricky's own state of mind and statements about others' false beliefs can be explained by examining more closely what is involved in making the two kinds of statements. The early contrastives were about his own prior belief that had changed in response to new experience or knowledge. Thus, they involved two states of belief in his mind, one of which was an inaccurate representation of reality and the other an accurate representation, the second following in time upon the first. Ricky's first statement about another's false belief was also about a prior state of belief that was at odds with reality. The difference was that, instead of experiencing the two states himself, he had to make an inference about my prior belief state, based on our joint earlier experience and the kinds of questions I had asked him. The statement about my false belief was more sophisticated than his contrastives about his own states because he had to infer what my state of mind was as opposed to experiencing the inaccurate state himself. Moreover, the belief state he inferred for me was different from the one he himself had. Nonetheless, the reasoning about the false beliefs of self or other may have been very similar: A prior representation of reality was seen as inaccurate in light of the present reality. No direct comparison had to be made between my inaccurate belief state and Ricky's own accurate one. In essence, Ricky was explaining my behaviour in terms of false representations of reality; children find it easier to give such explanations than to predict behaviours on the basis of false beliefs (Bartsch & Wellman, 1989; Dunn et al., 1991).

Ricky's talk about false beliefs was only one manifestation of increased attention to the relation between reality and nonreality. A few months later, around age three, he began to use a plethora of hypothetical constructions such as, "If I had a ladder, I would climb up it and change that lightbulb." Hypotheticals and contrastives both require the speaker to think about and compare the actual state of affairs either to a nonactual state or to an inaccurate belief state. In both cases, the grammatical constructions chosen make clear the speaker's stance on the relation of the nonreal to reality. However, for hypotheticals, the nonreal state is not a past one but a possible or future one. Possibly children have to acquire a sense of the hypothetical before they can begin to *predict* others' actions on the basis of false beliefs.

Language practice allows even more flexible ways than contrastives and hypotheticals to talk about the nonreal, by the use of constructions that do not directly signal how the discourse relates to reality. For example, speakers often tell jokes and fantasies in "as if" discourse, using the same formal devices recruited for direct descriptions of reality. Speakers frequently signal they are entering such "as if" realms of discourse with intonation or facial cues. Children have to learn these cues and to recognise when such discourse is not mapping directly to reality. Ricky had generally been able to discover when he was being teased and had learned how to tease others in turn. Still, he would often insist on making explicit what realm of discourse he and his interlocutor were in. For example, when he started to recount a story about a fictional character who loses a button, his grandfather seemed to Ricky to be genuinely overly concerned about the animal's loss. Ricky reassured him, saying "It just tells about it" (meaning, "It's just a story"). Behaviours of this sort also show that he was focusing on the complex relations between mind, language, and reality.

Developing Concepts of Self and Other Selves

Social understanding involves knowing when people can be expected to behave in similar ways and when they can be expected to be different. For example, adults know that virtually all people would not step in front of an oncoming train, but some people dislike eating dandelions. This simple example belies the broad knowledge acquired about the behaviour of others over a lifetime. Young children develop both their concepts of themselves and of other people as they observe and reason about the motives for their own and others' behaviour. Not only do children have to learn that others do not necessarily like or want everything they themselves do, but they have to learn that others may not believe everything they do (Flavell, Flavell, Green, & Moses, 1990). Such knowledge depends in part on recognising that mental states are not just mirrors of reality, but are contingent on a host of factors such as experience and predilection. Thus, appropriate expectations about human behaviour rest on epistemological theory: Eventually, children must have a folk theory about how knowledge is acquired and used in reasoning in order to predict how others will behave in various circumstances. Ricky's early attention to states of ignorance versus knowledge and representations of nonreality versus reality demonstrates that toddlers are immersed in the effort to understand people's behaviour.

Ricky's contrastives were evidence that he was aware of his own belief states and that he had begun to recognise he could have misconceptions about reality. Moreover, he insisted on occasion that only he was able truly to characterise his internal states, often correcting others who would assign descriptors to him. He also began to talk explicitly about the possible selves (Markus & Nurius, 1986) he might have when he grew up. This suggests he had begun to see himself as an individual with both a history and a future, constant, albeit changing, across time. For example, at 38 months of age, he asked me to take a photograph of him holding up a picture of himself when he was a baby.

His dealings with others gave evidence of a growing understanding that others could be both alike and different from him. He would ask others about their preferences and would sometimes voice an opinion and then ask others, "What do you think?" Although recognising that people's opinions and tastes could differ, he nonetheless expected them to be held to a common level of rationality. He would ask people to justify their statements or behaviours and then question their logic if he was unconvinced by their answers. For example, he had been calling me to join him in play in the living room as I was cleaning the kitchen after dinner one night. My mother attempted to stop his badgering by telling him I was washing the dishes. He challenged her statement by saying, "I don't hear the water running." Thus, he recognised that some matters were not open to opinion but instead were subject to common logic. Even his own mother, who had previously been treated as a general knowledge store, was now occasionally questioned about her sources of knowledge, with Ricky asking her (albeit in a tone more quizzical than challenging) after she had made an assertion, "How you know that?"

Learning about how the self and others can differ as a consequence of experience was an everyday activity and involved even incidents of ordinary visual perception. Although Ricky had been thinking about visual perspective at 18 months of age, he still, at times, wanted to make explicit what others were seeing and how it related both to their actions and to his own perceptions. Moreover, he now used language to try to confirm his hypotheses about others' percepts and their subsequent actions.

As we played at a table in the den, I moved a lamp because its light was in my eyes, unintentionally putting it in Ricky's line of sight of the baseball game that I had hardly noticed on the TV. Ricky moved the lamp to the other side of the table, saying, "I move it back." Now its cord was in a precarious position, so I moved the lamp once again. Ricky asked, "You move it because it's blocking baseball thing?" At his words, I realised that the lamp would have been in my line of sight had I been watching the game, so I said, "yes." Only as he moved the lamp to a position that interfered with *neither* of our views and said, "So I move it back here, and it not block baseball," did I realise that I had inadvertently blocked *his* view of the TV by my actions.

Although Ricky had misinterpreted why I had moved the lamp in the first place, the subsequent interaction revealed that he was thinking about the differences in visual perception for people as a function of their lines of sight (Yaniv & Shatz, 1990). Moreover, the incident shows how a toddler can use language to help him understand how people relate to the world and to compare his place in that world with the place of others.

Sophistication and Naivety about Others

Children reach a new level of social sophistication when they realise that others do not necessarily possess the same knowledge they do; this understanding provides them with the opportunity not only to be more considerate of others, but also to be disingenuous. Often, their first efforts to deceive are naive because the children cannot always—or do not understand that they have to—assess accurately what other persons truly know or can infer about the truth of the matter at hand in order for their deceptions to succeed. Ricky's early "deceptions" moved from inadequate attempts at hiding to subtler linguistic fabrications, which nevertheless were insufficiently guileful to fool a wary adult. After dinner with me one day, he announced with feigned innocence, "My mommy gives me chocolate ice cream every day." Ricky did indeed get his ice cream that evening, but only after I questioned the absoluteness of his claim.

Increasing sophistication coupled with lingering naivety about the particular status of others was also observed in incidents involving social rules. Especially with the start of preschool, Ricky became attentive to explicit social rules and prohibitions, but he was unworldly with regard to their scope. For example, his 28-year-old step-uncle told him he liked watching Mario Brothers cartoons. In amazement, Ricky, whose own TV-watching was severely restricted, asked incredulously, "Your mother lets you?"

Thus, Ricky's social knowledge was still fragile. It was not always available in novel situations, and awareness of the social roles and status of others was limited. Even while lacking some of the components required for felicitous outcomes, he engaged in interactions with the bits and pieces of knowledge he had, thereby providing opportunities for more learning. By the start of his fourth year, he had acquired enough of the knowledge necessary to think and talk about the behaviour of self and others in terms common to his discourse community. The rudiments of a burgeoning social-linguistic intelligence were in place.

CONCLUSIONS

Ricky had spent two years learning the language of his social group and using it to learn still more about people, as he practised, questioned, and experimented in social settings. In that time, he had observed others, compared himself to others, and elaborated his representation of himself and of those around him. Language learning and self–other comparisons had bootstrapped one another to create an increasingly complex understanding of mind.

The picture of the child painted in this chapter assumes some continuity of development over time. However, I do not mean to imply by the mention of continuity that the 15-month-old already essentially has a "theory" of mind. Surely there are some basic building blocks in place by then: 15-month-olds know a great deal about what makes a social being; they know they can create joint foci of attention with other humans (and maybe even some animals), and they can recognise when they have not created a mutual focus. Yet, the understanding of *mind* is richer than that. Just how rich we make it, and the behavioural criteria we set up to decide whether and when children have a theory of mind, depends on the definitions we give to our terms—what is meant by "understanding, " "mind," and "theory." I have argued that a minimal criterion is the demonstration of rudimentary social-linguistic intelligence, the ability to interpret the behaviours of self and others in language common to the members of one's discourse community. In Western societies at least, that means recognising that there are both differences and commonalities between self and others and using the language of mental states to express those relations and to rationalise behaviour.

Surely, the development of the understanding of mind continues beyond the toddler years, as Ricky's story and the work of others indicate. As noted, Ricky was still ignorant of many aspects of social knowledge, and there are many social or mental reasoning tasks that children fail (see Flavell, 1988, for a review). Yet, it may be too restrictive to argue that children under age four do not understand the representative nature of mind but instead believe the mind to have only a direct cognitive connection to reality (Flavell, 1988). The lamp-moving incident illustrates that Ricky understood that two people could simultaneously have two different perspectives, and the dry-pyjamas incident shows that he understood something about the role of both experience and inference in the formation of belief. Together, the incidents suggest that the three-year-old is capable of something more than a copy theory of mental representation. Three-year-olds may not know all there is to know about the mind's influence on the representation of reality, but they apparently are working on gaining a better understanding of it. Indeed, it is difficult to understand where the four-year-old's prowess comes from without assuming a serious effort on the part of the younger child to acquire social-cognitive knowledge. Moreover, it is not surprising to find the early evidence for this nascent representational understanding in spontaneous conversations in natural settings before seeing it in the laboratory. In sum, this case study demonstrates that the toddler period is the time when children actively work to understand themselves and others around them in communicable terms, when they develop a social-linguistic intelligence, without which theories of mind would be impoverished theories indeed.

ACKNOWLEDGEMENTS

This chapter is based on a paper presented as part of the symposium, "Early theory of mind competencies," at the biennial meeting of the Society for Research in Child Development, New Orleans, March 1993. The data come from a case study to be published by Oxford University Press (Shatz, 1994).

REFERENCES

Bartsch, K., & Wellman, H.M. (1989). Young children's attributions of action to beliefs and desires. *Child Development, 60*, 946–964.

Bruner, J.S. (1972). Nature and uses of immaturity. *American Psychologist, 27*, 1–28.

Dunn, J. (1988). *The beginnings of social understanding.* Cambridge, Mass.: Harvard University Press.

Dunn, J., Brown, J., Slomkowski, C., Tesla, C., & Youngblade, L. (1991). Young children's understanding of other people's feelings and beliefs: Individual differences and their antecedents. *Child Development, 62*, 1352–1366.

Flavell, J.H. (1988). The development of children's knowledge about the mind: From cognitive connections to mental representations. In J.W. Astington, P.L. Harris, & D.R. Olson (Eds.), *Developing theories of mind* (pp. 244–267). New York: Cambridge University Press.

Flavell, J.H., Flavell, E.R., Green, F.L., & Moses, L.J. (1990). Young children's understanding of fact beliefs versus value beliefs. *Child Development, 61*, 915–928.

Flavell, J.H., Shipstead, S.G., & Croft, K. (1978). Young children's knowledge about visual perception: Hiding objects from others. *Child Development, 49*, 1208–1211.

Gelman, R., & Shatz, M. (1977). Appropriate speech adjustments: The operation of conversational constraints in talk to two-year-olds. In M. Lewis & L. Rosenblum (Eds.), *Interaction, conversation, and the development of language* (pp. 27–61). New York: Wiley.

Golinkoff, R.M. (1993). When is communication a "meeting of the minds"? *Journal of Child Language, 20*, 199–207.

Gopnik, A., & Wellman, H.M. (1994). The theory theory. In L.A. Hirschfeld & S.A. Gelman (Eds.), *Mapping the mind: Domain specificity in cognition and culture* (pp. 257–293). New York: Cambridge University Press.

Harris, P.L. (1994). Thinking by children and scientists: False analogies and neglected similarities. In L.A. Hirschfeld & S.A. Gelman (Eds.), *Mapping the mind: Domain specificity in cognition and culture* (pp. 283–304). New York: Cambridge University Press.

Hickling, A. (1993, March). *The mind's "I": Children's conception of the mind as an active agent.* Paper presented at the Biennial Meeting of the Society for Research in Child Development, New Orleans.

Lempers, J.D., Flavell, E.R., & Flavell, J.H. (1977). The development in very young children of tacit knowledge concerning visual perception. *Genetic Psychology Monographs, 95*, 3–53.

Markus, H., & Nurius, P.S. (1986). Possible selves. *American Psychologist, 41*, 954–969.

Mayer, J., & Valian, V. (1977, October). *When do children imitate? When imitate? When necessary.* Paper presented at the Boston University Conference on Language Acquisition, Boston.

McTear, M.F. (1978). Repetition in child language: Imitation or creation. In R. Campbell & P. Smith (Eds.), *Recent advances in the psychology of language* (pp. 293–311). New York: Plenum.

Ruffman, T., Olson, D.R., Ash, T., & Kennan, T. (1993). The ABCs of deception. Do young children understand deception in the same way as adults? *Developmental Psychology, 29*, 74–87.

Shatz, M. (1994). *A toddler's life: Becoming a person.* New York: Oxford University Press.

Shatz, M., & Ebeling, K. (1991). Patterns of language learning related behavior: Evidence for self-help in acquiring grammar. *Journal of Child Language, 18*, 295–313.

Shatz, M., & O'Reilly, A. (1990). Conversational or communicative skill? A reassessment of two-year-olds' behavior in miscommunication episodes. *Journal of Child Language, 17*, 131–146.

Shatz, M., Wellman, H.M., & Silber, S. (1983). The acquisition of mental terms: A systematic investigation of the first reference to mental state. *Cognition, 14*, 301–321.

Woolley, J.D., & Wellman, H.M. (1990). Young children's understanding of realities, nonrealities, and appearances. *Child Development, 61*, 946–961.

Yaniv, I., & Shatz, M. (1990). Heuristics of reasoning and analogy in children's visual perspective taking. *Child Development, 61*, 1491–1501.

16 Before Belief: Children's Early Psychological Theory

Henry M. Wellman
University of Michigan, Ann Arbor, USA

Karen Bartsch
University of Wyoming, Laramie, USA

INTRODUCTION

When do children understand what about the mind—about the mental lives of persons and about such mental states as thoughts, dreams, wishes, and desires? This question has been much researched over the past few years and our picture of young children's understanding has been transformed and clarified by that research. In contrast to earlier characterisation (e.g. Piaget, 1929), it is now clear that probably by three and certainly by four years of age most children understand that people's external actions are in part the products of their internal intentions, ideas, emotions, and goals (see such volumes as Astington, Harris, & Olson, 1988; Butterworth, Harris, Leslie, & Wellman 1991; Frye & Moore, 1991; Whiten, 1991). One way to characterise this naive psychological understanding of preschoolers, older children, and adults, is to describe it as roughly a belief-desire mentalism (see, e.g. D'Andrade, 1987; Wellman, 1990). The basic idea is that we see persons as engaging in certain actions, exploits, or deeds because they *desire* certain things and *believe* some act will help achieve that desire. Or, people experience certain feelings and express certain reactions because their beliefs and desires have been satisfied or undermined in various ways.

Most of the many studies on this general topic have concentrated on children's understanding of beliefs, and have focused on three- and four-year-olds' understanding. Why has there been such emphasis on beliefs? One

331

reason is that an adequate understanding of belief manifests a key feature of our everyday understanding of mind: That mind represents the world and that in turn these representations determine actions. It is because John believes it will rain, for example, that he takes his umbrella with him. The workings of false belief nicely illustrates this feature: John's action is determined by his belief that it will rain even if his belief proves false and the weather remains sunny and clear. Children must at some point come to understand that people's actions are based on representations of the world and not the world directly. Hence, considerable attention has been focused on children's understanding of beliefs and false beliefs, and considerable interest has been generated by research demonstrating that four-year-olds easily and consistently understand persons' false beliefs, whereas three-year-olds do so either never, less often, or only under certain conditions (see, e.g. Lewis, this volume).

We take for granted that by three or four years of age children understand about beliefs and engage in belief-desire reasoning much like adults do (e.g. Wellman, 1990). Our focus concerns earlier ages and the origins of such a preschool achievement. Is there a time when very young children reason about people without an understanding of such mental states as thoughts and beliefs? If so, how can we characterise that earlier understanding, before belief? Are very young children generally ignorant and confused about mental life; perhaps just fixated on the external actions, behaviours, and expressions of people? Or do they have some simplified or alternative but nonetheless mentalistic understanding of people? If they do, what is that understanding like? In previous reports and presentations, we have hypothesised that very young children do possess a cogent understanding of people in advance of an understanding of belief—a naive psychology based in part on a simplified conception of mental states of desire (Bartsch & Wellman, 1989; Wellman, 1990; Wellman & Woolley, 1990). In this chapter, we briefly articulate and elaborate this account. Our main argument is that there is an early period—typified by two-year-olds—in which children lack a conception of belief or representation but, nevertheless, construe persons in mentalistic and subjective fashions. We will concentrate primarily on a positive description of very young children's understanding of mental states, captured in their understanding of desire.

Besides being focused on older children's understanding of belief, most prior research also shares the feature of having been conducted primarily through laboratory questioning tasks such as unexpected transfer and deceptive box false belief tasks (Perner, Leekam, & Wimmer, 1987; Wimmer & Perner, 1983). We have been exploiting a different, more naturalistic method; our principal findings come from children's everyday talk. The findings outlined here, and others as well, are presented more fully in Bartsch and Wellman (in press).

OVERVIEW OF THE RESEARCH

For several years we have been examining longitudinal natural language transcripts from ten English-speaking children aged two to five years. These transcripts are part of the CHILDES database, organised and made available by Brian MacWhinney and Catherine Snow (1985; 1990). The transcripts include, for example, those of Adam, Eve, and Sarah from Roger Brown's research program (Brown, 1973), and similar data from seven other children. We systematically searched the more than 200,000 child utterances in these transcripts for terms referring to thoughts, beliefs, and desires—all the terms listed in Table 16.1.

The transcripts contained approximately 12,000 utterances using these terms—mostly variations on *want*, *think*, and *know*. We were not interested just in children's use of these terms but in what children meant in using them. Children might, in certain cases or at certain ages, use such terms to refer genuinely to the psychological states of self and others, as adults often do. But they might use the terms in merely uninterpretable fashions, or simply in direct repetitions of adult speech, or for conversational, not referential uses (see, e.g. Shatz, Wellman, & Silber 1983). As an example of conversational use, a child might say "You know what?" merely to get the listener's attention, without really making reference to someone's mental state. Moreover, children might use terms such as *think* or *know* and *want* to refer to people's observable behaviours rather than to their inner subjective states. However, our examination revealed that many child utterances did convincingly reveal a genuine understanding of psychological states. Table 16.2 contains several examples.

The larger context of an utterance was crucial for coding whether it encompassed genuine reference to mental state. For instance, in the first

TABLE 16.1
List of Terms Examined[a]

Thoughts and Beliefs	Desires
Think	Want
Know	Wish
Expect	Hope
Wonder	Afraid (that)
Believe	Care (about)
Dream	

[a] All possible variants of a term were included. Thus *want* included want, wan', wants, wanna, wanted; *think* included think, thinks, thinked, thought; *believe* included make-believe, and so on.

TABLE 16.2
Genuine Psychological References

Thoughts and Beliefs

Abe (3:3):	I didn't get you a surprise.
Adult:	You didn't. I'm sad.
Abe:	No, don't be sad. I thought I would, 'cept I didn't see one for you.
Adam (3:3):	Can I put dis in de mail? Can I put my head in de mailbox ... so de mailman can know where I are?
Ross (3:3):	He was trying to rip it up, right?
Adult:	No, he won't rip it.
Ross:	But I know he could rip it.
Sarah (4:4):	You put it ... see? You don't know where the pieces go. I know. An' that goes there, right?

Desires

Adam (2:7):	Eat mommy.
Mother:	Eat?
Adam:	Yeah.
Mother:	I'm not hungry.
Adam:	Want spoon?
Mother:	No thank you.
Adam:	OK. You don't want a spoon. You don't want a spoon.
Ross (2:6):	He scratched me.
Adult:	Didn't it hurt?
Ross:	Yeah. I want a band-aid. The boy hurt me.
Adult:	The boy hurt you? How did the boy hurt you?
Ross:	The boy wanted to.
Sarah (2:8):	My new book.
Adult:	A new book.
Sarah:	New book. Wan' go read it? go ... see new book?
Abe (2:10):	You want ... you want to talk on the telephone?
Adult:	To who?
Abe:	Edna and John. You talk on the phone and they want to come over.
Adult:	You want me to find out if they want to come over?
Abe:	Yeah.
Adult:	OK. I'll try.
Abe:	You call on the telephone.

---

example in Table 16.2, if we knew only that Abe said "I thought I would," it could be argued that he was only using *thought* as a politeness marker, or to ask permission for some behaviour (e.g. "Would it be OK if I did?"). However, the larger context fairly convincingly shows that Abe was talking about an idea or plan that he had had but did not actualise. Similarly, in the first example for desire in that table, perhaps saying "want spoon" just signals a behavioural request (e.g. "give me the spoon"). But again the larger context indicates that Adam is not just making a request, or referring to behaviour; rather, he seems genuinely to be commenting on what Mommy wants. Our identification of genuine psychological references of these sorts was highly reliable, with better than 90% agreement between two independent coders.

Initial findings

Using this broad initial coding scheme, we charted the pattern of children's genuine psychological references to thoughts, beliefs, and desires. Such references are shown in Fig. 16.1 as a proportion of children's total utterances using any of the terms in Table 16.1. As Fig. 16.1 indicates, genuine references to thoughts and beliefs appear at just about the third birthday. By the fourth birthday, such references constitute about 25% of children's total psychological talk. In contrast, genuine reference to desire is apparent much earlier, in the talk of very young children.

Figure 16.1 portrays the data summed across all children, but the same general pattern was apparent in the data for each individual child. Four of the children contributed most of the data, about 70% of all utterances in the

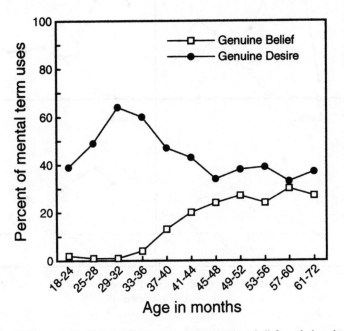

FIG. 16.1 Genuine psychological references to desires, and to beliefs and thoughts (from Bartsch & Wellman, in press).

entire dataset. The individual patterns for those children are shown in Fig.
16.2, where it is clear that individuals' data replicated the grouped data quite
closely.

We became aware of this general picture several years ago (e.g. Bartsch &
Wellman, 1989), and it helped form the basis for our hypothesis that there is
an early period in which children view people through a simplified
incomplete psychology, one that includes a core notion of desire but not
beliefs. A similar general picture emerges from other natural language
studies, such as those of Bretherton and Beeghly (1982) and Furrow,
Moore, Davidge, and Chiasson (1992). This picture and our related
hypothesis raise several important questions. We will concentrate on two of
these questions in this chapter. First, how credible is the conclusion that
children progress from first talking and conceiving of mental states of desire
to only later talking and conceiving of thoughts and beliefs? That is, would a

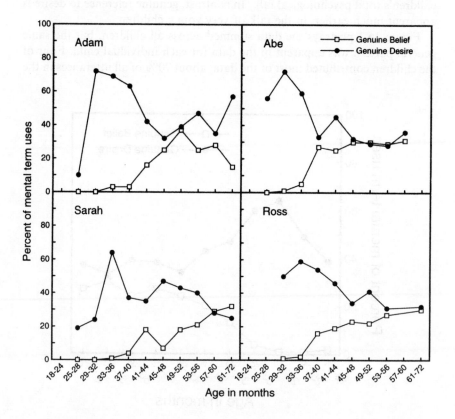

FIG. 16.2   Genuine psychological references for the four individuals contributing the most
data (individual figures from Bartsch & Wellman, in press).

closer or more rigorous look at their talk about the mind reveal that an early attribution to young children of an understanding of desires is a mistake; or relatedly, that an attribution of an understanding of thoughts and beliefs to only older children is a mistake? Second, if there is an earlier period, before children understand beliefs, in which they nonetheless construe people in terms of mental states such as desires, what can we say about the nature of that early psychological understanding? Several other sorts of analyses allow us to address both these questions.

Contrastives

A recognition critical to an appropriate understanding of mental states is that such states are independent of the physical world—desires are different from outcomes or from actions themselves, and thoughts or beliefs are different from the world that they are about. Similarly, mental states differ between individuals—my desires and thoughts are often different from yours. Following a method pioneered by Shatz et al. (1983), we looked for utterances in which children explicitly contrasted one of these alternatives with another—specifically, utterances in which children acknowledged or verbalised the distinction between mental states and the world, or between the mental states of different people. Example contrastives are presented in Tables 16.3 and 16.4 under the headings of Thought–Reality, Desire–Outcome, and Individual Contrastives.

Figure 16.3 shows the occurrence of these sort of contrastives (again portrayed as a proportion of all utterances using any of the focal terms). Obviously, the same developmental pattern emerges with regard to contrastives as that which came from the more general coding scheme. Two-year-olds are contrasting desires with outcomes and actions and contrasting the desires of different persons, but it is not until about three years of age that any such talk about thoughts and beliefs is evident. An examination of individuals' data again replicated the group data.

These findings for contrastives do two things. First, they corroborate the general picture obvious in Fig. 16.2, but this time with a more conservative and explicit analysis. That is, the data show that very young children can talk quite cogently about mental states—they do so for desires. Yet at the same time the data show that children begin to refer to thoughts and beliefs only later, at about three years of age. Second, the data indicate some of the ways in which very young children have a genuine understanding of mental states, in this case, desires: They seem to recognise that desires are not the same as outcomes or actions, and that they differ across individuals.

An adult understanding of mental states such as desires (or thoughts and beliefs), however, goes still further. With regard to differences between people, for instance, we adults not only know that mental states are different

TABLE 16.3
Belief Contrastives

Thought-Reality Contrastives

Adult:	Hey, it works. See?
Abe (3:4):	I thoughted it was busted.

Adult:	Do you really think it was haunted? By real ghosts? You think those were real ghosts who did it?
Mark (3:11):	I thought they were ... that ... there was a real man.

Ross (4:8):	Now she knows that I know. She used to think that I don't know when I really did.

Individual Contrastives

Adult:	I thought you were downstairs.
Ross (3:3):	I thought me was upstairs.

Adult:	Oh I think so. I think it goes in mommy and daddy's room.
Peter (3:1):	I think it goes right here.

Adult:	What are you making?
Sarah (4:9):	Something good out of this paper. An you don't know but I know.

Ross (3:7):	Do you think God is good?
Adult:	Yes.
Ross:	But we think God is mean.
Adult:	Why?
Ross:	Because he spanks me.

---

for different individuals, we know that people can have different attitudes about the very same thing—that is, we recognise that mental states are subjective. Do young children understand this subjective quality of mental states? To address this question, we identified specifically those contrastives that seemed to indicate an appreciation of subjectivity—those that expressed an acknowledgement, for example, that while I might want to eat that slightly over-ripe banana, you wouldn't want it at all. In our analysis of the subjectivity of desire, we included contrastives in which children used words like *want* and additionally the term *like* to express recognition of subjectivity. We found over 50 such conversations, exemplified in Table 16.5, in the talk of 2-year-olds, representing 9 of the 10 children. They were first found at an average age of about 2½ years.

We compared this talk about subjective desires with comparable talk about beliefs, such as:

Adult:	It's kind of orangish red.
Abe (3:1):	Orangish red?
Adult:	Yeah.

TABLE 16.4
Desire Contrastives

Desire-Outcome Contrastives

Adam (2:7):	I don't want it to leave it. Momma, why it leave?

Adult:	Don't push that button.
Naomi (2:11):	I want to push on this one.
Adult:	No, that's the one you're not supposed to.

Ross (3:0):	He (toy cookie monster) gonna eat my other raisins and I'm gonna eat these raisins. I want some cookies.
Adult:	We don't have any.
Ross:	My cookie monster wants my mommy to make some cookies for him.

Individual Contrastives

Adult:	I want you to tell her about this book.
Adam (2:8):	Don't want book.
Adult:	You don't want to tell her about the book.
Adam:	No.

Adult:	I'd like to see you draw on one.
Naomi (2:7):	No, I don't want to.
Adult:	No? I'd like to see you draw so much.
Naomi:	No.

Sarah (2:11):	Eat ... you eat water?
Adult:	No I don't want any water.
Sarah:	I want some.

Abe:	I don't think it's orangish red.
Adult:	You don't think it is?
Abe:	Uh huh. I don't think so, because it's orange, not red.

This is an especially forceful sort of comparison of belief and desire talk because of the similarity in the examples we looked for—for belief, the child had to acknowledge that one person believes "x" whereas someone else does not believe "x" or believes "not-x," for desire, that one person wants "x" whereas someone else does not want "x" or wants "not-x." Other subjective contrastives for beliefs and thoughts are shown in Table 16.6. Again, although two-year-olds talked about desires in this subjective fashion, talk about the subjectivity of thoughts and beliefs was found only about eight months later, essentially in children aged over three.

Subjectivity is one important feature of an adult understanding of mental states; another is the independence of mental states from the physical world that they "intentionally" point to. We looked at this generally in the Thought-Reality and Desire-Outcome Contrastives mentioned earlier, but

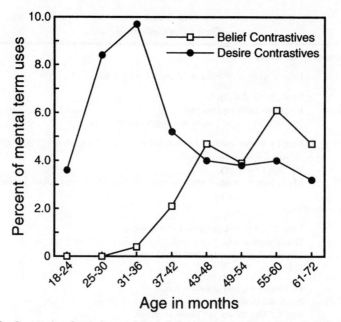

FIG. 16.3   Contrastives for desires, and for beliefs and thoughts (from Bartsch & Wellman, in press).

we also looked at it in several more precise ways. As just one example, consider that because mental states are independent of the world, they can be experienced and talked about before their worldly counterparts are encountered—for example, we can talk about desires that will be satisfied only in the future, and beliefs that can only be confirmed at a later time. We called this Advance Desire and Advance Belief talk and identified instances of it, like those in Table 16.7. Talk about desires that will not be acted on or satisfied until later appeared consistently in the talk of two-year-olds, beginning at about age two-and-a-half. In contrast, similar talk about beliefs and thoughts was virtually never found before age three.

Thus far, we have argued that very young children possess a mentalistic conception of people; specifically, that they construe people as having desires that are both subjective and independent of the world. An important additional question concerns whether young children's references to mental states are simply the mention of their own internal experiences or whether children also refer to the internal and hence unobservable states of others. One possibility is that, at some young age, children are merely reporting their own states rather than using mental state concepts or understandings to reason systematically about people in general (see, e.g. Smiley &

TABLE 16.5
Subjective Contrastives for Desires

Abe (2:10):	No.
Adult:	You don't like it?
Abe:	You like it?
Adult:	Yes. I do.
Abe:	But I don't like it.
Adult:	No, I don't want any (water poured on her).
Sarah (2:11):	Why?
Adult:	Because I don't like to get wet.
Sarah:	Huh. Don't like to get wet? Swim? You want you swim?
Adult:	No, I don't wanna swim.
Sarah:	OK. I like swim.
Adam (3:0)	I don't like shaving cream.
Adult:	You don't like shaving cream?
Adam:	No. Daddy like shaving cream.
Ross (3:3):	Do you like mushrooms?
Adult:	Yes. Do you like mushrooms?
Ross:	No. I hate them.

Huttenlocher, 1989). However, our data show that, at least by about two years of age, children are indeed referring to the internal states of both themselves and others. According to our initial coding scheme, which identified children's genuine references to desire, such references, although tending to be about the speakers themselves, are also about others. In fact, on average, two of each child's first ten genuine references to desire in our samples were attributions to others. This is, of course, further supported by two-year-olds' production of subjective contrastives, as mentioned earlier. How could young children acknowledge differences between themselves and others, with regard to wanting versus not wanting the very same object, unless they were indeed attributing to others unique and independent states of desire?

The analyses reviewed so far begin to fill out the picture of young children's understanding of mental states, before belief. Quite young children seem to understand that people possess internal mental states, at the least in the form of desires or wants. Talk about desires at this young age is not just talk about external behaviours or outcomes; children refer to desires for self and for others that are distinctively contrasted with parallel states of the world itself—for example, desires as different from the outcomes they point toward or the actions that would satisfy them. Moreover, young children refer to desires that differ across individuals and that are subjective.

TABLE 16.6
Subjective Contrastives for Thoughts and Beliefs

Adam (3:3):	What is that for, huh? Can I put some sugar in this? Does you think have sugar ... some sugar in here?
Adult:	I don't have any sugar.
Adam:	I think you have sugar.
Abe (3:4):	... Mommy, what is this kind of plate?
Adult:	A round one.
Abe:	I think it's a square plate.
Sarah (3:7):	Where's the bed?
Adult:	Whose bed?
Sarah:	Her bed.
Adult:	I don't know.
Sarah:	I think it disappeared. You think it does?
Adult:	Yeah, I think it disappeared.

Explanations and Arguments

If even very young children understand persons in psychological fashions, and if that psychological understanding changes in the years from two to five as children move from an understanding of states such as desires to an enlarged understanding encompassing thoughts and beliefs, then what sort of impact do these understandings and developments have on children's lives? For example, does a psychological construal of people affect children's causal reasoning about people's actions and reactions, and does it influence how children interact with others? Surprisingly, the wider ramifications of children's understanding of minds have been little studied (see also Dunn, this volume; Chandler, Lalonde, Fritz, & Hala, 1991). Our data allow us to begin to address these larger questions.

Explanations

It could be that young children understand that people have mental states, but do not appeal to such states to explain why people do things. That is, children might fail to incorporate a concept of mental states into something like a coherent causal-explanatory system. An intriguing question, therefore, concerns children's explanations of and causal reasonings about human behaviour. To address this issue we looked at children's use of the terms listed in Table 16.1 to explain action explicitly. Table 16.8 shows several examples of the sorts of explanations we found. Figure 16.4 shows the overall data with regard to children's explanations. That figure shows that children explain people's actions by appeal to their mental states quite early; they do so specifically by citing a person's desires. Children certainly do not

TABLE 16.7
Advance Desire and Advance Belief

Advance Desire

Abe (2:6):	Get a circle one for me (a kind of telephone).
Adult:	No, I won't get you a (telephone).
Abe:	I want one. When I grow big, I get one.

Sarah (2:9):	(In a talk about birthdays) Dere.
Adult:	Yes. Would you like one of those?
Sarah:	I want have one of dose.
Adult:	Tell Daddy. (said by mother)
Sarah:	I want have dose.
Adult:	For your birthday?
Sarah:	Yeah, for my birthday.

Adam (2:10):	More milk.
Adult:	You don't need more milk.
Adam:	Why not? Want milk in it.

Advance Belief

| Adult: | Jack is hiding |
| Naomi (3:5): | Yup. I think he's going to open the door and walk along. |

Sarah (3:5):	In here, mommy?
Adult:	Maybe. Let me see.
Sarah:	Maybe see. I think it's in here.
Adult:	Let me see.
Sarah:	I think it's in here, mommy.

Ross (3:11):	I'll pour it. Can I pour this?
Adult:	Will you be able not to spill?
Ross:	I think I won't.

await the advent of an understanding of belief, and hence belief-desire explanations, in order to employ mental state constructs explanatorily. The figure additionally shows that children's mentalistic explanations of actions change dramatically. Children begin to explain a person's actions by appeal to his or her desires; explanatory appeals to thoughts and beliefs appear only much later. It is also clear from other work, such as the experimental work of Wellman and Woolley (1990), that two-year-olds are capable of causal reasoning centring on a person's desires.

Arguments and Conflicts

Does children's developing theory of mind, moving from an early desire-oriented psychology to a later theory involving beliefs, affect not only children's reasoning about the social world but also their interactions in it?

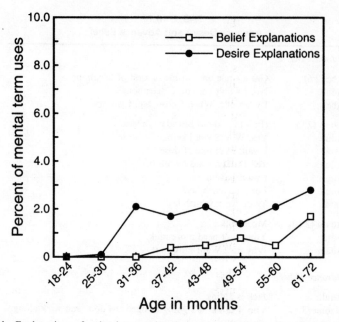

FIG. 16.4 Explanations of action by appeal to desires versus beliefs or thoughts (from Bartsch & Wellman, in press).

Although our investigation was limited to children's talk, we began to explore this issue by examining children's verbal conflicts. Some verbal disputes revolve around the physical aspects of persons (e.g. who is bigger or stronger) and some around aspects of social interchange (e.g. whose turn it is), but others involve specifically psychological aspects of persons (e.g. whose desires will prevail, or whose beliefs are correct). If young children are acquiring basic psychological construals of people then they are also acquiring the fodder for psychological disputes. Table 16.9 illustrates some of the sorts of disputes we found. In examining children's psychological disputes, we analysed their use of the terms from Table 16.1 but added some new terms as well. For example, with regard to disputes about beliefs, we looked at use of terms such as *think* and *know* but also children's use of simpler words such as *so*, *right*, *wrong*, etc. to engage in such disputes, such as in the following example:

Adam (3:7): That is so fingerpaint.
Mother: No. It's not fingerpaint.
Adam: It is fingerpaint!
Mother: You're silly.

TABLE 16.8
Explanations

Desire

Adult:	Why do you keep saying "why?"
Ross (2:7):	I want to say "why."
Adult:	You want to say "why?" Why do you want to say "why?"
Ross:	I just want to.

Adult:	Did he have breakfast?
Sarah (3:1):	No.
Adult:	No? Why not?
Sarah:	He don't wanna.

Ross (2:10):	Look, there's a car up in the air.
Adult:	Oh. Why is it up there?
Ross:	Man put it up there.
Adult:	Why did he put it up there?
Ross:	He want to fix it.

Belief

Abe (3:11):	Rufus (the dog) is barking so loud.
Adult:	Why do you think she's barking?
Abe:	Sometimes Rufus knows if somebody's outside.
Adult:	Is that why she barks?
Abe:	Yeah.

| Sarah (4:10): | I thought I saw his ugly-looking face, so I looked back. |

Ross (4:5):	Dad, why do they call Han Solo handsome?
Adult:	I don't know.
Ross:	Because they think he is?
Adult:	Yeah.

By including conversations that used these words (as opposed to just the thought and belief terms in our larger investigation), we were able to double-check our claim that reference to persons' desires precedes a construal of persons that involves belief. Conceivably, we could have found that disputes about belief via words such as *right* and *so* were present very early in life, even though children were not using the thought and belief terms of Table 16.1 at all. But we found no evidence for such a possibility. Figure 16.5 shows the overall data for desire disputes versus disputes about beliefs and thoughts. These expanded data, once again, show the now familiar pattern.

CONCLUSIONS

The emphasis in much current research on young children's understanding of belief and false belief has encouraged some simple and unfortunate conclusions: That a mentalistic understanding of persons is acquired in an

TABLE 16.9
Conflicts

Desire

Adam (2:10):	More milk.
Adult:	You don't need milk.
Adam:	Why not? Want some milk in it.

Abe (2:9):	I wanna, I wanna watch TV.
Adult:	You can in a little while.
Abe:	I wanna watch something now.

Belief

Abe (3:3):	They think they hace ... they are slimy.
Adult:	What do you think?
Abe:	I think they are good animals.
Adult:	You don't think they are very nice?
Abe:	I think they are, 'cept mean ones.

Adam (3:5):	Mr. Peanut Butter.
Adult:	Mr. Peanut. He's not peanut butter yet.
Adam:	He is so.
Adult.	Mr. Peanut.
Adam:	No.

---

all-or-none fashion at around three or four, and that an understanding of mind reduces to a single conceptual insight, that of false belief. Our research demonstrates that children's psychological understanding, their theory of mind, undergoes several extended developments in the years from two to five. Our findings confirm that in those years children do come to appreciate the existence and importance of representational mental states such as beliefs and false beliefs. More importantly, however, the data reveal that children understand several crucial aspects of people's internal mental lives—and several important relationships between inner states, outer events, and overt actions—long before they understand thoughts, beliefs, and false beliefs and long before the ages explored in current laboratory research. These earlier psychological conceptions are apparent in children's understanding of people's desires (and, relatedly, their understanding of certain emotions and certain perceptual or attentional states; see Baldwin & Moses, this volume; Bartsch & Wellman, in press; Baron-Cohen & Ring, this volume; Gopnik, Slaughter, & Meltzoff, this volume). Such an early psychological understanding, we believe, provides children with a remarkable facility for thinking about themselves and others: It encompasses an initial conception of subjective, mental life; it supports causal-explanatory reasoning about people's actions and expressions; and it influences

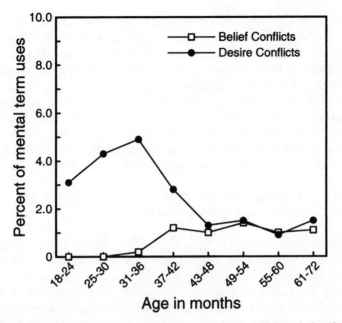

FIG. 16.5 Psychological disputes about desires versus about beliefs and thoughts (from Bartsch & Wellman, in press).

children's interactions with other people, as exemplified in their disputes and arguments with parents and siblings.

Like almost all developmental inquiry, examining children's developing understanding of mind requires us to address two basic questions. (1) Descriptively, what developments characterise children's understanding? What conceptions of mind appear earlier, what conceptions appear only later, and in what order? (2) Theoretically, how can we explain this developmental progression? What accounts for the nature of, and the changes in, children's understanding? These questions go hand in hand; theoretical accounts must explain the observed progressions. Currently, there are disagreements both about the descriptive course of children's understanding of mind and about how best to characterise and account for development in this domain. Our findings speak to both these debates. In what follows we will briefly discuss two broad families of descriptive accounts and, relatedly, two broad classes of theoretical positions, and outline the implications of our findings for both (for more comprehensive and detailed treatments see Bartsch & Wellman, in press; Gopnik & Wellman, in press).

Descriptively, a fundamental issue concerns whether children's basic conception of mental states does or does not change substantially in the years from two to five. Initial empirical demonstrations of changes in children's performance on false belief tasks (e.g. Wimmer & Perner, 1983; Perner et al., 1987) led to a very straightforward proposal: That children's understanding of mind changes quite dramatically as an initial belief-desire understanding is achieved, apparent by about age four but absent at about age three. More recently, there have been increasing demonstrations that even three-year-olds at times solve false belief tasks (e.g. Bartsch & Wellman, 1989; Chandler, Fritz, & Hala, 1989; Lewis, this volume; Robinson & Mitchell, 1992; Siegal & Beattie, 1991). In our data, three-year-olds also explicitly talk about false beliefs, as in this example:

Adult: I thought it was a bus.
Adam (3:3): It's a bus. I thought a taxi.

These newer demonstrations have led to the suspicion that perhaps no conceptual change takes place in this age range, but that instead a variety of performance factors are hindering young children's demonstration of an underlying appreciation of beliefs and desires. The suggestion is that an understanding of beliefs as well as other mental states is actually apparent in quite young children, certainly in young three-year-olds, and thus an understanding of both beliefs and desires must come on-line quite early (Chandler, 1988; Fodor, 1983), and indeed that even young children could not understand one of these mental states without understanding the other (Bennet, 1991; Fodor, 1992; Moses & Chandler, 1992).

However, our research, by extending the empirical focus to even younger children, supports the hypothesis of a substantial conceptual transformation in young children's thinking, and helps capture the nature and timing of that change. According to our data, the major change to account for is not from an absence of an understanding of false belief at age three to its presence at age four; rather, as described throughout this chapter, the change is from an early mentalism evident in two-year-olds' understanding of desires to later belief-desire understanding apparent in three-and four-year-olds. Although it is true that three-year-olds refer to beliefs and false beliefs, it is also true that younger children, two-year-olds, make no reference to such mental representational states as beliefs, or to thoughts, imaginations, or dreams.

It is extremely difficult to prove definitely that young children do not have some critical conception, say a conception of thoughts and beliefs, simply because that understanding is not demonstrated on various laboratory tasks or revealed in naturalistic observation. The possibility always remains that the young child appreciates the distinction or concept involved but simply does not employ it or talk about it. But in our data the absence of any reference to belief stands in stark contrast to young children's obvious understanding and fluent reference to desire. This allows us to address several alternative explanations. For example, one possibility might be that young children's failure to refer to thoughts and beliefs indicates that, although they understand that people possess mental lives, children just do not talk about such mental states, preferring instead to describe people's overt behaviours and external appearances. But, of course, our data make clear that young children regard people's mental states and experiences as an important topic of conversation; this is evident in their frequent references to desires and to emotional states. In the presence of such mental state discourse, the complete absence of talk about thoughts and beliefs becomes more striking and more interpretable. Alternatively, it might have been argued that talk about beliefs is particularly linguistically complex, requiring complex sentence forms referring to predicate sentential propositions, as in "You don't *know where the pieces go*" (Table 16.2). However, a closer examination reveals that reference to desires and reference to beliefs employ very similar sentence forms and language competence; both include use of propositional complements, such as "You *want to talk on the telephone*" (Table 16.2). Children demonstrate the competence needed to talk about beliefs before they do so: They demonstrate that competence in their talk about desires.

Consider one final alternative account of our data, showing that an early mentalistic reference to and understanding of desire precedes a later belief-desire understanding. Perhaps such a developmental progression merely reflects how adults talk to children, rather than children's conceptual understanding. Specifically, perhaps adults simply do not talk to children about beliefs until they are about three years' old. In that case, children's talk might also show the patterns we have observed. We tested this possibility by coding adult talk in the transcripts from the four children contributing the most data. We found that adults frequently used terms referring to beliefs and thoughts in talking to very young children—more than 25% of the mental term talk to 2-year-olds used belief and thought terms such as *think*. Moreover, in their use of such terms to talk to very young children, adults predominantly make genuine reference to thoughts and beliefs. More than 60% of all thought and belief term uses from parents were genuine references to thoughts and beliefs, even in talk to 2-year-olds. Thus, at a very young age children hear people described in terms of beliefs as well as their desires, yet such young children describe and reason about people in terms of desires, not beliefs. In short, our data give us ample reason to hypothesise that a substantial conceptual transition takes place in children's understanding of the mind in the years from two to five as children move from an initial desire psychology to a later appreciation of the existence and role of mental states such as thoughts and beliefs as well.

Let us suppose that, indeed, a substantial change in children's understanding of the mind takes place in the years from two to five. How shall we characterise and account for this change theoretically? At the extreme, a variety of different accounts are possible (see, e.g. Astington & Gopnik, 1991). We will concentrate briefly on two broad families of account. One sort of account is implied by the now common phrase used to describe this area of inquiry, the child's theory of mind. This phrase has been adopted by many writers because the term "theory" can loosely be used to refer to almost any sort of knowledge, and children's understanding of mind is by definition whatever knowledge children have about the mind and mental states. However, as part of a general characterisation of cognitive development in terms of theory development (e.g. Carey, 1985; Karmiloff-Smith, 1988; Wellman, 1990), it is possible to argue more precisely that children's understanding of mind provides them with a coherent conceptual system that functions in distinctly theory-like fashions, analogical to, but distinguishable from, scientific theories (e.g. Gopnik & Wellman, in press; Forguson & Gopnik, 1988; Perner, 1991; Wellman, 1985; 1990). Our characterisation of two-year-olds as having an early (perhaps initial) psychological theory centring on desire followed only later by a belief-desire theory, is framed by the larger proposal that children's understanding evolves through a series of theories, a succession of coherent and related reasoning systems.

This sort of theory-theory account can usefully be contrasted with another family of accounts, one that suggests that a theory metaphor provides a seriously misleading characterisation of children's understanding of minds. A strong contender of this sort is simulation theory. Simulation theorists (Goldman, 1992; Gordon, 1992; Harris, 1989; this volume; Johnson, 1988) argue that it is unnecessary to attribute to the child a theoretical system of constructs, such as the concepts of belief and desire, in order to explain their understanding of minds. When reasoning about minds, they contend, we do not resort to concepts, rather we simply resort to our own first-hand experience of mental life. Humans are organisms who have mental states—beliefs, desires, dreams, emotions, and more—and in our own case we need not conceive of such states but simply experience them. When it comes to attributing mental states to others, we need only imagine what our mental experience would be like if we were in the other's situation, and then attribute that experience to them—a process of simulating mental states rather than conceptualising mental states.

As stated by Gopnik and Wellman (in press, pp. 13–14):

> For both theory theory and simulation theory we can predict that there will be development: there will be initial "easy" problems solved correctly before later "hard" ones. But the notion of what will be easy and hard dramatically differ between these two accounts. For simulation theory the critical difference is between states that are directly reported [one's own current state] versus those that must be simulated ... In contrast, for theory theory the critical difference concerns states that are easy or difficult to conceive of.

Consider beliefs and desires as constructs, not as experiences. Such constructs are generic theoretical ones, applicable to self and other. If children's understanding of mind rests on such mental-state conceptions, then such constructs, once acquired, would be applied to the understanding of both self and others. But, of course, such theoretical constructs might well differ in nature or complexity such that one is conceived of in advance of the other. Indeed, our account predicts that a simple conception of desires is considerably less complex than an ordinary conception of representational mental states such as beliefs (Bartsch & Wellman, in press), and hence an understanding of desires should precede one of thoughts and beliefs. In contrast, in a simulation theory both beliefs and desires are experienced by the organism itself, as states of its own mind. This should mean that, at least when no simulation is required, it should be equally easy to experience and report beliefs as desires. Indeed, a prominant simulation theorist, Harris (in press), makes just this prediction. Harris (in press, pp. 13–14) goes on to argue that:

> ... simulation theory holds that young children ... should be relatively accurate at reporting their own current states... The theory theory makes no claim to such privileged access arguing instead that mental states, whether belonging to self or other, must all be filtered through the same theoretical lens... To the extent that theory-theorists argue that children's accuracy varies only with the nature of the mental state, ignoring their privileged access, they cannot explain children's relative accuracy in reporting their own states.

Our data have several implications for the debate between these contrasting theoretical positions. Most obviously, they are at odds with this last prediction of Harris's. Young children, two-year-olds, do refer to and reason about their own current states, as evident in their references to their own desires. But in our data they never mention or report on their own thoughts, beliefs, or imaginings. On simulation theory, young children clearly experience such states, both beliefs and desires. So, on that theory, why should the child's reports at first involve desires but not belief? On theory theory, however, there is a good reason why children's talk, about themselves and equally about others, first includes desires but excludes beliefs, thoughts, and dreams. Young children have yet to come to a theoretical conception of such representational mental states. Reference to such states requires more than simply experiencing and reporting them; children must also develop a conceptual understanding of such states and accord such states a conceptual role in their larger naive psychological framework.

To be clear, we do not deny an important role for the child's own first-hand experience in their developing understanding of mind. As Moore and Barresi (1993) have recently put it: "knowledge of the psychological states of self and others is not only theory-laden but also data-driven." But we do contend that such experience is theory-laden; it is marshalled and understood by the child through a conceptual framework that changes substantially in the years from two to five. What children say about the mind is in accord with this characterisation of mental state knowledge, and with the characterisation of an early desire-based theory changing to a later belief-desire theory. Our findings can not address all current controversies regarding children's theories of mind. However, we believe that they do add significantly to our descriptive knowledge of children's developing understanding of minds, and that they constrain and inform theoretical debate.

ACKNOWLEDGEMENTS

Conduct of the research outlined here has been supported by NICHD grant HD-22149 to Henry M. Wellman and support from the Centre for the Study of Child and Adolescent Development of Pennsylvania State University to Karen Bartsch.

REFERENCES

Astington, J.W., & Gopnik, A. (1991). Theoretical explanation of children's understanding of the mind. *British Journal of Developmental Psychology, 9*, 7–31.

Astington, J.W., Harris, P.L., & Olson, D.R. (Eds.) (1988). *Developing theories of mind*. New York: Cambridge University Press.

Bartsch, K. (1990). *Everyday talk about beliefs and desires: Evidence of children's developing theory of mind*. Paper presented at the meeting of the Piaget Society, Philadelphia.

Bartsch, K., & Wellman, H.M. (in press). *Children talk about the mind*. Oxford: Oxford University Press.

Bartsch, K., & Wellman, H.M. (1989). *From desires to beliefs: First acquisition of a theory of mind*. Paper presented at the Biennial Meetings of the Society for Research in Child Development, Kansas City.

Bennet, J. (1991). How to read minds in behaviour: A suggestion from a philosopher. In A. Whiten (Ed.), *Natural theories of mind* (pp. 97–108). Oxford: Basil Blackwell.

Bretherton, I., & Beeghly, M. (1982). Talking about internal states: The acquisition of an explicit theory of mind. *Developmental Psychology, 18*, 906–921.

Brown, R. (1973). *A first language: The early stages*. Cambridge, Mass.: Harvard University Press.

Butterworth, G., Harris, P.L., Leslie, A.M., & Wellman, H.M. (Eds.). (1991). *Perspectives on the child's theory of mind*. Oxford: Oxford University Press.

Carey, S. (1985). *Conceptual change in childhood*. Cambridge, Mass.: MIT Press.

Chandler, M. (1988). Doubt and developing theories of mind. In J.W. Astington, P.L. Harris, & D.R. Olson (Eds.), *Developing theories of mind*. New York: Cambridge University Press.

Chandler, M., Fritz, A.S., & Hala, S. (1989). Small-scale deceit: Deception as a marker of two-, three-, and four-year-olds' early theories of mind. *Child Development, 60*, 1263–1277.

Chandler, M., Lalonde, C., Fritz, A., & Hala, S. (1991). *Children's theories of mental life and social practices*. Paper presented at the meetings of the Society for Research in Child Development, Seattle.

D'Andrade, R. (1987). A folk model of the mind. In D. Holland & N. Quinn (Eds.), *Cultural models in language and thought* (112–148). Cambridge: Cambridge University Press.

Fodor, J.A. (1983). *Modularity of mind*. Cambridge, Mass.: MIT Press.

Fodor, J.A. (1992). A theory of the child's theory of mind. *Cognition, 44*, 283–296.

Forguson, L., & Gopnik, A. (1988). The ontogeny of common sense. In J.W. Astington, P.L. Harris, & D.R. Olson (Eds.), *Developing theories of mind* (pp. 226–243). New York: Cambridge University Press.

Frye, D., & Moore, C. (1991). *Children's theories of mind: Mental states and social understanding*. Hillsdale, NJ: Lawrence Erlbaum Associates Inc.

Furrow, D., Moore, C., Davidge, J., & Chiasson, L. (1992). Mental terms in mothers' and children's speech: Similarities and relationships. *Journal of Child Language, 19*, 617–631.

Goldman, A.I. (1992). In defense of simulation theory. *Mind & Language, 1*, 104–119.

Gopnik, A., & Wellman, H.M. (in press). The theory theory. In L. Hirschfeld & S. Gelman (Eds.), *Domain specificity in cognition and culture*. New York: Cambridge University Press.

Gordon, R.M. (1992). The simulation theory: Objections and misconceptions. *Mind and Language, 7*, 11–34.

Harris, P.L. (1989). *Children and emotion*. Oxford: Basil Blackwell.

Harris, P.L. (in press). Thinking by children and scientists: False analogies and neglected similarities. In L. Hirschfeld & S. Gelman (Eds.), *Domain specificity in cognition and culture*. New York: Cambridge University Press.

Harris, P.L., Johnson, C.N., Hutton, D., Andrews, G., & Look, T. (1989). Young children's theory of mind and emotion. *Cognition and Emotion, 3*, 379–400.

Johnson, C.N. (1988). Theory of mind and the structure of conscious experience. In J.W. Astington, P.L. Harris, & D.R. Olson (Eds.), *Developing theories of mind* (pp. 47–63). New York: Cambridge University Press.

Karmiloff-Smith, A. (1988). The child is a theoretician, not an inductivist. *Mind and Language, 3*, 183–195.

MacWhinney, B., & Snow, C. (1985). The child language data exchange system. *Journal of Child Language, 12*, 271–296.

MacWhinney, B., & Snow, C. (1990). The child language data exchange system: An update. *Journal of Child Language, 17*, 457–472.

Moore, C., & Barresi, J. (1993). Knowledge of the psychological states of self and others is not only theory-laden but also data-driven. *Behavioural and Brain Sciences, 16*, 61–62.

Moses, L.J., & Chandler, M.J. (1992). Traveler's guide to children's theories of mind. *Psychological Inquiry, 3*, 286–301.

Perner, J. (1991). *Understanding the representational mind*. Cambridge, Mass.: MIT Press.

Perner, J., Leekam, S.R., Wimmer, H. (1987). Three-year-olds' difficulty with false belief. *British Journal of Developmental Psychology, 5*, 125–137.

Piaget, J. (1929). *The child's conception of the world*. London: Routledge & Kegan Paul.

Robinson, E.J., & Mitchell, P. (1992). Children's interpretation of messages from a speaker with a false belief. *Child Development, 62*, 639–652.

Shatz, M., Wellman, H.M., & Silber, S. (1983). The acquisition of mental verbs: A systematic investigation of first references to mental state. *Cognition, 14*, 301–321.

Siegel, M., & Beattie, K. (1991). Where to look first for children's understanding of false beliefs. *Cognition, 38*, 1–12.

Smiley, P., & Huttenlocher, J. (1989). Young children's acquisition of emotion concepts. In C. Saarni & P. Harris (Eds.), *Children's understanding of emotion*. New York: Cambridge University Press.

Wellman, H.M. (1985). A child's theory of mind: The development of conceptions of cognition. In S.R. Yussen (Ed.), *The growth of reflection*. New York: Academic Press.

Wellman, H.M. (1990). *The child's theory of mind*. Cambridge, Mass.: MIT Press/Bradford Books.

Wellman, H.M. (1991). From desires to beliefs: Acquisition of a theory of mind. In A. Whiten (Ed.), *Natural theories of mind: The evolution, development, and simulation of everyday mindreading* (pp. 19–38). Oxford: Basil Blackwell.

Wellman, H.M., & Woolley, J.D. (1990). From simple desires to ordinary beliefs: The early development of everyday psychology. *Cognition, 35,* 245–275.

Whiten, A. (Ed.) (1991). *Natural theories of mind.* Oxford: Basil Blackwell.

Wimmer, H., & Perner, J. (1983). Beliefs about beliefs: Representation and constraining function of wrong beliefs in young children's understanding of deception. *Cognition, 13,* 103–128.

17

What People Say, What They Think, and What is Really the Case: Children's Understanding of Utterances as Sources of Knowledge

Elizabeth J. Robinson
University of Birmingham, UK

INTRODUCTION

Much of our knowledge about the physical world is acquired indirectly from other people: We are often told about things without having first-hand experience of them. But what people tell us is also one of the most direct sources of information about their beliefs. Sometimes talk about mental states is explicitly marked as such—"I thought it was in there"—but often it is not. Whenever somebody makes a statement about an aspect of the outside world, the statement simultaneously reveals the speaker's belief about that.

Often, there is consistency between what is said, what the speaker believes, and what is really the case: The Head of Department's secretary tells me he is in, I knock on his door, and I find he is indeed there. The speaker's belief was true, her message reflected her belief accurately, and there was no problem when I acted on the basis of what she told me.

On some occasions, though, things are not so simple: I see the Head of Department making for his office but, shortly after, the secretary tells me he is not in. Do I simply disbelieve her and knock on his door anyway (if I can manage that without offending her)? If I do this, acting on the basis of what I saw, do I assume the secretary failed to notice him come past, or do I wonder if she knows he is there but wants me to believe he is not? On the other hand, if I believe what I am told, how do I reconcile that with what I think I saw? Was it not him I saw? Or did he go into his room and immediately leave again?

The interpretation we make in apparently contradictory situations like this will depend on contextual cues, sensitivity to which is likely to develop over a number of years. Sometimes we treat what we are told as unreliable, and discount it in favour of what we saw. We might assume we misheard or misinterpreted what was said, or that the speaker had a false belief, intended to deceive, or made a slip of the tongue. Sometimes, on the other hand, we treat what is said as trustworthy, and try to resolve the contradiction by re-interpreting what we saw.

In attempting to explain the mismatch between knowledge obtained from direct sources and knowledge obtained from what somebody tells us, we are likely to make an inference about the speaker's intention or belief. Resolving the contradiction involves making a decision about whether the error lies in our own mind's processing of information, or whether it lies in the other person's mind. If the secretary's belief is accurate and her intention was to inform rather than to deceive, then maybe my interpretation of what I saw, or of what she said, was wrong. If her belief was false, or she intended to deceive, then my interpretation of what I saw and heard may be accurate. There are likely to be links between the explanatory frameworks people have available to make sense of apparent contradictions between what they are told and what they experience for themselves, and the way those contradictions are resolved.

We know that between the ages of around three to five years there are great changes in children's understanding about people's mental states. Interesting developmental questions arise about children's handling of the dual informative nature of utterances: How do children deal with the complex interplay between knowledge about the world obtained directly and indirectly via other people's utterances, between what people say and what they believe, between what people believe and what appears really to be the case?

We might expect to see age-related differences in the way children deal with contradictions of the kind described here. Such differences could be symptoms of an increasingly elaborate theory of mind. On the other hand, they could be causes of development of a more elaborate theory of mind. I shall speculate a little about these possibilities at the end of the chapter.

The rest of the chapter falls into three main sections, on utterance-world relationships, on utterance-belief relationships, and on the dual informative role of utterances.

UTTERANCE-WORLD RELATIONSHIPS

Do Children Discriminate Between Knowledge Obtained Directly and Knowledge They are Told?

From very early on, infants treat what people say as being about the world. They acquire knowledge about the world directly from what people tell them, as well as directly by seeing or feeling. But do they treat information obtained via other people as being equivalent to that acquired directly, or do they discriminate between knowledge obtained from these two types of source? Discriminating between knowledge from direct and indirect sources could be a first step in developing a category of "knowledge obtained via another's mind"—a category which, as adults, we may make use of implicitly when trying to resolve the kinds of contradiction mentioned in the previous section.

Perner (1988; 1991) argues that we should expect children from the outset to treat linguistic input differently from direct input (1988, p. 145): "... (it) would be disastrous if (the knowledge base) were linked (causally) to symbolic input, like language. Because linguistic statements can be unreliable (mistakes, lies) and are subject to frequent errors of interpretation, the child's knowledge base would become alarmingly unstable." Perner argues that young children treat symbolic input as a different kind of situation, which can mismatch the directly perceived situation. In support of his position, Perner cites Pea's (1980) evidence that young children are prepared to reject an incorrect description of an object. For example, on being asked "Is that a biscuit?", one child replied "No, apple." The implication in Perner's account is that not only do infants discriminate between knowledge acquired directly via their own senses and knowledge acquired from other people's utterances, but that they treat the latter as potentially unreliable.

However, a child could answer "No" to the question "Is that a biscuit?" without treating as unreliable utterances in statement form that are unaccompanied by cues that the speaker is joking. Suppose the child said "Doggy" when referring to a horse, and the adult said "That's a horse." Would the child reject that statement as unreliable, and continue to believe that the object referred to was really a dog? If she did, I suggest she would have little hope of achieving mastery over language. Furthermore, if children are to function effectively within a communicative network, surely they must assume (implicitly) that speakers normally conform to basic co-operative principles, and are truthful and informative. If they do assume this, then it is likely that they make the related assumption that what people say is normally a reliable source of knowledge about the world.

At some point, though, children will come across circumstances in which knowledge obtained directly, such as by seeing, contradicts what somebody tells them. I observed a nursery teacher say to a three-year-old "Sam is in the cloakroom, can you go and get him please?" The child went to search, but failed to find Sam even though he was, in fact, in the cloakroom. How did this child deal with the contradiction between what he was told and what he could see? Did he assume that the teacher was wrong, and return to the class with that information? Or did he assume that Sam must be in the cloakroom and continue to search? The child I observed just stood in the cloakroom, apparently unsure what to do, and eventually another child had to be sent to collect both him and Sam.

In this example, the teacher's statement was accurate, though it initially appeared not to be to the child listener. However, perhaps it is more common for people to be misinformed by what other people say than by what they experience directly. Even a speaker who intends to be truthful and informative can misinform through making a slip-of-the-tongue, or as a result of being mistaken about the matter to which she is referring.

Furthermore, whether or not it is more common to be misinformed by being told than by direct sources, it could be that knowledge obtained directly has a special salience, in that it appears to be reality rather than a comment on reality. We may for this reason give more weight to what we experience for ourselves than to what we are told. That is, we may be inclined to ignore the fact that what we know by seeing is subject to interpretation.

Whether or not we generally weight knowledge obtained directly as more reliable than knowledge obtained indirectly, as adults we have many potential ways of resolving contradictions between them, as my example at the beginning illustrated. In what follows I describe two series of investigations in which children were faced with contradictory information from direct and indirect sources. First we looked at how children dealt with these contradictions and, in the second series, we looked at their judgements of how another person would deal with them.

Do Children Treat What They are Told as Unreliable in Comparison with Seeing for Themselves?

In a series of studies carried out with Peter Mitchell and Rebecca Nye, three- to five-year-olds experienced contradictions between knowledge obtained directly (by seeing or by inference) and knowledge obtained via somebody else (by being told or shown a picture). Which source did the children choose to believe? Our procedure was based on the first part of the standard deceptive box task (Gopnik & Astington, 1988; Wimmer & Hartl, 1991), in which the child forms an expectation about the contents of the box by looking at the outside (e.g. Smarties), then sees that the true contents are something different (e.g. crayons). In our procedure, a teddy or a second experimenter then appeared and the child told him what was in the box. Of course, children answered on the basis of what they saw, updating their belief and abandoning their prior expectation. But what happens when they are told by the experimenter what is inside the box, instead of seeing for themselves?

In our initial studies we tried to make it plausible that the message should be believed: The children experienced the experimenter telling the truth on warm-up trials, in which they saw the contents for themselves after the experimenter had said what they were, and the experimenter feigned surprise on the test trials when he saw the unexpected contents, without giving any cues that he was joking or tricking. Finally, children saw the experimenter look inside the box before he gave his message. We do not know whether children were sensitive to these indicators of reliability, but we do know that, despite their presence, some children did not treat the experimenter's utterance as a trustworthy source of knowledge. Most children did update their beliefs in the message condition, but they were significantly less likely to do so than they were when they saw the true contents for themselves: In one of our studies, 78% updated on the message trials, compared with 95% on the seeing trials. The children who failed to update their beliefs in accordance with the message could usually report what the experimenter had told them.

It seems, then, that when children had only been told about the box's contents, they sometimes chose to maintain their prior belief, which was itself inferred on the basis of a picture on the outside of the box. Apparently, some of the children were inclined to distrust the knowledge obtained indirectly, even though their prior belief was based on rather flimsy evidence, and we had tried to indicate that the utterance was trustworthy.

There are circumstances under which children are much less likely to believe what they are told. In studies carried out by Kevin Riggs, described later, three-year-olds saw what colour mug was being put under a cloth, then heard Richard, who had not seen, say it was a different colour. Of course, the children believed what they had seen and not what Richard said. Similarly, in a small-scale study carried out by Rebecca Nye, children saw what was inside a box, then a second experimenter looked inside and said, incorrectly, that there was something different inside. As we might expect, the preschool children refused to believe what he had said. In another condition, the children's initial belief was based on a logical inference about the box's contents: They saw two different objects, one of which was transferred to the box in question, and the children then saw the one that was left behind, so could infer which was now in the box. The second experimenter then looked inside and gave a contradictory message about the box's contents. Interestingly, children were just as likely to disregard the utterance as they were when they had seen for themselves what the box's contents were. The great majority of the children gave greater weight to knowledge acquired directly via their own minds than to knowledge acquired indirectly via somebody else's, even though the direct knowledge was based on a logical inference.

This result suggests that there is nothing especially powerful about knowledge acquired by seeing, and that conclusion is supported by the results of a further condition. This time children formed an incorrect expectation about a box's contents by looking at the outside, then the experimenter looked inside and, instead of saying what she had seen, she showed a picture. Children saw something, but it was not the real object that they saw. The incidence of updating in this condition was very similar to that in the message condition I described first of all; as in the message condition there was significantly less updating than when the children saw the contents for themselves.

From all these results, it is clear that preschool children do not blindly disregard knowledge acquired via another mind when it contradicts knowledge acquired directly via their own mind alone. Rather, they show some flexibility in that they are less ˙ .ely to disregard the utterance when it contradicts a belief based only on having seen the exterior of the box, but more likely to disregard it when it contradicts a belief based on a logical inference or on direct seeing. Furthermore, our results so far suggest that it makes no difference whether the indirect knowledge comes via an utterance or a picture, so it does not seem as if linguistic input, rather than any input which comes via another mind, is treated as potentially unreliable. It seems possible, rather, that young children have implicit categories of knowledge obtained directly and knowledge obtained indirectly.

However, we cannot conclude from their behaviour that these children treat indirect knowledge as potentially unreliable because it comes via another mind. That is, although their behaviour is superficially consistent with implicit understanding that minds are subject to error, it may not really be a symptom of such understanding. Children may be behaving in ways consistent with explanatory frameworks that they do not yet possess. If the children were tested under more stringent conditions they might behave in ways inconsistent with implicit understanding about the unreliability of other minds. We do not yet know, for example, whether children are more likely to disregard the experimenter when she has not looked inside the box (and apparently has no prior knowledge of its contents), than when she looks before telling the child what is inside. That is, do children believe an utterance from a well-informed mind more readily than one from a poorly informed one? If they do, this would be more convincing evidence of implicit understanding.

Do Children Judge that Somebody Else Will Believe What They Have Seen Rather than What They Were Told?

Next, we went on to find out whether children could reflect on sources of knowledge if asked to judge what another person would think when somebody told him something that contradicted what he had seen for himself.

There is already evidence that children younger than about four years have difficulty reflecting on sources of knowledge, whether these are direct or indirect. O'Neill, Astington, and Flavell (1992) report that three-year-olds made errors choosing whether they need to see or feel an object to identify it, and several studies have shown that three-year-olds sometimes cannot report their sources of knowledge, whether these are direct (seeing) or indirect (being told) (Gopnik & Graf, 1988; O'Neill & Gopnik, 1991; Wimmer, Hogrefe, & Perner, 1988). Our focus of interest was slightly different from theirs, in that our children were not asked to choose or report a source of knowledge, but to judge what a person thought once he had received contradictory input from different sources.

In a study carried out with Peter Mitchell, Rebecca Netley, and Josephine Isaacs, each child watched two videos on a small personal video player. The first video showed a standard false belief story (along the lines of Wimmer & Perner's, 1983, procedure), and was used as a yard-stick to categorise children into those who did and did not acknowledge false belief. In the video, Clare and Alex put some sweets in a big tin, Alex goes outside, Clare takes a sweet and then puts the rest back in a small tin, and then she leaves. Alex returns for a sweet. There were various memory check questions and the video was replayed if necessary, then children were asked where Alex thought the sweets were. A realist error, failing to acknowledge false belief, was to judge that Alex thought they were in the small tin.

In the second video, Kevin and Rebecca enter their kitchen with some biscuits they have just bought. During the course of the video the biscuits are first put into a white cupboard, then removed and put into a green cupboard. There were two versions of the video, which differed in the point at which Kevin left the room: either before the biscuits were put away, so Kevin had no belief about where they were (no belief version), or after they had been moved to the second cupboard, so he had a true belief (true belief version). After the biscuits had been put in the second cupboard, Rebecca (who knew the true location but was described by the narrator as being mixed-up about where the biscuits were) subsequently called to Kevin, while he was out of the room, "The biscuits are in the white cupboard." Rebecca then left, Kevin returned, and the narrator announced that Kevin wanted a biscuit. Children were given memory checks and saw the video again if necessary. Then, with both cupboards on the screen, the narrator asked the test question about where Kevin thought the biscuits were.

We tried to make it plausible that Kevin would believe what he was told: Rebecca was alone in the kitchen with the biscuits, and subsequently called to Kevin, telling him where they were. She knew what Kevin knew about the biscuits, and could have had good reason to tell him something different. Nevertheless, when we showed the videos to a group of 36 18-year-old school pupils, 18/18 judged that Kevin thought the biscuits were where he had been told they were in the "no belief" condition, but 17/18 judged that he thought they were where he had seen them in the "true belief" condition.

We might then argue that the "correct" adult answer is to judge that Kevin will discount the message when it contradicts what he has previously seen. (Note that from these data we cannot be sure that people would judge in the same way if Kevin's belief was false, and Rebecca's message true.)

How did the three- to five-year-olds judge? As expected, most (70%) of those who failed the Clare and Alex false belief test judged, in both conditions, that Kevin thought the biscuits were where they really were: They made the usual realist error. Also as expected, most (96%) who passed the false belief test judged that Kevin thought what he had been told in the "No belief, false message" condition: Kevin's only information about the biscuits' location came from the false message, so he believed that. However, among those who passed the false belief test, 47% judged that Kevin would ignore Rebecca's message when he had previously seen the biscuits in the green cupboard. That is, false belief passers were more likely to judge that Kevin would believe what he had been told when he had no prior information, than when he had seen the biscuits put away. Although this pattern of responding was not as extreme as the one we found among the 18-year-olds, it seems that some of these children could reflect on sources of knowledge sufficiently to judge that another person would treat being told as less reliable than seeing for themselves. Perner and Davies (1991) report a similar result.

Next, we made another set of videos in which children would find it hard to make a realist error, since they did not see the true state of affairs. We wanted to find out whether even children who failed a classic false belief test would now show that pattern of responding, giving greater weight to what Kevin saw than to what he was told.

This time Kevin and Rebecca had a big jug in their kitchen. There were three distinct scenes. In one, Kevin saw (incidentally) inside the jug and the narrator announced that he saw orange juice. Either in an earlier or a later scene, Rebecca, without looking, told Kevin there was milk in the jug. In a final scene, Kevin and Rebecca are about to pour the contents of the jug. Children were asked to judge what Kevin thought was in it, and what Rebecca thought. Children also saw the Clare and Alex false belief video, with the order counterbalanced. When Rebecca's message precedes Kevin's seeing orange juice, we can assume that the correct answers are to judge that Kevin thinks there is orange juice in the jug, but that Rebecca thinks there is milk. However, when Rebecca's message follow Kevin's seeing, it is not obvious what Kevin thinks. Rebecca presumably again thinks milk, but this time Kevin could reasonably believe what Rebecca tells him since the contents could have changed since he looked.

A sample of adults, however, judged in just the same way whether Kevin's seeing preceded or followed Rebecca's message. Altogether, 89% judged that Kevin thought there was orange juice in the jug, 100% that Rebecca thought milk.

Neither did it make any difference to children's answers whether Kevin's seeing preceded or followed Rebecca's message. This result allowed us to dismiss a possible interpretation of the first study (and of Perner & Davies'), that children simply judged Kevin's belief on the basis of his first input, whether it was seeing or being told. Since seeing always preceded being told in those studies, we could not be sure that children based the listener's belief on what he had seen, rather than just on what he had experienced first.

Surprisingly, there was no difference between false belief failers and passers in the accuracy of judgements about what Kevin and Rebecca thought: Similarly to the adults, the majority said that Kevin thought there was orange juice (what he had seen) whereas Rebecca thought milk (what she had said). These results suggest that children who failed the false belief test could accept that Kevin and Rebecca had different beliefs about what the jug contained, and they based the belief judgements on the knowledge each had obtained.

This is consistent with Flavell (1988), who suggests that children may find it easier to consider two different mental representations of something that is not yet known. It seems, then, as if both the false belief failers and passers, like the adults, tended to base Kevin's belief on his direct rather than on his indirect knowledge. An alternative interpretation is that the children made simple associative links between Kevin and orange juice and between Rebecca and milk, and ignored the information about seeing or being told. We carried out a further study to check on this: This time Kevin had a drink of coke from a bottle as well as seeing orange juice in the jug, so he was associated with both coke and orange juice. Only 1 child out of 44 judged that Kevin thought there was coke in the jug, whereas 28 of them judged that Kevin liked coke. It seems as if the children's judgements were not based on simple associations, but that they were taking into account Kevin's informational access when judging his belief.

Summary So Far

In my invented example at the beginning, I heard the Head of Department's secretary say something which contradicted the evidence of my own eyes. I suggested a number of possible ways of resolving the contradiction; some implied that my own mind was in error, and others implied that the error lay in the other person's mind. In our investigations we exposed children to similar contradictions, which they experienced directly in the deceptive box series, and which they saw Kevin experience in the video studies. We know how they dealt with the contradictions: The results suggest that what was said was treated as less reliable than what was seen. However, we do not know why they did this, nor whether the children could have justified their responses. Given that three- to five-year-olds reported difficulty reflecting on their sources of knowledge (Gopnik & Graf, 1988; O'Neill et al., 1992; O'Neill & Gopnik, 1991; Wimmer et al., 1988), it would be surprising if they could. Furthermore, we do not know whether our children tended to discount what was said because the information came via another mind, which could be in error. If they did, they may be at risk of ignoring the interpretive aspects of indirect experience. That is, they may place too much reliance on what they have seen for themselves, failing to suspect that appearances are deceptive. Perhaps they tend to treat what people say as offering a comment on reality (which can be wrong), in contrast with what they experience directly, which may appear to be reality itself.

However, the adults may have tended to do that too. To our surprise the adults in both video studies placed greater weight on what Kevin had seen than on what he was told even though we tried to create circumstances in which it was reasonable to believe what was said. In the video studies, children, even false belief failers, showed quite similar patterns of judging to the adults.

If children (and adults) do treat utterances as providing a comment in reality, then this allows not only the possibility of a mismatch between utterance and the real-world referent, but also the possibility of vagueness: Utterances can provide inadequate clues to the real-world referent. Utterances that are vague might be interpreted in different ways by different listeners. Understanding that different people can make different interpretations of the same input is an important milestone in the child's developing theory of mind. Children who realise this show clearly that they assume (implicitly) that minds interpret incoming information and do not just copy it directly (and accurately).

Some of the work carried out in the 1970s and '80s on children's understanding about verbal ambiguity takes on a new importance when placed within this framework.

Do Children Understand that What People Say Can Provide Inadequate Information about a Referent in the Real World?

In the 1970s and early '80s a number of studies were carried out using a "communication game" procedure, in which a speaker described one of a set of referents, and the listener tried to pick the correct one. On some trials the description was ambiguous, in that it referred to more than one of the potential referents. Sometimes children were asked to evaluate the messages. Some studies focused on aspects of children's performance as speakers and listeners, and some looked at the relationship between performance and evaluations. Results suggested that children under the age of around six years seemed not to understand that verbal messages can be ambiguous, but seem instead to assume that so long as a verbal message fits the intended referent then the message is adequate, even if it also fits other potential referents.

However, children who failed to identify ambiguous messages as adequate were nevertheless often aware of a problem when they attempted to interpret such messages: Children reported that they were unsure that their interpretation of an ambiguous message was correct, despite judging that the message is inadequate (Beal & Flavell, 1982; Flavell, Speer, Green, & August, 1981; Robinson & Robinson, 1983). These children apparently detected a problem but did not know why the problem had arisen. Sodian (1988) went further and showed that children who judged ambiguous messages to be adequate could nevertheless say that a listener would not know the correct interpretation. (Incidentally, correct judgements of ignorance do not seem to be based on awareness of uncertainty: Mitchell & Robinson, 1990; 1992; Robinson & Mitchell, 1990; in press).

Young children can, then, report uncertainty about the correct interpretation of an ambiguous message, and can judge that a listener does not know the correct interpretation, but can apparently still fail to understand that the problem lies with the message itself. They apparently fail to realise that the message provides an inadequate clue to the real-world referent. Furthermore, they apparently fail to realise that it is impossible to tell which of the possible interpretations is the correct one. Robinson and Robinson (1983) found that encouraging children to make two interpretations of an ambiguous message (on behalf of two doll listeners) did not increase children's uncertainty that they themselves knew the correct interpretation. Many children made both possible interpretations but remained sure that they knew which was correct.

Following up this result, I carried out a series of investigations with Benedict Leigh and Fiona Palfrey, in which we looked at five- and six-year-olds' willingness to make explicit the two possible interpretations of an ambiguous utterance, and how that related to their knowledge judgements and their message evaluations. Children watched toy vehicles (go-karts, racing cars, and tricycles) run down a steep slope marked with three runways. At the bottom of the slope was a cliff edge, and the vehicles could career over this, causing the driver to fall out. These accidents could be prevented by the placement of cotton-wool mats at the foot of the relevant runway. The child acted on behalf of a doll safety person whose job was to place cotton wool mats in the appropriate places. On each trial, the child heard a message about which one of the three vehicles placed at the top of the slope was going to come down on this particular trial. Sometimes the message was unambiguous, so the safety person knew exactly which runway to protect with a mat. On other trials the message was ambiguous in that it referred to two vehicles, so two runways had to be protected.

In all our studies, in which we tried out variations of this basic procedure, it was clear that many children were loathe to put out more than one protective mat when the message was ambiguous, even though they judged that they did not really know which vehicle was going to run on that particular trial. Even following training, in which children were required to consider placing a mat at the bottom of each of the three runways in sequence, so it was absolutely clear that it was correct on some occasions to place more than one mat, they still failed to do that on subsequent test trials. We found that children who did place mats correctly at the foot of each runway to which an ambiguous message referred also gave correct message evaluations when asked: "Did I tell you exactly which car was going to run?": There was a significant correlation between scores gained for correct judgments to the "exactly which" evaluation question, and scores for correct mat placements.

It seems from these results, and from the earlier work on ambiguous utterances, that by around the age of six years children accept that an utterance can be inadequate in that it is not possible to identify which of a set of potential referents is the correct one. They realise that utterances can provide vague comments on reality. Younger children can be aware of a problem when they try to interpret such utterances, and can judge that they leave the listener ignorant of the correct referent, but apparently have difficulty identifying the utterance itself as intrinsically inadequate.

Understanding that the Same Input Can be Interpreted in Different Ways

It is not only what people say that can be ambiguous—direct input can be, also. If we are looking through a window and see only part of an object, we might not know exactly what it is. If I was correct earlier in arguing that young children do discriminate between direct and indirect sources of knowledge, treating utterances as potentially unreliable compared with visual input, we might predict that it is easier for children to acknowledge ambiguity in utterances than in visual input. There is weak evidence to suggest that this may be the case (Robinson & Robinson, 1982), though there is inconsistency between studies about young children's success at judging that an ignorant observer might not be able to interpret ambiguous visual information (Chandler & Boyes, 1982; Perner & Davies, 1991; Ruffman, Olson, & Astington, 1991; Taylor, 1988).

As I pointed out before, understanding that different people can make different interpretations of the same input, whether this is an utterance or something seen, is an important symptom of the child's developing theory of mind. Children's judgements about the informative value of ambiguous visual input place the attainment of this milestone at around six to seven years (Chandler, 1988). However, Perner and Davies (1991) argued that even four-year-olds had an interpretive theory of mind, on the basis of evidence similar to that I reported earlier, in our video study involving Kevin's thoughts about where the biscuits were. Children judged that one particular message—in our study, "The biscuits are in the green cupboard"—was believed by Kevin when he had not seen where the biscuits were, but ignored when he had seen. However, as in our study, Perner and Davies used a between-groups design, so no one child judged that a listener who had not seen anything contradictory believed the message, but a listener who had did not.

A stricter criterion for imputing understanding that the same input can be interpreted differently by different people could be based on the procedure used in Robinson and Robinson's (1983) study, in which individual children were invited to make different interpretations of an ambiguous message on behalf of two toy listeners. The children in this study were aged between five and seven years, and about half of them made different interpretations for the two listeners. Similarly, in the experiments in which children placed protective mats at the end of runways, those who placed two mats when the message was ambiguous clearly recognised that a particular utterance had two possible interpretations, though this time there was only one listener. In these studies about a quarter of the five-year-olds and about half the six-year-olds gained the maximum score for mat placement, showing clearly that they held in mind both possible interpretations of the message.

All the studies I have mentioned so far focused on children's understanding of relationships between utterances and the real world. We have seen that even three-year-olds behave in ways consistent with believing that what people tell them about the world can be less reliable than what they experience directly, but that at this age understanding about utterance-world relationships is far from complete.

In the next section, I focus on links between utterances and beliefs. Do children understand that what people tell them about the world reveals the speakers' beliefs?

UTTERANCE-BELIEF RELATIONSHIPS

Do Children Take the Speaker's Belief into Account When They Interpret What is Said?

I have placed work on children's understanding of message ambiguity in the section earlier on "utterance-world relationships." Yet, according to most of the published literature on understanding of message ambiguity, this is misplaced, and the research should have appeared in this section, on utterance-belief relationships. Young children's failure to understand that verbal messages can be ambiguous has been interpreted as a sign that they do not treat what somebody says as a clue to what that person thinks, a clue that can be inadequate. Conversely, understanding about message ambiguity has been seen as a sign that the child distinguishes what is said from the speaker's internal representation, and treats the ambiguous message as an adequate clue to the latter (Robinson, Goelman, & Olson, 1983; Robinson & Robinson, 1982; Robinson & Whittaker, 1986). Beal (1988) and Bonitatibus (1988) make similar arguments.

However, Robinson and Whittaker (1987) suggest there is a flaw in this argument. They point out that in the communication games used to assess children's understanding of ambiguity, when a speaker gives an ambiguous message there is a perfect match between the speaker's internal representation of the intended referent, and that referent in the outside world: The speaker's belief is an accurate representation of reality. Given the perfect match between the speaker's internal representation and external referent, how can we tell whether the child is considering the relationship between the message and the speaker's internal representation, or between the message and the real-world referent? Moreover, as mentioned earlier, children have difficulty realising that visual input can be ambiguous, yet in that case there is no equivalent of a speaker's internal representation. Robinson and Whittaker (1987) conclude that studies that were seen to be investigations of children's conceptions of meaning-message relationships may, in fact, have been investigations of object-message relationships.

Robinson and Whittaker argued that if we are to examine children's understanding of message-belief relationships, we need to use a procedure in which there is a mismatch between what the speaker believes, and what is really the case, so that we can tell which the child focuses on when she interprets the message. Robinson and Mitchell (1992) devised a procedure that meets that specification, in that the speaker held a false belief about the location of the object she wanted. Do children take the speaker's belief into account when they calculate which real-world referent the message refers to? We used three different stories. In one, a speaker doll (Mum) put a bag of multicoloured material (A) in a red drawer and a bag of different material, (B) in a blue drawer, then went into another room. In Mum's absence, another doll, Jane, swapped the bags around so that A was now in the blue drawer and B in the red one. Then Mum needed a particular (unspecified) bag of material to finish her sewing. She called through to Jane, "Jane, I need some more material, it's the bag in the red drawer." Children were asked "Which bag does Mum really want?"

We called this a "message-desire discrepant" task, since the bag that Mum thinks is in the red drawer is now in the blue one, so Mum really wants the bag in the blue drawer. If children interpreted the message in this way, we could infer that they treated the message as arising from the speaker's beliefs.

We can make this interpretation only if children judge that Mum really wanted what she said in a control, message-desire consistent, version, in which Jane took the bags out of their drawers but returned them to the same places. We included this control in our studies, and most children answered correctly. Leslie and Surian (personal communication) point out that we need to include a further control, in which Mum sees the bags swapped over before giving her message. Children should judge that Mum now wants the bag she refers to, and Leslie's and Surian's initial results suggest that by the time children pass a standard false belief task, they make no errors on that new control.

Our results showed clearly that children as young as four years of age did answer correctly in both the message-desire discrepant and message-desire consistent tasks, so apparently could take into account the speaker's belief when they worked out what the speaker really wanted. In our original study (Robinson & Mitchell, 1992), we reported that children performed better in the message-desire discrepant task than in a classic false belief task, but with a better-matched procedure we found no difference in difficulty between the two tasks (Robinson & Mitchell, 1994; see also Mitchell & Robinson, in press). Treating utterances as expressions of beliefs was apparent at the same time as acknowledging false belief, and was not a late-developing aspect of theory of mind, as had previously been argued by myself and others.

Do Children Read off Beliefs from Utterances?

In contrast with the suggestion I have just made, that children treat utterances as expressions of beliefs at about the same time as they acknowledge false belief in a classic task, Leslie and Thaiss (1992) state that say–think links are particularly easy to make. They argue that children normally have an inbuilt "theory of mind mechanism" (ToMM), whose task is to understand agents' behaviour in terms of their mental states. To do this, the mechanism infers from a representation of behaviour to a representation of the agent's associated propositional attitude (for example, believing something about the world). Although the ToMM is inbuilt, the Selection Processor (SP), which feeds in the correct information for the inference machine, matures over the first four years or so of life. Until SP is fully mature, current reality has a tendency to intrude. Sometimes, according to Leslie and Thaiss, the agent communicates the mental content directly in a verbal message, making it especially easy for the child to infer the agent's mental state. It is slightly more difficult for the ToMM if the agent behaves in a way consistent with the mental state, as when, for example, the puppet looked in the empty band-aid box in Bartsch and Wellman's (1989) study, but more difficult still if the child has only the agent's exposure history to go on, as in a standard false belief prediction task.

Leslie's assumption is, then, that children from a very early age use what people say as a guide to what they believe.

The results of Roth and Leslie's (1991) study suggest that three-year-olds can do this. Roth and Leslie (1991, p. 318) assumed that: "the ability to metarepresent could enable the very young child to conceive an utterance as expressing a speaker's mistaken belief and to separate it from her/his own representation of reality."

In Roth and Leslie's study, children watched a story in which Yosi and Rina go out to play. Yosi leaves some chocolate on the ground while they play ball. While he runs to get the ball, Rina takes the chocolate and hides it by the tree, telling the child that she wants to eat it all herself. Yosi returns and asks where the chocolate is. Rina lies that the dog took it and left it in the kennel. Children were asked where Rina thinks the chocolate is, and where Yosi thinks it is. The child knows that the chocolate is really by the tree. Only 4% of three-year-olds made a realist judgement (which in fact is the correct answer in this task), and most of them answered that both Rina and Yosi thought the chocolate was in the kennel.

These children, then, as expected on the basis of Leslie's account, used what the speaker said as a guide to what she thought, even when the child herself held a different belief. There was no comparison task in which children had to make a link between an action and a belief, so we cannot be sure that the utterance had the special status that Leslie assigns it. Whether or not this is the case, the absence of realist judgements among the three-year-olds is surprising, and is inconsistent with other results; for example, Flavell, Flavell, Green, and Moses (1990).

Riggs and Robinson (1993) also obtained results that were inconsistent with Roth and Leslie's. In our study, three- and four-year-olds had the opportunity to work out that a speaker had an out-of-date belief about the colour of a mug. Would they be better at judging what colour the speaker thought the mug was if they had the additional clue of an utterance that stated the colour? We compared judgements in two conditions in which child and experimenter played a game of hiding objects under a cloth and then saying what colour they were. They then played a trick on the experimenter's confederate (Richard): While he was out of the room, they exchanged a hidden red mug for a white one. In one condition, when Richard returned, the experimenter asked Richard what colour the mug was, and Richard replied that it was red, thereby providing an explicit clue about what he thought. Children were then asked what colour Richard thought the mug was. In the other condition, no message was given and Richard's belief could only be inferred from the fact that he was absent when the mugs were swapped. We found that the message did not help children at all: The incidence of realist errors was 60% in both conditions.

At present, then, Roth and Leslie's result seems to be an anomaly (though see a suggested interpretation in Perner, Baker, & Hutton, this volume), and it seems likely that what we have to explain is why young children continue to make realist judgements even when they have an explicit verbal clue about what the speaker thinks.

Why Don't Children Read off Beliefs from Utterances?

Perhaps children simply do not connect what people say with what they think, and see no contradiction in judging that a speaker thinks one thing but says something else. This seems unlikely, just as it seems unlikely that young children make no links between how a person behaves and what they think. In the video study described earlier, involving Kevin and Rebecca's jug, 74% of false belief failers judged that Rebecca thought there was milk in the jug, as she had said, even though orange juice was available as an alternative response. These children apparently used Rebecca's utterance as a guide to her belief.

Another possible reason for realist errors is that young children, under the age of around four, fail to understand that people can hold false beliefs, do not understand the possibility of misrepresentation of reality, and so cannot be said to have a representational theory of mind. This is a widely accepted view (e.g. Flavell, 1988; Gopnik & Wellman, 1992; Perner, 1988; 1991; Wellman, 1990). If children do not understand the possibility of false belief, then no wonder a verbal statement of such a belief does not help children to judge correctly what the speaker thinks.

However, an alternative interpretation of the evidence is that young children do accept the possibility of misrepresentation but that this is masked by a tendency to focus on real events in preference. The chapter by Peter Mitchell in this volume offers a more detailed (and stronger) version of the masking view; see also Robinson and Mitchell (1994). A weak version of the masking view is expressed by Russell, Mauthner, Sharpe, and Tidswell (1991, p. 343): "for the young child physical knowledge is more salient than mental knowledge so that in circumstances where the two are in competition, the former wins out." Russell et al. (1991) point out that the masking account need not necessarily imply that children do have an effective theory of mind before they can succeed on a classic false belief task: A requirement for imputing children with such a theory might be that they demonstrate an ability to direct attention away from knowledge of physical reality when asked to judge about belief.

In several investigations, children have been protected from the salience of reality to see whether this makes it easier for them to acknowledge false belief. The belief may be given a physical counterpart, either in the form of the protagonist's behaviour, or in the form of a picture, and both these forms of protection appear to be effective in helping children to acknowledge false belief, at least under some conditions (Bartsch & Wellman, 1989; Mitchell & Lacohée, 1991; Moses & Flavell, 1990; Robinson & Mitchell, submitted). Another way of offering protection is to remove the real object from the scene, and this again seems to be effective (Russell & Jarrold, 1991; Wimmer & Perner, 1983), although Perner (1991) points out the risks of obtaining false positives with procedures such as these: Has the child any opportunity to make a realist error if there is no longer a "real" location to refer to? A less extreme variation is for the child to experience current reality only indirectly, by being told, rather than directly by seeing. This is what happened in our deceptive box study, which I described earlier, in which children either saw the unexpected contents for themselves or were told or shown a picture by the experimenter. On the basis of the masking account, we would predict that children who accepted the new information would report their false belief more frequently in the message and picture conditions than in the direct seeing condition, because the indirect conditions offer protection against reality. We found this predicted effect in some of our studies but not in all (Robinson, Mitchell, & Nye, 1992). Similarly, Zaitchik (1991) reports that children found it easier to acknowledge another's false belief when they were only told about the true location of the desired object, though Zaitchik's interpretive framework is different from ours. In their chapter in this volume, Chandler and Hala summarise results that are also consistent with the masking account. This evidence suggests, then, that children who fail the classic false belief prediction task may really accept that people can have false beliefs, and reveal this when they are protected from the salience of reality.

We should note, though, that protecting children from reality in the ways just described does not ensure that they will correctly acknowledge false belief. There have been failures to replicate both Mitchell and Lacohée's (1991) facilitatory effect of giving one's false belief a physical counterpart in the form of a picture (e.g. Robinson & Goold, 1991), and the effect of indirect knowledge (see earlier). Given the difficulty of publishing failures to replicate, it is likely that there are others we do not know about. Even when group comparisons show significant effects, performance in the protected groups is by no means at ceiling. However, when it is effective, protection from the salience of reality seems to be sufficient to increase the incidence of correct acknowledgements of false belief; the success of the indirect knowledge conditions shows that additional clues to belief are not necessary to help the child.

Furthermore, some clues clearly do not help even if they are explicit. To come back to utterance-belief links and children's judgements about what colour Richard thought the mug was, why did the utterance "It's red," which expressed Richard's belief about the colour of the mug, not help children to focus on Richard's belief rather than on current reality? To interpret this finding within the masking framework: Perhaps an oral message, because of its transience, fails to offer protection from the salience of reality. The procedures that have been successful have either provided the belief with a physical counterpart so that it can compete on more equal terms with reality, or they have reduced the salience of reality directly. An oral message does neither of these, and at the moment children are asked the false belief test question, nothing is there at that time to help the child avoid making a realist error. The suggestion is, then, that children do not need clues to help them work out what the false belief is; what they need is protection from the salience of immediately perceptible reality, and oral messages offer no such protection.

If children make realist errors when judging what somebody thinks, and if they do connect what people say with what they think, they are faced with a potential contradiction when a person makes a comment about the world which the child believes to be untrue: Richard says "The mug is red," the child believes it really is white, and judges that Richard also thinks it is white.

One way of dealing with the contradiction is to distort one's memory of the utterance, so that one recalls a true statement about reality rather than a false statement. In the mug task, the child could recall that Richard said: "The mug is white." Misremembering does occur: Wimmer and Hartl (1991) found that, in a standard deceptive box task, children made realist errors about what they had originally said. That is, on seeing that there were really pencils in a Smarties tube, the child says: "I said pencils," just as in many studies it has been found that the child says: "I thought pencils." Kevin Riggs and I replicated this aspect of Wimmer and Hartl's result. However, we found that 23 children who misremembered their own false statement in a deceptive box task nevertheless remembered accurately what Richard said in the mug task, compared with a single child who showed the reverse pattern. Furthermore, children recalled accurately what Richard said despite making realist errors about what he thought (he thinks it's white). Twenty-two children erred in answer to the think question but not the say question, compared with one who showed the reverse pattern.

Did the children not see the judgements: "He thinks white, he said red" as contradictory? If not, why not? I shall discuss this further in the final section which deals with understanding of relationships between what is said, what is really the case, and what is believed.

Summary So Far

To summarise what I have suggested so far about children's understanding of utterances as sources of knowledge about the speaker's belief: By the time children pass a classic false belief prediction task, they are able to interpret what people say, taking into account their belief state (as in the message-desire discrepant task). They can treat utterances as expressions of speaker's beliefs. Children who fail a classic false belief task are not helped to acknowledge a speaker's false belief when he announces it (in the study involving Richard's mug). This could be because they simply do not accept the possibility of false beliefs.

However, I argued against this suggestion, since when children are protected from the salience of reality they may acknowledge false belief more readily than they can in the classic task. Protection is offered when reality is absent or known about only indirectly, or when the belief has a physical counterpart in behaviour or a picture. Utterances, having no contemporary physical reality, apparently do not offer the child protection from the salience of reality at the crucial time of judgement, and so do not help even though they had provided explicit clues to belief. Hence what somebody says is not used as a basis for judging what that person thinks when the utterance mismatches reality as known to the child.

Yet it seems unlikely that children who fail a classic false belief task see no connection between what people say and what they think. If they do make a connection, then they are faced with a potential contradiction when a speaker whom the child thinks holds a true belief, says something which the child considers to be false.

THE DUAL INFORMATIVE ROLE OF UTTERANCES

Judgements Involving Utterance, Reality, and Belief

To return for the last time to the imaginary occasion when my belief about the Head of Department's location, based on direct knowledge, was contradicted by what his secretary told me: Possible ways of resolving the contradiction took into account my judgements about what the secretary believed, what she intended me to believe, what was in fact the case, and what she actually said or intended to say. For an adult, the contradiction is resolved when we can create a consistent account of all these variables. We presented similar contradictory inputs to the children in our studies, but we do not yet know what inconsistencies between variables children are sensitive to, let alone what range of explanations they have available.

Nevertheless, there is some relevant evidence. I mentioned one relevant finding in connection with the study involving Richard's mug. Recall that the children saw the mug being swapped while Richard was outside, and when Richard returned he announced his belief about the mug's colour. Children who made realist errors about what they themselves had said in a standard deceptive box task also made such errors about what Richard thought, yet they recalled accurately what Richard had said. Why did children misremember their own false statement, but recall accurately Richard's false statement?

We considered two possibilities. The first, and perhaps the more interesting, is that the difference in accuracy of recall of the child's own false statement, compared with Richard's, is related to the child's knowledge state at the time the utterance was made. When the child says Smarties are the contents of the Smarties tube, she intends to make a true statement about reality, and assumes that it is indeed true. In contrast, when Richard says "It's red," the child assumes that this statement is false. Perhaps children mis-recall what they themselves said, when they assumed the utterance was true at the time it was made, but recall accurately what Richard said, when they assumed his utterance was false as he made it.

This first suggestion is consistent with Perner's (1991) argument that young children have no concept of statements that misrepresent reality, and so they update them on recall. On the other hand, he argues, they have no difficulty remembering statements which are designed to be counterfactual, such as jokes or pretend statements.

However, the second possibility is that there is a self–other difference when recalling false statements. Evidence against this comes from Wimmer and Hartl's (1991) study. They found that children mis-reported what a puppet, who shared their false belief, had said in a deceptive box task. However, using a similar deceptive box procedure, Riggs and I have failed to replicate this result. We found that children were much more accurate at recalling what another person had said was in the deceptive box than they were at judging what he had thought: 15 children answered the "say" question correctly but the "think" question wrongly, compared with 3 who showed the reverse pattern. We found no difference between judgements given in two conditions; in one children shared the other person's perspective and so assumed his utterance was true when it was made, and in the other condition children knew that the other's statement was false as it was uttered. It seems, then, that it is only when recalling one's own prior statement that distortions occur, and other people's false statements are recalled accurately.

In both the standard deceptive box task and the "Richard's mug" task, children who do not acknowledge false belief are faced with an impossible situation: a speaker whose belief is true, who apparently intends to make a true statement about reality, but who in fact makes a false one. Children deal with their own error by mis-remembering what they said. But for other people, they report the false message accurately, while making a realist error about the other's belief, apparently leaving the contradiction unresolved. Are the children aware of a contradiction, or could they at least become aware of it if questioned further? Would they then misjudge the speaker's intention, judging that he deliberately made a false statement despite really knowing the truth? Or would the child judge that the speaker simply made a performance error, a slip of the tongue? If children take either of these options, why do they not do the same when asked to recall their own false statement in a deceptive box task? These are some of the questions we shall attempt to answer in future studies.

Possibly, young children simply do not integrate information about belief, utterance, and real-world referent, and the consistency between "say" and "think" judgements for self in the deceptive box task give a misleading impression. Perhaps the consistency arises because the child makes a realist error independently for beliefs and for utterances, and fails to link what is said with what is thought. The possibility that nursery-aged children may not even detect the inconsistencies I have described is supported by results of a series of studies by Peter Mitchell (Mitchell & Russell, 1989; 1991; Mitchell, Munno, & Russell, 1991), which involved children aged between about five and nine years. At five, children seemed to have difficulty using cues that would have helped them resolve contradictions between utterance, referent, and belief. Children were told stories in which a speaker misdescribed an object, and children judged how the listener would interpret the utterance and what the speaker really meant. For example, Mary asked John to fetch her book, and described it as having a picture of a dog on the cover. John found what appeared to be the required book except that it had a picture of a cat on the cover. Using stories like this, Mitchell and Russell (1989) report that five-year-olds were just as likely as older children to judge that the item found by a listener, which only approximated to a description given by the speaker, was the one the speaker intended. However, five-year-olds, unlike older children, were not influenced by information about the accuracy of the speaker's memory for the intended object. Nine-year-olds, in contrast, judged more frequently that the found object was the one intended when the speaker's memory was depicted as bad than when it was depicted as good. These older children seemed to have a better grasp than did five-year-olds of the link between inaccurate representation and misdescription. Similarly, Mitchell and Russell (1991) found that nine-year-olds judged more often that the found object was the one the speaker tried to talk about when the discrepancy between described and found objects was small rather than gross. Five-year-olds' judgements were not influenced by the size of the discrepancy.

On the basis of the studies reported in the section on utterance-belief relationships, we can assume that the five-year-olds could treat utterances about the world as expressions of speakers' beliefs. However, this knowledge may be of limited use in complex real-life settings when the child is still ignorant of the appropriate cues to use when attempting to deal with a mismatch between utterance and reality. An implication of this is that the somewhat peculiar situations we have used in our experimental studies, in which, for example, children had privileged access to the speaker's belief, may allow children to demonstrate understanding of links between utterance, reality, and belief in a way in which they could not in more complex and obscure everyday situations. The child I described earlier, who came to a stop in the cloakroom when faced with a contradiction between what had been said ("Sam is in the cloakroom") and what he saw (no sign of Sam), may not be typical. Nevertheless, if we are to trace and explain the developmental course of understanding of the dual informative role of utterances, we should check experimental data against naturalistic evidence. Normally this action is recommended in the expectation that naturalistic data will reveal levels of understanding not apparent in experimental evidence. On this occasion, however, we might find the reverse pattern.

Further Questions

Much more work is needed before we can really link the development of children's understanding about utterance-world relationships to that of utterance-belief relationships, so that we can give an account of the development of understanding of the dual informative role of utterances. The results I have presented hint at the possibility that children treat utterances as potentially unreliable without yet understanding that utterances are expressions of beliefs. That is, in the section on utterance-world relationships, we saw that false belief failers tended to discount what was said in favour of what was seen, even in their judgements on behalf of Kevin. In contrast, in the section on utterance-belief relationships, false belief failers in the message-desire discrepant task showed little evidence of treating utterances as expressions of beliefs. One developmental possibility is that, as children gain reflective understanding of utterances as potentially unreliable sources of knowledge about the outside world, they gain the possibility of coming to understand why utterances are unreliable, namely because they come via another's mind, and minds can not only joke or lie but can also hold false beliefs. That is, children may go through the following sequence:

1. They unthinkingly treat knowledge obtained from an utterance as potentially unreliable relative to knowledge obtained directly, such as by seeing (as shown in the deceptive box studies). In doing this, their behaviour is superficially consistent with, though not yet symptomatic of, acceptance of the possibility of misrepresentation.

2. Children gain reflective understanding of differences between sources, and demonstrate this in their judgements (as in the video studies). Karmiloff-Smith (1986) and Clark and Karmiloff-Smith (in press) discuss this kind of representational redescription.

3. Children are then in a strong position to achieve understanding of why utterances can be unreliable: Speakers who intend to make true statements about reality can hold false beliefs.

I speculate, then, that coming to understand about utterance-world relationships may not be a mere symptom of a developing theory of mind, but may actually play a causal role in development. The particular route I have outlined is probably an oversimplification of the intertwining of development of understanding about each informative role of utterances, but may nevertheless provide a useful working framework. If the masking account presented earlier is correct, and children's early understanding of false belief can be masked by the salience of reality, then another factor needs to be included in the developmental scheme: Children's growing ability to acknowledge false belief even when the true state of affairs is strongly apparent.

An appealing possibility is that children move from level (2) to level (3) as a result of being told by parents and teachers about misunderstandings, and about other people's ignorance or false beliefs. Children with siblings apparently develop a theory of mind more quickly than those without (Perner, Ruffman, & Leekam, in press), and this could be because of the way parents talk to them about family conflicts (Dunn et al., 1991). That is, children who already treat what people say as potentially unreliable may be helped, by what people say, to understand why that is the case.

ACKNOWLEDGEMENTS

Much of the research reported here was carried out as part of an ESRC-funded project jointly directed by myself and Peter Mitchell, and with Rebecca Nye and Josephine Isaacs. I would like to thank Peter Robinson for his detailed comments on an earlier version of this chapter, and I am also grateful for the editors' comments.

REFERENCES

Bartsch, K., & Wellman, H. (1989). Young children's attribution of action to beliefs and desires. *Child Development, 60*, 946–964.

Beal, C.R. (1988). Children's knowledge about representations of intended meaning. In J.W. Astington, P.L. Harris, & D.R. Olson (Eds.), *Developing theories of mind*. Cambridge: Cambridge University Press.

Beal, C.R., & Flavell, J.H. (1982). Effect of increasing the salience of message ambiguities on kindergarteners' evaluations of communicative success and message adequacy. *Developmental Psychology, 18*, 43–48.

Bonitatibus, G. (1988). What is said and what is meant in referential communication. In J.W. Astington, P.L. Harris, & D.R. Olson (Eds.), *Developing theories of mind*. Cambridge: Cambridge University Press.

Chandler, M. (1988). Doubt and developing theories of mind. In J.W. Astington, P.L. Harris, and D.R. Olson (Eds.), *Developing theories of mind*. Cambridge: Cambridge University Press.

Chandler, M.J., & Boyes, M. (1982). Social-cognitive development. In B. Wolman (Ed.), *Handbook of developmental psychology*. Englewood Cliffs, NJ: Prentice-Hall.

Clark, A., & Karmiloff-Smith, A. (in press). The cognizer's innards: A psychological and philosophical perspective on the development of thought. *Mind and Language*.

Dunn, J., Brown, J., Slomkowski, C., Tesla, C., & Youngblade, L. (1991). Young children's understanding of other people's feelings and beliefs: Individual differences and their antecedents. *Child Development, 62,* 1352–1366.

Flavell, J.H. (1988). The development of children's knowledge about the mind: From cognitive connections to mental representations. In J.W. Astington, P.L. Harris & D.R. Olson (Eds.), *Developing theories of mind* (pp. 244–267). Cambridge: Cambridge University Press.

Flavell, J.H., Flavell, E.R., Green, F.L., & Moses, L.J. (1990). Young children's understanding of fact beliefs versus value beliefs. *Child Development, 61,* 915–928.

Flavell, J.H., Speer, J.R., Green, F.L., & August, D.L. (1981). The development of comprehension monitoring and knowledge about communication. *Monographs of the Society for Research in Child Development* (Serial No. 192).

Gopnik, A., & Astington, J.W. (1988). The development of children's understanding of representational change. In J.W. Astington, P.L. Harris & D.R. Olson (Eds.), *Developing theories of mind* (pp. 193–206). Cambridge: Cambridge University Press.

Gopnik, A., & Graf, P. (1988). Knowing how you know: Young children's ability to identify and remember the sources of their beliefs. *Child Development, 59,* 1366–1371.

Gopnik, A., & Wellman, H.M. (1992). Why the child's theory of mind really is a theory. *Mind and Language, 7,* 145–171.

Karmiloff-Smith, A. (1986). From metaprocesses to conscious access: Evidence from children's metalinguistic and repair data. *Cognition, 23,* 95–147.

Leslie, A.M., & Thaiss, L. (1992). Domain specificity in conceptual development: Neuropsychological evidence from autism. *Cognition, 43,* 225–251.

Mitchell, P., & Lacohée, H. (1991). Children's early understanding of false belief. *Cognition, 39,* 107–127.

Mitchell, P., Munno, A., & Russell, J. (1991). Children's understanding of the communicative value of discrepant verbal messages. *Cognitive Development, 6,* 279–299.

Mitchell, P., & Robinson, E.J. (1990). What determines the accuracy of children's judgments of their own knowledge? *Journal of Experimental Child Psychology, 50,* 81–101.

Mitchell, P., & Robinson, E.J. (1992). Children's understanding of the evidential connotation of "know" in relation to overestimation of their own knowledge. *Journal of Child Language, 19,* 167–182.

Mitchell, P., & Robinson, E.J. (in press). Discrepant messages resulting from a false belief: Children's evaluations, *Child Development*.

Mitchell, P., & Russell, J. (1989). Young children's understanding of the say-mean distinction in referential speech. *Journal of Experimental Child Psychology, 47,* 467–490.

Mitchell, P., & Russell, J. (1991). Children's judgments of whether slightly and grossly discrepant objects were intended by a speaker. *British Journal of Developmental Psychology, 9,* 271–280.

Moses, L.J., & Flavell, J.H. (1990). Inferring false beliefs from action and reactions. *Child Development, 61,* 929–945.

O'Neill, D.K., Astington, J.W., & Flavell, J.H. (1992). Young children's understanding of the role that sensory experiences play in knowledge acquisition. *Child Development, 63,* 474–490.

O'Neill, D.K., & Gopnik, A. (1991). Young children's ability to identify the sources of their beliefs. *Developmental Psychology, 27,* 390–397.

Pea, R.D. (1980). The development of negation in early child language. In D.R. Olson (Ed.), *The social foundations of language and thought* (pp. 156–186). New York: W.W. Norton.

Perner, J. (1988). Developing semantics for theories of mind: From propositional attitudes to mental representation. In J.W. Astington, P.L. Harris, & D.R. Olson (Eds.), *Developing theories of mind* (pp. 141–172). Cambridge: Cambridge University Press.

Perner, J. (1991). *Understanding the representational mind.* London: MIT Press.

Perner, J., & Davies, G. (1991). Understanding the mind as an active information processor: Do young children have a "copy theory of mind"? *Cognition, 39,* 51–69.

Perner, J., Ruffman, T., & Leekam, S.R. (in press). Theory of mind is contagious: You catch it from your sibs (who are close to you). *Child Development.*

Riggs, K., & Robinson, E.J. (1993). *What people say and what they think: Children's judgments of false belief in relation to their recall of false messages.* Paper presented at British Psychological Society Developmental Section Conference, Birmingham.

Robinson, E.J., Goelman, H., & Olson, D.R. (1983). Children's understanding of the relation between expressions (what was said) and intentions (what was meant). *British Journal of Developmental Psychology, 1,* 75–86.

Robinson, E.J., & Goold, J. (1991). *Young children's ability to report their own superseded beliefs: Facilitation via physical embodiment.* Unpublished manuscript, University of Birmingham, UK.

Robinson, E.J., & Mitchell, P. (1990). Children's judgments of undecidability when they are ignorant. *International Journal of Behavioral Development, 13,* 467–488.

Robinson, E.J., & Mitchell, P. (1992). Children's interpretation of messages from a speaker with a false belief. *Child Development, 63,* 639–652.

Robinson, E.J., & Mitchell, P. (in press). Children's judgments of ignorance on the basis of absence of experience. *British Journal of Developmental Psychology.*

Robinson, E.J., & Mitchell, P. (1994). Young children's false belief reasoning: Interpretation of messages is no easier than the classic task. *Developmental Psychology, 30,* 67–72.

Robinson, E.J., & Mitchell, P. (submitted). *Masking of children's early understanding of the representational mind: Backwards explanation versus prediction.*

Robinson, E.J., Mitchell, P., & Nye, R. (1992, September). *Young children's understanding of indirect sources of knowledge.* Paper presented to the Developmental Section of the BPS Conference, Edinburgh.

Robinson, E.J., & Robinson, W.P. (1982). Knowing when you don't know enough: Children's judgements about ambiguous information. *Cognition, 12,* 267–280.

Robinson, E.J., & Robinson, W.P. (1983). Children's uncertainty about the interpretation of ambiguous messages. *Journal of Experimental Child Psychology, 36,* 81–96.

Robinson, E.J., & Whittaker, S.J. (1986). Children's conceptions of meaning-message relationships. *Cognition, 22,* 41–60.

Robinson, E.J., & Whittaker, S.J. (1987). Children's conceptions of relations between messages, meanings and reality. *British Journal of Developmental Psychology, 5,* 81–90.

Roth, D., & Leslie, A.M. (1991). The recognition of attitude conveyed by utterance: A study of preschool and autistic children. *British Journal of Developmental Psychology, 9,* 315–330.

Ruffman, T., Olson, D.R., & Astington, J.W. (1991). Children's understanding of visual ambiguity. *British Journal of Developmental Psychology, 9,* 89–102.

Russell, J., & Jarrold, C. (1991). *The role of the object in deception and false belief tasks.* Unpublished manuscript, University of Cambridge, UK.

Russell, J., Mauthner, N., Sharpe, S., & Tidswell, T. (1991). The "windows task" as a measure of strategic deception in preschoolers and autistic subjects. *British Journal of Developmental Psychology, 9,* 331–350.

Sodian, B. (1988). Children's attributions of knowledge to the listener in a referential communication task. *Child Development, 59,* 378–385.

Taylor, M. (1988). The development of children's ability to distinguish what they know from what they see. *Child Development, 59,* 703–718.

Wellman, H.M. (1990). *The child's theory of mind*. London: MIT Press.

Wimmer, H., & Hartl, M. (1991). Against the Cartesian view on mind: Young children's difficulty with own false beliefs. *British Journal of Developmental Psychology*, 9, 125–138.

Wimmer, H., Hogrefe, J., & Perner, J. (1988). Children's understanding of informational origins as a source of knowledge. *Child Development*, 59, 386–396.

Wimmer, H., & Perner, J. (1983). Beliefs about beliefs: Representation and constraining function of wrong beliefs in young children's understanding of deception. *Cognition*, 13, 103–128.

Wimmer, H., & Perner, J. (1990). Young children's memory for false statements: Separating sense from reference. Unpublished manuscript, University of Sussex.

Zaitchik, D. (1991). Is only seeing really believing?: Sources of the true belief in the false belief task. *Cognitive Development*, 6, 91–103.

# V MISREPRESENTATION

18 Early Deception and the Conceptual Continuity Claim

Beate Sodian
University of Munich, Germany

INTRODUCTION

The emergence of children's ability to deceive others has recently attracted much attention in theory of mind research. A lively debate centres around the issue of whether three- or maybe even two-year-old children are capable of intentional deception or whether this ability only develops around the age of about four years. Why does this seem so important?

The core issue behind the apparently futile controversy about the age of onset of deceptive action is whether or not there is conceptual change in the child's understanding of the mental domain, where "conceptual change" refers to a fairly radical type of restructuring of the child's conceptual system such as that postulated by Carey (1985; 1991) for the domains of intuitive biology and physics: The older child's and adult's conceptual systems are not just enriched versions of the young child's, but core conceptual distinctions are drawn along different lines in the two systems. For example, Carey (1991) argues for the domain of common-sense physics that the young child has an undifferentiated concept of weight and density. Such an undifferentiated concept cannot be expressed in terms of the adult's conceptual system. In fact, from the point of view of the adult's conceptual structure such a concept is incoherent, and can only be explained through an analysis of its role within the context of related concepts and the theory in which they are embedded.

For the mental domain, proponents of the view that there is conceptual change in the child's theory of mind have claimed that

385

children below the age of about four years do not possess a concept of belief, that is, that they fail to draw the basic distinction between beliefs and reality. Since this distinction is fundamental to our adult understanding of the mental world, a system that lacks this distinction cannot just be an impoverished version of ours, but must be at least partially incompatible with ours. The main source of evidence for such a conceptual difference between four-year-olds and younger children is young children's failure to attribute false beliefs to other people when shown or told that these people lack access to relevant information. In such situations (e.g. the famous "Maxi-and-the-chocolate" task by Wimmer & Perner, 1983), three-year-olds mistakenly claim that the other person thinks what they know to be true. This finding has proved to be robust, and not attributable to trivial factors such as memory overload (see Perner, 1991, Chapter 8, for a review).

Critics of the conceptual deficit view have argued, however, that three-year-old children's failure on tasks requiring them to make belief attributions may be due to a variety of performance factors, rather than a conceptual deficit. Chandler, Fritz, and Hala (1989) argue that children may have difficulty dealing with the narrative structure of the standard false belief tasks that require hypothetical reasoning; children may be able to engage actively in belief manipulation long before they become able to comment on others' beliefs in hypothetical story tasks. Therefore, acts of deception should be a good indicator for the presence of a concept of belief in the deceiver, since deception involves the manipulation of others' behaviour by influencing their beliefs about reality. If it could be shown that children are capable of *intentionally* inducing false beliefs in others at a considerably earlier age than they pass "standard" false belief tasks, then the conceptual change view would be seriously threatened. It would then seem likely that children show an understanding of belief as early as we can test for it, and thus share the core concepts of our adult common-sense belief-desire psychology from early on. This would support the conceptual continuity view, as proposed by Fodor (1992), who claims that the adult's folk psychology is merely an enriched version of the young child's "Very Simple Theory of Mind" that is essentially innate.

Proponents of the conceptual continuity view claim that recent findings on the development of deception in children support their position in showing (1) a capability of active deception in children as young as two-and-a-half or three years (Chandler et al., 1989; Hala, Chandler, & Fritz, 1991), and (2) an explicit, statable understanding of the effects of deception on a person's beliefs in children who fail "standard" false belief tasks (Sullivan & Winner, 1991; Winner & Sullivan, 1993). If this is the correct interpretation of the findings on early deception, then the conceptual change view is indeed in serious trouble.

In the present chapter I will argue that these claims are unwarranted on a careful analysis of the available evidence. My interpretation is that, on the contrary, the findings from the deception studies give strong support to the conceptual change view. I will first show that the evidence on the development of deceptive *action* converges with the earlier findings on belief attribution in indicating that children below the age of three-and-a-half years do *not* possess a concept of belief. In the second part of the chapter, I will discuss recent claims that three-year-old children *understand* the effects of deception on a victim's belief, even though they may not actively engage in deceptive action. Based on recent findings by Peskin (1993) and Perner, Baker, and Hutton (this volume), I will argue that three-year-olds appear to have a specific misconception of the effects of trickery and deceit rather than an adult-like understanding.

THE CASE FOR A CONCEPTUAL DEFICIT

Age Trends in Deceptive Action

In the past two years, a considerable number of empirical studies have addressed the question of whether three-year-old children are capable of deception (Brooks, Samuels, & Frye, 1993; Chandler et al., 1989; Hala et al., 1991; LaFreniere, 1988; Peskin, 1992; Ruffman, Olson, Ash, & Keenan, 1993; Russell, Mauthner, Sharpe, & Tidswell, 1991; Sodian, 1991; Sodian, Taylor, Harris, & Perner, 1991). The answer given in the large majority of these studies is negative. Young three-year-olds typically fail to misinform a competitor even under very conducive conditions. A paradigm example is the task originally designed by Woodruff and Premack (1979) for the study of deception in chimpanzees: The subject watches while a reward is hidden in one of two opaque containers. Then a competitive partner appears who will keep the reward for himself when shown where it is. Will the subject point to the empty container to mislead the villain? Four-year-olds and older children will do so spontaneously on the first or second trials, whereas three-year-olds truthfully inform the competitor (LaFreniere, 1988; Sodian, 1991), and keep pointing to the baited box for trial after trial despite mounting frustration at losing the reward (Russell et al., 1991)[1]. Even when children are not under pressure to perform, but are asked to "advise" a story

---

[1] A recent study by Samuels and Brooks (1993) did not replicate Russell et al.'s finding that three-year-olds consistently fail to point to an empty box in order to obtain the content of a baited box. However, as opposed to Russell et al., who found a strong correlation between performance on the "windows" task and performance on a standard false belief task, Samuels and Brooks found that performance on their task was unrelated to performance on other theory of mind tasks, indicating that their subjects may have adopted a non-mentalistic strategy for solving the "windows" task.

figure, who does not want a villain to find the reward, on what to do or say, they choose to give truthful information. They do so even when a false description is modelled for them (Sodian, 1991).

Three-year-olds' reluctance to misinform a competitor is not limited to artificial situations like the deceptive pointing tasks. Joan Peskin (1991) tested children in a situation of high affective involvement that resembles real-life conflict situations between children. In her experiment, children faced the familiar problem of an opponent's always desiring exactly the same object that the child herself preferred. Since the opponent got the first choice, the only way of securing the desired object for herself was for the child to tell him that she wanted a different one from the one she in fact preferred. More than half of the 4-year-olds and about 80% of the 5-year-olds used this strategy, but less than 20% of the 3-year-olds did. Whereas 4-year-olds' performance improved over a series of trials, 3-year-olds continued to tell the truth despite mounting frustration.

Similar findings were reported by Ruffman et al. (1993), who studied children's use and understanding of a strategy of using deceptive clues to mislead an opponent, and by Brooks et al. (1993), who explicitly encouraged children to trick an experimenter so that he would not be able to find a sticker upon his return. Both studies report no (or minimal) attempts at deception in the majority of the three-year-olds, and a dramatic improvement at around the age of four years. Furthermore, Ruffman et al. (1993) were able to rule out that three-year-olds failure was due to pragmatic problems or to task complexity.

Thus, results of research on active deception closely parallel findings from belief attribution tasks in indicating dramatic improvement between the ages of three and four years. Interestingly, these findings from experimental research are consistent with adults' intuitions about the age at which children become capable of deliberate deception. Stouthamer-Loeber (1986) found that although day-care teachers' and mothers' intuitive judgements about the age of onset of this ability varied, there was a leap at the age of four years. Similarly, Clara and William Stern (1909) concluded from their analysis of diary data that children become able to tell genuine lies around the age of four years.

The parallel between the age trends in standard false belief and in deception tasks is more than a chance co-occurrence of unrelated age trends. Within-subject comparisons showed that performance on both types of tasks is strongly correlated (Ruffman et al., 1993; Russell et al., 1991; Brooks et al., 1993), and that this effect persists even when chronological age is partialled out (Sodian, unpublished data). Thus, it appears that young children's competence in understanding belief was not underestimated in false belief attribution tasks but that three-year-olds' failure on these tasks is indicative of a conceptual deficit.

The Underestimation–Overestimation Debate

It is still possible, however, that both deception and false belief attribution tasks have underestimated children's true competence because the same—unspecified—performance factors operate in both. Subtle variations in task features could therefore reveal true competence. When Chandler et al. (1989) reported the spectacular finding that children as young as two-and-a-half years employed deceptive strategies in a competitive hiding game, it appeared that they might have been successful in revealing true competence. In their experiment, a treasure was hidden by a puppet, which left visible tracks to the hiding place (one of four boxes). The child's task was to make it difficult for another person to find the treasure. Many two-and-a-half and three-year-olds used the obvious strategy of wiping out the tracks. Moreover, Chandler et al. report that three-year-olds, after some prompting, laid false tracks to empty locations, and that they pointed deceptively when questioned. Thus, three-year-olds and maybe even two-year-olds appear to be able to engage in deceptive action and therefore do seem to possess a concept of belief.

However, before we can accept this conclusion, it should be shown that young children apply deceptive strategies *selectively* to mislead an opponent. In their original study, Chandler et al. did not include a co-operative control condition. Therefore, it is impossible to tell whether children employed the "deceptive" strategies with deceptive intent or whether they merely enjoyed the activity of wiping out tracks and painting new ones. We ran a close replication of Chandler et al.'s study with the addition of a co-operative control condition, in which the child's task was to make it easy for a friendly person to find the treasure (Sodian et al., 1991, Experiment 2). In both the co-operative and the competitive conditions (in which the child was instructed to make it difficult for the other person, since the opponent would keep the treasure if he found it) children were given the option of either wiping out the tracks or reinforcing their clarity by adding an extra line.

Our results were clear-cut. Less than a third of the 3-year-olds whom we tested applied the strategies of reinforcing and wiping out tracks in the correct selective way, whereas almost all 4-year-olds did. Moreover, whereas 6 (of 20) 3-year-olds correctly wiped out for the opponent and reinforced for the co-operator, 3 3-year-olds showed exactly the opposite pattern. Thus, 3-year-olds did not seem to choose their strategy with the objective of the game in mind. We also tested whether children employed and understood the strategy of laying false tracks to an empty container. We found very little evidence of spontaneous laying of false tracks in children younger than 4 years, but we were fairly successful in getting children to accept this technique as a "good idea" when we modelled it for them. However, only 3 (of 14) 3-year-olds used the technique for the competitor only; the others either used it for both the co-operator and the competitor or for the co-operator only. In contrast, 10 (of 16) 4-year-olds showed the correct selective use. Similarly, whereas most 4-year-olds pointed to an empty location when questioned by the competitor, only very few 3-year-olds did so spontaneously. When "deceptive" pointing was observed in the younger children, it only occurred after they were prohibited by the experimenter from uncovering the treasure to the competitor.

Similar findings were obtained by Speer, Sullivan, and Smith (1992), who conducted another replication study of Chandler et al.'s experiment. They found that children younger than four years practised both seemingly deceptive and counter-deceptive behaviours indiscriminately in a deception condition and a co-operation conditioning. Thus, the results of two methodically improved replication studies indicate that three-year-old children can be led to produce deceptive ploys, but that they show no clear understanding of their effect. The finding that children younger than four used deceptive and informative strategies indiscriminately, whether asked to mislead a competitor or to inform a collaborator, seriously undermines the view that these young children possess a genuine understanding of belief.

This conclusion was rejected by Hala et al. (1991) on the grounds that they have gathered more evidence in support of their position that three-year-olds show a genuine understanding of deception. They report that three-year-olds are just as good as four-year-olds in selecting an appropriate response according to whether they are asked to help or hinder an experimenter in finding a treasure. At first sight, this result is puzzling, since their procedure appears to be very similar to ours. However, close scrutiny reveals that Hala et al. created a confounded assessment of children's selectivity: When children were asked to deceive the experimenter, a track to the hiding place was already in place. In contrast, when children were asked to help the experimenter, no track was in place. This difference may have biased children to produce "false tracks" more often in the deception condition. Although they could obviously lay new trails in either condition, the option of laying a new trail to the actual hiding place had been pre-empted in the deception condition, but not in the co-operative condition. In the deception condition, any new trail must therefore be a "false" one. Moreover, children were systematically warned against providing accurate information in the deception condition only (Hala et al., 1991, p. 87): Throughout this procedure '... subjects were cautioned not to blurt out the true hiding location." Thus to date there is no evidence that children younger than four years engage in intentional deception, that is, that they actively deceive other persons with the *intention* of inducing a false belief about reality in the opponent.

The Specificity of the Deficit

Demonstrations of young children's failure to deceive others are not sufficient to make the case for a specific conceptual deficit in children's understanding of belief. Three-year-olds' problems in deception tasks could also stem from a variety of other sources. It is possible, for instance, that three-year-olds differ from four-year-olds in their under-standing of the competitive nature of deception tasks, or that they are simply not motivated enough to try to win in such situations. Another possibility is that three-year-olds differ from older children in their ability to inhibit a response towards a salient object (see Russell et al., 1991, for such a proposal). They may be "irresistibly drawn" to pointing towards the location where the object actually is (or to describing truthfully the object they have in mind) even though they understand that it would be possible in this situation to manipulate the other person's belief. Thus, their problem on both false belief attribution and deception tasks may be a lack of executive control of behaviour rather than a conceptual deficit in the representation of belief.

Therefore, to support the assumption of a specific conceptual deficit in young children's understanding of belief it is necessary to show that these children succeed on control tasks that pose similar requirements to the deception tasks except that they do not involve the manipulation of *beliefs*. I have employed this method in a study of deception and sabotage (Sodian, 1991, Experiment 3).

If young children's failure on deception tasks is specific to the manipulation of *beliefs*, then they should be able to hinder an opponent from attaining a desire object by blocking his physical access to this object, while failing to do so by manipulating his beliefs. First evidence in favour of this assumption was gathered by Peskin (1992), who observed that, whereas almost all three-year-olds failed to misinform the opponent, they knew how to exclude him from the game physically. Consistent with her results, I found that three-year-olds are able to employ quite sophisticated physical manipulation ("sabotage") strategies, despite failing to use even simple deceptive tactics. I contrasted a deception with a sabotage condition in two tasks (see Table 18.1 for an overview).

In the first task, "sabotage" consisted in hindering the opponent from taking the desired object out of a box by locking it. Three-year-olds discriminated proficiently between an opponent and a friendly person in this task. Over 70% locked the box for the opponent and left it open for the friend on the first pair of trials, and only 2 (of 26) children failed to do so on the second trial pair. In contrast, when there was no lock available (deception condition), only 26% of these 3- to 4-year-old children lied to the opponent ("the box is locked") when asked whether

TABLE 18.1
Design of Deception/Sabotage Tasks and Correct Responses[a]

	Deception		Sabotage	
	Competitor	Co-operator	Competitor	Co-operator
One box	say that box is locked	say that box is open	lock box	leave box open
	tell lie	*tell truth*	*hinder*	*help*
Two boxes	point to empty box	point to full box	lock full box	lock empty box
	deceptive pointing	*correct information*	*hinder*	*counter intuitive action to help*

[a] Reproduced from Sodian and Frith, 1992, with permission.

they wanted to (truthfully) say that it was open or whether they wanted to say it was locked; even though it was explicitly pointed out to them that the opponent could not see that the box was unlocked, and that, being lazy, he would not bother coming all the way to the candybox if he thought it was not worth the effort anyway. Intuitively, it appears that sabotage was very simple in this task, whereas deception was more sophisticated, requiring children to tell a lie (even though the lie was modelled for them). Thus, the task conditions may have been biased towards producing an effect in the hypothesised direction.

Therefore, we designed a second task in which a quite sophisticated form of sabotage was contrasted with a simple deception strategy—deceptive pointing. In the deceptive pointing condition, the child was asked which box (the full or the empty one) she wanted to point to for the opponent or the friend, respectively. In the parallel sabotage condition, she was given the choice of which one of the two boxes to lock. In the competitive task version, the decision to lock the full box to hinder the opponent from getting the reward is fairly straightforward. In the co-operative version of this task, it would appear reasonable to leave both boxes open. However, if one is required to lock one of the boxes, then it only makes sense to lock the empty one so that the friend (who will give the child the candy if he can find it) will not look into the empty one and leave, disappointedly. Note that to pass this task, the child has to operate on the empty box, just as she is required to point to the empty box in the deception task. Therefore, if it can be shown that children lock the empty box in the co-operative physical manipulation condition, although they fail to point to the empty box in the deception condition, then it would appear unlikely that children's failure to point deceptively is due to a lack of executive control of behaviour, that is, to a problem in inhibiting a response towards a location where a salient object is hidden[2].

The results support the view that children's failure on the deceptive pointing task is, in fact, specific to deception. Figure 18.1 shows that even in the youngest age group (3:0 to 3:6) about half the children performed correctly on *both* sabotage trials, i.e. they locked the full box to hinder the competitor from gaining the reward, *and* they locked the empty box to help the friend attain the reward. In contrast, less then 20% correctly pointed to the empty box in the deception condition. As expected, the complex sabotage task did pose some difficulty for 3- to 4-year-old children. Only about 60% correctly distinguished between opponent and friend on the first trial pair. However, as Fig. 18.1 shows, even on this complex sabotage task performance was significantly better at all ages than in deceptive pointing. This finding was replicated for three-year-old children by Sodian and Frith (1992).

These results support the assumption of a specific conceptual deficit in three-year-old children's understanding of the mind. The results of the sabotage tasks indicate that three-year-olds certainly understand that they can hinder an opponent from winning a reward in a competitive game, and that they are quite motivated to do so. In fact, many three-year-olds spontaneously tried to hinder the opponent from opening the box by physical means even when there was no lock available (i.e. they truthfully indicated where the treasure was hidden, but at the same time tried to hold the box shut with their hands, to remove it from the table, etc.). In particular, the finding that three-year-olds can employ a quite sophisticated behavioural manipulation strategy that requires them to operate on an empty container indicates that their failure to engage in simple deceptive action is not due to a lack of executive control of behaviour.

Research on the development of deceptive action thus appears to support the view that there is conceptual change in children's developing understanding of the mind: Sharp developmental progression between the ages of three and four years was found in various deception tasks (as well as in real-life observations), and there is evidence that three-year-olds' failure on these tasks is *specific* to the manipulation of beliefs.

---

[2] One might argue that operating on the empty box may not be as difficult, from the point of view of executive control of behaviour, as pointing to the empty box. Strictly speaking, to control for this possibility adequately, the same (pointing) response should be asked for in both deception and sabotage conditions (e.g. pointing to where the competitor should "go").

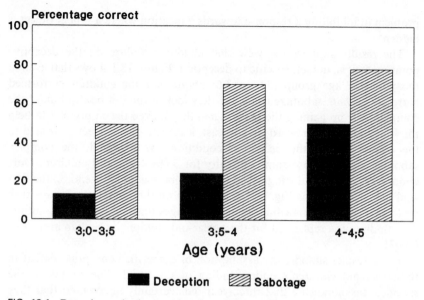

FIG. 18.1 Deception and sabotage (data from Sodian, 1991, Experiment 3; figure adapted from Sodian & Frith, 1993).

THREE-YEAR-OLDS' UNDERSTANDING OF TRICKERY: A CHALLENGE TO THE CONCEPTUAL DEFICIT VIEW?

Sullivan and Winner (1993) have recently presented a new challenge to the conceptual deficit view by claiming that even though three-year-olds may be reluctant to carry out deceptive acts themselves, they understand the effects of deception on a deceived person's beliefs (see also Winner & Sullivan, 1993). At first sight this proposal seems surprising, since the study of deceptive *action* was originally motivated by young children's poor performance on belief *attribution* tasks. Why should we expect three-year-olds to attribute a false belief to a deceived person, given that dozens of studies have shown that children of this age fail to do just this?

Sullivan and Winner's argument is that what may have made the standard false belief tasks difficult is not belief attribution per se but the fact the actors' mental states were not sufficiently highlighted in these tasks. This idea is motivated by a theoretical proposal made by Fodor (1992), who claims that young children do not lack a concept of belief but that their true competence is masked in most false belief tasks by a "reality correspondence bias," that is, the default assumption that beliefs correspond to reality. If children's errors in false belief tasks are attributable to such a bias, then performance should improve when the correspondence bias is weakened.

One way of weakening such a bias is to design tasks that highlight mental states rather than reality. Trickery and deceit should be ideal for highlighting mental states, since the whole point about deception is to manipulate others' beliefs. If three-year-olds have a concept of belief, then, so the argument goes, they should be more likely to attribute a wrong belief to a person who has been explicitly "tricked" or deceived than to a person who inadvertently received false information, since the context of deceit should help them over-ride their reality bias.

This assumption gains some support from everyday observations of young children's pleasure in witnessing and participating in playful trickery, and their enjoyment of fairy tales that contain episodes of deceit. It has been argued that young children could not show such interest in trickery and deceit if they had no understanding whatsoever of deception. However, it remains to be shown that children's enjoyment of such situations indicates that they understand these situations in the same way as adults do.

Understanding the Effects of Deception on the Victim's Belief

Children's understanding of the effects of deception on the victim's beliefs has been assessed in several experimental studies. The results are contradictory: Although Hala et al. (1991) report that most three-year-olds correctly answered that the deceived person would think that the treasure was hidden under the box to which the (false) trail pointed, we were unable to replicate this result (Sodian et al., 1991, Experiment 1). Similarly, Ruffman et al. (1993) found no evidence of an understanding of the effects of deception in three-year-olds.

Proponents of the early competence view could explain the negative results by arguing that in these studies the deceptive context may not have been made sufficiently salient and engaging. To test such an explanation, a deceptive context should be contrasted with a nondeceptive one.

This was done in a recent study by Sullivan and Winner (1993). They compared a neutral and a "trick" version of the so-called Smarties (deceptive box) task (Hogrefe, Wimmer, & Perner, 1986). In the neutral version, the child was shown a familiar box that had some unexpected contents, and was asked to predict what an uninitiated person would think the box contains. In the trick version, the contents were switched by the child and Experimenter 1 with the explicit purpose of playing a trick on Experimenter 2. This was done in a conspiratorial fashion, and much was made of how funny it was to be playing tricks.

Sullivan and Winner found that only 17% of their 3-year-olds correctly predicted that the uninitiated person would think there were Smarties in the box in the neutral version, whereas 69% correctly predicted the false belief of the person who had been tricked. Thus, 3-year-olds' ability to make correct inferences about others' false beliefs seems to be greatly enhanced by creating an explicit deceptive context (even though their performance was still far from ceiling).

In a second study, Winner and Sullivan (1993) showed that this effect did not depend upon the child's active participation in the deceptive action, but extended to a "witness only" task in which children were told a story about someone else's deceptive action, e.g. the story of Little Red Riding Hood, in which the wolf disguises himself as the grandmother. Fifty percent of a group of young three-year-old children (2:10 to 3:6) answered the question "Who does Little Red Riding Hood think is in the bed?" correctly, whereas no child in this age group was correct on the corresponding question in a neutral false belief task.

If children's responses to the question of what a deceived character will "think" reflect an adult-like understanding of thinking in the sense of believing something to be true, then these findings are strong evidence against the conceptual deficit claim. However, there are reasons to doubt this interpretation.

First, children could give correct answers in the trick condition based on their knowledge that people who have been tricked will be wrong (in what they say, do or think), without any deeper understanding of why this is so. Second, and more importantly, recent findings by Peskin (1993) indicate that 3-year-olds may misconstrue trickery and deception as a form of pretend play. Peskin presented children with classic tales of deception (like Little Red Riding Hood). Like Winner and Sullivan, she found that about 50% of the 3-year-olds answered the "think" question correctly (e.g. in a story about a girl who is deceived by a mean goblin who dresses up like a nice boy, children answered the question "Who does Leslie think he is?" correctly with "a nice boy"). However, only 25% of the 3-year-olds (but 90% of the 4-year-olds) grasped the deceit. The majority of the 3-year-olds thought that the purpose of the disguise was pretend play (the mean goblin won't play mean tricks because he is pretending to be a nice boy). This became even clearer in a second experiment in which Peskin phrased the "think"-question in a way so as to distinguish between "thinking within the pretend scenario" and "really thinking": "Does Leslie think he is really a boy or does she think he is pretending to be a boy?" When given this option, the large majority of the three-year-olds answered that the deceived story character thought that the goblin was *pretending* to be a nice boy. That is, three-year-old children did not understand that the point of the deceptive ploy was that the victim thought that the villain really was what he was pretending to be.

These findings indicate that three-year-olds' apparently correct responses to questions about a deceived character's intentional state do not reflect an understanding of deception, but indicate an interesting misconception: Three-year-olds misinterpret tales of deception as stories about pretend play.

An Undifferentiated Concept of Belief and Pretence

Peskin's study addresses only one specific type of deception, in which the purpose of an act of pretence is to deceive. Just as in pretend play, the wolf in Little Red Riding Hood puts on a false appearance and acts as if he were the grandmother; however, other than in pretend play, he does not do so in order to play with Little Red Riding Hood, but in order to deceive her. One might argue that in such special cases children may confound pretence with deception more easily than in more prototypical instances of deception.

However, Perner, Baker, and Hutton (this volume) have shown that three-year-olds' failure to differentiate between pretending and falsely believing is a more general phenomenon. In their tasks, children were shown actions that had to be interpreted as mistakes or as acts of pretence depending on whether or not the protagonist knew about a critical state of affairs. For instance, a story character acted-as-if feeding a rabbit in a box when the box was actually empty. In one condition, the protagonist knew that the box was empty whereas in the other condition he had not witnessed that the rabbit had been removed from the box and therefore mistakenly thought that it was still there. Children were asked whether the protagonist acted as he did because he was pretending that there was a rabbit in the box or because he really thought there was a rabbit in the box. Two experiments using this paradigm showed that children below the age of four years cannot differentiate between pretence and false belief. Thus, children below the age of four years appear to engage in pretend play without an understanding of the difference between pretence and belief. In Perner et al.'s (this volume) analysis, to engage in pretend play one merely has to differentiate between reality-adequate action (acting-as-is) and reality-inadequate action (acting-as-if).

Taken together, Peskin's and Perner et al.'s findings suggest that young children's correct responses to "think" questions in contexts of trickery and deceit may not reflect an understanding or belief but may be based on a more primitive understanding of "acting-as-if." Take, for instance, Sullivan and Winner's trick version of the Smarties task. Three-year-olds may well understand the "trick" scenario as some form of a pretend game. As in the familiar pretend games in which one acts as if an empty cup contained tea, the participants in this game act as if a Smarties box contained Smarties, whereas it really is empty except for a little useless piece of string. A third person who joins into the pretend scenario will also be expected to act as if the Smarties box contained Smarties. Thus, if children interpret the question of what the other person "thinks" is in the box as a question about "thinking within the as-if-scenario," then they will correctly judge that the other person thinks there are Smarties in the box, since this is obviously the accepted convention in this "trick" or as-if game.

This interpretation rests on the assumption that three-year-olds fail to understand the significance of a person's access to relevant information for her mental state. This has been shown by Perner et al. (this volume) for the distinction between pretence and mistaken action: Three-year-olds did not take into account whether or not the protagonist had witnessed the critical event. I realise that no parallel test has been done for the distinction between deceit and pretence. If the suggested interpretation is correct, then three-year-olds, in their judgements of what another person "thinks," should fail to distinguish between a "trick" condition, in which the deceived person lacks a critical piece of information, and a pretence condition, in which all participants know the true state of affairs.

Thus, based on Peskin's and Perner's theoretical analyses and empirical findings, my tentative interpretation of the findings on three-year-olds' understanding of deception is that children of this age do not differentiate between deceit and pretence, but that they assimilate deceptive acts to their understanding of "acting-as-if" as in pretend play. This interpretation may also account for some real-life observations of deceptive-looking acts by children well below the age of four years (see Newton, 1992, for an impressive collection of such episodes from children who showed no belief understanding on standard false belief tasks). In most of these anecdotes, there is no convincing evidence that the child acts with the *intention* to induce a false belief in another person. On the other hand, many of the deceptive-looking acts by young children are too creative and original to be explained by the assumption that children are merely mindlessly employing a behavioural routine. A third possibility is that children engage in deceptive-looking behaviours in a similar way as they engage in joint pretence: They create an as-if scenario and invite others to join in with them.

Speculations about Mechanisms of Development

To date, research on the development of deception has almost exclusively been concerned with the question of whether or not young children understand deception in the same way as older children or adults. I have argued that there are good reasons to believe that they do not and that their (mis)understanding of deception is embedded in an alternative conceptual framework in which pretence and belief are not differentiated[3]. This leaves us with the question of how children can ever come to understand trickery and

---

[3] I refer to Perner's work for a detailed account of how an undifferentiated concept of belief and pretence could function within the young child's understanding of the mental domain (Perner et al., this volume; Perner, 1993).

deceit in the way we do. How is it possible that, within a relatively narrow age range, the child can work out the distinctions between pretence and belief and between belief and reality along the lines of our conceptual system, if she starts off with a system that is partially incompatible with ours?

This question has hardly ever been addressed in theory of mind research, and there are certainly no adequate answers to it at present. If experiences from social interaction play a role in the child's intuitive theory building and revision, then one might speculate that the unintended effects of young children's deceptive-looking actions may provide an important learning experience on the way to the acquisition of a concept of belief. Children may be alerted to the fact that "acting-as-if" may have serious consequences if an uninitiated other person takes to be true what the child knows to be false. That is, young children may initially act in a potentially deceptive way without having formed a deceptive intent; however, occasionally such actions may have the effect of inducing a false belief in another person. If the child has not yet formed a concept of belief, she will not be able to understand, in our terms, what has happened. However, the experience that her action provoked some surprising reaction may focus her attention on discovering the causes for this reaction. Several such experiences may eventually lead children to construct a causal connection between what they told or showed another person and what this person thinks, and this may become the driving force in forming a mature concept of belief.

This speculation about relevant learning experiences is based on the assumption that the driving factor behind developmental progress in the child's theory of mind is an emerging understanding of informational causation. This proposal was originally made by Wimmer, Hogrefe, and Sodian (1988), who claimed that three-year-olds' difficulty with false belief is primarily due to a failure to understand the causal relation between a person's access to information and their epistemic states. For a revised version that takes into account recent criticism, see Wimmer and Weichbold (1993). The finding that there is sharp developmental progress in children's competences in deceptive action between the ages of three and four years fits nicely with this proposal, since strategic interaction (as in deception and in hide-and-seek games) depends crucially on an understanding of informational causation. The view that an understanding of informational causation is crucial to children's acquisition of a concept of belief would gain additional support if effects of concrete experiences with strategic interaction on belief understanding could be demonstrated empirically.

SUMMARY AND CONCLUSIONS

My main conclusion from this review of research on the development of children's ability to deceive others and to understand the consequences of deception is that research on deception does not support the claim that there is conceptual continuity in young children's understanding of the mind. On the contrary, the data give strong support to the view that the concept of belief is not acquired before the age of four years. I have first tried to show that research on deception supports the assumption of a specific conceptual deficit in three-year-old children's understanding of the mind. This leaves us with the task of specifying exactly *how* the three-year-old's conceptual system differs from the four-year-old's. Recent research on deception has made some contributions to answering this question. In particular, a study by Peskin (1993) indicates that a misunderstanding of acts of deception as acts of pretence may be a precursor to a mature understanding of deception. I have argued that this proposal can account for findings on early deception both in laboratory tasks and in real-life situations, and that it leads to some interesting speculations about possible mechanisms of conceptual change in the child's understanding of the mind.

ACKNOWLEDGEMENTS

My research on deception was supported by a grant from the *Deutsche Forschungsgemeinschaft*. I wish to thank the editors of this volume, and Josef Perner and Heinz Wimmer, for many helpful comments and suggestions on an earlier version of this chapter.

REFERENCES

Brooks, P.J., Samuels, M.C., & Frye, D. (1993). *Are three-year-olds capable of deception?* Paper presented as the meetings of the Society for Research in Child Development, New Orleans.

Carey, S. (1985). *Conceptual change in childhood.* Cambridge, Mass.: MIT Press.

Carey, S. (1991). Knowledge acquisition: Enrichment or conceptual change. In S. Carey & R. Gelman (Eds.), *The epigenesis of mind: Essays on biology and cognition* (pp. 257–292). Hillsdale, NJ: Lawrence Erlbaum Associates Inc.

Chandler, M., Fritz, A.S., & Hala, S. (1989). Small scale deceit: Deception as a marker of 2-, 3-, and 4-year-olds' early theories of mind. *Child Development, 60,* 1263–1277.

Fodor, J.A. (1992). A theory of the child's theory of mind. *Cognition, 44,* 283–296.

Hala, S., Chandler, M., & Fritz, A. (1991). Fledgling theories of mind: Deception as a marker of 3-year-olds' understanding of false belief. *Child Development, 61,* 83–97.

Hogrefe, G.J., Wimmer, H., & Perner, J. (1986). Ignorance versus false belief: A developmental lag in attribution of epistemic states. *Child Development, 57,* 567–582.

LaFreniere, P.J. (1988). The ontogeny of tactical deception in humans. In R.W. Byrne & A. Whiten (Eds.), *Machiavellian intelligence. Social expertise and the evolution of intellect in monkeys* (pp. 238–252). New York: Oxford University Press.

Newton, P. (1992). *Theory of mind in practice.* Paper presented at the European Conference on Developmental Psychology, Seville, Spain.

Perner, J. (1991). *Understanding the representational mind.* Cambridge, Mass.: Bradford Books/MIT Press.

Perner, J. (1993). *The many faces of belief: Reflections on Fodor's and the child's theory of mind.* Unpublished manuscript, University of Sussex.

Peskin, J. (1992). Ruse and representations: On children's ability to conceal information. *Developmental Psychology, 28,* 84–89.

Peskin, J. (1993). *When the purpose of pretence is deception: Preschoolers' understanding of intentional states.* Paper presented at the meetings of the Society for Research in Child Development, New Orleans.

Ruffman, T., Olson, D.R., Ash, T., & Keenan, T. (1993). The ABCs of deception: Do young children understand deception in the same way as adults? *Developmental Psychology, 29,* 74–87.

Russell, J., Mauthner, N., Sharpe, S., & Tidswell, T. (1991). The "windows task" as a measure of strategic deception in preschoolers and autistic subjects. *British Journal of Developmental Psychology, 9,* 331–350.

Samuels, M.C., & Brooks, P.J. (1993). *Strategic game playing in children through the "windows" task.* Paper presented at the meetings of the Society for Research in Child Development, New Orleans.

Sodian, B. (1991). The development of deception in young children. *British Journal of Developmental Psychology, 9,* 173–188.

Sodian, B., & Frith, U. (1992). Deception and sabotage in autistic, retarded, and normal children. *Journal of Child Psychology and Psychiatry, 33,* 591–605.

Sodian, B., & Frith, U. (1993). The Theory of mind deficit in autism: evidence from deception. In S. Baron-Cohen, H. Tager-Flusberg, & D. Cohen (Eds.) *Understanding other minds: Perspectives from Autism.* Oxford: Oxford University Press.

Sodian, B., Taylor, C., Harris, P.L., & Perner, J. (1991). Early deception and the child's theory of mind: False trails and genuine markers. *Child Development, 62,* 468–483.

Speer, J.R., Sullivan, G.M., & Smith, N. (1993). *Hiding paradigm affords no evidence of deceptive intent in 2½-year-olds.* Paper presented at the meetings of the American Psychological Society, San Diego.

Stern, C., & Stern, W. (1909). *Erinnerung, Aussage und Lüge in der ersten Kindheit.* Leipzig: Barth.

Stouthamer-Loeber, N. (1986). *Adults' perception of verbal misrepresentation of reality in four-year-olds.* Unpublished manuscript, University of Pittsburgh.

Sullivan, K., & Winner, E. (1993). *Three-year-olds' understanding of mental states: The influence of trickery.* Unpublished manuscript, University of Massachusetts.

Wimmer, H., Hogrefe, G.J., & Sodian, B. (1988). A second stage in children's conception of mental life: Understanding informational accesses as origins of knowledge and belief. In J.W. Astington, P.L. Harris, & D.R. Olson (Eds.), *Developing theories of mind* (pp. 173–192). Cambridge: Cambridge University Press.

Wimmer, H., & Perner, J. (1983). Beliefs about beliefs: Representation and constraining function of wrong beliefs in young children's understanding of deception. *Cognition, 13,* 103–128.

Wimmer, H., & Weichbold, V. (1993). *Children's theory of mind: Fodor's heuristics or understanding informational causation.* Unpublished manuscript, University of Salzburg.

Winner, E., & Sullivan, K. (1993). *Young three-year-olds understand belief when observing or participating in deception* Unpublished manuscript, Boston College.

Woodruff, G., & Premack, D. (1979). Intentional communication in the chimpanzee: The development of deception. *Cognition, 7,* 333–362.

19

The Role of Personal Involvement in the Assessment of Early False Belief Skills

Michael Chandler and Suzanne Hala
University of British Columbia, Vancouver, Canada

INTRODUCTION

Flooding the market of current claims concerning children's earliest theories of mind is a cluster of aggressively promoted, and still widely subscribed "one miracle" views—a stern and withholding family of heavily inbred accounts, according to which the years both before and after four are largely dismissed as wastrel years; slack times seen to make no real substantive contributions to the supposedly singular, stand-alone insight that minds, by their very nature, are representational (for a recent review, see Moses & Chandler, 1992). Although specifically tailored to fit the increasingly dated findings of an older, first generation of "theories of mind" research, such economy models of mental life, we will argue, never really suited what is otherwise known about the fabric of cognitive development, and provide an even poorer fit for the more up-to-date results of a second generation of better-measured research efforts. In the place of all such scant and increasingly outmoded one-miracle views, this chapter aims at substituting an alternative and, we hope, less withholding vision that sees children's progress toward a mature conception of mind as altogether more spread out, as starting sooner, as going on longer, and as marked by more in the way of qualitative transformations than has been widely supposed.

The flood of publications devoted to supporting this single watershed view already amounts to more than a hundred journal articles and at least a half-dozen recent volumes, leaving little hope of squeezing successfully into this short chapter a still fuller account of what might lie to either side. In grudging acknowledgement of these constraints we have reluctantly adopted the piecemeal strategy of restricting attention here primarily to three-year-olds and what they may or may not know about the possibility of false belief. Our central point about these young persons will be that, quite apart from what you may have heard elsewhere, when freed to interact in those purposeful ways that ordinarily lead adults to wonder about each other's mental states, children as young as three already evidence a clear working understanding of the fact that ignorance promotes false beliefs. Predictably set against our own "early onset" view (Chandler, Fritz, & Hala, 1989) are the increasingly strident claims of those whose nervous insistence upon the double security of both methodological belts and braces has led them to the cautious claim that persons younger than four must suffer some previously undetected cognitive deficit that wholly blocks them from understanding the possibility of false belief. In what follows, we plan to report upon a body of recent evidence meant to support further our own sunnier views on these matters and to leave those who think otherwise standing there in short pants.

Before getting down to the more particular business of laying out our version of what three- and four-year-olds do and do not understand about belief entitlement, however, it still seems to us useful to first spend a few introductory moments trying to situate the achievements of such young preschoolers in a somewhat broader interpretive context. With luck, such an opening move may also help to blunt the otherwise ready and pointed criticisms of those colleagues who, having apparently grown weary of what is widely perceived to be the theory of mind literature's inflated sense of self-importance, seem more than ready to remind us how little real light actually separates the claims of those currently quibbling over precisely where the goalposts of metarepresentational competence ought to be located. Following a few preliminary remarks about an alternative framework for reinterpreting such otherwise trivial threshold questions, we mean to return quickly to the more immediate business of deciding just how far one so-called miracle can be reasonably stretched in an effort to cover what preschoolers know and don't know about mental life.

THE BIG(GER) PICTURE

As just outlined, our main goal in what follows will be to assemble evidence—our own as well as that of others—meant to persuade you that four-year-olds do not, as has been widely reported, sit astride some singular, either-or, once-in-a-lifetime watershed irrevocably separating those that do and do not hold to a representational theory of mind (see also chapters in this volume by Lewis; Siegal & Peterson). The primary reason that they do not do so, we will argue, is that there is no such unique watershed, and that of the several natural inflection points that actually do mark off meaningful junctures in the course of children's maturing views of mental life, none appears to fall at or even especially near the much over-rated age of four. Instead, we will contend, it is both still younger two- and three-year-olds and considerably older six- and seven-year-olds who, if anyone, would seem to come closest to occupying whatever naturally occurring transitions do divide up the developmental course of children's changing views of mental life. If this is so, that is, if four-year-olds (who are routinely held up as being the first to acquire any real understanding of mind) are in fact better understood as marked by a confused admixture of early and late arriving abilities, then at least the question of whether it is two- or three- or four-year-olds who first grasp the possibility of false belief might take on some real theoretical weight. Having come that far, however, we should resist the temptation to lose ourselves once again in some overly detailed preoccupation with the exact timing of children's first "either-or" insight into the mind's metarepresentational nature, and set our focus instead on the altogether more feasible and interesting job of working out the general whereabouts of all of those several joints that do appear to divide the body of children's social-cognitive development. One way of getting such an inquiry off the ground, we suggest, is by first trying to decide, on strictly conceptual grounds, what a minimally complex but nevertheless recognisably adult reading of mental life would actually have to look like.

By our own lights, any minimally acceptable view of mental life would need to include, at the very least, the idea that minds somehow function as two-way streets, allowing for what Searle (1983) has described as both a "world-to-mind" and a "mind-to-world" direction of fit. That is, any reasonably grown-up version of mental life would seem to require the idea that minds not only conform themselves to an independent reality, but must also successfully alter or deform that reality in whatever interpretive ways are required to make life intellectually digestible by those working to absorb it. By this account, then, anything elaborate enough to match the tacit theories of mind already in place in the folk psychology of your usual young adolescent would also need to allow somehow for the fact that persons not only accommodate their understanding to new-found realities, but also assimilate experience to their own inbuilt structures or frameworks of understanding.

According to the provisional model we want to advance here, the progress of preschool and early school-age children toward a mature theory of mind ordinarily moves along a path marked, at the very least, by two distinctive junctures. At the first of these, young two- and three-year-old children typically advance their early careers as apprentice theorists of mind by initially subscribing to only the first half of Searle's larger double-barrelled account. They do this, we suggest, by first proceeding as though minds need only be made to "fit" the world, that only exogenous factors orchestrate mental life, and that we only passively copy or accommodate to the reality that helps to shape our lives (Chandler, 1988; Chandler & Boyes, 1982). That is, by our way of reckoning, young preschoolers begin their fledgling attempts to make explicit sense of mental life by initially adopting an only half-baked *copy theory* view of knowledge and belief, a view according to which minds are seen as somehow capable of accommodating themselves to the world, but which does not yet go on to include the contrapuntal idea that minds also deform or assimilate experience to fit their own structures. By these same lights, the other of these insights is not seen to put in a first appearance until sometime during the early primary school years, where it expresses itself as the novel realisation that two persons can and often do interpret one and the same stimulus event differently. In short, then, the earlier of these junctures, on which we are meant to focus here, involves realisations first in evidence, not among four-and five-year-olds, as has often been supposed, but rather among children as young as two or three, and is distinctively marked by an appreciation of the fact that persons who are systematically kept in the dark will ordinarily get things wrong. The second in this potentially long list of insights—the insight that things can be gotten wrong in more than one way—is similarly said to find its rightful place at six, seven, or eight years, and not during some Hollywoodised four-year transition.

If anything like the version of early epistemic development just outlined proves to be correct, that is, if early progress toward a mature conception of mental life does in fact proceed through at least the two separate steps or stages we have suggested, then all those monocular, one-miracle views that mistakenly conflate these separate accomplishments into one blurred composite image will naturally fall into each of two distinct types of errors. On the one hand, they will tend to trivialise the real accomplishments of six- and seven-year-olds and still older children by wrongly supposing that their genuinely new insights into the interpretive nature of mind—an achievement that necessarily presupposes what Searle calls a "world-to-mind" direction of fit—really amounts to no more than the simple recognition of the possibility of false belief. On the other hand, advocates of these same monopolistic, one-miracle views will also be grudging and slow to grant still younger two- and three-year-olds any legitimate understanding of the mind until they can successfully acquit themselves on whatever psychometrically inhospitable measures of false belief under-standing happen to be in vogue. They do this first by wrongly imagining that those who pass standard "Unexpected Transfer" and "Unexpected Contents" (or "deceptive box") measures of false belief already successfully grasp what Flavell (1988) has called the "one-many relation" that obtains between events in the world and their possible interpretation. Secondly, by playing upon two- and three-year-old children's weaknesses rather than their strengths, these same assessment procedures do not, as advertised, succeed in marking off some absolute lower limit of children's early understanding of false belief.

In the end the present chapter is perhaps best seen as an attempt to back only the second of the foregoing claims—the idea that the idea of belief entitlement first begins at four—whereas the task of better detailing what is required if one is to get at what is minimally involved in an interpretive view of mental life needs to be set aside for another occasion (see Lalonde, Chandler, & Moses, 1992). For present purposes, then, we will have done what we set out to accomplish if we manage to persuade you that most three-year-olds, and perhaps still younger children, already possess a well-oiled understanding of the fact that ignorance promotes mistaken beliefs, and that the routine failure of such young persons to demonstrate this ability on various well-known measures of false belief understanding is an indictment of various measurement procedures in common use, and not of those young preschoolers whom they systematically mislabel.

REREADING THE EVIDENCE ON FALSE BELIEF UNDERSTANDING

What must be credited as one of psychology's best-replicated findings is that, when pressed by strange adults to comment upon the hypothetical mental states of various only partially informed puppet figures, children younger than four or five usually lose track of certain of these computationally complex matters and so confuse "reality" with what these story characters mistakenly suppose it to be. Responding in this wrong-headed (if understandable) fashion has been christened "the reality error," and is widely taken as proof that, as a group, three-year-olds, and still younger children, have absolutely no appreciation of the fact that people are often mistaken in their beliefs. As of this writing there can be no fewer than half a hundred studies, all of which are held out as proof of two supposedly iron-clad conclusions: The first of these is the claim that two- and three-year-olds, but not still older children, are marked by some cognitive deficit that leaves them categorically unable to distinguish reality from its representations. The second is that the four- and five-year-olds who, against all odds, manage to consistently pass such Unexpected Transfer and Unexpected Contents measures of false belief understanding, also demonstrate by doing so that they already subscribe to a "constructivistic" or "interpretive" theory of mind (Perner, 1991; Perner & Davies, 1991; Ruffman, Olson, & Astington, 1991; Wellman 1990) and, as Flavell (1988) has put it, demonstrate an understanding of the "one-many" relationship between things in the world and their possible representation. Against these formidable odds, we mean to hold out for the spoiler claim that the evidence just pointed to supports neither of these two extravagant conclusions. If we are right about this, that is, if still younger children already appreciate the possibility of false belief, and only much older six- and seven-year-olds really begin to grasp the interpretive nature of the knowing process, then the ages of four and five years are emptied of much of their supposed uniqueness, and once again take up their more democratic place between one, two, and three years, on the one hand, and still older age periods on the other.

As already signalled earlier, this is not the place to attempt an empirical assault upon what we take to be the mistaken idea that four- and five-year-olds already subscribe to an interpretive theory of mind. There is perhaps room enough, however, to run the more straightforward conceptual argument that may amount to the same thing. Our point, for the moment, is simply that if one hopes to demonstrate that persons of any age already understand that one and the same stimulus event can support more than a single interpretation, then it is necessary to document that fact by first creating an assessment context in which different persons are actually exposed to one and the same stimulus event. To be generous, there is some legitimate room for confusion here. In Wimmer and Perner's (1983) much replicated "Maxi" task, for example, Maxi and his mother do, in some real sense, end up knowing different things about the singular matter of the whereabouts of the chocolate. At the same time, however, the whole point of this complexly orchestrated assessment task is to work things out in just such a way that Maxi remains ignorant of certain key details shown to be available to his mother. On reflection, it should be clear, we think, that young four- and five-year-olds' talent for keeping these confusing matters straight really succeeds in telling us nothing about their grasp of the prospect that minds might also have a "world-to-mind" direction of fit—a mind-world relation that still allows persons who are playing with precisely the same informational deck to construe their objectively identical experiences differently. It fails to instruct us in such matters precisely because the experience of the two story characters just isn't, and wasn't ever meant to be, objectively identical. Without taking the time to unwind all of the parallel details, we hope you will judge it to be equally obvious that both the much practised Unexpected Contents measure (Gopnik & Astington, 1988; Hogrefe, Wimmer, & Perner, 1986; Perner, Leekam, & Wimmer, 1987) and the false belief version of "appearance-reality" tests (Gopnik & Astington, 1988) also turn on the same device of gerrymandering evidence so that none of the target persons whose views are at issue have equal access to precisely the same stimuli. The intended effect of all of this is hopefully to bring you along to our view that there is nothing about the mountain of evidence arising from the application of these standard false belief measures that would allow anyone to reach any conclusion whatsoever about whether four- and five-year-olds do or do not as yet harbour an interpretive theory of mind. Data that does speak to this issue is currently being collected (Lalonde et al., 1992; Pillow, 1991), and so far it looks anything but good for children as young as four or five. Still, that is a story for another time and place.

The prior question, of whether only four- and five-year-olds but not still younger children understand the even simpler possibility that beliefs may be false, is more directly pertinent to the business of this volume and more answerable by appeals to research evidence. The short answer is that, running counter to the initial wave of findings primarily gathered in the 1980s, there has recently emerged a newer, second generation of research findings, many of which offer telling evidence to support the idea that three-year-olds, and perhaps even still younger children, may already have some firm grasp upon what it means to hold to a false belief (e.g. Chandler, Fritz et al., 1989; Freeman, this volume; Freeman, Lewis, & Doherty, 1991; Fritz, 1991; Hala, Chandler, & Fritz, 1991; Lewis, 1993; Lewis & Osborne, 1990; Moses & Flavell, 1991; Mitchell & Lacohée, 1991; Reddy, 1990; Robinson, Mitchell, & Nye, 1992; Sheffield, Sosa, & Hudson, 1993; Siegal & Beattie, 1990).

Whereas some of these newer studies have introduced novel assessment strategies in what otherwise seems to have been a highly root-bound research tradition, others have employed only slightly modified versions of the same classic Unexpected Transfer and Unexpected Contents tasks that initially gave rise to the suggestion of possible cognitive deficits among otherwise intellectually sound three-year-olds. Whatever their precise format, all of these alternative assessment strategies have generally shared the common goal of trying to get at abilities that may have been inadvertently obscured by an earlier reliance on inopportune assessment strategies. An early clue suggesting that some such corrective measures might be in order actually came from work carried out by the original developers in the now routinised Unexpected Transfer and Unexpected Contents measures. Early modifications to these original procedures, which included, for example, memory probes to ensure that subjects were following the story, proved successful in reducing the so-called threshold age of false-belief understanding from the earlier reported six years to a much younger four years of age (e.g. Perner et al., 1987). Subsequent attempts to pursue something of this same corrective strategy further, although much railed against by the "Mayflower" group, whose interests in the theories-of-mind arrived on the first boat, have included a variety of approaches ranging from merely simplifying the wording of the test questions (e.g. Lewis & Osborne, 1990; Siegal & Beattie, 1990) to the adoption of rather more radical changes meant to rationalise the task better for subjects. Despite these and other differences, the bulk of such alternative measurement efforts still can be usefully sorted into three broad categories, each of which is briefly detailed.

Answering the Right Question

The first of these categories is illustrated by a range of studies (e.g. Freeman et al., 1991; Lewis & Osborne, 1990; Siegal & Beattie, 1990) that have all proceeded on the assumption that the poor showing of young preschoolers on more standard false belief measures may have been due to the fact that the subjects of these earlier studies may simply have failed to understand precisely what they were being asked to do. Contributors to studies of this sort argue, for example, that in responding to questions about where Maxi "will look for his chocolate," three-year-olds may very well cut to the chase and so end up answering quite different questions about where Maxi "will *eventually* look," or about where Maxi "*should* look" for his chocolate. The obvious guard against this possibility is to introduce into the standard false belief assessment procedures whatever variations in emphasis or wording are required in order to ensure that experimenters and subjects are actually on the same page. The common finding reported by those who have attempted such methodological revisions is that when three-year-olds are further helped to understand what question they are meant to be answering, then the majority of them typically give evidence of already understanding the possibility of false beliefs.

Matters of Salience

The second general category of studies concerns the work of a further group of investigators who have proceeded on the somewhat different assumption that the routine failures of two- and three-year-olds on standard measures of false belief understanding may well be artefacts arising as a result of the fact that the measurement procedures in common use somehow prejudice their case by inadvertently attaching more saliency to the various "realities" that are presented than to their possible "mental representation." Advocates of such ideas have attempted to support their views by introducing special steps meant to ensure that "reality" (about, for example, the real current location of Maxi's chocolate) is somehow made less disarmingly salient, or that its mental representation (i.e. Maxi's poorly informed view on this matter) is somehow given greater weight.

In one example of such a corrective strategy our colleague Anna Fritz (1991) has undertaken to off-load some of the weight that usually adheres to the concrete realities of standard Unexpected Transfer and Unexpected Contents tasks by substituting, in one case, "pretend" chocolate for the real mind-grabbing chocolate ordinarily employed in Wimmer and Perner's (1983) classic Maxi problem. In a parallel study she also arranged an alternative version of the Unexpected Contents task in which the surprising fact about the typical Smarties box was not that it unexpectedly contained pencils, but rather that it was unexpectedly empty. The idea obviously at work in these studies was that "pretend chocolate" wouldn't have the same imperious saliency as does the real thing, just as "no contents" would prove to be somehow less salient or attention-grabbing than would the reality of actually finding real pencils where sweets had been expected. As it turned out, these straightforward saliency manipulations were enough to allow some 75% of the 3-year-olds tested to pass otherwise entirely standard false belief measures.

In a related program of study, Zaitchik (1991) also attempted to reduce the impact of witnessing some highly salient Unexpected Transfer by arranging that her subjects only heard rumours about—but did not actually witness—the fact that the location of various target objects was being changed. As had been the case in Fritz's studies, Zaitchik also found that the lion's share of her three-year-olds, who had only heard about—but did not actually see—a toy being moved, were remarkably good at recognising that, although they themselves knew about the crucial transfer, some other less well-informed onlooker would not. The general conclusion promoted by these several studies (as well as a study by Robinson et al., 1992) is that, if "reality" is not somehow made to seem overweening, and if mental events are allowed to assume anything like the importance ordinarily accorded them, then even young three-year-olds will regularly distinguish the truth from what those less well informed than themselves would mistakenly take it to be.

The flip-side of this same strategy is taken up in a pair of studies by Mitchell and his colleagues (Mitchell & Lacohée, 1991; Stevenson & Mitchell, 1992), in which efforts were made, not to somehow reduce the salience of reality, but to find ways of adding fresh salience to those ordinarily best-forgotten beliefs that experience has shown to be mistaken. For example, in the first of these studies, which utilised an otherwise standard version of the usual Unexpected Contents task, Mitchell and Lacohée (1991) found that the simple act of marking children's original beliefs, by "posting" a pictorial account of them in a post box, was enough to allow the large majority of their three-year-old subjects to remember accurately their own, now evidently mistaken, beliefs regarding the likely contents of a well-marked box. These studies, along with those reported earlier, offer strong support for the view that the poor showings ordinarily turned in by three-year-olds on standardised measures of false belief understanding can be laid off, in some large measure, to the fact that, in standard measurement procedures, the usual importance attached to mental events is somehow artificially eclipsed by other pressing realities of the moment.

Matters of Relevance

The third and final group of studies to be considered here find their fault with standard false belief measures, not so much in their particular phraseology or choice of stimulus materials, as in the fact that these procedures have typically turned upon matters that are often static, hypothetical, third-party, and of no immediate relevance or personal interest to the young subjects in question. As most developmentalists are generally well aware, if you hope to win the best of co-operative efforts from young preschool children, it is probably wise not to turn them into passive onlookers, but to engage them instead in some matter upon which they may freely act and about which they have some natural care and concern. Dunn (1988; 1991; see also this volume), for example, argues convincingly that if one wants to have a clear picture of young children's competencies, that it is essential to observe them acting on their own behalf. Similarly, Bruner (1990) argues that young children's earliest knowledge of mental life is *"enactive knowledge"* that first arises through participation in social interactions and is first evident in their efforts to regulate these interactions.

In one recent study, Freeman et al. (1991) attempted to put some of these principles to work by arguing that traditional false belief tasks have failed to promote an essential "need-to-know" in the story characters that are portrayed. Without some such incentive, they suggest, subjects are unlikely to take cognizance of the relevant mental representations of such story characters. To accomplish such purposes better these investigators devised a hide-and-seek scenario, in which one of the story characters badly "needed to know" the whereabouts of the other, and so cheats by peeking, only to have this ill-gotten information later rendered false as the result of a subsequent unforeseeable turn of events. Having taken these steps to attach real importance to the likely thoughts of their story characters, Freeman and his colleagues found that three-year-old subjects turned out to be quite good at keeping track of what such story characters might be thinking.

Although the studies by Freeman and his colleagues go an important distance toward according the measurement of false belief understanding a certain "human sense" (Donaldson, 1978), their aim was always to promote some "need to know" only within the minds of their story characters and not, as we ourselves have taken to do, to engage the cognitive motivation of our subjects directly. In one of their several studies, however, these investigators did come somewhat closer to our own approach to the problem by including a so-called "acting-out" condition. In this version of their task they proceeded, not by asking subjects to respond verbally as to where a protagonist might search in a hide-and-seek game, but by requiring them to use the puppet from the story narrative to demonstrate actively where he would search. In this way subjects were given a more active role in planfully working out what the protagonist might think and do. When combined with a testing context that also provided the protagonist with a "need to know," this active participation condition proved to be particularly effective in accessing the otherwise obscured false belief understanding of their young three-year-old subjects.

In contrast to the studies of Freeman and his colleagues, in which the beliefs of various story characters were especially highlighted by affording these protagonists some special "need to know," other investigators, ourselves included (e.g. Avis & Harris, 1991; Chandler et al., 1989; Hala, 1991; Hala et al., 1991; Sullivan & Winner, 1991), have sought somehow to cut out the middle man by directly engaging the interests of their child subjects in others' beliefs. For the most part, those who have pursued these research strategies have sought to increase their subjects' active interest in the mental experience of some protagonist by encouraging them to take steps to somehow mislead or deceive an opponent. By directly engaging the subject's own interests, such situations, it is argued, are more representative of the ordinary course of interpersonal life than are the passive onlooker roles into which subjects are typically cast in more standard false belief tasks (see Dunn, this volume). Although not everyone who has made use of such deception paradigms has had our theoretical reasons for expecting good things from three-year-olds, or has met with the same success in showing young persons to their apparent best advantage (e.g. Peskin, 1992; Russell, Mauthner, Sharpe, & Tidswell, 1991; Sodian, 1991; Sodian, Taylor, Harris, & Perner, 1991), enough hard evidence is available to warrant attempting to re-introduce such deceptive strategies back into the design of more standard Unexpected Transfer and Unexpected Contents tasks.

The results of one such effort can be seen in the findings of a recent cross-cultural study carried out by Avis and Harris (1991). These investigators sought to determine when young Baka children of East Africa come to the same understanding of the possibility of false belief manifest by Western European and North American children. Avis and Harris describe in great detail the initial difficulties they were forced to overcome in setting up a culturally appropriate testing situation that made real human sense to young Baka children. As in our own work, these investigators also finally settled on a procedure that involved subjects in a deceptive hiding task in a setting with which their young subjects were very familiar. Such efforts were deemed by Avis and Harris to be crucial to the success of their efforts to ensure that they obtained the best performance possible in a testing situation that might not otherwise allow their subjects to show evidence of their best abilities. Unfortunately, few investigators engaged in the study of Western children's theories of mind have shown comparable interest in devising such childcentred measures. Although it is difficult to compare the results of the Avis and Harris study directly with results based upon samples of Western children, because we do not know how the Baka children would have performed on more standard versions of false belief tasks, their results are nevertheless instructive. Based on their more interactive procedure, these investigators report that 65% of their 3-year-old Baka subjects correctly answered the false belief test question put to them. Although this performance falls somewhat short of the still better showing turned in by their 4-year-olds, it nevertheless exceeds results traditionally obtained in studies using standard false belief tasks with Western children.

Our own joint efforts to access young children's early insights about mental life also belong in this final category. Our working assumption in these recent studies has been that if traditional measures of false belief could be modified in ways that would give subjects an opportunity to be actively involved in intentionally bringing about another's false belief, then even young three-year-old subjects would have no difficulty in envisioning the false beliefs of those who were the targets of their own deceptive actions. The first two of these new studies were intended to provide an initial examination of whether, in fact, active involvement made any real difference in the ability of subjects to respond correctly to question about another's false belief. Study 1 accomplishes this through a modified version of the Unexpected Transfer or "Maxi" task, whereas Study 2 goes on to generalise these findings to an active version of the Unexpected Contents or "deceptive box" task. Study 3 is meant to provide a necessary control against alternate readings of the good results obtained for Studies 1 and 2. To this end, we set out in Study 3 to determine whether the facilitating effects found in Studies 1 and 2 might have alternatively been brought about as a result of other (to us) less theoretically interesting modifications to the standard task. Finally, in Study 4, we address more specifically the potential contributing role that participation solely in the *planning* phase of intentional actions might play in enabling subjects to perform at their best.

STUDY 1

In this study, 43 3-year-olds (m = 3:6) participated in an interactive version of the classic Wimmer and Perner (1983) Unexpected Transfer procedure, which modified otherwise standard procedures so that the subjects themselves took responsibility for bringing about the false belief of another. Of these original participants, three were later excluded because they incorrectly answered control questions that were meant to ensure that they adequately understood the task.

This assessment task, like the standard Unexpected Transfer task, involved the transfer of a treat from one location to another while a protagonist—in this case a second experimenter—was out of the room. In this more active version, however, subjects were drawn into a conspiracy with the experimenter (E1) in which they were assigned the task of hiding a treat from a second experimenter (E2). In order to assess their understanding of the consequences of their deceptive actions, subjects were then asked both where E2 would *look* for the object and where E2 would *think* the object was upon returning to the testing room.

Results

As can be seen in Table 19.1, performance was nearly at ceiling when subjects were asked to predict where E2 would *look* for the now hidden object. Overall, 87.5% of these 3-year-old subjects correctly responded that E2 would wrongly attempt to retrieve the object from the container in which it was originally kept. A Chi-square analysis indicated that this level of performance was significantly better than would be expected by chance if subjects were simply guessing (χ^2 [1, n = 40] = 22.5, P < 0.0001). As with the look question, the majority of subjects, 70% overall, also correctly responded that E2 would *think* the treat was in its original location, a difference that was again significantly different from chance (χ^2 [1, n = 40] = 6.4, P < 0.01).

It is clear from these results that young three-year-olds perform much better on this interactive version of the Unexpected Transfer task than on the more standard procedure after which it was patterned. This is true for both types of false belief test questions. Even if we adopt the most conservative stance and count as successful only those subjects who passed *both* the think and look question, the subjects of this study clearly outperformed those reported in previous studies using less interactive measures in which three-year-olds have consistently demonstrated a so-called *realistic* bias. No such realistic response bias was evident in the typical three-year-old tested in this study.

TABLE 19.1
Study 1: Active Unexpected Transfer
Task

Question Type	% Correct
Look	87.5
Think	70.0

Percent correct responses to belief questions. Age: 3 years, n = 40.

STUDY 2

Study 1 is modelled after most familiar measures of false belief understanding in which the Unexpected Transfer involves the *location* of an
object; Study 2 employed different measures, this time patterned after tasks
in which the false belief is brought about as a result of the *contents* of a box
being unexpectedly changed. This Unexpected Contents (or deceptive box)
procedure, developed by Hogrefe et al. (1986), typically proceeds by
presenting a subject with a familiar container, such as a Smarties box, which
in fact holds some unexpected contents, such as pencils. Like the standard
Unexpected Transfer task, consistently poor levels of performance have
been reported for three-year-olds, who mistakenly suppose that others will
somehow mysteriously know, as they know, about the box's unexpected
contents (e.g. Gopnik & Astington, 1988; Hogrefe et al., 1986; Perner et al.,
1987).

This second study employed procedures that again closely parallel
standard Unexpected Contents measures but, like Study 1, afforded subjects
the opportunity to create a false belief in another, this time by first hiding
the stereotypical contents of a box of cookies and then replacing these
original contents with some unexpected object which they chose from an
array of "joke" items such as rubber spiders and snakes. Test questions were
once again posed concerning both where E2 would *look* for the cookies and
what he or she would *think* was in the box.

Results

Of the 27 3-year-olds who participated in Study 2 (m = 3:6), 81%
responded correctly that E2 would *look* for the cookies in the box where he
or she had last seen them. This near-ceiling performance (shown in Table
19.2) closely corresponds to that found in Study 1 and is again significantly
different from what would be expected by chance (χ^2 [1, n = 27] = 10.70,
$P < 0.001$). Similarly, when asked what E2 would *think* was in the box, 81%

TABLE 19.2
Study 2: Active Unexpected Contents
Task

Question Type	% Correct
Look	81
Think	81

Percent correct responses to belief
questions. Age: 3 years, n = 27.

of the subjects again responded correctly that E2 would expect to find only cookies in the box, and so would be taken aback to discover the rubber spider or snake substituted in its place. Chi-square analysis again indicated that this level of performance is significantly different from what would be expected if subjects were responding at random (χ^2 [1, n = 27] = 10.70, $P < 0.001$).

Although the good performance of the young subjects who participated in our first two studies is being held out here as the result of having drawn them into the task of planfully framing their own goal-directed action, it still could be argued that these good results are due to other additional differenes that divide these action-based measurement strategies from the more standard measures. In the more standard Unexpected Transfer task, for example, subjects are not only relegated to a passive observer role, but the scene they observe is portrayed through the use of dolls or puppets. In contrast, the action-based Unexpected Transfer procedure employed in Study 1 made use of real people, including the subject, who played out the various roles. It could be argued, therefore, that it was this substitution of people for puppets, and not the fact that subjects were required to act planfully, that tipped the scales in the direction of better performance.

A second potentially important difference that distinguishes the interactive tasks introduced here from more standard Unexpected Transfer tasks is the use of deception. It is possible that simply introducing the theme of deception might, in and of itself, serve to facilitate young three-year-olds' ability to answer false belief questions correctly. To date, few studies have employed real people in deceptive tasks with young subjects (e.g. Russell et al., 1991; Sullivan & Winner, 1991), and so some test of this possibility also seemed warranted. Study 3 was designed to determine whether passively observing other real people behave deceptively is itself sufficient to facilitate performance on modified versions of standard false belief tasks.

STUDY 3

The procedure for Study 3 was a close replication of Study 1, with the key exception that rather than have the subject actively orchestrate the deception, the subject simply observed E1 perpetrating a deception on E2. In order to assess any potential facilitating effects that might be due to the use of real persons rather than puppet figures, Study 3 also included a standard version of the Unexpected Transfer task by way of comparison.

Of the 21 3-year-old (m = 3:6) subjects who participated in this study, only 1 responded incorrectly to the necessary control questions. All the remaining subjects first participated in an *observer-only* version that closely matched the procedures of Study 1, except for the fact that here the Unexpected Transfer was brought about through the deceptive efforts of an

TABLE 19.3
Study 3: Observer Unexpected
Contents Task

Question Type	% Correct
Deceptive Condition	
Look	40
Think	35
Standard Condition	
Look	40
Think	40

Percent correct responses to belief questions. Age: 3 years, $n = 20$.

experimenter and directed towards another real person (a second experimenter). This procedure was then followed by a standard version of the Perner et al. (1987) Unexpected Transfer task, in which puppet figures were used and deception played no motivating role. The control questions and the critical test questions were comparable across the two tasks. As was the case in Study 1, the test questions included both a "look" and a "think" version.

Results

Observer-deceptive Condition. As can be seen in Table 19.3, the proportion of subjects' correct responses to the crucial test questions after passively observing an act of deceptive hiding fell substantially short of the performance of their counterpart subjects in Study 1, who were actively engaged in bringing about the deception themselves.

In contrast to the results obtained in Study 1, only 40% of these 3-year-olds correctly answered the "look" question, a performance that was not significantly different from what would be expected by chance if subjects were responding randomly ($\chi^2 [1, n = 20] 0.8, P = 0.37, ns$). A similar level of performance was found for the "think" question which only 35% of the subjects answered correctly. Again this level did not differ from that expected by chance ($\chi^2 [1, n = 20] = 1.8, P = 0.18, ns$). When performance across the 2 test questions was combined, 60% of these 3-year-old subjects were found to have failed both test questions ($\chi^2 [1, n = 20] 13.07, P < 0.001$). Performance on the 2 crucial test questions for the standard control task was remarkably similar to performance on the observer-deception task. As shown in Table 19.3, only 40% of these 3-year-old subjects correctly answered the "look" question with an identical level of performance for the "think" question. Not surprisingly, a within-subject McNemar test of proportions demonstrated no significant difference between performance on the standard task as compared to that on the observer-deceptive task.

The results obtained in this study suggest that the procedural manipulation of simply using real people in a deceptive context is not sufficient to account for the good performance obtained by subjects in Study 1. It appears, then, that having subjects engage in goal-directed action does indeed make a difference to the performance of three-year-olds on false-belief test questions. What remains at issue, however, is exactly what it is about subjects' active involvement in these tasks that allows them to succeed at predicting the likely actions and beliefs of another accurately.

What we supposed as that the good results obtained in Study 1 were primarily due to our having provided subjects with the opportunity to generate a plan of action meant to manipulate another's beliefs, and that the physical act of actually carrying out this plan by placing the object in a new location did nothing to enhance their performance further.

Study 4 was designed to test these expectations by developing a testing situation in which the subjects were given responsibility for *deciding on a plan* to deceive another, but were not themselves responsible for physically carrying out that plan. In order to provide a direct basis for comparison of performance levels on this planning task, Study 4 also included an *active* and an *observer* condition. In this way, Study 4 served the additional purpose of allowing of a replication for the results obtained in Studies 1 and 3.

STUDY 4

Of the 64 3-year-olds ($m = 3:5$) who participated in this study, 4 were later excluded due to incorrect responses to the control questions. Subjects were randomly assigned to 1 of 3 conditions: an *active* condition; a *planning only* condition; and an *observer only* condition (all $m = 3:5$).

All three conditions closely follow the procedure used in Study 1 up to the point of E2's departure from the testing room. After E2 has left the room, subjects in the *active* condition, like their counterparts in Study 1, were invited to hide a treat by transferring it from its original location to a second location. In this way they participated in both planning and physically carrying out the plan to deceive E2. In contrast, subjects in the *observer-only* condition, like those in Study 3, simply watched E1 transfer the object with the purpose of hiding it from E2. Finally, in the *planning only* condition, subjects were first asked where they wished to hide the object and then watched while E1 went on to carry out the actual transfer of the object.

Results

Like their counterparts in Study 1, the 3-year-old children who participated in the *active* condition of Study 4 were near ceiling, with 80% successfully predicting where E2 would *look* for the object (see Fig. 19.1). Comparable performance was found for the *think* question, with 70% of the subjects responding correctly. Subjects were generally consistent in their responses and 70% were correct on both test questions, a performance that was significantly better than what would have been expected if subjects were responding randomly (χ^2 [1, n = 10)] = 21.6, P < 0.001).

In contrast to the good performance found for subjects who participated in the active condition, but in line with the results from Study 3, subjects in the *observer only* condition typically responded incorrectly to the false belief test question. As can be seen in Fig. 19.1, only 35% of subjects in this condition correctly answered the *look* question and a comparable 30% correctly answered the *think* question. As with other conditions, subjects tended to be consistent in their responses to the *look* and *think* questions, with 65% of subjects in the observer condition responding incorrectly to both, a performance that is significantly lower than would be expected by chance (χ^2 [1, n = 20] = 17.07, P < 0.001).

Whereas inclusion of the active and the observer conditions was meant to generalise the earlier findings from Studies 1 and 3, the addition of the *planning only* condition was introduced to help further specify the role that participating in such goal-directed planning might play in contributing to subjects' good performance. As can be seen in Fig. 19.1, subjects'

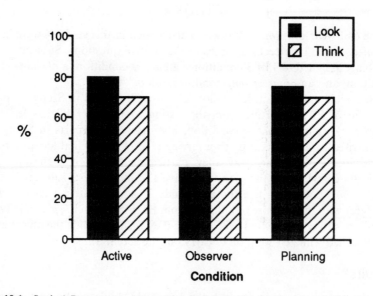

FIG. 19.1   Study 4: Percent correct responses to belief questions across three conditions (age = 3 years).

performance on the critical test questions in the planning condition was comparable to the performance of the three-year-olds who not only planned but actively implemented their plan to hide an object. A total of 75% of the subjects correctly answered the *look* question, with an identical proportion correct on the *think* question. Again subjects were mainly consistent in their responses, and 70% were correct on both the think and the look questions, a result that was significantly better than would be expected by chance (χ^2 [1, $n = 20$] = 21.6, $P < 0.001$).

To compare levels of performance across the three tasks, logistic regressions were carried out for performance on the *look* and the *think* questions with type of task as the independent variable. For the *look* question there was a significant effect for task (χ^2 [2, $n = 60$] = 9.55, $P < 0.01$). Subsequent paired contrasts indicated that there was no significant difference between levels of performance for the *active* and the *planning* conditions. In contrast, performance on the *observer* task was significantly different from performance on both the *active* and the *planning* tasks (χ^2 [1, $n = 40$] = 7.55, $P < 0.01$ for *active*; χ^2 [1, $n = 40$] = 6.06, $P < 0.01$ for *planning*).

Similarly, for the *think* question, a logistic regression indicated a significant effect for task (χ^2 [2, $n = 60$] = 9.16, $P < 0.01$). Once again, paired contrasts demonstrated no significant difference when the *active* and *planning* conditions were compared, whereas the *observer* condition was shown to be significantly different from both the *active* and *planning* conditions (χ^2 [1, $n = 40$] = 6.03, $P < 0.01$ for *active*; χ^2 [1, $n = 40$] = 7.50, $P < 0.01$ for *planning*).

SUMMARY AND DISCUSSION

Taken altogether, what these four studies go some important distance toward demonstrating is that, when allowed to go about the ordinary planful business of orchestrating their own lives, even young three-year-olds give every evidence of understanding that others often hold to and act upon beliefs that are manifestly false. Although such a demonstration does, of course, fly directly into the face of anyone still committed to the increasingly suspect view that children of less than four are constitutionally incapable of envisioning such false belief, it is, just as obviously, completely consonant with other lines of recent evidence of the sort summarised earlier and reported elsewhere in this volume. What we ourselves have made of all this, and hope to have persuaded you of as well, is that it is simply wrong and unjustifiably withholding to go on supposing that persons younger than four are altogether ignorant of the possibility of false belief. That is easy for us to say, however, because we have not just spent the better part of the last decade publicly militating for just the opposite conclusion. What about those who have attempted to wear this shoe on the other foot? That is, what, you may well ask, is to be made of these new findings by those whose reputational cap already rests firmly upon the claim that children younger than four all suffer some cognitive deficit that categorically disallows just those abilities so clearly demonstrated here? And, perhaps more interestingly, what different sorts of conclusions might suggest themselves to anyone not in the grip of such a representational deficit theory? What remains to be done as a final act for this chapter is to get the corpses of these last two questions off the stage.

It is still a bit early, perhaps, to get an altogether reliable reading of the common response of your average theory-theorist to our own and others' demonstrations of three-year-olds' competent understanding of false beliefs. This seems especially the case in view of the fact that, so far, the modal response to these embarrassing findings appears to be no response at all. That is, although one can scarcely turn around without bumping into yet another recent summary of the theory-of-mind literature, the most common picture still being painted is that of an unbroken line of evidence seamlessly supporting the idea that children younger than four are wholly ignorant of the possibility of false belief (see Russell, 1992, for an interesting exception to this trend).

Beyond these early stonewalling efforts, what perhaps constitutes the most serious response to our own and related forms of evidence have been those efforts to somehow marginalise such findings by urging that whenever three-year-olds succeed in demonstrating any understanding of the possibility of false belief it is only because they somehow have been propped up artificially by some unnatural form of social scaffolding. Although deciding what is and what is not "natural" very likely goes beyond the scope of this chapter, a compelling case can perhaps still be made to the effect that it is the so-called "standard" Unexpected Transfer and Unexpected Contents measures in common use that have gotten things the wrong way around. That is, it is arguably when children are allowed to plan and act in ordinary interpersonal situations that we are offered the best window onto their emerging understanding of mental life, and not when they are measured by their disinterested commentaries upon the arbitrary comings and goings of various puppet characters.

Finally, there are those who, perhaps seeing the tide of evidence running against them, have begun to suggest that the question of whether three- as well as four-year-olds are capable of grasping the possibility of false belief may not be the right sort of question to be asking. Although such arguments would seem less ingenuous coming from those whose own careers were not built upon having earlier championed the idea that four- and five-year-olds already possess abilities previously thought reserved for children of six or seven, there nevertheless would appear to be some real merit to such claims.

This is especially the case, we propose, for programs of research such as our own, in which the aim has never been the location of some unique watershed in the course of coming to a mature understanding of mental life. Instead, we feel that evidence of the sort that we have presented here not only serves to relocate children's first ideas about belief entitlement much closer to the very beginnings of their representational competence, but also clears out space for the addition of a whole new train of as yet unspecified intermediate theories of mind.

ACKNOWLEDGEMENTS

This research was supported by a research grant held by M. Chandler from the Natural Sciences and Engineering Research Council and by a doctoral fellowship held by S. Hala from the Social Sciences and Humanities Research Council of Canada. The research presented in this chapter forms part of the dissertation work of S. Hala.

REFERENCES

Avis, J., & Harris, P. (1991). Belief-desire reasoning among Baka children: Evidence for a universal conception of mind. *Child Development, 62,* 460–467.

Bruner, J. (1990). *Acts of meaning.* Cambridge, Mass.: Harvard University Press.

Chandler, M.J. (1988). Doubt and developing theories of mind. In J.W. Astington, P.L. Harris, & D.R. Olson (Eds.), *Developing theories of mind* (pp. 387–413). New York: Cambridge University Press.

Chandler, M.J., & Boyes, M. (1982). Social cognitive development. In B. Wolman (Ed.), *Handbook of developmental psychology* (pp. 387–402). Englewood Cliffs, NJ: Prentice-Hall.

Chandler, M.J., Fritz, A.S., & Hala, S. (1989). Small scale deceit: Deception as a marker of 2-, 3- and 4-year-old's theories of mind. *Child Development, 60,* 1263–1277.

Donaldson, M. (1978). *Children's minds.* London: Croom Helm Ltd.

Dunn, J. (1988). *The beginnings of social understanding.* Cambridge, Mass.: Harvard University Press.

Dunn, J. (1991). Understanding others: Evidence from naturalistic studies of children. In A. Whiten (Ed.), *Natural theories of mind: Evolution, development and simulation of everyday mindreading* (pp. 51–61). Oxford: Basil Blackwell.

Flavell, J.H. (1988). The development of children's knowledge about the mind: From cognitive connections to mental representations. In J.W. Astington, P.L. Harris, & D.R. Olson (Eds.), *Developing theories of mind* (pp. 244–267). New York: Cambridge University Press.

Freeman, N.H., Lewis, C., & Doherty, M.J. (1991). Preschoolers' grasp of a desire for knowledge in false-belief prediction: Practical intelligence and verbal report. *British Journal of Developmental Psychology, 9,* 139–157.

Fritz, A.S. (1991, April). *Is there a reality bias in young children's emergent theories of mind?* Paper presented at the Biennial Meeting of the Society for Research in Child Development, Seattle.

Gopnik, A., & Astington, J.W. (1988). Children's understanding of representational change and its relation to the understanding of false belief and the appearance-reality distinction. *Child Development, 59,* 26–37.

Hala, S. (1991, April). *The role of personal involvement in facilitating false belief understanding.* Paper presented at the Biennial Meeting of the Society for Research in Child Development, Seattle.

Hala, S., Chandler, M., & Fritz, A. (1991). Fledgling theories of mind: Deception as a marker of 3-year-old's understanding of false belief. *Child Development, 62,* 83–97.

Hogrefe, G.J., Wimmer, H., & Perner, J. (1986). Ignorance versus false belief: A developmental lag in attribution of epistemic states. *Child Development, 57,* 567–582.

Lalonde, C., Chandler, M., & Moses, L. (1992, May). *Early steps toward an interpretive theory of mind.* Paper presented at the Annual Meeting of the Jean Piaget Society, Montreal, Quebec.

Lewis, C. (1993, March). *Episodes, events and narratives in the child's understanding of mind.* Paper presented at the Biennial Meeting of the Society for Research in Child Development, New Orleans.

Lewis, C., & Osborne, A. (1990). Three-year-olds' problems with false belief: Conceptual deficit or linguistic artifact? *Child Development, 61,* 1514–1519.

Mitchell, P., & Lacohee, H. (1991). Children's early understanding of false belief. *Cognition, 39,* 107–127.

Moses, L.J., & Chandler, M.J. (1992). Traveler's guide to children's theories of mind. *Psychological Inquiry, 3,* 286–301.

Moses, L.J. (1991). Young children's understanding of belief constraints on intentions. *Cognitive Development, 8,* 1–25.

Perner, J. (1991). *Understanding the representational mind.* Cambridge, Mass.: MIT Press.

Perner, J., & Davies, G. (1991). Understanding the mind as an active information processor: Do young children have a "copy theory of mind"? *Cognition, 39,* 51–69.

Perner, J., Leekam, S.R., & Wimmer, H. (1987). Three-year-olds' difficulty with false belief: The case for conceptual deficit. *British Journal of Developmental Psychology, 5,* 125–137.

Peskin, J. (1992). Ruse and representation: On children's ability to conceal information. *Developmental Psychology, 28,* 84–89.

Pillow, B. (1991). Children's understanding of biased social cognition. *Developmental Psychology, 27,* 539–551.

Reddy, V. (1990). Playing with others' expectations: Teasing and mucking about in the first year. In A. Whiten (Ed.), *Natural theories of mind: Evolution, development and simulation of everyday mindreading* (pp. 143–158). Oxford: Basil Blackwell.

Robinson, E., Mitchell, P., & Nye, R. (1992, September). *Children's understanding of indirect sources of knowledge.* Paper presented at the Annual Meeting of the British Psychological Society, Edinburgh.

Ruffman, T., Olson, D., & Astington, J. (1991). Children's understanding of visual ambiguity. *British Journal of Developmental Psychology, 9,* 89–102.

Russell, J. (1992). The theory-theory: So good they named it twice? *Cognitive Development, 7,* 485–519.

Russell, J., Mauthner, N., Sharpe, S., & Tidswell, T. (1991). The "windows task" as a measure of strategic deception in preschoolers and autistic subjects. *British Journal of Developmental Psychology, 9,* 331–349.

Searle, J.R. (1983). *Intentionality: An essay in the philosophy of mind.* Cambridge: Cambridge University Press.

Sheffield, G., Sosa, B.B., & Hudson, J.A. (1993, March). *Narrative complexity and 2- and 3-year-olds' comprehension of false beliefs.* Paper presented at the Biennial Meeting of the Society for Research in Child Development, New Orleans.

Siegal, M., & Beattie, K. (1990). Where to look first for children's knowledge of false beliefs. *Cognition, 38,* 1–12.

Sodian, B. (1991). The development of deception in young children. *British Journal of Developmental Psychology, 9,* 173–188.

Sodian, B., Taylor, C., Harris, P., & Perner, J. (1991). Early deception and the child's theory of mind: False trials and genuine markers. *Child Development, 62,* 468–483.

Stevenson, E., & Mitchell, P. (1992, September). *The suggestibility of false belief*. Paper presented at the Annual Meeting of the British Psychological Society, Edinburgh.

Sullivan, J., & Winner, E. (1991). When 3-year-olds understand ignorance, false belief and representational change. *British Journal of Developmental Psychology*, 9, 159–171.

Wellman, H.M. (1990). *The child's theory of mind*. Cambridge, Mass.: Bradford Books.

Wimmer, H., & Perner, J. (1983). Beliefs about beliefs: Representation and constraining of wrong beliefs in young children's understanding of deception. *Cognition*, 13, 103–128.

Zaitchik, D. (1991). Is only seeing really believing?: Sources of the true belief in the false belief task. *Cognitive Development*, 6, 91–103.

20 Children's Theory of Mind and the Conversational Territory of Cognitive Development

Michael Siegal and Candida C. Peterson
University of Queensland, Brisbane, Australia

INTRODUCTION

In research on cognitive development, experimenters present children with tasks that adults are almost always likely to solve. By comparison, children frequently answer incorrectly, and the younger the children the more likely are their responses to be different from those given by adults.

In most accounts, it has been acknowledged that aspects of experimental situations are pertinent to age differences in performance. However, as Rogoff (1982, p. 125) has pointed out, context effects: "have generally been considered secondary to the examination of characteristics of the person." In this respect, models of cognitive development—particularly those that concern the development of a theory of mind—have often focused on children's abilities to process and retain information. Incorrect responses are commonly attributed to conceptual limitations or deficits (e.g. Flavell, Green, & Flavell, 1986; Perner, 1991; Perner, Leekam, & Wimmer, 1987).

Yet usually in experiments, adults are observers and children are actors. It is a well-documented finding, at least from research conducted in English-speaking countries, that the causal attributions of actors and observers frequently diverge (Fleming & Darley, 1989; Jones & Nisbett, 1972. Observers may attribute the behaviour of actors to their personal dispositions and may not fully consider the influence of the constraints of situations. Actors are more likely to attribute their own behaviour to the situation and they give greater recognition to situational effects that prevent

427

the display of their competence. These actor-observer differences can extend to experimental settings. Although well-meaning adult observers of children's behaviour may believe a conceptual limitation or deficit has been uncovered, children can answer incorrectly not because of some conceptual difficulty but because they do not share the purpose and context of an experimenter's questions. For this reason, their behaviour may be attributed instead to the inscrutable characteristics of the conversational environment provided by the experimenter. Therefore to formulate a comprehensive model of cognitive development requires investigations of children's abilities as conversationalists.

Our aim in this chapter is not merely to offer yet another reminder of the importance of conversational factors; it is to highlight the central attention that these factors deserve with respect to approaches that have viewed development primarily in terms of conceptual limitations and deficits. In focusing on theory of mind research that has so often been interpreted recently to reflect limitations in preschool children, we challenge the interpretation that three-year-olds' performance often reflects a conceptual deficit. As will be shown, recent research findings that have made strong claims about conceptual deficits can be reinterpreted in terms of the pragmatic use of language. Previous evidence that has been used to support the existence of a conceptual deficit is attributed to a clash of conversational worlds between children and adults.

Scientific and Pragmatic Concerns in a Clash Between the Conversational Worlds of Adults and Children

As Hilton (1990) has shown, causal explanations require forms of conversations between persons and therefore are subject to rules of conversation. To give an explanation in science requires answers that are often irrelevant to the pragmatic, localised concerns of the lay person (Hart & Honore, 1985). For example, in conservation experiments, a major concern of scientists is to determine how certain children are of their initial answer. After having been told that another child had said the opposite of this answer, the children are then often given the opportunity to change their minds. The question for research on cognitive development is, "Now does that row have more than that row?" or "Now do you think that this glass has more water than the other?" (Answer: "If nothing is added or taken away following a transformation, the quantities remain the same as before.") However, in this context, children may not identify the scientific relevance of the experimenter's inquiry. As lay persons, they may believe that they are expected to use information about another child because the experimenter had provided it and would not have done so if it were irrelevant. The implicit question for children in importing relevance from their own experience may be: "Is the child who said that smart or dumb and is that supposed to change my answer (even though I was sure the first time)?"[1] When children do not share the scientific nature of the experimenter's question, they may fail to block the inference that repeated questioning should be followed by answer switching. They may choose a different response to satisfy what they perceive are the situational constraints within the conversational environment (Poole & White, 1991; Rose & Blank, 1974; Siegal, 1991a; 1991b; Siegal, Waters, & Dinwiddy, 1988).

The recognition that adult forms of communication in experimental settings can obscure an authentic understanding is hardly new (Bruner, 1986; Donaldson, 1978; 1982; Flavell & Wohlwill, 1969; Gelman, Meck, & Merkin, 1986; Hughes & Grieve, 1983; Light, Buckingham, & Robins, 1979; McGarrigle & Donaldson, 1974; McGarrigle, Grieve, & Hughes, 1978; Rommetveit, 1979; Siegel, 1978; Siegel, 1974). In one of the most important statements from this standpoint, Donaldson (1978, p. 69) concluded: "When a child interprets what we say to him his interpretation is influenced by at least three things (and the ways in which these interact with each other)—his knowledge of the language, his assessment of what we intend (as indicated by our non-linguistic behaviour), and the manner in which he would represent the physical situation to himself if he were not there at all." Moreover, Vygotsky (1962) assigned a central role to shared word meanings in his views on thought and language which, as Wertsch (1991) has shown, has been amplified to an individual's "voice" or world-view perspectives in interpreting utterances. Yet despite the longstanding recognition that has been accorded to conversational influences on children's answers to questions, this perspective has not gained widespread consideration in research on cognitive development, possibly owing to the absence of a consensus on a framework for identifying what aspects of conversation can account for answers across a range of tasks. This may also be due to a current disenchantment with grand developmental theories that have been eschewed in favour of smaller-scale minitheories whose scope is limited to specific settings (Parke, 1989).

All the same, there is little doubt that shared relevance and informativeness is a fundamental aspect of coherent, causal explanations that are governed by rules of conversation. According to Grice (1975, p. 45), a "Cooperative Principle" underlies effective communication: "Make your conversational contribution such as is required, at the stage at which it occurs, by the accepted purpose or direction of the talk exchange in which

---

[1] We are grateful to Anne-Nelly Perret-Clermont for this insight.

you are engaged." To produce conversation that is in accordance with this principle, Grice lists four rules or conventions that may be described, in short, as the Maxims of *Quantity:* "Say no more or no less than is required," *Quality:* "Try to say the truth and avoid falsehood," *Relevance* (or *Relation*): "Be informative," and *Manner:* "Avoid obscurity and ambiguity." These are promissory notes or "conversational rules of thumb" that precede a general theory of collective action (Clark, 1987). Nevertheless, the general Gricean framework provides important insight into the nature of communication processes (Brown & Levinson, 1987; Hilton, 1990; Levinson, 1989).

In conversations between adults, it is mutually understood that the rules may sometimes be flouted to create what Grice has termed "conversational implicatures." Such nonconventional forms of language are used, for example, where the rules contradict (e.g. in cases where to be relevant and informative would violate the quantity rule to speak no more than is required) or where irony is intended through an uninformative statement of the obvious or where there is a politely motivated desire to ensure, through repeated questioning, that the listener understands. However, even in adult conversations, the listener is liable to be misled if a rule is broken quietly.

To probe the depth and certainty of children's understanding, experimenters may set aside conversational rules and pose questions where the answer is obvious or repeated when an answer has already been given. But unlike older children and adults, young children have just acquired language skills that permit them to participate in conversation. They have been engaged in verbal interaction with caregivers who are attentive to the need to adjust their speech to the characteristics of a young child unfamiliar with the complexities of adult conversation. Speakers to children under the age of three years generally shorten their utterances and do not say more or less than is necessary to sustain conversation; they are clear, relevant and informative in referring to objects and events in the here and now, and they are concerned to correct truth value in the child's speech rather than errors of syntax (Brown & Hanlon, 1970; De Villiers, 1978, pp. 192–198). In short, children's early conversational habits are consistent with the speech input of caregivers who, for the most part, have not set aside conversational rules.

Thus young children may not appreciate an experimenter's purpose if his or her questions emanate from within an adult conversational world that contains many unspoken implications. Just because they demonstrate substantial ability in adjusting their speech to the characteristics of the listener (Gelman & Shatz, 1977) does not mean that they can be addressed as if they had the conversational experience of adults. In the main, they may not share an experimenter's assumption that the general purpose underlying departures from these rules is the scientific one of establishing their understanding of concepts. Consequently, in response to the implications arising from forms of well-meaning questioning that are understood by adults who are experienced in conversation, young children may misinterpret the experimenter's purpose. They may answer incorrectly not because they do not know the answer but because the conversational worlds of adults and children clash. In some cases, communication may be jeopardised by children's perception that an experimenter is not even observing the basic principle that speakers cooperate with the listener.

APPRAISING THE QUANTITY AND QUALITY OF QUESTIONS AND THE PHYSICAL SETTING OF THE EXPERIMENT

From a conversational standpoint, the characteristics of the situation are pivotal in interpreting their lack of success on cognitive tasks. In inadvertently setting aside the quantity rule, an experimenter may say less or more than is necessary to enable children to share the purpose underlying the test questions. In contravening the quality rule, well-meaning experimenters may present tasks that children approach without critically evaluating the sincerity underlying the questioning. In either case, the relevance of the task may not be shared by children, who are liable not to share the conversational implications of questions and offer uncritical or pretend responses instead of correct ones that reflect their knowledge. Aside from shortcomings in the quantity and quality of conversation, there is another explanation for children's lack of success that goes beyond Gricean examples of ambiguity and obscurity in speech ("manner"). It is that children and experimenters differ in the manner in which they represent the physical territory to which questions refer.

To give due regard to the effects of situational characteristics requires consideration of how young children interpret and answer questions. We contend that, once children are induced to share the purpose and territory of questions that do not set aside conversational rules, they are more likely to respond in a manner that reflects their theory of mind and to disclose what they know about mental states. From this perspective, we address six questions of our own: (1) Can children predict the consequences of others' false beliefs? (2) Can children understand the nature of their own false beliefs? (3) To what extent are inconsistently correct answers evidence for a conceptual deficit? (4) To what extent are consistently incorrect answers evidence for a conceptual deficit? (5) Are children unable or unwilling to use deceptive tactics? (6) How extensive are children's difficulties in representation?

Can Children Predict the Consequences of Others' False Beliefs?

A common proposal is that young children's answers on tasks that require them to predict the consequences of the false beliefs of others amount to a deficit or limitation in their theory of mind when beliefs clash with desires. For example, in a notable series of studies, Wellman and Bartsch (1988) have found that three-year-olds and young four-year-olds do poorly on stories that require an understanding of "explicit false beliefs." In these tasks, a story character's desire to find an object is explicitly mentioned, the object is said to be really in one location, and the character is said to believe that the object is in another (wrong) location (e.g. "Jane wants to find her kitten. Jane's kitten is really in the playroom. Jane thinks the kitten is in the kitchen. Where will Jane look for her kitten?" Correct answer: kitchen; three-year-olds' common answer: playroom). In a fashion that is reminiscent of Piaget's (1970) emphasis on egocentrism, Wellman and Bartsch have proposed that three-year-olds do not fully appreciate that desires can be unfulfilled owing to the location of identities in the external world. Though they can often determine how behaviour follows from beliefs, they weight desires over beliefs when these are in conflict in false belief tasks. In support of this explanation, Wellman and Woolley (1990) report that two-year-olds and young three-year-olds succeed on tasks that involve predicting behaviour on the basis of desire despite failing false belief tasks.

However, for children to succeed on explicit false belief tasks, they must understand that the scientific purpose is to test whether they can detect how others' thoughts may be initially mistaken. It is assumed that children follow the implications of the language used by the experimenter and infer that the question, "Where will a person (with the false belief) look for the object?" means "Where will the person look first?" If this assumption is unwarranted, children who can predict the consequences of holding false beliefs may not reveal their knowledge because they do not share the experimenter's purpose in questioning rather than because they weight desires over beliefs. Instead the purpose may appear to be something more familiar and straightforward: to test whether children can predict the behaviour of others in achieving a goal. Therefore, "Where will Jane look for the cat?" may simply be interpreted as "Where will Jane have to look (or go to look) for the cat in order to find it?" rather than "Where will Jane look for the cat first?", which is the implication intended by the questioner who has assumed that the child shares the purpose of the task.

In experiments designed to examine this issue (Siegal & Beattie, 1991), even three-year-olds often responded correctly when asked to predict the initial behaviour of a story character with a false belief. Although these studies were restricted to one type of situation (i.e. the conversational implications of *look* questions) and did not extend to research bearing on children's understanding of the consequences of other aspects of the mental world such as pretending, remembering, and feeling, false belief tasks provide an illustration of how conversational rules may be inadvertently contravened in conversations with children. In this case, the experimenter is speaking less than is required—a violation of the quantity rule that necessitates that children make an inference that is critical to their success. Once the question is amply enriched to dispense with the inference, children can predict the consequences of holding false beliefs. It has been maintained (Siegal & Beattie, 1991; Siegal & Sanderson, 1989; see also Lewis & Osborne, 1990) that a similar analysis can apply to other related research (e.g. Harris et al., 1989; Perner et al., 1987; Perner & Ogden, 1988).

In other theory of mind research, efforts have been made to avoid the need for children to make conversational inferences and consider the forms of questions addressed to children. But in these cases, the conversational territory to which questions refer remains problematic. The materials may be so attractive or the story so wordy that children may ignore the temporal aspects of the situation or even neglect what the experimenter is saying to focus on what is physically present.

For instance, Robinson and Mitchell (1992) sought to meet the point that false belief tasks are vague as to time. Using playpeople and scenery, they gave three-year-olds from mainly working-class backgrounds a task that required them to indicate where a story character would look first:

> This is a story about a boy called Peter, and this is his dad. Peter's playing in his go-kart. Now it's time to go to school, so Peter puts his go-kart away behind the settee. Now Dad comes in, and he's going to check the go-kart over to make sure it's safe. He takes the go-kart and checks that it's all right, and then puts Peter's go-kart back here (in the other room). So it's in a different place now. Does Peter know his go-kart has moved? No, he doesn't. Now Peter comes home from school and he wants to play with his go-kart.
>
> Where does he go to look for his go-kart first of all, here or here? (order of pointing counterbalanced)

This situation is considerably longer than the short two-sentence story descriptions given to the middle-class children in the Wellman and Bartsch and Siegal and Beattie studies (e.g. "Sam thinks his puppy is in the bathroom. Sam's puppy is really in the kitchen. Where will Sam look (first) for his puppy?"). Had Robinson and Mitchell's subjects simply reproduced the last location of the go-kart without following other details in the story, they would have been scored as lacking an understanding of false beliefs in answering the test question. Moreover, unlike in the Siegal and Beattie experiments, the children were not asked to predict behaviours based on the true beliefs of story characters and thus may not have identified occasions in the story when Peter's beliefs would have led to finding the go-kart.

Can Children Understand the Nature of their Own False Beliefs?

Despite these issues, according to Gopnik and Slaughter (1991), children are so preoccupied with their own current mental states that, not only do they lack an understanding of others' beliefs, but they have little insight into their own past beliefs. In a belief task devised by Gopnik and Slaughter, three-year-olds were shown a closed crayon box. They initially reported to the experimenter that the box contained crayons. The experimenter then demonstrated that birthday candles were inside. The children scored no better than chance on the experimenter's questions, "When I first asked you, before I opened up the box, what did you think was in the box then? Did you think there were candles inside or crayons inside?" But as one of us has noted elsewhere (Siegal, 1993), having just viewed the candles inside the box, children are likely to use this single piece of physical information (candles in the box) to answer rather complex "double-barrelled" questions about beliefs that require the simultaneous consideration of two possible choices. In reconciling the relevance of the context to the question, they may regard the introduction of the information as pivotal. After all, they might reason, why would an adult go to the trouble to create and disclose the information unless the implication was to use it in answering the test questions? In doing so, children would simply reinterpret the questions about beliefs as the straightforward question, "What do you think is inside the box?" The three-year-olds would likely have answered more correctly had they received the single, short question, "What did you first think was in the box?" with care taken to ensure that they regarded each alternative as equally relevant.

Gopnik and Slaughter contrast responses on their belief task to those on a pretend task where three-year-olds easily answered questions about pretending that a stick was first a spoon and then a magic wand, "When I first asked you, before we moved over here, what did you pretend the stick was then? Did you pretend it was a spoon or a wand?" However, from an early age, children recognise that pretending is detached from physical reality, unlike thinking, which can be either detached or nondetached and continuous. They could not incorrectly reinterpret the questions about pretending to mean "What do you pretend the stick is?" because of their detachment from the two induced states and because the experimenter had not highlighted physical information that could lead one of the pretend states to be construed as more relevant to the answer.

Similarly, in a series of studies carried out by Wimmer and Hartl (1991), most three-year-olds who saw *one* unexpected physical object in a deceptive box task gave incorrect responses to the test question: "Listen, when in the beginning he took the box out of my bag and showed it to you, what did you think was in here?" However, when in a "change of state" task, the children were shown *two* pieces of physical information, in which the expected contents (matches) were replaced by unexpected ones (sweets), most children answered the test question correctly, possibly because either alternative could now be regarded as relevant.

Because false beliefs arise from a sequence of events, test questions often refer to the past or future. Yet young children do not easily recognise the purpose underlying questioning about false beliefs and their habit is to assume from previous conversational experience that questions refer to the present. Thus they may still have a strong inclination to reinterpret test questions in this fashion unless special efforts are taken to align their initial interpretation with that intended by the experimenter through simple, clear messages.

For example, Pratt and Bryant (1990) have shown that double-barrelled questions (e.g. Do you know what is in the box or do you not know what is in the box?") used in tasks such as those devised by Gopnik and Slaughter are hard for children to comprehend and are prone to interruptions and responses before the experimenter poses the second alternative. Children may assume that, because an experimenter has gone to the trouble of mentioning an alternative, it must be relevant and therefore worthy of choice. Yet even fairly advanced or cumbersome questioning forms may reveal an understanding of false beliefs if these are accompanied by a physical setting that is attractive and relevant. Mitchell and Lacohée (1991) gave three-year-olds practice in "posting" a pictorial representation of their predictions of the contents of deceptive boxes. When the posting was relevant to the representation of their initial belief, most children responded to the test question: "When you posted your picture in the postbox, what did you think was in here (the deceptive box)?" by distinguishing false beliefs from reality. By contrast, when the posting procedure was irrelevant to their initial representation and thus irrelevant to the test question, most did not succeed. Mitchell and Lacohee interpret this result as demonstrating that children's understanding of beliefs is dependant on physical representations and that such understanding dissipates when beliefs are not accompanied by a physical counterpart. However, the relevant posting procedure may have also conveyed to the children the importance of using their initial representation to answer the test question, thus clarifying the relation of the temporal aspect of the question to their previous belief and enabling the children to answer correctly. If this is the case, their previous understanding of beliefs may endure even in the absence of a relevant physical representation. Yet it may not be disclosed in response to forms of questioning that appear to focus on the contents of a deceptive box.

As Pratt and Bryant point out, children *act* as if they understand their own beliefs as well as those of others. This observation is consistent with reports by Bretherton and Beeghly (1982) that two-year-olds often talk about internal states in conversation with their mothers and by Woolley and Wellman (1990) that three-year-olds spontaneously distinguish between the real and nonreal properties of objects and actions. Of course such observations do not demonstrate that young children have an adult-like ability to understand the nature of beliefs and to distinguish between reality and appearance. Nevertheless, there is a striking discrepancy between these findings and the results of many theory of mind studies, which require children to understand the purpose and implications of questions if they are to succeed. This discrepancy is shown clearly in a study by Sullivan and Winner (1991) in which children's spontaneous comments contrasted with their answers to experimental test questions. For example, when asked to substitute unexpected contents such as string in a box of crayons or pencils in an "M & Ms" candy bag, children aged three to three-and-a-half years frequently made comments such as "No one will know we put pencils in here!" But these same children often responded incorrectly to a series of probes: "What did you think was in the bag before we looked at it, pencils or M & Ms? (Representational change question). When (name of a playmate who has not witnessed the change of contents) sees this bag all closed up will he know what's really in the bag, yes or no? (Ignorance question.) What will (name) think is in the bag, M & Ms or pencils?" On such "deceptive box" tasks, the oblique and wordy reference to the new contents might have confused the children. For instance, they could have jumped from the mention of "really" in the ignorance question to the thought that: "There really are pencils in the bag and that the playmate will understand this information once it is shared," and interpreted the ignorance and false belief questions to mean: "What will the playmate see when he looks inside?"

Is Inconsistency in Children's Correct Responses Evidence for a Conceptual Deficit?

Although an examination of the evidence suggests that children have an understanding of the nature of their own and others' beliefs, an inconsistent pattern of responses has often been seen as support for a conceptual deficit in children's theory of mind. In one study, Moses and Flavell (1990) presented children with movies that portrayed false belief scenarios. For example, three-year-olds were shown a child named Mary who hurt her finger, saw a band-aid box on the table, and found a toy car inside instead of band-aids. In response to the false belief question: "What did Mary think was gonna be in the box before she opened it?' the children often chose a car. In response to a subsequent question on true beliefs, "What does Mary think is in the box now?" they often unexpectedly said band-aids. The account favoured by Moses and Flavell is that many of the chihldren knew little about beliefs and responded with whatever seemed most salient at the time the questions were asked. Another is that children's understanding of beliefs was not disclosed under conditions involving repeated questioning that is liable to set aside the quantity rule. The children first heard a false belief question that they may have interpreted as: "What does Mary think is in the box when she opens it?" This was followed by a question (on true beliefs) that could have been regarded as highly similar, prompting children to switch their answers.

The latter alternative gains support from an examination of the basis for children's poor performance on the "Sally-Anne" task devised by Baron-Cohen, Leslie, and Frith (1985). In brief, the procedure consists of two trials, each involving a doll named "Sally" who has a basket and a doll "Anne" who has a box. In the first trial, Sally hides a marble in her basket and leaves the scene. While she is gone, Anne shifts the marble to her box. Sally returns and the child is asked: "Where will Sally look for her marble?" followed by two control questions: "Where is the marble really?" and "Where was the marble in the beginning?" The purpose of the first control question is to ensure the child has attended to the marble's true location, and the second checks for memory of the original hiding place. For children who answer both control questions correctly, the test of an understanding of false beliefs is to indicate that Sally will search the basket for the marble. However, as there are only two possible places where the marble could be, a child who merely points randomly would be correct at a chance level of 50%. To lessen the possibility that children could be correct by chance alone, Baron-Cohen et al. (1985) included a second trial identical to the first except that Anne now hides the marble in the experimenter's pocket. Here the odds of making a correct false belief inference by chance are only 33%. It has been the approach of Baron-Cohen et al. (1985) and others who have followed their procedure to require consistent success on both trials as evidence of a "theory of mind."

However, the second trial may have inadvertently produced a side effect. Some children may not share the experimenter's purpose for questioning on a second trial that is liable to set aside the quantity rule to say no more than is necessary for effective communication. They may import their own relevance to the situation. They may believe that Sally on Trial 2 will know better than to search the basket for her marble because Anne, as shown by her mischievous behaviour on Trial 1, will surely have snatched it away from there. If children do answer on the basis of this assumption, they will be scored as failing to understand that other people may entertain false beliefs according to Baron-Cohen et al.'s criteria for success. Thus failure on the "Sally-Anne" task may reflect children's inexperience with the conversational environment rather than a deficient understanding of false beliefs.

To test this hypothesis, we carried out an experiment in which the participants were 121 children who attended kindergartens and preschools located in middle-class areas of Brisbane, Australia. These were divided into 3 age groups consisting of 41 3-year-olds (mean = 3:5; range, 3:2 to 3:11), 58 4-year-olds (mean = 4:6; range 4:0 to 4:11), and 22 5-year-olds (mean = 5:2; range, 5:0 to 5:5).

Each child was tested individually by a female experimenter in a procedure identical to Baron-Cohen et al.'s (1985) except for two minor modifications designed to minimise demands upon memory and syntactic skills. First, we replaced the doll "Anne" by a teddy bear to eliminate the need for memorisation of the names of two dolls. Second, as in the Siegal and Beattie (1991) study, Baron-Cohen's original belief question: "Where will Sally look for her marble?" was replaced by: "Where will Sally look first for her marble?" This was done in order to prevent the children from interpreting the question in a manner different than that intended by the experimenter, such as: "Where will Sally have to look for her marble to find it?"

In our experiment, the children were given the two trials in two different orders. Each order was presented to approximately half of the subjects at each age level. Order 1 was identical to the procedure that had been used by Baron-Cohen et al. and was given to 53 children. Order 2 was given to the remaining 68 children. In this format, the order of the two trials was reversed by having the bear, who had been introduced to the children following Baron-Cohen et al.'s procedure as the owner of the box, hide the marble in the experimenter's pocket on Trial 1. Thus there were three possible hiding places on both trials of Order 2 in contrast to Order 1, which had only two hiding places on Trial 1 and three on Trial 2. To test Eisenmajor and Prior's (1991) suggestion that the ease of the task may be influenced by the within-trial order of the belief and control questions, half the children received the control questions ahead of the belief question on either Trial 1 or Trial 2 and the other in the order used by Baron-Cohen et al.

Table 20.1 shows the numbers of children in each age group who made correct false belief inferences on the 2 trials in responding that Sally would search first in her basket. A one-way analysis of variance on the numbers of correct answers over the 2 trials indicated that there was a significant difference among the age groups, $F (2, 118) = 4.50$, $P < 0.013$. Newman-Keuls comparisons at the $P < 0.05$ level indicated that both the 4- and 5-year-old groups outperformed the 3-year-olds. However, on Trial 1, even most of the 3-year-olds (26 out of 41, or 63%) were correct. As predicted, compared to the numbers of children who erred on Trial 1, the numbers who erred on Trial 2 were significantly larger than would be expected by chance, $\chi^2 (1) = 7.35$, $P < 0.01$. Of the 23 children who made an error on only 1 of the 2 trials, 18 did so on Trial 2 compared to only 5 on Trial 1.

TABLE 20.1
Performance on the Two Trials of the Modified Baron-Cohen et al. False Belief Task

Age Group	Pattern of Answers on the Two Trials				
	Both Right	Both Wrong	Trial 1 Only Wrong	Trial 2 Only Wrong	Total
3-year-olds	19	12	3	7	41
4-year-olds	40	6	2	10	58
5-year-olds	18	3	0	1	22

We conducted several further analyses on the data. A comparison of performance on the two trial orders revealed no significant order effects in the numbers of children correct or incorrect on the two trials or those erring on either Trials 1 or 2 alone, $\chi^2 (3) = 1.04$, ns. Thus the reduced likelihood of chance accuracy owing to the greater number of Trial 1 hiding places within Order 2 had no appreciable effect on the children's answers. Among the 23 children who made an error on only one trial, whether the true location of the marble was the pocket ($n = 9$) or the box ($n = 14$) on that trial made no difference to the numbers of errors, $\chi^2 (1) = 1.09$, ns. Similarly, among the same 23 children, the order of questions within the trial that produced the error had no significant impact upon error rate, $\chi^2 < 1$. Of the 23 children, 13 made their sole error on a trial where the belief question preceded the control questions while 10 did so on a trial where control questions came first. Thus the significantly higher rate of errors on Trial 2 than Trial 1 cannot be explained by any features of the procedure other than a deterioration under subsequent questioning. Not sharing the scientific purpose of the experimenter's questions may have led the children on Trial 2 to assimilate the events of Trial 1 to their own experiences of hiding games. In our experiment, only 15 of the 41 3-year-olds were incorrect on the first trial. This result contradicts the claim that young children's inconsistent answers on the original Baron-Cohen task provide compelling evidence that they do not understand the nature of beliefs.

Apart from research with normal preschoolers, a conceptual deficit has often been invoked to account for the poor performance of children with autism on false belief tasks (Baron-Cohen, 1988; 1992; Baron-Cohen et al., 1985; Frith, Morton, & Leslie, 1991; Leslie & Frith, 1990). But, owing to the nature of their handicap, autistic children are less likely than normal children of the same age to appreciate the reason behind adult experimenters' violations of familiar conversational rules for the purpose of assessing children's knowledge. Two of the critical diagnostic features of autism, according to both DSM-III-R and the World Health Organisation (Frith, 1989, p. 11), include: "qualitative impairment in reciprocal social interaction" and "qualitative impairment in verbal and nonverbal communication, and in imaginative activity". The first of these problems severely restricts the autistic child's active participation in dialogue. Thus even though all autistic children with normal hearing are superficially exposed to adult speech, and many of them do even manage to acquire a reasonable vocabulary of individual word meanings, their social aloofness is likely to preclude their attention to, and hence mastery of, any but the most basic of conversational rules. As Perner, Frith, Leslie, and Leekam (1989) have noted, school-aged autistic children and adolescents frequently lack even such elementary pragmatic communication skills as gaze direction, informing, initiating, or adjusting to the listener's needs. Furthermore, in their own research, Perner et al. found not only that autistic children performed poorly on a communication-adjustment task, but also that there was no significant correlation in the autistic group between success on this task and the size of the child's receptive vocabulary of individual word meanings (as assessed by the British Picture Vocabulary Test). Thus, even when researchers selectively recruit autistic subjects with wide vocabularies (as shown, for example, by verbal mental ages above four years on receptive vocabulary tests), there is no necessary guarantee that the child has a sufficient grasp of the pragmatics of adult conversation to succeed on tasks where familiar assumptions about conversation are deliberately violated for scientific ends. At the same time, the other features of autism—impaired imagination and deficient verbal and nonverbal communication skills—undoubtedly serve to restrict the exposure with children with autism to the varied conversational experiences offered to a normal child of four years. In view of these handicaps, the styles of conversation that parents, teachers, and other caregivers use with older autistic children are likely to be very similar to those used by parents of normal children who are just beginning to participate in dialogue. Therefore, it is probable that even high-functioning older autistic children and adolescents with adequate vocabularies and no intellectual handicaps other than autism are no more capable of comprehending the scientific purpose for departing from conversational rules in experiments than are normal children under four years. If so, then the questions put to autistic participants in false belief tasks undoubtedly require the same attention to rules of conversation that can serve to facilitate the performance of normal three-year-olds (e.g. Siegal & Beattie, 1991).

From this perspective, older individuals with autism are similar to normal three-year-old children. Both have had limited conversational experience except that, for individuals with autism, their understanding of conversational rules and the physical setting of the experiment reflects their disability rather than their age. Should steps be taken to avoid the need to make conversational inferences, they should be more likely to answer correctly.

In support of this interpretation, Eisenmajor and Prior (1991) gave children with autism who had failed Trial 1 or Trial 2 of Baron-Cohen et al.'s Sally-Anne task a third trial where the belief question was changed to: "Where will Sally *first* look for the marble?" from: "Where will Sally look for the marble?" As in the Siegal and Beattie study, this change dispensed with the need for the children to infer that the question related to Sally's initial search behaviour. It led to a significant improvement in performance, with 9 of the 18 children with autism who failed on the earlier 2 trials succeeding on the third one.

Some basic level of language ability is undoubtedly a prerequisite for participation in sophisticated dialogue with an experimenter and, as Eisenmajor and Prior demonstrate, the success of children with autism on belief tasks is strongly related to their scores on measures of pragmatic skills. Consequently, before attributing the performance of children such as those with autism who are likely to be developmentally delayed to a deficit in their theory of mind, it is important to examine the conversational demands of these tasks. Further research is also needed to determine whether conversational supports like the one used by Eisenmajor and Prior improve performance on the many recent measures that have been creatively devised to examine the false belief knowledge of children with autism (e.g. Roth & Leslie, 1991; Russell, Mauthner, Sharpe, & Tidswell, 1991; Sodian & Frith, 1992).

Is Consistency in Children's Incorrect Responses Evidence for a Conceptual Deficit?

On other belief tasks, children can be *consistently* incorrect—a result that is incompatible with an answer-switching or "local concerns" explanation in reaction to questioning on two or more trials. Thus a consistently incorrect pattern might be regarded as stronger evidence for conceptual deficit. For example, Flavell, Mumme, Green, and Flavell (1992) carried out a large-scale investigation of three- to five-year-olds' understanding of beliefs. In their Study 1, they elicited children's own moral beliefs about the behaviour of a story character who had harmed another child (e.g. by hitting or biting). The children were then required to indicate whether the story character believed that such behaviour was acceptable. The procedure of Study 2 was similar and involved a wider range of situations. First, children's own beliefs about situations with factual, value, moral, and social conventional content were elicited; then they were asked to reiterate a story character's own beliefs. In Study 3, the task was to reiterate others' deviant beliefs in these four domains, immediately after these had been presented in stories, without offering one's own beliefs. Finally, in Study 4, children had to infer the moral beliefs of two story characters in dispute about the ownership of property (e.g. story characters named Jane and Peter who argue about the ownership of a jacket, each stating a belief that it belonged to him or her with the intention of taking it home).

In all four studies, three-year-olds had considerable difficulty in representing clashes between their own and others' beliefs, in contrast to the four- and five-year-olds, who appeared to recognise how conflicting or deviant beliefs can underlie behaviour. However, as Flavell et al. recognise, the procedure used in Studies 1 and 2 may have rendered children's own beliefs so salient that these may have masked their understanding when asked to report on the beliefs of others. In Studies 3 and 4, designed to rule out this possibility, the children were questioned about story characters' beliefs without first having been asked to report their own beliefs. The stories in Study 3, for example, consisted of items such as "This is Hank. Hank thinks cats do read books. He thinks cats do do that. Does Hank think that cats do or don't read books?" The three-year-olds often refrained from reiterating such deviant beliefs even after the question was repeated following corrective feedback ("Actually, Hank thinks cats do read books. Does Hank think that cats do or don't read books?"). They responded that Hank thinks cats do not read books, leading Flavell et al. to join researchers such as Perner (1991) in claiming that three-year-olds have little or no ability to represent the nature of beliefs in particular and mental states in general.

Nevertheless, despite their poor performance on the measures used by Flavell et al., young children often do not share the experimenter's scientific purpose in questioning—in this instance to determine the extent to which children understand beliefs. Consequently, stories such as those about a boy who believes that cats can read books are liable to seem so incredulous that these may be interpreted as a violation of the quality rule in conversation, which enjoins speakers to be sincere and avoid falsehood. To reconcile the departure from the quality rule with the relevance of the story and to maintain the assumption that the experimenter is co-operating with the listener in communication, children may instead have interpreted the question to mean: "Does Hank really think that cats do or don't read books?" rather than: "Does Hank think that cats do or don't read books?" Similarly, the children may have interpreted questions about disputed ownership in Study 4 as: "Who does the jacket belong to?" rather than: "Who does Jane (or Peter) think it belongs to?" because it was seen in terms of a request to assist an adult to arbitrate conflicts between the ownership claims of peers. In either case, the three-year-olds may be seen as consistently incapable of distinguishing others' beliefs from their own, not because of some conceptual limitation but because they reinterpret the questions. Their answers reflect their own local concerns instead of the scientific purpose of the experimenter and are to questions different than those that were intended.

Although acknowledging conversational influences on children's answers, Flavell and his colleagues note that in their studies children's responses are consistent and significantly correlated across task domains. For this reason, they maintain that three-year-olds not only lack an understanding of beliefs but are sure of their answers. Flavell et al. (1992, p. 970) proceed to contend that their data demonstrate the opposite of our thesis. According to Flavell et al., we hold the simple view that children's poor performance reflects their inexperience with conventions of conversation, which results in changing their answers in response to repeated questioning.

These remarks fall far short of an accurate portrait of our position. Whether children switch or retain their original answers is an outgrowth of conversational processes that are complex and involve their knowledge of how rules of conversation are used in the adult world as well as their interpretation of the physical setting of the experiment. Both answer-switching and answer consistency are present in experiments in which children's lack of performance can be seen in terms of their answers to questions that were not intended by the experimenter.

As one of us has pointed out (Siegal, 1991a; 1991b), response consistency may in fact mask children's authentic knowledge of the distinction between appearance and reality in the earlier research conducted by Flavell and his colleagues (Flavell et al., 1986). For example, to questions such as: 'When you look with your eyes right now, is it a bear or is it Ellie?' and "Is it a bear really and truly," three-year-olds may respond that an experimenter who wears a bear mask may not only look like a bear but be a bear really and truly in order to compliment an investigator on the effectiveness of his or her deception. In effect, they may be answering the question: "How good is this disguise?" twice. A similar explanation can be proposed for children's responses when they clearly regard a story character's behaviour to be incredulous, as in the stories used in Flavell et al.'s (1992) Studies 1, 2, and 3. Children's conviction in the correctness of their responses to their *own* interpretation of the experimenter's question (e.g. "Does Hank really think that cats do or don't read books?") will result in repeating their first answer when the question is repeated. However, in some instances, children interpret the question as intended and are certain of their answers. But they may come to attach little importance to the questions and switch their response in the hope of concluding the conversation with the experimenter (Siegal, 1991b, p. 77).

Another limitation to Flavell et al.'s position rests upon their apparent acceptance of the proposition that individuals infer mental states of thinking and wanting simply from observing behaviour. As we noted in the introduction to this chapter, in societies where adults are expected to follow their individual thoughts and desires, this may be often the case. Yet irrespective of their mental states, the behaviour of young children and of adults in collectivist societies is often dictated by external constraints. For example, we have reported that the belief in consistency between attitudes and behaviour in collectivist societies such as Japan is not as strong as that in individualist Western societies such as Australia (Kashima, Siegal, Tanaka, & Kashima, 1992); Japanese adults are more likely than Australians to attribute behaviour to the constraints of situations rather than to individual mental states.

Similarly, preschoolers who have had little contact with others outside their home may be reluctant to indicate that another child's behaviour is due to a genuinely unorthodox belief. Their beliefs in the correctness of responses to questions about behaviour are coloured by situational constraints. In the domain of social conventions, for example, their answers to questions about the appropriateness of behaviour across contexts are dependent upon the extent and variety of their contact with others. Those who are veterans at daycare are presumably relatively experienced in conversation with peers and adults outside the family. By contrast, newly enrolled children are liable to misunderstand the scientific purpose of a question that aims to gather information about the expression of an individual's beliefs. Their answers may amount to a compliant echoing of beliefs that are dictated by adult authorities in the home. Consequently, newly enrolled children who have been reared at home are less likely to indicate instances where the very behaviour that they believe is right in one situation is wrong in another (Siegal & Storey, 1985). Once more there is reason to conclude that the comparative proficiency of older children in Flavell et al.'s studies to recognise deviance and discrepancy in beliefs is due to their increasing skill in understanding the implications of conversations as a result of diversity in their conversational experience.

Are Children Unable or Unwilling to Use Deceptive Tactics?

The position that young children have a deficit in their theory of mind has provided a basis to hypothesise that they should be unable to use deceptive tactics. Sodian, Taylor, Harris, and Perner (1991) take this view in claiming that three-year-olds are so severely limited in their theory of mind that they cannot enact simple deceptions to create false beliefs in others. In a first experiment, children aged two, three and four years were given a sandpit, a toy truck, and a toy driver that could be hidden under one of five cups. They were told to move the driver from the truck, hide him under one of the cups, and prevent a second (adult) experimenter from finding him. It was explained that this could be done by smoothing over the sand. Children under four years rarely laid down false tracks spontaneously and required several hints to ensure that they would perform a deceptive act. They had considerable difficulty in answering questions such as: "Where will the (second experimenter) look when he/she comes back?" In a second experiment, three- and four-year-olds participated in a hide-and-seek game. The task was to use a felt-tip pen in the form of a puppet to produce thick tracks that would enable a king to find a "treasure" of small yellow stickers in one of four boxes and to use a paper towel to wipe out the existing tracks in order to prevent a robber to find the treasure. The 4-year-olds clearly outperformed the 3-year-olds; only 6 out of the 20 3-year-olds wiped the tracks out for the robber only, while thickening them for the kings, as opposed to 14 of the 16 4-year-olds. In fact, 9 of the 20 3-year-olds, in contrast to none of the 4-year-olds, thickened the tracks for both the king and the robber. On this basis, Sodian et al. (1991) have claimed that 3-year-olds are constrained by a conceptual deficit that precludes the ability to understand how actions can lead to deceptive beliefs and outcomes.

Again, however, these results may reflect children's lack of conversational experience. In the first experiment, it is likely that they interpreted the questions such as: "Where will the (second experimenter) look to find the toy when he/she comes back?" as "Where will he/she have to look to find the toy?" Indeed, three-year-olds might want to please an adult by revealing the source of a desired object. Moreover, in the procedure of the second experiment, three-year-olds might find a pen that takes the form of a puppet more attractive to use than a paper towel, and thus would be likely to use the pen indiscriminately.

Despite Sodian et al.'s contention that the younger children did "agree" to the experimenter's request to make it "easy" for the king and "hard" for the robber, the children's answers indicated that they might not have shared the purpose of the experiment. In other studies (Sodiam, 1991), about half of three-year-olds responded negatively to the question: "Do you want the robber to find the treasure?" only after the question was repeated. Regardless of whether described as a robber or king, children may be reluctant to assign a negative evaluation to any attractive puppet or, for that matter, any attractive person (Siegal & Rablin, 1982). Because of a puppet's attractiveness, children may be unwilling to use deceptive tactics to thwart him from achieving a goal, and it may be necessary to have children choose only one puppet to be given access to a reward in order to ensure that they are not indulgent with both. In essence, Sodian (1991, Experiment 3) did conduct such an experiment and found that in a task where children were asked to make a clear choice without engaging in the attractiveness of a dialogue with a puppet (instructions: "Make it hard for the robber; make it easy for the king"), children now were likely to succeed. By contrast, when asked to respond directly to the presumably entertaining question asked by each puppet ("Where is the treasure?"), the children now complied in both instances, regardless of the injunction of the experimenter to make it hard for the robber.

The procedure used in Sodian's research is similar to that in a study conducted by Peskin (1992), who begins her report by an anecdote: Jeremy (aged three): "Mommy, go out of the kitchen." Mother: "Why, Jeremy?"

Jeremy: "Because I want to take a cookie." The 3-year-old's conversation is said to demonstrate young children's inability to understand the significance of beliefs in concealing information about intentions. Peskin then proceeds to describe what she regards as support for this claim. In her study, an experimenter gave various stickers to children aged three to five who were asked to voice their preferences. The children were asked to conceal information about these preferences from a naughty puppet who "always chooses the sticker that you want. He doesn't care if you're sad." Unlike the older children, most of the three-year-olds did not conceal their true preferences through refusing to tell or by providing the puppet with misinformation.

Nevertheless, the younger children may not have had a strong preference for a sticker in the first place. By responding in a subsequent "exclusion procedure" that only the "good" puppet should have a sticker, they may have indicated that the bad puppet should do without, not that they themselves have a definite preference. Moreover, the lack of deceptive tactics displayed by the children may be due to their unwillingness to mislead or obstruct actively using verbal messages rather than a theory of mind deficit. Anyone who knows the reaction of three-year-olds in experimental situations recognises that they are often unwilling to volunteer any information. The anecdote used by Peskin can now be easily reinterpreted. The three-year-old may want to draw attention to how much he wants a cookie by stating that he would even want to take one while his mother is out of the kitchen.

How Extensive are Young Children's Representational Difficulties?

Many investigators have attempted to make the case that children's difficulties are limited to the representation of beliefs and do not generally extend to include other mental states such as pretences, images, and desires (e.g. Gopnik & Slaughter, 1991; Gopnik, Slaughter, & Meltzoff, this volume). Such views are mild when compared with those of other investigators. For example, in a series of five experiments reported by Zaitchik (1990), preschoolers were given questions that took the form of a "belief format" (Actor A places object in location x and then leaves. Actor B moves object to location y. Test question: "Where does A think the object is?") and a "photo format" (Actor A places object in location x and takes a photo of it. Actor B moves object to location y. Test question: "In the picture, where is the object?"). The children had considerable difficulties with tasks constructed along both formats. However, they may have interpreted the belief question: "Where does A think the object is?" to mean "Where will A think the object is once it has been located?" Similarly they may have interpreted the question on the photo: "In the picture, where is the object?" as "Where is the object in the puppet show (that would appear in a photo)?" rather than the intended adult interpretation: "Where was the object in the photo that was taken before?"

Although Zaitchik (1990, p. 58) is evidently aware of the difficulty of saying more than is necessary, the experimenter in the photo research instead may have set aside the quantity rule by saying less than is necessary for effective communication. Children who have learned language from speakers who have referred mostly to the here and now are expected to make the inference that they are to be tested on a question that refers to an action that has been completed in the past and endures in the present, even though the question is framed in the present tense only. In fact, the photo tasks were so difficult that many four-year-olds who easily succeeded on belief tasks did not on photo tasks. Yet in making some strong statements about the dispositional nature of the child, Zaitchik (1990) stakes out a rather extreme position. Using evidence from preschoolers' responses on tasks that involve the understanding of information contained in photographs, she has contended that children's conceptual problems are not just restricted to mind (i.e. the representation of false beliefs) but extend to representation in general: "... young children's failure on the false belief task is not due to an inadequate epistemology (though they may have one) and is symptomatic of a larger problem with representations" (p. 41) "... none of the properties of beliefs which have been taken to cause the child's problems apply to the photos. Photos are not immaterial, they are not intangible, they are not private and internal ... Nevertheless, (children) fail" (p. 62).

Children's difficulties in experiments that involve representation are certainly large and general. However, from a conversational perspective, we propose again that these apparently extensive difficulties can be attributed to the characteristics of an experimental situation in which speakers have inadvertently departed from conversational rules[2].

---

[2] In describing the results of two experiments, Leslie and Thaiss (1992) have recently reported that, although children with autism do poorly on false belief tasks compared to normal four-year-olds, they show an advantage in understanding pictorial representations. On this basis, Leslie and Thaiss claim that the performance of children with autism on the types of problems used by Zaitchik (1990) rules out linguistic explanations for their lack of success on related false belief tasks. However, an inspection of Leslie and Thaiss's data reveals that the difference between the two groups of children on the photograph tasks used in their Experiment 1 was not significant; a majority in both groups succeeded. In Experiment 2, both normal children and those with autism performed at a level that did not differ from what would be expected by chance, with 10 out of 15 children with autism who were successful ($P = 0.151$, by a one-tailed binomial test) in contrast to 7 out of 21 normal children ($P = 0.095$, by a one-tailed binomial test). The "marked advantage" in this experiment attributed to normal children was also not significant, $\chi^2 (1) = 2.678$, $P > 0.05$. Older children with autism may be as familiar as normal children with conversations that concern photographs and pictures. Understanding a speaker's reference to photographs would not appear to require the same pragmatic communication skills as gaze direction and adjusting to the listener's needs that are necessary in following discourse about mental states.

CHILDREN AS CONVERSATIONAL NOVICES AND THE TENSION BETWEEN CONVERSATIONAL AND SCIENTIFIC INFERENCES

Transitions in Children's Answers to Questions

Because young children have just acquired language from caregivers who have been implicitly attentive to conversational rules, they are liable to misconstrue the unspoken implications of well-intentioned questions when these rules have been set aside in experimental settings for scientific purposes. These implications require children to have experience in recognising that a question can refer to the past or future, that it does not necessarily require any more than a restatement of a previous answer, or that it may take the form of an attempt to examine their understanding of deception. Apart from these issues, children may not answer questions correctly because they do not share the physical setting of the experiment and do not view persons and objects in the same way as investigators. In all six of the questions that we have addressed, children's difficulties in theory of mind research can be attributed to their lack of familiarity with the conversational territory of the experiment rather than to a conceptual deficit or limitation.

Conversations that take place in experimental settings where the purpose and contextual relevance are not apparent can create considerable bewilderment in young children who are often caught in a power imbalance. They know that the experimenter already has the right answer and has the language to express it with ease and that, even if the purpose was shared and the answer was within their grasp, they could not respond as gracefully. In these situations, an atmosphere of confrontation may emerge that can prevent children from expressing their knowledge (Freeman, Sinha, & Condliffe, 1981). To facilitate their performance, special planning in questioning methods and materials is needed that maintains the "conversational peace" between children and experimenters.

What, then, can account for the shift from apparent failure at three years of age to an appreciable success at four years in the many theory of mind experiments that have assumed children's ability to share the implications of questions and the physical representation of the situation? One factor is change in the conversational environmentt of the home. Brown and Dunn (1991) made audio-recordings of family conversations in which children aged 24 to 36 months participated. They discovered an abrupt and statistically significant increase between 30 and 36 months in the mother's reference to her own mental states while speaking to her child. Of course, mothers may introduce the demand for conceptualising their own discrepant viewpoints as a function of recognising a budding awareness of false belief in their offspring. But it is also likely that increasing familiarity with conversing about what goes on in the mind of another person prepares the child, as a four-year-old, for success on standard false belief tasks.

In a related study, Dunn et al. (1991) tested a group of three-year-old second-born siblings on false belief tasks requiring predictions and explanations of puppets' searching for objects in misleadingly marked containers. Using longitudinal data on family conversations gathered when the children were two years nine months old, they found that the frequency of mother-child dialogues about feeling states and causality predicted the three-year-olds' success in explaining puppets' actions on the basis of false beliefs. Moreover, co-operative interaction with an older sibling at age two was an additional significant predictor of the ability to generate false belief explanations seven months later. Dunn et al. suggest that early false belief knowledge may have its roots in family conversation. Children who play co-operatively with an older sibling may gain insight into others' beliefs. Moreover, children are better able to explain than to predict puppets' actions on the basis of false beliefs because at home explanations involving false belief undoubtedly arise more frequently than predictions. Dunn et al. cite examples from mothers' dialogue with children that was spontaneously triggered by protests or conflict between siblings such as "He thought it was his turn" and "She didn't know I had promised it to you." In contrast, a mother would generally have to interrupt ongoing dialogue in order to request predictions of future behaviour involving false beliefs. As such references about the future are infrequent, children would be inexperienced in identifying the purpose and implications of false belief prediction tasks in experimental settings.

Between the ages of three and four years, the understanding of the adult conversational world that occurs at home is accompanied by increasing exposure to teachers and peers in daycare and preschool. There children become better equipped to share the conversational world of adults who are seeking answers to scientific questions rather than to local concerns (Sharp, Cole, & Lave, 1979, pp. 56–58) and can begin collaboratively to generate and explain solutions to problems (Hatano & Inagaki, 1991; Rogoff, 1990). They become acquainted with modes of narratives and story-telling that convey the canonical mental models for interpreting language. They strive to make the appropriate inferences in serious conversation as well as in humour, which is a key aspect of social acceptance (Masten, 1986). Engaging in such activities requires the exercise of symbolic "meta-pragmatic" abilities that involve the use of personal pronouns and definite articles as well as explicit references to forms of speech (Hickmann, 1987; Karmiloff-Smith, 1987; Wertsch, 1985, pp. 145–150). Within this environment, children become more adept at answering questions in experimental settings.

Towards Revealing What Children Know Through Concern for the Conversational Environment

Conceptual deficits or limitations have often been invoked to account for children's lack of success on measures of their theory of mind. Nevertheless, the pragmatic, local concerns of children may not coincide with the scientific purposes of experimenters. Although children may still not be granted a complete, adultlike understanding, if tasks are tailored to their experience in conversation and care is taken to formulate questions that do not set aside conversational rules, they should be more likely to disclose their knowledge without inadvertently answering the wrong question or importing their own variety of relevance. When experimenters phrase their questions in accord with conversational rules and the task itself is organised around a purpose the child can share, three-year-olds can be capable of displaying an understanding of false beliefs and the nature of deception. To this end, a conversational framework provides a guide to examine situational characteristics that contribute to their performance. By no means do we wish to suppress the position that cognitive development in general can be examined in terms of conceptual limitations or deficits; future research may, in fact, point in this direction. However, with regard to the proposal that children's early understanding of beliefs reflects a conceptual limitation, the current evidence is not convincing. In fact, in our sceptical view, the notion of a conceptual limitation or deficit that has been invoked to explain the results of theory of mind research may prove similar to the now discredited notion of "instinct" that was once commonly used to explain animal behaviour—especially when scientists were unable to posit any external agent of change (Hinde, 1974, p. 24)[3].

Through focusing on the conversational territory of cognitive development, we aim to provide a fresh, more precise model of what children know in specific domains. In the case of children's theory of mind, which lies within the domain of psychology, our position is that differences in conversational experience are reflected in the differences between the poor

---

[3] This is not to say that increasing social interaction is all there is to the conversational understanding that is necessary for success on many belief tasks. Sodian et al. (1991) speculate that young children's difficulties may have a neuropsychological underpinning. Similarly, Thatcher (1992, p. 44) notes that a "milestone" in children's performance on theory of mind tasks at four years of age concurs with a surge of growth in the right frontal lobe, and Frith et al. (1991) have proposed that the performance of children with autism in theory of mind research reflects neuropsychological processes. These observations may be seen as unduly reductionist (Putnam, 1988). But it is worthwhile noting that there is also a neuropsychological basis to pragmatic development in which the right hemisphere influences the interpretation of conversation (Kaplan, Brownell, Jacobs, & Gardner, 1990; Kasher, 1991; Zaidel, 1978). Thus the success on theory of mind tasks that comes about with increased age may reflect the developmental neuropsychology of pragmatic abilities as well as the effects of social interaction.

performance on belief tasks of three-year-olds, whose answers reflect their own local concerns, and the dramatic changes exhibited by older children, who are more apt to recognise and share the scientific purpose of an experimenter's questions, which can set aside the quantity, quality, relevance, and manner rules in conversation. This explanation accounts for young children's difficulties in answering questions about beliefs once they start to converse and the comparative proficiency of older children. If questioned as if they possess the knowledge of language use that is possessed by a speaker well-versed in the adult conversational world, who shares the implications of departures from conversational rules, young children will be unlikely to display their understanding on belief tasks. If care is taken to remove children's dependence on understanding the implications of conversations by avoiding repetitive or overly brief forms of questioning, as well as to ensure that they share the physical setting of the experiment and the purpose of asking about a deception, even three-year-olds are often likely to answer correctly and to demonstrate what they know.

ACKNOWLEDGEMENTS

Some of the results reported here were presented at the Fourth Annual Convention of the American Psychological Society, San Diego, June 1992. We thank Jane Mackelworth for her work in data collection, and are grateful to the Ashgrove West, Hillsdon, Ironside, and St. Thomas Riverview Kindergartens and Preschools for their fine co-operation.

REFERENCES

Bakhtin, M.M. (1981). *The dialogic imagination: Four essays by M. M. Bakhtin*. M. Holquist, Ed., C. Emerson & M. Holquist, Trans. Austin: University of Texas Press.

Bakhtin, M.M. (1986). *Speech genres and other late essays*. C. Emerson & M. Holquist, Eds; V.W. McGee, Trans. Austin: University of Texas Press.

Baron-Cohen, S. (1988). Social and pragmatic deficits in autism: Cognitive or affective? *Journal of Autism and Developmental Disorders, 18*, 379–402.

Baron-Cohen, S. (1992). The theory of mind hypothesis of autism: History and prospects of the idea. *The Psychologist, 5*, 9–12.

Baron-Cohen, S., Leslie, A.M., & Frith, U. (1985). Does the autistic child have a theory of mind? *Cognition, 21*, 37–46.

Bartsch, K., & Wellman, H.M. (1989). Young children's attribution of action to beliefs and desires. *Child Development, 60*, 946–964.

Bretherton, I., & Beeghly, M. (1982). Talking about internal states: The acquisition of an explicit theory of mind. *Developmental Psychology, 18*, 906–921.

Brown, J.R., & Dunn, J. (1991). "You can cry, mum": The social and developmental implications of talk about internal states. *British Journal of Developmental Psychology, 9*, 237–256.

Brown, P., & Levinson, S.C. (1987). *Politeness: Some universals in language usage*. New York: Cambridge University Press.

Brown, R., & Hanlon, C. (1970). Derivational complexity and the order of acquisition in child speech. In J.R. Hayes (Ed.), *Cognition and the development of language* (pp. 155–207). New York: Wiley.

Bruner, J.S. (1986). *Actual minds, possible worlds.* Cambridge, Mass.: Harvard University Press.

Clark, H.H. (1987). Relevance to what? *Behavioral and Brain Sciences, 10,* 714–715.

De Villiers, J.G., & De Villiers, P.A. (1978). *Language acquisition.* Cambridge, Mass.: Harvard University Press.

Donaldson, M. (1978). *Children's minds.* Glasgow: Fontana.

Donaldson, M. (1982). Conservation: What is the question? *British Journal of Psychology, 73,* 199–207.

Dunn, J., Brown, J., Slomkowski, C., Tesla, C., & Youngblade, L. (1991). Young children's understanding of other people's feelings and beliefs: Individual differences and their antecedents. *Child Development, 62,* 1352–1366.

Eisenmajor, R., & Prior, M. (1991). Cognitive linguistic correlates of "theory of mind" ability in autistic children. *British Journal of Developmental Psychology, 9,* 351–364.

Flavell, J.H., Green, F.L., & Flavell, E.R. (1986). Development of the appearance-reality distinction. *Monographs of the Society for Research in Child Development, 51* (Serial No. 212).

Flavell, J.H., Mumme, D.L., Green, F.L., & Flavell, E.R. (1992). Young children's understanding of different types of beliefs. *Child Development, 63,* 960–977.

Flavell, J.H., & Wohlwill, J.F. (1969). Formal and functional aspects of cognitive development. In D. Elkind & J.H. Flavell (Eds.), *Studies in cognitive development* (pp. 67–120). New York: Oxford University Press.

Fleming, J.H., & Darley, J.M. (1989). Perceiving choice and constraint: The effects of contextual and behavioral cues on attitude attribution. *Journal of Personality and Social Psychology, 56,* 27–40.

Freeman, N.H., Sinha, C.G., & Condliffe, S.G. (1981). Collaboration and confrontation with young children in language comprehension testing. In W.P. Robinson (Ed.), *Communication and development.* London: Academic Press.

Frith, U. (1989). *Autism: Explaining the enigma.* Oxford: Blackwell.

Frith, U., Morton, J., & Leslie, A.M. (1991). The cognitive basis of a biological disorder: Autism. *Trends in Neuroscience, 14,* 433–438.

Gelman, R., Meck, E., & Merkin, S. (1986). Young children's numerical competence. *Cognitive Development, 1,* 1–29.

Gelman, R., & Shatz, M. (1977). Appropriate speech adjustments: The operation of conversational constraints on talk to two-year-olds. In M. Lewis & L.A. Rosenblum (Eds.), *Interaction, conversation, and the development of language* (pp. 27–61). New York: Wiley.

Gopnik, A., & Slaughter, V. (1991). Young children's understanding of changes in their mental states. *Child Development, 62,* 98–110.

Grice, H.P. (1975). Logic and conversation. In P. Cole & J.L. Morgan (Eds.), *Syntax and semantics, Vol. 3: Speech acts* (pp. 41–58). New York: Academic Press.

Harris, P.L., Johnson, C.N., Hutton, D., Andrews, G., & Cooke, T. (1989). Young children's theory of mind and emotion. *Cognition and Emotion, 3,* 379–400.

Hart, H.L.A., & Honore, T. (1985). *Causation in the law* (2nd edn.). Oxford: Clarendon Press.

Hatano, G., & Inagaki, K. (1991). Sharing cognition through collective comprehension activity. In L.B. Resnick, J.M. Levine, & S. Teasley (Eds.), *Perspectives on socially shared cognition* (pp. 331–348). Washington, DC: American Psychological Association.

Hickmann, M. (1987). The pragmatics of reference in chihld language: Some issues in developmental theory. In M. Hickmann (Ed.), *Social and functional approaches to language and thought* (165–184). Orlando: Academic Press.

Hilton, D.J. (1990). Conversational processes and causal explanation. *Psychological Bulletin*, *107*, 65–81.

Hinde, R. (1974). *Biological bases of human social behaviour.* New York: McGraw-Hill.

Hughes, M., & Grieve, R. (1983). On asking children bizarre questions. In M. Donaldson, R. Grieve, & C. Pratt (Eds.), *Early child development and education* (pp. 104–114). Oxford: Blackwell.

Jones, E.E., & Nisbett, R.E. (1972). The actor and the observer: Divergent perspectives of the causes of behaviour. In E.E. Jones, D.E. Kanouse, H.H. Kelley, R.E. Nisbett, S. Valins, & B. Weiner (Eds.), *Attribution: Perceiving the causes of behaviour* (pp. 79–94). Morristown, NJ: General Learning Press.

Kaplan, J.A., Brownell, H.H., Jacobs, J.R., & Gardner, H. (1990). The effects of right hemisphere damage on the pragmatic interpretation of conversational remarks. *Brain and Language*, *38*, 315–333.

Karmiloff-Smith, A. (1987). Function and process in comparing language and cognition. In M. Hickmann (Ed.), *Social and functional approaches to language and thought* (pp. 185–202). Orlando: Academic Press.

Kasher, A. (1991). On the pragmatic modules: A lecture. *Journal of Pragmatics*, *16*, 381–397.

Kashima, Y., Siegal, M., Tanaka, K., & Kashima, E.S. (1992). Do people believe that attitudes are consistent with behaviour? Towards a cultural psychology of attribution processes. *British Journal of Social Psychology*, *31*, 111–124.

Leslie, A.M., & Frith, U. (1990). Prospects for a cognitive neuropsychology of autism: Hobson's choice. *Psychological Review*, *97*, 122–131.

Leslie, A.M., & Thaiss, L. (1992). Domain specificity in conceptual development: Neuropsychological evidence from autism. *Cognition*, *43*, 225–251.

Levinson, S.C. (1989). A review of relevance. *Journal of Linguistics*, *25*, 455–472.

Lewis, C., & Osborne, A. (1990). Three-year-olds' problems with false belief: Conceptual deficit or linguistic artifact? *Child Development*, *61*, 1514–1519.

Light, P.H., Buckingham, N., & Robins, A.H. (1979). The conservation task in an interactional setting. *British Journal of Educational Psychology*, *49*, 304–310.

Masten, A.S. (1986). Humor and competence in school-aged children. *Child Development*, *57*, 461–473.

McGarrigle, J., & Donaldson, M. (1974). Conservation accidents. *Cognition*, *3*, 341–350.

McGarrigle, J., Grieve, R., & Hughes, M. (1978). Interpreting inclusion: A contribution to the study of the child's cognitive and linguistic development. *Journal of Experimental Child Psychology*, *25*, 528–550.

Mitchell, P., & Lacohée, H. (1991). Children's early understanding of false belief. *Cognition*, *39*, 107–127.

Moses, L.J., & Flavell, J.H. (1990). Inferring false beliefs from actions and reactions. *Child Development*, *61*, 929–945.

Parke, R.D. (1989). Social development in infancy: A 25-year perspective. *Advances in Child Development and Behavior*, *21*, 1–48.

Perner, J. (1991). *Understanding the representational mind.* Cambridge, Mass.: Bradford Books/MIT Press.

Perner, J., Frith, U., Leslie, A.M., & Leekam, S.R. (1989). Exploration of the autistic child's theory of mind: Knowledge, belief, and communication. *Child Development*, *60*, 689–700.

Perner, J., Leekam, S.R., & Wimmer, H. (1987). Three-year-olds' difficulty with false belief: The case for a conceptual deficit. *British Journal of Developmental Psychology*, *5*, 125–137.

Perner, J., & Ogden, J.E. (1988). Hunger for knowledge: Children's problem with representation in imputing mental states. *Cognition*, *29*, 47–61.

Peskin, J. (1992). Ruse and representations: On children's ability to conceal information. *Developmental Psychology*, *28*, 84–89.

Piaget, J. (1970). Piaget's theory. In P.H. Mussen (Ed.), *Carmichael's manual of child psychology, Vol. 1* (pp. 703–731). New York: Wiley.

Poole, D.A., & White, L.T. (1991). Effects of question repetition on the eyewitness testimony of children and adults. *Developmental Psychology, 27*, 975–986.

Pratt, C., & Bryant, P. (1990). Young children understand that looking leads to knowing (so long as they are looking into a single barrel). *Child Development, 61*, 946–961.

Putnam, H. (1988). *Representation and reality.* Cambridge, Mass.: MIT Press.

Robinson, E.J., & Mitchell, P. (1992). Children's interpretation of messages from a speaker with a false belief. *Child Development, 63*, 639–652.

Rogoff, B. (1982). Integrating context and cognitive development. In M.E. Lamb & A.L. Brown (Eds.), *Advances in developmental psychology: Vol. 2* (pp. 125–170). Hillsdale, NJ: Lawrence Erlbaum Associates Inc.

Rogoff, B. (1990). *Apprenticeship in thinking.* New York: Oxford University Press.

Rommetveit, R. (1970). On the relationship between children's mastery of Piagetian cognitive operations and their semantic competence. In R. Rommetveit & R.M. Blakar (Eds.), *Studies of language, thought, and verbal communication* (pp. 457–466). London: Academic Press.

Rose, S.A., & Blank, M. (1974). The potency of context in children's cognition: An illustration through conservation. *Child Development, 45*, 499–502.

Roth, D., & Leslie, A.M. (1991). The recognition of attitude conveyed by utterance: A study of preschool and autistic children. *British Journal of Developmental Psychology, 9*, 315–330.

Russell, J., Mauthner, N., Sharpe, S. & Tidswell, T. (1991). The "windows task" as a measure of strategic deception in preschoolers and autistic subjects. *British Journal of Developmental Psychology, 9*, 331–349.

Sharp, D., Cole, M., & Lave, C. (1979). Education and cognitive development: The evidence from experimental research. *Monographs of the Society for Research in Child Development, 44* (Serial No. 178).

Siegel, M. (1988). Children's knowledge of contagion and contamination as causes of illness. *Child Development, 59*, 1353–1359.

Siegal, M. (1991a). A clash of conversational worlds: Interpreting cognitive development through communication. In L.B. Resnick, J.M. Levine, & S. Teasley (Eds.), *Perspectives on socially shared cognition* (23–40). Washington, DC: American Psychological Association.

Siegal, M. (1991b). *Knowing children: Experiments in conversation and cognition.* Hove: Lawrence Erlbaum Associates Ltd.

Siegal, M. (1993). Knowing children's minds. *Behavioral and Brain Sciences, 16*, 79–80.

Siegal, M., & Beattie, K. (1991). Where to look first for children's understanding of false beliefs. *Cognition, 38*, 1–12.

Siegal, M., & Rablin, J. (1982). Moral development as reflected by young children's evaluation of maternal discipline. *Merrill-Palmer Quarterly, 28*, 499–503.

Siegal, M., & Sanderson, J.A. (1989). Do children have a concept of mental representation: A comment on Perner and Ogden's position. *Cognition, 31*, 277–280.

Siegal, M., & Share, D.L. (1990). Contamination sensitivity in young children. *Developmental Psychology, 26*, 455–458.

Siegal, M., & Storey, R.M. (1985). Day care and children's conceptions of moral and social rules. *Child Development, 56*, 1001–1008.

Siegal, M., Waters, L.J., & Dinwiddy, L.S. (1988). Misleading children: Causal attributions for inconsistency under repeated questioning. *Journal of Experimental Child Psychology, 45*, 438–456.

Siegel, L.S. (1978). The relationship of language and thought in the preoperational child: A reconsideration of nonverbal alternatives to Piagetian tasks. In L.S. Siegel & C.J. Brainerd (Eds.), *Alternatives to Piaget: Critical essays on the theory.* New York: Academic Press.

Siegel, I.E. (1974). When do we know what a child knows. *Human Development, 17*, 201–217.

Sodian, B. (1991). The development of deception in young children. *British Journal of Developmental Psychology, 9,* 173–188.

Sodian, B., & Frith, U. (1992). Deception and sabotage in autistic, retarded and normal children. *Journal of Child Psychology and Psychiatry, 33,* 591–605.

Sodian, B., Taylor, C., Harris, P.L., & Perner, J. (1991). Early deception and the child's theory of mind: False trails and genuine markers. *Child Development, 62,* 468–483.

Sullivan, K., & Winner, E. (1991). When 3-year-olds understand ignorance, false belief and representational change. *British Journal of Developmental Psychology, 9,* 159–171.

Thatcher, R.W. (1992). Cyclic cortical organization during early childhood. *Brain and Cognition, 20,* 24–50.

Vygotsky, L.S. (1962). *Thought and language.* Cambridge, Mass.: MIT Press.

Wellman, H.M., & Bartsch, K. (1988). Young children's reasoning about beliefs. *Cognition, 31,* 239–277.

Wellman, H.M., & Woolley, J.D. (1990). From simple desires to ordinary beliefs: The early development of everyday beliefs. *Cognition, 35,* 245–275.

Wertsch, J.V. (1985). *Vygotsky and the social formation of mind.* Cambridge, Mass.: Harvard University Press.

Wertsch, J.V. (1991). The problem of meaning in a sociocultural approach to mind. In A. McKeough & J.L. Lupart (Eds.), *Towards the practice of theory-based instruction: Current cognitive theories and their educational promise.* Hillsdale, NJ: Lawrence Erlbaum Associates Inc.

Wimmer, H., & Hartl, M. (1991). Against the Cartesian view on mind: Young children's difficulty with own false beliefs. *British Journal of Developmental Psychology, 9,* 125–138.

Woolley, J.D., & Wellman, H.M. (1990). Young children's understanding of realities, nonrealities, and appearance. *Child Development, 61,* 946–961.

Zaidel, E. (1978). Lexical organization in the right hemisphere. In P. Buser & A. Rougeul-Buser (Eds.), *Cerebral correlates of conscious experience* (pp. 177–197). Amsterdam: Elsevier.

Zaitchik, D. (1990). When representations conflict with reality: The preschooler's problem with false beliefs and "false" photographs. *Cognition, 35,* 41–68.

21

Episodes, Events, and Narratives in the Child's Understanding of Mind

Charlie Lewis
Lancaster University, UK

INTRODUCTION

A popular British television detective series, *Inspector Morse*, involves the exploits of a thoughtful police officer who, each week, finds himself in search of a murderer. Even on its re-showings, an estimated 18 million British viewers attempt to construct the reasons why a victim has been killed. As an audience we are given many false leads along the way and our task is to work out which of the many possible candidates committed the crime. The series works so well because the author plays with our understanding of the protagonists' intentions. As the plot unfolds we constantly update our "theories" about likely murderers. In doing so we often become misled about the importance of some of the evidence. We hear, for example, that the wife of the deceased has a lot to gain from her husband's death, hated him, and has lied to the Inspector. This often leads us to disregard the crucial piece of evidence to implicate another potential perpetrator—after many a false lead we find the wife has been murdered or that she has a solid alibi. It is such "errors" in grasping a plot as it unfolds that will form the basis of this chapter, albeit with a focus on young children's understanding of much simpler texts.

I mention *Inspector Morse* because the success of the series relies upon the dynamic way in which the audience casts and recasts the storyline that might account for the protagonists' (and the author's) intentions. In many respects viewers reveal their own susceptibilities to misread the mental states of the

457

protagonists, thus demonstrating adults' problems in grappling with the many levels of text comprehension. I wish to make a claim that however simplified a false belief task might be, it still requires the child to construct contrasting interpretations of the author's (i.e. the experimenter's) aim. Before focusing upon young children I will cite some evidence to show how subtle is the process of negotiation between story-teller and listener over the status of a third entity, the text, by showing how adults can easily be led to misconstrue an experimenter's aims/intentions. As Gopnik, Slaughter, and Meltzoff (this volume) suggest, there is a danger of becoming obsessed with methodological detail in false belief tasks. Yet experimental traditions often unfold like an episode of *Morse*, in that researchers are all too prone to follow false leads and adhere to one theoretical account over others before the evidence is fully in. Far from being neurotic about task fixation, I suggest that the various researchers who are exploring the child's many possible points of access to false belief are at the same time measuring the boundaries of the false belief tasks as an indicator of the development of social-cognitive skills. I hope to establish clear reasons why the issue of narrative is central to our understanding of children's understanding of mind, by starting with a brief mention of experimental data that reveals some of the problems witnessed in the adult viewer's self reflections while performing tasks analogous to watching *Inspector Morse*. In contrast to Gopnik and her colleagues I will then put a case, made elsewhere in this volume (see e.g. the chapters by Chandler & Hala; Freeman; Siegal & Peterson), that the traditional approach to theory of mind competence has all too readily overlooked alternative interpretations of young children's failure to provide the "correct" answer. By implication I will suggest that there is much value in gazing intently into the entrails of the false belief procedure as it lies on the dissection table.

TEXT AND THE ADULT'S MISPERCEPTION OF INTENTIONALITY

Over a diversity of tasks, older children (see, e.g., Smith, 1978) and adults (e.g. Kvavilashvili, 1987; Subbotsky, 1990) have been shown to misinterpret critical mental state information. Our understanding of intentionality may be misconstrued as a result of at least three factors.

First, cognitive load seems to influence our ability to link mental states with action. In an elegant demonstration, Kvavilashvili (1987) examined adults' prospective memories for their own intentions. She set up an experiment in which participants were instructed to convey an important message to the experimenter, who was supervising the next part of a laboratory task in another room. Given their involvement in the "filler" task, many subjects forgot to do this.

Second, we are likely to change our recall events as a result of the ways in which we reconstruct the available evidence. In an interesting series of experiments, Spiro (e.g. 1980), asked subjects to recall a narrative either two days or some weeks after being told it. If they had originally been unaware of a need to recall the story later, the adults tended to add information, usually by confirming that the actors' intentions had been fulfilled. Such "additions' are not unusual in research requiring individuals to relate stories (e.g. Feldman, Bruner, Renderer, & Spitzer, 1990).

Third, within negotiations with others involving a high processing load, we are likely to construct a "story" of events that fits the data, even if this involves attributing magical powers to the experimenter, or reordering our memories of the passage of events over time. So, cognitive load and the process of organising information interact. For example, Subbotsky (1993) asked adults at the start of an experiment to fetch a toy from the corner of the room. He then conducted a task in which participants sat down and placed an object into a box. Then this object "miraculously" disappeared when they reopened the box (the box had a false bottom that was ingeniously disguised). Subbotsky investigated the adult's interpretation of this "miracle" to examine the relationship between memory for events and intentions in such circumstances. Seventeen per cent of subjects spontaneously claimed that Subbotsky had removed the object when they fetched the toy, even though not only was there a clear delay between fetching the toy and placing the object in the box, but the temporal order of these events was clearly marked out. Then, when directly questioned about whether the experimenter might have done this, 42% of the undergraduate respondents answered in the affirmative. Subbotsky's experiment demonstrates neatly how, when reconstructing an understanding of intentions, even adults can be induced to reorder the events in an episode and endorse a credible account of magical causality.

We[1] would not wish to argue that adults lack any theory of mind competence on the basis of Kvavilashvili's subjects' lapses in memory, Spiro's participants' inventiveness, and Subbotsky's adults who temporarily suspend their recall of events in time or allude to the magical powers of the experimenter. Yet analogous claims are often made within developmental psychology concerning issues of competence. For example, in the theory of mind tradition the critical question concerns the time at which children come to gain the representational capacity to perform the "litmus test" (Chandler, 1988) experiment, the false belief task. The goal of the work presented here is twofold, centring around the theme of the false belief task

---

[1] I write "we" here as this work was conducted in collaboration with Norman Freeman and the help of others who are cited all too briefly in the text. The research was supported by a grant from the Economic and Social Research Council (No. R-000-23-2330).

as a narrative. In the first place, we wish to examine the cognitive demands placed on the child who has to recall a series of events, linked together into a coherent storyline. The "standard" (i.e. unexpected transfer) task (Wimmer & Perner, 1983), in which all that happens is that Maxi's chocolate is removed from the cupboard where he expects it to be, actually contains a rich tapestry of "plots" and events. Even the deceptive box experiment (see Mitchell & Lewis, this volume) can be seen to contain two easily confusable storylines—about the contents of the box on the one hand and the actors' mental states on the other. We wish to examine the issue of memory load upon the young child's ability to hold contrasting plots in mind at the same time. This analysis will be considered after the next section. Our second goal of this research is to shift the metaphorical emphasis, by using the issue of narrative to depict those skills that the child acquires. Narratives are part of a culture's everyday activity (Carrithers, 1991). Not only do they have high ecological validity, they are also grounded in social practices—they have to be understood in terms of narrator and listener, plot and sub-plot, and traditions concerning the outcomes of particular storylines. We turn now to address the issue of the false belief task as narrative.

WHY LINK NARRATIVE AND FALSE BELIEF?

Whatever their structures, the procedures of conventional false belief tests develop narrative themes. It is not by accident that characters like Maxi in the most famous task (Wimmer & Perner, 1983) are billed as "protagonists." If we consider the task as a narrative, the higher-order issue (Maxi's uncertainty) takes place within a context of sub-plots (i.e. the individual events, in which the chocolate is moved to various locations). Of course, the topic of the episode could concern the location of the displaced object rather than the protagonist's mental state. Indeed, it might concern any number of possible issues, like the struggles between mothers and children over tidiness in the home, one child's addiction to chocolate, or whatever the listener/reader takes it to be about. The two limiting factors are the individual's ability to generate a storyline (often limited by familiarity with a particular genre) and the business of constructing the salient events from the text base. Most contemporary accounts of the three-year-olds' performance at the task assume that the failure to *disambiguate* these "plots" is caused by an intellectual incapacity to understand propositions about mental states. Irrespective of whether the fundamental issue concerns young children's understanding of the causes of action (Wellman, 1990) or the representational status of mental states (Perner, 1991), the common focus has been upon the child's understanding of the relationship between such "atomic" *individual* propositions. The false belief task is taken to be one in which the premises of a logical syllogism unfold before the child, who only has to retain and process such premises in order to arrive at their natural conclusion. However, it is clear that an account based upon narrative comprehension is equally as plausible.

Over the past several years linguists (Griemas & Courtes, 1976) and psychologists (Astington, 1990; Bruner, 1990) have pointed out that texts, narratives, and discourse have to be understood in terms of distinct layers of meaning. The most obvious division, according to these authors, is between the two "landscapes" of action (e.g. where the chocolate is at any time) and consciousness (e.g. Maxi's grasp of the events). In addition, commentators (e.g. Lucariello, 1990; Olson, 1990) point out that a grasp of narrative is no longer regarded as fixed—we also have to come to terms with the narrator's stance within the storyline. As Chafe (1990, p. 92) puts it: "Language could not function as it does if the speaker were not constantly creating his or her own version of the addressee's processes." Listeners/readers are thus faced with a complex task of reconstructing stories and discourse in such a way that they can be understood and committed to memory. Likewise with narrative, Kintsch and van Dijk (1978) propose that an understanding of stories is dynamic—the individual extracts propositions and these become integrated into a short-term memory buffer in cycles while the text is presented. Information is thus organised into a series of chunks (cf. Chi, 1978), particularly where it is repeated or if it is predicted that it will be useful for subsequent integration.

However, as a dynamic process, grasping such inputs involves two types of mental work. The first is very much what contemporary theoreticians of mind focus upon. It is the microstructural relationship between the individual propositions within a sequence. In passing it is worth noting that much debate on text understanding in the 1980s concerned the way in which individuals process such relations (Garnham, 1985). However, there is a second level of such text understanding, which we suspect has escaped the notice of current theoreticians of mind. This is termed "macrostructural" because it refers to the individual's constructions of the text as a whole (Kintsch & van Dijk, 1978, pp. 365–366): "the propositions of a text base must be connected relative to what is intuitively called a topic of discourse ... Relating propositions at a local manner is not sufficient. There must be a global constraint that establishes a meaningful whole, characterised in terms of a discourse topic." This is carried out by the process of reorganising the story as a whole—for example in reconstructing an argument for suspecting that a new character is the murderer in *Morse*, or, in Subbotsky's subjects, building an obviously spurious account of the events in his "magic" experiment discussed earlier. People, old and young, reorganise their account of events by deleting (i.e. no longer actively processing) information regarded as not of use, or by making generalisations that act as a superset guiding a reorganised group of propositions.

Utilising this approach to the processing of stories, it would be predicted that three-year-olds may fail the false belief task because such general macrostructural processing is immature. They do not integrate mental state information into their "plot," either because they lack the working memory capacity to maintain all the details, or because they do not regard such mental state information as worthy of integration. Thus, when faced with the test question, they cannot reconstruct information because all but the essential details linking the protagonist and the displaced object have been erased. Since Perner, Leekam, and Wimmer (1987), false belief tasks have built-in control questions to test the child's memory of the premises necessary for an inference about a protagonist's mental state. Thus the children's problems do not derive from simple failure to recall individual events. Yet the traditional task does not give clear guidelines to the child about what is to be memorised and how—events might be easy to recall, whereas actors' intentions, which have to be constructed by recalling the causal fabric of those events, may be regarded as less important.

WHY IS MEMORY AN ISSUE IN THE FALSE BELIEF TASK?

As Astington and Gopnik (1991) point out, many versions of the false belief task have yielded a consistent picture. At age three children can correctly recognise that another person is ignorant of the true state of affairs—e.g. that a domino box actually contains another object—by answering the question: "Will he know what is really in the box?" (Hogrefe, Wimmer, & Perner, 1986). They can also explain why a protagonist acts upon a false belief (Bartsch & Wellman, 1989). Likewise, if their prediction that a matchbox contains matches is confirmed, and then the contents of the box are subsequently changed, children can remember their previous thoughts about the contents (Wimmer & Hartl, 1991). Yet when children have to pit one belief against another (i.e. if their belief is at odds with that of another) then three-year-olds usually fail. They do so even when explicitly told that the protagonist's belief is false (Wellman & Bartsch, 1988) or when the protagonist can be seen on a "frozen" video screen to be expressing surprise that a box does not contain its usual contents (Moses & Flavell, 1990). Unlike previous authors, we contend that three-year-olds show such patterns of performance because they fail to grasp the causal texture of the false belief narrative. Ordinarily events pass children by and they cannot retrace vital links between the landscapes of action and consciousness when asked to retrace the protagonist's mental state. We suggest that if the events are more firmly established then young children should show greater skill. For example, they might pass the Wimmer and Hartl task described earlier because the memory "matches in box" is enhanced through repetition—the child's initial "story" being confirmed when the box is opened. Likewise with false belief, a collection of recent experiments has suggested that if the means of accessing the memory base is in some way guided by the experimenter, the three-year-old can respond correctly—that the critical question refers to the protagonist's mental state and not the location of the (sweet in many cases) object of desire. These studies reduce the child's search load using three different, yet complementary techniques.

First, there is evidence to suggest that three-year-olds can identify others' mental states if the narrative base, from which the child has to draw, is reduced. Zaitchik (1991) conducted a false belief task where, since neither the protagonist nor the child saw the objects that gave rise to contrasting belief states, the object was less central to the narrative. In this condition, 70% of 3-year-olds correctly identified the protagonist's false belief. Second, three-year-olds' performance can be boosted if they are given props to help them reconstruct their understanding of events that lead an actor to formulate a false belief. This has been demonstrated in two ways. Retrospectively, a "highlight statement" in which the experimenter prompts the child to "Remember people can be wrong about what is in the (now empty location)," leads to a significant improvement in three-year-olds' performance (Sullivan & Winner, 1991). Prospectively, if children post a picture of their to-be-falsified belief while it is being established then again their performance over-rides the salience of their knowledge of the current state of affairs if the experimenter prompts them to recall the posting exercise (Mitchell & Lacohée, 1991; see also Freeman, this volume). Third, it has been contended that three-year-olds might fail to demonstrate an understanding of another's mental state simply because they are unclear about the intent of the experimenter's question. Two studies have demonstrated that if three-year-olds are asked more explicitly about the actor's *initial* searching place, then they are more likely to succeed (Lewis & Osborne, 1990; Siegal & Beattie, 1991). These locate the child's problems within the communication about the task itself, rather than a domain-specific problem with mind. Such conclusions are not without their detractors (Astington & Gopnik, 1991; Mitchell & Lacohée, 1991), but further work suggests that three-year-olds might simply misunderstand much of what experimenters ask of them. For example, Freeman, Lewis, and Doherty (1991) produced a contrast between young children's chance responses to standard false belief questions and their much improved performance in a condition in which they had to act out the protagonist's search pattern. In this latter procedure, more three-year-olds took this protagonist to the empty location than would be expected by chance. Again the data suggest that the child's problems lie beyond the confines of a simple inability to understand mental representations.

A common link between these studies is that they all attempt to boost the child's performance when *reconstructing* the protagonist's false belief. Even the "posting" task of Mitchell and Lacohée, cited earlier, was conducted to facilitate children's subsequent performance in hindsight, in that the child was asked to recall the event of posting in order to gain access to mental state information. In order to examine the role of broader narrative comprehension and production skills, we need a procedure that bolsters children's performance by securing their knowledge of the narrative base prospectively, without attempting to boost later recall through retrospective prods. In a series of experiments described later, the standard false belief task is transformed into a picture-book format for two inter-related reasons. Firstly, most children have a familiarity with the narrative structure of picture books. Binding the story into a coherent framework might in itself be sufficient to enhance preschoolers' performance. Secondly, having the task in book format enables a child to learn about the text in a diversity of ways. Books are read many times over during normal adult–child interaction (Tucker, 1981). They can be read by the adult, told by the child, or discussed by both, and thus the telling can be directed by the child in a self-paced way. Such manipulations of the way in which information is presented might have a crucial bearing upon how the child links mental state inferences and real-world knowledge.

EXPERIMENT 1: THE STANDARD PROCEDURE CONTRASTED WITH A NARRATIVE VERSION

In order to examine the efficacy of a false belief task presented in book form, our initial task was to compare it with a more standard version. Thus the first experiment conducted (with Charlotte Hagestadt) presented the traditional version as a screening procedure, with the same design of problem subsequently administered as a picture book. In this the child told the story back to the experimenter before the test question was asked. Three contrasting predictions may be made. Firstly, theory theory accounts (e.g. Perner, 1991) would maintain that preschoolers would perform equally poorly in the two conditions. Similar patterns have been produced in a variety of settings and no effect has been demonstrated by presenting the task in a variety of formats (Astington & Gopnik, 1991). Secondly, it might be that the child's problem with false belief lies within the procedures that have been used. Here, the book task might present the critical information in a highly structured and ecologically valid way. If such a speculation were true then any presentation of the book task would produce greater success than the standard procedure using dolls. Thirdly, it might be that if children are given greater familiarity of the storyline they will grasp the test question more readily.

To discriminate between these three predictions the following procedures were employed. Firstly, preschoolers aged three to four years were tested on a standard task using dolls. Two weeks later they were given the picture-book version. Children were allocated to one of two conditions, labelled "one run" and "two runs." Half were "read" the false belief book on "one run" through and were asked the test question in the same way as they would perform a standard task. The other half were given the book task, but here the pictures revealing the story were shown to them (minus the critical test page—see later) and then they were asked to describe the pictures back to the experimenter (E) on a second run through—hence the term "two runs." Preschool children are well used to immersing themselves in the same book repeatedly with an adult. This condition gave the child more opportunity to knot together the critical storyline before being confronted with the false belief problem. Only after the second run through the book were these children shown the final page and asked the test question.

We tested 3- to 4-year-olds ($n = 116$; mean age 48 months [sd = 6; range = 36–60]) of mixed ethnicity and socioeconomic status in two inner-city nursery schools. For the screening phase we used two Playpeople dolls, enacting a scene that was as close as possible to the most common variants of the task (e.g. Wimmer & Perner, 1983; Baron-Cohen, Leslie, & Frith, 1985). Here, one doll puts the cow into the container and leaves the room (E puts it out of sight). The other doll "places" the cow in the other pot and stands halfway between the two pots. The child is then asked the critical false belief question: "Where do you think Red/Blue (the first doll) will look for his toy cow?," and two control probes to ensure that the child has grasped the information required to make the critical false belief inference: "Where is the cow now?" (Reality Control) and "Where did Blue/Red put the cow in the beginning?" (Memory Control). We found that 40 passed the test, whereas 42 failed it and a further 22 children failed 1 of the control questions. As would be predicted from previous experiments, success at this screening task was closely related to age. Of the 40 who passed, 33 were over 4 years old, whereas of the 42 who failed only 13 were 4 years old (χ^2 [1, $n = 80$] = 20.5, $P < 0.0001$).

Two weeks later the children performed the book task. This contained a false belief problem equivalent to the standard screening task. Since this is a novel mode of presenting the problem it is described in full:

Page 1 shows a girl and her cat in their living room standing next to her television, between the bedroom and kitchen doors. The child was introduced to the characters and asked to decide what to call the girl (the name specified was used throughout the task: We use Kiki by way of example). The child was shown the two adjoining rooms and asked to identify them.

Page 2 shows Kiki putting the cat into a basket in the bedroom. The child was told that Kiki was getting the cat to sleep in its basket.
Page 3 shows Kiki back in the sitting room watching TV "all afternoon."
Pages 4, 5, and 6 reveal the cat quietly leaving by the bedroom window, entering the kitchen window, and going to sleep on a chair.
Page 7 shows Kiki turning off the TV, about to go and look for her cat.

The two groups of children, who passed or failed the standard task, were each rank-ordered by age and then divided into the two groups described earlier; the 1 run group (20 had passed screening, 21 had failed; mean age 49 months) and the 2 runs group (20 had passed screening, 21 had failed, mean age 49 months). In the latter condition, on each page E ensured that the child recited the critical information needed to grasp the protagonist's false belief, using prompts like "What is the little girl (cat) doing now?" We recorded and transcribed the children's narrations to measure their verbal fluency. Having completed one of these procedures E then turned over to the seventh page for the first time and asked, "Now, which room will Kiki go into to get her cat?" followed by the control questions in counterbalanced order: "Where is the cat now?" (Reality Control) and "Which room did Kiki put her cat in at the beginning?" (Memory Control).

Does Consolidation of the Narrative Enhance Performance?

Comparison of the one and two runs conditions allows us to consider whether familiarity with the narrative is important in influencing performance at the task. Figure 21.1 presents a breakdown of success/ failure in the book task in relation to condition (one run vs. two runs) and passing vs. failing the screen task. The two left-hand columns show the one run condition (which is essentially a standard theory of mind task in book format). The results indicate a close correspondence between children's performance in the two tasks. The two columns on the right display the results for the two runs condition. The data contrast with those in the one run group since a majority of children who failed the screening test now passed the book task.

Statistical analysis revealed two significant main effects on performance[2]. Those who passed at screening were more likely to succeed at the book task. There was also a superior performance of the two runs group over the one run condition. Unlike the screening task, age (i.e. being three or four) did

---

[2] A log linear analysis was performed to discern the impact of age, performance at screening, and condition upon success/failure at the book task. The effect of screening was significant: χ^2 $(1, n = 80) = 5.04, P < 0.05$, as was the effect of one vs. two runs through the book: $\chi^2 (10, n = 80) = 4.12, P < 0.05$).

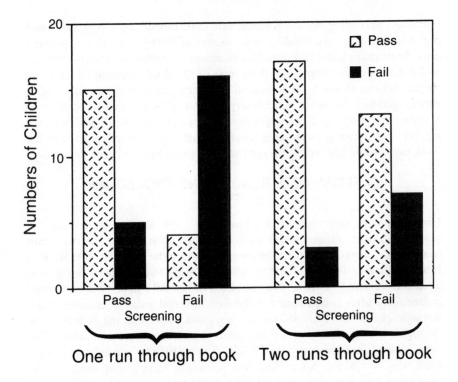

FIG. 21.1   False belief performance in the "one run" and "two runs" conditions compared with success at "standard" false belief screening.

not have an effect on success or failure. A similar pattern of results in the book task was found in 22 children who had failed a control question in the screening test, but were nevertheless tested on the two runs procedure. Six failed the memory control question again and were dropped from the analysis. Of the rest 9/16 correctly answered the false belief question.

It thus seems from these results that when the two runs condition is taken into consideration the traditional age-related pattern of children's performance in the false belief task is not found. Clearly, a majority of subjects who failed the standard task were able to answer the test question correctly having retold the story. However, one swallow does not make a summer, so we conducted a series of follow-up experiments to replicate and extend the procedure. Experiment 2 (conducted with Joanna King) firstly allows us to see if the existence of a pretest somehow exerted an influence on the two runs procedure of the book task, so that preschoolers might "succeed" but for the wrong reasons. Secondly, it explored the two runs procedure more closely to identify why it might enhance performance.

Certainly, according to the Kintsch/van Dijk model, both repetition and organisation of the material have a positive effect upon story comprehension. To examine these two possible influences in relation to one another, a 2 × 2 factorial design compared the effects of the child "reading" the text on the second run-through (i.e. replicating Experiment 1, in which the child is encouraged to construct a richer interpretation of the text) with the effect of E telling the story twice (i.e. repetition through chunking). In addition, the second "run" through was manipulated so that half were taken through the book twice while half went through the book once, but read each page twice.

EXPERIMENT 2: READER AND PROCEDURE EFFECTS

Using the same materials as in Experiment 1, 68 children (mean age: 46 months, sd = 5; range 36–55) were randomly allocated to the two main conditions (a replication of Experiment 1 in which the story was told back to E by the child and one in which E "told" the story twice). These two groups were further subdivided in two. Subjects either told/were told each page immediately after it was read for the first time, in order to enhance recall through chunking (Chi, 1978), or they told/were told the whole book through a second time. The test and control questions were presented in the same way as in Experiment 1. Of the 67 subjects who passed the control questions, 41 (61%) passed the test question. Given that none of the conditions matched the standard false belief task, separate analyses were conducted to estimate performance in the two conditions. Each manipulation—the child telling the story on the second run and either participant "reading" each page twice—produced above-chance success (24/34 = 71% correct; $P < 0.01$ binomial), whereas the experimenter reading the book twice and the act of reading the complete book twice produced chance results (17/33 = 51% correct).

In both these experiments the ages of the participants were in the main between 3:5 and 4:2 years. Given the success of the children, the next logical step would be to investigate whether the same procedure can be used to demonstrate successful false belief reasoning in younger children. Therefore, Experiment 3 was designed to combine the most facilitative methods in Experiment 2 and test them on a group of children aged, in the main, less than 3:6.

EXPERIMENT 3: HOW DO YOUNG THREE-YEAR-OLDS FARE?

Forty-nine children were tested in four playgroups (with Paul Daly, Heather Douglas, and Jim Turner). The mean age was 39.7 months (sd = 5.7; range 29–52). In this experiment not only did the children each describe the page immediately after the experimenter had done so, but they also told the complete story by themselves immediately afterwards, with prompts if necessary. If the 47 children, 32 passed the test question ($P = 0.018$, 2-tailed, corrected binomial). However, 27 failed 1 of the control questions and were excluded from subsequent analyses. This number is high, but is to be expected given the age of the subjects. In keeping with the research of Lucariello (1990), which found that preschoolers embellish the text in their retellings of stories, many of these children appeared to treat the control questions as a means of demonstrating their creativity. Some simply updated the storyline (e.g. "the cat is in the soil"; "he's outside on the digger") when asked where the cat was now (the reality question)! Nineteen of the 20 children who answered the control questions "correctly" made the correct false belief attribution. Fourteen of these were under three years six months. Indeed, all the children under three were successful (binomial $P = 0.031$, one-tailed). The one child who failed the task was aged 3:4. So, in addition to replicating the effect demonstrated in the first two experiments, these data show that when they are in full command of the narrative, even children around their third birthdays appear able to link events that are discrepant with a known state of affairs.

EXPERIMENTS 4 AND 5: LIMITS OF THE PROCEDURE

Having established the reliability of this effect we felt it was necessary to test it to its logical conclusions. We added extra events to the episode and examined the effects of different questions upon performance. For the sake of brevity we collapse discussion of two experiments on different samples (from Bristol and Lancaster, respectively), since they employed comparable procedures.

Experiment 4 was designed to put narrative access to a more stringent test by adding an event at the start of the story. Here the two protagonists start the episode in the garden, before Kiki decides to watch TV while the cat sleeps. The story then proceeds as before, with the two in the sitting room for the next scene. This event was included partly to see whether the addition of an extra event overloaded the child's memory too much for successful performance, and also to overcome a potential criticism of the original design. It might be the case that children learn to reproduce the story recursively, since the technique of getting them to go through the text a number of times might encourage such an approach to it. If this was the case then a question about the next action in the story might prompt children unknowingly to give the correct answer. If all they do is remember where Kiki and the cat went first, they might simply reiterate the story from the beginning and arrive at the correct answer. We predicted here that if children were simply rehearsing Kiki's movements in the book, then some at least would state "garden" in response to the test question in this condition. In this version we collected data from 47 children who passed the control questions (mean age 46.2 months, range 31–58).

In Experiment 5 we decided to be well and truly mean to the children and entice them into confusing the contents of their memory for previous beliefs. Here we added an alternative first picture, which corresponds with the end point of the story. So the story starts with the cat happily in the kitchen. Clare Smith tested 35 children in 2 inner-city nursery schools. Their mean age was 48 months (range 38–55).

As well as having a different additional picture in the story, some of the children in each experiment were asked the test question: "Where does Kiki think her cat is?" when the author turned over to the final page, instead of the usual "Where will Kiki go to find her cat?" Some previous studies have found no effect of questions about action vs. mental states on performance, whereas others suggest that the "think" question is the harder (see Freeman, this volume). However, we wished to check further whether asking a question about the protagonist's thoughts, having immersed the child in a narrative about action, might prevent the child from accessing the protagonist's false belief.

Taken together, the two experiments allow us to comment upon some conditions that constrain preschool children in the book-format-with-memory-enhancement. In Experiment 4 the "Where will Kiki go..." question, asked in Experiments 1–3, produced the predicted above-chance performance: 71% (20/28) were successful (binomial, $P = 0.02$). In contrast, only 31% (5/16) passed the "think" question. Age (3- vs. 4-year-olds) had no effect, nor did the interaction of age by question. However, the "main effect" of the question was significant[3]. In Experiment 5 all of the children were at chance. Half (12/24) of those asked the "think" question and 55% (6/11) of those asked the "go" question correctly identified the protagonist's false belief.

Thus Experiments 4 and 5 show that preschoolers can be as confused by the events in the book task as they can in the standard Maxi procedures. An additional episode that adds a benign detail to the story does not necessarily confuse children, whereas the purposefully complicated procedure of Experiment 5 does. In many respects the act of making the start of the story correspond with the end point produces problems of separating out the various layers of the text—by including the kitchen twice, we supposed that the event "cat in kitchen" would assume centrality in the child's recall

---

[3] A log linear analysis was conducted to examine the effects of age (3 vs. 4) and question (think vs. go) upon successful vs. unsuccessful recall of Kiki's belief. The effect of question was significant (χ^2 [1, $n = 43$] = 5.7, $P < 0.02$).

of events. This raises the questions of just how stable the ability to understand false belief is, which we will discuss in the next experiment, and why children err when it comes to questions about the protagonists' thought, which we will postpone until the discussion of narrative production.

EXPERIMENT 6: OLDER CHILDREN'S UNDERSTANDING OF AN OVER-FAMILIAR NARRATIVE

In our final experiment, we explore the problem of understanding the event structure of a narrative from a different angle, but one which complements the earlier experiments. Having demonstrated competence on the most straightforward task in children around their third birthdays (Experiment 3), and yet having designed tasks that children entering the fifth year of life find problematic (Experiment 5), it seems relevant to find a design that even older children find complex, just because they find it difficult to unravel the various layers of story line within a clear causal structure. We thus carried out a range of tasks that set the false belief problem into a context that makes such "human sense" (Donaldson, 1978) to older children in which, paradoxically, they fall foul of the same problems faced by younger children in the false belief task.

We set the false belief problem into a fairy tale that no streetwise four-year-old could possibly have missed and of which such a child could not imagine that you or I would be ignorant. We set up exactly the same book-reading procedure with two samples. One contained children at a playgroup, with a mean age of 51 months (range 41–58 months); the second, in the first year of primary school, was a year older (mean age 60 months). Here, the story was of Goldilocks and the Three Bears in a format simplified to resemble the Kiki story, whereby the child repeated the story back to E on a second run through. The text was as follows:

Page 1: Here are the three bears ... This is Daddy bear ... This is Mummy bear ... This is Baby bear.
Page 2: Mummy bear makes porridge for breakfast (in piloting we discovered that many children did not know what porridge was, so we substituted this with a popular cereal eaten with hot milk if, in pretesting, children did not understand the term).
Page 3: The porridge is too hot ... so the bears go out for a walk.
Page 4: Here is Goldilocks ... "No one is home," says Goldilocks ... She goes into the bears' house.
Page 5: Goldilocks wants some porridge ... She tastes Daddy bear's porridge ... Oh! It's too hot.
Page 6: She tastes Mummy bear's porridge ... Yuk! It's too cold.

Page 7: She tastes Baby bear's porridge... Mmm! It was just right ... Look! It's all gone. Goldilocks has eaten up all Baby bear's porridge.
Page 8: Goldilocks is tired... She goes to sleep in Baby bear's bed.
Page 9: Here are the bears coming home... They're just about to open the door...

Two test questions were asked, with appropriate memory and reality control questions: "Do the bears think that anyone is in their house?" and "What does Baby bear think is in his bowl?" Given that the watershed for theory of mind competence has repeatedly been found to be somewhere around the child's fourth birthday, standard accounts would predict that most four-year-olds and certainly those aged five would sail through this task. In the younger sample 15 children answered the control questions correctly, but only 2 stated correctly that Baby bear thinks that there is porridge in his bowl—13 answered that he thinks there is nothing there, a figure significantly above chance (binomial, $P = 0.002$). Similar patterns were also obtained (by Helen Upright) in the older children. For example, 32 of the 45 children affirmed that the three bears knew that Goldilocks was in their house as they strolled up the path (binomial, $P = 0.04$). These data suggest that children aged four and five can fall foul of problems concerning which macrorules to employ in tasks like this.

GENERAL DISCUSSION OF NARRATIVE RECALL AND FALSE BELIEF REASONING

To summarise the earlier experiments; they appear to show that, under certain conditions, preschoolers seem to display an understanding of false belief. This is demonstrated particularly in the contrast between the "standard" and "book" procedures in Experiments 1–3, which stretched the procedure down the age scale and found the same pattern of results for children as young as two years, nine months. Experiments 4–6 showed that, although the effect was erased by a "confusing" event or question type beyond the scope of the narrative (e.g. asking the child about the protagonist's thoughts when the story is purely about her actions), simply adding a benign event did not deter children. Success of three-year-olds in tasks involving two runs through the book appears hard to account for in the more traditional interpretations of the false belief task. These assume that the three-year-old cannot perform a critical inference contrasting two mental states on the same issue. The evidence presented here appears to show that young children's failure in the false belief task lies in a specific problem they have in *reconstructing* the protagonist's mental state from memory.

A claim that difficulties in understanding false belief stem in the main from a problem of recall seems unlikely on initial consideration. As stated earlier, memory for the facts (where Kiki put her cat and where the cat is now) is known not to be at issue, since children who cannot remember these facts are excluded (cf. Perner et al., 1987). Yet the successful conditions in the book task need to be explained in terms of how these procedures influence the nature of recall: Something about the way in which their memories were constructed seems to have assisted the children.

Taken together, the experiments show that recall of the narrative base is necessary for success. They suggest that failure arises from problems in grasping the causal texture of the task. Mere familiarisation with the events within a novel text enhances performance, as we see in the contrast between the one run and two runs conditions in the book task in Experiment 1. The success of this apparently very slight modification clearly suggests that the "standard" (i.e. one run) procedure produces false negative results. Research on the development of scripts and events has long shown both that events which occur together tend to be "schematised" into a semantic structure and also that repetition increases recall (see e.g. Hudson, 1986). Although repetition is a feature of the effect demonstrated in the experiments here it is not sufficient to increase the child's likelihood of recalling mental state information—the experimenter reading the story twice, for example, in Experiment 2 does not raise the child's performance above chance. Rather, the data suggest that younger children's problems in false belief tasks lie in their abilities to schematise the premises into a consistent storyline.

Using a narrative framework to understand this storyline in false belief performance, the success of children can be interpreted as follows. Those who fail the task by using a reality-based judgement do not do so because they have a slavish adherence to reality (Russell, Mauthner, Sharpe, & Tidswell, 1991), but because the "story" they construct is limited to a misplaced understanding of the individual events that unfold. According to such an interpretation, in "traditional" variations of the experiment, like the screening task in Experiment 1, for example, three-year-olds "read" the discourse as being about the whereabouts of the displaced person or object (the cow in the screening task, or Maxi's chocolate in the standard procedure), since that object/person is the linking focus of the events—it appears more often than any of the protagonists. One of the basic elements of story comprehension is that repeated items tend to be constructed as being more central in the individual's reconstruction (Kintsch & van Dijk, 1978). Two runs through the book *may* allow the child to construct a more complex narrative, either by "chunking" the elements on each page through its repetition or by the child having publicly to reconstruct the events back to the experimenter (cf. Bartlett, 1932). Both procedures enrich the database upon which the child acts.

However, if the wrong location is emphasised in the story (e.g. the kitchen in Experiment 4), children can easily be persuaded to revert to a judgement based upon reality because of the salience of their own true belief. Taken one step further, we believe that failure of the older children in the fairy story adds a further layer of textual analysis that needs to be considered. We realise that more work is needed further to test the reasons behind the data presented in Experiment 6, particularly given contrasting findings obtained by Winner and Sullivan (1993). However, the fact that older children failed this task can best be explained by an assumption that no one could possibly be ignorant of the Three Bears Story—not even the bears themselves! The same influences operate upon adult viewers of *Inspector Morse* when, presented with a storyline that is accentuated in the drama, they imagine that the only possible killer is the one to whom the "evidence" points.

NARRATIVE PRODUCTION AND FALSE BELIEF REASONING

Asking children to recall the storyline of the false belief task might not be the only means of gaining access to their understanding of how mental state information fits into their grasp of events. In the conditions in which children related the story to us in each of the experiments here, we transcribed their versions of the story to see whether they might predict success/failure at the task. Such a relationship would add further evidence for the argument that false belief comprehension is embedded within an understanding of the various layers of a text. As a means of gauging children's general production skills, the transcripts from three of the experiments discussed earlier were rated by two independent judges according to the "fluency" of their narrative; based on elaboration, clarity and coherence, length of utterances, and prompting needed. In each task narrators were divided into three groups by two independent raters. Reliability was up to 97% in Experiment 2. The first group was rated as *poor* at recalling the story even with prompts from E. Here is a typical example of conversation as each page was examined. It will be seen that up to page 4 the child did not convey any information about the picture and needed prompts on page 6:

Page 1: Exp: What is happening in the first picture?
           Sub: She watches ... cat.... TV.
Page 2: Exp: Now what is happening? ... [pause] ... she puts the cat to bed.
Page 3: Exp: And then what does she do? ... She's watching television.
Page 4: Exp: And now what happens?
           Sub: He got through window.
Page 5: Sub: And in through kitchen window.

Page 6:   Exp: What is he doing now?
             Sub: Sittin' on chair.
             (Experiment 1: Subject 14: Age 4: 1 years)

The majority of children were defined as *average* narrators. These recalled
the gist of the story, often, but not always, without prompts. In this example
the child was scored as average largely because she did not supply sufficient
information or textual bridges. Given that the text was relatively coherent
and she volunteered information about what was happening on the test page
(no. 7), she was just below the borderline for good narration (see following):

Page 1:   Sub: Watches telly.
Page 2:   Sub: She ... what was her name?
             Exp: Carla.
             Sub: Carla puts the pussy in the bed.
Page 3:   Sub: An' Carla ... um ... watches telly.
Page 4–5: Sub: Carla ... the cat goes to that window and he goes in this
                  kitchen window.
Page 6:   Sub: And on the chair.
Page 7:   Sub: Um ... Carla wants to find the pussy.
             (Experiment 1: Subject 61: Age 3: 6 years)

The third group was classified as *good* narrators. These children
demonstrated a clear grasp of the story's content and structure, plus they
connected the themes of the story, as we see in this example:

Page 1:   Sub: She's watching telly with her cat.
Page 2:   Sub: And she went to her bedroom and put the cat into the
                  basket.
Page 3:   Sub: And then she went back into the room and watched telly all
                  afternoon.
Page 4:   Sub: But the cat got out the bedroom window.
Page 5:   Sub: And went in the ... went in the kitchen window.
Page 6:   Sub: And if the cat went to sleep on the chair.
Page 7:   Sub: And the girl standed up.
             (Experiment 1: Subject 19: Age 4: 3 years)

Figure 21.2 shows the relation between fluency in narrative recall and
success/failure in the book task in Experiments 1 and 2. It reveals a linear
relationship between narrative fluency and success in the false belief
question that followed: Poor narrators were largely unsuccessful, average
children largely successful, and good narrators were at ceiling (χ^2 [2, n = 85]
= 29.2, P < 0.0001).

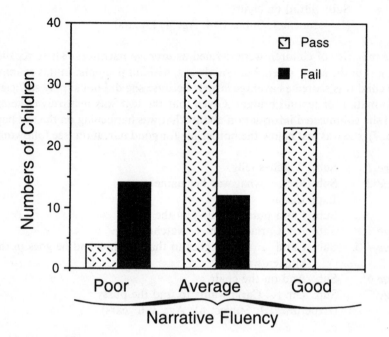

FIG. 21.2   Narrative fluency and false belief performance.

IS NARRATIVE PRODUCTION SUFFICIENT FOR
SUCCESSFUL FALSE BELIEF REASONING?

The narrative fluency data suggest that being able to reconstruct the events into a coherent story is sufficient to predict successful response to the critical question. This close relationship is in line with current theoretical analyses of the way in which narratives are constructed by speakers. These models closely resemble those of story comprehension, which were discussed at the start of the chapter. For example, Bamberg and Marchman (1991) maintained that schematic structures are organised in a hierarchical fashion, so that less relevant schemes are embedded within more relevant ones. Likewise Peterson and McCabe (1991) point out the importance of children learning how to connect discrete utterances into a coherent narrative. In the case of the Kiki story tested in these experiments, this involves the construction of the theme that grasps the protagonist's intentions/beliefs, which with only one run fail to become consolidated into the storyline. The patterns of data presented in Fig. 21.2 suggest that good narrators linked their description of the text into a coherent whole.

In three different experiments good narrators could predict where Kiki would go when confronted by a new event. A problem that the earlier account of false belief comprehension has to overcome concerns the fact that in Experiment 5 there was no obvious relationship between narrative skill and false belief prediction when the test question involved predicting Kiki's thoughts (even though the predicted relationship was evident where Kiki's action was under consideration). Although further work needs to be done, both to consolidate these findings and to clarify them, we assume that children's failure in this condition indicates a limitation in their ability to generalise from one narrative state (the narrative of action depicted in the plot) to another (the story of Kiki's inner mental world). Such a conclusion is inferred bearing in mind research on more general narrative skills. The ability to organise discrete episodes into a thematic whole appears in these domains from age three onwards. Research on children's understanding of picture books, for example, shows that when recalling quite lengthy stories (i.e. 24 pages), three- and four-year-olds tend to recall events in isolation (Berman, 1988; Trabasso & Nickels, 1992). Trabasso and Nickels found that three-year-olds focus predominantly upon state changes with neutral outcomes (e.g. "he fall down") and settings (e.g. where the action on a particular page takes place). Only at the age of four did they find evidence for a sensitivity to the actor's "goal plans" and the links between characters, but even then the story characters' reasons for acting were not made explicit.

The data presented here support the finding that preschoolers' narratives rarely describe actors' mental states. The example of subject 61, who said "Carla wants to find the pussy," was relatively rare. In Experiment 1, for example, only 9 (7.7%) children made such references and these were not predictive of success—subject 61 failed a control question, and 3 of the remaining 8 failed the test question. Such patterns caution us against using language production data as a means of gauging the child's comprehension of mental state terms.

CONCLUSIONS

The data from these experiments suggest that domain-general problems concerning the recall of interlinked events provide the basis of young children's failure at false belief tasks. With their focus upon the nature of specific developmental shifts in the preschool period, theory theory accounts appear to be closed to the possibility that young children face, in a more vivid way, problems of understanding others' mental states that extend far beyond this age span (Chandler, 1988).

Further work needs to explore the nature of the link between narrative comprehension and false belief understanding. For example, being able to formulate and access detailed and enmeshed accounts of stories might allow individuals to perform a number of tasks. If this were the case then the measure of narrative fluency would predict superior performance on a variety of tasks not centrally concerned with understanding mental state information. Alternatively, it might be the case that an understanding of narrative gives specific access to theory of mind capabilities, since stories are quintessentially about such information—an argument made by Lucariello (1990).

At the very least, the data presented here reveal the problems inherent in testing three-year-olds' capabilities—they are notoriously difficult to assess and we quite easily forget that the data from false belief experiments are the product of complex negotiations between often distracted or unwilling children with none-too-perfect experimenters. The chapter has attempted to pinpoint two levels of understanding. Firstly, there are the child's limitations as a memoriser/information processor. The success of children in the novel book task can be explained in Trabasso and Nickels's (1992, p. 272–273) words: "The more knowledge children have about goal plans, the more information they can include and organise into the same number of narrative units." Secondly, the preschooler needs help with constructing a view of events that comes close to that of the experimenter. Negotiation between the two has a direct influence upon the child's "ability" to display an understanding of false belief (Trabasso & Nickels, 1992, p. 251): "the content and the structure of a narration is determined as a result of an interaction between a person's model of physical and psychological causation and the events to which the model is applied."

REFERENCES

Astington, J.W. (1990). Narrative and the child's theory of mind. In B.K. Britton & A.D. Pellegrini (Eds.), *Narrative thought and narrative language* (pp. 151–171). Hillsdale, NJ: Lawrence Erlbaum Associates Inc.

Astington, J.W., & Gopnik, A. (1991). Theoretical explanations of children's understanding of mind. *British Journal of Developmental Psychology, 9*, 7–31.

Bamberg, M., & Marchman, V. (1991). Binding and unfolding: Towards the linguistic construction of narrative discourse. *Discourse Processes, 14*, 277–305.

Baron-Cohen, S., Leslie, A., & Frith, U. (1985). Does the autistic child have a "theory of mind?" *Cognition, 21*, 37–46.

Bartlett, F.W. (1932). *Remembering: An experimental and social study*. Cambridge: Cambridge University Press.

Bartsch, K., & Wellman, H.M. (1989). Young children's attribution of action to beliefs and desires. *Child Development, 60*, 946–964.

Berman, R.A. (1988). On the ability to retain events in narrative. *Discourse Processes, 11*, 269–499.

Bruner, J. (1990). *Acts of meaning*. Cambridge, Mass.: Harvard University Press.

Carrithers, M. (1991). Narrativity: Mindreading and making societies. In A. Whiten (Ed.), *Natural theories of mind* (pp. 305–317). Oxford: Blackwell.

Chafe, W. (1990). Some things narratives tell us about the mind. In B.K. Britton & A.D. Pellegrini (Eds.), *Narrative thought and narrative language* (pp. 79–111). Hillsdale, NJ: Lawrence Erlbaum Associates Inc.

Chandler, M. (1988). Doubt and developing theories of mind. In J.W. Astington, P.L. Harris, & D.R. Olson (Eds.), *Developing theories of mind* (pp. 387–413). Cambridge: Cambridge University Press.

Chi, M. (1978). Knowledge structures and memory development. In R. Siegler (Ed.), *Childhood thinking: What develops?* (pp. 73–96). Hillsdale, NJ: Lawrence Erlbaum Associates Inc.

Donaldson, M. (1978). *Children's minds*. London: Fontana.

Feldman, C.F., Bruner, J., Renderer, B., & Spitzer, S. (1990). Narrative comprehension. In B.K. Britton & A.D. Pellegrini (Eds.), *Narrative thought and narrative language* (pp. 1–78). Hillsdale, NJ: Lawrence Erlbaum Associates Inc.

Freeman, N.H., Lewis, C.N., & Doherty, M. (1991). Preschoolers' grasp of a desire for knowledge in false-belief prediction: Practical intelligence and verbal report. *British Journal of Developmental Psychiatry. 9*, 139–158.

Garnham, A. (1985). *Psycholinguistics: Central topics*. London: Methuen.

Griemas, A., & Courtes, J. (1976). The cognitive dimension of literary discourse. *New Literary History, 7*, 433–447.

Hogrefe, G.J., Wimmer, H., & Perner, J. (1986). Ignorance versus false belief: A developmental lag in attribution of mental states. *Child Development, 57*, 567–582.

Hudson, J. (1986). Memories are made of this: General event knowledge and development of autobiographical memory. In K. Nelson (Ed.), *Event knowledge: Structure and development* (pp. 97–118). Hillsdale, NJ: Lawrence Erlbaum Associates Inc.

Kintsch, W., & Van Dijk, T.A. (1978). Toward a model of text comprehension and production. *Psychological Review, 85*, 363–394.

Kvavilashvili, L. (1987). Remembering intention as a distinct form of memory. *British Journal of Psychology, 78*, 507–518.

Lucariello, J. (1990). Canonicality and consciousness in child narrative. In B.K. Britton & A.D. Pellegrini (Eds.), *Narrative thought and narrative language* (pp. 131–149). Hillsdale, NJ: Lawrence Erlbaum Associates Inc.

Lewis, C., & Osborne, A. (1990). Three-year-olds' problems with false belief: Conceptual deficit or linguistic artifact? *Child Development, 61*, 1514–1519.

Mitchell, P., & Lacohee, H. (1991). Children's early understanding of false belief. *Cognition, 39*, 107–128.

Moses, L.J., & Flavell, J.H. (1990). Inferring false beliefs from actions and reactions. *Child Development, 61*, 929–945.

Olson, D.R. (1990). Thinking about narrative. In B.K. Britton & A.D. Pellegrini (Eds.), *Narrative thought and narrative language* (pp. 99–110). Hillsdale, NJ: Lawrence Erlbaum Associates Inc.

Perner, J. (1991). *Understanding the representational mind*. Cambridge, Mass.: MIT Press.

Perner, J., Leekam, S., & Wimmer, H. (1987). Three-year-olds' difficulty with false belief: The case for a conceptual deficit. *British Journal of Developmental Psychology, 5*, 125–137.

Peterson, C., & McCabe, A. (1991). *Developing narrative structure*. Hillsdale, NJ: Lawrence Erlbaum Associates Inc.

Russell, J., Mauthner, N., Sharpe, S., & Tidswell, T. (1991). The "windows task" as a measure of strategic deception in preschoolers and autistic subjects. *British Journal of Developmental Psychology, 9*, 331–349.

Siegal, M., & Beattie, K. (1991). Where to look first for children's knowledge of false beliefs. *Cognition, 38*, 1–12.

Smith, M.C. (1978). Cognizing the behavior stream: The recognition of intentional action. *Child Development, 49,* 736–743.

Spiro, R.J. (1980). Accommodative reconstruction in prose recall. *Journal of Verbal Learning and Verbal Behavior, 19,* 84–95.

Subbotsky, E. (1990). The preschooler's conception of the permanence of an object (verbal and actual behavior). *Soviet Psychology, 28,* 42–67.

Subbotsky, E. (1993). *Foundations of the mind.* Cambridge, Mass.: Harvard University Press.

Sullivan, K., & Winner, E. (1991). When 3-year-olds understand ignorance, false belief and representational change. *British Journal of Developmental Psychology, 9,* 159–172.

Trabasso, T., & Nickels, M. (1992) The development of goal plans of action in the narration of a picture story. *Discourse Process, 15,* 249–275.

Tucker, N. (1981). *The child and the book.* Cambridge: Cambridge University Press.

Wellman, H.M. (1990). *The child's theory of mind.* Cambridge, Mass.: Bradford/MIT Press.

Wellman, H.M., & Bartsch, K. (1988). Young children's reasoning about beliefs. *Cognition, 30,* 239–277.

Wimmer, H., & Hartl, M. (1991). The Cartesian view and the theory view of mind: Developmental evidence from understanding false belief in self and other. *British Journal of Developmental Psychology, 9,* 125–138.

Wimmer, H., & Perner, J. (1983). Beliefs about beliefs: Representation and constraining function of wrong beliefs in young children's understanding of deception. *Cognition, 13,* 103–128.

Winner, E., & Sullivan, K. (1993, April). *Deception as a zone of proximal development for false belief understanding.* Poster presented at the Society for Research in Child Development, New Orleans.

Zaitchik, D. (1991). Is only seeing really believing? Sources of true belief in the false belief task. *Cognitive Development, 6,* 91–103.

Author Index

Subject Index